Marx's Ethical Vision

Marx's Ethical Vision

VANESSA CHRISTINA WILLS

OXFORD
UNIVERSITY PRESS

Oxford University Press is a department of the University of Oxford.
It furthers the University's objective of excellence in research, scholarship,
and education by publishing worldwide. Oxford is a registered trade mark of
Oxford University Press in the UK and in certain other countries.

Published in the United States of America by Oxford University Press
198 Madison Avenue, New York, NY 10016, United States of America.

© Oxford University Press 2024

All rights reserved. No part of this publication may be reproduced, stored in
a retrieval system, or transmitted, in any form or by any means, without the
prior permission in writing of Oxford University Press, or as expressly permitted
by law, by license or under terms agreed with the appropriate reprographics
rights organization. Inquiries concerning reproduction outside the scope of the
above should be sent to the Rights Department, Oxford University Press, at the
address above.

You must not circulate this work in any other form
and you must impose this same condition on any acquirer

Library of Congress Cataloging-in-Publication Data
Names: Wills, Vanessa, author.
Title: Marx's ethical vision / Vanessa Christina Wills.
Description: New York : Oxford University Press, [2024] |
Includes bibliographical references and index.
Identifiers: LCCN 2023050544 | ISBN 9780197688144 (hardback) |
ISBN 9780197688151 (epub)
Subjects: LCSH: Marx, Karl, 1818–1883—Ethics. | Socialist ethics.
Classification: LCC B3305.M74 W485 2024 | DDC 171/.7—dc23/eng/20231226
LC record available at https://lccn.loc.gov/2023050544

DOI: 10.1093/9780197688175.001.0001

Printed by Integrated Books International, United States of America

The manufacturer's authorised representative in the EU for product safety is Oxford University Press España S.A. of El Parque Empresarial
San Fernando de Henares, Avenida de Castilla, 2 – 28830 Madrid (www.oup.es/en or product.safety@oup.com). OUP España S.A. also acts as
importer into Spain of products made by the manufacturer.

Contents

Preface ix
Acknowledgments xiii

1. Introduction 1
   Why Think About Marx and Ethics? 3
   Analytical Marxism and Dialectical Method 6
   Précis of a Marxist Ethics 9
   The Structure of the Argument 13

2. Ideology Critique and the Critique of Morality 16
   "Ideology" is Not a Wholly Pejorative Concept 18
   Rival Analyses of Marx's "Ideology" Concept 28
   Moral Suasion and Marx's Anti-Utopianism 38

3. A Historical Materialist Account of Human Nature 46
   Biological and Social Being in Marx's Account of Human Nature 50
   Human Needs 61
   The "Rich Individual" in Marx's Ethical Vision 66

4. Alienation 72
   "Alienation" in Marx's Early Writings 78
   "Alienation" in Marx's Later Works 84

5. Radical Chains (Marx on Freedom and Determinism) 95
   Marx on "the Difference Between the Democritean and the Epicurean Philosophy of Nature" 101

6. Individuality 117
   Interests, Individuals, and Egoists: Marx on Max Stirner 129
   Defending Marx's Methodological Holism 136

7. "Bourgeois" Freedom and Equal Right 141
   Freedom 144
   Justice and Equal Right 149
   Rights and/in Communism 161

8. Marx's Critiques of Rival Moral Theories 166
   Marx and Christianity 172
   Marx and Kantian Morality 177
   Kantian Ethics 179

Marx's Rejection of Kantian Ethics	182
Eduard Bernstein and Social Democracy's Embrace of Kant	186
Later Attempts to Reconcile Kantian Ethics and Marxist Theory	190
Marx on Utilitarianism	194
Marx and Bentham	195
Marx and J. S. Mill	203
Marx and Malthus	208
Conclusion	210
9. "No Particular Wrong": The Abolition of Morality	213
The End of Sacrifice	215
Meanings of Morality's Abolition	219
Progress and Perfectibility	236
10. Conclusion	239
What Now?	242
Coda: "The Ruthless Criticism of All that Exists," Yesterday and Today	244
Notes	247
Bibliography	279
Index	289

... the only immutable thing is the abstraction of movement—mors immortalis.
—Karl Marx

Preface

When the United States invaded Iraq in the spring of 2003, I was a philosophy graduate student at the University of Pittsburgh. I was preparing myself for a career as what Karl Marx might have called a "bourgeois ideologist." Of course, I simply called it "training to be a moral philosopher."

At that point in my life, I believed the liberal, capitalist institutions that ruled the world were more or less well-equipped and qualified to do so; I thought all they really needed were more smart people with good ideas about how to make the world a better place. I did not think them perfect—far from it. But neither did I expect that far from navigating humanity out of crisis, they would needlessly plunge us into one. And so you could say I had my own crisis of liberal faith. It became suddenly clear to me that "freedom," "reason," "rights," and "humanitarian intervention" were not what they seemed. Our leaders were not acting rationally and they were clearly not acting as though they had the interests of humanity in mind.

Amidst this uncertainty, I was sure of one thing: the invasion of Iraq, the 2001 invasion of Afghanistan, and the so-called war on terror as a whole, were grave moral wrongs. So I threw myself into local antiwar activism; this would be the first context in which I ever met socialists. Today, to be an open socialist is hardly uncommon; but in 2003, it was still widely regarded as incredibly anachronistic and passé to admit to being a Marxist.

I noticed that the Marxists seemed almost preternaturally steadfast in their commitment to political struggle and building mass movements. I grew more interested in knowing what it was they thought about the world that led them to have this steadfast disposition. And so I became increasingly intrigued by the ideas of Karl Marx.

Reading Marxist theory offered me a theoretical framework that would explain the bizarre death drive of the imperialist war on terror. I could get the idea that we lived in a system that prioritized private accumulation over the well-being of people. But I did not feel much closer to a theoretical argument to support my conviction that this was objectively morally wrong. I wanted to know, what did a Marxist theory entail about the nature of morality? The answers I encountered in my studies did not satisfy me, either because they were overly naive and uncharitable about liberal morality or because they simply did not offer a thorough enough interpretation of the full massive scope of Marx's writings on the subject. So I changed my topic of academic study and made this my project: to articulate, as fully as possible, a distinctively Marxist approach to ethics.

In the intervening years, I have written from a Marxist perspective on topics including race, gender, atheism, false consciousness, admiration, policing, political violence, and more. Much of the brutal fallout I and others predicted would come from the war on terror has indeed come to pass. The United States' 2021 withdrawal from Afghanistan revealed the whole endeavor as a cruel ruse. It is not "freedom" and "democracy" that the US has left behind in its wake, but rather profiteering adventurism and casualties of war. Meanwhile, fascist movements are on the rise worldwide, sprouting like mushrooms in the fetid soil of racism and imperialism that capitalist wars require.

Still, especially as an enduring response to the 2008 Great Recession, interest in left ideas is greater than it has been in many decades. In the 2000s, my project was regarded as quaint yet decidedly quixotic. Today, it is clearer that this effort was prescient. Working-class struggle is on the rise. There is much more widespread clarity regarding the dim prospects that our current way of doing things can lead us out of crisis, especially as the world faces the twin disasters of climate change and the still-ongoing COVID-19 global pandemic with its terrifying revelations about the world's unpreparedness to manage public health emergencies in a rational and humane way.

My reasons for doing this work are several. They include my own endless scholarly curiosity about this book's topic and my desire to contribute to the broader scholarly understanding of ethics and of Marx's place in the history of philosophy in particular. But I also do this work in order to give courage to revolutionaries, in and out of the academy.

We humans under capitalism are inundated in ideology that seeks to lull us into complacency about social ills or worse, to seduce us into perpetuating them. We are subjected to countless and relentless attempts to convince us that this is all there is and that "there is no alternative." We are told that we must respect the liberty of our oppressors and exploiters to grind us under. If my book has a single message, it would be this:

If you think that another world is possible . . . if you think that this is not how we are supposed to live . . . if you think that human beings are so much more than what we appear to be today . . . if you think that we ought to take up the struggle against all conditions that demean us, that turn us against one another, and that squander our precious creative human potential . . . you are right.

Washington, DC
May 2023

Acknowledgments

My name appears alone as author of this book, and yet it would hardly have been possible without an expansive community of family members, friends, mentors, colleagues, and comrades who have loved, uplifted, and encouraged me in various ways.

I would like first of all to acknowledge the decades of care, hard work, encouragement, and devotion given to me by my parents, Andrea Beaumonte and Walton Wills. They were my first teachers, my first audience, and my first constructive critics. One does not typically get to choose one's parents, but if it were up to me, I would go back again and choose these two witty, kind, and vibrant people to be mine.

My community includes a large network of beloved friends whom I met as an undergraduate at Princeton University and then as a PhD student in philosophy at the University of Pittsburgh. I have friends from my childhood in Philadelphia and friends I've met through my travels, through my love of music, through activism, and through shared interests of all kinds. I count myself deeply fortunate to be loved by such excellent human beings who have known me so well and for so long, supporting me in my adventures, helping me remain true to myself, and allowing me to feel at home in far-flung places.

I have held two faculty positions in the time since I began the line of research leading to this book. I am deeply grateful to my supportive and encouraging colleagues at both St. Joseph's University and the George Washington University. Academia can be a hostile space; if I feel at home in my chosen profession, camaraderie with my peers is most of the reason why. I thank my co-editors at *Spectre Journal*. Especially in what has been a time of disorientation and disorganization for much of the political left, I've treasured *Spectre* as an intellectual home and counted myself extremely fortunate to have such brilliant, committed comrades to work alongside. Friends, family, and colleagues have all cared for me and given me strength.

Some of the research for this book began its life as part of my doctoral dissertation. My dissertation committee—Michael Thompson, John McDowell, Tommie Shelby, and the late Peter Machamer—supported me in my determination that I would write not just a dissertation about Marx but an *actually*

Marxist dissertation, proceeding from the working hypothesis that Marxist theory has much to offer us and that Marxist method constitutes a viable approach to philosophical inquiry. I have also benefited greatly from the mentorship of senior scholars who were generous enough with their time and attention to encourage me in what, especially at the beginning, must have seemed a rather quixotic philosophical project. These include Olúfẹ́mi Táíwò (author of *Legal Naturalism* and currently at Cornell University), John Exdell, Ruth Groff, and Janine Jones, among others.

I am grateful to colleagues, comrades, and students over the years who have raised questions and objections that helped push my thinking as I developed this book's arguments. I would especially like to thank Jeffrey Stout, Molly Farneth, and James Wetzel for their kind, careful, and critical engagement with an earlier version of this manuscript. Their generosity and enthusiasm in volunteering valuable time and attention to this project came at a crucial moment, giving me courage when I needed it most. I am thankful to Rob Tempio for his advice, encouragement, and support, and to anonymous reviewers who have provided feedback on earlier versions of this book, as well.

This book is the culmination of many years of research and study that has been generously supported by a number of institutions. These include the Fulbright US Student Program, the German Academic Exchange Service, Humboldt-Universität zu Berlin, the Northeast Consortium for Faculty Diversity, the Department of Philosophy at the University of Rochester, the Munich Center for Ethics at Ludwig-Maximilians-Universität München, and the Dresher Center for the Humanities at University of Maryland Baltimore County. I have also had the opportunity to present portions of the material in this book at conferences, workshops, and invited lectures too numerous for me to name here.

If I have expressed myself clearly in this book, it is thanks in part to the many hundreds of students I have taught over the years. The opportunity to be part of their learning journeys has been immeasurably enriching to me as I pursue my own, and their questions push me all the time to think more deeply and to explain more simply. This book would not be what it is without years of standing in classrooms, explaining complex ideas to curious and interested students excited to tackle big questions, challenge old assumptions, and develop new perspectives. Similarly, I am extremely grateful to the many university professors whose student I have been. I could not hope to have approached this book's complex subject matter without the guidance, encouragement, and wisdom my philosophical training has given me.

I wish to thank and honor activists, revolutionaries, and freedom-fighters past and present, the world over. Thank you for your example.

Finally, I would like to thank Peter Ohlin and Oxford University Press for their support of this project and for bringing it out into the world. That is the point of all this, after all—that this attempt to interpret the world might be available and of use to all who seek to change it. I am thankful to everyone along the way who has helped to make this happen.

1
Introduction

Between the fall of the Soviet Union and the fall of Lehman Brothers, if the Anglophone academy could be said to have arrived at any consensus about the value of Marxist theory, it would be that Marxism was a quaint historical curio at best and a world-historically hubristic folly at worst.[1] Today, however, well on our way through the first half of the twenty-first century, we live in a moment of greatly renewed interest in Marxist ideas. This curiosity is stoked by, among other factors, the worldwide economic shocks of 2008 and, in more recent times, by impending climate catastrophe, incipient fascisticization, and the still-ongoing global COVID-19 pandemic.[2] Any of these on its own would stand out as a rebuke to the neoliberal triumphalism of the 1990s, famously crystallized in Francis Fukayama's assertion that humanity had arrived at "the end of history," there to find permanently expanding capitalist prosperity.[3] Taken together, they present at least strong prima facie evidence for what Karl Marx identified as the inherently and ineluctably crisis-ridden nature of capital and, therefore, good reason to encounter his writings anew.

The time is ripe to challenge the core assumptions of our age and to analyze how and why it might be that all has not been as it seemed; the time is ripe, in other words, for gadflies.[4] And yet if in 1845 Karl Marx thought it necessary to remind philosophers that the point is to *change* the world, he might be astonished to survey our current state of affairs and find many philosophers unsure as to whether it is even within our remit to *interpret* it.[5]

This book is one small attempt to take up the questions of our age. My project in the following pages is, first of all, to offer a critical reconstruction of Marx's approach to ethical critique of what is; second, to show how that approach relates to, and troubles, a host of still-dominant assumptions about the character, role, and content of ethical theory; and third, to demonstrate how such a perspective can improve both our theories about the world and our attempts to make the world better.

I write from the point of view of those who have become convinced that there is something—perhaps many things—deeply *ethically* wrong with the current arrangement of our social world and who suspect that the root of this wrong is to be found in the ways that we as human beings collectively produce and reproduce our lived, material conditions of existence within circumstances shaped by the logic of capital. If our crumbling world is one that we have brought about through the sum of our activity as a species, then perhaps some glimmer of hope remains that we might remake it in the image of our fully realized selves.[6]

And yet to be both a Marxist and an ethicist is a stance rife with tension; it is Marx and his collaborator, Friedrich Engels, who write, in what was posthumously published as their *Critique of the German Ideology*, that "the Communists do not preach morality at all."[7] Indeed, Marx famously seems to call for the abolition of morality altogether. And yet Marx's writings are shot through with what certainly seem like normative, distinctly ethical evaluations of people, actions, regimes, economies, and political states of affair. "Vampire," "serpent," "barbarous"—these are only a few of the unflattering descriptions Marx applies to capital and, notably, these all occur in his later writings, supposed by many of his interpreters to be his most thoroughly *amoral*.[8]

This situation presents a handful of interpretive possibilities. Perhaps, as G. A. Cohen and Allen Wood suggest, Marx incongruently, and in spite of himself, held ethical commitments that were untenable and incompatible with his materialist, deterministic claims about the lawlike development of history. Or perhaps, as argued by Louis Althusser and Daniel Brudney, Marx's earlier humanistic writings should be thought of as youthful romantic inclination, which Marx took to be superseded by later works after his "Theses on Feuerbach," which in turn are taken to represent a mature and distinctly amoralist view. Or, perhaps Marx's tendency to ethical expression betrayed his own sentiment that his theory required an ethical dimension which it lacked: one that could be supplied by Kantian ethics, as suggested by Eduard Bernstein, Max Adler, and Philip Kain, among others. Or still yet, perhaps Marx had no overarching ethical picture to offer, but instead endorsed a radical historicism of the type Cornel West attributes to him in his 1991 book on the subject, *The Ethical Dimensions of Marxist Thought*.[9]

I adopt none of these approaches to understanding Marxism's ethical dimensions (or lack thereof), although each has something to recommend it. I argue instead that Marx's writings reveal a single, coherent ethical perspective that evolves and deepens over the course of his intellectual life.[10] This perspective is always rooted in the aim to develop human beings' capacity to intervene rationally and purposively into their natural and social conditions of existence. Such agency over the production of their life circumstances would allow human beings to create those conditions conducive to the in-principle limitless proliferation of human talents, capacities, and diverse forms of life—to the emergence of "rich individuality." He describes this latter concept in the 1857 *Grundrisse*, an unpublished manuscript in which Marx asserts the desirability of

> the development of the rich individuality which is as all-sided in its production as in its consumption, and whose labour also therefore appears no longer as labour, but as the full development of activity itself, in which natural necessity in its direct form has disappeared; because a historically created need has taken the place of the natural one.[11]

About this, I will have more to say in Chapter 6, where I discuss the role of individuality in forming a central, defining element of Marx's ethical perspective. Here, I will say a bit about the reasons for interesting ourselves in Marxism's ethical dimensions, at all.

Why Think About Marx and Ethics?

What I offer here is an explication of Marx's own ethical positions as expressed in his writings over the course of his life—from his youthful philosophical poetry up through his magnum opus, *Capital*. It is also an elucidation of his oft-misunderstood and often quite illuminating critiques of other moral theories and of bourgeois morality as a whole. But as students of Marx will already be aware, any attempt to explain the ethical content of Marx's philosophy cannot be simply a faithful rendering or summation of views on the matter already plainly stated by him. So my project is not only to highlight and clarify aspects of Marxist theory that often go unrecognized or misunderstood. It is, crucially, to offer a critical reconstruction of Marx's approach to ethics, one that is as fully consistent with and grounded in Marx's writings as possible.

Although Marx had significantly more of substance to say about ethics than he is generally given credit for, it is also true that he left behind explanations of his historical materialist method, analyses of the commodity-form that remain unmatched in their breadth and detail, manuscripts on mathematics, and even the satirical and surprisingly lengthy *Heroes of the Exile*, in which he relates, in comic pastiche, the experiences of exiled participants in Germany's 1848 uprising. At the end of his life, Marx intended a study of the anthropologist Lewis Henry Morgan's findings and their implication for the materialist conception of history that he and his collaborator, Friedrich Engels, described in what was posthumously published as their *Critique of the German Ideology*.[12] (Engels would later continue this study of Morgan's work and publish it as *The Origin of the Family, Private Property, and the State*.)

Danny Goldstick states the case very plainly in his 2022 article "Marx, Marxism, Ethics": "You are not going to get a treatise on normative ethics from Karl Marx."[13] In fact, Marx seemed to make time for almost anything and everything *but* to craft a sustained treatment of a distinctively Marxist, historical materialist approach to ethics. So why is it that nearly two centuries later, Marx's interpreters (such as myself) persist in attempting to piece one together on his behalf?

There is no transcendent answer to the question "Why concern ourselves with ethics?" I will not offer one in the course of this book. Ethics concerns questions about what we ought to do, how we ought to live, and how we ought to treat one another. For communists, that "ought" is intrinsically connected to a conception of the essential nature of human beings and the conditions of our flourishing. There is no "something higher" than human beings, no greater cause, value, or power in service to which we dedicate our minds, bodies, creativity, and time. To be a communist is to seek to approach the world from the perspective of the species and to adopt the active furtherance of humans' well-being and creative potential as one's subjective aim.

In capitalist society, this is an inherently ethical posture. Most people do not live in a society that is organized so as to simply produce individuals who recognize themselves as human and recognize all that is human as one with themselves. Quite the contrary: in capitalist society, as in all class society, to insist on the realization of human freedom and equality as something more than an idle ethical phrase is to court ridicule as a dreamer and persecution as a threat.[14]

Since this species self-recognition, this full active awareness of oneself as a human being who is of a kind with every other human being, is not yet a materially realized fact of human life, we need theory to grasp it. This is not to say that ethical theory ought to be some retreat into pure abstraction, idealism, or utopianism. A Marxist approach to ethics takes stock of the already really existing social element that both embodies the society to come and has the means and the motive to bring that society about. These are capitalism's gravediggers—the working class. Marxist ethics is intrinsically part and parcel of a theory of proletarian revolution.

Marxism, as is well known, sees in capitalist society a social landscape overwhelmingly defined by the battle between workers and their exploiting bosses. It is this class struggle that produces the social history of capitalist society. The class struggle is a struggle over material resources, a struggle for human survival, a struggle for domination or self-determination—it is a struggle for power. The outcome of the struggle will not be determined by which side is ethically "right" or "wrong," but rather by the respective sides' practical effectiveness in guarding and promoting their material interests. Given that this is so, what is or is not "ethical" might seem utterly beside the point, in which case, Marxism would be of a piece with a kind of radically subjective nihilism; it would be the proletariat's battle plan, but not anything more than that.[15] This interpretation of Marx's theory of class struggle undergirds readings of Marxism as an "amoralist" theory, one that licenses any behavior whatsoever in the name of proletarian revolution and is ultimately silent on universal questions about the good of humanity at large.

This "amoralist" reading is a misapprehension that loses sight of one of the most central and enduring lessons of Marx's work, one to which he returns again and again: transforming the world and having universally valid scientific knowledge of its objective character are linked together in praxis. Transforming the world requires some antecedent knowledge of its workings, grants further insight into its essential character, and renders increasingly thin the seeming membrane between our inner mental representations of the world and the objective world itself. Proletarian struggle's centrality to the future of humanity inheres precisely in that it has a universal character. As Marx put it in an early work, the proletariat is

> a sphere which has a universal character by its universal suffering and claims no *particular right* because no *particular wrong*, but *wrong generally*, is perpetuated against it ... a sphere, finally, which cannot emancipate itself without emancipating itself from all other spheres of society and thereby emancipating all other spheres of society, which, in a word, is the *complete loss* of man and hence can win itself only through the *complete re-winning of man*.[16]

Marx takes himself to have developed a method capable of uniting into a single pursuit all forms of human inquiry about the natural and social world. As he and Engels wrote, "We know only a single science, the science of history."[17] Demonstrating their theory's capacity to account for the apparent ethical aspects of human social being is a crucial test of that claim. And while Marx and Engels denied that strictly moral appeals were themselves of any great use in transforming the world for the better, to understand how such matters as the relationship between freedom and determinism, the concept of human nature, and the idea of human flourishing all figure into Marxist theory is indispensable in developing and applying the materialist conception of history as a theory of social change.

Analytical Marxism and Dialectical Method

Over the last several decades, there have been numerous initiatives to "recontextualize," "resituate," "reevaluate," and "rethink" Marx, some of them, of course, quite salutary. But I greatly suspect there is value yet to be found in "*thinking Marx*," a principle I apply throughout the current study.[18] To that end, I take seriously Marx's claim to have developed a worthwhile and novel theoretical method, that of historical materialism. So while, as I say, the project here is one of critical reconstruction, I proceed from the working assumption that Marx had something sensible and illuminating to offer us.

An assumption fatal to many attempts to make sense of Marx, or to evaluate Marxist arguments and theorizations today, is the comfortable certainty that we already know what he said. But Anglophone philosophers, especially those working in the analytical tradition, are in many ways hamstrung in our reception of Marx's ideas. One of the reasons for this has to do with the circumstances of analytical philosophy's very inception as a repudiation of British Idealism.[19] To understand Marx's theoretical commitments, one must be willing to entertain certain Hegelian precepts, such as: the notion that all existing things are united as parts of a single, internally differentiated totality; the claim that an object can develop in a manner which comes to annihilate its present form and convert it into its opposite, and that this process is always already unfolding so that any object that is, also is what it is not; and the view that things have essential natures which only come to be knowable in the course of their dynamic historical development over time.

Analytical philosophers' understanding of Marx is deeply shaped by, among other factors, the field's legacy of hostility to Hegelian dialectics and to that theory's insistence that the world is knowable in and through contradictory aspects of existence: contradictions that cannot be reconciled in thought, unless also reconciled in history. This is to say: dialectics sees contradiction not primarily as a sure sign of confused or unclear *concepts* which must be rendered conceptually unambiguous so as to describe a static, "clear and distinct" reality. Rather, dialectics regards contradiction as a real, ontological, and objective feature of the complex, dynamic, internally conflictual, and ambiguous world, itself. The task of philosophers, then, is to develop concepts that capture this real, dialectical restlessness.

When analytical philosophers have treated the subject of Marx and ethics, they have tended to put the question in stark, undialectical terms: "Did Marx have an ethical theory or did he not?" The answer? Marx had an analysis of how human beings are essentially beings that produce themselves and their own conditions of existence, and he had a critique of class society's incapacity to permit human beings to live in full accordance with this essential nature, so that they might finally be what they are. This is, on the one hand, of a kind with virtue theoretical ethical critique in the mode of Aristotle's *Nicomachean Ethics*. On the other hand, Marx constantly downplays the prescriptive aspect of his critique and presents it as a fundamentally descriptive project; only, the object under description is itself inherently and irreducibly normative, since human striving and progress toward greater human development (even if only in fits and starts and with frequent reversals) is already part of Being.

Analytical philosophers frequently dismiss this kind of answer as mysticism. The most well-known and influential form of this dismissal comes from the Analytical Marxist school of the 1970s and 1980s. These figures, such as G. A. Cohen, Jon Elster, John Roemer, and Erik Olin Wright, also occasionally described themselves as engaged in "No Bullshit" Marxism—this to signal the degree of respect they felt dialectics ought to be accorded. Denying that Marx's theoretical method was of any value, they sought instead to place (what they took to be) his conclusions upon (what they also took to be) the firmer methodological foundations of analytical philosophy.

The Analytical Marxists denied the two central pillars of Marx's method: dialectics and methodological holism. The emphasis instead on sentential truth also had a rather striking interpretive implication: it is common among Analytical Marxists to pluck individual sentences from

Marx's corpus and submit them to conceptual analysis of what they *could* most "reasonably" mean, taken on their own and polished clean of dialectic.

I will allow the reader to draw their own conclusions as to whether this form of Analytical Marxism was in fact a species of Marxism, at all; there is a robust debate about this question.[20] What's clear, however, is that if we want to know whether the materialist conception of history *as Marx understood it* has an ethical content, then familiarity with the Analytical Marxist academic movement is not going to cut it. We need to go back, find what Marx had to say, and try to understand him on his own terms.

Most of the leading practitioners of Analytical Marxism eventually abandoned the movement, declaring Marxist theory unsalvageable not only in its precepts but perhaps also in its conclusions. Yet as James Furner writes in his 2018 book *Marx on Capitalism*, "Analytical Marxism has long ceased to be a live movement, of course. But it is one thing for Analytical Marxism to cease as a live movement, and another for its influence on how Marx is read or viewed to die out."

In a January 2021 plenary speech delivered to the Eastern Division meeting of the American Philosophical Association, Tommie Shelby identified himself as an Analytical Marxist, making him likely the best-known living philosopher to continue to wear the mantle. However, Shelby's variant of Analytical Marxism differs in that it emphasizes more of what is useful in analytical philosophical method than it does what is purportedly useless in Marxism. In defending the "analytical" aspect of this orientation, Shelby cites such virtues of analytical method as "the high value it places on conceptual clarity, logical rigor, and detailed argumentation" and "its reliance on careful scientific studies for its empirical premises."[21]

I am in agreement with Shelby that these are vitally important conventions of analytical philosophy. I seek to help show, however, that to embrace Marxist method is not to abandon the best of what philosophy offers our attempts to cognize the world. Marx's critique of Enlightenment reason is not a wholesale rejection of objectivity, universality, and reason, as such, and is to be clearly distinguished from those critiques that are. Marx saw himself as *both* preserving what was truly rational and scientific in the best bourgeois thought of the age *and* demonstrating how it fell short of its pretensions to objectivity and universality; this failure, Marx thought could be corrected by attending more closely to the conflict, dynamism, and restlessness of existing, concrete reality and by seeking to represent that dynamism in thought and in ways that nondialectical approaches cannot do. To the extent that the methods of analytical philosophers still instantiate some of the highest intellectual virtues of Enlightenment reason, these are not rejected, but rather already incorporated, subsumed, and surpassed in Marx's materialist conception of history.

Précis of a Marxist Ethics

Marx's and Engels's "materialist conception of history" stands in a centuries-long tradition of philosophical engagement with the question "What makes scientific knowledge of the world possible, if it is possible?" What necessary connection, if any, exists between our ideas of the world and the world "itself," making our ideas count as ideas that are about the world as such? In the second of his 1845 "Theses on Feuerbach," Marx wrote,

> The question whether objective truth can be attributed to human thinking is not a question of theory but is a practical question. Man must prove the truth, i.e. the reality and power, the this-worldliness of his thinking in practice. The dispute over the reality or non-reality of thinking that is isolated from practice is a purely scholastic question.[22]

Normative, ethical matters are knowable and objective in just the same way that any other aspect of existence is knowable for Marx—they are revealed in the course of our practical engagements with the world. They are not timeless, abstract, ahistorically given truths, but rather are historically emergent products of human social existence as it has developed in time. In developing a kind of self-knowledge at the level of the species, we discover an inner movement and aim, one which we may then take up consciously as our own and strive to realize. In this sense, a human *ought* is derived precisely from what humans are, have been, and might become. As Marx and Engels wrote in one of the manuscripts later posthumously published as part of *The Critique of the German Ideology*,

> Communism is for us not a *state of affairs* which is to be established, an *ideal* to which reality [will] have to adjust itself. We call communism the *real* movement which abolishes the present state of things. The conditions of this movement result from the premises now in existence.[23]

The ethical aims of communism are not deduced through passive, abstract contemplation, but rather are drawn as conclusions from the already existing human aims that are posited in practice through activities ranging from securing subsistence to engaging in social movement activism and revolutionary struggle. In this sense, Marx's ethical vision of communism is based on an understanding of the conditions that would have to be brought about in order to promote aims of survival and self-realization that are already inherent in the movement of human history. The conditions that working class struggles seek to overthrow are precisely those which threaten all human existence on the planet, making their victory necessary not only for the interests of their class but for the future of humanity itself.

Friedrich Engels observed in his 1878 work *Anti-Dühring* that "universal emancipation is the historical mission of the modern proletariat." He went on,

> To thoroughly comprehend the historical conditions and thus the very nature of this act, to impart to the now oppressed proletarian class a full knowledge of the conditions and of the meaning of the momentous act it is called upon to accomplish, this is the task of the theoretical expression of the proletarian movement, scientific socialism.[24]

With this invocation of "scientific socialism," a phrase albeit borrowed from the French socialist, Pierre-Joseph Proudhon, Engels cemented the term's synonymity with the materialist conception of history—that is to say, with Marxism. Depending on whom you ask, Marxist theory's claim to scientificity is its chief virtue or a hubristic and "ideological" boast. When we say of a claim, theory, method, or perspective that it is "scientific," among many things we typically mean is that it is in some deep sense, objective, universal, and truth-tracking. What could justify Marxism—a theory that announces itself openly as one that represents the world from the interested perspective of just one subset of human beings, the working class—in laying claim to scientificity?

That Marxism is a "scientific" sort of socialism seems most immediately plausible in the case of its observations and predictions regarding economic matters. In the roughly one and three-quarters of a century since Marx and Engels wrote that "the history of all hitherto existing society is the history of class struggles," perhaps countless events have occurred to confirm the working assumption that in class societies, the course of human events is largely determined by conflicts between those who control the circumstances under which productive activity occurs and those who carry it out.

That Marxism is "scientific" strikes many as less plausible, however, with respect to its apparent normative commitments. One might think, with Louis Althusser, that Marx eschewed humanistic moral reasoning in roughly equal proportion as his engagement with economics and the critique of political economy deepened over the course of his later works.[25] Or one might argue, with Allen Wood, that to the extent Marx held onto moral commitments throughout his life, these were in tension and incompatible with an economic determinism to which he was committed.[26] More broadly, and especially in the Anglophone philosophical tradition, it is accepted as obvious that morality is not the sort of thing that lies within the purview of science at all, since science is a study of what *is* and morality pertains to what *ought to be*.

A Marxist worldview is at once ethical and scientific. It is simultaneously a view of the world from the interested perspective of the oppressed and exploited laboring masses *and* an objective and universally valid account of human existence. A key part of what has complicated many attempts properly to describe the normative character of Marxist theory is a set of assumptions regarding the limits of what is scientifically knowable—assumptions Marx did not share. Marx did regard some questions as in some sense "unaskable," or at least, as ones that could not be posed without courting a kind of rational incoherence. Yet it is hardly incidental that Marx took up as his motto the words of the ancient Greek playwright, Terence, who in his 163 BC play *Heauton Timorumenos* wrote, "*humani nihil a me alienum puto*" (or, "nothing human is alien to me"). Human existence is itself a thoroughly human product. For this reason it is knowable through, and subject to intervention by, the operation of human productive activity. It is in and through our human attempts to transform the world that we come to know the world and our place in it.

The bourgeoisie, in advancing its own aims as a class and remaking the world in its image, made previously unimaginable strides in advancing science, greatly expanding humanity's productive powers and transforming human understanding of our place in the world. Philosophical concepts of liberty, reason, equality, and individual right—themselves still mystifying and incomplete—were nonetheless ideological advances over doctrines such as the divine right of kings. But these at least ostensibly liberal concepts, and the social contractarian philosophies of which they are elements, betray the contradictions of bourgeois rule. The same capitalist ideologies employed to justify the capitalists' overthrow of feudalism also in turn serve white supremacy, patriarchy, imperialism, oppression, and exploitation; they function as tools of liberation but just as often, of domination. (These contradictions of bourgeois liberalism have been well discussed by authors including Jean Bricmont, Charles Mills, and Carole Pateman, among others.)[27]

As much as capitalist rule courts irrationalism in order to evade critique, ultimately it cannot dispense entirely with science.[28] For the working class, objective knowledge of the world is only more crucial. Whereas the capitalist class relies on mystification to conceal the nature of its rule, the proletariat as a class has no incentive to shrink away from the hard truths facing all of humanity as a species. Climate change is not imminent and still less it is illusory; it is here and it may well wipe us out. Imperialist war does not bring freedom or dignity to people on the planet—it degrades and destroys them. Increasingly, capitalism cannot even maintain the pretense of holding solutions to humanity's crises; it counsels that we acquiesce instead to their permanence.[29] In the mid-twentieth century, Margaret Thatcher advised that there was no alternative to capitalism and neoliberalism. More recently, we have been counseled to sacrifice our very lives for the economy.[30]

The working class contains the vast majority of human beings on the planet. In their struggle for greater freedom, power, and autonomy—for the conditions of fulfilling life—they battle for recognition that the world around them is one they have made through their laboring and that they can make anew. To reason about what the life of our species ought to be, about what we ought to do, and about how we ought to treat one another is ethical reasoning. It is necessary in order to imagine a world beyond the one we now know. And so against the capitalist insistence that there is no alternative, a working-class perspective reveals that another world is possible. But Marxist theory offers no creed of self-abnegation. That, it leaves to the bourgeois ideologues preaching "Patience."

Given the holistic character of Marxist theory, the attempt to articulate a Marxist ethical perspective brings us into conversation with other longstanding debates in Marx scholarship. Among these are the implications of Marxist ideology critique for ethical thought. Articulating a Marxist ethics and a Marxist critique of prevailing moral theories allows us to diagnose the hypocrisy of moralistic criticisms of Marxism. It allows us to better make sense of numerous complex themes in Marx's thought such as the relationship between freedom and determinism, the notion that the ruling ideas in a society are the ideas of its ruling class, and the Aristotelian view in Marx that human beings have a nature which determines their proper aims. It additionally sheds light on the role of ethics in our social discourse and poses distinct challenges for ethical theories that focus first and foremost on moral dictates addressed to individuals, which Marxist theory does not do. It has implications for individuals, but its primary addressee is the working class as a whole.

Marx did not simply dismiss capitalist morality and leave things at that. He returned to the subject of morality again and again, all throughout his career. If we neglect the project of articulating a specifically Marxist approach to ethics, we unnecessarily restrict our ability to make sense of that—of what Marx said at great length about morality and of why he found it so necessary to say.

The Structure of the Argument

The remainder of this book is organized around seven major themes in Marx's treatment of ethics. The progression of these themes is designed in such a way that their effect is cumulative, each building on the ones before it so that we gradually acquire an understanding of Marx's incredibly detailed philosophical system. I begin in Chapter 2, "Ideology Critique and the Critique of Morality," by considering the question of whether morality is a form of "ideology" and discuss what this would mean for Marxism as a form of "ideology critique" that reveals the often misleading and illusory characteristics of ideology. I argue there for a reading of Marx's "ideology" concept befitting morality as an ideal phenomenon that persists in class society but that would be "abolished" together with the abolition of capitalism. In this chapter, I address challenges from authors including Louis Althusser and Charles Mills who present differing and divergent accounts of "ideology" in Marx.

I then go on in Chapter 3 to explain Marx's method, what he and Engels called, "the materialist conception of history" and which is commonly referred to as "historical materialism." I argue that it is necessary to distinguish Marx's historical materialism from any "one-sided" or epiphenomenalist account of the relationship between matter and ideas. The materialist conception of history is one that regards humans' productive activity as central and fundamental in determining their form of life. I describe what Marx and Engels take their historical materialist method to reveal about the nature of human beings, and how their nature provides the basis for a normativity that emerges out of humans' social activity as they produce in order to satisfy an ever-expanding array of needs, both those based on subsistence and those which are socially produced.

Having an account in view of Marx's conception of human nature then situates us to investigate what it means, on Marx's theory, for human beings to be alienated from that nature. This is the subject of Chapter 4, along with the historiographical question, posed by influential French Marxist, Louis Althusser, of whether Marx eventually abandons his concepts of human nature and of alienation in his pursuit of a more "scientific" approach to understanding human history.

I introduce the concept of "dialectical compatibilism" in Chapter 5, to describe Marx's account of freedom and determinism as two mutually conditioning aspects of a single, historically developing unity. This dialectically compatible unity of freedom and determinism develops in a manner shaped and driven by humans' attempts to intervene into our natural and social existence. This account frees my interpretation of Marx from the trap set by a rigid opposition of freedom and determinism in human history. In keeping with the principle that all of human existence is a human product, human freedom is to be understood as a historically emergent product of human activity aimed at satisfying our needs.

In Chapters 6, 7, and 8, we delve more deeply into Marx's disagreements with various extant moral theories and principles. In Chapter 6, I take up the concept of "individuality" (which comes up also in Chapter 3's discussion of "human nature") and demonstrate the centrality of that concept for unpacking the ethical content of Marxist theory. Individuality is itself, like freedom, a human product, one that emerges as the outcome of humans' expanding range of capacities, powers, and ways of being. This is in contrast to what Marx calls "bourgeois" individuality—individuality as an abstraction of mutually hostile competitors. It is also here in Chapter 6 that we engage in a detailed discussion of Marx's engagement with Max Stirner's ethical egoism. I argue that since the overwhelming majority of what was posthumously published as Marx's and Engels's *Critique of the German Ideology* is dedicated to a refutation of ethical egoism, that collection ought to be thought of as containing an exhaustive work of moral philosophy with numerous insights for understanding Marx's relationship to ethics.

We come to Marx's critique of "bourgeois" freedom and "bourgeois" equal right in Chapter 7. Here, we find a striking example of ideology critique and the application of dialectics, as Marx analyzes these concepts and their deployment, showing that in practice, bourgeois freedom and right are the very opposite of what they seem to be in theory. In this chapter, we also extend our discussion of freedom from Chapter 5 and introduce the notion of transitional rights which early revolutionary societies would guarantee but that would lose their meaning in a communist society in which the flourishing of each is, and is understood to be, the necessary condition of the flourishing of all.

Chapter 8 treats Marx's critiques of a range of moral perspectives including Christian ethics, Kantianism, Utilitarianism, and, briefly, Malthusianism. Rather than simply dismissing these theories as counter to the class interests of the proletariat, Marx offers nuanced, detailed, and illuminating critiques of a range of moral views. This enriches our understanding of these theories and grants us deeper insight into Marx's own philosophical theory and method. I place special emphasis on exploring the relationship between Marxism and Kantianism, as these two theories are most closely related in terms of a shared philosophical tradition and the question of whether they might be brought together into a Marx-Kant synthesis has been raised again and again in the history of Marx interpretation.

While my aim throughout this book is to argue that there is a coherent ethical content in Marxist theory, I nonetheless also argue that Marx understands ethics as a transitory historical phenomenon. The conditions for its abolition have not yet obtained, but in a fully developed communist society, they would. In Chapter 9, I present various interpretations of what it could mean to say that morality would be "abolished." Drawing on the tradition of virtue ethics, I offer an account of what it would be to exist and to socially interact in such a society.

Chapter 10 is the book's conclusion. There, I draw together the book's major themes and make a final case for assessing human social existence as first and foremost, itself a human product. Beyond the conclusion, readers will find a Coda to this book. There, drawing on the historical example of Angela Davis in 1969, I offer brief reflections on the past, present, and future of radical scholarship in the academy.

2
Ideology Critique and the Critique of Morality

Among Marxist theory's most important influences upon the academy has been the critique of ideology, which is essential to such fields as Cultural Studies, Critical Theory, Critical Legal Studies, and Critical Race Theory, among others. The core of Marxist ideology critique is to acknowledge the material and sociohistorical determinants of our forms of consciousness and especially to identify how the exercise of power determines which ideas become widely held. In identifying the sources of our theoretical (or, more often, *pretheoretical*) ideas, we gain greater insight into their content and into the role they often play in justifying our social, economic, and political status quo. Ideology critique permits us to demonstrate how it is that a given concept might seem transparent and simple at first blush; but when we examine how the object corresponding to that concept exists and unfolds in history, we may realize that in practice, it is the very opposite of what it announces itself to be in theory. (This is a theme to which we shall return in Chapter 5, on freedom and determinism, and in Chapter 7, on freedom and rights.)

There has been significant debate regarding whether the centrality of ideology critique in Marx's theory entails his wholesale rejection of any form of consciousness that could reasonably be described as "ideological." This question of whether or not Marx eschews ideology altogether is of the utmost importance to a study of Marx's moral thought. If Marx regards all ideology as inherently and uniformly reactionary, then his theory can hardly be supposed to support the view that morality, which is a species of ideology, can have a revolutionary content in some cases.

I argue that to say, as Marx does, that moral commands are a form of "ideology" is not by itself to reject all moral reasoning out of hand. It is however to insist, as Marx writes in *The German Ideology*, that "Consciousness can never be anything else than conscious being, and the being of men is their actual life-process," and that like other forms of thought, it has "no history, no development; but men, developing their material production and their material intercourse, alter, along with this their real existence, their thinking and the products of their thinking."[1] For this reason, to evaluate and understand the content of moral theorizing cannot be solely the purview of abstract contemplation; we must understand the emergence and application of these theories within their historical, economic, and sociopolitical context.

Over the course of the present chapter, I first present a positive account of how "ideology" is best understood on Marx's view. Hesitation to take the Marxist concept of "ideology" seriously often stems from concern that to do so will lead to a "doctrinaire" or "dogmatic" and rigid opposition of uniformly false, mystifying, and illusory bourgeois consciousness on the one hand, to Marxist theory on the other. But not only does this not square with Marx's often glowing assessments of the historical role of bourgeois theory, but the concern itself reveals the degree to which mainstream approaches to Marxist theory tend to present it in caricature. Marx advocated "the ruthless criticism of all that exists," not mindless arson. Therefore, we need an "ideology" concept that allows us to make sense both of Marx's critique of what is illusory and mystifying in bourgeois thought and of what Marx felt ought to be preserved in a more highly developed form.

I then go on to describe three competing analyses of Marx's "ideology" concept: Louis Althusser's, Nicholas Abercrombie's and Bryan S. Turner's, and Charles Mills's. Althusser's is the most well-known of the three and easily the most influential, arguing that ideology is "thought devoid of history." I argue that whatever the merit of such a concept, it cannot be Marx's. Abercrombie's and Turner's is the least well known of the three; I address it here because it lays out, in an illuminating way, a common misconception about the nexus of ideology, class interest, and class consciousness.

Charles Mills's analysis of Marx's "ideology" concept underwent key changes over the course of his writings on the subject. Initially, he takes ideology to be theory that mystifies its own origins and efficacy; later, he takes it to be a synonym, in Marx's work, for "superstructure." Although a staunch critic of Marxism, for several decades, Mills remained one of the most prominent Anglophone political philosophers consistently to engage with Marxist ideas, making his analysis relevant for us here. This is especially so, given the role of a form of ideology critique in animating the argument of one of his most well-known works, his 1997, *The Racial Contract*.

I conclude this chapter with a discussion of Marx's critique of moral suasion and of what he took to be the voluntaristic moralism of "utopian" socialism. Understanding Marx's critiques of utopianism sheds light on what he took to be the limits of moral injunction and how these limitations follow from central precepts in his historical materialist critique of ideology in general.

"Ideology" is Not a Wholly Pejorative Concept

In the current section, I will focus on two arguments in *defense* of ideology or at least, in defense of certain aspects thereof. These are both arguments that Marx himself makes, but which have received little attention in treatments of this subject. The first argument, appearing in the *Manifesto*, is that ideology has a potentially revolutionary character and can assist even its bourgeois practitioners in seeing the need to switch their allegiances to the working class. The second argument hangs closely together with the explanation of Marx's historical materialist method. Because ideology is the form in which human beings become conscious of "the existing conflict between the social productive forces and the relations of production" and "fight it out," it would be wrongheaded to advocate purely "nonideological" modes of thought in a class society.[2]

Before addressing either of these arguments directly, however, I will first address three interrelated questions. These are: What is bourgeois ideology? What is proletarian ideology? What is the relation between them?

Put briefly, bourgeois ideology is the view of nature and society from the class standpoint of the bourgeoisie. Its specific perspectives on the desirability of existing economic relations, the mutability or lack thereof of human characteristics and personality traits, and the best explanations of change and development in nature, to name just a few of countless possible questions for human beings, are shaped and determined in different ways by the bourgeoisie's conception of itself and of bourgeois society as the highest possible form of human social development. This is not to say that it is impossible to see from within a bourgeois standpoint that there may well be significant room for improvement on existing conditions. However, bourgeois ideology, and the class standpoint within which it is produced, are distinguished by a conviction that any further human progress can be achieved only through the leadership of the bourgeois class and its institutions, and upon the economic basis of capitalist exchange.

As Marx writes in 1859, it is human beings' "social existence that determines their consciousness."[3] The economic interests of the capitalist class, together with its actual dominance in existing class society, lead its members to confuse wittingly or unwittingly the conditions necessary for the promotion of their class's interests with the conditions necessary for the advancement of humanity as a whole. As Georg Lukács writes of bourgeois thought in *History and Class Consciousness,*

> The veil drawn over the nature of bourgeois society is indispensable to the bourgeoisie itself. For the insoluble internal contradictions of the system become revealed with increasing starkness and so confront its supporters with a choice. Either they must consciously ignore insights which become increasingly urgent or else they must suppress their own moral instincts in order to be able to support with a good conscience an economic system that serves only their own interests.[4]

This tendency can be overcome with a complete change of class allegiance, in which an individual bourgeois or bourgeois ideologist comes to identify with the interests of the working class and attempts to theorize from within the proletariat standpoint. Such an achievement can at times take place when there is a great preponderance of evidence telling against significant elements of bourgeois ideology together with a personal commitment on the part of the individual to reflect reality in their thinking as faithfully and as clearly as possible.

It is important, when speaking of what Marx refers to as bourgeois ideology, to recognize its limits but also to appreciate the huge scope of possible expression within those limits. There is a diversity of opinion across the contemporary political spectrum of bourgeois thought, and, as it is also important to note, elements of bourgeois ideology can take on a different character at different points in history. Thinkers as diverse as John Locke, Maximilien Robespierre, Irving Kristol, and Kofi Annan each develop and promote bourgeois ideology, albeit in drastically different forms and with fundamental disagreements on key questions. And even a central tenet of that ideology, such as that the bourgeoisie represents the interests of humanity and is its rightful leader, was revolutionary and progressive in the eighteenth century and now deeply conservative, today.

A key feature of bourgeois ideology and of the bourgeois mode of production at its inception, as opposed to the feudal society that it opposed and replaced, was that it gave pride of place to science and to materialism. Rationality, materialism, and a scientific worldview free from the backwardness and superstition of feudalism facilitated the major advances in production that laid the basis for the rise of the bourgeois class. Huge advancements have been made in human beings' theoretical understanding of the world and in their capacity to master it and subordinate it to their ends, all within an ideology that takes capitalist class society to be the highest form of human social organization. As Marx and Engels write in *The Communist Manifesto*, "Whereas past industrial classes depended on maintaining production unchanged, the bourgeoisie must constantly revolutionize production and therewith, society."[5] And it is capitalism and the need of the bourgeoisie to constantly change and revolutionize society which have in turn produced a need for higher levels of human consciousness, making it possible for human beings to have a more accurate and scientific knowledge of their social existence than was possible in previous class societies. In Marx's words, the bourgeoisie has removed the "sentimental halo" from relations of exploitation and "man is at last compelled to face with sober senses, his real conditions of life, and his relations with his kind."[6]

However, although that interest in science remains an important part of bourgeois thought today, it exists often in a narrow or distorted form, and frequently takes a backseat to this class's historical need to compromise with feudal and religious forces and/or to defend itself against working-class challenges to its rule.[7] Whereas criticism of religion was once a defining aspect of bourgeois ideology, religious mysticism now finds itself quite at home within it.[8] The Enlightenment ideal which held up science as a form of thought and practice in which the deepest and most fundamental questions could be answered through the work and intelligence of human beings, has given way to a conception of science as merely the art of manipulation, often divorced from a deeper inquiry into the nature of reality.

Bourgeois ideology is by no means a form of consciousness that exists only among members of the bourgeoisie or among its ideologists. As Marx wrote in *The Communist Manifesto*, "The ruling ideas of each age have ever been the ideas of its ruling class," and not only does the ruling class hold these ideas, but throughout the history of a class society, it is usually the case that *most* of its members also hold those ideas.[9] These ideas are developed and promulgated by the ruling class in large part because they bolster the reign of that class, and the ruling class has the best infrastructure at its disposal to disseminate those ideas. But this alone is not enough to ensure broad assent. In a capitalist society, bourgeois consciousness finds widespread acceptance in large part because it actually does reflect and explain, if only in a distorted and limited manner, the world in which members of that society find themselves. As Marx writes in *On the Poverty of Philosophy*:

> Social relations are just as much produced by men as linen, flax, etc. Social relations are closely bound up with productive forces. . . . The same men who establish their social relations in conformity with the material productivity, produce also principles, ideas, and categories, in conformity with their social relations.[10]

To find "proof" that a woman's labor is less valuable than a man's, one need look no further than the fact that women earn roughly eighty cents on the dollar when compared with men. The "evidence" that Blacks are inherently dangerous and must be controlled can be found in the high proportion of them who are ensnared in the criminal justice system. Much about the real social relations in which human beings stand to one another under capitalism seems to confirm the "ruling ideas" of that society, which in turn provide an ideological bulwark for the maintenance of those social relations. It is with this in mind that, in *The Communist Manifesto*, Marx replies to the charges of an imagined bourgeois interlocutor:

> But don't wrangle with us so long as you apply, to our intended abolition of bourgeois property, the standard of your bourgeois notions of freedom, culture, law, &c. Your very ideas are but the outgrowth of the conditions of your bourgeois production and bourgeois property, just as your jurisprudence is but the will of your class made into a law for all, a will whose essential character and direction are determined by the economical conditions of existence of your class.[11]

However, within capitalist society, not all ideology is bourgeois ideology. Within class societies there exist not only the ideas of the ruling class, but also the ideas of the class that is ruled, but in the process of coming to power. In the struggle between bourgeoisie and proletariat, the ideas of the proletariat are capable of bringing the blurry view of the world through bourgeois ideology into sharp focus, revealing what appeared to be the essential and eternal social relations of capitalist society as rather historical, transient, and susceptible to abolition through the active intervention of the masses and the production of new economic relations. As Marx writes in *On the Poverty of Philosophy*:

> The same men who establish their social relations in conformity with the material productivity, produce also principles, ideas, and categories, in conformity with their social relations. Thus the ideas, these categories, are as little eternal as the relations they express. They are *historical and transitory products.*
>
> There is a continual movement of growth in productive forces, of destruction in social relations, of formation in ideas; the only immutable thing is the abstraction of movement—*mors immortalis.*[12]

Insofar as there is a substantial amount of thought within bourgeois ideology that is useful and accurate in reflecting reality, proletarian ideology does not totally discard it and it would be mistaken to label the whole of bourgeois ideology throughout its history as worthless. The working class is itself a part of bourgeois society and seeks to transform its relations of production, building socialism upon a material basis formed by the forces of production developed under capitalism. Similarly, proletarian ideology is in part the attempt to identify and preserve what is best in bourgeois thought. Proletarian ideology seeks to transform intellectual production so that further progress can be made in developing a theoretical understanding that both provides the most accurate possible reflection of reality and the ideal tools necessary for human beings to transform nature in accordance with their needs. The transition from bourgeois to proletarian ideology is succinctly described by Marx when he writes:

> When people speak of the ideas that revolutionise society, they do but express that fact that within the old society the elements of a new one have been created, and that the dissolution of the old ideas keeps even pace with the dissolution of the old conditions of existence.[13]

We can come now to the first of two principal arguments I will advance in this section against understanding all ideology as inherently reactionary: the argument that ideology, as an attempt to grapple with the conflicts between the relations of production and the forces of production, can play a progressive role in revealing to its practitioners the need for a society led by the working class in the interests of humanity.

Marx's views with regard to the potentially progressive role of ideology are clearly expressed in his remarks on the phenomenon of bourgeois ideologists who shed their class allegiance to the bourgeoisie and join the proletariat in its struggle. For Marx, the reality of the historical situation under capitalism is most clearly appreciated from the point of view of the proletariat, but is by no means accessible only to actual proletarians. It is possible in principle for any person to adopt this standpoint and to identify with the aims of the working class. In these cases, members of other classes, for instance, of the bourgeoisie or petty bourgeoisie, recognize that the proletariat is the force in society capable of advancing the interests of humanity as a whole. Marx and Engels describe this process in the *Manifesto*:

> Finally, in times when the class struggle nears the decisive hour, the progress of dissolution going on within the ruling class, in fact within the whole range of old society, assumes such a violent, glaring character, that a small section of the ruling class cuts itself adrift, and joins the revolutionary class, the class that holds the future in its hands. Just as, therefore, at an earlier period, a section of the nobility went over to the bourgeoisie, so now a portion of the bourgeoisie goes over to the proletariat, and in particular, a portion of the bourgeois ideologists, who have raised themselves to the level of comprehending theoretically the historical movement as a whole.[14]

As I mentioned earlier in the present section, at least two factors come into place in cases where members of the bourgeoisie join the proletariat: (1) a preponderance of evidence emerges which throws fundamental tenets of bourgeois ideology into question; and (2) a commitment on the part of the individual person to the pursuit of truth and, we can add, to the continued existence and development of humanity. Here, both of these factors figure prominently in Marx's description of how members of a ruling class may go over to the side of a revolutionary class, and of how such defections took place in the conflict between feudal nobility and the bourgeoisie, and now take place in the conflict between the bourgeoisie and the proletariat. In a time of crisis, bourgeois ideology, and its commitment to the necessary and desirable permanence of capitalist society and of the bourgeoisie's leadership of humanity, becomes increasingly difficult to maintain alongside a commitment to understanding reality. As the contradictions within capitalist society become more "violent" and "glaring," it becomes easier to see that a continued existence and development for human beings will require a fundamentally different type of society in which these glaring contradictions have been resolved.

In this passage then, far from denigrating ideology or assigning it a purely reactionary role, Marx expresses the progressive potential of ideology. It should be stressed, however, that it is a limited potential—only a "small section of the ruling class" will see the need to support the struggle of the revolutionary class. But Marx emphasizes that in the case of bourgeois ideologists who side with the working class, it is precisely their ideological accomplishments that allow them to see clearly that the proletariat is "the class that holds the future in its hands."

Were it the case that on Marx's view ideology is always false consciousness and always obscures reality, it would be impossible to make good sense of Marx's statement that "in particular, a portion of the bourgeois ideologists" become radicalized in great part through their own theoretical work and ability to capture and reflect a historical moment in which the victory of the proletariat is required in order for human progress to continue. Additionally, Marx also writes that as members of the bourgeoisie switch allegiances and join the working class, this provides the proletariat "with fresh elements of enlightenment and progress."[15] This underscores the point that not all bourgeois thought is inherently reactionary; rather, what is valuable and progressive in it can be incorporated and further developed in proletarian ideology, and in a socialist society, in a way that is no longer possible in a society based on capitalist relations of production.[16]

This brings us now to the second argument in defense of ideology: because ideology is the form in which human beings become conscious of "the existing conflict between the social productive forces and the relations of production" and "fight it out," it is simply wrongheaded to expect there to be an abolition of ideological modes of thought in a class society, and Marx does not make this mistake.[17]

Famously, Marx envisions a future society in which ideological forms such as morality and religion would be abolished. Communism is the theory of the existing elements within capitalist society that aim to produce a new society based on democratic control of society's resources, the satisfaction of human needs, and the development of human powers. But the society aimed at in Communism is not merely a new form of class society with the proletariat as the ruling class: rather it is the abolition of class society altogether and with it, class domination and class struggle. Communism does not propose for this new society a new moral, political, or legal order because these forms of thought have their basis and their application in class society, where they express the class struggle and function as ideological weapons with which to wage it. For Marx, ideological forms of thought would indeed cease to exist in a fully developed communist society. However, this does not mean that Marx thinks it is either possible or desirable to think "nonideologically" in the present instance.

At the moment, we still live in class society and the working class must wage its struggle within it. Marx does not argue that moral theory, philosophy, political science, and so on are already impotent and outdated. Nothing could be further from the truth, as he himself engages in exactly these forms of thought. Moreover, because a transitional socialist society would also be a class society, there, too, the working class would use ideology to theorize its historical situation and assert its leadership in society.[18]

As Marx asks (rhetorically):

> Does it require deep intuition to comprehend that man's ideas, views, and conception, in one word, man's consciousness, changes with every change in the conditions of his material existence, in his social relations and in his social life? What else does the history of ideas prove, than that intellectual production changes its character in proportion as material production is changed?[19]

Proletarian consciousness and socialist consciousness will therefore differ greatly in content from bourgeois consciousness. Yet they will share in common with bourgeois consciousness the fact that they are distinctively ideological, because they occur in class societies and reflect an ongoing class struggle.

Now that I have provided the two principal arguments against conceiving of ideology as inherently reactionary, I would like to say a bit more about Marx's view that consciousness in a fully developed communist society *would* be nonideological, and in particular about his rejection of the idea that there are any eternal moral truths. Marx imagines an interlocutor's retort to these views:

> "Undoubtedly," it will be said, "religious, moral, philosophical, and juridical ideas have been modified in the course of historical development. But religion, morality, philosophy, political science, and law, constantly survived this change. There are, besides, eternal truths, such as Freedom, Justice, etc., that are common to all states of society. But Communism abolishes eternal truths, it abolishes all religion, and all morality, instead of constituting

them on a new basis; it therefore acts in contradiction to all past historical experience."[20]

This charge provides Marx with an opportunity to counterpose his own historicized understanding of morality, et al., to the idea that such forms of thought are ahistorical, eternal, and unchanging. That certain moral concepts have been common among various historical epochs need not entail that the concepts are valid independently of the historical circumstances from which they are drawn or to which they are applied. Marx points out that the "states of society" mentioned by his interlocutor have all been marked by the existence of classes and of class conflict. It is this class conflict which has made these forms of thought valid as reflections of reality or as intellectual tools with which to understand and/or transform it. Marx replies,

> What does this accusation reduce itself to? The history of all past society has consisted in the development of class antagonisms, antagonisms that assumed different forms at different epochs. But whatever form they may have taken, one fact is common to all past ages, *viz.*, the exploitation of one part of society by the other. No wonder, then, that the social consciousness of past ages, despite all the multiplicity and variety it displays, moves within certain common forms, or general ideas, which cannot completely vanish except with the total disappearance of class antagonisms. The Communist revolution is the most radical rupture with traditional property relations; no wonder that its development involved the most radical rupture with traditional ideas.[21]

Since social consciousness is determined by historical reality, it is entirely to be expected that societies conditioned primarily by class conflict would have certain ideas in common. But Communism is a movement which abolishes class society and seeks to produce a new society based not on class conflict but on human solidarity. "In place of the old bourgeois society, with its classes and class antagonisms," Marx writes, "we shall have an association, in which the free development of each is the condition for the free development of all."[22] Marx does not think that a future communist society would produce a new moral code since, firstly, it would already be a society based on the needs of human beings and secondly, it would be developed, as Marx argues, out of a long revolutionary process in which values such as solidarity would become realized in normal human practice through habituation and education. This does not mean that at present, in our class society, there is not genuine morality, genuine moral facts of the matter about what human beings ought to do, or the resources to make factive moral judgments about existing states of affairs. A world in which class antagonism exists is a world that still has a place for genuine morality. Not only is there a role for morality in capitalist society, but Marx also believes there will be a role for morality in a transitional socialist society, as well, even as the gap between what is and what ought to be grows smaller.

Marx attempts to expose what he sees as the hypocritical posturings of bourgeois morality. Most of all, he criticizes the tendency of bourgeois morality to justify the existing state of affairs as desirable and necessary, and also to see morality itself as fixed and unchanging. Yet Marx shows no sign of shying away from negative moral judgments of bourgeois society. These judgments are based on what I argue is the crux of Marx's condemnation of capitalism: that capitalism degrades and limits human beings, thwarts the development of their capacities, fails to satisfy their existing needs, and prevents them from producing more sophisticated modes of social interaction and metabolism with the natural world that would in turn engender in them new needs and lay the material basis for an unlimited human progress and development.

It should be noted that Marx readily accepts the interlocutor's charge that Communism seeks to abolish political science, among other ideological forms of thought. And it goes almost without saying that Marx thought it was important to carry out theoretical work in politics as an aid to revolutionary action. The subtle point lies in understanding that one of the goals of Communism as a theory and as a movement is to use political means to abolish man as a political animal and to abolish the basis for politics altogether. "In the beginning," Marx writes, "this cannot be effected except by means of despotic inroads on the rights of property."[23] However, over time, as class distinctions disappear, "the public power will lose its political character" and the proletariat will have "abolished its own supremacy as a class."[24] The desired end is a society without politics and class domination. The prescribed means are political organization and what Marx refers to as the democratic and revolutionary dictatorship of the proletariat.[25]

In much the same vein, philosophy is a necessary tool in order to bring about a world in which philosophy no longer exists as a separate, specialized enterprise divorced from human beings' everyday existence. And similarly, as long as there is a gap between how human beings ought to relate to one another and how they actually do relate to one another, there will continue to be a role for a genuine human morality and for moral theory in working out answers to the questions, "What ought we to do?" and "How ought we to live?" The need for this role to be filled can only disappear in a future Communist society based on the needs of human beings and in which human beings have interactions with one another that are based on relations of human solidarity. But at the moment, there is still plenty of need for moral theory.

Rival Analyses of Marx's "Ideology" Concept

In making sense of the influential reading of Marx provided by the mid-Twentieth Century French Communist, Louis Althusser, it is critically important to note that Althusser's own Marxian or Marx-*inspired* ideology concept is not itself meant to be a rendering of Marx's concept. In his essay "Ideology and Ideological State Apparatuses," Althusser clearly distinguishes between Marx's ideology concept and his own, writing,

> While the thesis I wish to defend formally speaking adopts the terms of *The German Ideology* ("ideology has no history"), it is radically different from the positivist and historicist thesis of *The German Ideology*.

Althusser reads Marx's "ideology" concept, at least in Marx's later writings beginning with those published as *The Critique of the German Ideology*, as having a content in line with what I have called the "pejorative" interpretation thereof. That is to say, Althusser's interpretation of Marx is heavily informed by the supposition that for Marx, ideology is more or less identical with "false consciousness." He writes,

> Ideology, then, is for Marx an imaginary assemblage (*bricolage*), a pure dream, empty and vain, constituted by the "day's residues" from the only full and positive reality, that of the concrete history of concrete material individuals materially producing their existence.[26]

Althusser goes on to claim that for Marx, "ideology has no history." Continuing the passage cited above, Althusser writes,

> It is on this basis that ideology has no history in *The German Ideology*, since its history is outside it, where the only existing history is, the history of concrete individuals, etc.

In *The German Ideology*, the thesis that ideology has no history is therefore a purely negative thesis, since it means both:
(1) ideology is nothing insofar as it is a pure dream (manufactured by who knows what power: if not by the alienation of the division of labour, but that, too, is a negative determination);
(2) ideology has no history, which emphatically does not mean that there is no history in it (on the contrary, for it is merely the pale, empty and inverted reflection of real history) but that it has no history of its *own*.[27]

But Marx never says that ideology "has no history," not even in the qualified sense of its being nothing more than an "empty and inverted reflection of real history." For Marx, the historical development of ideology is determined by the practical activity of human beings producing and reproducing their conditions of existence. Marx, as a materialist, of course does not think *any* idea of any type has a history that is in some way independent and unmoored from the material circumstances under which it is thought. But in fact, no part of Being has "a history of its own"; ideology is no worse off in this regard than a field or a herd of cattle. Althusser distorts Marx's text and mystifies the concepts of history and historicity, obscuring far more than he illuminates about Marx's own use of the concept of "ideology."[28]

Althusser further mischaracterizes Marx's historical materialist critique of ideology by insisting that for Marx, ideology is best understood as "imaginary," giving us no insight at all into the objective relations of production in a given society. Althusser writes, "all ideology represents in its necessarily imaginary distortion not the existing relations of production (and the other relations that derive from them), but above all the (imaginary) relationship of individuals to the relations of production and the relations that derive from them."[29] In other words, according to Althusser, ideology for Marx provides no evidence about the real, objective nature of things; it is necessarily wholly separate from science.

In an attempt to "materialize" the ideology concept and correct the positivism he claims to detect in Marx, Althusser coins the term "ideological state apparatuses." These are sociopolitical structures that call upon and activate (or, in Althusser's terminology, "interpellate") individuals to behave in ways determined by their social roles. But when he goes on to write that "all ideology has the function of 'constituting' concrete individuals as subjects," Althusser comes dangerously close to practicing exactly that method which Marx already rejects as a doomed attempt to "set out from what men say, imagine, conceive... in order to arrive at men in the flesh."[30]

Althusser's theory of ideological state apparatuses is designed to correct for what he considers the inert, because insufficiently material, character of ideology in Marx's development of the concept. Ideology, for Althusser, plays a role in history because it is not properly understood as an ideal substance but rather as a set of always-already embodied practices, responses, and reflexes. But in attempting to go "beyond" Marx, Althusser comes around full circle to the same questions of (material) determinism and (ideal) spontaneity that animated the German Idealist tradition, and in response to which Marx offered a more plausible and complex answer than the one Althusser proposes in its place.

Already in his *Critique of Hegel's* Philosophy of Right, Marx writes,

> The weapon of criticism cannot, of course, replace criticism by weapons, material force must be overthrown by material force; but theory also becomes a material force as soon as it has gripped the masses.[31]

Of course, what it means exactly for theory to "grip the masses" is left vague, here. But by the time we get to the writings posthumously published as Marx's and Engels's *Critique of the German Ideology*, the historical materialist account of the relationship between ideas and matter is far more sophisticated than Althusser lets on in his description of it. Althusser is not wrong to note that if ideology, for Marx, is nothing more than an "empty" "bricolage" of "residue," and admits of no internal development, then it must remain mysterious how such spiritual detritus could ever play a causal role in determining the course of history and affecting material circumstances. However, Althusser's materialism itself has more in common with the "one-sided" materialism Marx rejects than it does with the historical materialist approach of "setting out from real, active men, and on the basis of their real life-process demonstrating the development of the ideological reflexes and echoes of this life-process."[32] This is an approach, Marx and Engels argue, "which conforms to real life, it is the real living individuals themselves, and consciousness is considered solely as their consciousness."[33]

It is mistaken to construe this perspective as one of matter, taken abstractly on the one hand, strictly deterministically producing a kind of abstract ideal echo, on the other. For Marx, the solution to philosophy's puzzle about the relation of ideas to matter is found in the active labor process in which human beings are necessarily always involved (albeit in more or less alienated ways). This is why, for Marx and Engels, we must start with "real, active" human beings engaged in the process of producing and reproducing their means of subsistence. In the process of labor, the distinction between ideal and material aspects of Being can be made only in abstraction: labor is the active combination and integration of ideal forms with matter, and the practical realization of ideas in matter. The philosophical puzzle, then, is one that cannot be resolved in a purely contemplative mode; for Marx, it is resolved practically, in the activity of labor.

The materialist conception of history is, in turn, a perspective on the world from the point of view of the active laborer. It is "materialist" not in the sense of denying the distinctively ideal character of thought, consciousness, or ideology, or in the sense of reducing it to some cluster of strictly determinist mechanisms. The materialism of Marx's critique of ideology inheres in that it is only by proceeding from human beings as material, biological beings, intervening in their material world in order to satisfy their material needs, that one may arrive at this resolution of the puzzle about how to understand the relationship of ideas to matter.

Let us turn now to Nicholas Abercrombie and Bryan S. Turner, who in their 1978 paper "The Dominant Ideology Thesis" argue that Marx actually presents two conflicting theories of ideology. The first theory (implied, they argue, by Marx's and Engels's claim that "social being determines consciousness"), "suggests that each class forms its own system of belief in accordance with its own particular interests which will be basically at variance with those of other classes. The second suggests that all classes share in the system of belief imposed by the dominant class."[34]

Abercrombie and Turner argue that if it is the case that the ideology of a class is determined by the interests of that class, then it cannot also be the case that the ruling ideas of an epoch are the ideas of the ruling class, as Marx and Engels claim in their *Critique of the German Ideology*. This is so, Abercrombie and Turner write, because if the ruling ideas of the epoch are the ruling class's ideas, then we should expect their ideas to also be the ideas of the working class. However, if that were so, then it would seem to rule out the possibility that the working class's ideas are determined by their *own* class interests, interests that are in turn antagonistic to those of the bourgeoisie.

This is an error into which one falls if one fails, as these authors do, to understand class conflict as an interactive and evolving system in motion. The "social being" of the working class does not manifest in isolation from the bourgeoisie but rather is shaped by it, the class with the greater social power to craft those material conditions within which the working class develops its consciousness of the world. The working class does not simply osmotically soak up bourgeois ideas. It is one's life that determines one's consciousness and the proletariat lives in bourgeois society. Its class consciousness is the consciousness of itself as a class conditioned by material circumstances arranged about as far as possible to produce and reproduce the rule of the bourgeoisie.

Under these circumstances, the consciousness produced is therefore not usually *Das Kapital*, sprung fully formed from the head of each and every worker. It is rather a mix of ideas, attitudes, and sentiments shaped by the experience of living under capital. There is no irreconcilable tension between what Abercrombie and Turner take to be Marx's two theories because Marx's point about the "ruling ideas" in society is not to be construed so simplistically as they present it. Capital cannot rule except in a world made by labor. Therefore, when we speak of the ruling class and of ruling ideas, we must not lose sight of the fact that just as workers' consciousness is forged under capitalism, so the rule of capital does not take place in a vacuum. It is shaped in ways that are determined in part by its pitched battles with labor.

To give a concrete example of what I mean when I say that class conflict is interactive and evolving, we can look, for example, at the ebbs and flows of labor militancy in various capitalist economies. In times of rising labor militancy, workers are able to raise their consciousness of their own interests and fight for them, chipping away at the often seemingly absolute hegemony of exploitative capitalist domination. It is worth noting, as well, that key aspects of social justice organizing tend to be explicitly educational in focus, whether in the form of teach-ins, reading groups, lectures, pamphlets, shared syllabi, and so on. Demands that may have previously seemed unthinkable are suddenly pressed into the public discourse, finding their way onto the bargaining table. In other periods of history, when the labor movement is more quiescent, they lose this ground. Without the opportunities created by a rise in mass struggle, opportunities for political education also tend to shrink. My point is that if Abercrombie and Turner expect to find in Marx a diagram, valid for all historical circumstances, that can universally describe the exact balance of bourgeois and proletarian influence on the emerging and developing consciousness of members of the working class, they will be disappointed. This is not a shortcoming of Marxist theory, but rather an appropriate reflection of the dynamic character of the object under analysis.

Charles Mills, in his 1994 article "Marxism, 'Ideology,' and Moral Objectivism," offers a far more nuanced and sensitive analysis. Mills argues that in identifying morality as a form of ideology, Marx and Engels are not making a claim about the falsity of moral statements themselves, but rather a claim about the falsity of what morality purports to be, namely, objectively true and also efficacious in improving humans' circumstances. To say that morality is ideology in Marx's and Engels's sense, Mills writes, is to say that it "characteristically misunderstands its own genesis, is unrealistic about its psychological capacity to motivate, correspondingly inflates its causal significance, and thus systematically over-estimates its actual ability to transform the socio-economic order."[35] Mills identifies as a chief merit of his interpretation that on his rendering, Marx's "ideology" concept would provide better support for the project of articulating a Marxist ethics than do other rival interpretations of "ideology."

That Marx and Engels think of morality as an ideal phenomenon whose character is explained by the material base, and that they rebuke moral philosophers' tendency to overexaggerate the usefulness of extolling moral principles and pronouncements, is unquestionably the case. Perhaps quite unsurprisingly, I agree with Mills (1994) that these views held by Marx and Engels are perfectly compatible with the attempt to seek "an objectivist revolutionary morality that self-consciously *recognizes* its material roots in the economic 'revolutionary tendencies' of a situation, and that has no propensity to exaggerate its likely causal efficacy."[36] Mills argues that his account would have the virtue of leaving the door open for a Marxist morality touting itself as *non*ideological and therefore not subject to the harsh criticism Marx doles out to morality at numerous points throughout his corpus. The defense would be that Marx was strictly discussing those varieties of morality that happen to be ideological and was not speaking out against nonideological forms of morality.

But even with accord reached on some of these points regarding the nature of Marx's and Engels's critique of morality, the question still remains whether Mills is correct that "ideology" is best understood as a term used to describe theory that is deluded about its own sources and the rather narrow limits upon its socially transformative possibilities, rather than as a more neutral descriptor of consciousness and of systems of ideas that emerge within class societies.

The problem for Mills's 1994 interpretation of Marx's ideology concept, however, comes when we notice that the account Marx gives of the development of ideology is *also* his account of the emergence of *any* and *all* ideal aspects of social Being. In a writing later published posthumously as part of

The Critique of the German Ideology, Marx and Engels write that, "We set out from real, active men, and on the basis of their real life-process we demonstrate the development of the *ideological* reflexes and echoes of this life process. The phantoms formed in the human brain are also, necessarily, sublimates of their material life-process, which is empirically verifiable and bound to material premises."[37]

If what makes a certain idea or system of ideas count as ideological is that it is an idea that obscures its own basis in materiality, and that it is an idea that appears to be much more causally efficacious than it actually is, these are sufficient conditions satisfied by the vast majority of ideas in the vast majority of heads in the great, vast majority of people. And that tendency toward idealism is not simply a matter of maintaining better or worse theoretical hygiene on an individual level; the lesson we are to draw from Marx's and Engels's critique of ideology is that the world of capital is set up *precisely* in a way that reliably and necessarily produces exactly this mystifying effect.

Mills's proffered solution to the problem, his suggested path toward a "nonideological" Marxist morality, is itself, in the end, idealist. It falls into the very trap it promises to help us navigate our ways out of. If we have the right *ideas* about revolutionary morality, if we develop a morality that "self-consciously *recognizes* its material roots," then we can free ourselves from the material circumstances' tendency to produce ideology and in fully escaping the mystifying tendencies of capital, we can thereby land upon a morality that is nonideological. I submit that this solution succumbs rather readily to the familiar pitfall of which Marx tried, perhaps here in vain, to warn us.[38] It places entirely too much faith in the power of the right ideas to free us from the mystifying effect that our alienated material conditions of life have upon our consciousness. And so while Mills's 1994 discussion of ideology is in numerous respects quite clarifying and sharp, its central argument does not make it seem any less like folly to speak of nonideological consciousness within the context of class society.

In a later work, his 2003 *From Class to Race*, Mills rejects his 1994 account of Marx's ideology concept and argues in its place that all aspects of the superstructure are inherently ideological. Mills points to a passage in *Theories of Surplus Value* where Marx speaks of "state officials, military people, artists, doctors, priests, judges, lawyers" as workers who produce "'immaterial' [in other words, *ideal*] commodities." In light of this, Mills updates his position so that his "claim now is that for Marx and Engels all of these can be described as 'ideologists,' since they work in the 'ideal' superstructure and produce 'ideal' products."[39] They work in fields, and under conditions, that tend to foster the illusion that their ideas spring from their own genius, when in fact, their ideas are shaped by external material processes of which they persist largely unaware.[40]

One of Mills's targets in this later treatment of the ideology concept is a view he attributes to Joe McCarney, among others, which holds that "ideology" is a neutral and not pejorative concept in Marx's theory.[41] It is one we brought under consideration earlier in the present chapter. In his 1859 preface to *A Contribution to the Critique of Political Economy*, Marx writes that when studying social revolution, "it is always necessary to distinguish between the material transformation of the economic conditions of production . . . and the legal, political, religious, artistic or philosophic—in short, ideological forms in which men become conscious of this conflict and fight it out."[42] And as we noted earlier, this passage seems to support an analysis of the "ideology" concept on which ideological forms are not inherently reactionary just in virtue of their being classed and ideological.

Throughout the 2003 piece, Mills seems to conflate two different senses in which "ideology" could be a pejorative concept. On the one hand, one might mean that "ideology" is identical with thoroughgoingly reactionary bourgeois consciousness. On the other hand, one might mean that "ideology" captures the sense in which ideas sometimes obscure and mystify the reality of material relations. In reaching his later conclusion about Marx's concept of ideology, Mills concludes that if all aspects of the superstructure are ideological for Marx, then (a) "ideology" is an unhelpful concept for distinguishing bourgeois from proletarian consciousness because they are both ideological, and (b) ideology is not to be understood as mystification since *all* consciousness is ideological including ostensibly true and clarifying proletarian consciousness.[43]

But Mills reaches each of these conclusions too quickly. He points to rather crude and doctrinaire attempts to denounce the "ideological" character of bourgeois consciousness. He argues, sensibly enough, that this charge is meaningless if proletarian consciousness is *also* necessarily ideological, as would follow from the claim that *in general*, all superstructural forms in class society are inherently and necessarily ideological. In this, Mills suggests that to reject "the one-dimensional, class-reductionistic, and ultimately quite absurd polarization of (Marxist proletarian) science versus (non-Marxist bourgeois) ideology" would be a novel move in the legacy of Marxist thought, a kind of theoretical advance in the tradition. But this is not the case; in Marx himself we see serious and sensitive engagement with bourgeois theory, famously, for example, in the cases of Georg Wilhelm Friedrich Hegel and of Adam Smith. Marx's hours upon hours in the Reading Room of the British Museum were spent poring through the writings of precisely those bourgeois producers of "immaterial commodities," often to critique and at least as often, to gather insight into the real nature of capitalist relations. Many a Marxist has been known to read a bourgeois newspaper or two—critically, yes, but not simply to dismiss every word within its pages as so much nonsense. As I detailed in the first part of the present chapter, there is just not much evidence for the claim that the Marxist tradition discards *all* bourgeois thought production as worthless mystification.

As for the second conclusion, that ideology is not to be understood as mystification, this is also too quick. Ideology does, in part, mystify. One of the chief lessons of *Capital* is that capitalism's economic relations of production necessarily mystify our understanding. This is not a doctrine that ought to plunge us into skepticism and despair. It is a call to action, a reminder that passive contemplation makes us especially susceptible to these mystifications and that therefore, as Marx noted in the second of his *Theses on Feuerbach*,

> The question whether objective truth can be attributed to human thinking is not a question of theory but is a practical question. Man must prove the truth—i.e. the reality and power, the this-sidedness of his thinking in practice. The dispute over the reality or non-reality of thinking that is isolated from practice is a purely *scholastic* question.[44]

As much insight into the nature of existence as it is possible for us to gain today, the conditions do not yet exist for fully objective knowledge of the world. The correct way to understand the relationship between bourgeois and proletarian consciousness is not as a distinction between "ideological" (uniformly empirically false) and "nonideological" (uniformly empirically true) thought. The distinction is instead a theoretical confrontation between the consciousness of a class whose interests are *served* by mystification, and the consciousness of that class of people who, if they are ever to be free, must come to see the world just as it is.[45] This contradiction finds expression in thought but it cannot be resolved in thought. As I have written elsewhere,

The movement from fracture to wholeness, from particularity to universality, is something that must be eventually produced; and that product will be the result of a political project accomplished by the proletariat as a revolutionary subject in the course of human history, seeking emancipation from its own exploited, alienated, and degraded condition. In the Communist Manifesto, Marx and Engels refer to the proletariat as "the class that holds the future in its hands." It is the proletariat's specific capacity to dissolve social antagonisms and produce a society in which the flourishing of each conduces to the flourishing of all, that lends the character of universality to its perspective. In the proletariat's historical task, the opposition of particular and universal interest is not merely theoretically and philosophically, but practically and politically overcome.[46]

One legacy of the Analytical Marxist tradition that is represented not only in Mills's reading of Marx but in *most* Anglophone academic work on Marx, is the refusal to encounter Marx on his own methodological terms. Indeed, the Anglophone academy has by and large regarded such refusal as a *prerequisite* for any mature philosophical engagement with Marx's ideas, all with predictable results. Writing in 2000 of the methodological approach taken in his 1978 book *Karl Marx's Theory of History: A Defence*, Cohen explains,

> All analytical Marxism is analytical in the broad sense, and much is analytical in the narrow sense. In each sense of "analytical," to be analytical is to be opposed to a form of thinking traditionally thought integral to Marxism: analytical thinking, in the broad sense of "analytical," is opposed to so-called "dialectical" thinking, and analytical thinking, in the narrow sense of "analytical," is opposed to what might be called 'holistic' thinking. The fateful operation that created analytical Marxism was the rejection of the claim that Marxism possesses valuable intellectual methods of its own. Rejection of that claim enabled an appropriation of a rich mainstream methodology that Marxism, to its detriment, had shunned.[47]

Some members of the Analytical Marxist current that coalesced around G. A. Cohen in the late 1970s went so far as to dub themselves scholars of "No-Bullshit" Marxism.[48] The "bullshit" in question? None other than the beating heart of Marxist theory and practice: dialectics. It is by neglecting the central role of dialectics in Marxist theory—that is, by attempting to excise from Marxism his attention to the whole inner conflict and development of existence, and by regarding apparent theoretical contradictions mainly as philosophical puzzles to be dissolved through abstract conceptual analysis, that one flattens Marxism into pat, platitudinal nonsense, then finally to dismiss it from the halls of "serious" philosophical endeavor. Unsurprisingly, this was precisely the trajectory of most of the key figures in the Analytical Marxist school.

James Furner diagnoses the collapse of Analytical Marxism quite correctly in his 2018 book *Marx on Capitalism*. He writes,

> One reason to undermine the self-told narrative around Analytical Marxism's disappearance is to embolden other Marxist projects. Cohen's account of Analytical Marxism's disappearance is that Analytical Marxism's Marxism led to its undoing. By contrast, . . . the analytical constraints of Analytical Marxism led to its undoing.[49]

So, of course it is absolutely correct that Marx does not dismiss all ideology as inherently bourgeois in character, always upholding and legitimizing the dominance of the ruling class. Rather, Marx argues that in capitalist society, the bourgeoisie and its class nature play a primary role in shaping the ideas of the age. This does not mean, however, that Marx thinks it is either possible or desirable to function or to think "nonideologically" in a class society.[50] An ideology is a system of ideas developed in order to make sense of social contradictions. As such, it is completely necessary that the proletariat develop its own ideology and engage with such ideological forms as morality and political theory. In the *Manifesto*, Marx writes that "the proletarian movement is the self-conscious, independent movement of the immense majority, in the interest of the immense majority."[51] For the proletarian movement to be self-conscious is precisely for it to work out, ideologically, its present situation, its aims, and the best means by which to attain its ends.

Moral Suasion and Marx's Anti-Utopianism

One way in which Marx's approach to ethics differs from others is that, since historical materialism predicts that people are likely to do that which they perceive to be in their own material interest, the making and accepting of ethical arguments is not very effective on its own for producing real change and for that reason is not, in and of itself, a priority.[52] *Worse*, to the extent that ethical arguments do tend to be persuasive when made, it is because they ratify and reflect a dehumanizing reality and demand that those in whose interest it would be to revolutionize society sacrifice themselves before it, instead.

These criticisms of morality's role in class society receive special attention in Marx's critiques of utopianism. In contemporary literature, Marxism is often referred to as a utopian theory. However, both Marx and Engels were very vocal about the distinctions between their scientific and revolutionary method, and the idealist methods of what they considered to be utopian forms of socialism, such as those espoused by the so-called True Socialists. Instead of engaging in political activity and looking to the existing economic and social situation to identify which elements in the existing society are in a position to change society, utopianism, Marx and Engels charge, depends on the greatness of an idea to compel people to action through its own intellectual appeal.

In his 1948 article "German Utopianism: 'True' Socialism," Auguste Cornu writes,

> The "true" socialism which arose in Germany between 1843 and 1847 was the specific form which utopian socialism took in that country. It came into being when modern capitalism was taking shape in Germany and was closely related to French socialism, which had arisen half a century previously, at the time of the bourgeoise's coming to power in France. . . . Utopian socialism did not perceive the internal contradictions of capitalism, which engender economic and social crises, nor was it able, in view of the weakness of the proletariat, to envisage the class struggle as a means of emancipation. It therefore failed to find in society itself the source of the solution for the problems raised by the development of society. . . . Instead of showing how the future emerges out of existing society, it set up a sharp contrast between the present, which is nothing but disorder and injustice, and the future, in which harmony will reign. . . . While thus contrasting a future ideal society to existing society, utopian socialism endeavored to show how that ideal society must of necessity realise itself merely as a result of its rational and moral superiority.[53]

As Marx writes in *The Communist Manifesto*, the "True Socialists"

> consider themselves far superior to all class antagonisms. They want to improve the condition of every member of society, even that of the most favored. Hence, they habitually appeal to society at large, without distinction of class; nay, by preference, to the ruling class. For how can people, when once they understand their system, fail to see in it the best possible plan of the best possible state of society? Hence, they reject all political, and especially all revolutionary, action; they wish to attain their ends by peaceful means, and endeavor, by small experiments, necessarily doomed to failure, and by the force of example, to pave the way for the new social Gospel.[54]

The True Socialists (Karl Grün, Hermann Semmig, Edgar and Bruno Bauer, and others) are exemplars of this sort of utopianism, arguing that the communism of Marx and Engels is inferior to their theories because Marxist theory does not rely solely on moral motivation as a means to bring about communism. Semmig, for instance, argues for socialism as an "anarchic system" which would rely on "the moral core of mankind," and accuses communists of having failed to achieve "free moral activity." However, this "moral core of mankind" is left completely unexplained and undefined. How exactly it would bring about communism in a historical situation in which so many factors militate against it, is anyone's guess, especially as the True Socialists opposed the kind of liberalizing bourgeois reforms that could serve to overthrow feudalism and produce conditions within which communists could more effectively organize.[55]

The appeal to a "moral core" fails to explain the real process through which socialism might be achieved. In this way, Semmig's *mere moralism* provides cover for a lack of political clarity. The "free moral activity" that he looks to as a way for human beings to effect the transition from class society to socialism is activity undetermined by the real concrete historical situation. Semmig "abandons the real behaviour of the individual and takes refuge in his indescribable, inaccessible, peculiar nature."[56] However, while human beings can imagine themselves as totally free, undetermined beings, in fact, they act in conditions and in circumstances that do not at all depend on their free choice, and their actions are in this way therefore partially determined by external, concrete historical circumstances which must be taken into account in any conception of how communism might be attained. The particular circumstances in question, in the context of Marx's disagreements with the True Socialists, were those of the German bourgeoisie's struggle against feudalism, and for liberal reform, in the early part of the nineteenth century.

In refusing to extend conditional support to the German bourgeoisie's struggle against the German aristocracy and for democratic reform, the True Socialists, Marx argued, had merely attempted to warm over an approach to social change that was already inadequate when developed earlier, and in a more sophisticated manner, by utopian French socialists such as Charles Fourier and Henri Saint-Simon. Marx described Semmig et al. as writers "who have absorbed a few French and English communist ideas and amalgamated them with their own German philosophical premises."[57] But in the absence of a vibrant workers' movement in Germany at the time of their writings, the attempt to transform the ideas of utopian French socialism into a distinctively "German" ideology could only deteriorate into an abstract, petit bourgeois retreat from struggle and into pure theoretical abstraction reflecting the "petty circumstances of the artisan."[58]

Marx and Engels respected the work of "critical-utopian" socialists such as Fourier, Saint-Simon, and Robert Owen, but thought it crucial to understand the latter's work as both visionary and yet limited in that the conditions they sought to interpret were ones in which working-class struggle remained in its nascency. In the *Manifesto*, Marx writes that "the proletariat, as yet in its infancy, offers to [Saint-Simon, Fourier, Owen, et al.] the spectacle of a class without any historical initiative or any independent political movement."[59] As such, the French utopian socialists of this period could well be forgiven for theorizing the proletariat as "the most suffering class" and not as an active, transformative force capable of revolutionizing society. Still, Marx insists, the Utopians were mistaken to reject revolutionary action; the mistake is compounded as class struggle heightens and sharpens, and yet certain thinkers—such as the True Socialists—cling to a perspective that omits the self-activity of the working class and relies instead on the persuasive power of reason alone, intending to win the ruling classes over to the cause of socialism.

In his 2002 paper "Marx's Critique of the Utopian Socialists," Roger Paden argues that Marx's critique of the Utopians is nonetheless unsuccessful. Paden refers to the view that Marx and Engels criticized the Utopian socialists for indulging in mere moralism as the "Strategic Criticism." He writes,

On this interpretation, the Marxist criticism of the Utopian socialists is based on the idea that, while Marx and Engels shared their ends (their vision of the general shape of the ideal society) and were, therefore, Utopians themselves, they believed that the means the Utopian socialists proposed to attain those ends were insufficient. . . . There are a number of problems with this criticism of the Utopian socialists. Perhaps most important, it overestimates the possibility that violent revolution can produce a truly ideal society, while underestimating the power of moral criticism. Moreover, it falsely portrays people as simple victims of the dominant ideology and/or as completely controlled by their narrow economic and class interests. However, this rejection of the power of moral argument to motivate people has been shown to be false by the history of Marxism itself, as it has been moral arguments that have moved many people from a variety of social classes to join this cause. It also underrates the ability of Utopian visions—including Marxist utopias—to cause people to seek political change. History suggests, therefore, that, although small scale utopias are perhaps doomed to failure and although sudden violent revolutions can sometimes succeed, there are no good political reasons to reject in principle gradual, morally-motivated utopianism.[60]

I will address the problems Paden sees in the criticism of mere moralism as a strategy for social change one at a time. Paden's first objection, that criticizing the Utopian socialists for indulging in mere moralism gets things wrong about the relative efficacy of violent revolution and moral criticism, has at least two problems as far as I can see. The first is that the revolutionary means Marx prefers to mere moralism cannot simply be boiled down to "violent revolution." Paden effectively indulges in a sleight of hand, replacing what is in Marx's and Engels's writings a description of a long and difficult process, with the idea of a "sudden violent revolution" which Paden invokes as though such an event is to contain within itself all that would be required for a transition to communist society. In doing so, Paden dramatically oversimplifies the political program that Marx and Engels promote in their writings and practice in their own political activism. This program includes the organization of masses of people to enter into a political fight for legal reforms, as well as struggles within the workplace for better wages and working conditions, and of course, efforts at political education and the dissemination of revolutionary ideas. It is true that it would be a mistake to assume that *mere* "violent revolution" would be any more effective at bringing about communism than issuing moral commands to society at large would be, but this is also not what Marx is saying and the interpretation on which his critique of Utopianism criticizes the Utopian socialists for their mere moralism need not be committed to such a view. In fact, as mentioned above, Marx's critique of the "True" Socialism, French Utopianism's intellectual descendant in Germany, was rooted precisely in the fact that its adherents were insufficiently *supportive* of liberal, bourgeois reforms.

When Marx and Engels write of the need for revolution, their point is that only the proletariat can radically restructure society in the way that is necessary for communism to be achieved. Thus, the argument for political revolution—a transfer of political rule from one part of society to another—as a means to achieve communism is tied together with Marx's and Engels's identification of the proletariat as the progressive, existing force within society that can realize communism. Paden would be well within his rights to disagree with Marx and Engels that this is true of the proletariat. Yet insofar as he provides no argument to that effect, he does not provide adequate support for his decision to dismiss out of hand the idea that revolution might be necessary for communism to be realized and that mere moralism might not do the job.

Additionally, with respect to Paden's first objection, Paden seems to overlook that Marx's and Engels's belief that revolution may involve violence is based on the fact that the bourgeoisie is quite certain to violently oppose and suppress any attempts to infringe upon private property and bourgeois rule. It is not that Marx and Engels think violent revolution, taken abstractly, has some inherently progressive potential, considered in isolation from specific historical circumstances. (A "violent revolution" undertaken by a small, politically isolated sect would be nothing more than foolhardy adventurism.) Rather, Marx and Engels do both seem to think that for the working class to be successful in its revolutionary or often, even in its merely reformist aims, it must be prepared to survive the brutally and violently reactionary forces that have historically been deployed to defend capital, from the Freikorps in Germany, to the Pinkertons in the US, to Pinochet's DINA in Chile. I can see no reason to think it prima facie just up for grabs, as Paden seems to, that "the power of moral argument" might be enough to see the working class through such tough times.

Paden's second criticism of the kind of view I attribute to Marx and Engels is that it wrongly assumes that people's actions and beliefs are strictly determined by their economic class interests. Who, after all, is to say that a member of the bourgeoisie might *not* be swayed by moral argument alone? But I don't think that reading Marx and Engels as critics of the mere moralism of the Utopian socialists in any way commits one to the view that moral argument can *never* bring a person around to the view that communism is desirable unless she already has economic interests that would be served by it. Certainly, Paden is quite right that historically, people from a range of social classes have been convinced of the need for communism and sometimes through moral argument. Marx and Engels may have been better aware than most that one need not actually be a member of the working class in order to be convinced of the need for communism. But Marx and Engels do think it is a mistake to advocate mere appeal to human beings' moral sentiments without taking into account what their economic interests are and whether those interests are better served by the maintenance of the status quo or a transition to a different type of society. To interpret Marx's and Engels's critique of mere moralism as a criticism of the view that moral argument alone can bring about communism does not require one to show that no one ever responds to moral reasons even where they go against one's self interest. Rather, the question is whether mere moralizing alone can ever galvanize the majority of society in the way that would be required for a transition to communism; anyone who believes that it might owes us some argument for that.

Marx distances himself from the issuance of moral injunctions as ways, in and of themselves, to close the gap between what "is" and what "ought" to be. His and Engels's "scientific socialism" does not share the same difficulties as "true" or utopian socialism when it comes to the question of rational motivation because it is not opposed to the needs of individuals, but rather is theorized as a means of recognizing and satisfying those needs. It identifies as the revolutionary class that class which, because of its position in economic production, is already brought into conflict with the forces of capitalism through its struggle for its own continued existence. Moral calls for altruistic sacrifice become necessary for a political theory when the link between rational self-interest and the prescribed course of action can no longer be demonstrated through reason.

The flourishing, development, and well-being of human individuals guides Marx at every stage of his philosophical work and is the basis of his outlook on morality. He argues both that it is the highest goal for human beings, and that it provides the standard by which moral theories should be judged. When Marx criticizes specific moralities, it is not because he has abandoned any moral conception whatsoever. Rather, what rival theories represent abstractly as a desirable state of affairs is, for Marx, a goal to be aimed at through practical revolutionary activity, not merely wished for in systems of moral injunctions. As he writes of Max Stirner, the mistake is in thinking that

> the communists want to "make sacrifices" for "society," when they want at most to sacrifice existing society; in this case he should describe their consciousness that their struggle is the common cause of all people who have outgrown the bourgeois system as a sacrifice that they make to themselves.[61]

So, if all of that is the case, then what is the role of a book about the Marxist approach to ethics—an approach that, in Marx's own work, was tinged with everything ranging from indifference to outright disdain? My aim is not to produce an absolute calculus of right action, a decision procedure spitting out moral judgments about every conceivable human dilemma. In fact, insofar as what I offer in these pages is a guide to action, it will be because part of what I offer is an outline of how we might determine which actions are such as to further the cause of human emancipation. But which ones will or will not is itself an empirical question to which a definitive answer can only be given in the course of revolutionary practice.

Throughout the present chapter, I have alluded to a distinctively proletarian perspective on the world. In Marxist theory, that perspective is the materialist conception of history, a perspective from the point of view of labor. This is the topic of Chapter 3, "A Historical Materialist Account of Human Nature."

3
A Historical Materialist Account of Human Nature

One of my central theses in this book is that according to a Marxist approach to ethics, we ought to do that which promotes human flourishing. It follows that in order to know precisely what we might be called upon to do in practice, we must know something of what it is to flourish *as* a human being. It further follows that we must have some account of what it is to be a human being in the first place. A Marxist account of human nature is therefore central and foundational for getting clear on Marx's vision of what it would be to abolish our alienation from that nature and achieve reconciliation with it.

However, if "human nature" is the sort of thing that can be resolved into a discrete list of fixed traits and dispositions had by all human beings at all times, then Marxist theory offers no such thing. Marx consistently and vehemently rejects what he sees as earlier attempts to characterize human existence in such a fixed and abstract manner: he is highly critical of doctrines that mistake specific determinate historical expressions of human potential as eternal, unchanging, universal features of human beings. And yet as I will argue over the course of this chapter, Marx does offer what we may reasonably consider to be his own account of essential human nature, a rival to those he rejected. In fact, Marx's entire theoretical framework is rooted in, and made sensible by, his historical materialist account of what it is to be human.

One might—especially if one has been raised in the modern Anglophone philosophical tradition—reasonably wonder how an account of human nature could be relevant to morality. By going down that road we might, after all, find ourselves in grave peril of committing a naturalistic "is–ought" fallacy of a kind with what David Hume, among others, are taken to have so strenuously warned us against.[1] "What *is*," one might protest, "is war, strife, competition, egoism, poverty, and want!" Human nature, as actually expressed throughout history, often does not look very good. So it is not unreasonable to maintain skepticism that what *is* might give us any real guidance as to what *ought* to be.

But this insistence upon a stark disconnect between what *is* and what *ought* to be is itself utterly alien to Marx's theoretical method. It is precisely denied by his and Engels's materialist conception of history, itself an heir to Hegelian dialectics which has as one of its tenets that actually obtaining conditions already contain within them the possibility of their overthrow (their "negation," to adopt Hegel's term). The dialectical method that Marx and Engels adapted from Hegel has, as another of its tenets, that a thing's phenomenal appearances express a nature that can be known by observing the alteration of those appearances under changing conditions in history, and drawing valid conclusions about what determinate nature might give rise to such appearances. ("Essence," Hegel tells us in the *Science of Logic*, "appears."[2]) Thus, Marx and Engels emphasize attention to movement, dynamism, process, and history as the absolute cornerstone of scientific inquiry into the real nature of things. It is, according to the materialist conception of history, impossible to know a thing except by observing it in motion and dynamic interaction.[3]

As for what *is* today, what exists is not just sheer capitalist dystopia. We do not exist in a world that is shaped *only* by capitalists promoting capitalist ideas, building capitalist institutions, and enforcing capitalist property relations. We live in a world in which capitalists have an overwhelmingly significant role in determining human reality; but try as they might, their rule over humanity is no settled fact. It is an ongoing, unfolding battle they must wage every day against the working classes who, in resisting capitalist domination and struggling for the conditions of human survival, play their own key role in determining the course of human history. Of all capitalism's innovations, its greatest historical achievement is to have forged the proletariat that digs class society's grave. It is this practical contradiction between capital and labor, its dynamic unfolding under changing historical circumstances, that increasingly draws the whole of humanity into a single, central conflict. The sharp, ever more all-encompassing character of this battle creates, as a material reality, the possibility of observing the species as a totality in motion, one riven by internal conflicts whose expression under different circumstances over time grants us insight into the nature of the species as one whole. What do we see?

For Marx, it is always an error to attempt to develop an account of what human beings are by essentializing and universalizing their habits, interests, and values just at some particular given point in time. Any of these is a particular contingent *appearance*, just one way among many in which human nature might manifest. When we speak of a Marxist conception of human nature, it is not any particular appearance to which we refer, nor even to some large set of these separate appearances taken together. Essential human nature is a complex of *all* these myriad appearances and of the process that yields these separate appearances and makes such a wide and varying array of them possible at all. That process is labor: human beings' goal-directed intervention into their natural and social environment, an intervention that humans initiate in order to satisfy their needs, and through which they necessarily transform their environment and themselves in the process.[4]

Human nature, for Marx, is best understood not just in terms of what we are at some given moment in time, but crucially, in terms of the generative activity through which we produce, reproduce, and necessarily transform and expand what it is that we are and might become. This is what he has in mind when he writes, in the third of his *Theses on Feuerbach*, that "the coincidence of the changing of circumstances and of human activity or self-changing can be conceived and rationally understood only as *revolutionary practice*."[5] What human beings essentially are cannot be understood by us except by engaging in the process of transforming ourselves and, in doing so, realizing it is precisely our capacity to consciously self-change that constitutes and gives rise to our conditions of existence. And this is an activity that is only made possible through social coordination, interaction, and interdependency. Hence, as Marx continues in the sixth of his *Theses*, "the human essence is no abstraction inherent in each single individual. In its reality it is the ensemble of the social relations."[6]

As much as it has become something of a truism of moral philosophy in the analytical tradition to insist that it is always fallacious to deduce an "ought" from an "is," this notion descends precisely from a Humean positivism that is directly at odds with Marx's dialectical materialism. (For that matter, we don't even have to get all the way to Marx to find key figures in the history of philosophy who would have found this view strange—the insistence that there is an "is–ought fallacy" doesn't much square with Aristotelian virtue ethics, either, given that the latter rests on a theory of human nature and of the conditions of flourishing for beings with that nature.)

If, for all we know, what *is* bears no necessary connection to what precedes or follows it—if all we can say of what *is* is to describe what *appears to be* at some one particular time-slice—then indeed it would be quite a mystery how we could derive normativity from that. But if aiming, striving, goal-directedness—if *generation*, *life*, and *process* in fact *are* part of what *is*, then at least one cannot be so sure that it is simply a kind of category mistake to suggest that what is already contains, even if only in embryo, what ought to be. In this sense, a Marxist approach to ethics can be understood as an attempt in part to recoup the loss, described for example in Alasdair MacIntyre's *After Virtue*, inflicted by liberalism's repudiation of the Aristotelian notion that there is a shared, universal, objective, and knowable human nature from which normative claims can be derived about how human social life ought to be arranged.

Indeed, arguments for the purportedly "amoralist" character of Marxist theory frequently diagnose it as embracing a Nietzsche-esque nihilism. This is a point MacIntyre raises and that Paul Blackledge later revisits in his 2012 book *Marxism and Ethics*, a very much MacIntyrean reconstruction of Marxist ethics. There, Blackledge argues that rather than nihilism, "Marx's ethics amounts to a modern version of Aristotle's account of those practices underpinning the virtues through which individuals are able to flourish within communities."[7] The failure to appreciate the normative character of Marx's theory is then diagnosable as a consequence of the relative sidelining of Aristotelianism within the modern moral tradition, a circumstance that renders many frankly unable to know ethical theory when they see it.

The brief sketch provided above, of a defense for deriving an "ought" from an "is," might strike some as excessively teleological. We will address that concern at length in Chapter 5, on freedom and determinism. But here, as we move into the next sections of the present chapter, I will explain the character of human nature as it figures within Marx's ethical vision. First, I will explain what distinguishes Marx's account of human nature from crudely biologistic accounts that really would be irrelevant to ethical questions. Next, I will demonstrate how one incorporates a historical materialist account of human nature into ethical reasoning. Lastly, I will address the objection that perhaps communism simply demands much more than what is made possible by essential human nature. It is true that human beings as we exist now would be very ill-suited to a fully developed communist society, indeed. But the promise of communism lies precisely in that we might yet make of ourselves more than what we so far have been.

Biological and Social Being in Marx's Account of Human Nature

In keeping with Marx's methodological materialism, his ethical vision is derived in the first place from an assessment of what human beings are and what, given their nature, is beneficial to their flourishing.[8] But Marx does not believe it is possible to determine morality based merely on humans' *biological* being and *biological* needs. So when I say that Marx's ethical vision takes human nature as its starting point, I certainly do not mean to reduce human nature to a collection of merely biological facts about members of the species *Homo sapiens*. Such a crass form of biologism would conceive of human nature and of human needs too statically and narrowly. It would not account for the ways human beings continually transform their conditions of existence by altering their material production and thus their own consciousness, and in turn their own nature and their needs.

However, neither would it be right to say that the biological nature of *Homo sapiens* is irrelevant to morality. Social being (human existence as it is produced and transformed historically by human activity)—and natural, biological being, form two moments of a single dialectical unity of human nature. Yet natural being plays a fundamental and ontologically prior part.[9] In his book *Ontology of Social Being*, Georg Lukács puts this point in the following way:

> Social being cannot be conceived as independent from natural being and as its exclusive opposite ... The objective forms of social being grow out of natural being in the course of the rise and development of social practice, and become ever more expressly social.[10]

Humans are natural beings in the sense that they are biological beings of a certain sort. In particular, they are mammals, with a particular anatomy, particular metabolic processes, and particular history of evolutionary development that has led to their emergence as a distinct biological species. As natural beings, humans require such basic materials as food, water, shelter, breathable atmosphere of a particular chemical composition, and so on, in order for their biological processes to go on—that is of course to say, they need these things in order to live. Insofar as human beings require food, water, and the like, human beings are largely indistinct from animals. But the respects in which they are distinct matter quite a lot. Marx writes:

HISTORICAL ACCOUNT OF HUMAN NATURE 51

> The first premise of all human history is, of course, the existence of living human individuals. Thus the first fact to be established is the physical organisation of these individuals and their consequent relation to the rest of nature. Of course, we cannot here go either into the actual physical nature of man, or into the natural conditions in which man finds himself—geological, oro-hydrographical, climatic and so on. All historical writing must set out from these natural bases and their modification in the course of history through the action of men.
>
> Men can be distinguished from animals by consciousness, by religion or anything else you like. They themselves begin to distinguish themselves from animals as soon as they begin to *produce* their means of subsistence, a step which is conditioned by their physical organisation. By producing their means of subsistence men are indirectly producing their material life."[11]

Marx argues that the essence of human existence is the labor process. Labor is the essential activity through which human beings intervene consciously and purposively into the natural world and the processes unfolding within it. It is the activity through which they intervene in and transform their own relationships to nature and to one another as human beings.[12] In *Capital*, Marx describes the labor process in the following terms:

> Labour is, in the first place, a process in which both man and Nature participate, and in which man of his own accord starts, regulates, and controls the material re-actions between himself and Nature. He opposes himself to Nature as one of her own forces, setting in motion arms and legs, head and hands, the natural forces of his body, in order to appropriate Nature's productions in a form adapted to his own wants. By thus acting on the external world and changing it, he at the same time changes his own nature. He develops his slumbering powers and compels them to act in obedience to his sway.... We pre-suppose labour in a form that stamps it as exclusively human. A spider conducts operations that resemble those of a weaver, and a bee puts to shame many an architect in the construction of her cells. But what distinguishes the worst architect from the best of bees is this, that the architect raises his structure in imagination before he erects it in reality. At the end of every labour-process, we get a result that already existed in the imagination of the labourer at its commencement. He not only effects

a change of form in the material on which he works, but he also realizes a purpose of his own.[13]

Unlike animals, which engage in their animal behaviors without conscious awareness of what it is to act *as* members of their species, human beings are what Marx calls "species-beings." Humans possess a conception of themselves as a species and are able to act in accordance with it.[14] Humans can understand what necessary conditions must be fulfilled in order for their species to survive and, more than that, to thrive, realizing its present capacities and developing new ones. Further, human beings can also produce in accordance with the standards of other species, understanding their conditions of flourishing and providing for them accordingly. From agriculture to pet care, humans are able to behave in such a way as to promote and direct the processes of nutrition, growth, and reproduction that occur within other animals. What's even more, humans can self-consciously direct their activity so as to produce in accordance with conceptual abstractions such as beauty, as for example, when they produce art. In his 1844 "Estranged Labour" manuscript, Marx explains the difference between animal and human activity thus:

> The animal is immediately one with its life activity; it is that activity. Man makes his life activity itself an object of his will and consciousness. He has conscious life activity. It is not a determination with which he directly merges. *Conscious life activity directly distinguishes man from animal life activity. Only because of that is he a species-being.*[15]

As a dynamic process, as an activity, human nature is not some ghostly *something* lurking in the heart of every person, or standing "behind" the myriad appearances of human existence. Rather, it inheres in the complex of that whole wide range of appearances that human activity assumes. As we saw in the previous chapter, Marx raises the point that "the essence of man is no abstraction inherent in each single individual. In its reality it is the ensemble of the social relations."[16] In order to determine the essence of human existence, Marx assesses a concrete totality of determinate instances of human activity and social relations. Through analyzing these varied examples as they appear in the course of history, Marx determines what is common to each of those instances and what gives rise to them and explains their emergence and decay.

As we have already noted, central to Marx's ethical vision is a thesis that contemporary moral philosophers frequently reject out of hand: that from a claim about what *is* the case for essential human nature, we may derive claims about what *ought* to be the conditions of human existence. Essential human nature—which is for Marx, the labor process—is itself not neutral with respect to its outcome. Its aim is always already the satisfaction of human needs and the preservation of human life. We ought, Marx argues consistently throughout his writings, to recognize this aim as our own and act so as to realize it. Ethical questions are always ultimately grounded in empirical investigation as to what conditions are in fact likely to promote the flourishing of creatures such as us.

Since for Marx, human nature is the complex of all human activity, everywhere, past and present, taken as one whole, it is therefore dynamic, constantly developing and constantly transformed as human beings act and produce in different ways. Marx writes in *Capital*, in "acting on the external world and changing it, [man] at the same time changes his own nature."[17] Out of this concrete totality of human activities and social relations, it is possible to develop an abstraction that is valid for each of these concrete appearances. That abstraction is the labor process. Marx sees labor as the conscious intervention of human beings into the world, setting causal processes into motion in order to realize ends that they first posit in thought.[18] Marx argues that this teleological realizing of ends is the essence of human existence—it is what distinguishes human beings from other forms of life not just theoretically but in the practical sense that it is through this process that human beings make their form of life more and more distinct from any other species'. It is the practical basis upon which human existence develops in its diverse and dynamic appearance.[19]

Alan G. Nasser, in his 1975 paper "Marx's Ethical Anthropology," writes of the connection between this conception of human nature and Marx's ethical critique of capitalism. According to Nasser,

> We are told that if the worker were to be functioning in an "exclusively human" way, his production would "[realize] a purpose of his own." But in fact, as a *wage*-laborer his ability to produce is used to realize the purposes of the capitalist, for whom the worker's life-activity is a use-value. Under capitalism, the teleological character of human labor is the private property of the capitalist class.

That the capitalists' pursuit of their class interests prevents workers from exercising their human *ergon* is regarded by Marx as an *unethical* state of affairs.[20] Indeed, what sort of condemnation other than *ethical* would be appropriate in this context, given Marx's adherence to a normative anthropology? For it has been the historical role of *ergon*-based anthropologies to support claims concerning what is ethically good and bad for men.... It has been suggested that "The slanted interest, charged language and acrid tone of *Capital* imply not moral indignation, but simply outrage at the conditions of exploitation."[21] But such "outrage," voiced in reference to an explicitly stated normative anthropology, and constituting a systematic network of commendations and condemnations, is precisely what counts in the Western philosophical tradition as *moral* indignation.

It should also be noted here that on Marx's view, capitalists are *also* alienated from their essential human nature. In pursuing their class interests, capitalists frustrate not only workers' human flourishing, but their own. Capitalists' scope for action is limited and determined by economic laws that operate beyond their control, even though those laws are themselves produced by human activity and social relations. (We will return to this point in the following chapter, where Marx's concept of "alienation" will be our topic.)

Whenever Marx evaluates the moral status of an economic formation, a political system, the role of a group or collective, or the specific actions of one individual person, he does so within the context of an abstract and universal conception of human social existence, that is in turn derived from an analysis of the concrete totality of human social being.[22] Marx asks whether or not the action, principle, political movement, etc. in question is such as to promote or to inhibit the expansion of human powers and the satisfaction of human needs. Put differently, in order to know the ethical status of a thing, one must know whether or not it helps human beings to realize their nature. And for Marx, humans are naturally social beings who satisfy their needs and transform their existence consciously through the labor process. However, to identify what will and will not promote human nature is no mean feat. I do not intend to make it sound obvious or apparent, simply on the basis of an abstract philosophical apprehension of human essence, which human actions will fit that bill.

Marx's account of human nature is in a certain sense, quite "thin." He does not think that human beings are necessarily or ineluctably selfish, altruistic, competitive, fallen, vicious, or any other of a whole host of characterizations that other theories have posited as necessary and permanent features of human nature. Technically speaking, everything a human being has ever been or done constitutes part of human nature. But then it is fair to ask: once we have ascended "from earth to heaven," as Marx and Engels put it in *The Critique of the German Ideology*, abstracting a very plastic and dynamic human essence out of the concrete totality of determinate appearances, how do we get back down again to make specific claims about how human beings *ought* to behave in the concrete?[23]

That move downward is mediated by different levels of abstraction between essential human nature that is universal to all human beings, and any given particular, concrete historical situation.[24] We approach historical questions assuming that human beings are always at least indirectly producing their own conditions of existence when they produce in order to satisfy their needs. However, that presupposition is obviously quite general and human production can take on any of a wide variety of specific forms. So in evaluating a concrete historical situation it is not enough to know merely that human beings produce their existence through the labor process.

No human being acts in conditions of absolute knowledge. Yet in seeking to determine what is morally right or wrong in a given situation, we must gather as much information as possible regarding moments of the concrete totality of social existence in which one acts. In short, a historical materialist appraisal of human social existence is a prerequisite for accurate normative judgments. Here is a nonexhaustive description of some of the most important aspects of reality that we must investigate, in order to determine what is morally required at a particular historical moment.

In addition to knowing that human beings produce their existence, we must also determine how that production is carried out. We must know the mode of production of the relevant society in which the ethical determination is to be made. We must know whether there is a division of labor and if so, how labor is divided. Furthermore, we must know what stage of development a society is at within that mode of production. This is an empirical question about the economic organization of a society. To answer that empirical question, we have to investigate such matters as: Who takes part in economically productive activity? Is this a hunter-gatherer society where people mostly consume what is found ready in nature? Are human beings actively intervening into nature to direct its processes, as in an agricultural society? Has production become more highly regimented and socialized, made vastly more efficient by the innovations of industrialization? We then need to examine how goods are distributed once they are produced. Is a surplus created? If there is a surplus, how large is it, and who controls it?

We also need to know what material resources society has at its disposal and how these might allow a transition to a higher stage of society—that is, one more amenable to the realization of human nature. It is merely utopian, Marx argues, to advocate a new type of society without properly identifying exactly which forces within the old society make such a transition and development possible and how those forces can be directed toward such a transition. A social transformation can only be genuinely moral at a point at which the elements exist with which to realize it.

We need to know what if any classes exist in the society and what the balance of forces are among them. The notion of economic class is itself an abstraction out of a totality of individual human actors within an economic system. In the case of capitalism, we often see this economic system depicted as one in which autonomous individuals interact with one another as equals, bringing different wares to market—sometimes corn, sometimes their own labor power. However, when we evaluate the dynamics of this system, we see that in fact, these individuals relate to the market in different ways. More closely examined, these "free" and "equal" individuals tend to belong, by virtue of their relation to the capitalist market, in one of two broad categories: those, on the one hand, who buy labor power, and those, on the other hand, who sell it. And whether you are the capitalist who buys labor power in order to produce commodities she can then sell to increase her profit, or the worker who has nothing to sell but his labor power in order to satisfy his private needs, your actions are not so "free." Instead, they are determined in significant ways by the economic laws that govern the movement of commodities in such a society. And these actors are not so "equal," because those who live by buying labor power and amassing profit tend to have the upper hand over those who live by selling their labor power daily and thereby building the store of accumulated dead labor which rests in the hands of the capitalist.

So in determining what an actor ought morally to do within a given historical situation, we must determine the class membership of the particular historical actor in question. We must then also ask whether her actions promote the interests of her class and how those class interests stand in relation to the interests of society or of humanity taken as a whole. We need to know the level of organization of that class, whether it has become conscious of its interests, and whether it has developed a political leadership capable of advancing its group interests.

We need to know the nature and breadth of the individual person's scope for action. To determine this, it is important to understand the historical factors that have led up to the moment in which she acts, as well as to know the individual's own personal qualities and capacities.

The investigation into each of these questions will proceed from an understanding that each of these aspects of social being has arisen out of a long process of human beings producing their own existence through their active adaptation to the world in which they live. However, in order to derive specific, concrete moral claims out of this abstract and general principle, we must understand the particular manner in which this essence is realized, and then the manner in which it is distorted, frustrated, or limited in the various historical formations that have arisen out of the process of human self-changing.

It may sound as though it is an awfully tall order, to need to know so much about the historical context in which an agent acts. But the point is that to say with a high degree of accuracy what is morally required in a given historical situation, we need to know as much of this context as possible *and* we need to understand it in a manner informed by categories such as "class" and "economic mode of production." Only then can we understand how all the parts of this totality interact with one another and form a developing whole into which human beings can consciously and rationally intervene. With regard to morality, what it means to say, as Marx does, that "when reality is depicted, philosophy as an independent branch of knowledge loses its medium of existence," is that we cannot make accurate moral claims without investigating the concrete historical situation as thoroughly and systematically as possible.[25] Philosophy continues to exist as part of our knowledge, but there is no longer a hard and fast border between philosophical knowledge and the scientific knowledge of society and nature. It is superseded and subsumed within historical materialism. And so I wholly disagree with, for example, Philip J. Kain's argument in his 1984 paper "Marx and the Abolition of Morality," that for Marx, "only science can be justified, not morality. Moral judgments cannot be empirically verified and they are not true or false." The question: What is to be done? is answered by determining what, in a particular situation, is most likely to promote the realization of human nature. This is something that can be determined empirically via the method I have sketched here.

What is moral at a given point in time depends on a whole range of determinate and historically emergent factors. While Marx does think that in the present historical moment, human beings ought to work to promote communism, this view does not entail or imply that the promotion of communism has been the morally right activity for humans to engage in at all historical times. To make such a suggestion would be to illegitimately abstract from the specific historical circumstances which first make communism possible only at a certain stage in the development of capitalist production. As Marx argues, to call for the immediate implementation of fully developed communism at a time when the historical forces do not yet exist with which to achieve it is hopelessly utopian. It is also merely utopian even to call for communism at a time when it might be achieved, but while proposing impotent means such as mere moral suasion, which is unequal to the task of realizing a communist society.

In order to draw the conclusion that human beings ought to promote communism, Marx does not abstractly imagine what ideal future society would best suit human beings as he imagines them to be. Instead, he examines how the alienation of humans from their essence leads to a debased, limited existence for human beings and even threatens continued human existence of any kind. He examines the economic tendencies already existing within capitalism that lead to greater rationalization and socialization of human production. These provide the basis for greater conscious control of human beings over their own powers. He looks to the existing workers' movement and its political and economic aims, and how the achievement of its aims would affect the entire society of which it is a part. Communism, as Marx tells us, is not an "ideal to realize," but an already real and existing movement within capitalist society, which human beings can and should work to promote.

Adopting Marx's ethical vision, it is possible to make moral judgments not just about what a class or society as a whole ought to do, but also about individual agents and their actions. Again, in evaluating the actions of a particular individual agent, in order to answer the question of what this person ought or ought not to do, we have to understand the relevant historical context. We need to know what paths for action are actually open to her, and how her individual actions are likely to make an impact on the historical situation in which she acts. The greater the historical import and potential of her action to either promote or inhibit the realization of unalienated human nature, the greater the moral significance of that action.

Early in his career, Marx writes that for human beings there is an imperative "to overthrow all relations in which man is a debased, enslaved, forsaken, despicable being."[26] Within human social arrangements that promote the domination of things over people and of man over man, it is always possible to ask what can be done to do away with this debasement, and how any particular action relates to the struggle to overthrow it. The answer to the question of how a person should act is determined by assessing empirically the conditions in which she acts, and the potential of her action to promote the further realization of essential human nature. This abstraction is itself determined empirically by assessing a concrete totality of human history and existing social relations. In this sense, Marx's method for determining what is moral or immoral at a given historical moment is a scientific method, and one that can provide guidance in individual action, a commonplace expectation of ethical inquiry.

In the 2018 edition of his *Why Marx Was Right*, Terry Eagleton writes,

> As far as religion goes, it is worth pointing out that there have been Jewish Marxists, Islamic Marxists, and Christian Marxists who champion so-called liberation theology. All of them are materialists in Marx's sense of the word. . . . Marxist materialism is not a set of statements about the cosmos, such as "Everything is made out of atoms" or "There is no God." It is a theory of how historical animals function.[27]

Well, yes and no. It is true that Marx's materialism is a theory of human beings in their historical development. It is also true that Marx does not explicitly espouse any version of atomism and that he is resolutely hostile to pronouncements on the existence or nonexistence of God. However, Marx's refusal to entertain metaphysical questions of that type does not imply that he was amenable to any answer whatsoever that one might wish to give them. If Marx saw little value in denying the existence of God (and indeed, he saw no value at all in statements of this kind), it is because he saw still *less* value in raising the question of God's existence to begin with. And *this* is a judgment from which positive assertions of God's existence can hardly escape.

Marx's impatience with atheism was based in his critique that it was *still too religious*. This is why Marx wrote in an 1842 letter to Arnold Ruge, "I desired that, if there is to be talk about philosophy, there should be less trifling with the label 'atheism' (which reminds one of children, assuring everyone who is ready to listen to them that they are not afraid of the bogy man)."[28] Atheism is "religious" because, like theistic belief, its assertions outstrip the possibilities of what, on Marx's view, can be scientifically known by human beings. In a contribution to the 2019 Routledge *Companion to Atheism and Philosophy*, I wrote,

> For Marx, not even the natural world has an existence independent of human beings, for it is so thoroughly conditioned by human action. As we saw earlier, for Marx it is this actuality of practical engagement with the natural world that makes it objectively knowable for human beings.[29]

So yes, it is true that Marx's materialist conception of history is a theory of how human beings, we "historical animals," to adopt Eagleton's phrase, inhabit the world and produce and reproduce ourselves in the world. But Marx's anthropocentrism commits him to the principle that a theory of worldly human social existence is, *a fortiori*, also a theory of the world. It is not simply that we cannot *know* what lies beyond. There is simply no "beyond" of which we can sensibly speak. It is for this reason that, in opposing his own materialism to Ludwig Feuerbach's, Marx writes in a passage on Feuerbach that was later published posthumously as part of *The Critique of the German Ideology*,

> Feuerbach speaks in particular of the perception of natural science ... Even this pure natural science is provided with an aim, as with its material, only through trade and industry, through the sensuous activity of men. So much is this activity, this unceasing sensuous labour and creation, this production, the basis of the whole sensuous world as it now exists, that, were it interrupted only for a year, Feuerbach would not only find an enormous change in the natural world, but would very soon find that the whole world of men and his own perceptive faculty, nay his own existence, were missing. ... The nature that preceded human history, is not by any means the nature in which Feuerbach lives, it is nature which today no longer exists anywhere (except perhaps on a few Australian coral-islands of recent origin) and which, therefore, does not exist for Feuerbach.[30]

If Marx's materialism leads him to a certain skepticism regarding humans' capacity to know the non–human-inhabited natural world, that alone puts us in a position to well imagine how he might regard supernatural claims about the eternal divine, or even attempts at inquiry into such matters. But does this make Eagleton incorrect to assert that there are Jewish, Muslim, and Christian Marxists? I don't think it does; historiographically, it would not be a very valuable endeavor to scour the record for all who have taken up the banner of Marxism, organized for workers' liberation, and understood and combatted capitalism's dehumanizing, exploiting destruction of humanity, and then use their relationship to religious tradition to rigidly impose some litmus test of strict Marxist orthodoxy. I think Eagleton is of course correct that there are countless Marxists in each of these traditions. But for those whose relationship to religious tradition involves some belief in the supernatural, or the rejection of the principle of "Man as the highest being for Man," no, it cannot be said that they are materialists *in Marx's sense of the word*. In this, anyway, they are at least in good company with most of the self-professed atheists who claim Marx's materialism.

Human Needs

The satisfaction of human needs is an important part of Marx's moral conception, so much so that Agnes Heller, in her 1974 book *The Theory of Need in Marx*, went so far as to suggest that in Marx's economic theory, "the concept of need plays one of the main roles, if not actually *the* main role."[31] Those needs, according to Marx, develop and expand as human powers and the sophistication of their social production increases. Marx regularly invites his reader to keep in mind that the prerequisite for any more complex or sophisticated form of social existence is that humans' basic natural needs for food, water, shelter, etc., first be satisfied. Yet as social beings, humans have not only their strictly biological needs, but also needs that come about as a result of humans' attempts to satisfy those biological needs and the complex of needs that arise historically out of that initial pursuit.[32] In producing according to their existing needs, human beings not only satisfy those needs, but also create new needs, the fulfillment of which impose new requirements, setting the process into further motion as human beings then develop new forms of production to meet their new needs. This relationship between the presence of human needs and their role as a spur to further creativity and thus, to further expansion of human powers, is what inspires Andrew Chitty's remark, in his 1993 essay "The Early Marx on Needs," that "human needs are constitutive of our essence as human beings."[33] If we take into account that for Marx, having a need is not a passive state but rather one moment in a mutually reinforcing and co-constitutive dialectic of needing and creating, then we will have the right picture in mind.

In the *Grundrisse*, Marx refers to these needs, "historic needs—needs created by production itself," "needs which are themselves the offspring of social production and intercourse," as "social needs." Social needs, the "needs created by production itself," have their basis in the natural needs toward which production was historically first directed and which must still at present continually be satisfied. As Marx writes in *The German Ideology*:

> The first premise of all human existence and, therefore, of all history, [is that humans] must be in a position to live in order to be able to "make history." But life involves before everything else eating and drinking, a habitation, clothing and many other things. The first historical act is thus the production of the means to satisfy these needs, the production of material life itself. And indeed this is an historical act, a fundamental condition of all history, which today, as thousands of years ago, must daily and hourly be fulfilled merely in order to sustain human life.[34]

And since those natural needs for food, drink, shelter, etc. are directly determined by the characteristics of humans as natural beings, it is right to say that human biological being plays a fundamental role in determining the development of social needs. However, it is not the case that social needs are in any way simply reducible to natural needs, and it would also be foreign to Marx to regard natural needs as the "real needs," and the social, historically arisen needs, as somehow less genuine. Marx provides a specific example of how basic, biological needs give rise to increasingly *social* needs in his discussion of a group of French workers.

> When communist *artisans* associate with one another, theory, propaganda, etc., is their first end. But at the same time, as a result of this association, they acquire a new need—the need for society—and what appears as a means becomes an end. In this practical process the most splendid results are to be observed whenever French socialist workers are seen together. Such things as smoking, drinking, eating, etc., are no longer means of contact or means that bring them together. Association, society and conversation, which again has association as its end, are enough for them; the brotherhood of man is no mere phrase with them, but a fact of life, and the nobility of man shines upon us from their work-hardened bodies.[35]

These workers' need for higher wages in order to ensure continued access to food and housing gave rise, in the struggle against their bosses, to a need for solidarity with fellow workers. This socially produced need is no less a genuine need for human beings than is the biological need for food. To the contrary, for Marx it is precisely such socially produced needs that *most* fully express a distinctly human character.

In his 2011 book *Why Marx Was Right*, Terry Eagleton summarizes the lesson of this passage in the following terms:

> The best things are done just for the hell of it. We do them simply because they belong to our fulfilment as the kind of animals we are, not out of duty, custom, sentiment, authority, material necessity, social utility or fear of the Almighty. There is no reason, for example, why we should delight in one another's company. When we do so, however, we are realising a vital capacity of our "species being." . . . Human solidarity is essential for the purpose of political change; but in the end it serves as its own reason.[36]

Of course, there are all sorts of good reasons that it belongs to our dynamic and evolving nature, as human beings, to be—or in any case, to come to be—the sort of creatures that crave sociality. In going about the business of creating and recreating the conditions of everyday material life, we produce and reproduce our longing for the company of one another. Eagleton's point is that Marx describes a form of life in which the question "Why be in fellowship with other human beings?" requires no other, further answer pointing beyond the intrinsic desirability of companionship, itself.

Marx writes that the significance of communism as a goal for human beings is that it will realize "a new manifestation of the forces of human nature and a new enrichment of human nature," thereby laying the material basis for the realization and development of existing capacities and the appearance of new ones, and corresponding needs.[37] Under capitalism, Marx argues, human beings are so separated from the natural world and from their own species-being (their own particularly human mode of interaction with the natural world, i.e., the labor process and interaction with its products) that their needs as human beings are limited to bare subsistence—and often, not even as much as this.

Under capitalism, a person's needs have no effective capacity to be fulfilled unless that person has money to fulfill the need. For workers, particularly, their needs are reduced to just those needs that must be fulfilled in order for their work to be done. As Marx writes, "It is not only that man has no human needs—even his animal needs cease to exist."[38] A central element of Marx's opposition to capitalism is that it limits the development of human beings by inhibiting the fulfillment of human needs and in so doing, also limits the range of existing human needs to needs only for the barest essentials. Capitalism bars humans from the kind of relationship to the natural world and the products of their labor that would create more sophisticated forms of human interaction with their environment, closing down the development of corresponding new needs, as well. As Lukács pointed out in his book *Ontology of Social Being*, this inhibition of needs is tantamount to the inhibition of human nature itself.[39]

Furthermore, Marx argues that in class society, human production is carried out in an alienated manner. Instead of being directed consciously and rationally by human persons, labor—what labor is performed and how it is performed, and who performs it—appears determined by economic laws that operate independently of anyone's control. In class society, and particularly in capitalism, this basic teleology in the conscious life activity of human beings is disrupted. The person who carries out the work of realizing a product may have no ideal representation of the work at all. The worker produces not in accordance with a standard that she has consciously set for herself, but rather produces as part of an extended process that appears not to be determined by any human rationality or human goal-positing at all, but instead, by abstract economic laws of supply and demand. The work, as a result, begins to lose its human character, a process accelerated by the character of work itself, which becomes increasingly odious to the worker—a denial and a sacrifice of her human existence, rather than a realization and expression of the human being in the external world.

This disruption of the basic teleology in the labor process occurs not only for the industrial worker producing in a fashion dictated by the laws of the market. Rather, it takes place in all manner of human activity, including intellectual and political activity. Operating within class society, human beings behave less as individual actors, and more and more as exemplars of this or that class. Class actors behave in manners dictated to a great extent by the economic and social system of which they are a part.

The question arises, then, of how that teleology is disrupted and how it comes to be the case that economic laws, rather than human beings, govern production. This result comes about as human beings produce and regularities begin to appear within that totality of human activity—regularities that are neither fully understood nor controlled and which come to develop the appearance of external laws of production. Thus, a world that human beings have produced actually appears to be independent from and hostile to human beings (we can say, human beings become alienated from their own product, the social world). The essence of social being, which is the labor process as conscious life activity, is mediated by social forms so that it no longer appears as the product of conscious life activity and the developing complex of teleological goal-positing and production by concrete human individuals. Instead, it comes to defeat the teleological aspect which is a normal part of the labor process and of conscious life activity. For an example of this, one might consider the demonstrated incapacity of humanity at this point in history even to cease sowing the seeds of its own impending destruction. Dominated as it is by the profit motive, our society refuses to address the environmental crisis that threatens to wipe out human beings on Earth altogether. Even the most simple, basic aim of human beings to safeguard our continued survival is thwarted by social arrangements that inhibit the ability of humans to act rationally and effectively in accordance with that goal.

The solution to this disruption, Marx thinks, is to bring the appearance of social being into accordance with its essence. This means that production must be brought under the rational, conscious control of human beings. And for that to occur, without regularities in human production taking on the appearance of disempowering and objectionably determining social laws, social production must be coordinated socially, and directed not toward profit, but instead toward the creation of a society in which the free development of each is the precondition of the free development of all. What I am describing here in Marx's thought is the transition from capitalism, to the transitional stages of socialism and, eventually, to fully developed communist society.

It is important not to interpret Marx's vision of this future society in which "the free development of each is the condition for the free development of all" as some Marxian "end of history." Instead, Marx argues that class society constitutes the *prehistory* of the human species, and that only with humanity's rational control over its own powers and over the natural world of which human beings are a part (which would itself include the abolition of the opposition between humans and the natural world), can an actually *human* history begin to unfold. Marx refers to this in the *Critique of Political Economy* when he writes:

> The bourgeois mode of production is the last antagonistic form of the social process of production—antagonistic not in the sense of individual antagonism but of an antagonism that emanates from the individuals' social conditions of existence—but the productive forces developing within bourgeois society create also the material conditions for a solution of this antagonism. The prehistory of human society accordingly closes with this social formation.[40]

With the resolution of this antagonism, the material basis for moral theory as a way to theorize the gap between human existence as it is, and human existence as it ought to be, will also disappear; morality and moral theory, as such, will no longer exist. We will return to this theme in Chapter 9, "The Abolition of Morality," so here, I will only note that although this doctrine may seem unusual, it should not seem at all surprising, given Marx's historical materialism. Morality as such is universal and objective, yet also thoroughly historical. It emerges at a certain point in the historical development of the world, and will eventually also pass away.

The "Rich Individual" in Marx's Ethical Vision

In addition to analyzing other moral theories, Marx, over the course of his writings, develops a distinctively historical materialist ethical vision based on human beings "in their actual, empirically perceptible process of development under definite conditions," and the requirements that must be satisfied in order to bring about the circumstances in which we might see what Marx calls the "all-sided development" of "rich individuality."[41] Marx examines the goals of such important struggles as the French Revolution and considers how they represent the highest consciousness about what is necessary in order for human beings to preserve the historical gains of class societies and move closer toward an "all-sided development." Based on his understanding of these struggles, their aims, and their historical role, together with his understanding of human nature, Marx draws the conclusion that man is the highest being for man and that human development itself is therefore the most important goal for human beings. In his criticisms of other moral theories and of existing class society, his standard becomes clear. A moral philosophy must promote the continued existence of humanity, the preservation of its cultural heritage in all its diversity and achievements, and the "rich individuality" and "all-sided development" of human needs and capacities.

In the *Grundrisse*, Marx asserts the desirability of

> the development of the rich individuality which is as all-sided in its production as in its consumption, and whose labour also therefore appears no longer as labour, but as the full development of activity itself, in which natural necessity in its direct form has disappeared; because a historically created need has taken the place of the natural one.[42]

Marx argues that one of the aims of human social existence is for human beings to bring increasingly much of the natural world and more of their own social relations under their conscious, rational control. That ability of human beings to extend greater control over themselves and over the natural world is a key aspect of bringing about their "all-sided development." The extent to which labor is carried out as a mere means to life or as life-activity itself is another key aspect of the all-sided development of human beings. In alienated labor, the essence of man's social being, labor, is converted into a mere means for the maintenance of his continued existence as a biological being with merely natural needs. The extent to which those natural needs, such as, say, the need to eat, have been transformed into social, historically arisen needs is a further marker of the extent to which this all-sided development has taken place. For instance, for an early human being, the need to eat may have had hardly any other appearance than the simple need for plain fruit or flesh. Today, after centuries of social development, it may appear as the need for adequate access to affordable grocery items and the tools to carry out appropriate culinary preparation. Here, we can say that a "historically created need has taken the place of a natural one."

When Marx refers to the "rich individuality" that could first be developed in communist society, he refers to the human being in whom human essence has been brought into accordance with human appearance. Instead of appearing as a debased, limited creature, hampered and controlled by economic laws, the human is an essentially social being with a capacity for in-principle unlimited development through the labor process. She also *appears* to be so in a society in which the natural world and the social sphere have been brought under human beings' conscious and rational control and directed on the basis of human needs. The existence of human persons as individuated beings at all, is itself the result of social production, a point Marx makes when he says that man "is not only a social animal, but an animal that can isolate itself only within society."[43] Only at a certain stage in the development of production can human beings emerge as individuals, rather than merely as "herd animals" pursuing goals and interests that are narrowly subordinated to the struggle for bare survival.[44]

It is on the basis of these aspects of Marx's view that Erich Fromm writes, in his, *Marx's Concept of Man*,

> Marx's aim was that of the spiritual emancipation of man, of his liberation from the chains of economic determination, of restituting him in his human wholeness, of enabling him to find unity and harmony with his fellow man and with nature. Marx's philosophy was, in secular, nontheistic language, a new and radical step forward in the tradition of prophetic Messianism; it was aimed at the full realization of individualism, the very aim which has guided Western thinking from the Renaissance and the Reformation far into the nineteenth century.[45]

Dynamism and processual development are key elements of essential human nature that is stunted in a society that does not allow human beings to satisfy their full range of needs and develop an unfolding array of human powers in the natural world. Marx calls for the abolition of human beings' alienation from essential human nature and more specifically, of their alienation from the world they themselves have produced. This is a call for labor to be carried out in accordance with human essence. As conscious, purposive activity that increases and develops humanity's command over the external world and over himself, and is directed toward the satisfaction of human needs and development of human powers, such a reconciliation of essence and appearance, Marx argues, would usher in the beginning of truly human history.

This view of human nature responds to one of the most common criticisms of Marxism's vision of a future world in which the flourishing of each is the precondition of the flourishing of all. That is the view that human beings are essentially selfish and competitive, in ways that make such a communist society utterly infeasible, and "idealistic" to even imagine. Political philosopher David Estlund has referred to this as "the human nature constraint." He characterizes this commonly held position (which he himself rejects) as follows:

A normative political theory is defective and thus false if it imposes standards or requirements that ignore human nature—that is, requirements that will not, owing to human nature and the motivational incapacities it entails, ever be satisfied.[46]

Leaving aside whether or not the constraint is legitimate in itself, let us nonetheless concede that for Marxism at least, it would be damning if it were to turn out that human nature ensured the practical recommendations of a Marxist normative political theory could never be realized. This is a special vulnerability of a Marxist moral theory, because its entire *raison d'etre* is not theory as an end in itself, but rather the concrete, practical, lived, bringing-to-fruition of those remedies which the theory recommends. Marxist moral theory is only meaningful when combined with practice in the dialectical unity of praxis. If Marxist theory cannot ever be realized because human nature is intrinsically such as to necessarily preclude it, then the theory is itself a failure, as its validity is rooted in its claim to a correct understanding of human existence in the world, from which claims about how humans *ought* to exist in the world, follow.

In navigating the challenge set forth by the "human nature constraint," we can see a great part of what hangs on the essence/appearance distinction. At least for those of us who live in present-day, capitalist, market-driven Western societies, it is disingenuous to pretend that skepticism about whether communism could ever work for people such as ourselves is always unjustified. In fact, *it couldn't* work for people like us; not even Marx thought that it could. The case for communism's feasibility hangs crucially on the question of whether the greed, antagonism, and selfishness that predominate in capitalist society are fixed and ineradicable features of human life.

Marx's argument for a communist society is that such a society is best suited to our nature. But how can this be, when even he acknowledges that human beings, as they exist in capitalist society, are not yet suited to communism? Again, we must appeal to the distinction between human nature at the level of essence, and at the level of appearance. On Marx's view, a communist society is morally desirable because it would allow human beings to develop their powers in a more all-sided manner than is possible today. The struggle for mere survival blocks many individuals from acting in ways that are not narrowly subordinated to the satisfaction of biological needs. Servicing the need for food, water, and shelter cuts them off from increasing their capacity to realize themselves in and through their natural and social environment.

Freeing humans from this struggle for survival (what Marx calls "natural necessity") would allow them to express their essential nature in a more developed and fully realized manner.

For Marx, the feasibility of communism, the plasticity of human nature, and the case for revolution are all intimately and inextricably linked to one another. In their *Critique of the German Ideology*, he and Engels wrote,

> Both for the production on a mass scale of this communist consciousness, and for the success of the cause itself, the alteration of men on a mass scale is necessary, an alteration which can only take place in a practical movement, a revolution; this revolution is necessary, therefore, not only because the ruling class cannot be overthrown in any other way, but also because the class overthrowing it can only in a revolution succeed in ridding itself of all the muck of ages and become fitted to found society anew.[47]

A common complaint lodged against socialist thought is that when we look around, we find people who are selfish, racist, misogynistic, and perhaps possessed of many other undesirable traits that render them generally antisocial. Today such people seem hardly fit to function productively within a society based on values of solidarity and cooperation. Marx might agree. The future communist society he envisions is one that makes a radical break with all existing social relations. For such a society to be possible, human beings suited to that society must be created. Happily, human beings are constantly creating and transforming themselves as a species. What remains is for that process of transformation to be carried out in a conscious and goal-directed manner, with the aim of promoting prosocial traits, discouraging antisocial ones, and forming practices and institutions conducive to social collaboration and individual well-being.

Understanding essential human nature as humans' own power to intervene into natural and social processes and, consequently, into their own development, allows us to make judgments about what is conducive or injurious to the flourishing of this essential nature while also acknowledging that specific human traits vary over time, and that this variation in appearance has consequences for morality. Communist revolutionary activity, for instance, is morally required just at that stage in human social development when it is made possible. Communism is justified when the conditions of its possible success are in place. This is not the case at a time when all human beings live as hunter-gatherers, Marx argues. But it is the case now that capitalism has transformed social production such that it is possible to produce enough to satisfy everyone's needs. In this sense, morality is "contingent" in that what is moral at a given time is in large part determined by existing material conditions and the current stage of human social development. What a communist morality requires of us today is not that we attempt to instantiate, today, the very habits and values that would prevail in that later society. This would be unfeasible, and at odds with Marx's entire approach. Rather, it requires that we act so as to transform our existing social relations, which we *are* capable of doing right now, as a correct understanding of essential human nature makes clear.

In Chapter 4, I explain Marx's account of what it is to be alienated from that human nature. Let us turn to that question now.

4
Alienation

If in Marxist theory, human nature is to be understood not as a set of fixed traits but rather as an ongoing and generative process of human self-making, then alienation may be understood as that same process gone awry. For Marx, the truth that "man is the highest being for man" functions as an ethical ideal. This phrase is one of several Marx uses to describe what it would be for human beings to live in an unalienated way—that is, to be in full possession of their creative capacities and to embrace the furtherance of the in-principle limitless expansion of human powers as their highest aim.

To understand the alienation concept and its centrality in Marxist moral thought, it is necessary to distinguish heavily psychologized depictions of disaffection and ennui, with which we might be more familiar, from the materialist concept Marx deployed. For Marx, alienation pertains to frustrated or misdirected human productive powers. Alienation bears important psychological features and symptoms—ones that play an important role in motivating the working class to seek its abolition. Yet alienation is primarily to be understood as a feature of relationships among material beings: the relationship of humans to their products, of humans to other humans or to the species in general, and of any given human to herself.

Human beings are essentially social beings who produce their own existence through conscious, purposive activity in the labor process. When human beings are alienated from their essence, this process in which they consciously and purposively direct and produce their own existence is frustrated. Human beings' products—material, social, and intellectual—take on a foreign and hostile character. Instead of furthering human aims, in alienation, the products of human labor thwart the intentions of their creators. Their products seem to exist independently, as though their emergence and development were not determined by human activity. The fact that these things have been produced through human activity, and can be controlled and directed through that activity, is partly or entirely obscured.

Alienation is contrary to, and impedes the development of, essential human nature.[1] Yet insofar as it is itself a result of human activity, alienation is also an aspect and outcome of that nature. (To put this in more Hegelian terms: alienation is the active, practical negation of essential human nature, but also at the same time, itself one moment of the expression and realization of essential human nature. Essential human nature thus contains its own negation. Communism, that movement which abolishes the present state of things, is the negation of this negation and thus the positive realization of essential human nature.) It will not be enough, then, to offer moral approval or disapproval on the simple basis of whether any given activity, or social arrangement, is properly understood to be part of human nature. *All human activities and products are aspects and expressions of human nature, including alienation itself as the frustration and distortion of that nature.* The relationship of human nature to moral evaluation is not to simplistically rule particular behaviors and social arrangements as compatible or incompatible with human nature. Rather, the question is whether or not a given object of moral evaluation furthers or hinders the ongoing full, free, and conscious development of human creative powers. Some human activities and social forms are consistent with this aim and others are not.

The goal of abolishing alienation—of realizing human essence as the unalienated activity of labor—is *moral* in the sense that it is a claim about how human beings ought to live, and how they ought to treat one another.[2] This is a contextual moral principle. It is not a timeless, ahistorical goal. It exists as a goal only once human beings become alienated from their species-being, and only until the moment when they come to fully realize their species-being once again. Yet we must be mindful not to characterize the abolition of alienation as a simple return to an unalienated past. For Marx, as for Hegel, it is only through alterations to human existence realized in (and through) the development of history that the abolition of alienation can be achieved. In some ways it is a return—to life without economic classes and their attendant division of labor.[3] And in other profound ways, it is something wholly historically new.

Whether Marx retained this alienation concept throughout his early and later work is a matter of perennial debate among scholars of his work. One of the most influential discussants of this question is the French socialist theorist, Louis Althusser, who argued that to retain the alienation concept as a central category of analysis was "un-Marxist." Althusser argued that in developing the theory of historical materialism and presenting it in his and Engels's writings on Feuerbach that were later published, posthumously, as part of *The Critique of the German Ideology*, Marx abandoned his early humanism and all of its trappings. Althusser asked: "Why do so many Marxist philosophers seem to feel the need to appeal to the pre-Marxist ideological concept of 'alienation'?"[4] He maintained that "Marx's youth did *lead* to Marxism, but only at the price of a prodigious break with his origins, a heroic struggle against the illusions he had inherited from the Germany in which he was born, and an acute attention to the realities concealed by these illusions," among these, the alienation concept.[5]

I argue that the abolition of alienation (or put otherwise, the practical realization of "man as the highest being for man," or the realization of essential human nature) is the highest ethical ideal for Marx. The question of whether Marx had a consistently ethical point of view throughout his career thus hangs on whether he consistently called for the abolition of alienation. In the coming pages, I will make the case that Marx remained consistently committed to the "alienation" concept as an ethical framework, even during those times when he shied away from calling it by that name.

Capitalism is not distinguished from earlier economic forms by the fact that the commodity-form exists. In earlier societies, human beings also produced items to profit from their sale. Capitalism, rather, is the economic system in which the commodity-form becomes the dominant mode of exchange (and eventually of human social existence altogether). There is a tendency under capitalism for absolutely everything to be converted into a commodity—up for sale, potentially alienable. The category of the alienable includes human beings' own capacity to perform labor, as the majority of human beings are compelled to take their labor power to market. In 2011, while arguing on the floor of the House of Representatives against wage protections for workers, United States Representative Steven King stated, "Labor is a commodity just like corn or beans or oil or gold, and the value of it needs to be determined by the competition, supply and demand in the workplace."[6] King was roundly—and rightly—criticized for justifying laissez-faire economic policies with this comment. However, it would be mistaken to deny that Rep. King made quite a succinct and accurate, if brutal, statement of a central principle of capitalist production. It is merely the approving formulation of what Marx had decried in 1844: that in capitalism, "the worker's existence is . . . brought under the same condition as the existence of every other commodity."[7]

The appearance of human beings as atomized individuals striving for the satisfaction of mere "egoistic need" develops hand-in-hand with the expansion and sharpening of alienation as a feature of the human condition.

Hungarian Marxist philosopher, István Mészáros, writes that in capitalist society:

> Alienation is therefore characterized by the universal extension of "saleability" (i.e. the transformation of everything into commodity); by the conversion of human beings into "things" so that they could appear as commodities on the market (in other words: the "reification" of human relations); and by the fragmentation of the social body into "isolated individuals" (*vereinzelte Einzelnen*) who pursued their own limited, particularistic aims "in servitude to egoistic need," making a virtue out of their selfishness in their cult of privacy.[8]

To satisfy one's needs in capitalist society, one requires money. And whether capitalist or worker, in order to make money, one must sell something. Marx writes in "On the Jewish Question":

> Selling [*Veräußerung*] is the practical aspect of alienation [*Entäußerung*]. Just as man, as long as he is in the grip of religion, is able to objectify his essential nature only by turning it into something *alien*, something fantastic, so under the domination of egoistic need he can be active practically, and produce objects in practice, only by putting his products, and his activity, under the domination of an alien being, and bestowing the significance of an alien entity—money—on them.[9]

However, the sale of labor power to satisfy private, "egoistic" needs is particularly alienating in that "estranged labour reverses this relationship [between conscious being and species-being], so that it is just because man is a conscious being that he makes his life activity, his *essential being*, a mere means to his *existence*."[10] Labor under capitalism alienates the human being from his own essence, and changes "the life of the species into a means of individual life."[11] Insofar as man's essential nature as a member of the species *Homo sapiens*, his ability to labor, is converted into a commodity to be sold in order to satisfy the private, egoistic needs of the individual, it is this inversion that Marx argues would (and should) be set aright in the transition to a communist society.

I focus my discussion primarily on the alienation of workers through the sale of their labor power. However, it is crucial not to ignore that both worker and capitalist are alienated in capitalist society. For Marx, everyone who lives under capitalism has a life governed by anarchic laws and processes that operate beyond anyone's conscious direction or control. (Again, think here of the economic laws of supply and demand. These not only determine the fate of the worker, but also dictate to the capitalist what and how much is to be produced, and under what conditions.) Under capitalism, both workers and capitalists take part in human activity that is directed at the accumulation of profit as its highest end. Therefore, both are alienated insofar as they fail to recognize human development (the realization of human essence as an active adaptation to the environment through the labor process, and the ongoing and limitless development of human powers) as the highest aim for human beings, or to engage in practices reflecting the status of that aim.

A question arises. If both capitalist and worker are alienated in capitalist society, then why does Marx focus on the working class as a potentially revolutionary force in society, and not on the capitalists who apparently hold so much more power? Is this not arbitrary? The answer is twofold. First, Marx argues that because of their role in production, workers are uniquely positioned to redirect society's resources and to make human development the conscious aim of human production. Capitalism socializes the labor process, prompting relations of solidarity and cooperation to develop among workers. It is precisely the further development of such relations that would help contribute to the production of a society based on human solidarity and democratic control of the means of production. Relatedly, while it is not possible for every person to be a capitalist, it *is* possible to have a society in which the only economic class is the working class. The worker's conditions of existence are thus generalizable in a manner that would allow for the abolition of class society, as for everyone to be a member of the same class is for there to be no classes at all. Marx argues that it is the abolition of class society, together with a preservation and further development of the productive capacities developed in capitalism, that can provide the material basis for the abolition of alienation.

Secondly, workers and capitalists both experience alienation, but they experience it in decidedly different ways. As Marx writes in *The Holy Family*:

> The propertied class and the class of the proletariat present the same human self-estrangement. But the former class feels at ease and strengthened in this self-estrangement, it recognises estrangement as its own power and has in it the semblance of a human existence. The latter feels annihilated in estrangement; it sees in it its own powerlessness and the reality of an inhuman

existence. It is, to use an expression of Hegel, in its abasement the indignation at that abasement, an indignation to which it is necessarily driven by the contradiction between its human nature and its condition of life, which is the outright, resolute and comprehensive negation of that nature.[12]

It is this indignation and awareness of her own abasement that impels the worker to abolish the conditions in which she exists and to forge new ones in which her human nature is affirmed and expressed, rather than "outright, resolutely and comprehensively negated." And as Marx writes in his essay "Comments on James Mill":

Labour to earn a living involves: 1) estrangement and fortuitous connection between labour and the subject who labours; 2) estrangement and fortuitous connection between labour and the object of labour; 3) that the worker's role is determined by social needs which, however, are alien to him and a compulsion to which he submits out of egoistic need and necessity, and which have for him only the significance of a means of satisfying his dire need, just as for them he exists only as a slave of their needs; 4) that to the worker the maintenance of his individual existence appears to be the *purpose* of his activity and what he actually does is regarded by him only as a means; that he carries on his life's activity in order to earn means of *subsistence*. Hence the greater and the more developed the social power appears to be within the private property relationship, the more egoistic, asocial and estranged from his own nature does man become.[13]

The working class, because of its position in capitalist society, is capable of overthrowing the existing relations of production and because of its subjective lived experience of capitalism, can be rationally motivated to do so on the basis of its economic interests.

It is true that throughout most of the history of capitalist society, we do not see the overwhelming majority of workers consciously struggling together to bring about communism. However, workers have attempted, in various ways, to resist the oppressive conditions of capitalist society. They still do so, for instance, when they strike against low wages, demand shorter workdays, or fight to keep their pensions. At crucial points, workers can and do become revolutionary. Marx examines the history of those working-class struggles through the economic, political, and social contexts in which they are waged. He also develops a conception of human nature and of human needs that is grounded in the real existence of individual human beings throughout history. Looking at human needs, and analyzing the content of workers' demands and determining what sort of society would be necessary in order for these needs and demands to be met, Marx argues that these needs and demands point toward the imperative to achieve a communist society.

Alienation under capitalism is a *universal* human condition. Workers, however, have a subjective experience of alienation as markedly oppressive and harmful in ways that those with greater access to society's resources do not typically experience. It is the universality of alienation as a human condition in class society that raises the class struggle between proletariat and bourgeoisie from a mere battle between particular classes to a fight for universal human emancipation, making workers' interests and aims representative of universal human ethical imperatives.

In the remaining pages of this chapter, I will trace Marx's development of the "alienation" concept from his earlier works such as the *Economic and Philosophic Manuscripts*, through his middle period including the writings that make up *The Critique of the German Ideology*, and finally to the concept's appearance in *Capital*. We will discuss in finer detail how Marx's alienation concept figures into his larger theory and into his moral thought in particular. This will answer those who argue that Marx abandoned the alienation concept in his later work, or that it is possible to grasp Marx's theory without it.

"Alienation" in Marx's Early Writings

The Economic and Philosophic Manuscripts of 1844 constitute the *locus classicus* for Marx's account of alienation, and so this is where we shall begin in exploring his use of the concept in his earlier works. To grasp Marx's invocation of the "alienation" concept, it is useful to recall the term's economic significance in describing the transition from feudal to capitalist property relations, especially with respect to the ownership and transfer of land. Marx captures this in the "Rent of Land" manuscript, where he notes that under capitalism it becomes necessary that the "romantic" appearance of feudal relations

> be abolished—that landed property, the root of private property, be dragged completely into the movement of private property and that it become a commodity; that the rule of the proprietor appear as the undisguised rule of

private property, of capital, freed of all political tincture; that the relationship between proprietor and worker be reduced to the economic relationship of exploiter and exploited; that all . . . personal relationship between the proprietor and his property cease, property becoming merely objective, material wealth; that the marriage of convenience should take the place of the marriage of honour with the land; and that the land should likewise sink to the status of a commercial value, like man. It is essential that that which is the root of landed property—filthy self-interest—make its appearance, too, in its cynical form. It is essential that the immovable monopoly turn into the mobile and restless monopoly, into competition; and that the idle enjoyment of the products of other people's blood and sweat turn into a bustling commerce in the same commodity. Lastly, it is essential that in this competition landed property, in the form of capital, manifest its dominion over both the working class and the proprietors themselves who are either being ruined or raised by the laws governing the movement of capital. The medieval proverb *nulle terre sans seigneur* is thereby replaced by that other proverb, *l'argent n'a pas de maître*, wherein is expressed the complete domination of dead matter over man.[14]

This is a key passage for us because keeping it in view will help stave off a tendency to psychologize the alienation concept and reduce it to merely personal subjective experience. Marx's alienation concept shares a lineage with that of thinkers such as Rousseau who wrote that "to alienate is to give or sell."[15] It also highlights the connection between alienation and the economic freedom that capitalism achieved as a victory against the constraints of feudalism. This was a precondition for the further historical achievements made by the bourgeoisie. This connection between alienation and freedom is a theme we will return to later when we address Marx's critiques of liberal morality. But let us now turn to what Marx does have to say about the worker's subjective experience of alienation under capitalism.

The economic concept of alienation takes on a distinctively normative significance when we note that on Marx's theory, alienation is not *merely* "to give or sell," but rather to be in a hostile confrontation with that which was formerly one's own. Instead of recognizing oneself in the alienated object, one encounters it as one does an enemy. We see this expressed in Marx's characteristically poetic style when he writes, in the "Estranged Labour" manuscript, that "the alienation of the worker in his product means not only that his labor becomes an object, an external existence, but that it exists *outside* him, independently, as something alien to him, and that it becomes a power on its own confronting him."[16]

In unalienated production, a person's products would be a confirmation and expression of individuality, free activity, and the ability to appropriate and transform nature to achieve human ends. Under capitalism, the worker's own product has an inimical character for him. It is produced not in accordance with the worker's own exercise of purposiveness and free agency, but rather as dictated by economic laws of supply and demand that operate in spite of him.

As a commodity, the product becomes added to the capitalist's store of "dead labor" of capital. Possessed now of a mass of stored-up accumulated labor, the capitalist is in a position to exercise even greater control over workers. Productive activity thus appears to worsen the worker's lot rather than improve it. His own essential power is at once also the engine of his degradation. As a result, "The worker becomes an ever cheaper commodity the more commodities he creates. The *devaluation* of the world of men is in direct proportion to the *increasing value* of the world of things."[17]

If the result of labor under capitalism is the worker's alienation from his product, then, Marx reasons, the activity of labor itself must be a process of active alienation, since "the product is after all but the summary of the activity, of production."[18] He writes that labor under capitalism is active alienation in several respects:

> First, the fact that labour is *external* to the worker, i. e., it does not belong to his intrinsic nature; that in his work, therefore, he does not affirm himself but denies himself, does not feel content but unhappy, does not develop freely his physical and mental energy but mortifies his body and ruins his mind. The worker therefore only feels himself outside his work, and in his work feels outside himself. He feels at home when he is not working, and when he is working he does not feel at home. His labour is therefore not voluntary, but coerced; it is *forced labour*. It is therefore not the satisfaction of a need; it is merely a *means* to satisfy needs external to it. Its alien character emerges clearly in the fact that as soon as no physical or other compulsion exists, labour is shunned like the plague. External labour, labour in which man alienates himself, is a labour of self-sacrifice, of mortification. Lastly, the external character of labour for the worker appears in the fact that it is not his own, but someone else's, that it does not belong to him, that in it he belongs, not to himself, but to another. Just as in religion the spontaneous

activity of the human imagination, of the human brain and the human heart, operates on the individual independently of him—that is, operates as an alien, divine or diabolical activity—so is the worker's activity not his spontaneous activity. It belongs to another; it is the loss of his self.[19]

In this description of the character of labor, Marx turns his attention from the worker's product as accumulated or "dead" labor, to the character of the labor process itself. Labor is the essential form of free human activity, and the process through which human nature can be fully expressed in history. However, under capitalism, labor is so odious that the worker performs labor only because through the sale of his labor power can he satisfy his private needs. What should appear as the intrinsic aim of human existence is converted into its means. As the worker's labor power is not his own, and belongs to a foreign power (the capitalist), labor appears as a denial and a sacrifice of the worker's existence, and as something to be studiously avoided whenever possible.

Because labor takes on such an unattractive character, workers rarely recognize the labor process as the essence of human activity. Instead, they come to feel they are truly themselves only when at leisure, or while satisfying those needs they have in common with animals:

> As a result, therefore, man (the worker) only feels himself freely active in his animal functions—eating, drinking, procreating, or at most in his dwelling and in dressing-up, etc.; and in his human functions he no longer feels himself to be anything but an animal. What is animal becomes human and what is human becomes animal.
>
> Certainly eating, drinking, procreating, etc., are also genuinely human functions. But taken abstractly, separated from the sphere of all other human activity and turned into sole and ultimate ends, they are animal functions.[20]

Insofar as humans are natural, biological beings, they have their natural needs more or less in common with other mammals. Their biological make-up is such that in order for the human species to persist and to flourish, human beings must have their biological needs for food, water, housing, and so on satisfied, and they must continue to propagate themselves as a species through sexual reproduction. But human beings are distinct from other natural beings in the means by which they satisfy these needs. Human beings, through socially mediated labor, intervene consciously and purposively into their environments in order to satisfy their natural needs. In so doing, they transform both their environments and themselves, produce new forms of social interaction, and develop new powers and in turn, new social, historically arisen needs. They produce themselves not merely as natural, but also as social beings. In unalienated labor, human beings recognize this continual process of satisfying social, historically arisen needs and developing new powers as an end in itself and as the realization of human beings' essential nature as natural and social beings who satisfy their needs through labor.

In alienated labor, natural and biological needs are not regarded as the ontological basis for a limitless development of social, historically arisen needs. Instead, they are "separated from the sphere of all other human activity and turned into sole and ultimate ends." The powers which have been developed in and through human history—capacities for language, for theorizing, for engineering, and so on—are converted into little more than new ways of satisfying man's natural, biological needs and of serving his "animal functions." As a result of the odious character of labor under capitalism, workers subjectively experience themselves in their "animal functions" as free and active, but experience themselves in their distinctively human functions as little more than animals.

While here Marx describes a subjective experience of alienation in labor under capitalism, it is important again to emphasize that alienation is not *merely* subjective. The objective relationship is between human beings and their essential nature as social beings who produce their own existence through the labor process. In alienation, this relationship is inverted and disturbed. The worker's subjective experience of alienation from his own essence as a conscious and freely active being arises from the real condition in which his activity is not his own. Marx writes of the alienation of labor:

> This relation is the relation of the worker to his own activity as an alien activity not belonging to him; it is activity as suffering, strength as weakness, begetting as emasculating, the worker's *own* physical and mental energy, his personal life—for what is life but activity?—as an activity which is turned against him, independent of him and not belonging to him. Here we have *self-estrangement*, as previously we had the estrangement of the *thing*.[21]

And if the worker is alienated from his product and from himself, then, Marx argues, these things must have been alienated to someone else—to other human beings. "Every self-estrangement of man, from himself and from nature, appears in the relation in which he places himself and nature to men other than and differentiated from himself. . . . [The worker] creates the domination of the person who does not produce over production and over the product."[22] Thus, what seemed to be a domination of things over human beings, turns out to be a social relation: the domination of capitalists over workers.

The alienation of the worker's labor results in the possession of that labor by another human being. Marx argues that every "self-estrangement" is realized and expressed as a relationship between human beings. The worker "creates the domination of the person who does not produce over production and over the product."[23] It is for this reason that the working class alone has the capacity to abolish the dominion of man over man, and heed the categorical imperative to "overthrow all relations in which man is a debased, enslaved, forsaken, despicable being."[24]

I have discussed alienation as the separation of human beings from human essence, and as a condition in which human beings' products appear to exist and to operate independently and in spite of human activity. The alienation of labor, for Marx, has both a subjective and an objective character. Workers labor under conditions that are odious and oppressive, and find themselves unable to direct their own activity freely, instead being compelled to sell their labor power in order to satisfy their needs. As a result, workers subjectively experience work as dehumanizing, and subjectively experience their "animal functions" as those in which they are really human and freely active. This subjective experience is based in an objective condition in which their labor belongs to and is directed by a foreign power: the capitalist.

Yet it must again be stressed that alienation does not only affect workers. Capitalists also experience alienation, albeit in a different form. They experience their decisions as dictated by economic laws of supply and demand, that appear to operate independently of human actors. However, because these economic laws can allow them to expand their financial wealth, capitalists tend to experience alienation as friendly and affirming, and as a phenomenon which affords them some "semblance of a human existence," to invoke Marx's remarks in *The Holy Family*.[25]

It is the sale of labor power and the proletariat's active self-alienation that produces alienation for both capitalist and worker. Hence, Marx writes, "the emancipation of the workers contains universal human emancipation."[26] The workers cannot abolish their own alienation as a class without also abolishing a society based on the separation of human beings from their essential human nature, or without abolishing the domination of one human being over another.

"Alienation" in Marx's Later Works

There is fairly broad consensus about the features of Marx's account of alienation in his early writings. However, the oft-invoked separation of Marx into an "early" and a "late" Marx is founded in large part on the notion that Marx abandoned the alienation concept partway through his career, along with the ethical implications that come along with it. A number of commentators have taken the absence of the word "alienation" in most of the works of this period to suggest that Marx jettisoned the concept, perhaps because he found it to be incompatible with historical materialism as that method is outlined in the writings which constitute *The Critique of the German Ideology*. The claim that Marx jettisons the alienation concept is also part of the argument that there might be a moral dimension to Marx's earlier work written prior to *The German Ideology*, but that this aspect of Marx's thought is purged in a turn toward economic determinism that is alleged to take place in that work. But as I will show, while "alienation" (*Entfremdung* or *Entäußerung* in Marx's German) does not appear in *The Communist Manifesto* or in most of Marx's other major works between 1847 and 1857, alienation as a phenomenon and as a problem continues to play a central theoretical role in Marx's thought.

While during this period, Marx does not often mention "alienation" by name, he does at many points between the years 1847 and 1857 describe the character of labor in terms almost identical to those he uses earlier when he calls that character "alienated." Therefore, we must draw a distinction between Marx's chosen *terminology* and his conceptual framework. He continues to invoke the alienation concept consistently to characterize and explain the ways in which human beings under capitalism are denied from pursuing an all-sided development of their nature. As Marx's understanding of the relationship between alienation and human nature remains consistent, so does the moral critique of class society that emerges from it. This can be demonstrated by comparing remarks Marx makes about labor in the *Economic and Philosophic Manuscripts of 1844*, in the 1847 document "Wage Labour and Capital," and in the 1848 *Communist Manifesto*.

As we have seen, the *Economic and Philosophic Manuscripts of 1844* contains some of Marx's clearest treatments of alienation in his early work. In the manuscript titled "Estranged Labour," for instance, we learn that the alienation of labor is constituted by at least three things. First, the worker does not experience her work as an expression of herself. It is rather the activity in which the worker feels least like herself. Since for Marx the labor process is the essence of human existence, this phenomenon of experiencing one's own work as foreign amounts to experiencing oneself—one's own active essence—as foreign. It is also a phenomenon in which one's relationship to the external world is disturbed. This is because the labor process is a process in which the human being realizes herself as distinct from nature, and yet a part of it; she appropriates natural resources and transforms them into extended parts of herself and means by which to realize her agency.

Second, her labor is not an end which she pursues for its own sake, but rather merely the means to other ends. This second aspect of alienated labor is meant to follow from the first: because work appears so hateful to the worker, she would not perform it unless absolutely compelled to do so. As Marx later puts it in the 1875 "Critique of the Gotha Programme," labor appears as "a means to life," rather than as "life's prime want."[27] In capitalist society, because the worker has nothing to sell but her own labor power, and must sell *something* if she is to have money to eat, house herself, and afford all the rest of life's necessities, she is then compelled to sell her labor power. She therefore enters into a contract with an employer and transfers the ownership of her labor power from herself to another person in exchange for money.

As a result of this sale, there arises the third condition that is part of the alienation of labor: the labor that the worker performs is not her own, but belongs instead to another person. It is not the worker who teleologically posits ends which are to be realized through her labor, but rather, the employer. This real separation of the worker from her labor and therefore, from her essence as a consciously producing human being, serves as the material basis for, and the confirmation of, her experience of that labor as a denial of herself rather than as an expression of herself. It is this phenomenon of the self-denying character of labor under capitalism that leads Marx to describe this alienated labor as "self-sacrifice" or as "mortification." He consciously chooses religious language to describe alienated labor, thereby emphasizing the similarities between them, and how in both of these phenomena, the "spontaneous activity" of human beings falsely appears to operate independently of the beings whose activity it is.

I argue that Marx continues to theorize alienated labor after *The Critique of the German Ideology*, supposedly the point at which he abandoned alienation as a concept with which to describe and explain the character of human existence in class society. For instance, in the 1844 passage from "Estranged Labour," which I have quoted above, Marx writes that the worker's labor power "belongs, not to himself, but to another." In the 1847 "Wage Labour and Capital," Marx writes that the worker's labor power is part of his life activity which "he sells to another person," and that it "is a commodity that he has auctioned off to another."[28] In both passages, Marx describes a condition in which a part of the worker's life activity has come to belong to an external person, who is not himself. This condition is realized through a sale of the worker's labor power. In "Wage Labour and Capital," Marx goes on to write,

> Labour-power is a commodity which its possessor, the wage-worker, sells to the capitalist. Why does he sell it? It is in order to live.
>
> But the putting of labour-power into action—i.e., the work—is the active expression of the labourer's own life. And this life activity he sells to another person in order to secure the necessary means of life. His life-activity, therefore, is but a means of securing his own existence. He works that he may keep alive. He does not count the labour itself as a part of his life; it is rather a sacrifice of his life. It is a commodity that he has auctioned off to another.[29]

Here, just as in the earlier "Estranged Labour" manuscript, work is not an end in itself, but a means by which to achieve ends which are external to it (namely here, simply maintaining one's bare existence). The worker sells his labor power to the capitalist and thereby makes "a sacrifice of his life." The strong parallels between this work, written after the writings that constitute *The Critique of the German Ideology*, and Marx's earlier writings in the *Economic and Philosophic Manuscripts*, are quite clear. In the 1844 passage, Marx calls this sale of the worker's labor power a "self-sacrifice," a "mortification," and "the loss of his self." In 1847, he calls it "a sacrifice of his life." In both cases, the word "sacrifice" is used in an unmistakably purely pejorative sense. In 1844, "the worker's activity is not his spontaneous activity" and "belongs to another." In 1847, the worker "does not count the labour itself as a part of his life."

Although labor power in action is life activity itself, for the worker, the exercise of that labor power comes not to be experienced or regarded as part of his life and it comes to seem to the worker that it is the enjoyment of creature comforts that constitutes his "real life." When labor is alienated, human beings experience themselves as most themselves and most human in precisely those activities in which they are least distinctively human. And why shouldn't they, when the character of work itself is often so odious and mind-numbing that it fails to develop the worker as a full human being, and rather converts them into little more than a part of a machine? Marx describes this phenomenon in "Estranged Labour" and he does so again in "Wage Labour and Capital":

> And the worker, who for twelve hours weaves, spins, drills, turns, builds, shovels, breaks stones, carries loads, etc.—does he consider this twelve hours' weaving, spinning, drilling, turning, building, shovelling, stone-breaking as a manifestation of his life, as life? On the contrary, life begins for him where this activity ceases, at table, in the public house, in bed. The twelve hours' labour, on the other hand, has no meaning for him as weaving, spinning, drilling, etc., but as earnings, which bring him to the table, to the public house, into bed. If the silkworm were to spin in order to continue its existence as a caterpillar, it would be a complete wage-worker.[30]

Labor is so boring, so stultifying, so one-sided that while it is in reality the most human of activities, it is converted into machine- or animal-like activity. As Marx writes in *The Communist Manifesto*:

> Owing to the extensive use of machinery, and to the division of labour, the work of the proletarians has lost all individual character, and, consequently, all charm for the workman. He becomes an appendage of the machine, and it is only the most simple, most monotonous, and most easily acquired knack, that is required of him.[31]

As a result, the only activities in which the worker truly does feel alive and "freely active" are in those activities which are not uniquely human at all, but which he shares with animals: eating, drinking, and procreating. And in "Wage Labour and Capital," Marx has a specific animal in mind: the silkworm, if a silkworm spun silk just in order to continue its worm-like existence.

While Marx does not use the word "alienation" in works such as the *Manifesto* or "Wage Labour and Capital," in continuing to refer to the worker's separation from his own labor as a "sacrifice," he does establish a clear terminological continuity between the two descriptions. There are also enough key similarities among Marx's description of labor in works before and after *The German Ideology* to bring into serious doubt whether it might be reasonably maintained that Marx jettisons the alienation concept his later work. It is far more likely that Marx made a terminological shift to avoid the possibility of his view being confused with those of others (such as Bruno Bauer and Max Stirner) who were also using the term "alienation" (*Entfremdung* or *Entäußerung*) at the time, but in different ways.

For Marx, the alienation that typifies class society can only be abolished once workers overthrow the existing relations of production, in which workers are compelled to "sacrifice" their labor power and to place it under the control of the capitalist class. In the place of capitalist production, Marx argues for a system in which workers would exercise democratic control over their own labor and regard labor itself as "life's prime want"—a realization of their essence rather than an affront to it.

In prioritizing production aimed at private accumulation for its own sake over the interests of human beings themselves, modern society gets things backward, and this is one of the senses in which it is an alienating society. If consciousness can only be consciousness of social being, as Marx argues, then we can understand how in a society organized on the basis of production for its own sake, even at the expense of human beings, certain absurdities become intelligible or even, common-sense and "obvious." For instance, that hundreds of workers should be condemned to misery and starvation because the factory can't use them, anymore, becomes not absurdity or obscenity but good capitalist "common sense." Capitalist society is alienating in that it deprives human beings of a correct understanding of their own place in the world and obscures the fact that "man is the highest being for man."

In the *Grundrisse*, prepared between 1857 and 1861, more than ten years after "Wage Labour and Capital," Marx argues that in the ancient world, human beings were taken to be the aim of production. "The enquiry," Marx argues, "is always about which form of property creates the best citizens." In the modern world, this relation has been reversed.[32] Human life, that is to say, human labor, human creativity, ingenuity, sociality, etc., are all instrumentalized and treated as means to production. "Production for production's sake," as Marx puts it in *Capital*, but more precisely, the creation of surplus value, of profit, become the organizing principle of modern society.[33]

However, it must be emphasized that this "production for production's sake" is not an unqualified bad, since it is that relentless drive toward production that has revolutionized society's forces of production to an extent not even imaginable under previous economic systems. Alienation has been a feature of human existence long before capitalism, but capitalism has made it possible for alienation to finally be abolished. It is possible again to have a society in which production is carried out in order to satisfy the needs of human beings: one in which not merely a narrow band of the lucky and the well-born would enjoy some semblance of a human existence, but rather, in which a genuinely human existence would be possible for all human beings. Hence, it would be a mistake to simply long romantically for a return to the productive relations of ancient society. As Marx writes in the *Grundrisse*,

> the old view according to which man always appears in however narrowly national, religious or political a determination as the end of production, seems very exalted when set against the modern world, in which production is the end of man, and wealth the end of production. IN FACT, however, if the narrow bourgeois form is peeled off, what is wealth if not the universality of the individual's needs, capacities, enjoyments, productive forces, etc., produced in universal exchange; what is it if not the full development of human control over the forces of nature—over the forces of so-called Nature, as well as those of his own nature?[34] What is wealth if not the absolute unfolding of man's creative abilities, without any precondition other than the preceding historical development, which makes the totality of this development—i.e., the development of all human powers as such, not measured by any previously given yardstick—an end-in-itself, through which he does not reproduce himself in any specific character, but produces his totality, and does not seek to remain something he has already become, but is in the absolute movement of becoming?
>
> In the bourgeois economy—and in the epoch of production to which it corresponds—this complete unfolding of man's inner potentiality turns into his total emptying-out. His universal objectification becomes his total alienation, and the demolition of all determined one-sided aims becomes the sacrifice of the [human] end-in-itself to a wholly external purpose. That is why, on the one hand, the childish world of antiquity appears as something superior. On the other hand, it *is* superior, wherever fixed shape, form and established limits are being looked for. It is satisfaction from a narrow

standpoint; while the modern world leaves us unsatisfied or, where it does appear to be satisfied with itself, is merely *vulgar*.[35]

To address the limiting and alienating aspects of production under capitalism, it would be insufficient to advocate a return to antiquity or to understand the good human life as one that instantiates the virtues of a privileged class within an economic form that no longer exists. Rather, we must comprehend the lack of a "predetermined yardstick" for human development as what it is: a condition in which it has become possible to see that human development is potentially open-ended and limitless, and not as cause to abandon the notion of the human being and of human development as an end in itself.

As we also see in the passage above, closely related to the failure of modern society to recognize human development as an end in itself is its inability to allow, on a general scale, individuals to engage in an expansive and expanding array of activities. Across the whole society, taken as a whole, and in the many different types of human pursuits we can detect what Marx calls the "absolute working-out" of man's "creative potentialities." Yet the individual worker simply "reproduces himself in one specificity," performing some particular task in the division of labor, while his capacity for other activities atrophies and withers away. In the first volume of *Capital*, Marx describes this tendency in arrestingly vivid terms when he writes that capitalism

> converts the labourer into a crippled monstrosity, by forcing his detailed dexterity at the expense of a world of productive capabilities and instincts; just as in the States of La Plata they butcher a whole beast for the sake of his hide or his tallow.[36]

This is another aspect of alienation: an individuals' scope of possible activity is narrowed under capitalism, unnecessarily and wastefully so. The machinery developed in capitalist society's relentless push for production and wealth reduces socially necessary labor to a minimum, thereby creating the conditions for the emancipation of labor.[37] However, instead of being liberated through this more efficient production, the worker becomes a mere accessory to the productive process and to the machine. In this way, objectified labor, in the form of capital, confronts living labor, in the form of the worker, as the power which rules it. "The activity of the worker, restricted to a mere abstraction of activity," Marx writes, "is determined and governed in every respect by the movement of the machinery, not vice versa."[38]

This form of alienation is also described elsewhere in *Capital*:

> At the same time that factory work exhausts the nervous system to the uttermost, it does away with the many-sided play of the muscles, and confiscates every atom of freedom, both in bodily and intellectual activity. The lightening of the labour, even, becomes a sort of torture, since the machine does not free the labourer from work, but deprives the work of all interest. Every kind of capitalist production, in so far as it is not only a labour-process, but also a process of creating surplus value, has this in common, that it is not the workman that employs the instruments of labour, but the instruments of labour that employ the workman.[39]

In his book *Karl Marx*, Allen Wood suggests that Marx's thought on alienation undergoes a shift between his earlier and later work. Namely, Wood suggests that in Marx's earlier work, alienation is an "explanatory concept," and that in the later writings it functions only as a "descriptive concept." Wood writes:

> We should look on alienation in Marx's mature thought not as an explanatory concept but as a descriptive or diagnostic one [and] view it as describing the condition of a person who lacks a sense of self-worth or of meaning in life, or else preserves such a sense only by being the victim of illusions or false consciousness.[40]

To be fair, Wood clarifies that this is only a "provisional" suggestion. But it is worth mentioning all the same that Marx in no way psychologizes alienation in the way that Wood suggests he does. Although alienation often does involve or lead to a sense of personal ennui, the concept of alienation in Marx's later work is by no means simply a description of a psychological state. It instead describes the real position of the human being with relation to the forces of production in a capitalist society. This plays an explanatory role insofar as it is impossible to understand, in Marx's theory, how the human being is diminished without deploying it.

Concerning alienation's conceptual character, I am in agreement with Eugene Kamenka, who writes,

In the economic *magnum opus* of his mature period—*Das Kapital*—he does not rely on the term "alienation" at all. Was it, then, one of the casualties of his tendency toward economic reductionism? Had it been dropped as a "philosophic" or "ethical" concept having no place in his new objective and scientific historical materialism?

The answer is no. The positive content which Marx gave to the term "alienation" remains central to the position he is expounding in *Capital*. The mental process of objectifying one's own product and allowing it to dominate one Marx now calls the *fetishism* of commodities; it remains the same process. Man's loss of control over his labour power Marx calls his *dehumanisation*; it, too, is the same process—a process which for Marx remains of central importance to the understanding of capitalism. Man's loss of control over the product of his work Marx now calls *exploitation*; a term which does not mean that Marx thinks the capitalist is getting too much—more than is *"reasonable,"* but which underlines his insistence that what belongs to one man, or to men in general, is being appropriated by others, or by some men in particular. Exploitation is made possible by the creation of surplus value; but its basic ground for Marx remains the alienation of man from his labour power, the fact that man's activity becomes a commodity. In the *German Ideology* and in Marx's economic notes and drafts made between 1850 and 1859 the connexion of all this with the term "alienation" is made specific. But we do not need to have the connexion made specific, to have the actual term flourished in the text, to see precisely the same theme in *Wage Labour and Capital*, the *Critique of Political Economy* and *Capital* itself.[41]

I do not think it is possible to seriously maintain that the concept of alienation undergoes any significant revisions at least from the time it appears in the *Economic and Philosophic Manuscripts of 1844* and through the rest of Marx's works following the *Manuscripts*. And I certainly do not think it is correct to maintain that Marx abandons the concept altogether. Consider the following passage from *Capital*:

> On the one hand, the process of production incessantly converts material wealth into capital, into means of creating more wealth and means of enjoyment for the capitalist. On the other hand, the labourer, on quitting the process, is what he was on entering it, a source of wealth, but devoid of all means of making that wealth his own. Since, before entering on the process,

his own labour has already been alienated from himself by the sale of his labour-power, has been appropriated by the capitalist and incorporated with capital, it must, during the process, be realised in a product that does not belong to him. Since the process of production is also the process by which the capitalist consumes labour-power, the product of the labourer is incessantly converted, not only into commodities, but into capital, into value that sucks up the value-creating power, into means of subsistence that buy the person of the labourer, into means of production that command the producers. *The labourer therefore constantly produces material, objective wealth, but in the form of capital, of an alien power that dominates and exploits him; and the capitalist as constantly produces labour-power, but in the form of a subjective source of wealth, separated from the objects in and by which it can alone be realised; in short he produces the labourer, but as a wage labourer.* This incessant reproduction, this perpetuation of the labourer, is the sine quâ non of capitalist production.[42]

This is remarkably close in content to passages about alienation that already appear in the 1844 "Estranged Labour" manuscript. What remains for today's readers is to understand more specifically how the phenomenon of alienation also relates to the inversion of bourgeois ideals and their conversion into their opposites, as when Marx writes in the *Grundrisse* that the worker

sells himself as an effect. He is absorbed into the body of capital as a cause, as activity. Thus the exchange turns into its opposite, and the laws of private property—liberty, equality, property—property in one's own labour, and free disposition over it—turn into the worker's propertylessness, and the dispossession [*Entäusserung*] of his labour, [i.e.] the fact that he relates to it as alien property and vice versa.[43]

Here, it is instructive to note Richard Gilman-Opalsky's remarks on the significance of Marx's *Grundrisse*, in his 2020 book *The Communism of Love*. There, Gilman-Opalsky correctly observes,

Grundrisse can only be understood as a sustained inquiry into the ways that capital and money disfigure and destroy healthy human community. Marx's overarching concern in *Grundrisse* is to understand the necessary devaluation, dehumanization, and alienation of the human being in capitalist society. The humanism of *Grundrisse* is scarcely obscure, and any reading that misses the central importance of this is a misreading. Those who categorically reject the basic premises of Marxist-humanism do not do so only by selectively reading the *Economic and Philosophic Manuscripts of 1844* but also by failing to read *Grundrisse* well or even at all.[44]

To understand more fully the meaning of Marx's *Grundrisse*, in Chapters 7 and 8, we will explore Marx's critiques of the limitations and hypocrisy of bourgeois morality. We will see how the process of alienation under capitalism lays a material foundation for the ideologies that reflect a world in which the ideals of liberal morality are expressed, in practice, as their opposites. But first, in Chapter 5, we will explore the relationship between freedom and determinism in Marx's thought. Much will hang on the character of the interrelation between the two, for one classic objection to the notion of a Marxist ethics is that Marx might be committed to a fatalistic determinism that rules out freedom and, ipso facto, morality. But this is not the case, as we will see.

5
Radical Chains (Marx on Freedom and Determinism)

If Marx's and Engels's materialist conception of history entails that human behavior is strictly deterministic and that socialism is guaranteed by the inexorable march of history, then it would seem to follow that human beings are not and could not be "free" in the way that the practice of moral judgment generally presupposes them to be. When we deem a person to be morally responsible—that is, to be the appropriate object of moral praise or blame—we generally presume that they have, in some deep sense, *chosen* to act as they did. We presuppose that they are the author of the event in question.

Strict determinism has it that actions which might seem at first blush to be "mine" in some deep sense were in fact fatalistically preordained by circumstances preceding even my very existence. "My" decisions would for that reason then be quite out of my control and not properly attributable to *me*, after all. A Marxist moral theory owes to its hearers an explanation of how it is that historical materialism is not strict determinism of this kind, a further explanation of what kind of determinism historical materialism *does* entail, and an account of how this can be compatible with the human emancipation Marx repeatedly identifies as the chief aim of socialist praxis.

If Marx's economic determinism requires that individual human beings always only behave just as the "laws of history" unavoidably compel them to, then moral praise and blame is no more appropriately applied to them than it is to inanimate objects dropped from heights. Numerous interpreters of Marx, presuming that historical materialism does entail a strict, mechanistic determinism, have gone on to reason that Marx's theory is therefore inhospitable to morality. However, historical materialism does not entail this.

We might here be appropriately reminded of Marx's oft-quoted observation that "men make their own history, but they do not make it as they please; they do not make it under self-selected circumstances, but under circumstances existing already, given and transmitted from the past."[1] What is meant by that famous line from Marx's 1852 *Eighteenth Brumaire of Louis Bonaparte*? For one thing, it expresses that human social existence is the product of human labor, and as such, it is susceptible to human intervention aimed at making it over and (re-)directing its course. I argue this principle is absolutely central to Marx's moral thought. Any given individual human being, while alienated from their human powers, has relatively little in the way of genuine authorship over their actions or even their entire lives, but not exactly none. By contrast, at the level of the species, it can be said that humanity truly is the author of its actions, and of the course of its own history. This is true even if only unconsciously so, and in an attenuated fashion prior to the realization of full human emancipation in fully developed communism.

Both Marx and Engels insist on multiple occasions that humanity itself is a human product.[2] However, "humanity" is an abstraction. To satisfy ourselves with the explanation that "humanity" is free in the desired sense (even while individual human beings are not) would be to content ourselves with a resolution of the antagonism between freedom and determinism that occurs only in the realm of thought. Yet our aim is not merely to discover a clever solution to a philosophical puzzle. It is rather to ascertain how this kind of self-making can be manifested by individual human beings, so that a given individual might more truly be said to be the author of her actions.

As such, the discussion of freedom and determinism in Marx is highly interwoven with our understanding of Marx's concept of the individual. For purposes of clarity and presentation, I treat these subjects in two separate chapters. (Chapter 6, "Individuality," directly follows the present one.) Here, I will set the stage for understanding the reconciliation of freedom and determinism in Marxist thought, but it will be more fully transparent once we've considered Marx's view of individuality. An explanation of the relationship between freedom and determinism in Marx's thought, and that of the relationship between individual and society, outline in parallel the same historical process through which human emancipation becomes realized.

In order to help orient our discussion, it is useful to say a bit about how Marx's proffered resolution to the antagonism between freedom and determinism relates to the positions that many readers will recognize as familiar from traditional Anglophone philosophy. "Incompatibilism" is the name given to views that hold freedom to be untenable in the presence of determinism. "Compatibilist" views maintain that this pair can coexist. If we were to map Marx's positions onto Anglophone/analytical-philosophical perspectives on the matter, then Marx is a compatibilist about freedom and determinism.

However, such a mapping must remain purely heuristic. If taken too literally, it will obscure what Marx takes to be two of the most important distinctions between historical materialism and the worldviews he associates with ideologically "bourgeois" approaches. Namely, one must not overlook the deep extent to which on a Marxist approach to thinking through freedom, agency, morality, and necessity, the precise relationship between freedom and determinism can be given no static or permanent description.

This antagonism is one that shifts dynamically over the course of human history, with each side of the contradiction conditioning and transforming the development of the other. There is no fixed and final answer to the question of how human freedom can exist in the presence of deterministic laws. This relationship is not a puzzle to be contemplated in thought, but a problem to be worked out concretely in the course of history. What's more, the impetus for this development is provided by human action, itself both free and determined.

Here, I use the term "dialectical compatibilism" to invoke both the ways in which Marx's approach to freedom and determinism is in conversation with traditional analyses of this pairing, and also the ways in which it is fundamentally divergent from them.[3] This position moves beyond the views typically arrayed along the axes of determinist or libertarian, compatibilist or incompatibilist. Much of the confusion surrounding Marx's positions on the relationship between freedom and determinism stems from the fact that for Marx this is an evolving and historically contingent relationship. One cannot issue timeless, universal statements about the degree to which external determining factors influence human behavior, or concerning the extent to which this behavior is the free and voluntary action of human beings.

It is true that humans have acted under conditions that, speaking for the most part, they have not chosen. Yet in so doing, they also bring those conditions increasingly under their conscious control. As humans develop greater control over their circumstances, they correspondingly broaden their capacity for free, self-directed agency. In this way, on Marx's account, freedom and determinism conflict with one another much as they do on the most well-known "incompatibilist" accounts. Yet deterministic economic forces also function as preconditions for human freedom and figure into the story of how that freedom comes about. Marx's picture is not of a compatibility between freedom and determinism that holds true in precisely the same way for all humans across time and space, but rather of a human freedom that grows, spurred in part by the operation of deterministic laws. In human activity, freedom and determinism are mutually conditioned in ways that produce their ever-greater dialectical compatibility, unfolding across time.

Karl Popper, whose influence in the Anglophone reception of Marx has been unfortunately large, writes that Marx adhered "to the false belief that a rigidly scientific method must be based on a rigid determinism."[4] Indeed, it has become something like conventional wisdom that Marx subscribed to a crude economic determinism that would make human freedom unintelligible. This view of Marx usually rules out, or at least declares incoherent and unintelligible, any genuinely moral content in his work. Hence, one work in micro-economics could claim that Marx's "economic determinism had consequences for the picture of human beings in Marxist theory, and for the freedom of action of economically acting individuals. They have no autonomy of action, they only carry out economic laws."[5] And Jules Townshend in his 1996 book *The Politics of Marxism: The Critical Debates*, could write,

> a potential conflict arose between Marx's economic determinism and his idea of human agency, which allowed individuals, and particularly classes, a certain autonomy of action, through 'practical-critical' activity. Marx's idea that communism was inevitable permitted him to avoid the question of whether it was morally desirable.... Yet what if the determinist theory, upon which this 'inevitability' rested, was flawed? Would this not then put the moral appeal of socialism centre stage?[6]

In a similar vein, Eugene Kamenka, in *The Ethical Foundations of Marxism*, argued that Marx did not see the proletariat as an active force in society, and instead

> stuck to his negative view of the proletariat as the *most suffering class* ... Marx chose to rely on "history," to hold out to the proletariat the vision of a classless society *made safe* for goods, where enterprise and freedom would be *guaranteed* by the economic foundations of society itself, where freedom would not lie in struggle, but follow from mere existence.

Kamenka writes that this conception had a "servile character," and that in following Marx, "Marxists were upholding a servile and unfree morality."[7]

It is, as we will find, an oversimplification to understand Marx's comments about the role of economic laws in shaping the prospects for and likelihood of communism as though they simply participate in a balancing act between the twin poles of deterministic inevitability and abstract moralistic voluntarism. It is a still more grave vulgarization to suggest that it collapses entirely into the mechanistic determinism Marx explicitly rejected.

Willis H. Truitt, in his 2005 book *Marxist Ethics: A Short Exposition*, wittily remarks on the critical reception of Marx's historical materialism: "It is odd that the issue of determinism in Marx should be brought up at this late stage of the development of Marxist thought. One might even suspect that all these years of academic anti-Marxist indoctrination which teaches that historical materialism is a deterministic system has worked."[8]

A final note before we proceed: although I speak here of "freedom," I do not argue that Marx defended the existence of "free will." In fact, he did not, and his references to free will are nearly always ironic. By "free will," Marx understood the self-determining, spontaneous, autonomous, cause of human actions that figures in the moral theory of philosophers such as Immanuel Kant. But Marx writes of Kant:

> Neither he, nor the German middle class, whose whitewashing spokesman he was, noticed that these theoretical ideas of the bourgeoisie had as their basis material interests and a *will* that was conditioned and determined by the material relations of production. Kant, therefore, separated this theoretical expression from the interests which it expressed; he made the materially motivated determinations of the will of the French bourgeois into pure self-determinations of "free will," of the will in and for itself, of the human will, and so converted it into purely ideological conceptual determinations and moral postulates.[9]

In *Capital*, Marx describes the worker as "the man who is compelled to sell himself of his own free will"; here, too, his words drip with irony.[10] Freedom in Marxist theory has little to do with the kind of spontaneity that requires we posit the will as an ideal/spiritual substance, wholly undetermined by material causes. It has much more in common with what Hegel, in *The Philosophy of Right*, calls "concrete freedom." Hegel writes,

> *concrete freedom* requires that personal individuality and its particular interests should reach their full *development* and gain *recognition of their*

> *right* for itself ... and also that they should, on the one hand, *pass over* of their own accord into the interest of the universal, and on the other, knowingly and willingly acknowledge this universal interest even as their own *substantial spirit*, and *actively pursue it* as their *ultimate end*.[11]

It would be a facile error simply to translate Hegel's terms into "materialist" concepts, in order to arrive at a Marxist concept of freedom. However, it is nonetheless illuminating to note here how little this kind of freedom has to do with the undetermined free will. This view of freedom is best expressed as a proliferation and mastery of one's own powers, a kind of individual flourishing that is made fully possible only in and through one's unalienated relationship to the species. Marx alludes to this in the *1844 Manuscripts*, where he writes,

> Just as through the movement of private property, of its wealth as well as its poverty—of its material and spiritual wealth and poverty—the budding society finds at hand all the material for this development, so established society produces man in this entire richness of his being—produces the rich man profoundly endowed with all the senses—as its enduring reality. We see how subjectivity and objectivity, spirituality and materiality, activity and suffering, lose their antithetical character, and thus their existence as such antitheses only within the framework of society; we see how the resolution of the theoretical antitheses is only possible in a practical way, by virtue of the practical energy of man. Their resolution is therefore by no means merely a problem of understanding, but a real problem of life, which philosophy could not solve precisely because it conceived this problem as merely a theoretical one.[12]

I give the name "dialectical compatibilism" to that view. Human beings are compelled to act so as to satisfy their needs within circumstances that they cannot fully control. But in so doing, they are determined—by biological need and by external circumstances—to respond to their need and their circumstances in ways that, in turn, expand their capacities to intervene into the world around them and direct its processes. They gain greater freedom precisely as a result of the deterministic forces to which they are subjected.[13] Human freedom is itself a human product, one that emerges gradually over the course of history out of human beings' goal-directed interactions with their natural and social environment. There is no inconsistency in Marx describing fairly law-like, deterministic regularities of human behavior on the one hand and speaking of a flourishing of human freedom, individuality, and creative potential on the other. If determinism is the negation of real human agency, then human freedom is the negation of that negation, one that can emerge only in the course of history.

In the following sections of this chapter, I trace Marx's treatment of the relationship between freedom and determinism. I consider how his approach to theorizing that relationship developed over the course of his life, with special attention paid to his doctoral dissertation on Democritus and Epicurus, the *Communist Manifesto*, and *Capital*.

Marx on "the Difference Between the Democritean and the Epicurean Philosophy of Nature"

Marx's doctoral dissertation is also an early treatment by Marx of the relationship between freedom and necessity, and an examination of the ontological status of abstract objects. Here, Marx studies the differences between the atomistic physical theories of the ancient Greek materialist philosophers, Democritus and Epicurus. Marx defends Epicurus against the charge leveled against him by Cicero, Leibniz, and others, that he is little more than a poor plagiarist of Democritus, arguing that not only does Epicurus make unique philosophical contributions of his own, but that his physical theory represents a theoretical advance beyond Democritean atomism. This advance consists partly in Epicurean physics' avoidance of the strict mechanistic determinism that is a hallmark of Democritus's view. On that basis, Marx credits Epicurus with formulating a materialist worldview that can accommodate freedom.

To understand the relationship between Marx's study of ancient Greek atomistics and his views on the relationship between freedom and determinism, it will be first necessary to introduce the physical systems of Democritus and Epicurus in a bit of detail.

Democritus argued that the fundamental physical structure of matter is composed of atoms—small, indivisible particles—that move in straight lines. The motion of atoms in Democritean physics is determined entirely by external forces on them. They move, impelled by the downward pull of gravity or by the force of collisions between atoms. Epicurus adopted the framework of Democritean atomism, with the following notable alteration: atoms did not simply move in a straight line, the path of which was strictly determined by external forces acting on the atom. Rather, atoms sometimes, but not always, "swerved" slightly from their original paths. This motion was determined not by the action of external forces, but by the atoms' own intrinsic natures.

As Walter Englert demonstrates persuasively in *Epicurus on the Swerve and Voluntary Action*, Epicurus developed his doctrine of the swerve as a response to a challenge from Aristotle. How could one explain the motion of animals—a self-movement that resisted explanation in terms of strict mechanistic determinism—using atomistic theory? This challenge left Epicurus with two choices:

> either to assert that living creatures only apparently had this power, and that all their motions could be explained in terms of the weight and collisions of atoms from which they are made, or to find a new motion in the atoms that could account for the property in animals.[14]

Epicurus chose the latter course. With the addition of the swerve to his atomistic physics, Epicurus posited a type of atomic motion that allowed for atoms to move in ways not determined purely by their weight and collisions. The apparently nondeterministic and voluntary motion of animals could then be explained in virtue of this property of the atoms that comprised them.

This "swerve" distinguishes Epicurus's physics from Democritus's. Since the motion of atoms is not completely determined by external forces, Epicurus's physics describes a world that is not strictly mechanistically deterministic and in which atoms as individual entities are not simply subject to external necessity. For Marx, this is a crucial and fruitful departure from Democritus. Marx sees the swerve as a natural physical explanation for the possibility of individuals to intervene into the material world beyond themselves, through activity determined by their own unique qualities. This allows for the "existence" of an atom to be in harmony with its "essence." This harmony of existence with essence constitutes the real expression of the atom, the reconciliation of the conflict between freedom and necessity. As Marx writes:

> The contradiction between existence and essence, between matter and form, which is inherent in the concept of the atom, emerges in the individual atom itself once it is endowed with qualities. Through the quality the atom is alienated from its concept, but at the same time is perfected in its

construction. It is from repulsion and the ensuing conglomerations of the qualified atoms that the world of appearance now emerges.[15]

The swerve allowed the atom to differentiate and distinguish itself in terms of its relationship to other atoms. But atoms as purely abstract objects are incapable of realizing themselves in matter in this way. Only concretely individual atoms with specific qualities can repel other atoms, thereby differentiating themselves and coming to exist in correspondence with their essences. As George McCarthy writes in his very lucid and detailed treatment of Marx on Epicurus:

> For the atom to exist and be real, it must have certain spatial qualities such as size, shape, and weight and thus take on a determinate existence. However, as a determinate being with material existence, the atom must take on qualities or properties that contradict its essence as pure immediacy and abstract individuality (alienation). It is this contradiction between material existence and essence (Concept) that lies at the heart of Epicurus's philosophy and his view of Greek society. Marx saw in Epicurus the first philosopher to incorporate the notion of the contradiction between essence and reality into his thought.[16]

Abstract unqualified objects cannot exist because they cannot affect matter, and cannot thereby bring about the expression of their essences. It is for this reason that Marx says "abstract individuality is freedom from being, not freedom in being."[17] Moreover, Marx argued, reasoning based on contemplation of such abstract objects will necessarily lapse into methodological idealism. Centering abstractions means eschewing material determinations as *mere* appearances that distract from a proper appreciation of the nature of reality, rather than being the absolute starting place for a proper understanding of it.

The Epicurean swerve was attacked by a number of ancient commentators on the basis that Epicurus provided inadequate philosophical justification for belief in such a property of atoms. Cicero notably complained that Epicurus's doctrine of the swerve was "rather to beg the question than to discuss it."

He argued that Epicurus's theory of the swerve had established

> A fortuitous concourse of atoms to help us out of our difficulty. [...] But you have not yet discovered that primitive power in nature from which your

atoms derive their motion. [. . .] You have not yet revealed to us any extrinsic cause which impresses each atom with that impulse which gives it its proper direction.[18]

Marx argues that this demand for a cause of the swerve is beside the point, since for it to be caused in the way that Cicero demands would be for it to be brought back into the domain of a mechanistic determinism. Marx writes, "To inquire after the cause that makes the atom a principle—a clearly meaningless inquiry to anyone for whom the atom is the cause of everything, hence without cause itself."[19]

Marx's defense of the Epicurean swerve is that on Epicurus's atomistic physics, the atom itself is the active principle in nature. Therefore, the movement of Epicurus's atom is very far from requiring an explanation in terms of the forces exerted upon it by the rest of the natural world. Instead the Epicurean atom itself determines that world. Marx admires in Epicurus's thought its lack of reliance, in contrast to Aristotle's "unmoved mover," upon an external source of motion in order to explain the existence and appearance of the natural world.

While for our purposes it has been necessary to present a general explanation of the doctrines in Epicurus that Marx chose to treat in his first extended philosophical work, what is crucial to notice in the doctoral dissertation is not so much this or that vagary of Epicurus's physics, and Marx's reaction to each bit of it, but rather Marx's overarching interest in defending what he recognizes as a brand of materialism that can accommodate freedom, conscious activity, and intervention into the material world. As James O'Rourke writes in his 1974 book *The Problem of Freedom in Marxist Thought*, "although Marx himself does not endorse the Epicurean position *en bloc*, it is clear from the text that he is in genuine sympathy with its leading principles, especially those which seem to be compatible with the Hegelian philosophy of spirit." This gives us some prima facie reason for skepticism that Marx himself endorsed a mechanistic determinism that would have far more in common with Democritus, whose physics he already rejects at this early stage in his philosophical development, than it does with Epicurus.

However, Marx is also critical of the role that atoms as abstract individuals continue to play in Epicurus's physics. As George McCarthy writes in *Marx and the Ancients*:

The radical individualism of Epicurus was necessary to undermine positivism and religion, but was not adequate to develop a real social anthropology or theory of society based on friendship, citizenship, and public participation. For this, a turn to Feuerbach's notion of species being and Aristotle's view of democracy and citizenship would become necessary.

It would be Marx's immediate task in his early writings to move from one level to the other, to move from abstract self-consciousness and freedom to concrete self-consciousness in the political economy. In order to overcome the contradictions of existence and essence—materialism and ethics—implicit in Epicurean physics, the alienation of the objective and physical world must be overcome through social praxis. The theoretical praxis and ethical critique of the philosopher must be transformed into effective action on the world and a change-over of the institutions of political economy. The *Dissertation* sets the path, the direction, and the priorities for Marx's earliest and later studies on the social relations of production. Just as the *Dissertation* begins with a critique of the foreign externality of nature, *Capital* begins with a critique of the "natural laws" of political economy. It is this relation between self-consciousness and nature in all its material forms—from physics to political economy—that is at the heart and soul of Marx's lifework.[20]

But before we get to our discussion of *Capital*, let us note that if there were a single text to which one might look for support in reading Marx as a strict determinist, it would likely be the *Communist Manifesto*. It is Marx's great rallying cry, in which he famously exhorts workers to revolution with assurances that they've "a world to win" and "only their chains to lose." However, on closer inspection we find that even in the *Manifesto*, Marx sees history trending in a direction that produces the increasingly greater possibility of communism—but not its inevitability.

In the *Manifesto*, Marx writes that "What the bourgeoisie . . . produces, above all, is its own grave-diggers. Its fall and the victory of the proletariat are equally inevitable."[21] This claim locates both the strength and the Achilles's heel of the bourgeoisie in one and the same historical force: the working class. Capitalists accumulate wealth by extracting surplus value from the human beings who are compelled to sell their ability to labor. At the same time that this relationship enriches and empowers the capitalist class, it also sows the seeds of what may become its eventual destruction. Marx makes this point in his criticism of feudal opposition to the bourgeoisie, writing, "What they upbraid the bourgeoisie with is not so much that it creates a proletariat as that it creates a revolutionary proletariat."[22]

Marx's claim that the bourgeoisie's fall and the proletariat's victory are "equally inevitable" ought to be understood in this context. They are "equally inevitable" because their sources are the same. Because the conditions of the bourgeoisie are mirrored in those of the working class, each is precisely as likely as the other. This is not to say that the proletariat's victory is inevitable, full stop, but rather to stress that the emergence and development of the proletariat, a necessary condition of the capitalist mode of production, is inextricably linked to the capitalist enterprise itself.

Marx speaks, especially in *Capital*, of the capitalist as "capital personified and endowed with consciousness and a will."[23] A capitalist is a person who acts in a manner that is to a great extent determined by economic laws that guide the movement of the capital she possesses. Marx also speaks, in *Capital* and elsewhere, of the actions of the proletariat understood in terms of what it is as a class and what, by virtue of that nature, it will be compelled to do.

As we discussed at the beginning of this chapter, numerous authors have taken this strand in Marx's thought to imply a crude economic determinism. Marx is (mis)characterized as professing human actions to be one-sidedly determined by economic laws that operate beyond their control. But what Marx describes when he addresses the way in which economic laws play a role in determining the actions of human beings, are tendencies of members of various social groups to act in circumstances shaped through those laws. These are not iron-clad predictions for particular individuals. Howard Sherman, in his 1981 paper "Marx and Determinism," puts this point very well:

> Marx pointed out that one can find regularities of human behavior, that on the average we do behave in certain predictable ways. This behavior also changes in systematic ways, with predictable trends, in association with changes in our technological and social environments. At a simpler level, the regularities of human behavior are obvious in the fairly constant annual numbers of suicides and divorces (although these also show systematic trends). If humans did not, generally, behave in fairly predictable ways, not only social scientists but also insurance companies would have gone out of business long ago. Any particular individual may make any particular choice, but if we know the social composition of a group, we can predict,

in general, what it will do. Thus, on the average, most large owners of stock will vote in favor of preferential tax rates for capital gains; most farmers will favor laws that they believe to be in the interest of farmers.[24]

As a rule, a capitalist will tend to maximize his profit irrespective of the social repercussions. A bourgeois intellectual will tend to develop theoretical justifications for the continuation of capitalism, often in spite of the glaring social contradictions. Within a bourgeois standpoint, and even while continuing to support the bourgeoisie as the class most suited to lead humanity economically, politically, and socially, it is possible for certain members of this class to develop a keen understanding of the social contradictions produced by class society. In some cases, bourgeois ideologists develop real commitments to such noble and crucial aims as human development or the eradication of ills such as global poverty and ecological destruction. Marx recognizes this phenomenon as a feature of the subjective consciousness of individual bourgeois theorists. For instance, in *Capital*, Marx notes that the capitalist "Robert Owen, soon after 1810, not only maintained the necessity of a limitation of the working-day in theory, but actually introduced the 10 hours' day into his factory at New Lanark," even though "this was laughed at as a communistic Utopia."[25]

Marx goes on to credit Owen with developing an approach to education that could serve as an early model for education in a communist society:

> From the Factory system budded, as Robert Owen has shown us in detail, the germ of the education of the future, an education that will, in the case of every child over a given age, combine productive labour with instruction and gymnastics, not only as one of the methods of adding to the efficiency of production, but as the only method of producing fully developed human beings.

According to Marx, the progressive aspects of Owen's thought were, in the end, limited by his failure to recognize the proletariat as the class best suited to lead humanity out of the contradictions produced by class society. For Marx, a bourgeois class position and standpoint tend to delimit the range of actions and opinions we are likely to see even from a reformer such as Owen. However, it would be wrong to ignore that within that position and perspective there remains a wide array of open choices for individual actors and they may formulate valuable insights and opinions, and that these views might strive to faithfully reflect reality and even to progressively transform it, pointing beyond that bourgeois perspective.

Another example of this can be found in the work of nineteenth-century French novelist and playwright Honoré de Balzac. Balzac of course had not bourgeois, but actually royalist sympathies, and was opposed to the bourgeoisie at a time when it played a historically progressive role. Yet he was one of Marx's favorite authors, an artist whom Marx describes in *Capital* as "generally remarkable for his profound grasp of reality."[26]

In an 1888 letter, Engels further elucidates the genius of Balzac's realism. Engels writes the letter in response to a request that he review a novel written by a socialist author. He concludes that the novel is not very good, criticizing it particularly for being unrealistic in its depiction of the working class as a passive mass. Engels goes on to illustrate his point with a discussion of the realism to be found in Balzac's work, a realism that is achieved in spite of the latter's royalist sympathies:

> Balzac was politically a Legitimist; his great work is a constant elegy on the inevitable decay of good society, his sympathies are all with the class doomed to extinction. But for all that his satire is never keener, his irony never bitterer, than when he sets in motion the very men and women with whom he sympathizes most deeply—the nobles. And the only men of whom he always speaks with undisguised admiration, are his bitterest political antagonists, the republican heroes of the Cloître Saint-Méry, the men, who at that time (1830–6) were indeed the representatives of the popular masses. That Balzac thus was compelled to go against his own class sympathies and political prejudices, that he saw the necessity of the downfall of his favourite nobles, and described them as people deserving no better fate; and that he saw the real men of the future where, for the time being, they alone were to be found—that I consider one of the greatest triumphs of Realism, and one of the grandest features in old Balzac.[27]

A figure such as Robert Owen demonstrates some of the most progressive viewpoints possible within a bourgeois perspective. More typically, there are persons such as John D. Rockefeller or John F. Kennedy, who simply seek mostly to rationally advance the interests of their class. (I am speaking of a narrowly instrumental "rationality" in these cases.) Additionally, there are individuals such as Joseph McCarthy who actively promote the most brazenly reactionary tendencies of their class.

In the face of this evident diversity in ruling class thought, Marx would argue that across this range of bourgeois actors, their identifications with that class inhibit them, from fully recognizing the progressive role of the proletariat and its fitness to lead society. So long as they maintain their bourgeois identification, they are unlikely to fully embrace the historical materialist perspective developed in Marx's thought. However, within that bourgeois perspective and bourgeois class identification, a wide range of thought and action is possible. The charge of crude economic determinism does not fully allow for this, as Marx does.

Furthermore, not only is a wide range of thought and action possible within a bourgeois class identification, but it is possible for individuals to choose to renounce that identification entirely. Already in *The Communist Manifesto*, Marx explains that confronted by the immense contradictions of capitalist society, an increasing number of individual members of the bourgeoisie (and of the petty bourgeoisie) may switch their class allegiance entirely to the camp of the proletariat. These virtuous turncoats come to the view that it is only the victory of the working class, leading a movement toward communism, that can safeguard the continued existence and development of humanity. Of course, one need look no further than Marx's collaborator, Engels, for an example of a bourgeois who chose this course. However, it would be deeply misguided to develop a theory of, and a program for, social and economic development that relied heavily on such occasional changes of camp. In a society based on profit, it is the profit motive, by and large, that dominates in the decision-making of capitalists, just as it is the conscious or unconscious struggle against the inhuman aspects of labor under capitalism that dominates in the decision-making of workers.

Marx argues that economic relations determine human action to a significant extent, but this by no means licenses interpreters to dub him a strict economic determinist who sees no room for freedom of human action. Marx is able to describe and account for a wide range of human action, even as he sees that action being constrained by economic factors. Marx's theory, as a theory of the emancipation of the human species through the self-emancipation of the working class, depends precisely on the struggle of human beings to realize themselves as free and conscious human actors, and further, to be more than "appendages to machines" or mere subjects of economic and social relations that dominate them instead of being directed by them.

In *Capital*, Marx discusses the economic trends that prepare the way for a fully human existence, but critics who accuse Marx of seeing communism

110   MARX'S ETHICAL VISION

as a matter of deterministic historical inevitability fail to appreciate that he also discusses how capitalism inhibits human progress. Left unchecked, capitalism would render progress ultimately impossible. In the first volume of *Capital*, Marx writes:

> Capital that has such good reasons for denying the sufferings of the legions of workers that surround it, is in practice moved as much and as little by the sight of the coming degradation and final depopulation of the human race, as by the probable fall of the earth into the sun. In every stockjobbing swindle every one knows that some time or other the crash must come, but every one hopes that it may fall on the head of his neighbour, after he himself has caught the shower of gold and placed it in safety. *Après moi le déluge!* [After me, the flood] is the watchword of every capitalist and of every capitalist nation. Hence Capital is reckless of the health or length of life of the labourer, unless under compulsion from society. To the out-cry as to the physical and mental degradation, the premature death, the torture of overwork, it answers: Ought these to trouble us since they increase our profits? But looking at things as a whole, all this does not, indeed, depend on the good or ill will of the individual capitalist. Free competition brings out the inherent laws of capitalist production, in the shape of external coercive laws having power over every individual capitalist.[28]

Several important themes are expressed in this passage. First, far from leading inexorably toward a communist future, capital—and of course, the capitalist class, taken as a whole—looks impassively at the "coming degradation and final depopulation of the human race." This prospect is treated as though it were merely some regrettable but ultimately unalterable natural certainty. (Relating this to the contemporary situation, we can consider the baleful shoulder-shrugging that typifies the attitudes of many of today's world governments toward impending and already unfolding catastrophes such as global climate change.)

It is only under "compulsion from society" that humanity can be taken off of its collision course with the destructive effects of capitalism. The conscious and active intervention of the masses into politics and into world history is ultimately all that stands between us and this "final depopulation." We can see that Marx agreed with this from his own political engagement with the workers' movement, not to mention his lifelong dedication to investigating how the social and economic gains of capitalism can be preserved and subsumed in a higher stage of social development, and his conviction that just this ought to be done and could only be done by the active masses. Marx prioritized the majority of society acting in the interest of the majority of society.

Second, we see mentioned in this passage the way in which the "free competition" of capitalist society reveals itself to be unfreedom in practice, taking on the "shape of external coercive laws having power over every individual capitalist." One important question to be asked of those who see here some ground to label Marx a crude economic determinist and therefore an amoralist, is whether they can really doubt that capitalists generally act in ways designed to preserve and multiply their capital. "Looking at things as a whole," the capitalist, no matter how noble he might be in his heart of hearts, whether his will be "good or ill," must extract as much labor as possible, at as little cost to himself as possible. This remains true if he wishes to compete in the marketplace and to remain a capitalist, at all. It is this general tendency of people in capitalist society to defend their economic interests that makes it possible to predict that class struggle between the bourgeoisie and the proletariat, whose interests are in conflict with one another, will take place. However, it does not by any means guarantee which side will win out in that inevitable conflict.

It is true that there are numerous occasions on which Marx expresses his conviction that human beings would achieve a communist society. I happen to think this view was reasonable, based on the historical vantage point available to Marx at the time. However, as Sherman writes in his 1981 paper "Marx and Determinism":

> Human beings are free to make (or not make) a revolution, but our actions are predictable by a knowledge of present and previous conditions, including our psychologies, and the laws or regularities of human behavior under these conditions. "To say that the revolution is inevitable is simply (in Marx's scheme) to say that it will occur. And it will occur... not in spite of any choices we might make, but because of choices we will make."[29] The prediction of socialist revolution, however, must be expressed as a probability rather than a certainty because of our limited knowledge of the conditions and the laws.

Under capitalism, the range of actions available to people are narrowed. And within that narrow range, people are most likely, "as a whole," to take the actions that defend their economic interests. Here we might cite again Marx's observation in *The Eighteenth Brumaire of Louis Bonaparte*: "Men make their own history, but they do not make it just as they please; they do not make it under circumstances chosen by themselves, but under circumstances directly found, given and transmitted from the past."[30] It is not possible to have a correct understanding of capitalist society without understanding the extent to which many factors, including economic laws, do delimit the range of actions available to people under capitalism, and do make some actions more likely to be taken than some other ones.

Though it is certain that under capitalism, workers will struggle against their conditions, it is by no means simply necessary or historically determined that their struggles will be victorious, or that communism will be achieved. It is not necessary that workers will recognize their class interests, will gain a theoretical understanding of the nature of capitalism, will organize themselves politically in such a way as to effectively promote their interests, or will recognize human development and "rich individuality" as the highest aim for human beings. Even if they achieve all these things, I would like to emphasize that from our historical vantage point today, it is plain to see that that they may not do so before the spoliation of the Earth under the capitalist mode of production is too far gone. We may not avert a premature "final depopulation" of the human race. Whether any of these things do take place, and in a timely way, depends in great part upon the actions of what Marx refers to as the most conscious elements of society setting a political direction and theoretical context for the struggles that emerge. And when they do so, they do so not merely as patients subject to inexorable economic laws, but as historical agents who through their activity, assist their fellows in realizing their historical agency as well. Marx recognizes that there is a space for free and conscious intervention even under capitalism. But he also recognizes that this scope is limited. One of the goals of a communist movement, then, is to intervene consciously into human history in the ways that are currently possible. While constrained by capitalism, the communist movement works to expand the sphere of free action and push necessity back to its furthest possible limit.

None of this is to negate the extent to which economic processes in class society, which are the result of human actions but which have developed spontaneously, without conscious human planning or direction, have led to a historical moment that points toward communism, and provides the material basis for communism. This is how alienated labor can function, over the course of history, to make its own abolition more possible, and create the conditions for human emancipation. For instance, as Marx points out, the forces of production are increasingly socialized even if the *relations* of production are not. It is for this reason that Marx could write in *The German Ideology* that "Communism is for us not a *state of affairs* which is to be established, an *ideal* to which reality [will] have to adjust itself. We call communism the *real* movement which abolishes the present state of things. The conditions of this movement result from the now existing premise."[31]

The whole development of human history is a movement toward a point at which the stakes for humanity become increasingly clear: "given and transmitted from the past," they boil down to a stark choice. This is the choice either to build a movement that preserves and develops the positive contributions of class society as the historical and material basis on which to create a society that satisfies human needs, or to allow the destructive aspects of capitalism to simply play themselves out, stamping out of existence countless achievements of human culture. Think here, for instance, of fascism and its historical appearance where capitalism has fallen into decay and the workers' movement has not been able to seize power. In this instance matters would be still more dire: unchecked climate change would quite likely bring about a hastened extinction as a result of ecological crisis.

Because of how capitalism has revolutionized production, it is possible for human beings to devote a vanishingly small amount of time to satisfying their biological needs. They can devote the majority of their lives instead to the intellectual, cultural, and artistic pursuits that enrich the social existence of humanity. These pursuits develop humanity's existence well beyond the merely biological. To use Marx's terminology, it is possible for human beings to free themselves in great part from the narrow requirements of "natural necessity." The capitalist mode of production is especially contradictory in this respect. Through the drive of capitalists to revolutionize the forces of production in order to relentlessly increase efficiency and profits, it has become possible to produce enough to satisfy a wide and expanding array of human needs, and with a minimum of human labor devoted to the satisfaction of subsistence needs. Under class society, however, the economic basis of society places great limits on that human development. As Marx writes in the first book of *Capital*:

> All methods for raising the social productiveness of labour are brought about at the cost of the individual labourer; all means for the development

of production transform themselves into means of domination over, and exploitation of, the producers; they mutilate the labourer into a fragment of a man, degrade him to the level of an appendage of a machine, destroy every remnant of charm in his work and turn it into a hated toil; they estrange from him the intellectual potentialities of the labour process in the same proportion as science is incorporated in it as an independent power; they distort the conditions under which he works, subject him during the labour process to a despotism the more hateful for its meanness; they transform his life-time into working-time, and drag his wife and child beneath the wheels of the Juggernaut of capital. . . . It establishes an accumulation of misery, corresponding with accumulation of capital. Accumulation of wealth at one pole is, therefore, at the same time accumulation of misery, agony of toil slavery, ignorance, brutality, mental degradation, at the opposite pole, i.e., on the side of the class that produces its own product in the form of capital.[32]

At the heart of capitalist production lies a contradiction between the immense wealth produced by this economic system and the immense privation and subjection also produced by it. This passage above puts forward the moral critique of capitalism which Marx levels against capitalism throughout his work. Capitalism produces all manner of human degradation, reducing the human being to the mere "appendage of a machine" and grinding down their intellectual and fully human potential. But at the same time that capitalism degrades the human being, it is also capitalism that produces the material basis for the "rich individuality" which forms the basis of Marx's moral outlook.

Marx's moral outlook and his approach to understanding human individuality are based in the historical materialist method that he first outlined in *The German Ideology*, but already employed well before that. The *Grundrisse* opens with the line, "To begin with, the subject to be discussed is *material production*."[33] How humans produce in the natural world in order to satisfy their needs is the basis for any scientific understanding of human beings. Marx goes on to write that socially determined production of individuals is the starting point for inquiry. Marx's conception of the individual, which plays a significant role throughout his work, takes on a more robust and concrete character in his later writings. This begins especially with the *Grundrisse*, as a result of the fact that here Marx brings the results of anthropology to bear more directly and to a greater extent than in his early work. Indeed, at the end of his life, Marx became interested in the work of American anthropologist Lewis Henry Morgan, and intended to write a treatment of Morgan's writings. Marx died before he could complete that project, a work Engels later adopted and published as *Origin of the Family, Private Property, and the State*. This gives us an indication of how Marx attempted to base his understanding of the individual on the results of science throughout his career. Marx's aim was to theorize concrete individuality based on the lived experiences of existing human beings, an improvement over the abstract, one-sided individual who, he charged, forms the subject of eighteenth-century philosophy (this is a theme to be taken up more fully in the following chapter, in which I discuss the concept of individuality in Marx's thought).

In the afterword to the second German edition of *Capital*, Marx describes his method of historical materialism:

> My dialectic method is not only different from the Hegelian, but is its direct opposite. To Hegel, the life process of the human brain, i.e., the process of thinking, which, under the name of "the Idea," he even transforms into an independent subject, is the *demiurgos* of the real world, and the real world is only the external, phenomenal form of "the Idea." With me, on the contrary, the ideal is nothing else than the material world reflected by the human mind, and translated into forms of thought. . . . The mystification which dialectic suffers in Hegel's hands, by no means prevents him from being the first to present its general form of working in a comprehensive and conscious manner. With him it is standing on its head. It must be turned right side up again, if you would discover the rational kernel within the mystical shell.
>
> In its mystified form, dialectic became the fashion in Germany, because it seemed to transfigure and to glorify the existing state of things. In its rational form it is a scandal and abomination to bourgeoisdom and its doctrinaire professors, because it includes in its comprehension an affirmative recognition of the existing state of things, at the same time also, the recognition of the negation of that state, of its inevitable breaking up; because it regards every historically developed social form as in fluid movement, and therefore takes into account its transient nature not less than its momentary existence; because it lets nothing impose upon it, and is in its essence critical and revolutionary.[34]

The critics who charge Marx with economic determinism attack him, by and large, for failing to conjure up in thought what does not already exist in reality—a world of human beings who act entirely freely, and a human society that allows ways of living undetermined by narrow economic pressures and interests. Marx does not offer that illusion or otherwise indulge the ideological demand for it.

What is necessary and inevitable is the impermanence of the existing state of things, but not what will replace it, assuming that human society actually does continue to exist and develop in the long term. Of course, it might not. But already to suggest that capitalism cannot go on forever is itself "critical and revolutionary," as Marx points out. It holds out the possibility that the existing state of things might be cast away in favor of something new, and for human intervention into the "fluid movement" of history. It is the certainty of such movement that allows Marx to conceive of a further development of the human individual.

Such a development can only occur upon an economic basis that has not yet been developed, just as the full freedom of the human person can only exist in a society in which "the free development of each is the condition for the free development of all," a society that has not yet been produced. In reading Marx as a crude economic determinist who cannot account for human freedom, his critics reveal only a very shallow engagement with the complexity of Marxist thought. Even while Marx refuses to attribute a range of freedom to human beings that does not yet exist in capitalist society, he sees how that sphere of freedom can be expanded upon a new economic base. A new and more robust freedom can be brought about through the activity of conscious human actors, leveraging existing social processes to achieve their goal.

6

Individuality

No concept figures more centrally into Marx's ethical thought than that of "individuality." Individuality is at stake both in his blistering condemnations of bourgeois egoism and in his positive vision of a world of freed human beings pursuing their individual and social self-realization in a society designed to promote it. The relevant methodological disagreements with classical liberal political theory turn largely on the question of what it means to premise political theory on the basis of human individuals' needs and natures. Marx's own theory of human individuality exemplifies his historical materialism, which understands the natural and social world as produced by (and susceptible to) human intervention in that world. The claim that human individuals are the products of human social activity and intervention into history anchors Marx's historical materialist critique of capitalism, his criticism of liberal political theory, his revolutionary program, and his vision of a better world.

Marx's preoccupation with individuality might appear curious, in certain quarters.[1] A kind of gray, nondescript collectivism has come over the years to be associated with Marxism in much of the popular imagination (although with the rise of left protest movements, antifascist struggle, and support for democratic socialism in recent years, this is rapidly changing). And indeed, his promotion of individuality as a value bears practically no resemblance to capitalism's atomizing, consumerist exaltation of the "individual." To clarify this distinction, it is helpful to turn to Marx's concept of a "social individual." The social individual is a being in whose person the antagonism between society and individual is reconciled. In capitalist ideology, the notion of "individuality" is invoked in order to reify and essentialize the separateness and mutual antagonism among persons. It represents shrinking away into the private sphere as a high expression of individuality and freedom. For Marx, conversely, individuality is the result of that practical social interdependency which continually produces novel avenues for self-expression and self-realization.

The tension between Marxist and capitalist conceptions of individuality is highlighted by Marx in the *Communist Manifesto*. In the following quote, he addresses an imagined bourgeois interlocutor's accusation that the Communists aim to do away with individuality:

> From the moment when labour can no longer be converted into capital, money, or rent, into a social power capable of being monopolised, i.e., from the moment when individual property can no longer be transformed into bourgeois property, into capital, from that moment, you say, individuality vanishes. You must, therefore, confess that by "individual" you mean no other person than the bourgeois, than the middle-class owner of property. This person must, indeed, be swept out of the way, and made impossible.[2]

By no means does Marx intend for individuality as such to also be swept away. For it is not stultifying, degrading, enslaving capitalism that instantiates the conditions best suited to the full flourishing of the individual human person. Yet capitalist ideology advertises individual self-realization as precisely one of its most notable achievements. It does this through presuming and naturalizing an opposition between individual and society, so that social cooperation is regarded with some suspicion as inimical to individual human expression, or at the very least, always ultimately in tension with it. As capitalism guards against democratic control of society's resources, it preserves the conditions under which capitalists arise and persist. Capitalists express their individual human agency through their domination of resources and people. Capitalism as a system thus prevents the individual flourishing of the majority of human beings, while affording even to the economic elite only a highly impoverished form of individuality predicated on the absence of mutual and authentic human social connections. Frustration of individuality, in Marx's sense of that term, is inevitably required by capitalist conditions.

Marx's conception of individuality represents a significant point of departure from the abstract, atomized individual of liberal theory. Instead of attempting to isolate actors from context, Marx proceeds from an understanding of human beings as concrete "social individuals" and looks to the results of natural and social science to form the basis of his theorizing about how human beings ought to live. Replacing the liberal picture of human beings as competitive individuals who produce society in order to satisfy their egoistic wants, Marx presents human beings as essentially social.

Human beings are able to individuate themselves, to devote time and resources to needs that are not the strictly biological needs of a mammal in the species *Homo sapiens*, and to develop capacities beyond those narrowly suited to satisfying biological needs. But this is only possible through the labor process. Moving beyond subsistence needs is a point in human history when social production has begun to reach a degree of complexity and sophistication such as to support such individuation. This process no doubt originates quite early in human history. Nonetheless, the fact of human individuality is not a timeless truth about human nature, but rather a historically emergent phenomenon produced by essentially social beings through the labor process.

In the writings collected into his 1857 *Grundrisse*, Marx reflects upon the abstract individualism of classical liberalism, writing that it is "stupid" for a conception of human beings to take "the isolated man as its starting-point." Marx continues:

> Man becomes individualised only through the process of history. Originally he is a species being, a tribal being, a herd animal—though by no means as a *zoon politikon* in the political sense. Exchange itself is a major agent of this individuation. It makes herd-like existence superfluous and dissolves it.[3]

It is not possible to have a fully accurate understanding of human individuality without also understanding the essence of human beings as productive beings. Humans produce their needs and transform their natures through social labor. Therefore, not only are the concepts of individuality, essential human nature, and labor interrelated, but their interrelation suggests the method that is best suited to successful inquiry into each of them. That approach is described by Marx and Engels in their *Critique of the German Ideology* as the "materialist conception of history." Historical materialism takes human production and the circumstances in which it takes place to be fundamental in conditioning human existence. The character of human social relations is produced and determined through their interactions with nature and with one another through the labor process. Labor is best understood as a process in which human beings interact with nature both as part of it and as distinct from it. In this light, it is possible to see how human existence becomes increasingly sophisticated. From this view, the history of human development is also the history of the emergence and development of distinct human personalities and what Marx later terms, "rich individuality," in *Capital*.

The capitalist mode of production in particular has contributed greatly to making it possible for there to be a greater proliferation of human powers and forms of being than existed in feudal society, or in any other previous societies. One of the most significant ways in which it does this is through the process of globalization. From a Marxist perspective, globalization is a result of capitalism's character as a system that must constantly seek out new markets for the commodities it produces, as well as new sources of raw materials and fresh labor.

As Marx writes, the capitalist system must "nestle everywhere, settle everywhere, establish connections everywhere."[4] This expansionist aspect of capitalism plays two roles that are each important here for our discussion of the development of human individuality. First, capitalism as an economic system tends to spread to more and more parts of the globe, fundamentally transforming societies wherever it goes. Second, capitalism brings people from disparate parts of the globe into contact with and interdependence upon one another. There is precious little production carried out today that uses resources or labor that only exist within the borders of one nation. In order to do so much as cook a dinner, we purchase spices from one country, vegetables from another, cookware from a third. We then sit down to eat at a table made in a fourth, while wearing clothing made in a fifth. Marx writes, "In place of the old wants, satisfied by the productions of the country, we find new wants, requiring for their satisfaction the products of distant lands and climes."[5] He continues,

> as in material, so also in intellectual production. The intellectual creations of individual nations become common property. National one-sidedness and narrow-mindedness become more and more impossible, and from the numerous national and local literatures, there arises a world literature.

These "wants" build and strengthen the connections among disparate parts of the globe and make a world culture possible. They lay down the basis for the sort of global cooperation which would be necessary to build communism as an economic system. More directly relevant for our purposes here, they achieve historical breaks. For instance, they take the provincial person of feudal society and transform her into the cosmopolitan of bourgeois society. These shifting contexts and progressions make a new wealth and diversity of human experiences and activities into live options for the individual person.

Marx observes that the creation of the material basis for such an individuality already exists as an ongoing and developing process in human history. Rich individuality can only be realized by means of advances in society. This form of individuality is constituted by the full development and proliferation of human capacities and entails the production of the human as an all-sided being rather than as a limited and degraded being. It depends upon increased efficiency and complexity in social production and the social existence of human beings. The history of human social development is intimately and necessarily connected with the history of the emergence and further development of human individuality. In fact, they are two moments of the same historical process. In positing the development of rich individuality as the highest aim for human beings, Marx does not simply conjure up a moral command out of whole cloth. Rather, he argues that human beings must work consciously to promote a process that is already developing in human history, but whose continued development depends entirely upon whether or not human beings will build a society with such human development as its guiding principle.

An understanding of human beings as concrete, specific, and potentially "rich" and fully social individuals is superior to classical liberal political philosophy's theorization of the human person as an isolated, and competitive, atomized individual. It better captures the reality of what it is to be a human being and is more consonant with the results of anthropology which reveal individuality to be a product of social labor. Rather than a reliable constant, this research has shown individuality to be a historically emergent phenomenon. This conception of concrete human individuality has greater explanatory power in analyzing how societies and individual human beings grow and develop. It is able to make sense of individuality not as a timeless and ahistorical fact, but rather as a result of human activity: initially as an unintended consequence of social production and then, with the transition to socialist relations of production, consciously promoted as the highest aim of social production.

What Marx describes in the *Grundrisse* and *Capital* as "rich individuality" functions as a standard for the ethical evaluation of people, actions, and circumstances. "Rich individuals" are persons liberated from *abject* dependency on other people and yet fully, consciously, and enthusiastically interdependent with them. The promise of communism's capacity to promote rich individuality, and the reality of capitalism's manifest incapacity to do the same, are two key premises in the case for socialism. The notion of "rich individuality" in *Capital* represents the development of a thread in Marx's thought that extends at least as far back as his doctoral dissertation on Democritus and Epicurus. Attending to Marx's use of the individuality concept allows us insight into how his body of work constitutes a coherent whole, and into how this concept coheres with those of human nature, alienation, and freedom in Marx's writing.

We have already explored how Marx's doctoral dissertation sheds light on the development of his thought on the dialectic of freedom and determinism. Marx's study of the atom also figures importantly in his philosophical development, more broadly. This commentary on atomism in ancient Greek philosophy has not attracted attention from very many of his interpreters. Yet as Peter Fenves observes in his treatment of Marx's doctoral thesis, "the dissertation foreshadows Marx's later work most of all in its many orientations, objectives, and methods of research."[6]

We can draw out a connection between the dialectic of freedom and determinism, and the nature of human individuality. This holds especially as pertains to individuals' capacities for self-directed action. In Kant, for example, freedom is closely linked to autonomy: my actions are free when they are caused just by me, and not by that which is alien to me and beyond my control. In those circumstances, a philosophical account of freedom hangs crucially upon the possibility of accurately describing the boundaries of my selfhood, of individuating me from the world of which I am a part, in hopes that with such knowledge in hand, one might correctly ascertain whether a particular action originated with me.

The relevance of Marx's early study of Greek atomistics to his conception of human individuality is also more exactly stated by a passage in *The Holy Family*. There, Marx criticizes liberalism's presupposition that the role of the modern state is to "hold together the individual self-seeking atoms." He argues, against this picture, that not only is this not the state's role (for human beings are already bound together by their organically interdependent social relations), but that human beings are not to be analogized to atoms at all. In this way, questions of political philosophy (what is the proper role of the state in mediating human relations?), social philosophy (how ought human beings to relate to one another?), and philosophical anthropology (what is it to be an individual human being, after all?), are linked with metaphysics in the question of to what extent human individuality can be accurately described as analogous with the singleness and independence of the atom.

In *The Holy Family*, Marx writes:

> Speaking exactly and in the prosaic sense, the members of civil society are not *atoms*. The *specific property* of the atom is that it has no properties and is therefore not connected with beings outside it by any relationship determined by its own *natural necessity*. The atom *has no needs*, it is *self-sufficient*; the world outside it is an absolute *vacuum*, i.e., it is contentless, senseless, meaningless, just because the atom has *all fullness* in itself. The egoistic individual in civil society may in his non-sensuous imagination and lifeless abstraction inflate himself into an *atom*, i.e., into an unrelated, self-sufficient, wantless, *absolutely full*, blessed being. Unblessed *sensuous reality* does not bother about his imagination, each of his senses compels him to believe in the existence of the world and of individuals outside him, and even his *profane* stomach reminds him every day that the world *outside* him is not *empty*, but is what really *fills*. Every activity and property of his being, every one of his vital urges, becomes a *need*, a *necessity*, which his *self-seeking* transforms into seeking for other things and human beings outside him.... It is therefore not the *state* that holds the *atoms* of civil society together, but the fact that they are *atoms* only in *imagination*, in the *heaven* of their fancy, but in *reality* beings tremendously different from atoms, in other words, not *divine egoists*, but *egoistic human beings*.[7]

This is not to deny the radicalism of classical liberal theory vis-à-vis the monarchist ideologies it opposed and supplanted; it would of course be mistaken to overlook that in the case of, for example, a figure such as John Locke. For Locke, the point is not for individuals to remain in their isolation but rather to form society with one another. In explaining why it might be that there exists no historical record of a "state of nature," Locke reasons that

> it is not at all to be wondered, that history gives us but a very little account of men, that lived together in the state of nature. The inconveniences of that condition, and the love and want of society, no sooner brought any number of them together, but they presently united and incorporated, if they designed to continue together.[8]

However, this Lockean explanation of the impetus to civil society incorporates two errors of liberalism. It presupposes a natural separateness and disunity of human beings, and it justifies political subjection and hierarchy as necessitated by natural antagonisms among human individuals. Marx references atomistics in his critique of political liberalism precisely because classical liberal political philosophy relies so heavily on the conception of the human being as an isolated being, who needs little from other human beings and from society besides perhaps some guarantee that it will be left alone to pursue its own happiness. Human beings are individuals, yes, but real, concrete individuals with needs that impel them constantly to seek out other human individuals and maintain relationships with them, and to make use of the natural world they metabolize as what Marx calls their "inorganic body." For individual human persons to flourish, develop, and maintain a continued existence, they must make their needs effective in the world outside themselves, and realize themselves in and through their connections with the outside world. It is in this way that an individual person's "self-seeking" can be transformed "into seeking for other things and human beings outside him."

Marx further clarifies his conception of individuality in *The German Ideology*. There, he writes,

> [under capitalism] the productive forces appear as a world for themselves, quite independent of and divorced from the individuals, alongside the individuals; the reason for this is that the individuals, whose forces they are, exist split up and in opposition to one another, whilst, on the other hand, these forces are only real forces in the intercourse and association of these individuals. Thus, on the one hand, we have a totality of productive forces, which have, as it were, taken on a material form and are for the individuals themselves no longer the forces of the individuals but of private property, and hence of the individuals only insofar as they are owners of private property.... On the other hand, standing against these productive forces, we have the majority of the individuals from whom these forces have been wrested away, and who, robbed thus of all real life-content, have become abstract individuals, who are, however, by this very fact put into a position to enter into relation with one another *as individuals*.... Things have now come to such a pass that the individuals must appropriate the existing totality of productive forces, not only to achieve self-activity, but, also, merely to safeguard their very existence.[9]

At this point in his career, Marx shied away from invoking the alienation concept by name. However, as we discussed earlier in Chapter 4, the concept is perfectly recognizable in his description of human individuals at odds with one another, and even with their own productive capacities. A concern with human emancipation and the flourishing of individual human beings continues to form the basis of Marx's normative condemnation of bourgeois society and his arguments for the creation of a new society based on the satisfaction of human needs, throughout his work. Marx writes in the *Manifesto* that in bourgeois society, "capital is independent and has individuality, while the living person is dependent and has no individuality."[10] On the other hand, in communist society, accumulated labor is "a means to widen, to enrich, to promote the existence of the labourer."[11] To promote the "existence" of the worker and, more broadly, of the human being, is to make it possible for this person to interact with the world outside of herself through a wide and expanding array of activities. Under communism, production will be carried out toward the end of promoting this increased development of human beings' capacities and satisfaction of their needs.

In the posthumously published *Grundrisse*, Marx terms this his "dialectic method." He contrasts his own focus on the socially determined production of human individuals in the natural world, with the work of economists such as Adam Smith and David Ricardo. These political economists, he charges, rely on a conception of human nature given to them by eighteenth-century philosophers who take the individual in the society of "free competition," the person who appears to be freed from any natural or social bonds, as the basis of their theorizing. Instead of understanding this type of person as a particular historical development, they instead understand the essence of this type of person as the essence of human nature itself and project it backward into the past, mistaking a social phenomenon at a particular historical moment for a natural and stable feature of mankind.

But according to Marx, this method of abstracting away from a contemporary appearance and mistaking it for a stable essence obscures a pertinent point concerning individuality. If we examine the anthropological record and attempt to understand what human beings have been over the course of their existence, we do not end up with a picture of human beings as essentially the atomized, isolated, competitive individuals of bourgeois society. Instead, "The further back we go in history, the more does the individual, and accordingly also the producing individual, appear to be dependent and belonging to a larger whole."[12]

Marx argues that to suppose that it is possible for human beings to have produced as "isolated beings apart from society" is as much of an absurdity as the development of speech without individuals living and speaking together. Production, he says, is always the production of "social individuals," and all production is the appropriation of nature by the individual within a particular form of society. To come back to his words in the introduction to the *Grundrisse*:

> The further back we go in history, the more does the individual, and accordingly also the producing individual, appear to be dependent and belonging to a larger whole. At first, he is still in a quite natural manner part of the family, and of the family expanded into the tribe; later he is part of a community, of one of the different forms of community which arise from the conflict and the merging of tribes. It is not until the 18th century, in "bourgeois society," that the various forms of the social nexus confront the individual as merely a means towards his private ends, as external necessity. But the epoch which produces this standpoint, that of the isolated individual, is precisely the epoch of the hitherto most highly developed social (according to this standpoint, general) relations. Man is a zoon politikon in the most literal sense: he is not only a social animal, but an animal that can isolate itself only within society. Production by an isolated individual outside society—something rare, which might occur when a civilised person already dynamically in possession of the social forces is accidentally cast into the wilderness—is just as preposterous as the development of language without individuals who live together and speak to one another.[13]

Later in the *Grundrisse*, Marx reiterates these ideas when he argues that "human beings become individuals only through the process of history," and that "exchange itself is a major agent of this individuation."[14] It is only in and through society that the human being becomes individualized, and so the existence of the human being as an individualized animal is one that is historically arisen and socially produced. As opposed to the picture of the human being as an essentially atomized or essentially individual being, "The human being is ... an animal that can only individuate itself in society."

Individuation, Marx argues, is a process that takes place only within society and only at a certain stage of social and economic development. Marx himself does not flesh out this claim in great detail, but it is possible to reconstruct the story nonetheless. For human beings to appear as individuals, and not merely as biological specimens of a certain type, requires that productive forces be developed so that she does not need to spend her entire waking life satisfying her merely biological needs for food, water, shelter and the like. Such a level of development in the forces of production is too great and complicated a task to be carried out by a single person. It is an inherently social project in that it requires a number of people working together, communicating with one another, and developing increasingly complex ways of organizing and dividing their labor. Sociality is hence *prior* to any individuation that takes place in human beings. That process of individuation is also a mark of how far human social development has progressed. The more efficiently a society satisfies biological human needs, and the more productive it is, creating new resources to satisfy the historically emergent needs that arise in an increasingly complex society, the more that its members are able to pursue activities determined more by their own expanding array of interests and less by mere biological necessity. In a phrase, we begin to see an emergence of the "rich individuality" that Marx regards as the highest aim for human beings.

It is the case that human beings appear more social the further in the past we look, but it is also true that if we take a clear look at human beings living today, we find that it also makes little sense to think of existing society as a mere aggregate of isolated individuals. Thus, Marx argues that "society does not consist of individuals, but expresses the sum of the relationships and conditions in which these individuals stand to one another."[15] Marx sometimes uses the phrase, "social individuals"; this is very apt to describing the types of actors we find in society and captures the dual aspects of human nature as inherently social and potentially "richly" individual.

In the capitalist mode of production, capitalists' profit is based on driving down the amount of labor necessary to satisfy the basic reproductive needs of their workers, as far as possible. Capitalism has massively reduced, through the division of labor and the industrialization, mechanization, and rationalization of production, the labor necessary to satisfy human needs. This would potentially free up the majority of human beings' hours for the pursuit of tasks not narrowly subordinated to the reproduction of the species.

Marx writes in the *Grundrisse*, capitalist production provides

> the material elements for the development of the rich individuality, which is as varied and comprehensive in its production as it is in its consumption, and whose labour therefore no longer appears as labour but as the full

development of activity itself, in which natural necessity has disappeared in its immediate form; because natural need has been replaced by historically produced need.[16]

Capitalism, in its drive to increase profits and productivity, revolutionizes and advances the capacity of society to satisfy a wide and expanding range of human needs. It thereby makes it possible for there to be a transition to a society in which rich individuality would be the "ruling principle" of the society and recognized as the highest good for human beings. As Marx says of the capitalist in the first volume of *Capital*:

> Fanatically bent on making value expand itself, he ruthlessly forces the human race to produce for production's sake; he thus forces the development of the productive powers of society, and creates those material conditions, which alone can form the real basis of a higher form of society, a society in which the full and free development of every individual forms the ruling principle.[17]

The obvious question that may be asked here is whether human flourishing—the development of "rich individuality"—really is the highest aim for human beings, and whether this understanding of human flourishing really can play the role of an ethical ideal in any moral theory worth the name. A further question is whether building a movement for communism really is the best way to realize this aim. I will treat the three questions separately, although they are closely related.

I will begin by restating the first question, which might be put: What is so good, anyway, about satisfying human needs and developing human capacities? Why should that be the basis of our moral theory? Why not maximizing happiness? Or instantiating the virtues? Or following divine commands, for that matter?

Though some will find this answer unsatisfying: we should care about the full flourishing of human beings because *they're us*. For Marx, the question "Why promote human flourishing?" doesn't arise unless a person already has a thoroughly alienated and un-human perspective on her own species and on the world. For such a figure, knowing that some path of action is most likely to preserve the continued existence of human beings and to further their full development in the natural world does not suffice. They regard it as still an open question whether that path ought to be taken. This would be similar to the mistake made by the person who wants to know the answer to the theological question "Why is there something rather than nothing?," to whom Marx replies:

> Since for the socialist man the entire so-called history of the world is nothing but the creation of man through human labour, nothing but the emergence of nature for man, so he has the visible, irrefutable proof of his birth through himself, of his genesis. Since the real existence of man and nature has become evident in practice, through sense experience, because man has thus become evident for man as the being of nature, and nature for man as the being of man, the question about an alien being, about a being above nature and man—a question which implies the admission of the unreality of nature and of man—has become impossible in practice.[18]

This line of thought can be applied to the question of whether or not "man is the highest being for man," as Marx says, which expresses the same idea as the statement that the development of rich individuality is the highest moral aim. For Marx, it is incoherent to talk about value in a way that does not posit human beings and their productive activity as the source and ontological basis of all value.

Elsewhere, I have referred to this as Marx's "radical irreligion," which I argued

> is best understood not primarily as an ontological stance on the existence or non-existence of God, but rather as part and parcel of a philosophical worldview radically committed to sweeping such questions aside, to ontologically and epistemologically centering the human perspective, to overthrowing "all relations in which man is a debased, enslaved, forsaken, despicable being," and to taking as its core principle that "man is the highest being for man."[19]

Interests, Individuals, and Egoists: Marx on Max Stirner

Although they are not typically regarded as such, the writings collected as Marx's and Engels's *Critique of the German Ideology* constitute a rich and detailed engagement with moral philosophy, and an important expression of Marx's moral outlook.[20] After all, roughly two-thirds of the hefty volume is devoted to a merciless critique of Max Stirner's 1845 defense of ethical egoism, *The Ego and Its Own*[21] (*Der Einzige und sein Eigentum*).[22] Harkening back to some of the major themes we addressed in Chapter 4 on the alienation concept, here I discuss Marx's disagreements with Stirner on the question of how to solve the problem of alienation, a question that figures importantly into Marx's moral thought. In countering Stirner's radically individualist, egoist, and nihilist proffered solutions to alienation, Marx expresses key aspects of his own ethical outlook.

Marx's polemic against ethical egoism has been largely ignored, partly due to the fact that the entire set of those manuscripts which we now know as *The German Ideology* were not published until 1933, nearly ninety years after their completion. Moreover, the collection of writings runs roughly seven hundred pages, and in its abridged form, the form in which it is most commonly read (especially by English-language readers), the four hundred pages of polemic against Stirner are excised. The polemic itself is challenging for even the most careful reader who has not also read Stirner's book, which was required reading among intellectuals in 1845 Berlin, but is far less well-known today. These factors have contributed to Marx's attack on Stirner being overlooked and deemed inessential at best, a condition which is little changed since Paul Thomas rightly pointed out in his 1975 paper "Karl Marx and Max Stirner," that *The German Ideology*

> has rarely been read in its entirety; the long section Marx devoted to a phrase-by-phrase dissection of Max Stirner's *Der Einzige und sein Eigenthum*, in particular, has been almost completely ignored. . . . The task remains both to credit Marx's critique of Stirner with the importance it deserves, and to consider this critique in its context.[23]

In *The Ego and Its Own*, Stirner rejects all morality on the basis that it demands the sacrifice of the individual for a good that is not his own. Of course, communism is included in this category of theories that posit a "good cause" for which the individual must sacrifice himself.[24] Stirner discovers that every "good cause," which has been thought to be a good in itself, is actually an egoistic cause, seeking its own good. (For Stirner, causes are quite capable of engaging in their own self-directed activity, not to mention, of duping human beings into servitude.)

In Stirner's view, the human pursuit of a "good cause" is always little more than a new brand of sacrifice and self-denial. Therefore, since every cause is itself an "egoistic cause," individuals should take the place of their own "good causes" and pursue only their own narrowest self-interest. Stirner writes:

> What is not supposed to be my concern! First and foremost the good cause, then God's cause, the cause of mankind, of truth, of freedom, of humanity, of justice; further, the cause of my people, my prince, my fatherland; finally, even the cause of mind and a thousand other causes. Only *my* cause is never to be my concern.... My concern is neither the divine nor the human, not the true, good, just, free, etc., but solely what is *mine* [*das Meinige*], and it is not a general one, but is—*unique* [*einzig*], as I am unique. Nothing is more to me than myself![25]

Stirner's writings might have been dismissed at the time of their publication had they not been quite so effective against their principal target: the ethical humanism of Ludwig Feuerbach. Feuerbach famously argued in *The Essence of Christianity* that "God" was merely an abstraction and personification of man's qualities. "The Divine Being," he wrote, "is nothing other than the being of man himself, or rather, the being of man abstracted from the limits of the individual man or the real, corporeal man, and objectified, i.e., contemplated and worshiped as another being, as a being distinguished from his own."[26] The oppressive, alienating nature of religion would be overcome once God was replaced by "Man" as a divinity for himself, and once human beings shed their pious attitude toward the abstraction, God, and took up a new one toward the abstraction, Man, recognizing that what had previously been regarded as a superhuman being was in fact only an objectification and deification of human qualities. Through the adoption of this new correct idea, "what is regarded as atheism today," namely, the denial of the existence of God, "will be religion tomorrow," a religion of Man.[27] But here, Thomas's 1975 paper is very clear in explaining the seriousness of the challenge Stirner posed to this view:

> The weakness in Feuerbach's argument that Stirner seizes upon is rooted in Feuerbach's conception of man's divinity, not as something man had to build or to create, but as something to be regained at the level of consciousness. Once it is regained, man must by implication give way before his new-found divinity. Stirner maintained that "divinity" will be as oppressive and burdensome a taskmaster as any other spirit or collectivity to which individuals, historically, have succumbed.... Feuerbach's celebrated

reversal of subject and predicate—his substitution of man for God as the agent of divinity—changes nothing; mankind as a collectivity is just as oppressive and sacred as God, because the real individual continues to be related to it in a religious manner.[28]

Feuerbach's humanism was developed to solve the problem of alienation, but in fact it only seemed to reproduce the problem, this time with the abstraction "Man" raised to the level of a divinity. Stirner argued that Feuerbach's humanism simply replaced a religious fear of God, and a Christian ethic of self-renunciation, with a religious sacrifice of the individual for the good of abstract "Man." Stirner rejected the problem of alienation, and also any quest for personal development or self-improvement, on the grounds that these cause individuals to adopt a religious, self-denying attitude to their possible, unalienated, better selves. Even to suggest that individuals should develop their own talents and capacities is to suggest that they sacrifice themselves in the interest of an alien "good cause."

Marx (as did many of the Young Hegelians) recognized the importance of Stirner's book as a critique of Feuerbach's ethical humanism.[29] A mere change in thought would not resolve the problem of alienation or do away with the self-renunciation of the individual which was characteristic of religious practice. However, Stirner himself made the same mistakes he accused Feuerbach of, lapsing into idealism and attributing to "causes" powers over human beings which they simply could not have (as though it were really the "causes," the "fixed ideas," that had led human beings astray, and not the real relations between human beings that had given rise to these ideas in the first place). Accordingly, Stirner's proposed solution to the problem was one that could be carried out entirely in the realm of thought: individuals had simply to choose to pursue their own narrow self-interest as an egoistic cause. "In the final analysis," Marx writes, Stirner

> arrives merely at an impotent moral injunction that everybody should himself obtain satisfaction and carry out punishment. He believes Don Quixote's assurance that by a mere moral injunction he can without more ado convert the material forces arising from the division of labour into personal forces.[30]

Marx's critique of Stirner's ethical egoism displays a philosophical continuity with his explication of the distinction between abstract and concrete individuality in his doctoral dissertation; the statement, "abstract individualism is freedom from being, not freedom in being" might be just as at home here as it is in that earlier work. For Stirner, the problem of alienation can simply be swept away through a further retreat of the private individual into herself as her only cause or concern, which she opposes to social concerns. Mutual dependencies and interrelations among human beings are regarded as illusory, at best, and dangerously deceptive, at worst. Not only does Stirner's brand of ethical egoism call on the individual to embrace asocial behavior and attitudes, but it argues that the individual should satisfy herself at her present level of development, whatever that may be, rather than strive to further that development. It posits the human person as a static, isolated atom, rather than as a concrete individual, developing and existing within society, for whom the problem of alienation can only be resolved through a transformation of society, brought about through coordinated human action aimed at common goals.

The connection between individual and society in Marx's thought is further clarified in Marx's defense of communism against Stirner's charge that communism calls for the subordination of individuals to the "good cause" of society. Stirner argues that for communists, "Society, from which we have everything, is a new master, a new spook, a new 'supreme being,'" for whom the individual must sacrifice himself.[31] Marx answers that far from denigrating the individual, the development of a communist society, and the practical activity required to achieve that society, are the only methods by which the well-being of individuals can actually be pursued, a goal which Stirner's "mere moral injunctions" cannot achieve. Stirner is mistaken in believing

> that the communists want to "make sacrifices" for "society," when they want at most to sacrifice existing society; in this case he should describe their consciousness that their struggle is the common cause of all people who have outgrown the bourgeois system as a sacrifice that they make to themselves.[32]

Stirner, on the other hand, offers no genuine solution to the real challenges that concrete individuals face. He argues against any organized political (much less, revolutionary) activity on the grounds that such coordinated, planned action would subordinate the individual to the needs of a collective. (Stirner does imagine that individuals might spontaneously form a "Union of Egoists" whose purpose is to restrict any social incursion into their egoistic pursuits, but provides no explanation as to how such a union might be achieved.)

Paul Blackledge writes, in his 2012 book *Marx and Ethics*:

> Against Stirner's claim that socialists had embraced a static model of human essence, which provided them with a moral basis for criticising existing society, Marx outlined a Hegelian historicised transformation of his earlier Feuerbachian materialism. In the modern world this process underpinned the emergence both of egoistic and more social forms of individualism. Morality, as it was understood by Stirner, was an essential authoritarian characteristic only of communities made up of the former. By assuming the universality of egoism, Stirner was unable to comprehend the concept of workers' solidarity. Conversely, because Marx recognized that solidarity had become a real need and desire for workers he concluded that it was unnecessary to impose the idea of community on them.[33]

Marx points to the workers' movement developing at the time of his writing, as a means by which the social conditions that limit the ability of individuals to flourish and pursue their own development as an end might be abolished. Stirner turns his back on this existing political current and retreats into the realm of ideas, thereby depriving himself of any genuine explanation of how the problem of alienation might be solved.

Characteristically of his and the Analytical Marxists' tendency to downplay, ignore, or outright revile the role of dialectics and historicity in Marx's thought, in his 2014 book *The Free Development of Each*, Allen Wood appreciates some key aspects of Marx's reply to Stirner but not several of those that are most crucial to articulating a correct understanding of Marx's approach to ethics. Wood writes:

> Marx accepted Stirner's idea that all interests, ideals, and principles that claim universal authority are to be rejected as ideology in a sense equated with "the dominion of thoughts" and are therefore false impositions on human freedom. This false universality is now interpreted by Marx and Engels as an expression of a society divided into warring classes; it is the way class interests try to impose themselves on us as having some sort of transcendent or sacred authority.[34]

Crucially, however, the universal authority of the working class, as "the class with the future in its hands," as the class against whom "no particular wrong" is done but "wrong generally," and as the sole class that can forge the key to humanity's self-emancipation from its "radical chains," is no "false imposition on human freedom" but rather the absolute ground of human freedom, which is a point Marx makes again and again (and again). Wood imposes a strict, mutually exclusive dichotomy between authority and freedom that is not Marx's (it is not even liberalism's, making it unclear why Wood reads Marx in this way). What Marx and Engels approvingly term, "despotic inroads on the rights of private property" and "the dictatorship of the proletariat" are no less authoritative for being, on their view, necessary for the historical emergence of realized human freedom and individuality. We can agree with Wood that the authority of the working class is not "transcendent or sacred," but to suggest that its universality is false in "a society divided into warring classes" is to fundamentally misunderstand the normative dimensions of Marx's project.

Charles Mills's 1994 essay "Marxism, 'Ideology,' and Moral Objectivism" puts the matter quite correctly when he writes that "a sympathetic reading" circumvents any nihilist reading of Marx's and Engels's claim that "the communists do not preach morality at all"; not only does Mills's interpretation evade the charge of nihilism, but it further clarifies why, still theorizing within the context of existing class society, Marx cannot be said to suggest that the working class has no universal principles to impose. Mills's tone is ironic at points, but the overall thrust of the analysis here is quite helpful:

> Their point is that the opposition of egoism and altruism is not immanent in the structure of things, but a product of class society. To "preach morality" in these circumstances (to moralize without understanding this material foundation) would be to tacitly endorse the permanence of this contradiction, when in fact it needs to be transcended by a new society in which (because of the communist cornucopia of goods) it will disappear. A purely moral critique, then (given their view of morality as tied to an idealist sociology), would be inadequate because it would fail to get to the root of things, the 'material source' rather than the "highflown ideological [read: idealistic] form," and would only address the superstructural symptom.[35]

As we saw earlier in Chapter 2, on ideology, the proletariat presages the abolition of morality because its class interests are identical with the interests of humanity and the development of those conditions within which human individuality may flourish. However, while recognizing the glimmers that workers' struggles offer us of a potential communist future, it is crucial not to forget that our present world remains rife with social antagonism. The proletariat has not made its conditions of existence general *yet*; that remains its historical task.

Defending Marx's Methodological Holism

I have so far approached the topic of individuality and individualism in Marxist theory primarily from the perspective of detailing Marx's understanding of what it is to be an individual human being, and his understanding of the relationship between the individual and society. Yet another important aspect of understanding individuality in Marxist theory has to do with methodology: How best to investigate and explain human social phenomena? Do we understand it by investigating the actions of group subjects such as economic classes or even, humanity itself, taken as a whole (methodological holism)? Or do we explain it as primarily the result of the aggregated actions of many discrete individual human actors (methodological individualism)?

What is at stake in the question of whether to understand Marx as primarily a methodological holist or a methodological individualist? Attributing methodological holism to Marx has the virtue of being more neatly fitted to his accounts of group agency. More specifically it fits his descriptions of the tasks, aims, and actions of the bourgeois and proletarian classes. There are also sections of Marx's writing that suggestively imply a strict holism: in the *Communist Manifesto*, Marx and Engels famously describe human history as predominantly the history of struggle between contending classes.

Methodological holism also makes the best sense of Marx's claims that class- and even species-level explanations account for the historic development of human beings. This becomes obscured if one attempts to admit, as the actions and interests of groups, only phenomena that can be reduced to the discrete actions and interests of separate and individual human beings. Put differently, social wholes exhibit emergent features that are irreducible to even the most detailed description of the specific features of the individual human beings that comprise them. Those posited wholes will be fundamentally impoverished and inadequate to the task of doing social philosophy, as would be any description of the social world that limits itself to only those social features that *are* fully reducible to the features and actions of individual human beings.

So what then, are the drawbacks of reading Marx as a methodological holist? For some commentators, the chief drawback seems to be that it is very hard to make Marx's methodological holism compatible with the more individualist presuppositions of much mainstream analytical philosophy. One of the most well-known attempts to reconcile Marxism with methodological individualism is "Rational Choice Marxism," itself a prominent variant of "Analytical" Marxism. This strand of Marxist interpretation emerged within Anglophone analytical philosophy in the 1980s. To motivate the need for such a reconciliation, Jon Elster writes in 1985:

> It is quite extraordinary, in my view, how Marx could shift from nearnonsense to profound insight, often within the same work. In the *Grundrisse*, for instance, we have on the one hand the most striking statements of methodological collectivism and dialectical deduction, and, on the other hand, equally striking analyses of the way in which micro-motives are aggregated into macro-behaviour, to use T. C. Schelling's phrase. It is my firm belief... that the central insights of Marx are so valuable that we would do him and us a disservice were we to accept *en bloc* the methodology in which they were embedded.[36]

In their treatment of the debates between "orthodox" Marxist methodological holism and analytical methodological individualism, Andrew Levine, Elliott Sober, and Erik Olin Wright summarize Analytical Marxism's attitude toward that holism:

> Authors such as Jon Elster, John Roemer, Adam Przeworski and G. A. Cohen have argued that what is distinctive in Marxism is its substantive claims about the world, not its methodology, and that the methodological principles widely held to distinguish Marxism from its rivals are indefensible, if not incoherent.[37]

Levine et al. conclude that while the rational choice Marxists are correct to prescribe a focus on the "microfoundations" of social phenomena, this does not necessarily indicate methodological individualism. Levine et al. argue, "It is one thing to call for the elaboration of microfoundations of macrotheory and another to specify the form such microfoundational analyses should take."[38]

In his 1987 paper "On Marx's Holism," Timothy Shiell argues that the approach to the holism/individualism debate that would be most compatible with Marx's views is a combination of metaphysical individualism and methodological holism. (Shiell does not purport to make any claims about what the historical Marx did in fact believe on this score, however.) Shiell takes what is at stake in the question of methodological holism in Marx to be this: "The question is not whether or not Marx actually made definitional reductions, but is, rather, whether or not anything Marx wrote implies or entails that the properties of social objects are wholly reducible definitionally to the properties and relations of individual persons and things."[39]

However, Shiell explicitly dismisses out-of-hand the possibility that in order to understand Marx's social ontology, we require a dialectical approach that incorporates aspects of both doctrines and resolves the contradiction between them. Shiell writes, "It might be natural to suppose that Marx would have rejected the individualist/holist dichotomy in favor of a third alternative elaborated along quite different lines due (perhaps) to his characteristically 'dialectical' way of thinking."[40] Shiell goes on to argue against this, that one should not assume that Marx was dialectical in every particular, and that one ought first to posit a more simple acceptance of "the two traditional alternatives," of either individualism or holism. This might serve as a general approach to understanding a philosophical figure. But it gets things backward with respect to Marx: surely, the default assumption ought precisely to be that his positions *are* dialectical. To presume that Marx understands the range of possible approaches to be exhausted by these two alternatives, misses the point that they both belong to a tradition that Marx makes clear it is his intention to upend.

Nonetheless, Shiell concludes with the following apt description of Marx's position:

> Marx's insistence on radical change in political economy forms the basis of his critique of methodological individualism. Because it provides only the simple determinations, the thin abstractions, methodological individualism cannot provide the sense of radical change which emerges from the full conception of the whole. Indeed, it systematically obfuscates the need

for such change. It is only when the abstracted parts are reconstructed back into the whole and the relations between them understood that the need and likelihood for radical change emerges.[41]

The debate over whether Marx's explanatory methodology is best described as "holist" or "individualist" dovetails with some of the concerns addressed in the preceding chapter, namely, whether one loses out on the ability to theoretically accommodate individual agency and freedom when offering social explanations in terms of inevitable clashes among classes.

Here, as with our earlier discussion of freedom and determinism, identifying a "dialectical compatibilism" in Marx allows us to make sense of what might initially appear to be irreconcilably opposite approaches. The insistence on treating individuals and their individual behaviors as the terrain on which social explanation bottoms out invariably leads to an incapacity to theorize the dynamics that give rise to those individual behaviors.[42] They are rendered conceptually invisible.

Methodological individualism might make better sense of social reality if human beings were themselves far more fully free and realized as individuals than they are under capitalism. But in a stratified, class-based society, the separate actions of individual human beings combine and produce social forces that in turn react back upon the members of society, directing their behavior differentially according to their economic class in ways that methodological individualism necessarily obscures.

The debate about methodologically individualist renderings of Marxism (as in "Rational Choice" or "Analytical" Marxism) brings us around full circle to Marx's insistence on doing away with "abstract" individualism and centering instead the real, concrete, individual human beings. This is so because it is in a sense quite odd—and sadly indicative of the shallowness that characterizes much of analytical philosophy's engagement with Marx's ideas—to *oppose* a methodologically "individualist" method to Marx's own "materialist" method, of which he wrote,

> The first premise of all human history is, of course, the existence of living human individuals. Thus the first fact to be established is the physical organisation of these individuals and their consequent relation to the rest of nature. Of course, we cannot here go either into the actual physical nature of man, or into the natural conditions in which man finds himself—geological, hydrographical, climatic and so on. The writing of history must

always set out from these natural bases and their modification in the course of history through the action of men.[43]

It is only in certain philosophers' imaginations that human individuals can be understood separately from the material conditions with which they interact and that produce them as particular persons in particular times. To assume a more methodologically "holist" approach is not to ignore the central role of human individuals in producing their social reality, but rather to allow that among the things human beings produce are social processes and categories that in turn affect human lives in ways that are rendered invisible by a reductive individualism.

One of the tasks of communism is for human beings to place themselves in more rational and conscious control of the social dynamics they create, a process that would in turn allow greater direct and indirect control over who we are and what we do, both as a species and as particular individuals. But this hasn't happened yet, and rendering it prematurely in pure thought, as methodological individualism does, impedes us in producing such a circumstance in reality.[44]

7
"Bourgeois" Freedom and Equal Right

> The civilization and justice of bourgeois order comes out in its lurid light whenever
> the slaves and drudges of that order rise against their masters.
> Then this civilization and justice stand forth as undisguised savagery and lawless revenge.[1]

Normative condemnations of bourgeois society and of bourgeois morality appear frequently throughout Marx's writings, not merely as casual asides, but as expressions of a coherent moral philosophy. In Marx's writings, the free and full development of the "rich individuality" of the human person figures as a standard against which to judge all social institutions and social relations. This is true not only of earlier writings such as *The Holy Family* and *The Economic and Philosophic Manuscripts*, but also of Marx's later work.

In writings such as the *Grundrisse*, *Capital*, and *The Critique of the Gotha Programme*, Marx also offers critical analyses of the concepts of "right," "freedom," and "equality" as they operate within classical liberal political theory. In unpacking Marx's critiques of these concepts, it is helpful to keep a key principle of Marxist ideology critique in view: "Consciousness can never be anything else than conscious existence, and the existence of men is their actual life-process." The meaning of "right," "freedom," "equality," and similar concepts in liberal theory therefore cannot be explicated by merely taking the pronouncements of liberal political theory at face value. They must rather be considered in light of the social, political, and historical context within which they emerge, and the (often hypocritical) theoretical and practical purposes to which they are put. In the preceding chapter, I presented Marx's distinction between "abstract" or bourgeois individuality and "concrete" or "rich" individuality that requires the conditions of communism to emerge. A similar distinction may be drawn between "abstract" or liberal bourgeois concepts of "right," "freedom," and "equality" on the one hand, and socialist versions of these concepts on the other.

It is useful to remind ourselves of what is conveyed by the adjective, "bourgeois." It is not some mere empty epithet or jibe. To say of a concept or of a theory that it is "bourgeois" is specifically to say that it emerges from, reflects, and reinforces the conditions that the capitalist class requires to maintain its position as the ruling class in society. The term is therefore not inherently pejorative, but simply descriptive. However, in recognizing the specifically bourgeois class character of certain concepts, we can discover that the value of realizing them is not to be taken for granted as obviously universally beneficial. (The freedom that capitalists require for profitable exchange, for example, also appears as the enslavement and domination of masses of people globally.)

Marx argues that bourgeois freedom, equality, and property only retain their validity within a specific form of activity under capitalism—commodity exchange, such as that which occurs with the sale and purchase of labor power. Abstracting away from the rest of social existence under capitalism, it is possible to believe that the worker is truly free insofar as she is able to make her will effective through contract; truly equal, because she receives in exchange for her labor power a wage of ostensibly equivalent value; and truly protected in her right to property, because she is able to dispose of her own labor power as she wills.

In the first volume of *Capital*, Marx writes:

> [The sphere] within whose boundaries the sale and purchase of labour-power goes on, is in fact a very Eden of the innate rights of man. There alone rule Freedom, Equality, Property and Bentham. Freedom, because both buyer and seller of a commodity, say of labour-power, are constrained only by their own free will. They contract as free agents, and the agreement they come to, is but the form in which they give legal expression to their common will. Equality, because each enters into relation with the other, as with a simple owner of commodities, and they exchange equivalent for equivalent. Property, because each disposes only of what is his own. And Bentham, because each looks only to himself. The only force that brings them together and puts them in relation with each other, is the selfishness, the gain and the private interests of each. Each looks to himself only, and no one troubles himself about the rest, and just because they do so, do they all, in accordance with the pre-established harmony of things, or under the auspices of an all-shrewd providence, work together to their mutual advantage, for the common weal and in the interest of all.[2]

But as soon as we leave this realm of abstraction we see, for instance, that the worker is denied access to the means of production. It now becomes possible to notice that he is not truly free to dispose of his labor power as he wills, but compelled to sell it so that he might continue to live. As these illusions of bourgeois morality become ever less tenable, the more concretely we understand the real situation of the worker and the real economic relations of capitalist society. The "Benthamite" notion that out of mere selfishness and private interest, the general commonwealth can be safeguarded, becomes harder to believe, and the hypocrisy and contradictions of capitalist society become clearer to see.

One might on this basis conclude that bourgeois society fails to live up to the promise of its liberal ideals, and that the situation calls for a "pure," unhypocritical realization of liberal "freedom" and the rest. This is a mistake, for their contradictory practical expression only reflects their contradictory theoretical content: they are not inadequately realized under the conditions of mature capitalism, but rather are fully expressed, their content laid bare. For this reason, the critical potential of liberal ideals as standards of evaluation against which to judge actually existing bourgeois liberal society is highly limited. We see Marx make this point in the *Grundrisse*, taking a dim view of the value of immanent critique in this context. Marx writes:

> Exchange value, or more precisely, the money system, is indeed the system of freedom and equality, and what disturbs [Proudhon et al.] in the more recent development of the system are disturbances immanent to the system, i.e. the very realization of *equality and freedom*, which turn out to be inequality and unfreedom.[3]

Bourgeois freedom is the freedom of the atomistic, individual agent to buy or sell a commodity, and bourgeois equality is the formal equality of individuals who expect to receive remuneration equivalent to the value of the commodities they enter into exchange. The worker and the capitalist *already* confront one another as formally free and equal in just this manner.[4] It is precisely this formal universal freedom and equality that forms the basis for the capitalist mode of production, which gives rise to the widespread de facto bondage of workers and the de facto social and economic inequality so characteristic of capitalist society.

Socialism cannot be conceived of as simply a realization of bourgeois ideals such as freedom, equality, and justice, because bourgeois freedom, bourgeois equality, and bourgeois justice are already realized *in bourgeois society*. They "who wish to prove socialism to be the realisation of the ideas of *bourgeois* society enunciated by the French Revolution," Marx writes, are therefore misguided.[5] Socialism cannot be justified purely as the real implementation of liberal principles. It requires rather that these be superseded.

In what follows, we will explore in greater detail first, Marx's remarks on liberal freedom, and then, his critique of liberal equal right. In the course of this discussion, we will address one influential argument for reading Marx as amoral: namely, that he does not seem at all concerned with justifying his prescriptions by appeal to a liberal conception of justice.

It is true, of course, that Marx wrote that the ruling ideas in a society are the ideas of its ruling class. But this in no way impugns the validity of insurrectionary ideas. If consciousness is conscious existence, then the existence of a revolutionary class produces its own attendant consciousness, every bit as valid as the ideas of the ruling class (and then some). It is this real revolutionary consciousness that Marx seeks to express in his theory and which he applies in the case for socialism. It should strike us as no surprise that just as capital and labor come into conflict, so will socialist and liberal ideals. And these conflicts appear even (or especially) with respect to such seemingly "pure" and essential matters as freedom and right. As Marx and Engels remind us in the *Manifesto*: "The Communist revolution is the most radical rupture with traditional property relations; no wonder that its development involves the most radical rupture with traditional ideas."

Freedom

To appreciate Marx's critique of liberal freedom, we must recall the lessons drawn from our earlier discussions of alienation and of the dialectic between freedom and determinism. Marx's analysis of liberal freedom will focus on its failure to capture the value of having and exercising those creative powers which allow one to participate actively in directing the forces that govern one's own conditions of existence. We also see here a specific application of how proletarian or socialist freedom must come into direct conflict with the guarantees of liberal freedom, as well as a more detailed presentation of how, in virtue of individuals' alienation from their creative powers, free capitalist competition gives rise to the practical unfreedom of human beings under capitalism. Our earlier discussion of alienation helps to shed light on Marx's analysis of the contradictory inner content of liberal freedom. Moreover, Marx's critiques of freedom, drawn here mostly from later works such as *The Communist Manifesto*, the *Grundrisse*, and *Capital*, will improve our understanding of how the alienation concept continues to play a key role in Marx's analysis throughout his mature works.

Recall that we have described alienation as a condition in which one is separated from, and opposed by, what is properly one's own. On Marx's account, individual freedom under capitalism has precisely this character. It would not be quite right to say that the picture of capitalism as a system that allows for freedom is totally illusory. It reflects a real freedom and a real historical achievement. Nevertheless, this is not the real human freedom of individuals, but rather the free and unfettered movement of capital.

"In free competition," Marx writes, "it is capital that is set free, not the individuals. As long as production based on capital is the necessary, hence the most appropriate, form for the development of society's productive power, the movement of individuals within the pure conditions of capital appears as their freedom."[6]

What is Marx saying here? A chief accomplishment of bourgeois revolutions across Europe was a political transformation that created the conditions in which commodity exchange could occur, without the limitations that had been placed on it by feudal property relations. Capitalists were now free to dispose of their private property in the manner most fitting to its internal logic of accumulation and expansion. The significance of this is captured well in Eric Hobsbawm's discussion of shifting property relations around land. Hobsbawm writes:

> Neither the political nor the economic revolution could neglect land ... The great frozen ice-cap of the world's traditional agrarian systems and rural social relations lay above the fertile soil of economic growth. It had at all costs to be melted, so that that soil could be ploughed by the forces of profit-pursuing private enterprise. This implied three kinds of changes. In the first place land had to be turned into a commodity, possessed by private owners and freely purchasable and saleable by them. In the second place it had to pass into the ownership of a class of men willing to develop its productive resources for the market and impelled by reason, i.e. enlightened self-interest and profit. In the third place the great mass of the rural population had in some way to be transformed, at least in part, into freely mobile wage-workers for the growing non-agricultural sector of the economy.[7]

This setting-loose of commodities conferred upon human beings the freedom to order their behavior in ways that corresponded to the capitalist mode of production, that they might best advance their private economic interests within it. This is an important freedom as capitalist exchange came to predominate as an economic system. But it is here that we can sense an inner contradiction in this concept of freedom. Freedom here amounts to freedom to act in accordance with economic laws that, though themselves the product of human social activity, seem to operate independently of human beings, dominating them. Marx writes of

> the absurdity of regarding free competition as the ultimate development of human freedom, and the negation of free competition as equivalent to the negation of individual freedom and of social production based upon individual freedom. It is merely the kind of free development possible on the limited basis of the domination of capital. This type of individual freedom is therefore, at the same time, the most sweeping abolition of all individual freedom and the complete subjugation of individuality to social conditions which assume the form of objective powers, indeed of overpowering objects—objects independent of the individuals relating to one another.[8]

The concept of alienation, then, is key to understanding the limitations of this capitalist freedom, which turns out to be human unfreedom in practice. It is the victory of "free competition" that paves the way for the complete subjection of individuals to market forces, which is to say, to their own products. What is necessary now in order to promote the full and expanding freedom of human individuals is not for this concept of bourgeois freedom to be more fully realized than it is. It is already fully realized together with all its inner contradictions. Only its supersession by a higher form of substantive social freedom could resolve them.

In his 1880 preamble to *The Programme of the French Workers' Party*, Marx writes that "the producers cannot be free unless they are in possession of the means of production."[9] Here, of course, Marx has in mind a substantive human freedom wholly incompatible with the capitalist system, which is in large part premised on producers' lack of ownership of the means of production. Capitalism dispossesses workers of those means further as it develops. Yet it would be mistaken to regard the ideal of this real human emancipation as some *mere* ethical abstraction. It is grounded in existing material reality as a form of freedom appropriate to a collective form of ownership of the means of production. This is a form of emancipation, Marx writes, "whose material and intellectual elements are shaped by the very development of capitalist society."[10]

The implementation of such a genuine, substantive freedom would entail what Marx and Engels earlier described, not disapprovingly, as "*despotic inroads* on the rights of property, and on the conditions of bourgeois production."[11] It would sit uneasily alongside Locke's classical liberal conception of men's natural "*perfect freedom* to order their actions, and dispose of their possessions and persons, as they think fit, within the bounds of the law of nature, without asking leave, or depending upon the will of any other man," as well as the principle that the proper role of the state is to protect these individual property rights so far as possible, and to hold them inviolable.[12] Should we then conclude from this that Marx was an amoralist, after all? Or that he thought the end of communism justified any means, whatsoever? No. That conclusion only seems compelling if we assume that the political morality of bourgeois liberalism has an absolute validity and that whatever challenges it must therefore be amoral. It would be more correct to say that socialism can be justified on these terms, no less and no more easily than bourgeois revolution might have been justified by appeal to ideologies that upheld the divine right of kings. Socialism is an economic system based on utterly different conditions of existence. For Marx, it is utterly unsurprising that its ideals should sometimes conflict with the old ones.

In the reformist struggles of workers under capitalism, we see a first inkling of how this genuine, substantive freedom comes into conflict with formal, bourgeois freedom. In the first volume of *Capital*, Marx writes:

> It must be acknowledged that our labourer comes out of the process of production other than he entered. In the market he stood as owner of the commodity "labour-power" face to face with other owners of commodities, dealer against dealer. The contract by which he sold to the capitalist his labour-power proved, so to say, in black and white that he disposed of himself freely. The bargain concluded, it is discovered that he was no "free agent," that the time for which he is free to sell his labour-power is the time for which he is forced to sell it, that in fact the vampire will not lose its hold on him "so long as there is a muscle, a nerve, a drop of blood to be exploited." For "protection" against "the serpent of their agonies," the labourers must put their heads together, and, as a class, compel the passing of a law, an all-powerful social barrier that shall prevent the very workers from selling, by voluntary contract with capital, themselves and their families into slavery and death. In place of the pompous catalogue of the "inalienable rights of

man" comes the modest Magna Charta of a legally limited working day, which shall make clear "when the time which the worker sells is ended, and when his own begins." Quantum mutatus ab illo! [What a great change from that time!—Virgil].[13]

Here, we find that the worker's freedom to enter into a contract and to dispose of his labor power as he wills is only a highly limited kind of freedom. In truth, the worker was never in this transaction a totally "free agent" at all, because he is not simply free to sell his labor power or not, but rather is compelled to sell it if he wishes to live. That compulsion makes the worker susceptible to the most brutal working conditions. The freedom to dispose of one's commodity (in this case, labor power) however one wishes ensures that, each standing alone, working people are ripe victims for "vampiric" capitalist exploitation.

The first step in bringing about substantive freedom from oppressive working conditions and exploitative relations of production is therefore for workers to combine together and push for laws that actually *curtail* the individual freedom of contract granted and guaranteed to them in bourgeois society. These measures on the part of workers are vehemently opposed by the bourgeoisie, not only with such concrete means as police violence and so on, but ideologically, as well:

> The same bourgeois mind which praises division of labour in the workshop, life-long annexation of the labourer to a partial operation, and his complete subjection to capital, as being an organisation of labour that increases its productiveness, that same bourgeois mind denounces with equal vigour every conscious attempt to socially control and regulate the process of production, as an inroad upon such sacred things as the rights of property, freedom and unrestricted play for the bent of the individual capitalist.[14]

As further illustration of this, Marx describes how in the French Revolution, the rights that could aid workers, such as the right of association, were subordinated in practice to the right of bourgeois property. As compared to all other forms of rights, property rights were granted absolute priority:

> During the very first storms of the revolution, the French bourgeoisie dared to take away from the workers the right of association but just acquired.

By a decree of June 14, 1791, they declared all coalition of the workers as "an attempt against liberty and the declaration of the rights of man," punishable by a fine of 500 livres, together with deprivation of the rights of an active citizen for one year. This law which, by means of State compulsion, confined the struggle between capital and labour within limits comfortable for capital, has outlived revolutions and changes of dynasties. Even the Reign of Terror left it untouched. It was but quite recently struck out of the Penal Code. Nothing is more characteristic than the pretext for this bourgeois coup d'état. "Granting," says Chapelier, the reporter of the Select Committee on this law, "that wages ought to be a little higher than they are, ... that they ought to be high enough for him that receives them, to be free from that state of absolute dependence due to the want of the necessaries of life, and which is almost that of slavery," yet the workers must not be allowed to come to any understanding about their own interests, nor to act in common and thereby lessen their "absolute dependence, which is almost that of slavery"; because, forsooth, in doing this they injure "the freedom of their cidevant masters, the present entrepreneurs," and because a coalition against the despotism of the quondam masters of the corporations is—guess what!—is a restoration of the corporations abolished by the French constitution.[15]

Bourgeois opposition to workers' attempts to exert social control on production further reveals the practical contradiction between formal bourgeois freedom and the real freedom that workers struggle for within capitalism, in political battles that necessarily point beyond capitalism. While the capitalist defends "sacred" bourgeois freedom, he is at the same time also perfectly willing to defend the real unfreedom of the worker, the "complete subjection" of the laborer to capital. These last several passages highlight, too, the intimate interconnections between "freedom" and "right." These are two concepts that I isolate from one another here abstractly but only for purposes of presentation and clarity. Let us turn now to Marx's critiques of liberalism, seen through the lens of his analysis of rights under capitalism.

Justice and Equal Right

Whether it has been termed a regrettable oversight or something of a scandal, it has been noted that Marx does not seem to justify communism by appealing to rights. Indeed, this supposed indifference to rights is sometimes cited as evidence of the amoralism of Marxist theory.[16] But throughout his early work, Marx presents a critique of rights in the modern state that demonstrates the inadequacy of bourgeois rights theory to address the needs of human beings. His critique of a liberal rights schema is informed by his ethical commitment to the satisfaction of human needs and the development and fulfillment of individual persons as the highest aim for human beings.

The cornerstone of Marx's critique is that bourgeois rights theory relies on an account of individuals as atomized competitors with rival interests, that serves as a holdover from the system of entitlements in feudal society. Rights function in the modern state to protect the privilege of the bourgeoisie. This role, Marx argues, is not an accidental one, but rather part and parcel of rights as such. Therefore, rights are an artifact of class society and the conditions of scarcity, competition, and domination that typify relations among human beings under capitalism. They would have no application in a society in which "the free development of each is the condition for the development of all," nor can they fully justify the transition to such a society.[17] So much the worse, Marx thinks, for rights.

Marx's first major work after his doctoral dissertation is a critique of Hegel's *Philosophy of Right*. In the *Philosophy of Right*, Hegel held that "what is rational is actual"—a pronouncement Marx interpreted to imply that the existing Prussian state represented the most rational form of society, and the resolution of all of the contradictions that had propelled the development of history up until its formation. This reading would imply that no further revolutionary political transformation was either desirable or possible. Marx argues that Hegel fell short of providing an objective account of the nature of right and morality, as such. Instead, Hegel had merely described the structure of the Prussian state and asserted it to be the highest level of social organization possible. In doing so, Marx argued, Hegel downplayed and overlooked the contradictions that still existed within the state. Marx writes:

> Hegel is not to be blamed for depicting the nature of the modern state as it is, but rather for presenting what is as the *essence of the state*. The claim that the rational is actual is contradicted precisely by an irrational actuality, which everywhere is the contrary of what it asserts and asserts the contrary of what it is.[18]

Marx nonetheless regards Hegel's work as extremely fruitful, if not for reasons that Hegel himself had in mind, observing somewhat wryly that "it was a great though unconscious service of Hegel to have assigned modern morality its true position" as intrinsically tied to, and flowing from, the ideological requirements of the modern capitalist state.[19] Marx's corrective is not to sweep Hegel's work aside altogether but to attempt a deeper and more perspicuous assessment of actually existing political reality.

Hegel's *Philosophy of Right* did succeed in demonstrating the manner in which the activity of the modern state is given a moral cover and justification. The government of the Prussian state declared itself to be concerned with public affairs and yet the bureaucracy safeguarded its own interests at the expense of the public. "The Estates," Marx objects, "are the sanctioned, legal lie of constitutional states, the lie that the state is the people's interest or the people the interest of the state."[20] This contradiction between the appearance of the modern state and its actual character belies its claim to rationality, suggesting that in order to make a scientific appraisal of the state, it will not be sufficient to evaluate only its ostensive, stated goals. It will be necessary to examine the real activity of the state, and its actual impact and consequences for the human beings who live and are affected by it.

The core of Marx's analysis of rights is his analysis of the relationship between right and privilege. For Marx, rights are a political expression of economic relations. The form that the state takes is determined by the dominant economic form of a society, and by the safeguards needed to protect the privileges of the class upon whom the state is based. Because of this, there is a tendency to transform into morally significant *rights* what already exist as privileges held by the ruling class. In addition to his critique of the Prussian state, it is largely in reference to the National Assembly of France's 1789 Declaration of the Universal Rights of Man that Marx develops his critique of rights, pointing out that the rights of man are historically arisen and contingent, not, as the Declaration asserts, "natural, inalienable, and sacred."[21]

Hans-Peter Jaeck observes further, in his work *Die französische bürgerliche Revolution von 1789 im Frühwerk von Karl Marx (1843–1846)* (The French Bourgeois Revolution of 1789 in the Early Writings of Karl Marx):

> Marx saw, as he had expressed in *The Holy Family*, in the constitutional representative democracy that had been created through the revolution of 1830, the present end-product of the "political expression" of the

bourgeoisie of their own class interests, the official expression of their exclusive power, the political recognition of their particular interests.[22]

The right to private property stands out for Marx as the prime example, the "specific mode of existence of privilege, of rights as exceptions."[23] This is so because the right to property is itself, *jus utendi et abutendi*, the entitlement to exclusive control over material resources, irrespective of (or at least with minimal possible concern for) the interests of other persons. Similarly, the right to liberty, which is guaranteed by the modern state, is "based not on the association of man with man but rather on the separation of man from man. It is the *right* of this separation, the right of the *restricted* individual, withdrawn into himself. The practical application of man's right to liberty is man's right to *private property*."[24] Marx continues:

> What constitutes man's right to private property?
> Article 16. (Constitution of 1793): "The right of property is that which every citizen has of enjoying and of disposing at his discretion of his goods and income, of the fruits of his labor and industry."
> The right of man to private property is, therefore, the right to enjoy one's property and to dispose of it at one's discretion (*à son gré*), without regard to other men, independently of society, the right of self-interest. This individual liberty and its application form the basis of civil society. It makes every man see in other men not the *realization* of his own freedom, but the *barrier* to it.[25]

Depicting the rights of man as *natural* rights, as the modern state does, obscures their basis in historically arisen social antagonisms and egoistic competition. Just as the ancient state had slavery as its economic basis, Marx notes in *The Holy Family* that the modern state is based on capitalism and the man of civil society, that is, "the independent man linked with other men only by the ties of private interest and unconscious natural necessity, the slave of labour for gain and of his own as well as other men's selfish need."[26]

Think here for instance of Rousseau's characterization of the natural liberty with which each man is born. Rousseau acknowledges that there is a natural tie between a child and its parent for the purpose of childrearing. Yet, he insists, "as soon as this need ceases, the natural bond is dissolved," that individuals may revert as soon as possible to their default state of natural independence. He goes on, "This common liberty is a consequence of man's nature. His first law is to attend to his own survival, his first concerns are those he owes to himself; and as soon as he reaches the age of rationality, being sole judge of how to survive, he becomes his own master."[27]

Locke earlier posits a similar form of natural independence:

> To understand political power right, and derive it from its original, we must consider, what state all men are naturally in, and that is, *a state of perfect freedom* to order their actions. And further to dispose of their possessions and persons, as they think fit, within the bounds of the law of nature, without asking leave, or depending upon the will of any other man.[28]

While it is necessary to demand that the rights recognized by the modern state and nominally guaranteed to all its citizens are respected and fulfilled, this demand is limited in that these rights are themselves formulated to protect privileges that by and large simply do not exist for the vast majority of persons. (One might consider, for instance, the gap between the formal freedom of speech guaranteed by the United States' constitutional democracy, and the actual, relatively meager, resources available to most individuals to disseminate their viewpoints in an effective way.) Therefore, when it comes to improving the situation of workers, and advancing not just political emancipation, but *human* emancipation (i.e., not merely negative freedom from interference, but also positive freedom to access society's resources and develop one's capabilities and talents), merely securing the rights guaranteed by the modern state remains inadequate. In her 2018 book *Marx and Hegel on the Dialectic of the Individual and the Social*, Sevci Doğan captures this contradiction when she writes,

> In civil society, man as an individual being is the foundation of this society and the presupposition of political life, which is a dilemma. It is a dilemma because on the one hand the individual is a presupposition and foundation of this new society and political state; on the other hand, the individuals exist without their self-activity or without acting both in civil society and in the political state.[29]

As Marx writes in his essay "On the Jewish Question," contrasting what he calls merely political emancipation from human emancipation, "The limits of political emancipation are evident at once from the fact that the state can free itself from a restriction without man being really free from this restriction, that the state can be a free state without man being a free man." Here, Marx refers to the fact that the state may not be a religious state, and yet the citizens of the state may remain in the grips of religion. Further:

> One should be under no illusion about the limits of political emancipation. The division of the human being into a *public man* and a *private man*, the *displacement* of religion from the state into civil society, this is not a stage of political emancipation but its completion; this emancipation, therefore, neither abolished the *real* religiousness of man, nor strives to do so.

In a condition of human, rather than merely political, emancipation, the strict division between the public and the private sphere disappears. The human being is able to act as a species-being—his activity is not the activity of an isolated atom, but rather the activity of an individual cooperating with other individuals, who has an understanding of himself as a member of the species, and who regards other persons as the source of his freedom, not as limiting barriers against it. The rights of man do not

> go beyond egoistic man, beyond man as a member of civil society—that is, an individual withdrawn into himself, into the confines of his private interests and private caprice, and separated from the community. In the rights of man, he is far from being conceived as a species-being; on the contrary, species-like itself, society, appears as a framework external to the individuals, as a restriction of their original independence.[30]

However, Marx's analysis of rights is not wholly negative and does not end with his observation that rights have their historical origin in the need to provide moral justification for existing privileges. Indeed, it is the proletariat's lack of privilege that prefigures a new society, one from which privilege is totally absent. Workers have no private property that allows them to compel or direct the labor of other human beings and therefore, Marx argues, no claims that conflict with the ability of other human beings to enjoy access to material resources, if those resources are allocated and employed in a social and rational way.[31] The proletariat satisfies the requirement that "only in the name of the universal rights of society can a particular class lay claim to universal dominance," and is "a sphere of society ... claiming no particular right because no particular wrong but unqualified wrong is perpetrated on it."[32]

So none of this is to say that Marx does not see a place for the discussion of rights and democratic demands in the pursuit of revolutionary ends. In fact, Marx argues that the appeal to rights plays a progressive role in preparing the proletariat to act as a united power.[33] In *The Critique of the German Ideology*, Marx even goes so far as to complain that Max Stirner, author of *The Ego and Its Own*, wrongly denigrates the role that discussion of rights can play in motivating and convincing workers to seize power, presenting proletarians as a "'closed society,' which has only to take the decision of 'seizing' in order the next day to put a summary end to the entire hitherto existing world order," when "in reality, the proletarians arrive at this unity only through a long process of development in which the appeal to their right also plays a part."[34]

Communism is the generalization of the situation of the proletariat, and so the "dissolution of society existing as a particular class is the proletariat."[35] While Marx argues that the proletariat has no "particular right," he does not mean that it has no rights at all, but rather that the rights of proletarians and of people in a transitional socialist society are quite distinct in content from the rights of man recognized in bourgeois society. They are rights that correspond not to the isolated citizen, guarding his private sphere in a world of competition, but instead, rights that correspond to a person who has no claim to private property and who survives and develops through cooperation with fellow persons with whom she shares a mutual dependence.

So it is an oversimplification to state, as for instance George Brenkert does, that "rights are not part of Marx's ethics."[36] We should also take issue with R. G. Peffer, who writes that one of Marx's criticisms "of justice and rights is based on his misconception that *all* moral theories are ideological in the sense that they *invariably* and *necessarily* support the social status quo."[37] Quite the contrary. Marx states:

> When the proletariat demands the negation of private property it merely elevates into a principle of society what society has advanced as the principle of the proletariat, and what the proletariat already involuntarily embodies as the negative result of society. The proletariat thus has the same right relative to the new world which is coming into being as has the German king relative to the existing world, when he calls the people his people and a horse his horse.[38]

Nonetheless, Allen Wood's influential study of Marx's moral views also argues that "Marx never claims that [goods such as physical health, comfort, etc.] ought to be provided to people because they have a right to them."[39] It is true that Marx is not in the habit of making moral appeals to capitalists, that they recognize the human rights of workers and "provide" goods to people. However, he does think that it is the proletariat's very lack of private property that entitles them to a society without private property as a defining aspect of social existence. Just as the bourgeois character of existing capitalist society consists in the bourgeoisie's capacity to implement and enforce these conditions that correspond to and serve its own economic interests, so the proletariat seeks to produce a society in which its own circumstances prevail. One key distinction lies in that the proletariat's conditions need not (and would not) appear as privilege: it is possible to make them perfectly general. In *Capital*, Marx lays out more specifically the inherent limits of rights talk as an aid to revolutionary and emancipatory politics, and why any gains made by the worker must be the result of struggle:

> The nature of the exchange of commodities itself imposes no limit to the working day, no limit to surplus labour. The capitalist maintains his rights as a purchaser when he tries to make the working day as long as possible, and to make, whenever possible, two working days out of one. On the other hand, the peculiar nature of the commodity sold implies a limit to its consumption by the purchaser, and the labourer maintains his right as seller when he wishes to reduce the working day to one of definite normal duration. There is here, therefore, an antinomy, right against right, both equally bearing the seal of the law of exchanges. Between equal rights force decides. Hence is it that in the history of capitalist production, the determination of what is a working day, presents itself as the result of a struggle, a struggle between collective capital, i.e., the class of capitalists, and collective labour, i.e., the working-class.

Marx's approach to rights and justice is similar to his approach to freedom and equality, insofar as bourgeois rights and bourgeois justice are also inadequate as theoretical resources to justify the substantive gains made by workers. However, capitalism does develop productive capacities which would make it possible to realize a higher form of justice, but one that can only be effectively realized with a revolution in the relations of production.

Again, we can recall that for Marx, "the producers can be free only when they are in possession of the means of production."

However, Marx's approach to rights has been largely oversimplified and misunderstood. Ziyad Husami raised a similar objection in 1978, lamenting that Wood (and also Robert Tucker) "collapse the Marxian moral theory into the Marxian sociology of morals and ascribe to Marx, by implication, a variant of moral positivism." Wood claims that "Marx positively denies that capitalist exploitation does the workers any injustice." Instead, according to Wood, Marx argues that any appeal to a notion of justice on the part of workers would be fundamentally misguided. Wood reads Marx as ruling out as invalid any moral critique of a society that does not appeal to standards that are in line with the existing economic system and serve to uphold it.

Wood believes that a section from Marx's *Critique of the Gotha Programme* supports his argument that Marx believes there is no right or justice beyond that which supports and belongs to the existing economic system.[40] Just as Marx argues for a higher form of socialist freedom which cannot simply be reduced to or understood as the realization of bourgeois freedom, so Marx argues for a higher and more substantive theory of human rights which would supersede bourgeois rights. This approach would subsume what is best in them and ultimately supplant them.

Wood quotes a single sentence from Marx's argument against the Gotha Programme's call for workers' "equal rights" to the surplus value and goods created by capitalist production: "Right can never be higher than the economic structure of society and its cultural development which this determines."[41] Marx's remarks, specifically directed at a draft political program for the United Worker's Party of Germany, are quoted out of that context in Wood's account, where Wood supposes that Marx's objection to the Gotha Programme is that it refers to rights at all.[42]

Marx's objection to the Gotha Programme's call for equal rights is not that it appeals to the concept of right, but that it calls for the same sort of limited formal equality that is entirely consistent with bourgeois ideology and bourgeois society, and that fails to address the needs of human beings as individuals with individual requirements. The Gotha Programme's calls for an equal distribution were a step forward, but not a step far enough, since merely to provide each person with an equal share of society's products would give rise to an effective inequality. Since each person has different needs unique to his or her condition, merely to give every person an equal share would result in some people having more than they can use, some having just enough, and some having not enough at all.

To avoid this result, "equal right" would have to be applied in such a way as to account for the differences among individuals and their specific needs. It would have to be "unequal" in its content and practical application. Equal right must actually be overcome in a socialist society and replaced with *unequal* right to the products of society.

It is worth reproducing the passage in its entirety:

> Right by its nature can exist only as the application of an equal standard; but unequal individuals (and they would not be different individuals, if they were not unequal) are measurable by an equal standard only insofar as they are made subject to an equal criterion, are taken from a certain side only, for instance, in the present case, are regarded only as workers and nothing more is seen in them, everything else being ignored. Besides, one worker is married, another not; one has more children than another, etc., etc. *Thus, given an equal amount of work done, and hence an equal share in the social consumption fund, one will in fact receive more than another, one will be richer than another, etc. To avoid all these defects, right would have to be unequal rather than equal.*
>
> But these defects are inevitable in the first phase of communist society as it is when it has just emerged after prolonged birth-pangs from capitalist society. Right can never be higher than the economic structure of society and its cultural development which this determines.
>
> In a higher phase of communist society, after the enslaving subordination of the individual to the division of labour, and thereby also the antithesis between mental and physical labour, has vanished; after labour has become not only a means of life but life's prime want; after the productive forces have also increased with the all-round development of the individual, and all the springs of common wealth flow more abundantly—only then can the narrow horizon of bourgeois right be crossed in its entirety and society inscribe on its banners: From each according to his abilities, to each according to his needs![43]

This is the context in which Marx's comment that "Right can never be higher than the economic structure of society and its cultural development which this determines" appears. It is impossible to understand this comment correctly without also considering this passage as a whole. Marx argues that the first phase of communist society would bear certain "defects" with regards to rights as a result of having been born of capitalism. He further refers to the "narrow horizon of bourgeois right" that only a "higher phase of communist society" can cross. Not only this, but Marx also has a conception in mind of what standard can replace that of bourgeois right. That standard is, famously, "From each according to his abilities, to each according to his needs."

This connects up with earlier criticisms of right in *On the Jewish Question* and *A Contribution to a Critique of Hegel's Philosophy of Right*. In those texts, Marx stresses the lineage of bourgeois right in a system of feudal privilege. This preserves the status of the right to private property as the *sine qua non* of bourgeois right as a whole. That right to private property as the *jus utendi et abutendi*, the right to use or misuse an item irrespective of the interests of others, is inherently antisocial. This is the right of an atomized individual who seeks only to have his private sphere of influence protected against incursions from others or from society as a whole. As such it would have no place in the social life of a system based on such principles as solidarity and communal democratic control over all of humanity's socially necessary resources.

In a 1979 reply to Husami's criticisms of his 1972 essay "The Marxian Critique of Justice," Wood does note that what he describes as "Marx's moralistic self-indulgence . . . contrasts strikingly with his abstemious and even contemptuous attitude toward the use of moral norms and values (such as right and justice) in the criticism or defense of basic social arrangements themselves." Wood does not offer an explanation for this contrast there, although he claims again in his 1999 book *Karl Marx*, that Marx "sees moral norms as having no better foundation than their serviceability to transient forms of human social intercourse, and most fundamentally, to the social requirements of a given mode of production."[44]

Marx certainly does believe that it is not possible to realize a given rights schema unless the appropriate material basis exists to support it. But Wood is mistaken in taking this to mean that for Marx it is illegitimate to criticize an existing society by appeal to any rights schema that does not itself uphold and legitimize the society in question. Indeed, the crux of Marx's criticism of capitalist society in his *Critique of the Gotha Programme* seems to be *exactly* this: that bourgeois right is narrow and defective when compared to the standard that would be realized in a communist society.

A further example of Marx's willingness to critique capitalist justice is found in the first volume of *Capital*. Here, Marx describes a scheme to reimburse landowners for the expropriation of their private property:

> Admire this capitalistic justice! The owner of land, of houses, the businessman, when expropriated by "improvements" such as railroads, the building of new streets, &c., not only receives full indemnity. He must, according to law, human and divine, be comforted for his enforced "abstinence" over and above this by a thumping profit. The labourer, with his wife and child and chattels, is thrown out into the street, and—if he crowds in too large numbers towards quarters of the town where the vestries insist on decency, he is prosecuted in the name of sanitation![45]

Wood argues that for Marx, "a higher mode of production is not 'more just' than a lower one; it is only just in its own way." Certainly, Marx might agree that capitalism is "just in its own way." However, not only can Wood's reading not account for the biting sarcasm with which Marx speaks of such "capitalist justice," but it cannot make good sense of Marx's indictment of bourgeois right as *defective* and *narrow* when compared with the "unequal" rights of a transitional socialist society, or with the conception of right whose content would finally be concretely realized in an abundantly productive communist society.

Why do commentators such as Brenkert, Peffer, and Wood make the error of suggesting that Marx denies the possibility of offering coherent ethical critique of capitalist values?[46] They recall that Marx tells us the ruling ideas in a society are always those of the ruling class, and they remember his observation that consciousness is always consciousness of concrete social existence. However, they forget something of vital importance, something one would not expect to have slip one's mind in a discussion of Marxist theory: namely, that the proletariat and its struggle also exist. Roughly three-quarters of a century before Peffer, Wood, and other Analytical Marxists engaged the question of Marx and ethics, precisely this mistake was being made by the German Social Democrat Eduard Bernstein. At the time, German communist and revolutionist Rosa Luxemburg reminded him, too, of the importance of Marx's dialectics. Without these, it is difficult if not impossible to make sense of the validity of proletarian values within a capitalist system. Luxemburg's words from well over a century ago still stand:

What is Marx's "dualism" if not the dualism of the socialist future and the capitalist present? It is the dualism of capitalism and labor, the dualism of the individuals, bourgeoisie and the proletariat. It is the scientific reflection of the dualism existing in bourgeois society, the dualism of the class antagonism writhing inside the social order of capitalism.[47]

The case for reading Marx as a theorist with a consistent ethical critique of capitalism is at once the case for reading him with his dialectical materialism intact. Without it, we are led away from his most key insight: that the better world of tomorrow is not some merely abstract utopian ethical ideal, but instead an already unfolding process that is already really existent in the present state of things.

Rights and/in Communism

Igor Shoikhedbrod, in his 2019 book *Revisiting Marx's Critique of Liberalism*, presents a reading of Marx on rights that would tend to complicate the account I have offered here. Shoikhedbrod argues against the view, held by many of Marx's detractors along with many who take up the Marxist tradition, that Marx conceived of fully developed communism as a form of society in which rights had, lacking the material basis they once had in the schisms of class society, "withered away." Shoikhedbrod presents a detailed account of Marx's evolving views on the nature of right, and his arguments are thought-provoking and lucid. While I think he is absolutely right about such claims as that communists ought to be champions of the rule of law in bourgeois society and ought not to indulge cheap cynicism about the role played by such legal doctrines, I will say a bit here about why I part ways with Shoikhedbrod's insistence that communist society would feature right and law as superstructural elements.

The notion of right that is relevant to our discussion is that found in the liberal political philosophy of John Locke, Jean-Jacques Rousseau, Immanuel Kant, John Rawls, and others in the social contract theory tradition. In this tradition, having rights—or not having them—is the difference between being someone to whom anything may permissibly be done and being someone with morally salient boundaries that others, who might be in a position to interact with you, must respect. Key to Shoikhedbrod's argument is that although historically and conceptually rooted in the conditions of bourgeois society, rights of this kind can outlast capitalist social relations, and that although the specific content may change, various prohibitions and entitlements bearing the *form* of a right can and should persist in communist society. "Rather than forecasting the 'transcendence' of rights in communist society," Shoikhedbrod writes, "Marx's new materialist theory points to the possibility of superseding the narrow horizon of bourgeois right."[48]

Shoikhedbrod continues,

> It is therefore a mistake to conclude that the historical achievements of capitalism, including the granting of formal legal rights, would be annihilated under communism. Abolishing elementary formal rights would mean reverting to pre-capitalist social relations, in which the direct domination of the master, lord, or patriarchal community actively inhibited the free development of individuals. Marx did not wish to return to the ruins of the past; rather, he maintained that some elements of the past would be preserved in a superseded form.[49]

But it is not so readily obvious that the withering away of right would have the effect Shoikhedbrod predicts; after all, it is not true that every previous form of human society in which the formal, individual rights of bourgeois society did not inhere, was one in which direct domination was the order of the day. For example, as I noted in Chapter 2, Marx intended a historical materialist treatment of anthropologist, Lewis Henry Morgan's findings on early societies in the Americas. This work was later taken up by Engels in his work *The Origin of the Family, Private Property, and the State*. Where philosophers in the liberal, social contractarian tradition reasoned from an account of individuals as rational abstractions seeking their own private self-interest within an imagined "state of nature," Marx and Engels emphasized the importance of proceeding from empirical facts about the real life-activity of human beings.

A great deal of Marx's and Engels's excitement regarding Morgan's work was what it revealed about the impermanence of various features of class society that others of their contemporaries tended to take for granted. Engels criticizes the assumption that patriarchy, for example, is a natural default for human beings, writing, "One of the most absurd notions taken over from 18th century enlightenment is that in the beginning of society woman was the slave of man." He goes on to emphasize that among hunter-gatherer and early agricultural societies, "the position of women is not only free, but honorable."[50]

Engels goes on to note that in some of the earliest recorded forms of human society in the Americas, "Within the tribe there is as yet no difference between rights and duties; the question whether participation in public affairs, in blood revenge or atonement, is a right or a duty does not exist for the Indian; it would seem to him just as absurd as the question whether it was a right or a duty to sleep, eat, or hunt."[51]

His arguments are drawn not only from accounts of the lives of Native people in the Americas (especially the Iroquois); Engels expands the empirical basis of his theorizing with observations on early Greek, Roman, and Germanic peoples. On this basis, Engels concludes that with the division of labor and the creation of a productive surplus, earlier, less hierarchical forms of human organization dissolved and the state emerged as a solution to social antagonisms brought about by economic changes. Engels uses the term "gentile" to refer to groups of tribes bound together by kinship ties:

> The gentile constitution had grown out of a society which knew no internal contradictions, and it was only adapted to such a society. It possessed no means of coercion except public opinion. But here was a society which by all its economic conditions of life had been forced to split itself into freemen and slaves, into the exploiting rich and the exploiting poor; a society which not only could never again reconcile these contradictions, but was compelled always to intensify them. Such a society could only exist either in the continuous open fight of these classes against one another or else under the rule of a third power, which, apparently standing above the warring classes, suppressed their open conflict and allowed the class struggle to be fought out at most in the economic field, in so-called legal form. The gentile constitution was finished. It had been shattered by the division of labor and its result, the cleavage of society into classes. It was replaced by the *state*.[52]

While it is true that, as Shoikhedbrod notes, "Marx did not wish to return to the ruins of the past," we ought not to infer from there that all Marx and Engels found in the past were ruins. There are early forms of communal life in which "rights" were not part of the social landscape, and which Marx and Engels see as examples of how greatly human social organization can diverge from what we have come to take for granted. These echoes of the past form part of a progression of chords, as it were, finding its resolution in a new historical form that does not merely repeat the past but that does find inspiration in it, relating to it as a part of the whole. And the example of early human societies gives us good reason to think it simply does not follow, from the absence of formal, legal right, that the inhibition of individuals' free development will ensue.

I have described already in earlier sections how Marx's theory of alienation is closely connected to his critique of bourgeois rights. We see this connection spelled out quite explicitly in the following passage from the first volume of *Capital*:

> At first the rights of property seemed to us to be based on a man's own labour. At least, some such assumption was necessary since only commodity-owners with equal rights confronted each other, and the sole means by which a man could become possessed of the commodities of others, was by alienating his own commodities; and these could be replaced by labour alone. Now, however, property turns out to be the right, on the part of the capitalist, to appropriate the unpaid labour of others or its product, and to be the impossibility, on the part of the labourer, of appropriating his own product. The separation of property from labour has become the necessary consequence of a law that apparently originated in their identity.[53]

Alienation is the predictable outcome of a society in which human labor power itself is a commodity to be bought and sold. It will reliably appear in a society where one is compelled by economic considerations to sell off the essential aspect of one's human being—one's capacity to produce—and make it the property of someone else to whom one stands in hostile relation. Marx quite clearly is critical of liberal values.

Philip Kain captures the issue succinctly in his book *Marx and Ethics*, where he writes,

> For Marx . . . to realize one's essence, one must do so consciously and this requires communal interaction. One must work consciously within and for the community, for the species, the universal. Rights, then, would be rights against others, against the community, and against one's essence, the universal.[54]

A right, we must recall, is a special kind of claim. And like any claim, it is a claim *against* some entity which is obliged—whether ethically, legally, or both—to honor it. In a fully developed communist society, everyone has a "right" to their conditions of flourishing in just the same way that everyone is a member of the same economic class. The political and historical conversion of proletarian class membership into a condition general to all human beings makes it the case that, while we are well at liberty to *call* that a class society, it is *not* a class society in any contentful sense of the term. This is what it means to say that in making its conditions of existence general, the proletariat abolishes itself as a class, abolishing class society with it. Similar is to be said of rights.

To have an individual, formal "right" to that thing which is absolutely required for the flourishing of every other person in society is conceptually and normatively superfluous. In a society in which the flourishing of each conduces to the flourishing of all, what discursive function can rights talk serve? In the communist society envisioned by Marxist theory, to say, "I have a right to those conditions which permit my flourishing" is exactly and directly the same thing as to say, "I have a right to *your* having those conditions which permit *your* flourishing." If my flourishing is also directly yours, which both of us seek to promote (as the "rich individuals" described in Chapter 3), what does it add to formulate my conditions of flourishing as a *right* to be defended (from whom)? I think the answer here is that it adds as much and as little as would be added by the insistence that communism is a class society just as capitalism is, with the only distinction being that it is a "class society" made up of a single class.

This is not, however, to dismiss Shoikhedbrod's well-taken points about the role of appeal to certain kinds of rights and entitlements in a class society. It is, however, to insist that at least as a reading of Marx, these insights ought to be taken as fully compatible with the claim that such right will wither away.

8
Marx's Critiques of Rival Moral Theories

> But capital not only lives upon labour.
> Like a master, at once distinguished and barbarous,
> it drags with it into its grave the corpses of its slaves,
> whole hecatombs of workers, who perish in the crises.[1]

In the previous chapter, we discussed Marx's critiques of specific theoretical concepts that figure largely in the social contractarian philosophies of figures such as John Locke and Jean-Jacques Rousseau. Namely, we surveyed Marx's criticisms of concepts of freedom, justice, and right that masqueraded as universal, but in the end were thoroughly and specifically bourgeois, reflecting the capitalist class's conditions of existence and its class interests. In the present chapter, we expand our lens and turn to Marx's critiques of four prominent ethical systems or perspectives. These are Christian ethics, Kantianism, Utilitarianism, and lastly, Malthusianism. In doing so, we both continue our discussion of Marx's critique of liberalism and find an opportunity to address one of the most important challenges to the notion that it could make sense to speak of a Marxist ethical vision: namely, that Marx is blisteringly hostile to more or less every ethical theory he ever takes into consideration.

Marx's critiques of rival moral theories have been taken as evidence that he regards ethical judgments and ethical theorizing as idle at best, inherently reactionary at worst. Especially if one misinterprets Marx as a strictly fatalistic economic determinist, then it might seem tempting to imagine him hostile to all normative theorizing in the realm of human values whatsoever and to conclude that Marxist theory offers no theoretical basis upon which to reason about what one *ought* to do and how humans ought to live. But Marx's critique of these rival moralities does not stem from any such simplistic mechanistic determinism. It flows from his historical materialist perspective with nuance that I will lay out here just in brief for the moment, for the purpose of introduction. To explore in greater detail his critiques of these theories and that critique's relationship to the method of historical materialism is the work of this chapter's remaining sections.

One aspect of Marx's approach to ethics, which has puzzled his interpreters, is that he accuses Christian and liberal moralities of being reactionary even (sometimes especially!) when they prescribe some of the very same prosocial forms of life that, according to Marx himself, human beings would express in a fully developed communist society. We cannot distinguish Marx's ethical vision from these other perspectives just in terms of what they each might regard as a desirable state of affairs for human beings to strive toward as their end. (We will find this to be especially apparent in Marx's criticisms of John Stuart Mill's utilitarianism.)

One key respect in which these noncommunist views differ—and in Marx's opinion, in which they err—is in commanding that human beings always act *now* as they might in that better world. A Marxist approach to ethics proceeds from the concrete reality of the matter, namely that such a world does not yet exist. It asks what we might do in order to really bring about that world of human beings acting humanely toward one another. Central to Marx's criticism of the rival views is that they each in their own way flee from materialism and into a realm of ahistorical ideal abstraction. In doing so, they frequently, paradoxically, command behavior that makes a really existing better world *less likely* if not outright impossible to achieve. They frequently prohibit precisely those actions and that behavior that would be necessary for the antagonism, alienation, domination, subjection, and suffering of our present world to be overcome. In this way, they function to prevent the very same norms and values they extol from ever actually being universally instantiated. (Here, as is so often the case, Marx's lesson is that we cannot accurately analyze a philosophical idea except by inquiring into how it really functions within the society from which it emerges and within which it holds ideological sway. We can abstractly push concepts around in our minds all day, but the real test is whether some form of thought aids human beings' capacity to intervene consciously and rationally into their existence so as to develop themselves as a species, or not.) For Marx, ethics is subsumed within "the science of history"—it is made a question of how to bring about, as a realized historical fact, that fulfillment toward which the species strives.

Although Marx presents numerous critiques of dominant moral theories throughout his writings, he devotes special attention to Christian ethics, to Kantianism, and to Utilitarianism (and therefore, in this chapter, so do I).

He argues that each depends, in one way or another, upon a mistaken conception of human nature. In the case of Christianity, we have a perspective that encourages human beings to turn away from worldly things and to sacrifice their worldly needs and material interests in service to God. Christianity gives theoretical and spiritual expression to the alienation that human beings experience, but the longing for unalienated life must make do with a promise of fulfillment in the world beyond. While among various forms of Christianity the details vary, they share the conviction that to be alienated, to live a form of life in which one exists out of alignment with what one "truly" is, is an ineluctable feature of worldly human existence. In Christian perspectives, alienation is a spiritual condition that can be overcome only with the destruction of the material body and the persistence of one's eternal soul freed from the anchor of the concrete—only in physical death and everlasting spiritual reunion with God. Moreover, whether one does achieve reunion with God in turn depends upon one's success in spurning the material world throughout one's years of spiritual exile in it. We might be put in mind here of the following lines from the Gospel of John:

> Do not love the world or the things in the world. If anyone loves the world, the love of the Father is not in him. For all that is in the world—the desires of the flesh and the desires of the eyes and pride in possessions—is not from the Father but is from the world. And the world is passing away along with its desires, but whoever does the will of God abides forever.[2]

Christian metaphysics thus recognizes the historicity and dynamism of the world while simultaneously regarding that impermanence as suspect; only the unchanging and eternal can be real and true. These can never be features of material existence, but they can with some immediate plausibility be imputed to the concept of God. Thus, while as previously stated, the particulars will vary among different Christian perspectives, in Christian ethical approaches, concerns with worldly matters will always be subordinated to and ultimately superseded by the demand to conform one's will with the will of God.

More to say about this later, but as we continue to set the stage, let us turn to a brief précis of Marx's critique of Immanuel Kant, which also brings us more squarely back to Marx's critiques of liberal moral and political theory generally. Kantian ethics' defining command is what Kant refers to in his 1785 *Groundwork of the Metaphysics of Morals* as "The Categorical Imperative," which is to "act only according to that maxim whereby you can at the same time will that it should become a universal law."

This imperative is categorical as opposed to merely hypothetical. That is to say, Kant presents it as a norm that follows logically from conceptual analysis of the nature of a will as such and not from any particular antecedent determinate *content* of that will. For Kant, to be in accordance with one's essential nature as a rational, willing subject is to resist the temptation of one's contingent, private concerns and desires and to conform one's will with that which reason commands of all rational, willing subjects.

Kant's ethics represent a specific engagement with longstanding philosophical debates regarding the relationship between the material and the ideal, and between subject and object, especially as these questions about agency and metaphysical substance apply to the interrelation between freedom and necessity. The apparent lawlikeness of the physical world makes it seem a hostile place for human agency, for if physical laws determine the order of the universe, what does this mean for physically embodied creatures such as ourselves who like to think ourselves free?

To set before human beings the task of aligning their will with the universal law is to propose that there is some part of them upon which the determining laws that appear to govern so much of the world do not, or at least need not, impinge. For Kant, then, to allow one's will to be determined by one's contingent material interests is to misuse it, for the essential nature of the will is to be active, agential, and wholly undetermined by that which is external to it. By abstracting away from any of the specific determinations that characterize a particular individual and her interests and render her an individual subject distinct from others, one realizes one's nature as a willing subject and instantiates one's essential freedom by willing in conformity with the universal law.

Here one also resolves, at least at the level of theory, the problem of multiple and conflicting particular interests which arise in a society of individuals each pursuing their own private good. By setting particular interests aside as inessential and inherently misleading with respect to the question of how one ought to act, Kantian morality offers a philosophical resolution to real social antagonisms that otherwise typically seem intractable and inadjudicable. Only that ought to be done which one can rationally and coherently will for absolutely everyone to do.

Almost needless to say, Kant's emphasis on the spontaneity of the undetermined free will is incompatible with the historical materialist insistence that human beings do not form their wills in a purely autonomous way. Human beings, Marxist theory insists, always exist within particular historical conditions that, to greater or lesser extents given the specific circumstances, determine them in ways they cannot directly control. As we saw in Chapter 5, this is not at all to say that human beings are unfree and do not exercise agency. Rather, it is to say that the notion of the wholly undetermined free will is a nonstarter. Human freedom comes not by retreating from worldly concerns and desires, but rather by engaging with the world in a way that allows one to realize one's aims in it, expand one's array of practical capacities, and recognize oneself as a member of a species for whom labor is the essential activity.

For Marx, the resolution to social antagonisms is not to scorn private interest in favor of universally valid moral law, nor to eschew the content of the will in favor of its abstract form. Rather, Marx's method is on the one hand, to analyze the content of the particular wills and interests that stand arrayed against one another in social conflict, and on the other, to reason about which of these is poised, through the pursuit of their really existing material interests, to reconcile the social antagonisms that make strife, domination, and chaos the likeliest outcomes of individual human beings all seeking to satisfy their individual desires within a class society. Put more succinctly: in Kantian ethics, the conflict between individual and society is resolved in thought with an ethical command to individuals that they abandon their private aims. Marxist theory proposes, as a practical task, that the world itself be rearranged by those in whose private interest it would be to create a world where all human beings could realize their aims in ways that do not impede, and rather facilitate, others doing the same.

Utilitarianism is the third ethical theory we will discuss in this chapter; it is also the most distinctively "capitalist" of the three and the one to which we will devote the most sustained attention. Utilitarianism is a species of consequentialism, that family of ethical theories which maintain that we ought to do that which brings about the best consequences. For utilitarian views, that means that we ought to do that which brings about the most utility, a principle which is expressed variously by utilitarianism's many proponents. Some examples of utilitarian formulations among its most famous advocates include that we ought to bring about "the greatest good for the greatest number" (Jeremy Bentham), that we ought to "maximize happiness" (John Stuart Mill), or that we ought to "minimize suffering" (Peter Singer).

Utilitarian theory does not demand—or at least, does not appear to demand—commitment to any particular robust metaphysical doctrine about the nature of human beings aside from what seems obvious at the phenomenal level; namely, that human beings have the capacity to experience pleasure and pain, and tend to prefer the former to the latter. One then proceeds from the fact of these preferences and, in the context of specific ethical questions and problems, reasons about what course of action is most likely to satisfy them. This apparent ecumenicism makes utilitarian ethics enormously popular in applications that require practitioners to reason ethically about situations involving diverse populations with values and worldviews that mutually conflict. Utilitarianism is, for all effects and purposes, the default morality of most liberal policymaking institutions, especially those that are internationalist in scope.

Marx focuses especially on two classical utilitarian theorists in the course of his writings: these are Jeremy Bentham and John Stuart Mill. His approaches to these philosophers are quite different, as we will see. But central to Marx's overall critique of utilitarianism is his view that utilitarianism substitutes one relation—usefulness—for an irreducibly infinite multiplicity of human social relations. Marx argues that for this reason, while utilitarianism claims ecumenicism, it in fact relies upon a distorted and narrow picture of human social being. In this sense, the concept of "utility" mirrors the abstraction of money by flattening, even obliterating, the *qualitative* differences in how things matter to us.

Let us be reminded that Marx writes of money, "Since money, as the existing and active concept of value, confounds and confuses all things, it is the general *confounding and confusing* of all things—the world upside-down—the confounding and confusing of all natural and human qualities."[3] We will keep this in mind when we turn again shortly to his critique of the concept of utility and its particular suitedness to the logic of capitalism.

Lastly, I will discuss Marx's critiques of Malthusianism. These are particularly useful for us because Marx regards Malthusianism as an especially odious version of the subordination of human beings to capital, where the actual concrete existence of human beings in the planet is deemed excessive where it might conflict with, or in any case, fail to further enable, private capitalist accumulation. This is of especial relevance as we countenance the impending threats to humanity posed, for example, by poverty, climate collapse, and pandemic illness.

Marx's critique is not just that these theories err with respect to human nature, but that they specifically err in ways that rationalize tolerance of hierarchy and domination in the present, lending ideological legitimacy to capitalism and disorganizing resistant movements against it. Over the course of this chapter, we will take each of these moral systems in turn and explore how this is the case. Analyzing Marx's criticisms of these approaches will in turn lend us further insight into the ethical content of his theory.

Marx and Christianity

Religion, according to Marx, is an expression of the alienation that is a hallmark of human life in class society. Religion is also a response to that alienation and even, at times, a kind of proto-rebellion against it. In the 1844 introduction to his *Critique of Hegel's Philosophy of Right*, Marx writes, "This state, this society, produce religion, an *inverted world-consciousness*, because they are an *inverted world*."[4] Myths and characters that human beings create appear as forces that exist independently of human beings. The causal relationship between human beings and their gods is inverted in religious belief; divine characters are believed to have created the very human beings who imagined them. In this way, religion is a symptom of a society in which human beings' active labor, and the products of that laboring, confront humans generally as independent entities that determine human existence quite apart from humans' capacity to intervene and direct them.

For these reasons, so long as the objective conditions giving rise to religion remain, it will be insufficient and largely futile simply to attempt (vainly, I might add) to "debunk" religious belief and provide supposed proofs of its logical incoherence or empirical falsity. It is the actual irrationality of human life in class society that gives rise to the irrationalism codified in religion and only a rational reordering of human life can abolish religion's real material basis.

At the same time, Marx recognizes that, as he puts it, "the miserableness of religion is at once the expression of real misery and the protest against real misery. Religion is the sigh of the oppressed creature, the heart of a heartless world, just as it is the spirit of spiritless conditions. It is the opium of the people."[5] Religion plays a significant social role as one of very few consolations available to the oppressed. It defers hopes for a better world to the world beyond; yet that it expresses and affirms the aspiration for an end to human misery and strife is no small virtue.

Marx in his early works was not alone among the Young Hegelians in criticizing religion. Ludwig Feuerbach, Bruno Bauer, Max Stirner, and others each devoted a great deal of philosophical attention to the falsity of religion, to its reactionary role in holding back social, intellectual, and political progress, and to the need for its abolition. What separates Marx from the other thinkers in his milieu is Marx's argument that the abolition of religion is not primarily a matter of irreligious materialists winning a battle of ideas against belief in the supernatural. Only once the real, oppressive, alienating conditions that give rise to religion and which are expressed in religion have been overthrown, Marx argued, could religion fade away.

Marx's specific criticisms of Christian morality are to be seen in this light. Once it is believed by human beings, religion does itself become a material force with a role to play in determining human social existence. However, religion is not itself to be identified as the ultimate *source* of human troubles. It is the other way 'round: when material conditions frustrate humans' capacity to recognize their form of life as their own historical product and to transform it, then human troubles and the possibility of their resolution come to be expressed in sublimated religious form.

The critique of religion in general and of Christianity in particular is necessary not merely as a tactical maneuver in some ideological battle, but because it helps to demonstrate and reveal what real change is necessary in the material conditions of human beings and in society. As Marx writes in his 1844 *Introduction to the Critique of Hegel's* Philosophy of Right, "The struggle against religion is therefore indirectly a fight against *the world* of which religion is the spiritual aroma."[6] He goes on:

> The weapon of criticism cannot, of course, replace criticism by weapons, material force must be overthrown by material force; but theory also becomes a material force as soon as it has gripped the masses. Theory is capable of gripping the masses as soon as it demonstrates *ad hominem*, and it demonstrates *ad hominem* as soon as it becomes radical. To be radical is to grasp the root of the matter. But for man, the root is man himself.... The criticism of religion ends with the teaching that *man is the highest being for man*—hence, with the *categoric imperative to overthrow all relations* in which man is a debased, enslaved, forsaken, despicable being.[7]

Marx's opposition to the particular morality espoused by Christianity is based in large part on the fact that he sees Christian morality as an ethic of servility and self-denial. As such, he takes it to be at odds with a moral outlook centered on the development and self-fulfillment of human beings. One of his most extended treatments of Christian morality in his early work appears as a little-discussed literary critique of Christian values as they are depicted and expressed in Eugene Sue's popular 1843 novel, *Les Mystères de Paris*. It is to this discussion that we will now turn.

In the final chapters of *The Holy Family*, Marx critiques the moral lessons drawn by the Young Hegelian "Szeliga" from Sue's novel. ("Szeliga" is a pseudonym of Franz Zychlin von Zychlinski, a follower of Bruno Bauer.) *Les Mystères de Paris* tells the story of Rudolphe, an aristocrat who disguises himself as a worker and goes on to "rescue" two working-class people from their fates. One of these is "Fleur de Marie," a sex worker who thinks of her situation as "inhuman," but who herself exudes strength and "preserves a human nobleness of soul."[8] Marie judges her own moral standing by the extent to which she has helped or harmed other human beings, and judges her situation as good or bad according to the extent to which it helps or hinders her in expressing her nature. Marx observes, "She measures her situation in life by her *own individuality*, her *essential nature*, not by the *ideal* of *what is good*."[9]

Our hero, Rudolphe, rescues Marie from life in the city and removes her to the countryside, placing her under the care of a Madame George.[10] Marie is taught Christian morality, and learns that in order to become worthy of her "rescue" she must give herself over to God:

> From this moment Marie is *enslaved by the consciousness of sin*. In her former most unhappy situation in life she was able to develop a lovable, human individuality; in her outward debasement she was conscious that *her human* essence was *her true essence*.[11]

She must sacrifice and deny herself, renouncing the joys and satisfactions of earthly life so that she might be worthy of heavenly life. She enters a convent and learns not to see other human beings as the ground of her fulfillment and satisfaction, but rather to seek validation and approval in a supernatural, alien God. She retreats from the world into the life of the convent where she eventually dies, fittingly (or in any case, melodramatically) enough, uttering a prayer with her final breath.

In his 1999 treatment of Marx on *Les Mystères de Paris*, Ricardo Brown writes,

> Marx puts forward the materialist view that it is through sensuous activity—in love and in labor—that humans experience the world. It is within sensuous activity that we experience the production of desire, the utilization of human impulses, and the historical materiality of human relations. This sensuous activity has, since the end of feudalism, been increasingly expressed in the production of the general ideological practices of capital, commodity fetishism and the concealment of bourgeois morality through the production of the "mystery of speculative love."[12]

I disagree with Brown's conclusion that Marx's ethical dimensions are grounded principally in finding "the ethical in the materiality of pleasure." However, Brown's *centering* of pleasure and desire in his careful reconstruction of a Marxist ethics is a salutary intervention into the conversation about Marxist ethics, most especially because it brings sharply into focus Marx's sharp hostility toward asceticism, self-abnegation, and *sacrifice* as ethical ideals.[13]

Marx's excursion into literary criticism is no mere digression. Where Szeliga presents this tale as an excellent bit of moral didactic, Marx means to show that the Christian morality which is supposed to redeem its adherents "saves" only by destroying the individual person who must renounce her earthly existence in exchange for heavenly life. We can recall Marx's discussion of the concrete individual in his doctoral dissertation. It is only in relation to the other concrete objects that exist in the material world that an individual can find development, expression, and existence. Marie's "Christian consolation," then, "is precisely the annihilation of her real life and essence—her death."[14] Her withdrawal from the world is the annihilation of her individuality and being.

Several years later, in an 1847 article for the *Deutsche-Brüsseler-Zeitung*, Marx is only more strident in his arguments for why Christian morality and its basis in a doctrine of original sin and redemption is inadequate as a theory of human liberation.[15] His argument is formulated against the claim made by a Prussian state functionary that there is no need for "all this tedious talk of communism, if only those who have the vocation for it develop the social principles of Christianity, then the Communists will soon fall silent." Marx's reply merits quoting at length:

> The social principles of Christianity have now had eighteen hundred years to be developed, and need no further development by Prussian Consistorial Counsellors. The social principles of Christianity justified the slavery of antiquity, glorifies the serfdom of the Middle Ages and are capable, in case of need, of defending the oppression of the proletariat, even if with somewhat doleful grimaces. The social principles of Christianity preach the necessity of a ruling and an oppressed class, and for the latter all they have to offer is the pious wish that the former may be charitable. The social principles of Christianity place the Consistorial Counsellor's compensation for all infamies in heaven, and thereby justify the continuation of these infamies on earth. The social principles of Christianity declare all the vile acts of the oppressors against the oppressed to be either a just punishment for original sin and other sins, or trials which the Lord, in his infinite wisdom, ordains for the redeemed. The social principles of Christianity preach cowardice, self-contempt, abasement, submissiveness and humbleness, in short, all the qualities of the rabble, and the proletariat, which will not permit itself to be treated as rabble, needs its courage, its self-confidence, its pride and its sense of independence even more than its bread. The social principles of Christianity are sneaking and hypocritical, and the proletariat is revolutionary.
>
> So much for the social principles of Christianity.[16]

Marx's point is that beyond the personal costs borne by the individual who practices a self-denying renunciation of earthly life, there is the role that Christianity has historically played on a broader social scale. Marx charges that it has preached accommodation to the status quo and inculcated in the masses of human beings traits that render them more easily governable by the ruling class, dissuading them from seeking a new social arrangement here on earth.

Marx concludes *The Holy Family*'s famous opium metaphor with the following observation:

> To abolish religion as the illusory happiness of the people is to demand their real happiness. The demand to give up illusions about the existing state of affairs is the demand to give up a state of affairs which needs illusions. The criticism of religion is therefore in embryo the criticism of the vale of tears, the halo of which is religion.[17]

Perhaps surprisingly, given Marx's frequent criticisms of religion, he repeatedly insisted that he was not an atheist, a denial I explicated in a 2019 paper on Marx and atheism. I explained there that Marx's critique of religion goes beyond the rejection of theistic traditions to encompass a rejection of all perspectives that subordinate the good of human beings to some supposedly higher end and obscure humanity's role as its own author. Moreover, Marx proposes no answer to the question "Does God exist?" and is far more concerned with demonstrating that the question itself is incoherent. And so, I argued that Marxism is best thought of not as an atheistic perspective, but as a "radically irreligious" one. I wrote,

> For Marx, atheism on its own does not go far enough. It makes a negative existential claim that there is no God. But to be irreligious, it is necessary to go further than this, to insist that not only is there no God, but there is no value whatsoever more important than that of human existence in its fullness, which encompasses the values of human welfare, human development, human agency, and human creative potential.
>
> Hence when it comes to religion, for Marx the defining question is not whether or not God exists. It is, rather, whether or not one irreligiously affirms the flourishing of human individuals in community with one another as the highest value for human beings, and engages in radical political practice aimed at the furtherance and concrete realization of this principle.[18]

Marx and Kantian Morality

> Kant und Fichte gern zum Aether schweifen
> Suchten dort ein fernes Land,
> Doch ich such nur tüchtig zu begreifen,
> Was ich—auf der Straße fand![19]

Karl Marx's theoretical work draws from, and stands within, several philosophical traditions that themselves intersect and overlap with one another. His emphasis on the life of the species and on humanity's conditions for flourishing and for realizing its essential nature, for example, situate him as an heir of Aristotelian virtue ethics, a point made by Alasdair Macintyre, Paul Blackledge, and John Gregson, among other commentators.[20]

Marx's relentless critique of the German Idealist tradition can obscure the fact, but importantly, he is heavily influenced by that tradition and occupies a special relation to it both within it and without. Just as, depending on how one draws the lines historiographically, Immanuel Kant is either the first German Idealist author or the author in response to whom the German Idealist tradition emerged, so Marx represents the rejection of that tradition—or, perhaps, we should rather say that the German Idealist tradition finds its culmination in his refusal and supersession of it.[21] Marx himself identified Hegel's philosophy as the highest expression of German Idealism and, ipso facto, of bourgeois philosophy as a whole. He famously described his and Engels's own materialist conception of history as the attempt to set Hegelian dialectics on its feet instead of on its head as they'd found it—to preserve the "rational kernel" bound within the "mystical shell" of idealist metaphysics.[22]

All of this makes it not particularly surprising that one perennial fascination among interpreters of Marx has concerned whether, and to what extent, Marx's theory might be compatible with the normative elements of Kant's system. The thought, typically, is something like the following: "If Marx's worldview lacks its own moral theory, why don't Marxists adopt the plausible one Kant came up with?"

But while the scholarship on Marx often addresses the relationship between Marx's and Kant's philosophies, only quite seldom did Marx himself mention Kant by name. What he does have to say about Kant is generally not complimentary, but it is illuminating. Marx's comments on Kantianism allow us to better understand what Marx took to be historical materialism's major points of divergence from Kantian philosophy. They also shed additional light upon Marx's criticisms of philosophical idealism as a whole.

My aim in this section is twofold. Firstly, it is to present Marx's critique of Kant and to discuss how this critique figures into Marx's perspective on the nature of ethics. Secondly, it is to answer the question posed above. Marx took his theory to be incompatible with Kantian morality, and I seek to show that—be it for better or for worse—he was correct in thinking so. Kantian ethics are not available for a Marxist theory to absorb. To make the case for the second point, I will evaluate the contours of early twentieth-century debates among leading figures in German Social Democracy who debated exactly this question. I will also address more recent attempts to synthesize Marxism and Kantian ethics and show how, in spite of themselves, these rather demonstrate the fundamental incompatibility of the two theoretical systems. If, as these advocates of synthesis tend to assume, Marxism is so wedded to a strict, fatalistic determinism that it cannot account for ethics, then the theory would be even worse off than they claim, because it admits of no supplementation from Kantian morality.

In what follows, I begin with an overview of Kantian ethics, followed by a presentation of Marx's critique of Kant. We will then be positioned to understand and evaluate the Marx-Kant debates of the early twentieth century and of today. So let us first present the outlines of Kant's moral philosophy, in brief.

Kantian Ethics

A central consideration for Kant, and for the figures of the German Idealist tradition sparked by his philosophical insights, is the attempt to arrive at a correct understanding of the relationship between material and ideal aspects of Being; namely, an understanding that would account both for the possibility of scientific knowledge about the world and for the possibility of human freedom in that world. One tension between the two desiderata is that scientific knowability can seem to hinge on a lawlikeness of the world that would tend to rule out the possibility of freedom in the world. In resisting, for example, David Hume's challenges to scientific and philosophical attempts to assert causation as an objective feature of external reality (as is the case, for example, in Newtonian physics), Kant embraced and defended the notion of lawlikeness in Being, which then left the problem of how to account for the sort of human freedom that would be compatible with a practice of moral judgment.[23]

Kant's solution to that problem was to suppose an autonomous, "rational free will," upon which notion his moral theory also rests. The free (ideal, abstract, spiritual) will differs from material (concrete, physical) objects that behave in a lawlike manner determined by the impact of external forces acting upon them. It is *like* the rest of Being in that it behaves and is determined in a lawlike way, and *unlike* the rest of Being in that the law by which it is determined is one that it gives to itself. Through its exercise of pure reason, the rational, free will ascertains universal Moral Law and binds itself to it. In this way, Kant sought to dissolve the puzzle for moral judgment that is posed by determinism about the physical world. All of Being behaves deterministically and all of Being is caused. But the objective and subjective aspects of Being are caused in importantly different ways. This solution both brings the will under the same conditions as the rest of Being and sets it apart as that aspect of Being which is determined only by itself, through reason.

We see this doctrine at work in Kant's *Groundwork of the Metaphysics of Morals*, where he writes,

> The will is a kind of causality belonging to living beings in so far as they are rational, and freedom would be this property of such causality that it can be efficient, independently of foreign causes determining it; just as physical necessity is the property that the causality of all irrational beings has of being determined to activity by the influence of foreign causes.[24]

In this way, Kant conceptually reconciles an apparent contradiction between freedom and determinism. He presents a metaphysical picture in which what appeared to be two opposing features of reality turn out, instead, to be two members of a kind: for the will to be free is not for it to be undetermined rather than determined. Rather, for the will to be free is for its content to be determined by the exercise of pure, unalloyed, a priori reason. In this vein, Kant asks,

> What makes a good will good? It isn't what it brings about, its usefulness in achieving some intended end. Rather, good will is good because of how it wills—i.e. it is good in itself.

Unlike the kinds of normative judgments we might make about a good table, a good song, or a good plan, a will is not to be judged by its fitness to be instrumentalized in the pursuit of some other good thing. A good will is not a will that is especially good *for* some purpose that is external to the act of willing. A good will is a will that conforms with the very concept of a will—one might even say, it is a will in which the *appearance* of the will is in alignment with its *essence* as an activity of rational self-determination. This is the case when the will is determined only by reason and it fails to be the case when the will is determined instead by private interest, which tempts agents constantly to instrumentalize the will as a means toward private, egoistic ends.

Kant presents the Moral Law, to which the will ought to conform itself, in the form of a "Categorical Imperative." "Categorical" because it is a command that remains valid for rational, willing subjects irrespective of whatever other antecedent aims and preferences they might or might not have. It is a law for the will that, Kant argues, follows from the very *concept* of a will. "The categorical imperative," Kant writes, "must abstract from every object thoroughly enough so that no object has any influence on the will; so that practical reason (the will), rather than catering to interests that are not its own, shows its commanding authority as supreme law-giving."[25]

Kant offers three separate formulations of this single Categorical Imperative. He first tells us that the Categorical Imperative is a command to "Act only according to that maxim whereby you can, at the same time, will that it should become a universal law."[26] In other words, when reasoning about what one ought to do, the Categorical Imperative prohibits one's engaging in practices that, if generalized, would undermine the social basis of the practice. He presents the example of promising, as a case in point. To ascertain whether it is morally permissible for one to knowingly promise in vain, one must consider whether it is coherent to will that everyone else do the same. But if vain promises became universally rampant, then everyone would also know not to put their faith in promises. The entire practice of making and accepting promises would collapse. By this, one comes to know that to knowingly make a promise in vain is to act in a way that is morally impermissible.

Kant's second formulation of the Categorical Imperative is that it is a command to "act in such a way that you treat humanity, whether in your own person or in the person of any other, always at the same time as an end and never merely as a means to an end."[27] It is important to clarify that this formulation of the Categorical Imperative does not actually bar one from treating a person as a means to an end; but it does bar one from treating any person, including oneself, in a way that instrumentalizes them, treating them with indifference toward their well-being. One must never treat any other person in a way that fails to recognize their humanity and their inherent worthiness of consideration as a being who matters. One may not sacrifice the well-being of another in the pursuit of some other aim. But more stringently, one also may not treat the improved well-being of another as some mere byproduct of another aim, as though it were merely some happy accident that the person affected happens to benefit. Any action that affects another human being must take up that human being's well-being as at least one of its explicit, direct, and intentional aims.

Kant then offers his third formulation of the Categorical Imperative, which is "to act only so that the will could regard itself as giving universal law through its maxim."[28] He arrives at this formulation after a brief discussion of what it is for a rational being to be in the "realm of ends." To exist in the realm of ends is to be a thing that has value and worth in its own right and not in virtue of some further effect that it brings. For one to will in a way that is in alignment with existence in the realm of ends, one must will in a way that sees the very act of willing *itself* as its own end. This entails willing in a way that is not subordinated to the furtherance of one's own private aims, but rather that is a will which could reasonably be had by all rational subjects in general, just in virtue of their being rational.

For Kant, the good will, so constituted as to be in conformity with the Moral Law, is the only thing that can be good without qualification. It then follows from this that the only proper object of moral judgment is the will. Concrete actions, in turn, are moral or immoral only insofar as the will that brings them about is either good or bad. As William James Booth writes in his 1997 essay "The Limits of Autonomy: Karl Marx's Kant Critique," this is a point of clear contrast between the two thinkers: "If Marx's idea of autonomy is best seen in the image of man as tool-user, Kant's core concept of autonomy must surely be expressed in the idea of the 'morality of intention,' of the good will."[29]

The sharpest contrast to be made here is with consequentialist views which maintain that an act is good or bad in accordance with its desirable or undesirable effects. But this, of course, would invoke *a posteriori* reasoning about the world, not to mention make the agent responsible for the outcome of causal pathways that she cannot entirely control. Kant's theory has the virtue of holding the agent responsible just for that which, on his view, she *can* control: her own spontaneous and rational free will.

I have presented Kant's moral theory here in outline. It will be illuminated further by our discussion of Marx's critiques of Kant, so let us turn to those now.

Marx's Rejection of Kantian Ethics

As we have seen, Marx is highly critical of the moral theories that were prominent within his time and philosophical milieu. Kantian ethics is no exception, with Marx mincing no words in his vehement rejection thereof. In *The German Ideology*, Marx diagnoses Kantian ethics as an ideological symptom of the late eighteenth-century German bourgeoisie's incapacity to impose its will upon reality. By this, he meant specifically that it had failed to do what the

French bourgeoisie had accomplished in its country: it had not yet carried out its own bourgeois revolution in Germany. "Kant's good will," Marx wrote, "fully corresponds to the impotence, depression, and wretchedness of the German burghers, whose petty interests were never capable of developing into the common, national interests of a class."[30] The irony Marx points out here is that in the theretofore failure of the German bourgeoisie to coalesce itself politically and act as a class, it had instead Kant's ethical admonitions to at least *think* like a collective subject with a will capable of making the world in its image. What we see here from Marx is, at least in sketch, an ideology critique of Kantian morality.

Again, Booth's "Limits of Autonomy" is helpful here to highlight the issue:

> The governing concept of autonomy that emerges from Kant's line of reasoning is one profoundly indifferent to the constraining impact of the world upon the will's causality. One reason for this we have already suggested: that given the particular, law-governed character of all phenomenal events (nature, human and inanimate), Kant's analysis is forced to search for the possibility of freedom in a domain that is not determined by the laws that rule space and time. What this means is that the world of the empirical agent must be put aside in order to disclose his or her true autonomy.[31]

Although Kant does not claim that his account is of a will free from *causation*, it *is* a will that is ungoverned by the same *type* of objective laws that govern objective reality. This on its own would seem to render it irreconcilable with Marx's materialist conception of history, which asserts the existence of general laws that govern all of human social life and its interaction with the natural world. However, this has not stemmed the tide of interpreters, from Eduard Bernstein in his 1909 work *Evolutionary Socialism*, to Philip J. Kain in his 1988 book *Marx and Ethics*, to more recent authors who have sought to find a home within Marxist theory for Kantian morality.[32] In this subsection, I will explain and assess Marx's critiques of Kantian morality, and discuss why a marriage of their two approaches has seemed appealing to some.

Some points in favor of the possibility of Kant-Marx synthesis are that Kant's conception of the good will is based in deriving what it is to be a *good* will from what Kant takes to be the essential character of a will. In this, it could conceivably be thought of as a kind of naturalist view sharing some key formal features in common with Marx's neo-Aristotelian view that human beings have a nature with conditions of flourishing that originate in and belong to that nature. One could, therefore, think of Kant and Marx as, respectively, idealist and materialist mirror images of one another in this way.

Moreover, Kant's admonition not to treat humanity as a mere means to an end, but instead as an end in itself, is not so very dissimilar—at least not in form or rhetoric—from Marx's claim that "man is the highest being for man."

Still and all, Marx puts forward at least two powerful critiques of Kantian morality. The first is that because of Kantianism's focus on the autonomous "free will" and on that will's conformity with the Moral Law as the central question for morality, and because of Kantianism's indifference to the practical consequences of acting upon that will, Kantian morality fails as a guide for social transformation. In this sense, Marx sees it as a weakness of Kantianism, and conversely, a relative strength of historical materialism, that the former lacks usefulness as a practical guide by which to actually bring about the world that it invites moral agents to represent conceptually in the course of moral reasoning.

"Kant," Marx charges, "was satisfied with 'good will' alone, even if it remained entirely without result, and he transferred the *realisation* of this good will, the harmony between it and the needs and impulses of individuals, to *the world* beyond."[33] Kantian morality, then, is for Marx a prime example of what he refers to elsewhere as "impotence in action," accommodating itself to powerlessness over reality and retreating into the realm of the private, internal, and ideal.[34] Furthermore, even regarding this autonomous "free will," Kant leaves wide open the gap between what "is" and what "ought" to be, arguing that the total conformity of individuals' wills with the Moral Law can only be realized in the "Realm of Ends," a condition that Kant argues cannot be realized in the material world. (We will return to this in the following chapter, which is about Marx's views regarding the "abolition of morality" once this gap is closed in the course of history.)

Marx's second argument against Kantian morality is that its focus on the free will belies the extent to which the will is itself determined by material conditions and material interests. The abstraction of the "free will" is illegitimate according to Marx because it attempts to prise apart the intellectual life of individuals from their economic, social, and historical context. A person with a will that is "wholly independent of foreign causes determining it," to adopt Kant's phrase, simply does not exist in reality, and therefore such a subject makes a rather poor starting point for moral theory. (Later, in 1853, Marx writes, there critiquing Hegel, "Is it not a delusion to substitute for the individual with his real motives, with multifarious social circumstances pressing upon him, the abstraction of "free-will"—one among the many qualities of man for man himself!")

This latter objection is also of a piece with Marx's critique of political liberalism, a critique that contains his second criticism of Kant's emphasis on the "free will." Classical political liberalism justifies and explains the authority of the state by maintaining that it is based upon the free will of the individuals who are governed by it. The French Revolution's *Declaration of the Rights of Man*, for instance, states that "law is the expression of the general will."

While drawing upon the French Revolution for inspiration, Kant, Marx argues, overlooked the fact that French republican ideas had their basis in specific economic and social conditions, and were developed by individuals whose wills were not "free" in the sense of being wholly undetermined by forces external to it, but rather were forged in specific historical circumstances and possessed content that changed in response to ongoing political developments. Marx writes,

> The characteristic form which French liberalism, based on real class interests, assumed in Germany we find again in Kant. Neither he, nor the German middle class, whose whitewashing spokesman he was, noticed that these theoretical ideas of the bourgeoisie had as their basis material interests and a *will* that was conditioned and determined by the material relations of production. Kant, therefore, separated this theoretical expression from the interests which it expressed; he made the materially motivated determinations of the will of the French bourgeois into *pure* self-determinations of *"free will,"* of the will in and for itself, of the human will, and so converted it into purely ideological conceptual determinations and moral postulates.[35]

The state arises from factors that exist quite independently of anyone's will, and has its basis in the economic and social development of a given society at a certain time. As Marx writes, "The material life of individuals, which by no means depends merely on their "will,"... is the real basis of the state."[36]

But as I have already stated above, although the rejection of Kantian morality very much permeates the whole of Marx's theory, he mentioned Kant by name and responded to him directly only rarely. To further explore the relationship between Marxist theory and Kantian morality, we will have to turn to Marx's later interlocutors in an ongoing debate about the possibility of Marxist–Kantian synthesis. On that note, let us turn now to our discussion of Eduard Bernstein's reformist neo-Kantian socialism.

Eduard Bernstein and Social Democracy's Embrace of Kant

Among the earliest and most influential of Marx's interpreters is Eduard Bernstein, a leading figure in the German Social Democratic Party at the turn of the twentieth century. Among his notable impacts on the development of socialism was his theory of "evolutionary socialism," presented throughout his writings of the late 1800s and early 1900s. Bernstein's "evolutionary" socialism was a reformist program that eschewed revolutionary activity, favoring instead gradual reform guided by an ethical commitment to socialism.

Bernstein interpreted Marx as an economic determinist who saw communism as the necessary result of a crisis-ridden capitalist society doomed to collapse. However, Bernstein took the relative prosperity of German society at the end of the 1800s to be proof that capitalism would continue to expand, workers' living standards would continue to rise, and it would therefore be preferable for the working class to limit its political program to gradual reforms of capitalism, rather than to embrace a revolutionary overthrow of the capitalist system. Over time, Bernstein reasoned, such gradual reforms could eventually add up to a communist society. But if communism was not inevitable, as Bernstein understood Marx to have assumed, then Bernstein believed it would have to be shown that it was a good moral choice. Since Bernstein understood Marx's theory to be deterministic, he argued that it did not have the resources for a moral philosophy on its own.[37] That moral philosophy would have to be lifted from somewhere—and Kantian morality might do.

We can already see that there are two important errors in Bernstein's argumentation. The first is that the fact of present economic expansion, taken by itself, by no means invalidates the thesis that capitalism is inherently crisis-ridden; Bernstein would not be alone in coming to realize this in the years following the 1899 publication of his *Evolutionary Socialism*. Secondly, Marx never subscribed to the crude economic determinism that Bernstein attributed to him. Although it is true that Marx thought crises were inevitable, he by no means committed himself theoretically to the view that communism was also inevitable.

In *Evolutionary Socialism*, we see how Bernstein's reading of Marx—a misreading, rather—set the stage for his reformism and embrace of Kantian ethics. Bernstein describes Marx's historical materialism in the following crudely deterministic terms:

> The question of the correctness of the materialist interpretation of history is the question of the determining causes of historic necessity. To be a materialist means first of all to trace back all phenomena to the necessary movements of matter. These movements of matter are accomplished according to the materialist doctrine from beginning to end as a mechanical process, each individual process being the necessary result of preceding mechanical facts. Mechanical facts determine, in the last resort, all occurrences, even those which appear to be caused by ideas. It is, finally, always the movement of matter which determines the form of ideas and the directions of the will; and thus these also (and with them everything that happens in the world of humanity) are inevitable. The materialist is thus a Calvinist without God. If he does not believe in a predestination ordained by a divinity, yet he believes and must believe that starting from any chosen point of time all further events are, through the whole of existing matter and the directions of force in its parts, determined beforehand.
>
> The application of materialism to the interpretation of history means then, first of all, belief in the inevitableness of all historical events and developments.[38]

In Chapter 5, I presented the notion of "dialectical compatibilism" to capture Marx's account of freedom and determinism as a historically developing dialectic, such that the relationship between freedom and determinism cannot be described in an ahistorically and universally valid manner. Freedom is a historically emerging product of human activity, guided by deterministic laws that weaken their hold as human beings' capacity to practically abolish the separation between humanity and nature develops in turn. Bernstein's misrepresentation of Marx's views regressively assimilates Marx's historical materialism to the earlier French materialism that Marx explicitly rejected.

As Pierre Broué recounts in his 1971 history of the German Revolution:

> The first serious attack on the theoretical level against the Marxist foundations of the Erfurt Programme started in 1898, and originated

from within the leading nucleus of the [German Social Democratic] Party, from a friend of Engels, an organiser of the illegal press in the time of the Exceptional Laws. This was the "revisionism" of Eduard Bernstein. He based himself upon his observations of the preceding twenty years, during which capitalism had developed peacefully, and he questioned Marx's perspective that the contradictions of capitalism would sharpen. At the same time, he questioned the philosophical foundations of Marxism, dialectical materialism. Bernstein believed that socialism was no longer the dialectical solution of these contradictions, imposed by the conscious struggle of the working class. He now saw socialism as being the result of the free choice of people, independently of their economic and social conditioning, as a moral option instead of a social necessity. He counterposed to what he regarded as outdated revolutionary phraseology the realistic search for reforms, for which the working class should sink itself into a broad democratic movement with important sections of the bourgeoisie.[39]

Bernstein's critique of Marx, and embrace of Kantianism, sets a template that numerous scholars and activists have followed. The argument contains three key moves: the first is to strip Marx of dialectic and substitute, in its place, a strict, one-sided, mechanistic determinism; the second is to assert that because Marxism is so mechanistic, it is first of all obviously wrong about human social existence and second of all, unable to accommodate moral theory; the third is to deny Marx's purportedly mechanistic determinism in the case of human activity and assert, in its place, Kant's moral conception and theory of freedom.

Bernstein's evolutionary socialism sparked a debate between him and Karl Kautsky, also then a leader in the German Social Democratic Party. Kautsky's 1906 work *Ethics and the Materialist Conception of History* further develops a Marxist critique of Kantian morality, largely in the form of a rebuttal to Bernstein's argument that Marx's theory required Kantian supplementation.

The core of Kautsky's argument for the fundamental incompatibility of Kantian with Marxist philosophy is the following. In a communist society, treating human beings as ends would already be embedded in social practices developed through revolutionary activity bringing about the transition from capitalist to communist society. There would then be no need for human beings to bind themselves to a Moral Law which contradicted their own interests and desires. The timelessness of the Moral Law is premised on the permanence of social contradictions that produce human solidarity as a merely ethical aspiration rather than as a concretely realized feature of lived experience. It presupposes metaethical commitments about the *ground* of morality that cannot be squared with Marxist philosophy's insistence that ethical problems and requirements emerge historically in the course of human practice and may eventually come to disappear within the same.

Kant argues that the Categorical Imperative is a universal and eternal maxim of reason. In this sense, Kautsky argues, Kant cannot account for the possibility of a future society struggled for on the basis of human solidarity. Kautsky writes,

> [The] timeless moral law, that man ought to be an end, and at no time simply a means, has itself only an "end" in a society in which men are used by other men simply as means to their ends. In a communist society, this possibility disappears and with that goes the necessity of the Kantian Programme for the "entire future world history." What becomes then of this? We have then in the future either no Socialism, or no world history to expect.[40]

Following Marx, Kautsky argues that Kantian morality ignores the ways in which historical, economic, and social factors can play a role in determining human consciousness and in particular, the formation of their wills. It substitutes the autonomous free will for the concrete and worldly human being as a moral agent. On the other hand, Marx also argues that Kantian morality is too easily reconciled to powerlessness over reality, making morality out as purely a question of "the good will," which is good without reference to its effects.

Kautsky articulates a third point of difference between Marxist and Kantian morality: because Kant thinks it is a permanent feature of human life that human beings' interests and desires will conflict with the Moral Law, he does not see morality as a historical phenomenon that can pass away in the course of human social development. Kant instead defers the resolution of this contradiction to the "Realm of Ends," which cannot be realized except through God. We will return to this theme in Chapter 9, where we discuss Marx's views regarding the possibility of morality ceasing to apply to human life at all, once relations of solidarity and human flourishing are practically instantiated.

Later Attempts to Reconcile Kantian Ethics and Marxist Theory

Since Bernstein, there have been more attempts to reconcile Kantian ethics with Marxist political philosophy. One notable example is Philip Kain's 1988 *Marx and Ethics*, where we find a more coherent and subtly argued Kant-Marx synthesis than was put forward by Bernstein. Kain draws our attention away from Kant's explicitly moral philosophical writings; with respect to these, he concedes the validity of the sorts of refutations raised by Kautsky. However, when it comes to the presupposition of a free, undetermined individual who is subject to a universally valid Moral Law, Kain argues,

> these are not Kant's assumptions in his writings on politics and philosophy of history. In these texts things are not just left to the individual. Individual choice is not enough to produce morality. The historical development of culture and social institutions is a necessary presupposition for the possibility of morality—for acting in accordance with the categorical imperative. This is where we find the similarity between Marx and Kant. Marx is seeking a historical agent that will make possible the realization of morality and in doing so is influenced by what Kant has to say about this sort of agency.[41]

In Kain's attempted synthesis of Marx and Kant we can hear some echoes of the legacy of Austro-Marxism, for which Max Adler's 1925 volume *Kant und der Marxismus* formed a key element of its theoretical basis. Adler argued for a reformulation of Marxism on the basis of Kant's concept of the free will. In his book *Marxist Conception of the State*, Adler writes,

> Through my critique one can see for the first time that the *Critique of Pure Reason* does indeed have a revolutionary meaning, inasmuch as the work was seminal for social science, and Kant can be seen as a terminal point of the old, and the beginning of a new, philosophy—the completion of the individualistic point of view and the founder of collective thought.[42]

Of course, Marx stands in a philosophical tradition with Kant or, at least, stands in close relation to that tradition and cannot be thoroughly understood except in conversation with it. About this, Kain is clearly right, just as Adler was. However, Kain's assessment of the relationship between Kant and

Marx is confused by his argument (influenced by Althusser's *For Marx*) that there is a sharp rift between Marx's writings before those published as his and Engels's *Critique of the German Ideology* and Marx's writings after it.

Kain argues that Marx's earlier writings represent a synthesis of Aristotle and Kant. This synthesis, Kain writes, gives rise to a distinction between moral obligation *simpliciter* and "burdensome" moral obligation. For Marx before the *Critique of the German Ideology*, humans in communist society would have moral obligations, but they would not experience these obligations as burdensome, because the obligations accord with their natural inclinations. Kain writes,

> Marx does, I think, have a theory of moral obligation, even though he does not put any emphasis on fulfilling burdensome obligations. This, I think, is because morality for Marx, at least in one respect, is not understood as it is for Christian morality or as for Kant, but much more as it was for Aristotle. . . . For Marx, as for Aristotle, the human being is exclusively natural and morality is the perfection of our nature. Virtue—the realization of our nature—is something we naturally seek. If our obligations appear as a burden, this is due to an opposition, or alienation, which has arisen within the natural social realm itself.[43]

But Kain then goes on to argue that "in the *German Ideology*, Marx's views on ethics begin to turn in a different direction." Kain continues, "His historical materialism . . . leaves no room for moral responsibility or moral obligation. Morality becomes ideology and it will disappear in communist society."[44]

This is so because Kain rightly sees Marx's historical materialism as rendering the free will of Kant's philosophy impossible. Kain's interpretation of Marx's later works hinges on a fundamentally Kantian assumption that any coherent account of ethics must presuppose a "free will," one that is not determined by anything external to it. Kain may have shown (I think, *did* show) that Marx's views on ethics cannot be assimilated to a Kantian frame, but this does not suffice to show that there is no ethical content in the historical materialism of Marx's later writings whatsoever. It would seem only still to suggest that what's there is more like Aristotle's virtue ethics than it is like Kant's Categorical Imperative.

More recently, a 2017 special issue of *Kantian Review* brought together scholars including Rainer Forst, Allen Wood, and Lea Ypi to reflect on the philosophical relationships between Marx and Kant. S. M. Love's contribution to this volume, "Kant After Marx," echoes Bernstein when she writes,

> If the revolution is not imminent as Marx predicted it would be, Marxism is left with a further problem: it is powerless to claim that we *should* bring the revolution about. Marx criticizes morality as ideology reinforcing the productive system of society. He attempts to make it clear that the claims of historical materialism are, as [G. A.] Cohen puts it, empirical and substantially value-free. History has shown that a transition to communist society was neither immanent nor inevitable. If we want social change to happen, we have to convince people that they should make it happen. Without the aid of morality, this will be a very difficult task.[45]

The main argumentative supports given for this fatalistic reading of Marx are Cohen's and Wood's strict-deterministic renderings of Marx's historical materialism. This account of Marx via Cohen and Wood follows an explanation of why serious engagement with Marx's theory is unlikely to find much value in the work of Marxist interpreters of Marx. The intellectual environment created by authors working in the Marxist tradition, Love warns, is too "ill-suited for growth." The key piece of evidence for this terminal ill-suitedness is Marxist theorists' purported tendency to "cling" to the view that communism is simply a fated historical inevitability, sure to take hold regardless of what actions human beings might or might not take along the way.

As we have seen in previous chapters of this book, this one-sided determinism does not follow from the materialist conception of history. That a communist outcome must be the self-conscious, purpose-driven, rationally guided result of organized and coordinated human activity, and that it depends, as Marx himself argued, on human beings making history but, alas, "not in circumstances of their own choosing" (so that the circumstances might well develop in such a way as to rule it out and bring common ruin in its stead), is a key tenet of Marx's theory. The premise that Marx presents a fatalistic determinism that cannot account for human agency and normativity is no more or less plausible than when Eduard Bernstein first proceeded from it in 1909. But this doesn't address the central pillar of Love's argument, which is that *without* the premise of communism as a strict deterministic outcome, Marx must appeal to the powers of moral suasion if communism is to appear as a potential outcome at all.

Setting aside the apparent separation between communism as an existing movement abolishing the current state of things, and communism as a result of conscious and agential human activity (a separation that doesn't exist in Marx's dialectically compatibilist account of freedom and determinism), there is the question of audience. The audience for Marx's ideas is made up of the world's working people—famously, it is the workers of the world whom he exhorts to "Unite!" The audience to whom the imperatives of communist thought are directed is made up of those who, as Marx puts it in his reply to Stirner's egoism, do not wish to make sacrifices for society but rather to place bourgeois society on the altar as a sacrifice they make to themselves.

Love writes that Marxism "is powerless to claim that we *should* bring the revolution about."[46] But there is, for Marx, no need to "preach morality" to those who cannot free themselves except by furthering the aim of human emancipation. It is possible then to speak directly of those things that realize the emancipatory aims of the working class and are in its interest. Marx's political project *always* crucially depends upon the subjective, self-conscious aims of human beings; this is not something that was left out of his view, that Kantian morality must now be marshalled to supply. The "abolition of morality," for Marx, comes in the form of the complete coincidence of the interests of the working class with the good of humanity. This is one of the many respects in which, on Marx's view, the condition of the working class under capitalism prefigures the universal condition of humanity in communism, such that wrongs committed against it are not merely particular, but universal wrongs.

Members of the capitalist class apprehend these imperatives as distinctly, ineluctably, and *merely* ethical in a way that allows Kantian ethics to seem common-sensical and eternal: from this perspective, if communism is what is necessary for the good of humanity, it is clear that it must entail some personal sacrifice that Marx seems unable to justify. But this is not a general, universal fact about the relation of the individual to society. It is a specific historical fact about the present-day relationship of capitalists to society.

Love's analysis is thus totally correct as a description of how those whose class interests run counter to the aims of Marxism are disposed to relate to its demands, if they are not part of that group of class traitors who defect from the bourgeoisie and recognize the proletariat as "the class with the future in its hands." The notion of class, however, must be centered in order to make sense of Marx's claim that the communists do not preach morality as such. This means, ironically, that Marxism resists Kantian attempts to "save" it by doubling down on good will. If moral suasion is ruled out as a revolutionary method, then we are left again with Marx's insistence that *only* the working class, whose class interest coincides with the interests of humanity, is suited to lead the struggle for human emancipation. There is no "Plan B"; the failure of the working class to emancipate itself would spell destruction for humanity and the eradication of any hope for communism.

Here we have detailed Marx's most important criticisms of Kantian morality and outlined Kantian ethics' incompatibility with Marxism. Let us now turn to Marx's critique of Utilitarianism.

Marx on Utilitarianism

In the writings later published as *The Critique of the German Ideology*, Marx and Engels dismiss James Mill's utilitarian moral philosophy as the "complete union of the theory of utility with political economy."[47] While they make reference there to the thought of Baron d'Holbach, Helvetius, Jeremy Bentham, and James Mill, the bulk of their criticism is aimed specifically at Jeremy Bentham, with whom Mill worked closely.

In this section, I provide a brief critical reconstruction of Marx's criticisms of utilitarian moral theory. A completely thorough treatment of Marx's analysis of utilitarianism lies beyond the scope of the present work and I do not, for instance, evaluate each of the many forms of utilitarianism that have been developed in response to objections sometimes similar in spirit to those that Marx raises. After studying Marx's criticisms of Bentham, we shall turn to his critique of John Stuart Mill. Marx's views on the younger Mill are most fully developed in his later works such as the *Grundrisse* and *Capital*. Whereas Marx had little use for Bentham, he regarded J. S. Mill as a serious thinker whose careful presentation of liberal responses to social problems shed clarifying light upon the limitations of liberalism, precisely because J. S. Mill developed it with such care.

Marx's criticisms of utilitarianism are twofold. He charges that utilitarianism is incapable of accommodating human individuality in all its concrete aspects, instead representing humans narrowly as sources or beneficiaries of utility. Secondly, Marx argues that utilitarianism functions in practice to justify the capitalist economic system that is itself the source of so much suffering it cannot alleviate.

Marx and Bentham

Karl Marx issued blistering condemnations of Jeremy Bentham's utilitarianism, rejecting it as "insipid" and dogmatic. Allen Wood, in his widely influential discussion of Marx, concludes that Marx's philosophical engagements with Bentham "exhibit even less substantive disagreement with Bentham's ['greatest happiness'] principle than comprehension of it."[48] Marx was not an incompetent theorist, so how can that be?

It isn't. Marx understood Bentham's utilitarianism better than most have, critiquing it cogently and substantively. But since Bentham's utilitarianism has fallen out of favor even among most utilitarians, one might well wonder whether vindicating Marx's critiques of him accomplishes anything more than to simply strike a dead horse a few more blows. Marx's engagement with Bentham is of historical interest, but as we will see, his critiques of Bentham also have important consequences for utilitarianism generally and for liberal moral theory more broadly as a whole. As such, they shed light on central debates in moral and political philosophy today. The dismissal of Marx's critiques of Bentham is part of a larger practice of neglecting or disparaging Marx's engagements with moral theory. Demonstrating the merits of Marx's critiques of Bentham's utilitarianism may encourage more open-minded approaches to understanding Marx's moral thought, a development that in my view would be salutary for contemporary moral philosophy.

According to Wood, "Marx's explicit statements about utilitarianism do not give us much to work with. They express contemptuous rejection of the doctrine, but give little evidence that Marx understands what he is rejecting."[49] Let us examine some of Marx's explicit statements about utilitarianism and consider whether this evaluation of them is fair.

One of Marx's most important critiques of Bentham's utilitarianism is that it is a conservative ideological justification for the status quo.[50] Whereas, Marx writes, utilitarianism had some egalitarian and revolutionary content in the works of Claude Adrien Helvetius and Baron d'Holbach, in Bentham's work it is "a mere apologia for the existing state of affairs, an attempt to prove that under existing conditions the mutual relations of people today are the most advantageous and generally useful."[51]

If Wood is right, then declarations of this sort betray a gross misunderstanding on Marx's behalf. And indeed, Marx's dismissal of Bentham as a "mere apologist" for the status quo will perhaps seem surprising to those familiar with Bentham's advocacy of progressive social causes. What's more,

Bentham's "Greatest Happiness" principle tells us that the most ethically desirable state of affairs is that which yields the greatest happiness for the greatest number of people.

It would be natural, then, to ask what prescriptions Bentham might have for societies with high levels of economic inequality, where the majority of the population scrapes by on very little and a small economic elite luxuriates in great excess. It seems at least arguably the case that in such a society, the maximization of utility would require the appropriation of wealth from the upper reaches of the social ladder, and its redistribution to improve, as much as possible, the lots of as many of society's members as possible. Indeed, it is likely the naturalness of this supposition that has given interpreters of Marx cause to wonder whether revolutionary socialism is not itself just a special version of utilitarianism.[52]

But consider Bentham's *Principles of the Civil Code*, published in 1843, only three years prior to the preparation of the writings that were later published as Marx's and Engels's *Critique of the German Ideology*. Bentham not only fails to draw the socialistic conclusions one might imagine could follow from the Greatest Happiness Principle, but he positions himself as an impassioned defender of the inviolability of private property and, yes, the economic status quo. He issues an impassioned plea against the redistribution of wealth, insisting that socializing private property could only decrease the quantity of happiness in the aggregate. Speaking with respect to the seizure of real estate, Bentham writes,

> The profit spread among the multitude divides itself into impalpable parts; the whole loss is felt by him who supports it alone.... Instead of one place suppressed, suppose a thousand, ten thousand, a hundred thousand: the total disadvantage remains the same. The spoil taken from thousands of individuals must be divided among millions ... The groans of sorrow and the cries of despair would resound on all sides: the shouts of joy, if there were any such, would not be the expression of happiness, but of the antipathy which rejoices in the misery of its victims.[53]

Bentham relies on some curious arithmetic to reach his conclusion that it is never permissible to violate the sanctity of private property. He argues that the subjective experience of property loss is so painful that no matter how great the wealth, its impact for those among whom it is distributed will necessarily be inconsequential compared to the individual's pain of losing it.

One might have thought that whether or not this were the case would depend entirely on the concrete facts of the matter—how much wealth? Distributed among how many? With what level of need?—and not the sort of thing one could simply pronounce a priori. But Bentham insists against this that it is always impossible to maximize happiness through encroachments on private property.

And if you were not keeping track, you might think "shouts of joy" emanating from the majority of human beings were as good a sign as any that happiness had been maximized. Bentham is on guard against such naive misconceptions. As he helpfully informs the reader, the joy of the masses does not count, because it is not real happiness, rather only the "barbarous," grasping *schadenfreude* of the have-nots.

Bentham is not yet satisfied, however, that he has done quite enough to impress upon the masses the importance of leaving class society just as it is. "I cannot yet quit this subject," he admits, "it appears so essential, for the establishment of the principle of security, to trace the error into all its retreats." He continues:

> Who, then, is the greatest egotist—he who desires to preserve what he has? or he who wishes to take, and even to seize by force, that which belongs to another? An injury felt, and a benefit not felt, such is the result of these fine operations in which the interest of individuals is sacrificed to that of the public.[54]

Whatever one might think about Bentham's stance on private property here, it would be hard to deny that Marx's critique of Bentham's utilitarianism as an "apologia for the existing state of affairs" is hardly unfounded. Wood's suggestion that Marx's criticism of Bentham is unintelligible except as a symptom of Marx's failure to understand Bentham is uncharitable, at best. Familiarity with Bentham's own stated views makes it no great secret why Marx would interpret him as he does.

In any case, these quotations from Bentham's work might all just be evidence that Bentham himself was a hypocrite. Perhaps they don't tell against Benthamite utilitarianism itself at all. But I don't think that is the case. I can only sketch here the kind of argument I think Marx might offer as further support for his claim that Bentham's Utilitarianism is "a mere apologia for the existing state of affairs." The sketch is inspired by George Brenkert's observation that the Utilitarian principle assumes a cleavage between the individual's interests and the general interests. It is for this reason one calculates individual utilities to find what is the greatest good. But it is just this cleavage that Marx condemns as characteristic of class society, and particularly bourgeois society. For man as man, as a species being, there is a harmony of personal and social interests because "he treats himself as the actual living species."[55]

Bentham's method in determining whether or not it would be permissible to appropriate a piece of private property is to quantitatively measure the pain caused to the erstwhile property-owner, as well as the pleasure brought thereby to the individual members of the public at large. And indeed, if his version of Utilitarianism is true, then this is precisely what he *should* do. But then, what matters in the end to the moral right- or wrong-ness of a particular state of affairs is something like the question "Just how badly do the people in power want to keep things the way that they are and how upset will they be if things are changed?" If the subjective discomfort of those in power is grave enough, then it turns out, just on this basis, that it is morally wrong to redistribute private wealth. A social question, of how resources necessary for the life and flourishing of the species ought to be allocated, is neatly converted into a conflict between individual and society. And act utilitarian calculations are based on the sum of calculable *individual* pleasure or suffering. Bentham is not merely hypocritically twisting hedonistic act utilitarianism to fit his arguments against the evils of wealth redistribution; he is correctly drawing the theory's natural conclusions.

Utilitarianism was first developed by Helvetius and Baron d'Holbach in something of a democratic spirit. By abstracting away from the particular person and focusing instead on utility, these authors could assert an equality among persons, since utility matters in whatever person you find it. As in the quote that James Mill attributed to Bentham, utilitarianism was the call for "everybody to count for one, nobody for more than one."[56] But that same version of utilitarian theory turns out to be profoundly undemocratic in practice.

If in *The German Ideology*, Marx is highly critical of Jeremy Bentham, then it would be fair to say that by the time it came around to the writing of *Capital*, Marx's opinion of Bentham had not improved. Marx's later criticisms of Bentham go beyond his critique of Benthamite utilitarianism which he put forward in *The German Ideology* and are here twofold: first, Bentham's moral theory is justified by a "dogma" that social wealth is finite, and second, Bentham illegitimately universalizes and essentializes the existence of "the modern shopkeeper" as though it were obviously right to assume that what is useful to this type of person is also useful to other people in different economic positions and at all historical times.[57]

Marx diagnoses as "dogmatism" Bentham's assumption that social productivity will remain at much the same level that it is now, or in any case, that it will not be possible to develop production so that it is possible to attain an abundance of products for human beings. The acceptance of this dogma gives rise then to the question of how to distribute social goods, *assuming scarcity*. Marx minces no words in his appraisal of this approach. He writes:

> Classical economy always loved to conceive social capital as a fixed magnitude of a fixed degree of efficiency. But this prejudice was first established as a dogma by the arch-Philistine, Jeremy Bentham, that insipid, pedantic, leather-tongued oracle of the ordinary bourgeois intelligence of the 19th century. . . . In the light of his dogma the commonest phenomena of the process of production, as, *e.g.*, its sudden expansions and contractions, nay, even accumulation itself, become perfectly inconceivable. The dogma was used by Bentham himself, as well as by Malthus, James Mill, MacCulloch, etc., for an apologetic purpose, and especially in order to represent one part of capital, namely, variable capital, or that part convertible into labour-power, as a fixed magnitude.[58]

This way of representing social wealth, Marx argues, leads to the notion that it is not possible to increase the portion of social wealth that is devoted to workers. Social production is conceived as fixed, when in fact it actually expands and contracts. Of course the relevant question is whether production can ever expand enough as to lead to an abundance of social wealth such that workers' living standards can be improved. But this is exactly the point Marx wants to emphasize: that it is illegitimate to simply assume a negative answer to this question and then to go on to theorize on the basis of that negative answer. To do so, Marx charges, is to lapse into dogmatic repetition of an economic truism that has not been demonstrated. Marx continues:

> The facts that lie at the bottom of this dogma are these: on the one hand, the labourer has no right to interfere in the division of social wealth into means of enjoyment for the non-labourer and means of production. On the other

hand, only in favourable and exceptional cases, has he the power to enlarge the so-called labour fund at the expense of the "revenue" of the wealthy.[59]

In arguing against the appropriation of private property for public use, Bentham seems to assume that it is not possible to increase production so that everyone has access to the resources they need to live rich and satisfying lives. This assumption allows him to cast any act of socializing private property as a misguided injury of the few, to no great benefit for the many. So Bentham writes that, "The profit spread among the multitude divides itself into impalpable parts; the whole loss is felt by him who supports it alone. The result of the operation is in no respect to enrich the party who gains, but to impoverish him who loses."[60] Bentham seems to assume that it is not possible to increase social wealth and that all that can be done is to distribute relatively finite wealth in different ways, in which case, Bentham argues, it can only seem arbitrary or cruel to diminish a few persons' utility and divide that utility up among a mass of people, each of whom will only benefit to a very limited extent as a result of it.[61]

For Marx, on the other hand, the socialization of wealth is not simply evaluated as an end in itself, which would simply be realized on the basis of existing production. Rather, it is conceived as one necessary part of a transition to an economic system in which production could be further advanced and a condition of abundance could be achieved, which would allow for a widespread, significant, and continuing improvement of living standards.

H. L. A. Hart, in his 1973 article "Bentham and the Demystification of the Law," succinctly and accurately describes the disagreement between Bentham and Marx on this question when he writes:

> Bentham was a sober reformer who examined society with the eye of a business efficiency or cost-benefit expert on the grand scale, and condemned the society of his day for its inefficient failure to satisfy, in an economic or optimal way, the desires that characterise human beings as they are. He contemplated no radical change or development in human nature and, though he thought things would be immensely better, if laws were reformed on Benthamite lines, he envisaged no millennium and no utopia. There would always, he thought, be "oppositions of interest" and "painful labour, daily subjection, and a condition nearly allied to indigence will always be the lot of numbers." . . . Marx condemned the existing forms of society not for mere inefficiency, but because its economic system stunted and

distorted human beings and prevented the exploited masses, and indeed also their exploiters, from developing their distinctively human powers. This could be rectified, not by the mere spread of ideas or enlightened education or piecemeal reform, but only by a radical and, if necessary, violent transformation of the economic and social structure of society. But with that transformation complete there would be conditions under which all men could achieve their full development in a form of society where men were humanly related to each other. Such optimism about the aftermath of revolution contrasts with Bentham's sober warning that "it may be possible to diminish the influence of but not to destroy the sad and mischievous passions."[62]

The debate between Marx and Bentham turns in large part not only on their different approaches to economics, but also on their different conceptions of human nature. Bentham regards human nature as relatively fixed, and destined to remain not appreciably different from its appearance in capitalist society. Marx, on the other hand, argues that on the basis of a transformation in production and a revolutionary change in society, human nature could develop and flourish in ways that capitalist relations render impossible.

This leads us to a second criticism of Bentham. Marx agrees with Bentham that a coherent moral theory will be based on a sound conception of human nature. But Marx charges that Bentham pursues this project of theorizing human nature in a limited and myopic way. According to Marx, Bentham not only reduces a wide diversity of distinct human relations and modes of experience to one single relation of utility. He also relativizes utility to one particular narrowly circumscribed form of human existence, that of the petty bourgeois small business owner. Marx writes:

> The principle of utility was no discovery of Bentham. He simply reproduced in his dull way what Helvétius and other Frenchmen had said with esprit in the 18th century. To know what is useful for a dog, one must study dog-nature. This nature itself is not to be deduced from the principle of utility. Applying this to man, he that would criticise all human acts, movements, relations, etc., by the principle of utility, must first deal with human nature in general, and then with human nature as modified in each historical epoch. Bentham makes short work of it. With the driest naiveté he takes the modern shopkeeper, especially the English shopkeeper, as the normal man.

Whatever is useful to this queer normal man, and to his world, is absolutely useful. This yard-measure, then, he applies to past, present, and future.[63]

Bentham, says Marx, mistakes one particular historical appearance for a human essence, wrongly taking the standard of the modern shopkeeper to be valid for all human beings, across all historical times, when in fact, whether or not a thing is useful depends on a whole host of contingent, historical factors which vary in each case.

Allen Wood, in his book *Karl Marx*, is strikingly disdainful toward Marx's critiques of Utilitarianism, but I'm not altogether convinced that Wood has brought those critiques clearly into view. He complains that "Marx's explicit statements about utilitarianism do not give us much to work with. They express contemptuous rejection of the doctrine, but give little evidence that Marx understands what he is rejecting."[64] Wood argues, for instance, that Marx is unfair to Jeremy Bentham when Marx writes that on Bentham's Utilitarianism, "the utility relation has quite a definite meaning, namely, that I derive benefit by doing harm to someone else."[65] But I'm not sure how else we are supposed to construe Bentham's comments when he likens the world of human beings to a receptacle that can hold only a limited amount of happiness:

> Take from your 2000 and give to your 2001 all the happiness you find your 2000 in possession of: insert in the room of the happiness you have taken out, unhappiness in as large a quantity as the receptacle will contain: to the aggregate amount of the happiness possessed by the 4001 taken together will the result be net profit? On the contrary, the whole profit will have given place to loss. How so? Because so it is that such is the nature of the receptacle, the quantity of unhappiness it is capable of containing during any given portion of time is greater than the quantity of happiness.[66]

Bentham really does seem to treat the distribution of utility as a zero-sum or perhaps more accurately, a *negative*-sum game; this in turn serves as his rationale for eventually abandoning the principle of "the greatest happiness to the greatest number" and coming to regard it as hopelessly naïve. Bentham assumes that there is a definite limit to the amount of happiness that can be divided among members of a community and that benefit to one person is harm to another. Bentham's conception of utility distribution is the reason that he argues that it is always morally wrong to appropriate the private property of the minority in order to distribute it among the majority—he argues that this can only amount to diminishing the happiness of the minority to an intolerable degree in order to achieve some almost unnoticeable increase of happiness to each member of the majority, so that the end result of such an operation is always an increase of unhappiness rather than of happiness. Such a view might well be worth rejecting out of hand, but as far as I can tell, it really is Bentham's considered view. If Wood has a reason for reading Bentham differently than this, he doesn't provide the argument for it or seem to address the fact that this is the view Marx has in mind. In any case, I think it is hardly accurate to say, as Wood does, that Marx's comments about Bentham "exhibit even less substantive disagreement with Bentham's principle than comprehension of it."[67] Marx appears to quite accurately describe Bentham's theory—more accurately than many of its expositors. Insofar as Bentham's utilitarianism relies on an assumption of perpetual scarcity and rules out any substantive redistribution of wealth as immoral, Marx's disagreement with Benthamite utilitarianism is, fair to say, at least not any less substantive than is Wood's criticism of Marx on this point.

Marx and J. S. Mill

John Stuart Mill fares much better in Marx's opinion. Marx says of "men like John Stuart Mill" that "it would be very wrong to class them with the herd of vulgar economic apologists" like Bentham. However, there is still a problem. Marx writes:

> J. St. Mill and many other political economists conceive the relations of production as natural, eternal laws, but regard relations of distribution as artificial, of historical origin, and subject to the control, etc., of human society.[68]

Marx criticizes J. S. Mill for taking the capitalist mode of production as the necessary economic basis for all future society, yet arguing for a new system of distribution on that economic basis. But, Marx argues, it is impossible to achieve a radical transformation in the distribution of goods without also revolutionizing the mode of production. In "Theories of Surplus Values," he writes,

> Profit, a form of distribution, is here simultaneously a form of production, a condition of production, a necessary ingrediency of the process of production. How absurd it is, therefore, for John Stuart Mill and others to conceive bourgeois forms of production as absolute, but the bourgeois forms of distribution as historically relative, hence transitory. . . . The form of production is simply the form of distribution seen *sub alia specie*. The *differentia specifica*—and therefore also the specific limitation—which sets bounds to bourgeois distribution, enters into production itself, as a determining factor, which overlaps and dominates production. The fact that bourgeois production is compelled by its own immanent laws, on the one hand, to develop the productive forces as if production did not take place on a narrow restricted social foundation, while, on the other hand, it can develop these forces only within these narrow limits, is the deepest and most hidden cause of crises, of the crying contradictions within which bourgeois production is carried on and which, even at a cursory glance, reveal it as only a transitional, historical form.[69]

Marx's argument is that capitalist production is aimed at and based in the accumulation of profit, which is an aspect of distribution. The capitalist requires a store of accumulated labor in order to make an outlay for the costs of production, and therefore requires that he receive as much of what is produced as possible. Without this, a capitalist venture will be unable to survive amidst competition from other businesses. Capitalists must reap a profit and reinvest it into the production process in order to keep the business running. Production and distribution are therefore, on Marx's view, two aspects of a single process within capitalism, and so it is incoherent to suggest that distribution can be radically transformed upon the economic basis of capitalist production.

Moreover, Marx argues, it is wrong to suppose that the capitalist mode of production is somehow fixed, necessary, or eternal, and not merely "a transitional, historical form," to adopt his phrase. Capitalism constantly revolutionizes the forces of production and yet as Marx notes here and elsewhere, the relations of production restrict human progress and limit the extent to which those productive forces can be fully unleashed. The products of capitalism, as Marx writes, are not merely the commodities that are produced under it, but also these relations of production and the social relations they give rise to: "It is not just this single thing that is produced, the commodity, a commodity greater in value than the capital originally advanced—but also capital and wage labour; or, the relation is reproduced and perpetuated."[70] It is this contradiction between the (developing, expanding) forces of production and the (narrow, restricting) relations of production that Marx believes will lead to an eventual passing away of the capitalist mode of production. Marx quotes Mill in *Capital*, pointing out that

> John Stuart Mill, in his "Principles of Political Economy," says: "The really exhausting and the really repulsive labours instead of being better paid than others, are almost invariably paid the worst of all. . . . The more revolting the occupation, the more certain it is to receive the minimum of remuneration. . . . The hardships and the earnings, instead of being directlyproportional, as in any just arrangements of society they would be, are generally in an inverse ratio to one another."[71]

So we can see why Marx does not wish to group J. S. Mill together with the "vulgar economic apologists," as Marx appreciates the fact that J. S. Mill argues that the existing distribution of goods under capitalism is unjust and ought to be abolished and replaced by a fairer system.[72] However, Marx also writes that "men like John Stuart Mill are to blame for the contradiction between their traditional economic dogmas and their modern tendencies." Marx recognized J. S. Mill as a thinker who was genuinely concerned with improving society and increasing the living standards of the masses of people. Marx also certainly recognizes that J. S. Mill is far and away from the apologist and "leather-tongued oracle" that Marx took Bentham to be. His criticism of J. S. Mill's utilitarianism is that without a fundamental change in the way production is organized, there can be no radical changes in distribution and therefore the ills which J. S. Mill quite rightly seeks to address can never be fully eradicated on the basis of capitalist production.

In *Marx and Mill: two views of social conflict and social harmony*, Graeme Duncan writes, describing Marx's objections to J. S. Mill:

> In a social order of the kind characteristically envisaged by liberals, the major liberal values could not be embodied or realised. Liberalism reflects and idealises, without transforming, the evil reality of capitalist society, which must be transformed if genuine individualism is to come into being. In its application to Mill, the charge is not hypocrisy, but that his vision of life, if it is assumed to have any relevance to the generality of the people,

would require much more far-reaching structural change, especially to the property and the class system, than those which he actually advocated.[73]

Marx's dispute with J. S. Mill, then, also touches upon broader issues about the differences between liberalism and Marx's communist theory and in particular on the central question of whether the realization of values such as individuality and freedom is possible upon the economic basis of capitalist production. Additionally, as we saw earlier in the section of this chapter on ideology, within bourgeois thought and among bourgeois thinkers there is still a wide range for different theories, viewpoints, and assessments of existing society. Marx recognizes this, distinguishing here between the "apologism" of Bentham and the sincere, if according to Marx, ultimately unrealizable progressivism of J. S. Mill.

G. A. Cohen argues that Marx overlooks the fact that J. S. Mill did suppose there might be some substantive changes in the way that production was organized, and therefore that Marx is unfair in charging J. S. Mill with seeing capitalist relations of production as fixed and permanent.[74] According to Cohen,

> [J. S.] Mill foresees the demise of wage labour. . . . True, he is not looking beyond commodity production. He envisages the persistence of a market economy, with capitalist firms replaced by co-operative enterprises, not a thorough socialization of the means of production. But this is not because he commits any such fallacy as the one Marx exposed.[75]

But I don't think this defense is quite enough to rescue J. S. Mill's brand of utilitarianism from Marx's critique of it. Even on this argument, Mill leaves intact what Marx identifies as the essence of the capitalist system—commodity exchange. Marx has no shortage of arguments for why it is problematically utopian to propose that commodity exchange could be the economic basis for what Mill would recognize as more just relations of distribution. "Co-operative enterprises," producing and exchanging commodities within a market economy, it must be said, *are* capitalist firms, and if they are to survive at all, they must operate in ways that are determined by the same economic laws of competition and supply and demand that, as Marx devotes so much attention to arguing, have had and continue to have a destructive social effect which must be overcome. This is the point of Marx's numerous critiques of the capitalist Robert Owen and the production of workers' co-operative enterprises as a way to be rid of the negative aspects of capitalism. It is not as though Marx were unaware that this was being proposed.[76] However, he is less than sanguine about the prospects because of cases like this one:

> *Equitable Labour Exchange Bazaars or Offices* (the name is given in English in the German original) were founded by the workers' co-operative societies in various towns of England in 1832. This movement was headed by Robert Owen, who founded such a bazaar in London. The products of labour at these bazaars were exchanged for a kind of paper "money" issued as labour "tickets," a working hour being the unit. These bazaars were an attempt by the Utopians to organise exchange without money in the conditions of capitalist commodity production and soon proved to be a failure.[77]

Co-operative enterprises within a system of capitalist commodity production have been attempted, but they have remained small experiments and have not shown themselves to be likely candidates as roads to socialism. What J. S. Mill leaves fixed, even by Cohen's lights, are features of the capitalist mode of production that Marx argues must be abolished if a rational distribution of goods is to be achieved.

I hope to have demonstrated here that Marx is both aware of and sensitive to the existence of different strands of utilitarianism, which he takes to be of differing degrees of merit. I also believe that Marx's critiques of Bentham and of J. S. Mill show the ways in which Marx's turn to economic questions in his later works informs a continuing engagement with moral theory. Marx's approach, and I think this is particularly clear in the case of his critique of J. S. Mill, is to examine the economic assumptions made by such theories and investigate whether the theories' positive proposals are realistic, given the specific limits that a society's modes of production can place on the ability of human beings to organize that society in a rational and moral way. But this is not by any means to suggest that moral concerns have been crowded out entirely by some strict economic determinism. Rather, Marx seems to agree in certain key respects with J. S. Mill's moral vision of what type of society human beings should strive to build. The main bone of contention here concerns the means by which such a society is to be achieved and the conditions that must be realized in order to produce it.

Marx and Malthus

Thomas Robert Malthus's 1798 volume *Essay on the Principle of Population* was written as a response to the view held by Enlightenment thinkers such as Jean-Jacques Rousseau, Thomas Godwin, and others that society and human beings were capable of considerable future progress toward a fully rational society. Godwin, one of Malthus's principal targets, opposed the idea of a fixed human nature, arguing that with a change in the structure of society, there could also be produced significant changes in human beings themselves.

Malthus aimed to show that such significant progress was impossible, taking aim at Enlightenment aspirations for a better and more rational society. Malthus claimed instead that the human population would grow exponentially and in doing so, put such strain on humanity's resources that overall, life would only become nastier, more brutish, and shorter. The situation could be ameliorated somewhat, Malthus offered, through abstinence from procreation, especially among the poor. Indeed, Malthus claimed that exponential population growth was produced by God so that human beings would be forced to learn such virtues as abstinence and restraint. According to him, it would always be the case that population growth would outstrip the resources available to satisfy the needs of society, and thus it was not possible to improve society by increasing production, since the population would always increase to catch up with and eventually outstrip it.

In "Wages," Marx targets Malthus's claim that world overpopulation is the cause of widespread poverty, as well as the promise of increased wages and marginally improved living conditions for the worker, if only the worker will limit his reproduction and cease to add to the "oversupply" of labor. Marx attacks what he refers to as the "utter stupidity, baseness and hypocrisy of this doctrine."[78] Malthusianism's advice to the worker is "stupid" because it is so totally impracticable. In fact, Malthus himself admits this and it constitutes part of the grounds for his pessimism about the possibility of greatly and permanently improving conditions for human beings.

Malthusianism is also hypocritical because the bourgeoisie cannot possibly desire for the working class to become smaller, since, as Marx writes:

> Big industry constantly requires a reserve army of unemployed workers for times of overproduction. The main purpose of the bourgeois in relation to the worker is, of course, to have the commodity labour as cheaply

as possible, which is only possible when the supply of this commodity is as large as possible in relation to the demand for it, i.e., when the overpopulation is the greatest.[79]

Even if it were the case that unchecked population growth was the cause of poverty, it would be impossible to address this effectively in an economic system that relies precisely on there being many more workers than there are jobs. It could only be addressed by overthrowing that system, but of course, this is not what the bourgeois intends when he adopts Malthusianism as an explanation of social woes, neither is it what Malthus himself prescribed, preferring instead to lay the blame for this suffering at the feet of the poor and their failure to be more sparing in their procreation.

This leaves us with the question of why Marx finds Malthusianism to be "base." Malthusianism is "base" because it places the moral blame for the worker's miserable condition upon the worker himself. If only the worker exerted greater self-control, the Malthusian can think, he would not be in such a sorry condition. It gives the bourgeois a license to observe widespread privation not as a product of capitalist society which could potentially be done away with, but rather as the natural and necessary, if lamentable, condition of human beings. As Marx writes, Malthusianism

> is the more welcome to the bourgeois as it silences his conscience, makes hard-heartedness into a moral duty and the consequences of society into the consequences of nature, and finally gives him the opportunity to watch the destruction of the proletariat by starvation as calmly as any other natural event without bestirring himself, and, on the other hand, to regard the misery of the proletariat as its own fault and to punish it. To be sure, the proletarian can restrain his natural instinct by reason, and so, by moral supervision, halt the law of nature in its injurious course of development.[80]

To relate this back to one of the main themes of this section, it is important to notice here that Marx is more than happy to reject a theory precisely on the basis that it merely serves to justify and uphold existing capitalist social arrangements which, in the light of how they needlessly damage or destroy a large section of humanity, are unjustifiable. The aim of Malthusianism as a doctrine is to lower expectations about what kind of society it is possible for human beings to achieve, and to thereby provide justification for the existing society with all of its faults. If the optimism of figures such as Rousseau and Corcoret represented some of the most progressive elements of bourgeois ideology, Malthusianism captures its conservative side that has reconciled itself to the limits of capitalist production. As Nicholas Churchich writes in his 1994 book *Marxism and Morality*:

> A movement of thought originating from Darwin's theory of evolution and inspired by writers like Malthus and Spencer gradually became a significant intellectual force destined to play a considerable role in the second half of the nineteenth century. This movement of thought was expressed in Social Darwinism which was essentially an attempt to justify the existing individualistic *laissez faire* and competitive system of class society. Both Marx and Engels reject the ideology of Social Darwinism....
>
> Social Darwinism, Marx contends, is characterised by the evils of unrestricted private enterprise. Instead of treating society as the organisational means by which men cooperate in the tasks of promoting their social and moral ends, Social Darwinists reduce it to the Hobbesian state of '*bellum omnium contra omnes*.'[81]

Marx's critique of Malthusianism is no mere historical sidenote. Rather, it provides us with an important source of insight into Marx's criticisms of bourgeois morality more generally. Marx's principal charge against Malthus is that he exonerates capitalist society in its role in producing human misery and closes the theoretical space for a systematic critique of capitalism by putting in its place a set of moral demands aimed at the poor and designed to blame them for their own suffering. This tactic is by no means the monopoly of Malthusianism, and in fact Marx criticizes Christian morality among other forms of morality for performing the same exculpatory task for bourgeois society. Also, Malthusianism is by no means a historical relic, and strong echoes of it can be heard today in the rhetoric of welfare reform, in certain corners of the environmentalist movement, and in other sectors across the political spectrum.

Conclusion

Marx's critiques of rival ethical approaches are not mere historical curios but have real implications for present-day debates about the prospects for social democracy and liberal solutions to contemporary social ills. After all, if revolutionary organizing is not actually necessary to bring about a better world of freedom, social harmony, individual fulfillment, and human progress—an aspirational vision that liberal political perspectives frequently share as their stated aim or at least, do not rule out as a potentially desirable outcome—then why not just spare everyone the trouble and vote it in, instead? All one would need, then, is the right ethical argument to persuade everyone, including those for whom considerations of private interest would move them to prevent such a better world from ever coming about. If the people are reasonable and the arguments are good, then it should be no trouble. Divert people away from the conflicts occasioned by competition for scarce resources; counsel them that they ought to set their self-interest aside and cease treating their fellow human beings as mere means with which to pursue their own private ends, even if this means going without. Keep the existing relations of capitalist production intact—they are there, anyway, creating an abundance of resources, the likes of which the world has never known before—and devise a system of ethical calculation to rationally determine who ought to receive what out of this great abundance. Remind the bosses that they ought to love their neighbor if they hope ever to receive their store in heaven.

The problem is that it is not so hard to construct a world of universal human fellowship in theory, but our work is cut out for us when it comes to the task of creating such fellowship in fact. Moral dictates might suffice for the spontaneous free wills that inhabit philosophers' theories, unencumbered by embodiment and material circumstance. But we as earthly, biological, material beings seek the promotion of our interests and the satisfaction of our needs. The system of capitalism is riven with conflicts, the most central and defining of these being the conflict between proletariat and bourgeoisie. In the rare circumstance that an individual capitalist succeeds in recognizing himself as a human being rather than a boss, he becomes capable of recognizing the proletariat's interests as aligned with the interests of the species as a whole. But this is atypical. Moral appeals only go so far. They might inspire charity, but no loosening on the reins of power. Or in the words of Frederick Douglass, "Power concedes nothing without a demand. It never did and it never will."

In seeking the overthrow of exploitative, oppressive, and alienating class relations, the proletariat carries the possibility of realizing those conditions in which human beings could truly relate to one another as ends in themselves and not as mere means to capital accumulation. But this cannot be achieved without a struggle, one in which capitalist classes will fight tooth and nail against the movement for human emancipation from class society's degradations.

Any ethical theory that would preach retreat and abstention from this struggle as a means to produce human emancipation, then, in practice also abandons emancipation as an end. This is the kernel of Marx's rejection of the ethical theories he critiques throughout his writings. It is not that there is no fact of the matter about what we ought to do, how we ought to live, and how we ought to treat one another. Rather it is that he is not content to sacrifice the project of creating real human freedom and a resolution to the conflict between private and public good, in order to maintain the ideal pretense that we've already got them now.

9

"No Particular Wrong"

The Abolition of Morality

Over the course of the preceding chapters, I have argued for the claim that Marx's theory has an ethical content which remains consistent throughout his work, though deepened and elaborated over the course of his life. Marx's materialism, his skepticism of bourgeois "justice," his criticisms of particular existing moral doctrines, and his rejection of moral suasion as a primary means of transforming society do not license the claim that his was an "amoralist" theory.

And yet those who read him this way are not entirely without rationale for doing so. Marx does describe the "abolition" of morality as one of the welcome achievements of the communist movement. He further indicates that a fully developed communist society would be without moral reasoning, as such. Without a firm grasp of the *historicity* of Marxist theory, it is all too easy to conflate Marx's predictions about what lies in the future with descriptions of the world at present. We are not yet living in the time of material abundance and full human realization envisioned by Marx and other communists. We cannot yet totally dispense with moral theory in the meanwhile. Morality is an attempt to theorize and close the gap between the world as it is and the world as it should be. Marxism is a theory that posits that the world can be *made* what it should be. But we are not there yet.

Therefore, it is both true that morality is valid, salient, and necessary in our current conditions, and that it will eventually lose this salience in a transition to fully developed communist society. If this claim seems odd, consider the person who announces that after careful moral analysis and contemplation, they have finally arrived at the conclusion that it would be wrong for them to harm an innocent stranger purely for their own private gratification. Compare them to another person to whom this desire, and the attendant moral question, simply never occurs. The fact that for the first person, it even comes up as a moral question at all, speaks unflatteringly to their character. In Marxist theory, this same comparison can be made on the level of the species. Morality is a contingent historical ideological form that has come into existence at a definite point in history and will pass out of existence once certain historical conditions are met, if they are met.

Responding to Hegel's *Philosophy of Right* and writing within the German context, Marx argues that human emancipation can be achieved in only one way:

> In the formulation of a class with *radical chains*, a class of civil society which is not a class of civil society, an estate which is the dissolution of all estates, a sphere which has a universal character by its universal suffering and claims no *particular right* because no *particular wrong*, but *wrong generally*, is perpetuated against it; which can invoke no *historical*, but only *human*, title; which does not stand in any one-sided antithesis to the consequences but in all-round antithesis to the premises of German statehood; a sphere, finally, which cannot emancipate itself without emancipating itself from all other spheres of society and thereby emancipating all other spheres of society, which, in a word, is the *complete loss* of man and hence can win itself only through the *complete re-winning of man*. This dissolution of society as a particular estate is the *proletariat*.[1]

Marx's claim is that the proletariat is unique in the complete coincidence of its interests with the interests of humanity. Hence, the wrongs committed against it are not simply contrary to any specific or "particular" interests it might have as a class. Wrongs committed against the proletariat are wrongs against humanity, itself: "wrong generally." This is why, from its own class perspective, the proletariat need not preach morality as such, nor have morality preached to it. In pursuing its emancipation from the dehumanizing, exploiting, and alienating reach of capital, it concretely constitutes the practical resolution of the most pressing ethical problem of our time. In this sense, workers' revolutionary activity also presages the "abolition of morality" that Marx foresees as a consequence of any future transition to a fully developed communist society, with its resolution of the contradictions between private interest and public good, and its forging of those conditions within which we might concretize into practice, and dissolve as an ethical imperative, the treatment of every person as though they were an end in themselves.

In the present chapter, I begin with a discussion of Marx's highly critical stance toward "sacrifice." Marx's insistence on the coincidence of individual with social interest, a coincidence which he sees not as merely theoretical but as already realized in workers' struggle, will help set the stage for making sense of his theory's implications regarding morality's abolition.

The End of Sacrifice

In writings both before and after those which make up his and Engels's *Critique of the German Ideology*, Marx distinguishes between, on the one hand, rational assessments of how human needs can best be satisfied and, on the other, moralistic calls for self-sacrifice. One key aspect of this distinction is that the two approaches must rely on different modes of motivation. The scientific communism developed by Marx depends on a correct assessment of the real needs of existing persons and aims to show rationally how the needs of people can be satisfied through effective political action and revolutionary activity. The Utopianism he criticizes (in the Bauer brothers and others), however, relies upon mere moralism—emotional appeals designed to make up for the fact that Utopianism lacks the resources to have motivational force on a pragmatic basis.

As we saw in Chapter 2, critiques of moralism play a key role in Marx's arguments against the "True Socialists." These are Utopian socialists who, Marx charged, rely upon the pronouncement of moral edicts to make up for their lack of a concrete political program by means of which socialism could be realized. This distinction between scientific communism—a theory derived using the method of historical materialism—and Utopianism is brought to bear most clearly in a document that Marx wrote with Engels, known as the "Circular against Kriege." This document critiques the rhetorical practices of Hermann Kriege, a socialist and editor of the New York-based, German-language newspaper, *Der Volks-Tribun*. Here, I will explain Marx's and Engels's criticisms of Kriege, and how these criticisms shed light upon Marx's approach to morality.

Der Volks-Tribun was produced and distributed in New York with the aim of representing the principles of the Communist Correspondence Committee to communists in the United States. Under Kriege's tenure as editor (or at least, so Marx charged), the editorial line of the journal began to deviate away from scientific communism and toward Utopianism and moralism, making irrational appeals to emotion in order to convince readers to take up the cause of communism. Finally, the editorial line of *Der Volks-Tribun* veered so sharply away from the principles of the organization it was supposed to represent, that Marx and Engels introduced a set of resolutions to a meeting of the Correspondence Committee, denouncing Kriege for what they referred to as "fantastic emotionalism" put forward under the guise of communism. These resolutions constitute the aforementioned circular in question.

A particularly important piece of evidence in Marx's and Engels's case against Kriege is what they regard as the latter's enthusiastic promotion of self-sacrifice as a communist virtue.[2] Instead of arguing for the coincidence of working people's self-interest with the interest of humanity, Kriege posits a moral sacrifice of setting one's own interests aside for the good of "others" who will benefit from a transition to socialism. This notion of sacrifice, of setting one's own interests aside, is totally at odds with Marxism. Marxist theory argues that all human beings have an objective interest in the realization of a communist society and of human emancipation. Further, Marxism addresses itself to that part of society whose subjective interest in surviving under capitalism aligns it with the cause of human emancipation. Marx and Engels charged that Kriege, instead, argued for communism not as a practical answer to the problems facing human beings, but rather as a moral imperative to be realized out of a sense of one's duty to humanity. In doing so, Kriege does precisely what, as we saw in previous chapters, critics such as Max Stirner accused communism of doing. This moralism posits "the common good," or "humanity," as an abstraction that demands sacrifices from real, concrete, human individuals, expressing alienation in a different form, rather than serving to abolish it.

The argument becomes yet clearer when Marx and Engels strike their final blow against the "sacrificing" Kriege.[3] They criticize Kriege because he expects to be praised for sacrificing himself for the good of others, instead of seeing revolutionary activity as something that he carries out for his own benefit as well as that of others. Kriege writes to the readers of *Der Volks-Tribun*, "We have other things to do than worry about our *miserable selves*, we belong to mankind." Marx replies:

> With this shameful and nauseating grovelling before a "mankind" that is separate and distinct from the "self" and which is therefore a metaphysical and in his case even a religious fiction, with what is indeed the most utterly "miserable" slavish self-abasement, this religion ends up like any other. Such a doctrine, preaching the voluptuous pleasure of cringing and

self-contempt, is entirely suited to valiant—*monks*, but never to men of action, least of all in a time of struggle. It only remains for these valiant monks to castrate their "miserable selves" and thereby provide sufficient proof of their confidence in the ability of "mankind" to reproduce itself!—If Kriege has nothing better to offer than these sentimentalities in pitiful style, it would indeed be wiser for him to translate his "Père Lamennais" again and again in each issue of the *Volks-Tribun*.[4]

Marx and Engels accuse Kriege of misrepresenting communism as "a religion of love," rather than presenting it as a science of human progress and development; to follow Kriege's reasoning would be essentially to take up a religious attitude toward humanity as a new god rendered into pseudo-materialist terms.[5] We do not "belong to mankind," to which we must constantly sacrifice our individual self-interest. One *should* be "worried about oneself"; it is in fact this concern with oneself and one's own circumstances that can be linked together with an argument for rational social control over society's resources. For those whose activity is the production and reproduction of society, there is no need for a moral leap across some perceived gap between individual self-interest and the general interest of society.

Marx and Engels are quite clear in separating their own theory from what they take to be Kriege's moralistic grandstanding. The point of communism is not for people to stop "worrying about themselves." Although Marx does not refer to "alienation" here, his comments here on sacrifice relate directly to the problem of alienation. To sacrifice oneself, after all, is to alienate oneself from oneself, to give oneself over to a being that is separate, for the satisfaction of aims that are considered more important than one's own. Marx does not think human progress can be aided by human self-denial, but rather, by human seeking for satisfaction and fulfillment. So what Kriege presents is not communist practice, but rather, as Marx and Engels call it, "a religion of love," an irrational and emotionalist call to self-alienation. Without a material link between self-interest and the general interest, Kriege retreats to an irrational appeal to emotion to make individuals do what is necessary for "society," an entity whose interests are imagined to be opposed to their own.

Sacrifice appears in Marx's work as an important theme as early as *The Holy Family* and shows up again in his polemic against Max Stirner, which makes up the bulk of what was later collected and posthumously published as *The Critique of The German Ideology*. There, Marx responds to Stirner's charge that communism is a so-called good cause, requiring human beings to sacrifice for a "greater good." Marx argues that far from requiring individuals to engage in sacrifice or altruism, his theory of communism is based on the needs and interests of people; it seeks to develop, confirm, and realize human individuals, not to promote sacrifice and self-renunciation. As Marx writes, Stirner's mistake in his critique of communism is in thinking that

> the communists want to "make sacrifices" for "society," when they want at most to sacrifice existing society; in this case he should describe their consciousness that their struggle is the common cause of all people who have outgrown the bourgeois system as a sacrifice that they make to themselves.[6]

As we saw also in our discussion of alienation (in Chapter 4 of this volume), Marx rejects sacrifice as a part of his communist theory. Therefore, Marx argues, Stirner is mistaken in his understanding of communism as a call to sacrifice and Hermann Kriege is mistaken in urging workers not to "worry about themselves." Marx has no need to urge the proletariat on with romantic appeals to sacrifice because he proposes a course of action that is consonant with people's interests, rather than at odds with them.

For Marx, unalienated human beings perform labor for one another not as a sacrifice but as an act of self-realization, in conditions of human emancipation, circumstances are arranged so that in satisfying the needs of others in society I am also directly satisfying my own needs. As Jan Kandiyali has pointed out, "This claim is philosophically distinctive. Philosophers before Marx emphasize self-realization (though they did not always use that term), but few saw meeting others' needs as constitutive of it."[7]

In Marx's private letters, he sometimes does praise the "sacrifice" of members of the Paris Commune and of other revolutionary struggles.[8] And he is perfectly aware that revolutionaries often do their work at great personal cost to themselves. Nothing in his arguments against Kriege or the Utopian Socialists can be taken to imply that Marx is unaware of the courage and dedication of such people, or that he is somehow stinting in his praise of them. But in attacking Kriege's "groveling," "self-sacrifice," and "religion of love," Marx's point is to thoroughly reject and distance himself from the moralism implicit in it. For Kriege, Marx argues, revolutionaries ought to act out of a sense of duty to the abstraction of "mankind," before which they are "nothing." This is anathema to Marx; it is not what he is praising in the revolutionaries who endure great risk and hardship to carry out their work.

Meanings of Morality's Abolition

It is in *The Communist Manifesto* that Marx most clearly articulates the notion of morality's abolition, defending it in the course of a debate he imagines between himself and a bourgeois interlocutor.[9] That interlocutor charges that "communism abolishes eternal truths, it abolishes all religion, and all morality, instead of constituting them on a new basis; it therefore acts in contradiction to all past historical experience."[10] The accusation here is (at least) twofold. First, that communism treats as merely historical and contingent what ought to be regarded as eternal and necessary. And second, that communism unjustifiably rejects the inductive hypothesis that the future will be like the past and that, therefore, morality will persist into the future, much as it has existed in the past. Marx responds that indeed communism *does* abolish morality, just as its critics charge. As it is the fact of class exploitation that gives rise to morality, it is only fitting that morality should "vanish" with the "total disappearance of class antagonisms."

Marx writes, representing the conversation between himself and the imagined bourgeois interlocutor:

> "Undoubtedly," it will be said, "religious, moral, philosophical and juridical ideas have been modified in the course of historical development. But religion, morality, philosophy, political science, and law, constantly survived this change."
>
> "There are, besides, eternal truths, such as Freedom, Justice, etc., that are common to all states of society. But Communism abolishes eternal truths, it abolishes all religion and all morality, instead of constituting them on a new basis; it therefore acts in contradiction to all past historical experience."
>
> What does this accusation reduce itself to? The history of all past society has consisted in the development of class antagonisms, antagonisms that assumed different forms at different epochs. But whatever form they may have taken, one fact is common to all past ages, viz., the exploitation of one part of society by the other. No wonder, then, that the social consciousness of past ages, despite all the multiplicity and variety it displays, moves within certain common forms, or general ideas, which cannot completely vanish except with the total disappearance of class antagonisms.
>
> The Communist revolution is the most radical rupture with traditional property relations; no wonder that its development involves the most radical rupture with traditional ideas.[11]

What does Marx mean here? One interpretive challenge for understanding Marx is presented by the heavy use of irony that is characteristic of his style throughout his written corpus. Brazilian Marxist and literary theorist, Ludovico Silva, writes in his 1971 book *Marx's Literary Style*, "Marx was a lifelong ideoclast, one of the fiercest and most fervent idea breakers of all time." Among Marx's most devastatingly "ideoclastic" weapons was his biting irony, perfectly calibrated to cut away the cloak around a thing and reveal it as its own dialectical opposite. The declaration that the realization of full human flourishing in the course of communist development would be coincident with the abolition of religion, morality, philosophy, political science, and law will strike many as so apparently outlandish on its face that perhaps we ought to interpret this bold claim in a highly deflationary and ironic way. Yes, Marx said it, but he couldn't have really *meant* it, such a reading would maintain. Perhaps he intended some hidden, subtler, meaning that is drenched here in irony.

To prefer a weaker, less radical reading where it is available is an entirely reasonable principle of textual interpretation. In this case, however, we have Marx insisting as explicitly and directly as he can that he fully intends the "most radical" meaning. He does so precisely to push back against and rule out weaker ones. In keeping with the "ideoclastic" nature of Marx's critique, it behooves us to entertain interpretations that render "abolition" in the strongest possible terms, so long as to do so is compatible with Marx's other claims and with his theoretical system as a whole. And indeed, it does follow immediately from the claim that morality is a form of the social consciousness of class antagonisms, that the total resolution and abolition of these antagonisms would produce material circumstances in which the forms of consciousness uniquely corresponding to class society could finally, in Marx's words, "completely vanish."

Marx's statements in the *Manifesto* regarding the abolition of morality, et al. do not appear in a vacuum. Rather, they are the culmination of a series of irony-inflected replies to various bad-faith accusations made against communists. In each case, irony is deployed as a kind of negation of the negation, through which Marx responds to communism's accusers by insisting pugnaciously that yes, the communist movement does intend to destroy that thing which it is accused of seeking to destroy. The irony, however, is that the thing in question—individuality, freedom, family, morality—isn't what it is declared to be and is already negated by capitalism's own destructive processes.¹² What communism seeks to abolish is the supposedly hallowed thing—private property, nation, etc.—as it actually exists, which is to say, as a decaying mockery of itself. The "destructive" role of communism in these examples is largely to dismantle illusion and pretension—to call a thing a thing, sweep aside the decay, and produce new social forms better suited to the real state of things. In each case, Marx proclaims that these features of class society must be done away with totally, not merely reformed and reconstituted.

As Peter Hudis writes in his 2015 essay "The Ethical Implications of Marx's Concept of a Post-Capitalist Society,"

> Marx's normative objection to the phenomenon of inversion informs his view of a post-capitalist society. Since Marx locates the central problem of capitalism in the dominance of the subject by products and activity of its own making, a new society represents the inversion of this inversion insofar as it abolishes any condition in which such a situation prevails.¹³

Take for example Marx's response to the charge that the communists wish to do away with countries and nationalities. It illuminates his statement that "in the national struggles of the proletarians of the different countries, they point out and bring to the front the common interests of the entire proletariat, independently of all nationality."¹⁴ I reproduce it here in full:

> The Communists are further reproached with desiring to abolish countries and nationality.
> The working men have no country. We cannot take from them what they have not got. Since the proletariat must first of all acquire political supremacy, must rise to be the leading class of the nation, must constitute itself the nation, it is so far, itself national, though not in the bourgeois sense of the word.
> National differences and antagonisms between peoples are daily more and more vanishing, owing to the development of the bourgeoisie, to freedom of commerce, to the world market, to uniformity in the mode of production and in the conditions of life corresponding thereto.
> The supremacy of the proletariat will cause them to vanish still faster. United action, of the leading civilized countries at least, is one of the first conditions for the emancipation of the proletariat.

> In proportion as the exploitation of one individual by another is put an end to, the exploitation of one nation by another will also be put an end to. In proportion as the antagonism between classes within the nation vanishes, the hostility of one nation to another will come to an end.[15]

Marx's response to the allegation follows a structure that appears in numerous iterations throughout the "Proletarians and Communists" section of the *Manifesto*. First, he states the allegation. Next, he counters that communists are hardly needed to destroy the object in question, since from the point of view of labor, that thing is already demolished and dismantled by capitalism and does not truly exist. In other words, only from a bourgeois perspective might it seem that the working class would experience the loss of nation as a loss to itself. Workers cannot lose what capitalism has already deprived them of. What remains is not to reconstitute some form of bourgeois nationalism for the working class, but rather for workers to develop and embrace class solidarity with one another across national borders. Capitalism has initiated the dissolution of national antagonisms and now it is up to the international working class to finish the job.

Marx highlights the inherent irony of the bourgeoisie's feigned anxiety about what the "loss" of nation-states would mean for workers, when it is the capitalist system that has set into motion those processes which make it so that working people already have no country to claim. Insofar as nation-states function undemocratically—facilitating the suppression of working people's autonomy, self-activity, and struggle for emancipation—the much-vaunted benefits of "citizenship" are, for all intents and purposes, already practically absent for workers. For working people to truly "have" a nation to claim, they must have political representation within that nation. True democratic representation for working people can be achieved only through proletarian self-organization and self-activity, conducted independently of bourgeois control. In its essential role as an instrument of class repression, this is precisely what the bourgeois state is organized to prevent. For working people to bring about full democracy, they must look beyond their national borders, distinguish their interests from those of the bourgeois state, organize internationally, and be in active solidarity with the working people of all countries. Those conditions in which the proletariat of a country might "constitute itself as the nation" are also precisely those that would ring the death knell for "national differences and antagonisms" already weakened by the homogenizing and universalizing process of global capitalist exchange.

We have already seen, in Chapters 6 and 7, how Marx makes analogous rhetorical moves in response to his imagined interlocutor's accusations that communists seek to destroy freedom and individuality. He writes,

> In bourgeois society, living labour is but a means to increase accumulated labour. In Communist society, accumulated labour is but a means to widen, to enrich, to promote the existence of the labourer.
>
> In bourgeois society, therefore, the past dominates the present; in Communist society, the present dominates the past. In bourgeois society capital is independent and has individuality, while the living person is dependent and has no individuality.
>
> And the abolition of this state of things is called by the bourgeois abolition of individuality and freedom! And rightly so. The abolition of bourgeois individuality, bourgeois independence, and bourgeois freedom is undoubtedly aimed at.[16]

Here, too, Marx deploys irony to present communism—the movement of workers' struggle against capitalist exploitation and for their own emancipation—as the negation of the negation. What communism seeks to destroy, he explains, are *bourgeois* individuality, *bourgeois* independence, and *bourgeois* freedom which, for working people, each exist concretely as the very opposite of what they announce themselves to be in theory. *Human* individuality, independence, and freedom would be produced in their place, but only in the course of sweeping away their sham, bourgeois impostors.

One might here reason that Marx's claims about the abolition of morality ought to be understood along similar lines: perhaps Marx does not mean that morality will be abolished *as such*, but rather only that *bourgeois* morality will be swept away and replaced with a new proletarian morality that would persist into fully developed communism, long after humans' alienated condition had already been overcome.

That reading has immediate plausibility but misses a key distinction between concepts such as freedom and individuality on the one hand, and morality, religion, and law on the other. The former, Marx regards as constitutive features of unalienated human social Being. Throughout his writings both before and after the *Manifesto*, Marx speaks of freedom and individuality as aspects of human life that develop over the course of human history in trajectories that partially co-constitute the fully realized flourishing of human beings themselves. Morality et al., on the other hand, which he and Engels describe as forms of ideology, also develop in ways that are determined by human history, but they belong specifically to a particular period within that history—the period within which human life is structured by domination, class conflict, and exploitation. Freedom and individuality in their human, rather than merely bourgeois form, are essential features of fully realized human nature. As such, while their bourgeois form will be abolished with the development of communism, they will nonetheless appear there in a *human* and unalienated form. Morality, by contrast, belongs to the "social consciousness" of a particular age—the age of class-based domination of some human beings over others, of external imperatives to which one is compelled to conform. The abolition of morality's bourgeois form—the form in which its contradictions are most fully expressed and beyond which lies not only the abolition of bourgeois domination, but of all domination and, in domination's place, the realization of true human emancipation—is therefore also morality's abolition *in toto*. There is no unalienated form which the abstract theorization of, and obedient submission to, an external moral law can take for beings who exist within "an association, in which the free development of each is the condition for the free development of all."[17]

As we saw in Chapter 8, even Kantian self-legislation counts, for Marx, as an external, alien command. This is in part because while Kant's account describes moral agents who are free to bind themselves (or not) to a priori moral law as they will, that law remains something eternal, unchanging, and undetermined by human history. Human beings can choose whether or not to obey it, but in obeying it, they subordinate themselves to it; an aspect especially highlighted by Kant's emphasis on the sacrificial character of morality and his insistence that human obedience to the moral law is all the more distinctively moral, the more it comes at a personal cost.

Consequentialist moral theories such as J. S. Mill's utilitarianism do not fare very much better and, Marx argues, also constitute alienated ways of relating to the world and the things in it. Just as capitalist exchange dissolves the manifold differences among things into the single category of money as universal abstract value, so utilitarianism, for Marx, is symptomatic of our incapacity to see objects for what they are. We do not see the world-in-itself and still less, the world-for-us; but rather, the world-for-capital. Commodity exchange conditions our perception of the world so that we never see or know things as they are, instead appreciating them only in light of their usefulness for yielding some further abstract end. Instead of apprehending things in their concrete fullness, we relate to them as so many interchangeable means to some abstract, empty form: money, in the one case, and utility, in the other.

Interpretive alternatives remain, however, for caching out fully what is meant by an "abolition of all morality instead of constituting it on a new basis." Let us consider two immediately plausible accounts of what this phrase might mean for Marx. The first interpretation of this claim would be that there is no genuine fact of the matter about morality in a fully developed communist society. The second is that there *would* be genuine facts of the matter about morality in such a society, but that the members of society would not engage in distinctively moral reasoning to ascertain those facts.[18] Let us consider these alternatives in order.

The first alternative is the one that construes Marx's prediction most radically and counterintuitively (but also, I think, most accurately). On this reading, for Marx, a fully developed communist society is a society without any fact of the matter at all about (what would be only so-called) moral requirements. For the members of fully developed communist society, prosocial ways of being are not obligations or claims made against them; they are simply their already fully inhabited and fully expressed ways of being. Human beings in such a society would be no more morally required to behave in prosocial ways than they are "morally required" to be primates. It is helpful here to think heuristically of morality as concerning a "gap" between the world as it is and the world as it ought to be.[19] No gap, no fact of the matter about what ought to be done to close the gap.

Consider again, in this context, Marx's and Engels's claim that

> morality, religion, metaphysics, all the rest of ideology and their corresponding forms of consciousness ... have no history, no development; but men, developing their material production and their material intercourse, alter, along with this their real existence, their thinking and the products of their thinking. Life is not determined by consciousness, but consciousness by life.[20]

To interpret the abolition of morality as a condition in which there is no fact of the matter about moral requirements at all best expresses historical materialist ideology critique. Morality is not some independent, abstract, external set of commandments handed down to humanity from the outside. It arises imminently from human conditions and forms of being. If the forms of alienated, exploited social being that give rise to morality go away, then morality as such goes with them.

The second interpretive possibility I presented above is that to say that morality is "abolished" in fully developed communist society is simply to say that while there might be facts of the matter about what is morally right or wrong, the members of such a society wouldn't engage in distinctively moral reasoning to arrive at those facts. Unlike the first alternative, there is no robust metaethical claim here about the standing or validity of moral claims as such. On the first alternative, no one in a fully developed communist society is, properly speaking, ever morally obligated. On the second alternative, the members of that future society might well be morally obligated to do all sorts of things. It is only that they do not represent those obligations to themselves in thought, and they do not *do* moral theory in order to ascertain moral obligations. They discharge their obligations because it is already embedded in their forms of life that they would do so. Unfortunately for this interpretation, it is ruled out by Marx's vehement insistence that "morality [*die Moral*, in his German]" is not simply "constituted on a new basis," but abolished altogether. In fully developed communism, there is no social form taking the shape of a command that human beings "follow," even if only unwittingly.

A third possibility, sharing similarities with each of the first two, is that we should seek recourse in Hegel's notion of *Sittlichkeit*, standardly translated into English as "ethical life." For Hegel, *Sittlichkeit* denotes a rational, well-ordered society with inhabitants who inhabit their social roles comfortably and readily, feeling at home in them. In the place of abstract moral commands to do, out of duty, what one would perhaps rather not do, individuals in conditions of *Sittlichkeit* actively embrace the activities associated with their roles. The private will of each individual is then coincident and in harmony with the good of society as a universal and collective whole. If the aim of communism is to be understood as the realization of *Sittlichkeit*, then a fully developed communist society would be one made of people for whom morally correct behavior has become habitual and customary. Importantly, these are not moral automata; their easy and comfortable embrace of their roles is the free, active expression of their fully realized selves.

In her book *Hegel on Second Nature and Ethical Life*, Andreja Novakovic writes that Hegel is to be understood as arguing that in *Sittlichkeit*,

> true conscience is no longer engaged in deriving objective content through its own resources or testing what is publicly recognized against the

measure of its subjective convictions. Its particular duties are prescribed by its specific position within the social order and it is committed to the requirements internal to its roles. So in an objectively rational social order the basic tension between social expectations and particular commitment is (for the most part) overcome, since I form my commitments within the context of institutional roles.[21]

Novakovic's characterization elegantly expresses that human beings in conditions of ethical life are not passive, automatic beings; they are rational, free, and active individuals who subjectively embrace their role expectations precisely because these expectations emerge from social arrangements that are themselves rationally ordered. We can also be put in mind of Karen Ng's observations about friendship in her book *Hegel's Concept of Life*, where she writes:

> The act of visiting your friend realizes good friendship, not because it is deduced from the practical syllogism, but because it is an act of self-determination, an act of self-determination that can only take place by reflecting the power of an objective universality or genus—in this case, the rational, ethical institution of friendship, which itself exists within the more encompassing objective universality of ethical life (*Sittlichkeit*).[22]

Yet crucially, to say that prosocial behavior is habitual among human beings for whom *Sittlichkeit* is realized as a fact of life is *not* to say that there will be no disagreement or conflict whatsoever. Molly Farneth illuminatingly presents this point in her book *Hegel's Social Ethics*, arguing that *Sittlichkeit* is best understood as a condition in which differences are resolved through democratic deliberation among rational agents who relate to one another through "full-fledged, reciprocal recognition," and for whom such mutual recognition and regard is not still an ideal to be aimed at, but an already realized fact about human social life.[23]

Communism as *Sittlichkeit* has significant immediate plausibility, especially given Marx's philosophical indebtedness to Hegel. The rub is that a Marxist conception of fully developed communism simply cannot incorporate Hegel's conception of stable social roles as part of unalienated human life; and yet the notion of such social roles grounds the very concept of *Sittlichkeit*. The notion that one would embrace a particular defined role (or even multiple roles) within a well-ordered society, inhabit it, and joyfully organize one's activity in accordance with the remit associated with that role, is too much akin to what Marx seeks to reject in capitalism's system of divided labor, which he believes artificially limits and stultifies humans' capacity to relate to the world directly, immediately, creatively, and expansively.[24]

The Critique of the German Ideology features a famous and brief sketch of daily life in communist society, which serves to help illustrate this point:

> As soon as the division of labour comes into being, each man has a particular, exclusive sphere of activity, which is forced upon him and from which he cannot escape. He is a hunter, a fisherman, a shepherd, or a critical critic, and must remain so if he does not want to lose his means of livelihood; whereas in communist society, where nobody has one exclusive sphere of activity but each can become accomplished in any branch he wishes, society regulates the general production and thus makes it possible for me to do one thing today and another tomorrow, to hunt in the morning, fish in the afternoon, rear cattle in the evening, criticise after dinner, just as I have a mind, without ever becoming hunter, fisherman, shepherd or critic.[25]

Freedom, for Marx, is not the subjective embrace of stable and defined social roles, but a life unmediated and undetermined, as far as possible, by any such roles at all. One is then simply a human being (or, as Marx puts it in the *Grundrisse*, a "rich individual"), shaping and reshaping one's interactions with the world and constantly reforging one's connections to it, and to the other people in it, *as* a human being—which is to say, as a dynamic and endlessly changing being whose relationship to the world can never be exactly what it was the day or year before. It is spontaneity unleashed. There is no principle to refer to, not the abstract universal principles of normative moral theory, nor even the "principle" of the defined social role that determines appropriate action for the person who inhabits it. The "rich individual" of communist society apprehends everything freshly, as the unique and particular object, person, or situation that it is. If such an individual can be said to inhabit and embrace any social role, that is simply the endlessly expansive role of a "human," which is to say, of a being fully engaged in the activity of in-principle boundless and ongoing self-change.

How does one approach the world in a human way? Clues are to be found in Marx's discussions, throughout his work, of how capitalism frustrates sense-perception and our subjective representations of the external world.

Commodity exchange and universal saleability, as we noted earlier, have conditioned our relations to other human beings such that we perceive them not directly, not as they are, but in terms of their abstract "usefulness" to us. Ruth Groff illuminates this point in her essay "Aristotelian Marxism/Marxist Aristotelianism," where she writes,

> The contention from a Marxist perspective is that the principled disregard for the particular, at the level of thought, expresses, *at* the level of thought, the principled disregard for the particular that is the mark of exchange-value. . . . If Kantian pure practical reason expresses the abstraction of exchange-value, the instrumental reason of utilitarianism can be seen to express the fact that commodified goods are produced not for their own sake, but instead as means—means to an end unrelated to their use-values.[26]

A consideration of *Capital* underscores the correctness of Groff's analysis. There, Marx writes,

> The expansion of value, which is the objective basis or main-spring of the circulation M—C—M, becomes [the capitalist's] subjective aim, and it is only in so far as the appropriation of ever more and more wealth in the abstract becomes the sole motive of his operations, that he functions as a capitalist, that is, as capital personified and endowed with consciousness and a will. Use-values must therefore never be looked upon as the real aim of the capitalist; neither must the profit on any single transaction. The restless never-ending process of profit-making alone is what he aims at.

The world of commodity exchange is structured such that, just as we approach labor as a mere means to biological subsistence—and not as the highest active expression of our species-nature as creative and "self-changing" beings—so do we approach one another as so many interchangeable means to the end of endless private accumulation. This disturbed relationship to our fellow human beings cannot be overcome through individual acts of willing our behavior to be in accordance with an abstract moral law that commands us to treat other people as ends in themselves. It requires a massive social transformation that abolishes those present conditions which incline us to regard everything and everyone as means to the limitless acquisition of, itself, empty and abstract value.

Marx, following Hegel, regards utilitarianism as a quite pure ethical expression of universal saleability and exchange. In the course of his arguments against Stirner, Marx writes,

> The extent to which this theory of mutual exploitation, which Bentham expounded *ad nauseam*, could already at the beginning of the present century be regarded as a phase of the previous one is shown by Hegel in his *Phänomenologie*. See there the chapter "The Struggle of Enlightenment with Superstition," where the theory of usefulness is depicted as the final result of enlightenment. The apparent absurdity of merging all the manifold relationships of people in the *one* relation of usefulness, this apparently metaphysical abstraction arises from the fact that in modern bourgeois society all relations are subordinated in practice to the one abstract monetary-commercial relation.[27]

In this critique of capital's tendency to flatten distinctions and obscure our perception of things, relationships, and people, Marx echoes earlier remarks, from his 1844 manuscripts, about vision, sense-perception generally, and epistemic access to the external world. In his "Private Property and Labor" manuscript, for example, Marx writes that "private property has made us so stupid and one-sided that an object is only *ours* when we have it—when it exists for us as capital, or when it is directly possessed, eaten, drunken, worn, inhabited, etc.—in short, when it is *used* by us."[28] He goes on:

> Although private property itself again conceives all these direct realisations of possession only as means of life, and the life which they serve as means is the life of private property—labour and conversion into capital.
>
> In the place of *all* physical and mental senses there has therefore come the sheer estrangement of *all* these senses, the sense of *having*. The human being had to be reduced to this absolute poverty in order that he might yield his inner wealth to the outer world....
>
> The abolition of private property is therefore the complete emancipation of all human senses and qualities, but it is this emancipation precisely because these senses and attributes have become, subjectively and objectively, human. The eye has become a human eye, just as its object has become a social, human object—an object made by man for man. The senses have therefore become directly in their practice theoreticians. They relate themselves to the thing for the sake of the thing, but the thing itself is an objective

human relation to itself and to man, and vice versa. Need or enjoyment has consequently lost its egotistical nature, and nature has lost its mere utility by use becoming human use.[29]

It would perhaps be tempting to gloss over Marx's references to organs of sense-perception, were it not for its connection to several themes that permeate his work and, most notably, to what we know about the keen interest Marx took early on in a study of Aristotle's *De Anima*, with its reflections on sense-perception, the nature of the soul, and the relationship between form and matter. As Scott Meikle notes in his book *Essentialism in the Thought of Karl Marx*, "Marx made the first German translation with commentary of *De Anima*," apparently with the initial intent of preparing this translation for publication.[30]

Perhaps the most-discussed passage in *De Anima* has to do with the relationships between form and matter, and between potentiality and actuality, in constituting the activity of sense-perception. Aristotle writes,

> It is necessary to grasp, concerning the whole of perception generally, that perception [*aisthêsis*] is what is capable of receiving perceptible forms without the matter, as wax receives the seal of a signet ring without the iron or gold. It acquires the golden or the metallic seal, but not insofar as it is gold or metal. In a similar way, perception is also in each case affected by what has the colour or taste or sound, but not insofar as each of these is said to be something, but rather insofar as each is of a certain quality, and corresponding to its proportion.
>
> The primary sense organ is that in which this sort of potentiality resides. The sense organ and this potentiality are, then, the same though their being is different.[31]

A long-standing interpretive puzzle about how to understand Aristotle's *De Anima* centers on Aristotle's physiology of sense-perception which has appeared, at least on its face, implausible to numerous of his commentators. In a famous line from the text, Aristotle writes that ensouled beings have a perceptive faculty which is initially unlike the object of perception but that, "on being affected it becomes like what has acted on it."[32] He goes on later in the text to say, "Perception is being affected in a certain way. Thus the active thing makes that which is potentially like it like it in actuality."[33] This view appears to account for sense-perception as a consequence of the organ of perception being affected by the object of perception in a manner that alters the sense-organ, making it like that which it senses so that in some sense, an eye literally *becomes* blue when in the presence of a blue object; it would then be this transformation of the eye from potentially blue, to actually blue, that counts as perceiving blueness with the organ of sight.

This is, needless to say, deeply puzzling. In his lectures on the history of philosophy, Hegel made sense of it in the following way. He argued that it would be mistaken to think simply that the form of "blueness," as an active principle, affects the material eye, which remains passive in the act of perception. Instead, he argued, one ought to think of the sense-organ as becoming like its object in the sense that the seeming separation between them is overcome so that there is not a passive, material subject on the one side and an active, ideal object on the other. Rather, "Sense-perception, as made like to itself, has, while appearing to be brought to pass by means of an influence working on it, brought to pass the identity of itself and its object."[34] Hegel continues:

> After the perceptive faculty has received the impression, it abrogates the passivity, and remains thenceforth free from it. The soul therefore changes the form of the external body into its own, and is identical with an abstract quality such as this, for the sole reason that it itself is this universal form.... Sense-perception is simply the abrogation of this separation [between subject and object], it is that form of identity which abstracts from subjectivity and objectivity.[35]

Our aim here is not to wade into the broader debate about how to understand *De Anima*. What is relevant for us is the relationship suggested in *De Anima*, with which Marx was deeply familiar, between epistemic access to the world and the interactive metaphysical oneness of a perceiving subject with the world as its object. Hegel challenged readings of Aristotle on which sense-perception was a question of active form and passive, inert matter, presenting in their stead a picture on which the activity of form produces activity in matter, so that the sense-organ is "like" its object and the body is "like" its soul in the sense that they are unified in an interactive process—one in which each acts upon, and is acted upon by, the other.

Hegel's dialectical idealist rendering of *De Anima*'s account of sense-perception emphasized the active role of matter, yet gave pride of causal place to form, the *idea*. Marx—never one to leave Hegel standing on his head when he could set him on his feet—incorporated into his own epistemology this notion of a mutual interaction between subject and object that forges an identity between them, rendering the objective, external world truly knowable to the human mind. For Marx, however, the dialectical interaction between mind and world that produces this happy outcome is precipitated not by abstract, universal forms acting upon human senses, themselves in attitudes of what would be initially passive contemplation.[36] Rather, it is an outcome produced by labor—human social activity directed toward satisfying one's needs through material interaction with the world outside oneself. Through this process, we humanize the world *and ourselves*, forging a unity between the two that both makes the world sensible and awakens our senses to the world.

While the few commentators who remark upon Marx's engagements with *De Anima* mostly do so to underscore Marx's neo-Aristotelian essentialism generally, in his "*Poiêsis, Praxis, Aisthêsis*," Henry Pickford gives sustained attention to what we might learn about Marx's views on sense-perception by reading them alongside Aristotle's discussion of sense-perception in *De Anima*. Articulating what he casts as a [Walter] Benjaminian model of Marxist aesthetics, Pickford writes:

> If virtuous action presupposes phronetic perception of the moral salience of a particular situation in its particularity, then virtuous practical-political action too requires such phronetic perception, and this ... model of Marxist *aisthêsis* is intended to cultivate the exercise and improvement of such perceptual capacities.[37]

The suggestion here is that Marx's conception of revolutionary activity is as a practice that transforms and refines the human faculty of perception (*aisthêsis*), allowing the normative dimensions of human social life to be apprehended more immediately and, as a result, responded to both more spontaneously and more appropriately.[38]

Let us return to the passage from "Private Property and Labor" which we addressed earlier. There, Marx writes that to overcome the institution of private property is also to bring about the "emancipation of all human senses." He continues:

> Only through the objectively unfolded richness of man's essential being is the richness of subjective human sensibility (a musical ear, an eye for beauty

of form—in short, senses capable of human gratification, senses affirming themselves as essential powers of man) either cultivated or brought into being. For not only the five senses but also the so-called mental senses, the practical senses (will, love, etc.), in a word, *human* sense, the human nature of the senses, comes to be by virtue of its object, by virtue of *humanised* nature. The forming of the five senses is a labour of the entire history of the world down to the present.... The dealer in minerals sees only the commercial value but not the beauty and the specific character of the mineral: he has no mineralogical sense. Thus, the objectification of the human essence, both in its theoretical and practical aspects, is required to make man's *sense human*, as well as to create the *human sense* corresponding to the entire wealth of human and natural substance.[39]

Marx's interest in ways of seeing, and their implications for our epistemic access to the world as it is, appears in his early writings and persists into his later work. In *Capital*, these themes are central in Marx's presentation of the concept of "commodity fetishism," a phenomenon in which things appear endowed with agency and independence that they do not have. Marx writes,

It is as clear as noon-day, that man, by his industry, changes the forms of the materials furnished by Nature, in such a way as to make them useful to him. The form of wood, for instance, is altered, by making a table out of it. Yet, for all that, the table continues to be that common, every-day thing, wood.[40]

Marx makes rather quick work here of discussing the relationships among form, matter, and function. What he takes to be the interesting problem is not that matter can take this form or that, but rather, that *qua* commodity, the object enters into relationships that are utterly indifferent to the thing as it *is*: indifferent to its form, material, or function. Marx continues,

The products of labour become commodities, social things whose qualities are at the same time perceptible and imperceptible by the senses. In the same way the light from an object is perceived by us not as the subjective excitation of our optic nerve, but as the objective form of something outside the eye itself. But, in the act of seeing, there is at all events, an actual passage of light from one thing to another, from the external object to the eye. There is a physical relation between physical things. But it is different with commodities. There, the existence of the things *qua* commodities, and the value relation between the products of labour which stamps them as commodities, have absolutely no connection with their physical properties and with the material relations arising therefrom.[41]

The infinitely myriad forms in which matter appears—all of the forms in which matter can be *made* to appear through the exercise of human labor—are elided in a single form that predominates in capitalist society and submerges all specificity and difference: the commodity-form. Because the activity of human labor is organized privately as the work of competing individuals or businesses and corporations, only the products of labor seem to interact and to express universality, and then, only when taken to market. Never mind that their universality—expressed as a universal exchangeability indifferent to their specific qualities—is only a kind of shadow of the universality of labor as essential human activity, expressed in definite moments, circumstances, and ways. Marx writes,

> Let us now picture to ourselves, by way of change, a community of free individuals, carrying on their work with the means of production in common, in which the labour power of all the different individuals is consciously applied as the combined labour power of the community . . . The life-process of society, which is based on the process of material production, does not strip off its mystical veil until it is treated as production by freely associated men, and is consciously regulated by them in accordance with a settled plan.[42]

In such a society, human beings would recognize their products as the outcome of their own practical activity; activity which could be regulated, redirected, and organized in conscious collaboration among all the members of society.

There is a temptation, here, that I will warn against. It is particularly seductive for those who approach Marxism from a mainly philosophical or otherwise theoretical angle. Metaphors of seeing, sense, and recognition—while true to Marx's conceptual schema—can easily incline one toward an *idealist* rendering of Marx's approach to morality. Perhaps, one might think, we can "see" right now, today, what specific sorts of action would be called for in a future communist society. If only we can rationally deduce the right communist principle, maybe theory can fit us today with the eyes of tomorrow.

This is, of course, exactly what Marx denies. He concludes the passage above by reminding his reader that the conditions under which society can "strip off its mystical veil" obtain only with the emergence of "a certain material ground-work or set of conditions of existence which in their turn are the spontaneous product of a long and painful process of development."[43] We might be reminded again of Marx's and Engels's earlier insistence that "for the success of the cause itself, the alteration of men on a mass scale is necessary, an alteration which can only take place in a practical movement, a revolution."[44] The only way to "create an appropriate human sense for the whole of the wealth of humanity and of nature" is to overcome the alienation of capitalist production and to successfully, and for the first time, usher in a self-conscious and truly human history. Philosophical problems can be represented abstractly in thought, but they cannot be solved there.

Should we then say that Marx's theory is itself totally without moral content or relevance because it presages a world without appeal to moral principle, as such? No. Such a world is not yet our world. Here, there remains much work to be done in order to do away with the alienation and economic exploitation that stifle human flourishing and solidarity. We cannot "think" ourselves into a form of consciousness that emerges only on the basis of social relations that do not yet exist.

We can, however, align ourselves with working people's struggles for freedom and human survival, today. Workers' struggles to resist and overthrow capitalist domination contain the germ of human emancipation. Thus, from the standpoint of workers under capitalism, morality is not an abstraction separate from class interest.[45] It both exists as an external command for the ruling classes, whose class interest disinclines them to follow it, and is already abolished as an external, alien command for those whose position is such that they cannot free themselves without freeing all of humanity, as well. This is an inner contradiction of capitalist society that can be resolved only once the highest moral imperative for human beings today is achieved: to secure the victory of working people over capital.

Progress and Perfectibility

Morality implies human imperfection. We engage in abstract moral reasoning largely because if we don't, we are more likely than not to get things wrong about how we ought to treat one another. One tradition of moral thought asks us to imagine human beings better than ourselves and to act as they would. Thus, for Aristotle, the figure of the *phronimos* is a practically wise being, one who acts well because they have been well brought up. Immanuel Kant proposes a similar thought experiment as a resource for moral guidance: we ask ourselves, what would we do if we lived in a "Realm of Ends," a condition in which everyone acted according to universal laws that they can will to others as maxims? We imagine creatures better than ourselves and seek to emulate them. But what if we could make ourselves into those better creatures? They do not imagine better selves and seek to emulate those in an infinite regress of moral imagination. They simply act in prosocial ways, as it is in their nature to do. They apprehend the objective world and act appropriately within it. As the early Marx might have put it, and the mature Marx would have agreed, "The senses . . . become theoreticians in their immediate praxis."

What makes Marx's approach importantly distinct is not that he thinks morality has validity only for those conditions in which there is no mutual recognition of one another's humanity and in which the world is not already arranged in a manner conducive to the universal satisfaction of human needs. This, he has in common with other moral theorists before and after him.[46] What makes Marx's view distinct is the claim that such conditions need not be a mere hypothetical dream. They are features of a world that can be achieved.

Marx's perfectionism is perhaps one of the most easily misunderstood aspects of his theory; it is, for example, what leads some to caricature his Hegelianism, suggesting that communism represents a kind of proletarian-inflected "end of history." It's not even clear that the "end of history" implies stasis of the sort often attributed to Hegel. But as far as understanding Marx, such caricatures overlook that far from announcing the end of history, Marx's theory heralds the possibility for a truly human history of conscious, open-ended, creative transformation to begin. This is what is meant when Marx says of bourgeois society, "The prehistory of human society accordingly closes with this social formation."[47] The human nature Marx would see perfected is labor itself—an inherently dynamic and ever-developing process of creation and self-changing.[48] There is no sense in which Marx can be understood as imagining that communism would bring human history to a close.

Critics who wonder whether the kinds of naturalized and habitual forms of prosocial human behavior Marx imagines for communist society could ever take place are quite right to point out that a human being is neither an angel nor a saint, nor could she be. But Marx's theory requires neither that she be nor that she become so. A human being is a natural being who, through socially mediated activity, is capable of intervening into her own nature so that it is her own product. Through the activity of labor, she can practically relate to her nature not as a fixed, given, and alien object but as her own concretized subjectivity. And this is made fully possible only through a process that brings about the social production of the human species as its own object on a grand scale, one with a shared intersubjectivity that creates the possibility of universal and objective consciousness about the natural and social world within which human beings intervene.

Marx holds out the possibility that when human beings alter their society to do away with the exploitation and degradation of human beings, they will also effect an alteration so profound that it will make prosocial forms of human interaction habitual, customary, and natural. If that is so, then it is not quite so puzzling why he would accept the charge that communism abolishes morality.

Such a world would be one in which universal human solidarity would be "no mere phrase" with us, "but a fact of life."[49] This in no way entails an end to obstacles, to divergent opinion, to all suffering, or to negotiation among various and conflicting individual perspectives. It does herald a world of people for whom the injunction to treat their fellow human beings as though they are ends in themselves is no more or less necessary than enjoining one's heart to beat.

10
Conclusion

The way out of the crises produced by capitalism is not backward to a simpler time, and so Marx is to be distinguished from romantic anti-capitalists who recognize only the negative consequences of capitalism. Marx theorizes the ways in which capitalism has *both* produced the conditions in which it is possible to see clearly that the highest aim for human beings is the "greatest possible development" of their "varied aptitudes" *and* made it possible to produce a society in which such a full and free development of human potential would be realized. The first volume of *Capital* features an explanation of capitalism's revolutionary and reactionary aspects in this regard, which is worth citing here in full:

> If, on the one hand, variation of work at present imposes itself after the manner of an overpowering natural law, and with the blindly destructive action of a natural law that meets with resistance at all points, modern industry, on the other hand, through its catastrophes imposes the necessity of recognising, as a fundamental law of production, variation of work, consequently fitness of the labourer for varied work, consequently the greatest possible development of his varied aptitudes. It becomes a question of life and death for society to adapt the mode of production to the normal functioning of this law. Modern industry, indeed, compels society, under penalty of death, to replace the detail-worker of to-day, grappled by life-long repetition of one and the same trivial operation, and thus reduced to the mere fragment of a man, by the fully developed individual, fit for a variety of labours, ready to face any change of production, and to whom the different social functions he performs, are but so many modes of giving free scope to his own natural and acquired powers.[1]

Under capitalism, "variation of work" tends to take the form of, on the one hand, the constant threat workers face of being thrown out of their current employment and forced to scramble for new work, or on the other hand, the drudgery and monotony of performing just one sort of task for the whole of their lives (while innumerable other workers are doing the same with regard to innumerable other tasks), so that labor in the case of each individual person takes on the character of a stultifying narrowness. Yet capitalism also makes human production, on a social scale, ever more varied, more dynamic, and more complex. What remains to be achieved, Marx argues, is for this variation, dynamism, and complexity to be made into features of the lives of individual persons and not merely of the society taken as a whole. This is a transformation that can only be achieved as a result of the revolutionary and modernizing processes of capitalism itself, and through the conscious, rational, and social intervention of human beings into those processes so that they become fully realized as human powers rather than powers over human beings.

At the same time that Marx identifies tendencies within capitalism that tend toward the socialization of production and the development of "rich individuals," he is by no means committed to any fatalism about the realization of socialism or of fully developed communism. Such an achievement will be the work of individuals cooperating consciously and socially to realize and exercise their historical agency. However, it would be wrong to think that because Marx is not a strict determinist, the field is open for voluntarism and moralism, or that whether or not communism will be achieved depends entirely on the presence and number of noble revolutionaries who, *purely* out of some personal sense of virtue and moral law, produce a new society at great cost to themselves. Communism may not be the only possible outcome, but Marx argues that when capitalism's crises become too significant for it to go on as a mode of production, the range of choices becomes strictly delimited. In the words of Rosa Luxemburg, they boil down to "socialism or barbarism" or as Marx puts it here, life or death.

As in his earlier works, here in writings such as those which make up the *Grundrisse* and *Capital*, Marx's conception of human individuals is a central focus in his worldview, along with his conviction that the development of human capacities and of "rich individuality" is the highest aim for human beings. He continues to base his criticisms of capitalism and his arguments for communism on the relative potentials of these two economic systems to allow for the exercise and expansion of human powers. In the *Grundrisse*, Marx writes that if achieved, communism would allow for the

> free development of individualities, and hence not the reduction of necessary labour time in order to posit surplus labour, but in general the reduction of the necessary labour of society to a minimum, to which then

corresponds the artistic, scientific, etc., development of individuals, made possible by the time thus set free and the means produced for all of them.[2]

Marx returns to this theme in the first volume of *Capital*, where he again addresses the way capitalism has developed the potential for individual human development to a historically unprecedented level—a potential that can only be realized with a transition to socialist relations of production:

> The intensity and productiveness of labour being given, the time which society is bound to devote to material production is shorter, and as a consequence, the time at its disposal for the free development, intellectual and social, of the individual is greater, in proportion as the work is more and more evenly divided among all the able-bodied members of society, and as a particular class is more and more deprived of the power to shift the natural burden of labour from its own shoulders to those of another layer of society. In this direction, the shortening of the working day finds at last a limit in the generalisation of labour. In capitalist society spare time is acquired for one class by converting the whole life-time of the masses into labour time.[3]

Capitalism has reduced socially necessary labor time to a minimum, but paradoxically, the more efficiently that reduction is accomplished, the more that dead labor rules over living labor, with stored-up surplus labor strengthening the hand of the capitalist against the worker. And as he writes in the third volume of *Capital*, capitalist production squanders human lives, or living-labour, and not only blood and flesh, but also nerve and brain. Indeed, it is only by dint of the most extravagant waste of individual development that the development of the human race is at all safeguarded and maintained in the epoch of history immediately preceding the conscious reorganisation of society.[4]

And with that "conscious reorganisation of society," Marx argues, the reduction of socially necessary labor would be a source of freedom for human beings. They would have more of their time available to them for pursuits beyond the mere struggle for survival; they would be able to exercise, develop, and expand their powers and develop as "rich individuals."

Marx argues for a transition to a new type of society in which human beings would develop as "rich individuals" who realize themselves in the external world through their conscious activity. Such a transition would, he writes, involve the achievement on the part of human beings of a better and clearer understanding of the relationship between themselves and their products. As Marx emphasizes in the *Grundrisse*, "Nature does not construct machines, locomotives, railways, electric telegraphs, self-acting mules, etc. They are products of human industry; natural material transformed into organs of man's will over Nature, or of man's activity in Nature."[5]

While of course everyone knows that one does not come across a locomotive in nature in just the same way one stumbles upon a frog or a ravine, it is important to fully recognize just how much promise such developments hold out for the immense ability of human beings to shape their natural and social world based on human understanding. Creations such as machines, railways, "self-acting mules" and, we can add, computers, airplanes, mRNA vaccines, and all the rest are, in Marx's words, "organs of the human brain, created by the human hand; the power of knowledge, objectified." He continues:

> The development of fixed capital shows the degree to which society's general science, knowledge, has become an immediate productive force, and hence the degree to which the conditions of the social life process itself have been brought under the control of the general intellect and remoulded according to it.[6]

There is an all-too-common tendency to caricature Marx as a dull mechanist, stubbornly insensible to the importance of ideas. But in examining Marx's views in the way that I have, I am convinced that quite the opposite is true. Marx is extremely clear and forceful about the power of human knowledge, and he is only *more* successful than idealist thinkers on this point because he is not forced to resort to mysticism in order to explain how it is that human beings can realize their ideas in the external world.

Far from themes of freedom, alienation, and individuality taking a back seat to a one-sided and untenable economic determinism in Marx's later works, they become the subject of an even deeper engagement during this period, as does the moral conception that they are a part of. It is here in these later works that Marx most clearly and explicitly theorizes the full development of "rich individuality" as the highest aim for human beings.

What Now?

A quarter of the way through the Twenty-First century, we live in a time of ever-deepening crisis. How do we find our way out? Capitalism does not have

CONCLUSION 243

the answer and it would much rather we didn't ask the question. A better world remains possible—for now—but only if we undertake and succeed at the monumental task of forging ourselves as a species, not only as biological fact but also as self-aware, sociohistorical force. Without this, we are doomed.

In these pages, I have argued for a particular way of interpreting Marx's writings. I have refused to dissect it for parts and insisted instead on situating it within its Hegelian tradition. I have attempted to retain and defend Marx's commitment to understanding all of Being as one dynamic, processual, and thoroughly interrelated whole.

Human self-recognition is species-awareness, but it is also more than that. It is awareness of ourselves as one with nature, with all of existence. It is awareness that our fortune is tied to that of the natural world. This awareness can help guide us toward a relationship with nature not merely as one more resource to exploit but as material existence that is continuous with our own.

Marx writes of labor as a kind of "metabolism" between human bodies and their environments. Understanding our relationship to nature in this way can help us to recognize its future as ours. We would do so neither as "masters" of it, nor in ascetic abstention from its abundance, and still less as lowly supplicants to it. Rather, through the metabolism of labor, we would forge our essential oneness with nature as its own living consciousness.[7]

As Marx famously put it, "The philosophers have only interpreted the world in various ways; the point is to change it."[8] But the rub is that we cannot do one except by also doing the other. This is the core of what it means to do theory from the point of view of labor. How does the world appear as it is changed by human hands? What light does our own collective power of creation cast upon us as we join our hands and set good things into motion? This book, a product of scholarship and struggle, is my contribution to a long-standing and ongoing human project of working out the answers to these questions and acting to change the world accordingly. Here, I leave my reader with these questions in the hope that you too may be moved.

Coda

"The Ruthless Criticism of All that Exists," Yesterday and Today

In mid-summer 1969, University of California Los Angeles had newly appointed the Black American Marxist philosopher, Angela Davis, as Acting Assistant Professor of Philosophy. On September 19, 1969—before Davis had so much as taught her first class—the University of California Board of Regents adopted a resolution calling for her contract to be terminated, in an effort championed by then-Governor of California, Ronald Reagan. The ostensibly fireable offense? Davis's membership in the Communist Party USA.[1]

This firing sparked a battle on multiple fronts: legal, political, and academic. Legally, Davis challenged the Regents' decision in court. She won in a case decided by California Superior Court Judge, Jerry Pacht, who described the arguments made by UCLA's legal counsel as a "terrifying" affront to academic freedom. Pacht cited the Regents' *own* policy that "no political test shall ever be considered in the appointment and promotion of any faculty member or employee," rejecting their claim that the right of political freedom ought to extend to everyone except, of course, Communists.[2] Davis was reappointed.

Academically, the movement to defend Angela Davis had a key lasting effect, with much of its momentum serving to help fuel the creation of Ethnic Studies departments at UCLA and on university campuses nationwide. Two thousand people arrived on the first day of lecture for Davis's first class, "Recurring Philosophical Themes in Black Literature," vividly demonstrating the widespread hunger to learn from and with her.

Politically, the Regents' firing of Davis sparked faculty organizing and student protests that served as a flashpoint of campus activism and struggle. In the months that followed, such political activity included massive anti-war rallies on campus, meetings of the Black Panther Party for Self-Defense, and events to defend the right of free speech. Davis was a frequent, highly sought-after, and highly effective speaker at many of these events.[3] When the Regents moved again in 1970 to dismiss Davis from her post—or rather, technically, when they opted not to reappoint her for another year—they cited her political speech as the basis for their decision. Ironically, they identified Davis and *her* ideas as a threat to academic freedom that had to be eliminated from the university environment. This time, the Regents were successful, and Davis was ousted. (It should be happily noted that later, however, Davis returned to the UC system where she was Professor of the History of Consciousness and of Feminist Studies at UC Santa Cruz, between 1991 and 2008. In a stroke of poetic justice, she also returned to speak at UCLA in 2014, where she was celebrated as a "Regents' Lecturer.")[4]

Angela Davis's is the most widely publicized case of a professional philosopher in the US being targeted for her commitment to Marxist theory and struggle, but she is very far from being the only one. Indeed, the stage for the drama was already set by the so-called California Oath Controversy in 1950, when passage of the Levering Act in the state of California required state employees—including faculty at the University of California—to swear among other things that they were not members of the Communist Party. Among those dismissed from the faculty were Jacob Loewenberg, a Hegel scholar who refused to swear out the oath. Of course, California was hardly alone; Senator Joseph McCarthy's campaign against "subversives" ushered in a period of artistic and intellectual repression that reached into all aspects of American society with predictably chilling effects for philosophy, a discipline that took the critique and subversion of dogma as its *raison d'être*.

The rhetorical strategy was patently sophistical, but devastatingly effective: the capitalist state would have to destroy free speech in order to save it. Communists, they argued, had no place in academia because they were not free inquirers at all, but rote dogmatists. Left to their own devices, the argument went, Communists could not be trusted to educate rather than indoctrinate their students and anyone else who would hear them. The academic enterprise of free inquiry, then, was incompatible with communism and required that any person committed to promoting communism be excised from the academic community.

In this respect, today we hear the loud echoes of yesterday, meant to drown out scholarly inquiry. The challenges that scholars face, which prevent a serious and productive engagement with Marx's ideas, come not only from conflicting theoretical commitments and internecine disputes over method, but also from the exercise of legal, economic, and political power aimed squarely at preventing it. Not only is this the case for thought about Marx, but also, as we see today, for myriad forms of anti-racist and anti-sexist theory, and indeed for all theory that seeks to critique oppressive and exploitative systems and ideologies. In this environment, it remains as important as ever to insist upon recontextualizing, resituating, reevaluating, rethinking, and yes, even *thinking* Marxism and other radical theories. My aim in this book has been to do just that: to contribute to the scholarly understanding of these ideas, to resist their misrepresentation and caricature, to stand in a tradition with those authors who have been doing this necessary work, and to inspire others to take up this urgent task, as well.

Notes

Chapter 1

1. For more about the 2008 collapse of the Lehman Brothers investment bank, see Mahmoud Mofid Abdul Karim's 2021 "Failure of Lehman Brothers."
2. A survey of periodicals over the past decade paints a picture of renewed mainstream engagement with Marxism. For example, in 2012, *The Guardian* published "Why Marxism Is On the Rise Again." In 2017, *The Atlantic* sought to explain "Why the Phrase 'Late Capitalism' is Suddenly Everywhere." And in 2018, *The Economist* exhorted, "Rulers of the World: Read Karl Marx!"
3. Fukuyama, *The End of History and the Last Man*. Interestingly, in his 2018 book *Identity*, Fukuyama argues that identity politics and their demands for respect and recognition have delayed the end of history a while longer.
4. The "gadfly" metaphor comes from Plato's *Apology*. Charged with corrupting the youth of Athens, Plato explains, "And now, Athenians, I am not going to argue for my own sake, as you may think, but for yours, that you may not sin against the God, or lightly reject his boon by condemning me. For if you kill me you will not easily find another like me, who, if I may use such a ludicrous figure of speech, am a sort of gadfly, given to the state by the God; and the state is like a great and noble steed who is tardy in his motions owing to his very size, and requires to be stirred into life. I am that gadfly which God has given the state and all day long and in all places am always fastening upon you, arousing and persuading and reproaching you. And as you will not easily find another like me, I would advise you to spare me." See also my 2016, "Philosophy as a Virtuous Irritation."
5. This is Charles Mills's challenge to ideal theory in Rawls and others. In his 2009 article "'Ideal Theory' as Ideology," Mills writes, "what distinguishes ideal theory is not merely the use of ideals, since obviously nonideal theory can and will use ideals also (certainly it will appeal to the moral ideals, if it may be more dubious about the value of invoking idealized human capacities). What distinguishes ideal theory is the reliance on idealization to the exclusion, or at least marginalization, of the actual."
6. I use the terms "ethics" and "morality" interchangeably throughout this book, and neither in an inherently pejorative manner. I do this for two closely related reasons. The first is that English-speakers, and even English-speaking philosophers, are in no widespread agreement at all about how these two terms ought to be disambiguated from one another or even if they should be. I find it preferable neither to assume nor imply any stable linguistic distinction between their meanings and instead to spell out any further necessary conceptual clarifications as they are needed. Secondly, Marx himself used an array of German terms interchangeably throughout his writing. In

The Communist Manifesto, "die Moral" seems to apply to the same thing he elsewhere calls "Sittlichkeit" in the course of his attacks on Max Stirner. He used "Moralität" similarly. Marx occasionally used "Ethik," a word drawn from Greek, to refer to the work of ancient Greek philosophers such as Epicurus and Diogenes, but did not do so in a way that suggested he meant to sharply distinguish it from die Moral. This being said, where I use the term "moralism" or variants thereof, I always mean to speak of the kind of sanctimonious imperatives that Marx abhors. "Moralism," for example, would apply to the cynical use of apparently moral language, directed at others, to produce in them a commitment to ethical ideals which come at a cost to them and some benefit to the speaker. It would also apply to attempts to change society purely through moral appeal.

7. Marx and Engels, *The German Ideology* in *Marx/Engels Collected Works* (hereafter, "MECW") 5:247.
8. Marx, "Wage Labour and Capital," MECW 9:197. Marx, *Capital*, MECW 35:306.
9. Jack Amariglio and Yahya M. Madra capture the situation well when they write, "Karl Marx is an unusual figure in the history of ethical and economic thought. Perhaps few such internationally influential thinkers have been so (apparently) contradictorily understood. He is variously interpreted as being a trenchant moral critic of the exploitation and alienation of the existing industrial capitalist social order (Buchanan, 1982; Geras 1985, 1992); an amoral historicist who relegated ethics to the realm of 'false consciousness'; a broadly conceived moralist who rejected 'the moral point of view' (Miller, 1984); a moral relativist who regarded ethical norms as incommensurable, culturally/locationally specific, and constantly changing along with transformations in concrete economic conditions; an ethical visionary who proposed one of the more enduring conceptions of economic and distributive justice over the past two centuries (DiQuattro, 1998); a strict economic determinist, who assigned to ethics a not-so-privileged place in the 'superstructure' of politics, law, religion, and ideology; a pre-Nietzschean nihilist, who saw 'values' as a blind for humans living fully (Ruccio and Amariglio, 2003); a one-sided ethical partisan, who reserved for the working classes an objective position within morality worth its historical weight; a transcendental humanist who believed that shared, communal ethical standards would triumph over the course of humanity's long haul (Kain, 1988); and much else besides." (Amariglio and Madra, "Karl Marx," in *Handbook of Economics and Ethics*, 325.)
10. As Ricardo Brown puts the point in his 1999 article "Marx and the Foundations of the Critical Theory of Morality and Ethics," Marx's early writings "should be seen as moments in Marx's overcoming and exposing of bourgeois morality . . . the results of this critique are to be found within a later work like the *Grundrisse*." Paul Blackledge has made a similar argument in his 2012 book *Marxism and Ethics*, as does Norman Geras in his 1983 book *Marx and Human Nature*, and as do others.
11. Marx, *Grundrisse*, MECW 15:251.
12. Terell Carver describes some of the history of the production of *The Critique of the German Ideology* as a single text in his 2010 article "*The German Ideology* Never Took Place."
13. Goldstick, "Marx, Marxism, Ethics," 95.

14. The capitalist state's outright hostility to communal ways of being is evidenced in the United States' destructive patterns of behavior toward Native cultures and communities. We see this, for example, in the Dawes Act of 1887, which privatized previously communally held Native lands and enjoined Native people to adopt "the habits of civilized life," which is to say, of life based on the principle of private property. See Emily Greenwald's 2002, *Reconfiguring the Reservation*.
15. Paul Blackledge's 2010 essay "Marxism, Nihilism, and the Problem of Ethical Politics Today" offers an illuminating discussion of the nihilist reading's career among interpreters of Marx such as Alasdair Macintyre and Simon Critchley. The question of Marxism's purported nihilism is also taken up in David B. Myers's 1976 essay "Marx and the Problem of Nihilism." Myers rightly concludes, "Far from opening the door to the "everything is permissible" dictum, Marx's criteria were in fact restrictive. What happens in history is good (i.e., human) (1) only if it involves the "self-liberation" of a hitherto oppressed class and (2) only if this class creates a classless society in which no one is allowed to develop his personality and satisfy his material needs in such a way as to prevent the human development of other individuals" (203–204).
16. Marx, *Contribution to the Critique of Hegel's Philosophy of Right*, MECW 3:186.
17. Marx and Engels, *Critique of the German Ideology*, MECW 5:28.
18. As William Briggs aptly puts it in his 2019 book *Classical Marxism in an Age of Capitalist Crisis*, "Marxist critiques flourish, not only of capitalism but of other Marxist theories. . . . Perversely there is one thing that unites a great many of these writers and theorists. It is the view that classical Marxism, while representing an important place in history, is pretty much a museum-piece" (12).
19. For more on the relationship between analytical philosophy and British Idealism, see W. J. Mander's *British Idealism*, Peter Hacker's "The Linguistic Turn in Analytic Philosophy," and Nicholas Griffin's "Russell and Moore's Revolt against British Idealism."
20. In his 1995 book *Self-Ownership, Freedom, and Equality*, Cohen himself allowed that it was probably more accurate to think of this school of thought as made up of "semi-Marxists" (144). The question is raised also in Michael Lebowitz's 1988 essay "Is 'Analytical Marxism' Marxism?," in Marcus Roberts's 1997 book *Analytical Marxism: A Critique*, and in Paul Blackledge's 2015 essay "G. A. Cohen and the Limits of Analytical Marxism."
21. Shelby, "Afro-Analytical Marxism and the Problem of Race."
22. Marx, "Theses on Feuerbach," MECW 5:3.
23. Marx and Engels, *Critique of the German Ideology*," MECW 5:49.
24. Engels, *Anti-Dühring*, MECW 25: 270–271. Here, Engels partially echoed Proudhon's coinage of the phrase, "scientific socialism" in the following passage from *What is Property?*: "In a given society the authority of man over man is universally proportional to the intellectual development which that society has reached, and the probable duration of that authority can be calculated from the more or less general desire for a true government, that is, for a government based on science. And just as the right of force and the right of stratagem retreat before the growing awareness of justice and must finally be extinguished in equality, so the sovereignty of the will gives

way to the sovereignty of the reason and ends up being replaced by a scientific socialism. Property and royalty have been crumbling ever since the beginning of the world" (Proudhon, *What is Property?*, 208–209).
25. Althusser, *For Marx*.
26. Wood, *Karl Marx*.
27. Bricmont, *Humanitarian Imperialism*; Mills, *The Racial Contract*; Pateman, *The Sexual Contract*.
28. The world's ruling classes' response to the COVID-19 pandemic is a case in point. Very few governments took the rational course of action to immediately initiate funded lockdowns during which people would have their basic material needs met so they could stay home and not spread the illness. The United States' ruling class continues to oppose universal healthcare—even in the midst of a global pandemic. Yet the pandemic also showed the capacity of governments and pharmaceutical companies to coordinate rapid development of safe, effective vaccines. It's worth noting that even so, science illiteracy among much of the general public after decades of miseducation and undereducation threatens to undermine the whole endeavor.
29. The continuing relevance of Marxist theory in our time is due to the fact that nearly 200 years later, we remain trapped in Marx's time and it is capitalism that keeps us there. As Terry Eagleton notes in his book *Why Marx Was Right*, "The final limit on capitalism, Marx once commented, is capital itself, the constant reproduction of which is a frontier beyond which it cannot stray. There is thus something curiously static and repetitive about this most dynamic of all historical regimes. The fact that its underlying logic remains pretty constant is one reason why the Marxist critique of it remains largely valid. Only if the system were genuinely able to break beyond its own bounds, inaugurating something unimaginably new, would this cease to be the case. But capitalism is incapable of inventing a future which does not ritually reproduce its present" (10).
30. Rodriguez, "Texas' Lieutenant Governor Suggests Grandparents Are Willing to Die for US Economy."

Chapter 2

1. Marx and Engels, *Critique of the German Ideology*, MECW 5: 36–37.
2. Marx, *Preface to A Contribution to the Critique of Political Economy*, MECW 29:263.
3. Marx, *Preface to A Contribution to the Critique of Political Economy*, MECW 29:263.
4. Lukács, History and Class Consciousness, 66.
5. Marx and Engels, *Manifesto of the Communist Party*, MECW 6:487.
6. Marx and Engels, *Manifesto of the Communist Party*, MECW 6:487.
7. Georg Lukács described this trajectory in nineteenth- and early twentieth-century German thought in his book *Destruction of Reason*, warning there that any land "with an imperialist economy, or any other bourgeois culture which is overshadowed by irrationalism" is at risk of being "taken over tomorrow by a fascist maniac compared to whom Hitler himself may have been only a clumsy novice" (91).

8. It is a useful exercise to consider how well or poorly the deism of the United States' "founding fathers" would have squared with the 1950s Red Scare's particular uses of religiosity as a bulwark against communism. Not incidentally, the addition of the words "under God" to the Pledge of Allegiance was championed by a minister, George M. Docherty, who believed that US patriotism should be more closely patterned on the United Kingdom's lingering feudalism. "I came from Scotland, where we said 'God save our gracious queen,' 'God save our gracious king,'" Docherty recalled in a 2004 interview. President Dwight Eisenhower approved the addition of these words to the pledge in 1954, at the height of the Red Scare (Siegel, "The Gripping Sermon That Got 'Under God' Added to the Pledge of Allegiance on Flag Day").
9. Marx and Engels, *Manifesto of the Communist Party*, MECW 6:503.
10. Marx, *The Poverty of Philosophy*, MECW 6: 165–166.
11. Marx and Engels, *Manifesto of the Communist Party*, MECW 6:501.
12. Marx, *Poverty of Philosophy*, MECW 6:166. Also, a note from the MECW: "Marx quotes these words from the following passage of Lucretius's poem *On The Nature of Things* (Book III, line 869): '*mortalem vitam mors cum immortalis ademit*' ('when mortal life has been taken away by immortal death')."
13. Marx and Engels, *Manifesto of the Communist Party*, MECW 6:503.
14. Marx, *Manifesto of the Communist Party*, MECW 6:494
15. Marx and Engels, *Manifesto of the Communist Party*, MECW 6:494.
16. In his 2003 essay "'Ideology' in Marx and Engels," Mills asserts that it is really "grasping at straws" to appeal to this passage as evidence of the contested character of ideology. "Obviously," Mills writes, "Marx and Engels' implication is that these individuals' being 'bourgeois ideologists' has been an *obstacle* to such comprehension, which is precisely why 'raising themselves' has been necessary" (25). But here, Mills conspicuously omits the section of this passage in which Marx *credits* bourgeois ideologists with contributing "fresh elements of enlightenment and progress" to the workers' movement. This statement is hardly ambiguous in its warm approval. Any plausibility that the "straw" insult might have had does not survive payment of attention to the remainder of Marx's sentence. While it is perfectly correct that these individuals had to "raise themselves" beyond bourgeois ideology, the internally contradictory nature of bourgeois consciousness itself, particularly of its liberal variants, does help prepare the ground for that leap.
17. Marx, *Preface to A Contribution to the Critique of Political Economy*, MECW 29:263.
18. Kai Nielsen, in his 1989 book *Marxism and the Moral Point of View*, observes correctly, I think, that morality "works to get people to accept the established order or, where it is a revolutionary ideology, to accept a new postulated revolutionary social order. It typically serves ruling class interests although sometimes it can also be an ideological weapon of a rising class in its struggle with the dominant class" (109).
19. Marx and Engels, *Manifesto of the Communist Party*, MECW 6:503.
20. Marx and Engels, *Manifesto of the Communist Party*, MECW 6:504.
21. Marx and Engels, *Manifesto of the Communist Party*, MECW 6:504.
22. Marx and Engels, *Manifesto of the Communist Party*, MECW 6:506.
23. Marx and Engels, *Manifesto of the Communist Party*, MECW 6:504–505.

24. Marx and Engels, *Manifesto of the Communist Party*, 6:505.
25. Marx, "Critique of the Gotha Programme," *MECW* 24:95. In his 2019 book *Marx on Emancipation and Socialist Goals*, Robert Ware explains, "Marx thoroughly embraced democracy . . . it is necessary to overcome strong ideological resistance to even thinking that Marx would contemplate democracy of any form in an ideal, or even good, society. . . . [A] misconception arises from an especially troubling bit of text from Marx (and Engels), a phrase that has been the brunt of attack but also the source of ideal models, that of the dictatorship of the proletariat. . . . Very simply, Marx's point was that the proletariat needs to form a democratic republic, through universal suffrage, in which the proletariat would rule politically, replacing the bourgeois dictatorship (or rule) by a dictatorship (or rule) of the proletariat" (161–162).
26. Althusser, "Ideology and Ideological State Apparatuses," 108.
27. Althusser, "Ideology and Ideological State Apparatuses," 183.
28. Consider for example Marx's rejoinder to Feuerbach that "the nature that preceded human history, is not by any means the nature in which Feuerbach lives, it is nature which today no longer exists anywhere (except perhaps on a few Australian coral-islands of recent origin) and which, therefore, does not exist for Feuerbach" (Marx, *Critique of the German Ideology*, MECW 5:40). On Marx's view, nothing, whether ideal or material, that exists for human beings exists independently of human history.
29. Althusser, "Ideology and Ideological State Apparatuses," 257.
30. Marx and Engels, *Critique of the German Ideology*, MECW 5:36–37.
31. Marx, *Critique of Hegel's Philosophy of Right*, MECW 3:182.
32. Marx and Engels, *Critique of the German Ideology*, MECW 5:37.
33. Marx and Engels, *Critique of the German Ideology*, MECW 5:37.
34. Abercrombie and Turner, "The Dominant Ideology Thesis," 151.
35. Mills, "Marxism, 'Ideology,' and Moral Objectivism," 378.
36. Mills, "Marxism, 'Ideology,' and Moral Objectivism," 393.
37. Marx and Engels, *The Critique of the German Ideology*, MECW 5:36. Emphasis mine.
38. In his 2011 essay "Karl Marx: Critique as Emancipatory Practice," Robin Celikates presents an analysis of Marx's critique of religion, and of Marx's critique of Young Hegelian critics of religion, that illuminates this point very clearly. Celikates writes, "Marx understands religion as a symptom of real social and political conflicts rather than as a mere delusion or an error for which the believers could be blamed . . . The critique of religion cannot be merely cognitive, for just appealing to the subjects' consciousness will not change the underlying reality" (110). What holds true here for religious ideology is the case for other forms, as well. If there is any lesson we are supposed to draw from Marx's critique of ideology, it is that mystification is a *sociopolitical* problem in the material structuring of our lives—it is not a philosophical puzzle to be dissolved through recognition.
39. Mills, "'Ideology' in Marx and Engels," 15.
40. One might imagine that a consequence of this is that the abolition of ideology implies, implausibly, the abolition of superstructure altogether. But of course this is not the case. It does, however, imply the abolition of the *ideological characteristics* of the superstructure in class society.

41. McCarney writes in his 1980 book *The Real World of Ideology*, "Now the general definition implicit in Marx's practice is that forms of consciousness are ideological if, and only if, they serve class interests" (8).
42. Marx, *A Contribution to the Critique of Political Economy*, MECW 29:263.
43. Mills, "'Ideology' in Marx and Engels: Revised and Revisited," 29.
44. Marx, *Theses on Feuerbach*, MECW 5:3.
45. In *History and Class Consciousness*, Georg Lukács writes, "The class consciousness of the bourgeoisie may well be able to reflect all the problems of organisation entailed by its hegemony and by the capitalist transformation and penetration of total production. But it becomes obscured as soon as it is called upon to face problems that remain within its jurisdiction but which point beyond the limits of capitalism" (54).
46. Wills, "PPE in Marx's Materialist Conception of History," 50.
47. It is worth noting that in accordance with such an approach, and having dismissed Marx's account of how ideological forms of thought arise as a necessary consequence of alienating, particularizing, and mystifying material conditions, Cohen substituted an idealist, psychologistic, and ahistorical explanation for the persistence of ideological forms of thought. "The disposition to generate ideology," Cohen wrote in his 1981 essay "Freedom, Justice, and Capitalism," "and the disposition to consume it, are fundamental traits of human nature." I will leave it to the reader to judge whether a richer methodology is in evidence here.
48. In a 2001 interview, Erik Olin Wright recalls, "I attended what came to be called the Analytical Marxism group (or more self-mockingly: the NBSMG, 'no-Bullshit Marxism Group'). This is a circle of ten or so scholars from several countries who have met once a year since 1979, originally in London and now in New York, to discuss work broadly relevant to radical egalitarian politics and social theory" (Kirby, "An Interview with Erik Olin Wright," 4).
49. Furner, *Marx on Capitalism*, 484–485.
50. This is the view that R. G. Peffer puts forward in his 1990 book *Marxism, Morality, and Social Justice*. In *Marx and Ethics*, Philip J. Kain argues, against Althusser, that Marx continues to be a humanist after *The German Ideology*, but defends his view by contending that he does "not think that humanism is ideological" (6). But I do not think that Marx espouses what would be a premature abolition of ideology, and I do not think that in order to show that an idea or system of ideas is progressive, one must first establish that it is nonideological.
51. Marx, *Manifesto of the Communist Party*, MECW 6:495.
52. As Charles Mills writes, "The recurrent theme in Marx and Engels's writings is . . . the 'impotence' of morality, the causal inefficaciousness of moral preaching" (Mills, "Marxism, 'Ideology' and Moral Objectivism," 389).
53. Cornu, "German Utopianism: 'True' Socialism," 97.
54. Marx and Engels, *The Communist Manifesto*, MECW 6:515.
55. In addition to their critique of Semmig, Marx and Engels also criticize Karl Grün on the grounds that Grün thinks all that is needed to transform human society is for consumers to be educated so as to consume in a "human" way (*The German Ideology*, MECW 5:518). Marx and Engels argue that this "moral postulate of *human*

consumption" is insufficient as it does not address the "real conditions of production" and the "productive activity of men." While there are numerous ways in which consumption takes on a distorted character in capitalist society, the idea that society can be transformed through simply lecturing people to consume less is thoroughly implausible. Furthermore, while consumption can be transformed, there is no need to limit overall human consumption because, Marx and Engels argue, production can be improved and revolutionized further so that higher, not lower, levels of consumption are possible and usual. This, they argue, would be possible in a different economic system that was consciously aimed at the satisfaction of human beings. The development and expansion of industry has played an enormously progressive role in human history and brought into existence innovations in production that make it possible for the first time in human history to produce enough for all human beings. The problem is not, at least not primarily or fundamentally, that human beings consume "inhumanly," but rather, that production is carried out in a wasteful manner and is not itself carried out with the satisfaction of human needs as its organizing principle. Marx and Engels add, "those economists who took consumption as their starting-point happened to be reactionary and ignored the revolutionary element in competition and large-scale industry" (*The German Ideology*, MECW 5:519).
56. Marx and Engels, *The German Ideology*, MECW 5:465.
57. Marx and Engels, "True Socialism" in *The Critique of the German Ideology*, MECW 5:478.
58. Marx and Engels, "True Socialism" in *The Critique of the German Ideology*, MECW 5:462.
59. Marx and Engels, *The Communist Manifesto*, MECW 6:514.
60. Paden, "Marx's Critique of the Utopian Socialists," 75.
61. Marx and Engels, *The German Ideology*, MECW 5:213.

Chapter 3

1. As it happens, whether or not this was Hume's intention is itself a matter of some philosophical debate. Daniel Singer, in his 2015 essay "Mind the Is–Ought Gap," argues that it is misleading to sum Hume's principle up as "no ought from an is." Alasdair Macintyre, in his 1959 essay "Hume on 'Is' and 'Ought,'" argues that to take "Hume to be asserting here that no set of nonmoral premises can entail a moral conclusion . . . is inadequate and misleading" (452). Indeed, MacIntyre takes Hume's moral theory to crucially depend on a central purported fact: that human beings have common interests. And MacIntyre takes Marx's theoretical move vis-à-vis Humean ethics to be the denial of that supposed fact and the insistence that human beings in class society do not have common interests; this denial is one MacIntyre himself endorses, arguing in his 1981 book *After Virtue* that "What Hume identifies as the standpoint of universal human nature turns out in fact to be that of the prejudices of the Hanoverian ruling elite" (231). But a precise accounting of how we ought to understand Hume's

views on the relation between "is" and "ought" is outside of the scope of this book and, in the end, not central to the point I wish to make here about Marx, which is that Marx's approach to ethics must be contrasted with what many moral philosophers take to be a cardinal rule of normative theory, one learned from Hume.

2. Hegel, *The Science of Logic*, 418.
3. For an in-depth discussion of the impact of Hegel's *Science of Logic* on Marx's dialectical method in works such as his *Grundrisse*, see Mark Meaney's 2013 *Capital as Organic Unity: the Role of Hegel's* Science of Logic *in Marx's* Grundrisse. Meaney's careful analysis of the two works' structures is itself anticipated by V. I. Lenin's observations in the course of his study of Hegel. Lenin concluded in his essay "Conspectus of Hegel's *Science of Logic*": "It is impossible completely to understand Marx's *Capital*, and especially its first chapter, without having thoroughly studied and understood the whole of Hegel's *Logic*. Consequently, half a century later none of the Marxists understood Marx!!"
4. As Robin Celikates notes in his 2011 essay "Karl Marx: Critique as Emancipatory Practice," for Marx, human nature "is subject to social conditions and historical changes, and in the final analysis has to be understood as the object of humanity's self-creation through labour" (104).
5. Marx, "Theses on Feuerbach," MECW 5:4.
6. Marx, "Theses on Feuerbach," MECW 5:4.
7. Blackledge, *Marxism and Ethics*, 3.
8. For a very interesting and useful further treatment of the similarities between Marx's moral naturalism and that of Aristotle, as well as of the important differences between them, see McCarthy, "German Social Ethics and the Return to Greek Philosophy: Marx and Aristotle."
9. In *The Critique of the German Ideology*, Marx writes:

> The production of life, both of one's own in labour and of fresh life in procreation, now appears as a double relationship: on the one hand as a natural, on the other as a social relationship. By social we understand the co-operation of several individuals, no matter under what conditions, in what manner and to what end. It follows from this that a certain mode of production, or industrial stage, is always combined with a certain mode of co-operation, or social stage, and this mode of co-operation is itself a "productive force." Further, that the multitude of productive forces accessible to men determines the nature of society, hence, that the "history of humanity" must always be studied and treated in relation to the history of industry and exchange. (*The German Ideology*, MECW 5:43)

10. Lukács, *The Ontology of Social Being* Vol. 2, 7.
11. Marx and Engels, *The German Ideology*, MECW 5:31. Emphasis in the original.
12. In his book *Marx's Concept of Man*, Erich Fromm summarizes the role of labor in the following apt terms: "Labor is the factor which mediates between man and nature; labor is man's effort to regulate his metabolism with nature. Labor is the expression of human life and through labor man's relationship to nature is changed, hence through labor man changes himself" (13).
13. Marx, *Capital*, MECW 35:188.

14. As James Furner puts this point in his 2015 essay "Marx with Kant on Exploitation," "As humans are aware of themselves as members of a kind, they interpret the exercise of their potentialities in light of a conception of the potentialities of the human species as an interdependent whole" (36).
15. Marx, "Estranged Labour," MECW 3:276. Emphasis mine.
16. For a book-length treatment of the concept of human nature in Marx's thought, see Sean Sayers, *Marxism and Human Nature*. Of possible further interest is Terry Eagleton's reply to Sayers's book, "Self-Realization, Ethics and Socialism," *New Left Review* 237, no. 1 (1999). Eagleton argues against Sayers that it is unsatisfactory to suggest that human nature is the totality of human activity. However, Marx does make an abstraction, the labor process, out of this concrete totality of appearances, as I argue here.
17. Marx, *Capital*, MECW 35:187.
18. In his 2019 book *Prolegomena to Any Future Materialism (Volume Two)*, Adrian Johnston writes, "A certain conception of the activity of labor obviously lies at the rock-bottom basis of the historical materialism of Marx throughout his intellectual itinerary. According to a materialist rendition of the dialectical interactions between subject and object, laboring praxis is the catalytic source of the immanent genesis of denaturalized history out of nature itself, the very origin of history as history proper. Put differently, human subjectivity, as fully an inner part of the physical universe, sets in motion trajectories of transformation by working upon and over its environments of surrounding objects (at first naturally given things, but, soon after these trajectories are launched, an additional teeming plethora, an ever-increasing swarm, of fabricated entities). In this internal torsion of a lone, Otherless nature that, as Hegel would put it, is not only substance but also subject, a single plane of material being comes self-reflexively to alter itself by giving rise to laboring subjects working in, on, and through material objects (themselves included)" (93).
19. In a 2002 paper, Ruth Abbey argues that Daniel Brudney is not sufficiently thorough in his presentation of Marx's conception of human nature. Abbey writes: "Brudney acknowledges that Marx had a conception of human essence: 'Marx's thought is that human beings are most essentially creatures who interact with the material world'. Brudney sees Marx as 'claiming that an obvious fact—that we transform the material world—reveals what is essential to our nature.' These tenets are correct, but do not go far enough. The significant omission lies in Marx's concern with how people work and transform their world. Because animals also interact with and transform the material world to ensure survival, Brudney's depiction of what is essential to humans does not capture their species distinction" (151–152).
20. According to Nasser, the *ergon* argument, found initially in Aristotle, "presupposes the following three claims: 1) that it makes sense, and is correct, to say that nature endows man qua man with a special function to perform, 2) that this function can be ascertained by determining the kind of activity that distinguishes *homo sapiens* (or, in Marx's case, as we shall see, *homo faber*) from every other species, and 3) that such activity is (the moral) *good* for man" ("Marx's Ethical Anthropology," 486).
21. Here Nasser quotes Donald C. Hodges, "Marx's Ethics and Ethical Theory," 231.

22. It will be seen that this reading of Marx puts me into stark disagreement with Allen Wood, who writes in his 1972 essay "Marx's Critical Anthropology" that "Marx seems ... to acknowledge no concept of man which could serve as a standard against which his present existence could be measured and criticized" (124).
23. Marx and Engels, *Critique of the German Ideology*, MECW 5:36.
24. The method I describe here is not explicitly laid out by Marx in the way that I have spelled it out. However, one instance in which Marx clearly applies this method is in *The German Ideology*. Marx writes that "the first premise of all human history is, of course, the existence of living human individuals" (MECW 5:31). He then goes on to a series of concrete determinations: how human beings produce to maintain their existence, and how they relate to nature, their division of labor, the emergence of exchange, the development of nations and the productive forces of those nations, and so on.
25. Marx and Engels, *The German Ideology*, MECW 5:37.
26. Marx, *Critique of Hegel's Philosophy of Right*, MECW 3:182.
27. Eagleton, *Why Marx Was Right*, 157–158.
28. Marx, "1842 Letter to Arnold Ruge," MECW 1:395.
29. Wills, "Marx," 49.
30. Marx, *Critique of the German Ideology*, MECW 5:40.
31. Heller, *The Theory of Need in Marx*, 25.
32. In his 1988 book *Marx and Ethics*, Philip Kain writes, "For Marx the human essence develops. Marx's concept of need is an important tool for understanding this development. New needs arise and are transformed in the context of evolving social conditions and relations. Moreover, new needs set the individual specific tasks and thus require transformation of the world if the need is to be satisfied. By following and understanding the reciprocal transformation of needs and of the world we can chart the development of the human essence" (25).
33. Chitty, "The Early Marx on Needs," 26.
34. The passage continues, and it is worth quoting at some length:

> The second point is that the satisfaction of the first need (the action of satisfying, and the instrument of satisfaction which has been acquired) leads to new needs; and this production of new needs is the first historical act....
>
> The third circumstance which, from the very outset, enters into historical development, is that men, who daily remake their own life, begin to make other men, to propagate their kind: the relation between man and woman, parents and children, the family. The family, which to begin with is the only social relationship, becomes later, when increased needs create new social relations and the increased population new needs, a subordinate one (except in Germany), and must then be treated and analysed according to the existing empirical data, not according to "the concept of the family," as is the custom in Germany. These three aspects of social activity are not of course to be taken as three different stages, but just as three aspects or, to make it clear to the Germans, three "moments," which have existed simultaneously since the dawn of history and the first men, and which still assert themselves in history today. (*The Critique of the German Ideology*, MECW 5:42)

258 NOTES

35. Marx, "Human Requirements and the Division of Labour," MECW 3:313.
36. Eagleton, *Why Marx Was Right*, 124.
37. Marx, *Human Requirements and the Division of Labour*, MECW 3:306.
38. Marx, *Human Requirements and the Division of Labour*, MECW 3:308.
39. Lukács writes, "the unfolding of human abilities and needs forms the objective foundation for all value, and for its objectivity . . . If any value whatsoever is investigated for its ultimate ontological foundation, then we unfailingly come up against the development of human abilities as the orientation governing it, as its adequate object, and this as the product of human activity itself" (*The Ontology of Social Being*, 80).
40. Marx, *Critique of Political Economy*, MECW 29:264.
41. For an interesting treatment of the concept of "rich individuality" in Marx, see Lebowitz, *The Socialist Alternative*.
42. Marx, *Grundrisse*, MECW 15:251.
43. *Der Mensch ist ein Thier, das nur in der Gesellschaft sich vereinzeln kann* (English: MECW 28:18, German MEW 13:616).
44. Marx writes, "Man becomes individualized only through the process of history. Originally he is a *species being*, a *tribal being*, a *herd animal*—though by no means a zoon politikon in the political sense. Exchange itself is a major agent of this individuation. It makes herd-like existence superfluous and dissolves it" (*Grundrisse*, MECW 15:420).
45. Fromm, *Marx's Concept of Man*, 2.
46. Estlund, "Human Nature and the Limits (If Any) of Political Philosophy," 208.
47. Marx and Engels, *Critique of the German Ideology*, MECW 5:52.

Chapter 4

1. There have been attempts to conceptualize alienation while rejecting the concept of human nature, with one of the most notable recent examples at this being Rahel Jaeggi's 2014 *Alienation*. As Frederick Neuhouser contends in an introduction to that work, the alienation concept must be "resurrected" because "traditional conceptions of alienation generally depend on substantive, essentialist pictures of human nature—accounts of 'the human essence'—that are no longer compelling" (xi). Jaeggi herself argues that "overcoming alienation does not mean returning to an undifferentiated state of oneness with oneself and the world," a tenet which she invokes to overcome what she takes to be two otherwise insuperable problems for the concept of alienation: "on the one hand, its essentialism and its perfectionist orientation around a conception of the essence or nature of human beings . . .; on the other hand, the ideal of reconciliation—the ideal of a unity free of tension—that seems to be bound up with alienation critique when it takes the form of social theory or of a theory of identity" (2).

   Yet Marxism is not committed to asserting the desirability of any "undifferentiated state of oneness with oneself and the world"—it is precisely the actively differentiating

role of history, in allowing for the proliferation of an ever-expanding array of new forms of social Being, that lies at the heart of a Marxist account of what it is to abolish our alienation from the productive powers which make such expansion and differentiation possible. For this reason and others, my treatment of the alienation concept is motivated by a commitment much like that which Chris Byron expresses in his 2016 article "Essence and Alienation," where he writes, "human nature is a *necessary* condition for demonstrating that alienation does occur in capitalist society, and presumably any other society that suppresses the better parts of species-being" (376).
2. And yet at the same time, Rainer Forst is exactly right to remind us that "the theme of *Entfremdung* in Marx must never be reduced to an ethical issue of being 'truly' and authentically oneself, as it first and foremost addresses relations of *Knechtung*, that is, of social domination in the form of economic exploitation and general political and legal oppression" (Forst, "Noumenal Alienation," 541).
3. In *Marxism and Ethics*, Paul Blackledge notes the relationship between alienation and the division of labor when he writes, "The necessary (social) aspect of the division of labour acts both as the material basis from our present (capitalist) alienation from the product of our labours, and the alternative potential that we might exercise real democratic control over society" (58).
4. Althusser, *For Marx*, 84.
5. For a detailed, book-length treatment of the continuity in Marx's concept of alienation, see Istvan Mészáros's, *Marx's Theory of Alienation*. Also, in Lawrence Wilde's 1998 book on Marxism and morality, Wilde argues that in *The German Ideology*, Marx "affirms his adherence to his earlier position in which communism was conceived as a struggle for the appropriation of the human essence" (Wilde, *Ethical Marxism and Its Radical Critics*, 22).
6. King, "King: Minimum Wage Increase Will Hurt Small Business."
7. Marx, *Contribution to the Critique of Hegel's Philosophy of Law*, MECW 3:65.
8. Mészáros, *Marx's Theory of Alienation*, 35.
9. Marx, *On the Jewish Question*, MECW 3:174.
10. Marx, *Economic and Philosophic Manuscripts of 1844*, MECW 3:276.
11. Marx, *Economic and Philosophic Manuscripts of 1844*, MECW 3:276.
12. Marx and Engels, *The Holy Family*, MECW 4:36.
13. Marx, *Comments on James Mill*, MECW 3:220.
14. Marx, "Rent of Land," MECW 3:266.
15. Rousseau, *The Social Contract*, 159.
16. Marx, "Estranged Labour," MECW 3:272.
17. Marx, "Estranged Labour," MECW 3:272.
18. Marx, "Estranged Labour," MECW 3:274.
19. Marx, "Estranged Labour," MECW 3:274.
20. Marx, "Estranged Labour," MECW 3:275.
21. Marx, "Estranged Labour," MECW 3:275.
22. Marx, "Estranged Labour," MECW 3:279.
23. Marx, "Estranged Labour," MECW 3:279.
24. Marx, *Introduction to a Contribution to the Critique of Hegel's Philosophy of Law*, MECW 3:182.

25. Marx and Engels, *The Holy Family*, MECW 4:36.
26. Marx and Engels, *The Holy Family*, MECW 3:280.
27. Marx, *Critique of the Gotha Programme*, MECW 24:87.
28. Marx, "Wage Labour and Capital," MECW 9:202.
29. Marx, "Wage Labour and Capital," MECW 9:203.
30. Marx, "Wage Labour and Capital," MECW 9:202.
31. Marx and Engels, *Manifesto of the Communist Party*, MECW 6:490.
32. Marx, *Grundrisse*, MECW 28:411.
33. Marx, *Capital*, MECW 35:591.
34. Marx's emphasis.
35. Marx, *Grundrisse*, MECW 28:411–412.
36. Marx, *Capital*, MECW 35:365.
37. Marx, *Grundrisse*, MECW 29:87.
38. Marx, *Grundrisse*, MECW 29:82–83.
39. Marx, *Capital*, MECW 35:425–426.
40. Wood, *Karl Marx*, 44.
41. Kamenka, *The Ethical Foundations of Marxism*, 144–145.
42. Marx, *Capital*, MECW 35:570. My emphasis.
43. Marx, *Grundrisse*, MECW 29:64.
44. Gilman-Opalsky, *The Communism of Love*.

Chapter 5

1. Marx, *The Eighteenth Brumaire of Louis Bonaparte*, MECW 11:103.
2. One place where this idea is most fully developed is in Engels's "The Part Played by Labour in the Transition from Ape to Man." For a modern expansion of this notion, one might look to the works of evolutionary psychologist, Michael Tomasello, whose work traces the sociohistorically situated origins and emergence of communication, cognition, and morality. Nowhere in his works does Tomasello cite Marx or claim to be engaged in a Marxist project. However, for one familiar with Marx's and Engels's writings on the natural and social development of the human species, it is striking just how very much Tomasello's conclusions are much as Marx and Engels would have predicted would be revealed in a careful study of the natural emergence of human sociality and its role in determining the development and expression of human nature. In his 2019 book *Becoming Human: A Theory of Ontogeny*, Tomasello presents his theory as "placing human sociocultural activity within the framework of modern evolutionary theory. Human children inherit a sociocultural context replete with cultural artifacts, symbols, and institutions, and their unique maturational capacities would be inert without a sociocultural context within which to develop. Normal human ontogeny thus requires *both* the maturation of species-unique cognitive and social capacities and also individual experience in such things as collaborative and communicative interactions with others, structured by cultural artifacts such as linguistic conventions and social norms."

Rather than taking the competitive individual as the basis of his conception of human nature, Tomasello argues that human beings distinguished themselves from giant apes through their sociality:

"The creation of a joint agent—while each partner maintains her own individual role and perspective at the same time—created a completely new human psychology, spawning new forms of both cognition and sociality" (Tomasello, *Becoming Human*, 15).

My point here is not that the two perspectives are exactly aligned. What is striking, however, is the importance of a key assumption: that human nature is itself a historically emergent product of human's being socially mediated productive activity, initially aimed at satisfying their needs of subsistence.

3. I began to use the term "dialectical compatibilism" as early as 2017 to describe Marxist theory's implications regarding the relationship between freedom and determinism. Since then, I am aware of one occurrence of the term in print: Adrian Johnston uses the phrase independently in his 2020 essay "The Triumph of Theological Economics." Of course, it's not surprising that two theorists would happen upon this phrase. It is important, though, to distinguish their uses. Johnston employs the phrase to illuminate how "Subjects write the very scripts they also play out" (32). My aim in applying the phrase "dialectical compatibilism" is to emphasize the historical co-constitution of free and deterministic elements in human agency, and the sense in which freedom is itself counterintuitively produced by deterministic processes in human history.
4. Popper, *The Open Society and Its Enemies*, 93.
5. My translation. Biesecker and Kesting, *Mikroökonomik*, 75.
6. Townshend, *The Politics of Marxism*, 19.
7. Kamenka, *The Ethical Foundations of Marxism*, 164–165.
8. Truitt, *Marxist Ethics*, 32.
9. Marx, *The German Ideology*, MECW 5:195.
10. Marx, *Capital*, MECW 35:753.
11. Hegel, *Elements of the Philosophy of Right*, 282.
12. Marx, "Private Property and Labour," MECW 3:302.
13. And as Kevin Brien has put the related point in his 1987 book *Marx, Reason, and the Art of Freedom*, "human beings are always more than antecedent conditions may have made them be, by virtue of their capacity to make what they become by their own activity" (40).
14. Englert, *Epicurus on the Swerve and Voluntary Action*, 55.
15. Marx, *Doctoral Dissertation on Epicurus*, MECW 1:61. This is Englert's translation of the text, and it appears in his *Epicurus on the Swerve and Voluntary Action*, 56.
16. McCarthy, *Marx and the Ancients*, 44–45.
17. Marx, *Doctoral Dissertation on Epicurus*, MECW 1:62.
18. Cicero, *On Fate*, 46–47.
19. Marx, *Doctoral Dissertation on Epicurus*, MECW 1:50.
20. McCarthy, *Marx and the Ancients*, 31.
21. Marx and Engels, *Manifesto of the Communist Party*, MECW 6:496.
22. Marx and Engels, *Manifesto of the Communist Party*, MECW 6:508.
23. Marx, *Capital*, MECW 35:164.
24. Sherman, "Marx and Determinism," 67.

25. Marx, *Capital*, MECW 35:304, Note 222.
26. Marx, *Capital*, MECW 37:44.
27. Engels, "Engels to Margaret Harkness in London; April, 1888," MECW 48:168.
28. Marx, *Capital*, MECW 35:275–276.
29. Here Sherman is quoting Laird Addis, "The Individual and the Marxist Philosophy of History," in Brodbeck, *Readings in the Philosophy of the Social Sciences*.
30. Marx, *The Eighteenth Brumaire of Louis Bonaparte*, MECW 11:103.
31. Marx and Engels, *The German Ideology*, MECW 5:49.
32. Marx, Capital, MECW 35:619.
33. Marx, *Grundrisse*, MECW 28:17.
34. Marx, *Capital*, MECW 35:19–20.

Chapter 6

1. This is by no means universally the case. Notable exceptions include treatments such as Sowell, "Karl Marx and the Freedom of the Individual"; Shaw, "Socialist Individualism"; and Forbes, *Marx and the New Individual*. Jon Elster, in attempting to capture this aspect of Marx's thought, also argues in his 1985 book *Making Sense of Marx* that whatever is valuable in Marx's theory of history can be cashed out in terms of methodological individualism, although I think this is going too far, about which I say more near the end of the present section.
2. Marx and Engels, *Manifesto of the Communist Party*, MECW 6:500.
3. Marx, *Grundrisse*, MECW 28:420.
4. Marx and Engels, *Manifesto of the Communist Party*, MECW 6:487.
5. Marx and Engels, *Manifesto of the Communist Party*, MECW 6:488.
6. Fenves, "Marx's Doctoral Thesis on Two Greek Atomists and the Post-Kantian Interpretations," 433.
7. Marx and Engels, *The Holy Family*, MECW 4:120–121.
8. Locke, *Second Treatise of Government*, 334.
9. Marx and Engels, *Critique of The German Ideology*, MECW 5: 86–87.
10. Marx and Engels, *Manifesto of the Communist Party*, MECW 6:499.
11. Marx and Engels, *Manifesto of the Communist Party*, MECW 6:499.
12. Marx and Engels, *Grundrisse*, MECW 28:18.
13. Marx and Engels, *Grundrisse*, MECW 28:18.
14. Marx and Engels, *Grundrisse*, MECW 28:420.
15. Marx, *Grundrisse*, MECW 28:195.
16. Marx, *Grundrisse*, MECW 28:251.
17. Marx, *Capital*, MECW 35:588.
18. Marx, *Economic and Philosophic Manuscripts of 1844*, MECW 3:305–306.
19. Wills, "Marx," in *A Companion to Atheism and Philosophy*.
20. In their 2014 book *Political History of the Editions of Marx and Engels's "German Ideology Manuscripts,"* Terrell Carver and Daniel Blank endorse an argument, made by Inge Taubert in her 1990 essay "Wie enstand der 'Deutsche Ideologie' von Karl

Marx und Friedrich Engels?," for the central importance of Marx's and Engels's writings on Max Stirner. Carver and Blank write, "Taubert's expositions illustrate once again how important Marx and Engels's critical examination of Stirner's *Der Einzige und sein Eigentum* was for the entire writing process of what is known to us as *The German Ideology*. Although Marx and Engels started out with an article on Bauer, it was in particular the critique of Stirner that became the basis not only for 'Sankt-Bruno,' but—more importantly—for most of the so-called manuscripts on Feuerbach. In conclusion, it must be stressed that there can be no understanding of 'Sankt Bruno' and the so-called Feuerbach manuscripts if one fails to study 'Sankt Max' first" (106).

21. Stirner, *The Ego and Its Own*.
22. This title is also sometimes translated into English, more aptly, I think, as "*The Individual and His Property*."
23. Thomas, "Karl Marx and Max Stirner," 159.
24. Nicholas Churchich seems to concur with Stirner's critique of Marx's communism. Churchich writes, "While it is debatable whether Marx is an individualist or an anti-individualist, in *The German Ideology* he definitely argues for the primacy and supremacy of collectivism. Like Rousseau, he starts with individualism but ends with the sacrifice of the individual to the collective and of private interests to the interests of the whole" (*Marxism and Morality*, 165). Churchich does not provide a clear argument for this view, but it seems to me that his reason for holding it is that he rejects Marx's claim that "abstract egoism" is a historical phenomenon produced by particular social and economic conditions, and not a necessary and ineliminable feature of human nature. Churchich writes that "Marx has failed to trace egoism to its real source within the personality of the human individual himself. He has also failed to understand that it is only by man's own moral effort that the harmonisation of self-interest and common interests is possible. The centre of man's moral and social life must be found within the self rather than outside it" (*Marxism and Morality*, 164). If that all is true, then Marx's solution to the antagonism between individual and society would indeed be unsatisfactory. If Stirnerian egoism is an ineliminable part of human nature, then all the social transformations in the world could not resolve the conflict between such egoistic individuals, and the interests of the community taken as a whole, and so realizing social, communal goods would indeed mean violating the private interests of Stirnerian egoists. However, (1) it strikes me as somewhat disingenuous to attribute to Marx the view that he espouses the sacrifice of the individual, because Marx pointedly does *not* think that egoism is a necessary feature of human beings, and argues that the transition to the sort of socialist society he espouses would be a transition in which this egoism fades away as an aspect of human life; and (2) Churchich means to put the burden of proof onto Marx to show that human nature is plastic and adaptable, but it seems to me that it is Churchich who is operating with the much more robust and "thick" conception of human nature. What one would need in order to agree with him that Marx's communism must necessarily involve the sacrifice of the individual's interests, is a very good argument to show that it can never be possible for human beings to exist without Stirnerian egoism. When Churchich does attempt to give such an argument, he refers to something that is much like a

soul—the immutable "personality of the human individual himself." Elsewhere, he writes that "Moral values, it must be recognised, are rooted in the endeavour of personal spirits and without this endeavour they could not be sustained" (*Marxism and Morality*, 99). Churchich is openly hostile to materialism, at one point even taking on a rather suspicious tone with regard to Marx and Engels's belief in evolution, "Assuming that men are the direct descendants of creatures which in the form of their bodies and brains were similar to apes, Engels indicates" (98). It seems to me that positing the existence of a "human personality" or of "personal spirits" which make Stirnerian egoism impossible to abolish involves much more controversial and tendentious assumptions than any that Marx can be accused of making.

25. Stirner, *The Ego and Its Own*, 5–7.
26. Feuerbach, *The Fiery Brook*, 111.
27. Feuerbach, *The Fiery Brook*, 130.
28. Thomas, "Karl Marx and Max Stirner," 161–162.
29. As Lawrence Stepelevich notes in his essay "Max Stirner and Ludwig Feuerbach," the debate between these two thinkers "exercised a powerful influence not only upon Feuerbach, but upon Marx as well" (451).
30. Marx and Engels, *The German Ideology*, MECW 5:342–343.
31. Stirner, *The Ego and Its Own*, 111.
32. Marx and Engels, *The German Ideology*, MECW 5:213.
33. Blackledge, *Marx and Ethics*, 80.
34. Wood, *The Free Development of Each*, 266.
35. Mills, "Marxism, 'Ideology,' and Moral Objectivism," 385.
36. Elster, *Making Sense of Marx*, 4–5.
37. Levine et al., "Marxism and Methodological Individualism," 68.
38. Levine et al., 82.
39. Shiell, "On Marx's Holism," 239.
40. Shiell, "On Marx's Holism," 240.
41. Shiell, "On Marx's Holism," 244.
42. As Sally Haslanger points out in her 2020 essay "Failures of Methodological Indivdualism," "An individualist social ontology places tremendous emphasis on the power of 'collective intentionality' to constitute the social world. But our powers are limited by material conditions, the complexity and fragmentation of societies, our embodiment, our ignorance, and the accidental bad effects of good intentions (not to mention the bad intentions). To understand societies, we must take all this into account. Understanding the multiple factors—material, cultural, historical, psychological—affecting our terms of coordination is necessary for critique, and for our efforts to promote social justice" (514).
43. Marx and Engels, *Critique of The German Ideology*, MECW 5:31.
44. As Luca Basso writes in his 2012 book *Marx and Singularity*, "Not only does Marx try to move beyond individualism and holism (to use sociological categories), he also brings to light their mutual implication: the individualist premiss of the debate, moving from the recognition of free and equal individuals, and their subsumption under an abstract social power, are two 'sides' of the same coin" (2).

Chapter 7

1. Marx, "The Civil War in France," MECW 22:348.
2. Marx, *Capital*, MECW 35:186.
3. Marx, *Grundrisse*, MECW 28:180.
4. "As far as the individual, real person is concerned, a wide field of choice, caprice and therefore of formal freedom is left to him" (Marx, *Grundrisse*, MECW 28:392).
5. Marx, *Grundrisse*, MECW 28:180.
6. Marx, *A Contribution to the Critique of Political Economy*, MECW 29:38.
7. Hobsbawm, *The Age of Revolution*, 150.
8. Marx, *Grundrisse*, MECW 29:40.
9. Marx, *The Programme of the French Workers' Party*, MECW 24:340.
10. Marx, "Preamble to the Programme of the French Workers' Party," MECW 24:340.
11. Marx and Engels, *Manifesto of the Communist Party*, MECW 6:504.
12. Locke, *Second Treatise of Government*, 269.
13. Marx, *Capital*, MECW 35:306.
14. Marx, *Capital*, MECW 35:361.
15. Marx, *Capital*, MECW 35:730–731.
16. This is very influentially the case, for example, in the interpretation of Marx that Allen Wood presents in his 1981 book *Karl Marx*, about which we will say more later on in the present chapter.
17. Marx, *Manifesto of the Communist Party*, MECW 6:506.
18. Marx, *Critique of Hegel's "Philosophy of Right,"* 64. Here I have preferred the translation found in the 1970 Cambridge University Press translation of Marx's *Critique of Hegel's "Philosophy of Right."* Marx's original German text reads as follows: "Hegel ist nicht zu tadeln, weil er das Wesen des modernen Staats schildert, wie es ist, sondern weil er das, was ist, für das Wesen des Staatsausgibt. Daß das Vernünftige wirklich ist, beweist sich eben im Widerspruch der unvernünftigen Wirklichkeit, die an allen Ecken das Gegenteil von dem ist, was sie aussagt, und das Gegenteil von dem aussagt, was sie ist" (Marx/Engels-Werke 1:267). The *MECW* translates the selection thus: "Hegel is not to be blamed for depicting the nature of the modern state as it is, but for presenting that which is as the *nature of the state*. That the rational is actual is proved precisely in the *contradiction* of *irrational actuality*, which everywhere is the contrary of what it asserts, and asserts the contrary of what it is" (MECW 3:63). "Essence" strikes me as a more natural and less ambiguous translation of "Wesen" than does "nature," which is what appears in the MECW translation.
19. Marx, *Contribution to the Critique of Hegel's Philosophy of Law*, MECW 3:108
20. Marx, *Critique of Hegel's "Philosophy of Right,"* 65. Again, the Cambridge University Press translation is preferable to the MECW translation. Marx's original German text reads: "Das ständische Element ist die sanktionierte, gesetzliche Lüge der konstitutionellen Staaten, daß der Staat das Interesse des Volks oder daß das Volkdas Staatsinteresse ist" (Marx/Engels-Werke 1:267). The MECW translation reads: "The *estates* element is the *sanctioned, legal lie* of constitutional states, the lie that the *state* is the *nation's interest*, or that the *nation* is the *interest of the state*" (MECW 3:65).

Translating the word "Volk" as "nation," instead of "people," is potentially obscure here, as Marx's aim is to distinguish between the state interests and the interests of the individual persons living under the state.

21. *Introduction to A Contribution to the Critique of Hegel's "Philosophy of Right,"* 142, Emphasis mine.
22. My translation. The original German text reads: "Marx sah, wie er in der 'Heiligen Familie' zum Ausdruck brachte, im *konstitutionellen Repräsentativstaat*, der durch die Revolution von 1830 geschaffen worden war, das vorläufige Endprodukt der 'politischen Aufklärung' der Bourgeoisie über ihre eigenen Klasseninteressen, den offiziellen Ausdruck ihrer ausschließlichen Macht, die politische Anerkennung ihres besonderen Interesses" (65).
23. Marx, *Contribution to the Critique of Hegel's Philosophy of Law*, MECW 3:109.
24. Marx, *On the Jewish Question*, MECW 3:162–163.
25. Marx, *On the Jewish Question*, MECW 3:163.
26. Marx and Engels, *The Holy Family*, MECW 4:113; Marx, *On the Jewish Question*, MECW 3:155.
27. Rousseau, *The Social Contract*, 156.
28. Locke, *Second Treatise of Government*, 269.
29. Doğan, *Marx and Hegel on the Dialectic of the Individual and the Social*, 300.
30. Marx, *On the Jewish Question*, MECW 3:164.
31. Of course, workers often do own small-scale property such as homes, cars, and so on. However, workers in general tend not to own much more than what is necessary to satisfy their own needs, construed narrowly. I am here contrasting personal private property with private property as capital. Capital is private property that gives its owner the ability to control the activity of others and subordinate it to one's own narrow ends. Workers may own small amounts of personal property, but this ownership does not allow them to purchase the labor power of others or to satisfy their needs by amassing capital. Moreover, workers do not own the means of production or society's natural resources and therefore are not in a position to bar other human beings from having access to them.
32. Marx, *Introduction to a Contribution to the Critique of Hegel's Philosophy of Law*, MECW 3:186.
33. For this reason among others, we ought to heed Bob Cannon's warning in his 2015 essay "Marx, Modernity and Human Rights," that "in rendering human rights a bourgeois phenomenon (restricted to exchange), Marxists risk colluding with capitalism's defenders in thwarting the critical potential of human rights" (168).
34. Marx and Engels, *The Critique of German Ideology*, MECW, 5:323.
35. Marx, *Introduction to a Contribution to the Critique of Hegel's Philosophy of Law*, MECW 3:186.
36. Brenkert, *Marx's Ethics of Freedom*, 89.
37. Peffer, *Marxism, Morality and Social Justice*, 323. Emphasis mine.
38. Marx, "*Introduction to A Contribution to the Critique of Hegel's 'Philosophy of Right,'*" 142. Emphasis mine.
39. Wood, *Karl Marx*, 121.
40. Husami, "Marx on Distributive Justice," 36.

41. Marx, *Critique of the Gotha Programme*, MECW 24:87.
42. Elsewhere, to support this view, Wood deploys reasoning that Ziyad Husami described as "bogus" in a 1978 reply to Wood's 1972 paper "The Marxian Critique of Justice." Husami argues that Wood relies overly much on a single ironic aside in *Capital* to the effect that the exploitation of labor power is "by no means in injustice to the seller"—the seller of labor power being, of course, the worker.
43. Marx, *Critique of the Gotha Programme*, MECW 24:87.
44. Wood, *Karl Marx*.
45. Marx, *Capital*, MECW 35:654.
46. William McBride also takes up this question—at least as regards Wood and also Robert Tucker—in his 1975 essay "The Concept of Justice in Marx, Engels, and Others." McBride largely explains it as a consequence of Wood et al. having distinguished too little between Engels's views on the matter, and Marx's. This is not the focus of my criticism here, but it bears consideration and McBride's article offers a compelling discussion of areas where their views on justice may have differed.
47. Luxemburg, "Reform or Revolution" in *The Rosa-Luxemburg Reader*, 151.
48. Shoikhedbrod, *Revisiting Marx's Critique of Liberalism*, 88.
49. Shoikhedbrod, *Revisiting Marx's Critique of Liberalism*, 87.
50. Engels, *The Origin of the Family, Private Property, and the State*, 113.
51. Engels, *The Origin of the Family, Private Property, and the State*, 217.
52. Engels, *The Origin of the Family, Private Property, and the State*, 228.
53. Marx, *Capital*, MECW 35:583.
54. Kain, *Marx and Ethics*, 79.

Chapter 8

1. Marx, "Wage Labour and Capital," MECW 9:228.
2. 1 John 2:15–17, English Standard Version
3. Marx, *"The Power of Money,"* MECW 3:326.
4. Marx, *Introduction to a Contribution to the Critique of Hegel's Philosophy of Law*, MECW 3:175.
5. My translation from the German, "Das *religiöse* Elend ist in einem der *Ausdruck* des wirklichen Elendes und in einem die *Protestation* gegen das wirkliche Elend. Die Religion ist der Seufzer der bedrängten Kreatur, das Gemüt einer herzlosen Welt, wie sie der Geist geistloser Zustände ist" (Karl Marx/ Friedrich Engels—Werke (Karl) Dietz Verlag, Berlin. Band 1. Berlin/DDR. 1976, 378). The English translation in the MECW reads, "*Religious* distress is at the same time the *expression* of real distress and also the *protest* against real distress. Religion is the sigh of the oppressed creature, the heart of a heartless world, just as it is the spirit of spiritless conditions" (*Introduction to a Contribution to the Critique of Hegel's Philosophy of Law*, MECW 3:175).
6. Marx, *Introduction to a Contribution to the Critique of Hegel's Philosophy of Law*, MECW 3:175.

7. Marx, *Introduction to a Contribution to the Critique of Hegel's Philosophy of Law*, MECW 3:182.
8. Marx and Engels, *The Holy Family*, MECW 3:168.
9. Marx, *The Holy Family*, MECW 3:170.
10. Chourineur's transformation into a "moral being" (MECW 4:163). He becomes doglike toward his new master, Rudolphe, even going so far as to say that "Je me sens pour vous, comme qui dirait l'attachement d'un bouledogue pour son maître" (MECW 4:164). Szeliga describes this transformation as the restoration of Chourineur to mankind, but really, he has become little more than what Marx refers to as a "moral bulldog."
11. Marx and Engels, *The Holy Family*, MECW 3:170.
12. Brown, "Marx and the Foundations of the Critical Theory of Morality and Ethics," 10.
13. Brown, "Marx and the Foundations of the Critical Theory of Morality and Ethics," 16.
14. Marx and Engels, *The Holy Family*, MECW 3:170.
15. It is worth noting that this article is written in September 1847, after Marx's and Engels's preparation of the manuscripts that form *The Critique of the German Ideology* and around the time he is supposed by some to have abandoned moral criticism. Yet when Marx condemns Christianity for having justified the "vile acts of the oppressors against the oppressed," this is a clear *ethical* critique of Christianity, as well as an indication of what values a revolutionary and liberating ethical vision would encourage, namely "courage, self-confidence, and pride."
16. Marx, *The Communism of the Rheinischer Beobachter*, MECW 6:231.
17. Marx and Engels, *The Holy Family*, MECW 3:176.
18. Wills, "Marx."
19. From Marx's early poem, "On Hegel," written prior to 1837 (Marx/Engels, Gesamtausgabe, Abt. 1, Hb. 2, 1929). In English, the text reads, "Kant and Fichte soar to the aether gladly/ Searching for a distant land/ But I only seek to grasp properly/ What I found on the street!" (my translation).
20. For more about this, see MacIntyre's *After Virtue*, Blackledge's *Marxism and Ethics*, and Gregson's *Marxism, Ethics, and Politics*.
21. I do tend to think of Kant as the second of these two options, but the point is not of special relevance here, so I leave it to the side. For more about the historiographical point, one may turn to Rudiger Bubner's *German Idealist Philosophy* where Bubner writes, "Though we have grown accustomed to calling ['the period delimited by the names of Kant and Hegel'] 'German Idealism,' this label is not altogether well chosen and is only partly valid in the case of Kant" (ix). The point is also made in Brian O'Connor's and Georg Mohr's 2006 anthology of writings in the German Idealist tradition. In the introduction to this volume, they write, "Kant might be seen to occupy the position of the philosopher who ends one epoch (rationalism, empiricism, enlightenment) and smoothes the way for a new 'critical' philosophy, which in its turn becomes the key reference point for the following generations of philosophers. . . . Kant's successors believed that his framework needed to be superseded in order to bring about what they regarded as the 'consistent realisation' of Kantian discoveries. But in so doing they departed ultimately from the basis of Kant's philosophy. . . . All of this would suggest that Kant is neither explicitly nor implicitly (in terms of

philosophical ambition) compatible with the post-Kantian direction of thought, designated as German Idealism, which Kant himself had nevertheless stimulated" (1–2).

22. Marx wrote, in the Afterword to the 1873 second German edition of *Capital*, "The mystification which dialectic suffers in Hegel's hands, by no means prevents him from being the first to present its general form of working in a comprehensive and conscious manner. With him it is standing on its head. It must be turned right side up again, if you would discover the rational kernel within the mystical shell" (MECW 35:19–20).

23. See Gordon Brittan's 1978 essay "Kant and Newton" for further elaboration of Kant's relationship to Newton and of his response to the challenge presented by Hume's Problem of Induction. There, Brittan outlines the history of the philosophical engagement and argues that while Kant's philosophy does not depend upon the truth of Newtonian physics, it is best understood as an attempt to develop a metaphysics that is *compatible* with Newton's laws. Also useful here is the background provided in Sheldon Smith's 2017 essay "Kant's Foundations for Newtonian Science."

24. Kant, *Groundwork of the Metaphysics of Morals*, 52.
25. Kant, *Groundwork of the Metaphysics of Morals*, 41.
26. Kant, *Groundwork of the Metaphysics of Morals*, 42.
27. Kant, *Groundwork of the Metaphysics of Morals*, 38.
28. Kant, *Groundwork of the Metaphysics of Morals*, 43.
29. Booth, "The Limits of Autonomy: Karl Marx's Kant Critique," 249.
30. Marx and Engels, *Critique of the German Ideology*, MECW 5:193–194.
31. Booth, "The Limits of Autonomy: Karl Marx's Kant Critique," 251.
32. Kain, *Marx and Ethics*, 15. Kain aims to show that Marx's moral outlook in his early work is broadly Kantian. He writes, "I hope to show that in many ways Kant and Marx agree and that in a very significant sense Marx is Kantian in his use of the categorical imperative."
33. Marx and Engels, *Critique of the German Ideology*, MECW 5:193.
34. Kant has been defended against the first sort of criticism that Marx makes: that Kantian morality is concerned only with the good will and not with actual outcomes. John Stuart Mill, R. M. Hare, and David Cummiskey are three notable commentators who have argued that the universalization principle amounts to consequentialism, in the end, since to ask whether or not a particular moral principle can be universalized is, these authors argue, just to ask what the consequences of such a moral principle would be.

I don't find this consequentialist reading of Kant very convincing. For one thing, it requires a great deal of doubt in Kant's own descriptions of his moral theory, as he seems to go to great pains to make it crystal clear that on his view, morality is not about ends or results, but rather purely focused on the self-determination of the autonomous will. This point is by no means decisive for rejecting the consequentialist reading of Kant, because he might have been wrong about the implications of the moral theory he developed. Still, I mention this issue because it is one that makes it prima facie more difficult to accept the consequentialist reading of Kant.

More significant, I think, is the fact that this reading seems to shift the meaning of "consequentialism" to an intolerable degree. Consequentialism, I take it, is the view that for a particular object of moral judgment, its moral goodness or badness depends on the consequences that result from it. Consequentialists might disagree about what types of consequences matter for the moral goodness or badness of the thing in question. But I don't think they can disagree about whether it matters or not that the consequences under consideration are ones that have any likelihood at all of actually happening. Yet on the type of "consequentialism" that these authors attribute to Kant, that notion would be discarded.

On Kant's theory, in deciding how I should act, I ask myself, What would transpire if everyone else were compelled to act just as I do, and because I have acted in such and such a way? But of course, that such a state of affairs might obtain is scarcely possible to imagine. The question Kant poses has nothing to do with the real consequences of my actions, and the fact that my individual actions may actually have precious little impact upon social practice has no significance whatsoever for the rightness or wrongness of the act about which I am deliberating. Instead, it is a useful device with which to determine whether the act I am contemplating is in conformity with the Moral Law, which is "the objective principle valid for every rational being," or not. The act turns out to be good or bad not in virtue of its consequences (which may in any case be negligible), but in virtue of its conformity with the Moral Law. So I don't believe that the consequentialist reading of Kant is successful or can defend him from Marx's criticism that his moral theory restricts itself, problematically, to the realm of the ideal, and does not provide a satisfactory treatment of the real outcomes of good or bad wills.

35. Marx and Engels, *Critique of the German Ideology*, MECW 5:195.
36. Marx and Engels, *Critique of the German Ideology*, MECW 5:329.
37. As an interesting historical note, Terrell Carver and Daniel Bank report, in their 2015 *Political History of the Editions of Marx and Engels's* German Ideology *Manuscripts*, that Bernstein did not exhibit any particular alacrity in facilitating the publication of the text which gives us our most thorough insight into Marx's and Engels's historical materialist method. Carver and Blank write that near the turn of the nineteenth century,

> almost all of the manuscripts that became known as *The German Ideology* were not in the archives of the SPD, but in the hands of Bernstein, who administered the manuscripts and unpublished works of the late Friedrich Engels. . . . According to a statement by David Borisovich Ryazanov (1870–1938), the eventual first publisher and editor of larger sections of *The German Ideology* in 1924/26, "[Franz] Mehring had asked for all the manuscript materials that have become *The German Ideology* from Bernstein but had failed to get them. Bernstein was evasive in his response . . . Ryazanov assumed that political differences between the 'revisionist' Bernstein and the more 'orthodox' Mehring would have played a role here" (10).

38. Bernstein, *Evolutionary Socialism*, 7.
39. Broué, *The German Revolution 1917–23*, 18.
40. Kautsky, *Ethics and the Materialist Conception of History*, 57–58.
41. Kain, "Aristotle, Kant, and the Ethics of the Young Marx," 16.

42. Adler, *The Marxist Conception of the State*, 98–99.
43. Kain, *Marx and Ethics*, 65–66.
44. Kain, *Marx and Ethics*, 83.
45. Love, "Kant After Marx," 583.
46. Love, "Kant After Marx," 583.
47. Marx, *The German Ideology*, MECW 5:412.
48. Wood, *Karl Marx*, 145.
49. Wood, *Karl Marx*, 145.
50. In fact, Bentham eventually abandoned the Greatest Happiness Principle, for reasons we will investigate here shortly. In an unpublished essay on Utilitarianism, Bentham wrote: "Greatest happiness *of the greatest number*. Some years have now elapsed since, upon a closer scrutiny, reason, altogether incontestable, was found for discarding this appendage. . . . Be the community in question what it may, divide it into two unequal parts, call one of them the majority, the other minority, layout of the account the feelings of the minority, include in the account no feelings but those of the majority, the result you will find is that of this operation, that to the aggregate stock of the happiness of the community, loss not profit is the result of the operation" (Bentham, "The Greatest Good for the Greatest Number," in Troyer, *The Classical Utilitarians*).
51. Marx and Engels, *The German Ideology*, MECW 5:413–414.
52. We see this in Wood, of course, with his claim that Marx ultimately has little substantive disagreement with Bentham. Derek P. H. Allen anticipated this view in his 1973 essay "The Utilitarianism of Marx and Engels." There, he wrote, "the arguments which support [Marx and Engels'] moral judgments are utilitarian in all but name" (189).
53. Bentham, *Principles of the Civil Code*, Pt.1, Ch.15, Sect. 6.
54. Bentham, *Principles of the Civil Code*, Pt.1, Ch.15, Sect. 6.
55. Brenkert, "Marx and Utilitarianism," 431.
56. Mill, "Utilitarianism," pg. 257.
57. And, as Michael Green notes in his 1983 essay "Marx, Utility, and Right," "What is wrong with the shopkeeper's view of utility is that one's very human abilities are considered merely as means to be exchanged for so many units of pleasure, satisfaction, or utility. Thus, each individual 'treats other men as means' " (434).
58. Marx, *Capital*, MECW 35:605.
59. Marx, *Capital*, MECW 35:606.
60. Bentham, *Principles of the Civil Code*, Pt.1, Ch.15, Sect. 6.
61. Of course, when in developed countries such as the US, roughly 1% of the population controls nearly 80% of the wealth, it would be hard to argue that the distribution of this wealth across a wider layer of society would not significantly increase the standard of living of an enormous number of people. But that is slightly beside the point, here.
62. Hart, "Bentham and the Demystification of the Law," 2–17.
63. Marx, *Capital*, MECW 35:65, Note 65.
64. Wood, *Karl Marx*, 145.
65. Marx and Engels, *Critique of the German Ideology*, MECW 5:409.

66. From "Excerpt on the Phrase 'Greatest Happiness of the Greatest Number,'" in Troyer, *The Classical Utilitarians*, 93.
67. Wood, *Karl Marx*, 145.
68. Marx, *Capital*, MECW 35:606.
69. Marx, *Grundrisse*, MECW 32:274.
70. Marx, "Transformation of Money into Capital," MECW 30:158.
71. Marx, *Capital*, MECW 35:606, Note 67.
72. This, even though of course Marx would point out that the current relations *are* just at least according to the tenets of capitalist justice.
73. Duncan, *Marx and Mill*, 295.
74. For a thorough accounting of Marx's engagements with Mill's ideas, see Michael Evans, "John Stuart Mill and Karl Marx."
75. Cohen, *Karl Marx's Theory of History*, 110.
76. In a draft of an article Marx was preparing for publication, he writes: "This much is however certain: the Americans, and particularly the poor workers in the large towns of New York, Philadelphia, Boston, etc., have taken the matter to their hearts and founded a large number of societies for the establishment of such colonies, and all the time new communities are being set up. The Americans are tired of continuing as the slaves of the few rich men who feed on the labour of the people; and it is obvious that with the great energy and endurance of this nation, community of goods will soon be introduced over a significant part of their country. However, it is not just in America but in England too that attempts have been made to realise community of goods. Here the philanthropist *Robert Owen* has been preaching this ideal for thirty years, he has sunk the whole of his large fortune in it and given everything he had in order to found the present colony at *Harmony* in *Hampshire*" (MECW 4:223).
77. Marx, "Proudhon," MECW 8:554.
78. "*Niederträchtigkeit*," in Marx's German; Marx, "Wages," MECW 6:428.
79. Marx, "Wages," MECW 6:433.
80. Marx, "Wages," MECW 6:433.
81. Churchich, *Marxism and Morality*, 229.

Chapter 9

1. Marx, *Contribution to the Critique of Hegel's* Philosophy of Right, MECW 3:186.
2. Marx and Engels, "Circular Against Kriege," MECW 6:45.
3. Marx and Engels, "Circular Against Kriege," MECW 6:49.
4. Marx and Engels, "Circular Against Kriege," MECW 6:49.
5. Marx and Engels, "Circular Against Kriege," MECW 6:46.
6. Marx and Engels, *The German Ideology*, MECW 5:213.
7. Kandiyali, "The Importance of Others," 573.
8. I discuss this further in my 2019 essay "Towards a Concept of Revolutionary Admiration."

9. The German term translated as "morality" in prominent English-language translations of the *Manifesto* is "*die Moral*," which typically carries the connotation of a system of moral commands.
10. Marx and Engels, *The Communist Manifesto*, MECW 6:504; The German word translated as "abolish" here is "abschaffen," which connotes a more complete doing-away-with than the German word "aufheben," which is also sometimes translated as "to abolish."
11. Marx and Engels, *The Communist Manifesto*, MECW 6:504.
12. One might wonder whether Marx speaks with tongue firmly in cheek when he accepts the charge that communists seek to abolish the institution of the family. But as Richard Weikart writes in his 1994 essay "Marx, Engels, and the Abolition of the Family": "While Marx once alluded to a higher form of the family in communist society, he and Engels usually wrote about the destruction, dissolution, and abolition of the family. The relationships they envisaged for communist society would have little or no resemblance to the family as it existed in nineteenth-century Europe or indeed anywhere else. Thus it is certainly appropriate to define their position as the abolition of the family. Only by making the term family almost infinitely elastic can they be said to have embraced merely a reformulation of the family" (658). See also Sophie Lewis's *Abolish the Family*. M. E. O'Brien explores similar themes in her book *Family Abolition*.
13. Hudis, "The Ethical Implications of Marx's Concept of a Post-Capitalist Society," 346.
14. Marx and Engels, *The Communist Manifesto*, MECW 6:497.
15. Marx and Engels, *The Communist Manifesto*, MECW 6:502–503.
16. Marx and Engels, *The Communist Manifesto*, MECW 6:499.
17. Marx and Engels, *The Communist Manifesto*, MECW 6:506.
18. Another proffered alternative is worth considering, but less likely and compelling. It is that people would continue to engage in forms of discourse that look awfully like the kind of thing that happens today in seminars and conferences about normative moral theory. However, it could be that such reasoning would not be properly "moral," just because in a nonexploitative society, that reasoning would of course not serve the role of grappling with actually existing exploitative social relations. Perhaps, since contingently, nothing in a fully developed communist society could be moral theory because it would have no subject matter to be about, such discourse would be more akin to a historical anthropology of past circumstances and moralities. It would be a little like attempting to go on doing film criticism in a world in which films had existed a very long time ago, but no one alive had seen one.
19. Only heuristically, because the world as it ought to be is not siloed away in some far-off utopian future. It is *already present*, albeit in a process of Becoming which exists materially as the proletariat's ever-present struggle for emancipation. This is why, as Marx puts it, communists do not "preach morality" to the workers' movement. The proletariat is the new world present in the old, struggling to transform Being in its own image—an image of free, active, fully realized humanity, which itself comes into clearer view in direct proportion as the world from which the proletariat emerges is overcome.

20. Marx and Engels, *Critique of the German Ideology*, MECW 5:36.
21. In *Hegel on Second Nature and Ethical Life*, Andreja Novakovic writes that Hegel is to be understood as arguing that in *Sittlichkeit*, "true conscience is no longer engaged in deriving objective content through its own resources or testing what is publicly recognized against the measure of its subjective convictions. Its particular duties are prescribed by its specific position within the social order and it is committed to the requirements internal to its roles. So in an objectively rational social order the basic tension between social expectations and particular commitment is (for the most part) overcome, since I form my commitments within the context of institutional roles" (41–42). Novakovic's characterization elegantly expresses that human beings in conditions of ethical life are not passive, automatic beings; they are rational, free, and active individuals who subjectively embrace their role expectations precisely because these expectations emerge from social arrangements that are themselves rationally ordered.
22. Ng, *Hegel's Concept of Life*, 240.
23. Farneth, *Hegel's Social Ethics*, 6.
24. In his, "Marx's Sketch of Communist Society in *The German Ideology*," Furner argues for the centrality of the "critical critic" sketch in Marx's and Engels's *Critique of the German Ideology*, as well as for the appropriateness of attributing this sketch to Marx rather than dismissing it as an addition from Engels that Marx would have preferred to omit. Furner writes, "The abolition of occupational confinement provides an argument for communism on grounds of individual autonomy, while the disappearance of occupational identity would permit life-activity a more universal and more individual form of recognition" (211).
25. Marx and Engels, *Critique of the German Ideology*, MECW 5:47. In his 2011 paper regarding this passage's importance and its relation to the rest of Marx's thought, James Furner challenges Terrell Carver's earlier contention that the sketch is a humorous aside revealing not much, if anything, about Marx's vision for a communist society. Far from being a few throwaway lines, Furner rightly concludes of this passage, "The abolition of occupational confinement provides an argument for communism on grounds of individual autonomy, while the disappearance of occupational identity would permit life-activity a more universal and more individual form of recognition" ("Marx's Sketch of Communist Society," 211).
26. Groff, "Aristotelian Marxism/Marxist Aristotelianism," 785.
27. Marx continues, "This theory came to the fore with Hobbes and Locke, at the same time as the first and second English revolutions, those first battles by which the bourgeoisie won political power. It is to be found even earlier, of course, among writers on political economy, as a tacit presupposition. Political economy is the real science of this theory of utility; it acquires its true content among the Physiocrats, since they were the first to treat political economy systematically. In Helvétius and Holbach one can already find an idealization of this doctrine, which fully corresponds to the attitude of opposition adopted by the French bourgeoisie before the revolution. Holbach depicts the entire activity of individuals in their mutual intercourse, e.g., speech,

love, etc., as a relation of utility and utilization. Hence the actual relations that are presupposed here are speech, love, definite manifestations of definite qualities of individuals. Now these relations are supposed not to have the meaning *peculiar* to them but to be the expression and manifestation of some third relation attributed to them, the *relation of utility or utilization*. This *paraphrasing* ceases to be meaningless and arbitrary only when these relations have validity for the individual not on their own account, not as spontaneous activity, but rather as disguises, though by no means disguises of the category of Utilisation, but of an actual third aim and relation which is called the relation of utility." (Marx and Engels, "Saint Max" in *The Critique of the German Ideology*, MECW 5:409.)

28. Marx, "Private Property and Labor," MECW 3:300.
29. Marx, "Private Property and Labor," MECW 3:300.
30. Meikle, *Essentialism in the Thought of Karl Marx*, 58. Excerpts from Marx's translation, along with his notes and marginalia thereon, are included in the *Marx-Engels-Gesamtausgabe*.
31. Aristotle, *De Anima*, 424a: 17–26.
32. Aristotle, *De Anima*, 417a.
33. Aristotle, *De Anima*, II.11.
34. Hegel, *Lectures in History of Philosophy*, 189.
35. Hegel, *Lectures in the History of Philosophy*, 191–192.
36. In his essay "Aristotle's *De Anima* and Marx's Theory of Man," David Depew writes, summarizing Marx's critique of Hegel's reading: "Just as worker and capitalist are captured in private and isolated worlds over against which objects seem external, abstract and not one's own, so too the modern intellectual is trapped in a world of abstract, private, and ungrounded conceptions which only problematically gain access and reference to trans-subjective reality" (177).
37. Pickford, "*Poiēsis, Praxis, Aisthesis*," 40–41.
38. Marx's early manuscripts suggest that when humans' alienation from their own creative powers is overcome—a process which can occur only through human appropriation and transformation of the external world, such that the separation between subject and object is overcome—the approach to what we think of now as moral questions might be somewhat akin to the kind of moral particularism described in John McDowell's 1979 essay "Virtue and Reason." There, McDowell describes an approach to moral questions that is best analogized to a special sort of vision. Virtue, McDowell argues, is not a kind of moral knowledge, but rather, "a disposition (perhaps of a specially rational and self-conscious kind) to behave rightly; the nature of virtue is explained, as it were, from the outside in" (331). McDowell goes on to recommend that we "give up the idea that philosophical thought, about the sorts of practice in question, should be undertaken at some external standpoint, outside our immersion in our familiar forms of life" (341).
39. Marx, "Private Property and Communism," MECW 3:302.
40. Marx, *Capital*, MECW 35:81–82.
41. Marx, *Capital*, MECW 35:83.

42. Marx, *Capital*, MECW 35:89–91.
43. Marx, *Capital*, MECW 90–91.
44. We might also be reminded again of Marx's and Engels's earlier insistence that "for the success of the cause itself, the alteration of men on a mass scale is necessary, an alteration which can only take place in a practical movement, a revolution." Marx and Engels, *Critique of the German Ideology*, MECW 5:52.
45. In this way, as in others, the class position of workers under capitalism hints at the universal condition for emancipated human beings in developed communism.
46. In his 2021 book *Communism, Political Power, and Freedom in Marx*, Levy del Aguila Marchena argues that it is a weakness of Marx's view not to constitute an even *more* radical break with bourgeois theory. Speaking here of Marx's related views on the abolition of politics as a feature of human life in the transition to communism, del Aguila Marchena writes, "Marx here subscribes to a variety of the fetishistic commitment of the bourgeois horizon in his understanding of the political reduced to technique: the fetishism of the 'invisible hand' of the market gives way here to the fetishism of the 'communist technique' which should be able to deal with the management of the common" (136). The plausibility of del Aguila Marchena's critique seems to turn on the question of what constitutes fetishism and it's worth noting that a "hand" and a "technique" are things of two entirely different kinds. The fetishistic character of ideology that represents economic developments as actions taken by the "invisible hand of the market" lies in its obscuring the reality that it is not any invisible hand acting upon us, but in fact *ourselves* as human beings acting upon our own social reality, that gives rise to economic developments. The agency we imputed to that "invisible hand" was always in fact our own. There can be no parallel drawn here with what del Aguila Marchena calls "communist technique" or what Engels might have called, "the administration of things," to be contrasted with "the government of man." It is not the unique, "fetishized" capacity of any anointed technique that accounts for the reconciliation of social antagonisms in communist society. Rather, it is the production of the human species as a universal subject, a process that is the task of revolutionary change. This task does not bring about the end of all disagreement or conflict. What it does away with is the domination of one part of society over another, so that confronting the challenges of human life is not a matter of one part of society opposing itself to another, but rather of genuinely democratic deliberation about how to address the needs of all.
47. Marx, *Critique of Political Economy*, MECW 29:264.
48. In *Capital*, Marx says of labor, "The labour process . . . is human action with a view to the production of use values, appropriation of natural substances to human requirements; it is the necessary condition for effecting exchange of matter between man and Nature; it is the everlasting Nature-imposed condition of human existence, and therefore is independent of every social phase of that existence, or rather, is common to every such phase" (MECW 29:194).
49. Marx, "Human Requirements and the Division of Labour Under the Rule of Private Property," MECW 3:314. For a detailed discussion of the connections between Marx's abolitionism and Kant's ethics, see Lea Ypi's 2017 essay "From Revelation to Revolution."

Chapter 10

1. Marx, *Capital*, MECW 35:490.
2. Marx, *Grundrisse*, MECW 29:91.
3. Marx, *Capital*, MECW 35:530.
4. Marx, *Capital*, MECW 37:92.
5. Marx, *Grundrisse*, MECW 29:92.
6. Marx, *Grundrisse*, MECW 29:92.
7. As pandemic illness, climate catastrophe, and food insecurity all threaten humanity, our current moment highlights the indispensability of Marx's approach to understanding our historical relationship to nature. As George Henderson and Eric Sheppard argue in their 2006 "Marx and the Spirit of Marx," "Our contemporary world, where climate, ecosystems, organisms and the landscape are profoundly reshaped by human activities, certainly is one where almost all aspects of nature have been transformed. Yet nature is also shaped by biophysical processes that continually break out of the boxes into which humans seek to cram nature (think of global warming, or mad cow disease), biting back in ways that show how second nature remains crucial to social life, and always partially beyond the control of capitalism. This ongoing, complex and interdependent relationship between societal and biophysical processes is well captured by applying Marx's favored dialectical analysis" (59).
8. Marx, *Theses on Feuerbach*, MECW 5:5.

Coda

1. It is worth noting the entirety of the Regents' September 19, 1969 resolution: "Whereas, on October 11, 1940, the Regents adopted a Resolution stating that 'membership in the Communist Party is incompatible with membership in the faculty of a State University'; and Whereas, on June 24, 1949, The Regents reaffirmed and amplified that policy with a resolution stating, in part, 'pursuant to this policy, the Regents direct that no member of the Communist Party shall be employed by the University'; and Whereas, in an action reported March 22, 1950, the Academic Senate, Northern and Southern Sections, concurred in the foregoing policy by adopting a resolution that proved members of the Communist Party are not acceptable as members of the faculty; and Whereas, on April 21, 1950, The Regents adopted a Resolution confirming and emphasizing their policy statements of October 11, 1940, and June 24, 1949; and Whereas, it has been reported to the Regents that Angela Y. Davis was recently appointed as a member of the University faculty, and subsequently she informed the University Administration by letter, stating, among other things, that she is a member of the Communist Party; Now, Therefore, The Regents direct the President to take steps to terminate Miss Davis' University appointment in accordance with regular procedures as prescribed in the Standing Orders of The Regents" ("Statement Issued

by Regent Higgs" in *University Bulletin: A Weekly Bulletin for the Staff of the University of California.*)
2. "U.C.L.A. Barred from Pressing Red's Ouster," *New York Times*, October 21, 1969, 35.
3. See also Daniel Gordon, "The Firing of Angela Davis at UCLA, 1969–1970."
4. For more on the California Oath Controversy, see John McCumber's 2016 book *The Philosophy Scare*. See also David P. Gardner's 1969 "By Oath and Association."

Bibliography

Abbey, Ruth. "Young Karl Does Headstands: A Reply to Daniel Brudney." *Political Theory* 30, no. 1 (2002): 150–155.

Abercrombie, Nicholas, and Bryan S. Turner. "The Dominant Ideology Thesis." *The British Journal of Sociology* 29, no. 2 (1978): 149–170.

Allen, Derek P. H. "The Utilitarianism of Marx and Engels." *American Philosophical Quarterly* 10, no. 3 (1973): 189–199.

Althusser, Louis. *For Marx*. London: Allen Lane, 1969.

Althusser, Louis. *On the Reproduction of Capitalism: Ideology and Ideological State Apparatuses*. New York: Verso Books, 2014.

Amariglio, Jack, and Yahya Madra, "Karl Marx." In *Handbook of Economics and Ethics*, edited by Irene van Staveren and Jan Peil, 325–332. Cheltenham, UK: Edward Elgar, 2009.

Aristotle. *De Anima*. New York: Oxford University Press, 2016.

Basso, Luca. *Marx and Singularity: From the Early Writings to the Grundrisse*. Leiden: Brill, 2012.

Bentham, Jeremy. *The Collected Works of Jeremy Bentham*. Edited by H. L. A. Hart and J. H. Burns. New York: Clarendon Press, 1996.

Bentham, Jeremy. *The Works of Jeremy Bentham, published under the Superintendence of his Executor, John Bowring*. 11 vols., Vol. 1. Edinburgh: William Tait, 1838–1843.

Bernstein, Eduard. *Evolutionary Socialism: A Criticism and Affirmation*. New York: Shocken Books, 1961.

Biesecker, Adelheid, and Stefan Kesting. *Mikroökonomik: Eine Einführung aus Sozialökologischer Perspektive*. Munich: Oldenbourg Wissenschaftsverlag, 2003.

Blackledge, Paul. "G. A. Cohen and the Limits of Analytical Marxism." In *Constructing Marxist Ethics*, edited by Michael J. Thompson, 288–312. Leiden: Brill, 2015.

Blackledge, Paul. "Marx in the Anglophone World." *Socialism and Democracy* 24, no. 3 (2010): 160–168.

Blackledge, Paul. "Marxism and Ethics." *International Socialism* 1, no. 120 (2008). Retrieved from https://isj.org.uk/issue-120/

Blackledge, Paul. *Marxism and Ethics: Freedom, Desire, and Revolution*. Albany: SUNY Press, 2012.

Blackledge, Paul. "Marxism, Nihilism, and the Problem of Ethical Politics Today." *Socialism and Democracy* 24, no. 2 (2010): 101–123.

Booth, William James. "The Limits of Autonomy: Karl Marx's Kant Critique." In *Kant and Political Philosophy: The Contemporary Legacy*, edited by Ronald Beiner and William James Booth, 245–275. 1997.

Brenkert, George G. "Marx and Utilitarianism." *Canadian Journal of Philosophy* 5, no. 3 (1975): 421–434.

Brenkert, George G. "Marx, Engels, and the Relativity of Morals." *Studies in Soviet Thought* 17, no. 3 (1977): 201–224.

Brenkert, George. *Marx's Ethics of Freedom*. New York: Routledge, 1983.

Bricmont, Jean. *Humanitarian Imperialism; Using Human Rights to Sell War.* New Dehli: Aakar Books, 2007.

Brien, Kevin M. *Marx, Reason, and the Art of Freedom.* Philadelphia: Temple University Press, 2006.

Briggs, William. *Classical Marxism in an Age of Capitalist Crisis: The Past Is Prologue.* New York: Taylor & Francis Group, 2019.

Brittan, Gordon G. "Kant and Newton." In *Kant's Theory of Science,* 117–142. Princeton, NJ: Princeton University Press, 1978.

Brodbeck, May (ed.), *Readings in the Philosophy of the Social Sciences.* London: Macmillan, 1968.

Broué, Pierre. *The German Revolution, 1917–1923.* Leiden: Brill, 2004.

Brown, B. Ricardo. "Marx and the Foundations of the Critical Theory of Morality and Ethics." *Cultural Logic: A Journal of Marxist Theory & Practice* 4 (1999): 1–20.

Brudney, Daniel. "Justification and Radicalism in the 1844 Marx: A Response to Professor Abbey." *Political Theory* 30, no. 1 (2002): 156–163.

Brudney, Daniel. "Justifying a Conception of the Good Life: The Problem of the 1844 Marx." *Political Theory* 29, no. 3 (2001): 364–394.

Brudney, Daniel. *Marx's Attempt to Leave Philosophy.* Cambridge, MA: Harvard University Press, 1998.

Bubner, Rudiger, ed. *German Idealist Philosophy.* New York: Penguin, 1997.

Buchanan, Allen E. *Marx and Justice: The Radical Critique of Liberalism.* Lanham, MD: Rowman & Littlefield, 1982.

Buchanan, Allen E. "Marx, Morality, and History: An Assessment of Recent Analytical Work on Marx." *Ethics* 98, no. 1 (1987): 104–136.

Buchanan, Allen E. "Revolutionary Motivation and Rationality." *Philosophy & Public Affairs* 9, no. 1 (1979): 59–82.

Byron, Chris. "Essence and Alienation: Marx's Theory of Human Nature." *Science & Society* 80, no. 3 (2016): 375–394.

Cannon, Bob. "Marx, Modernity and Human Rights." In *Constructing Marxist Ethics,* edited by Michael J. Thompson, 165–191. Leiden: Brill, 2015.

Carver, Terrell. "*The German Ideology* Never Took Place." *History of Political Thought* 31, no. 1 (2010): 107–127.

Carver, Terrell, and Daniel Blank. *A Political History of the Editions of Marx and Engels's "German Ideology Manuscripts."* New York: Springer, 2014.

Celikates, Robin. "Karl Marx: Critique as Emancipatory Practice." In *Conceptions of Critique in Modern and Contemporary Philosophy,* edited by Karin Boer and Ruth Sonderegger, 101–118. London: Palgrave Macmillan, 2012.

Chitty, Andrew. "The Early Marx on Needs." *Radical Philosophy* 64 (1993): 23–31.

Churchich, Nicholas. *Marxism and Morality: A Critical Examination of Marxist Ethics.* Cambridge: James Clarke & Co, 1994.

Cicero, Marcus Tullius. (tr. C.D. Yonge) "On Fate." In *The Treatises of M. T. Cicero.* London: H. G. Bohn, 1878.

Cohen, G. A. "Freedom, Justice and Capitalism." *New Left Review* 126, no. 1 (1981): 3–16.

Cohen, G. A. *History, Labour, and Freedom: Themes from Marx.* Oxford: Clarendon Press, 1988.

Cohen, G. A. *Karl Marx's Theory of History: A Defence.* Princeton, NJ: Princeton University Press, 1978.

Cohen, G. A. *Self-Ownership, Freedom, and Equality*. New York: Cambridge University Press, 1995.
Comninel, George. "Emancipation in Marx's Early Work." *Socialism and Democracy* 24, no. 3 (2010): 60–78.
Cornu, Auguste. "German Utopianism: 'True' Socialism." *Science & Society* 12, no. 1 (1948): 97–112.
Cummiskey, David. "Kantian Consequentialism." *Ethics* 100, no. 3 (1990): 586–615.
del Aguila Marchena, Levy. *Communism, Political Power and Personal Freedom in Marx: Beyond the Dualism of Realms*. New York: Springer Nature, 2021.
Depew, David. "Aristotle's *De Anima* and Marx's Theory of Man." *Graduate Faculty Philosophy Journal* 8, nos. 1–2 (1981–1982): 133–187.
Doğan, Sevgi. *Marx and Hegel on the Dialectic of the Individual and the Social*. Lanham, MD: Rowman & Littlefield, 2018.
Duncan, Graeme Campbell. *Marx and Mill; Two Views of Social Conflict and Social Harmony*. New York: Cambridge University Press, 1973.
Eagleton, Terry. "Self-Realization, Ethics and Socialism," *New Left Review* 237, no. 1 (1999): 150–161.
Eagleton, Terry. *Why Marx Was Right*. New Haven, CT: Yale University Press, 2018.
Elster, Jon. "The Case for Methodological Individualism." *Theory and Society* 11, no. 4 (1982): 453–482.
Elster, Jon. *Making Sense of Marx*. New York: Cambridge University Press, 1985.
Elster, Jon. "Rationality, Morality, and Collective Action." *Ethics* 96, no. 1 (1985): 136–155.
Englert, Walter. *Epicurus on the Swerve and Voluntary Action*. Riga: Scholars Press, 1987.
Estlund, David. "Human Nature and the Limits (If Any) of Political Philosophy." *Philosophy & Public Affairs* 39, no. 3 (2011): 207–237.
Evans, Michael. "John Stuart Mill and Karl Marx: Some Problems and Perspectives." *History of Political Economy* 21, no. 2 (1989): 273–298.
Farneth, Molly. *Hegel's Social Ethics: Religion, Conflict, and Rituals of Reconciliation*. Princeton, NJ: Princeton University Press, 2017.
Fenves, Peter. "Marx's Doctoral Thesis on Two Greek Atomists and the Post-Kantian Interpretations." *Journal of the History of Ideas* 47, no. 3 (1986): 433–452.
Feuerbach, Ludwig. *The Fiery Brook: Selected Writings of Ludwig Feuerbach*. New York: Anchor Books, 1972.
Forbes, Ian. *Marx and the New Individual*. New York: Routledge, 1990.
Forst, Rainer. "Noumenal Alienation: Rousseau, Kant and Marx on the Dialectics of Self-Determination." *Kantian Review* 22, no. 4 (2017): 523–551.
Fromm, Erich, and Karl Marx. *Marx's Concept of Man: Including "Economic and Philosophical Manuscripts."* New York: Bloomsbury Publishing, 2013.
Fukuyama, Francis. *The End of History and the Last Man*. New York: Simon & Schuster, 2006.
Fukuyama, Francis. *Identity: The Demand for Dignity and the Politics of Resentment*. New York: Farrar, Straus and Giroux, 2018.
Furner, James. *Marx on Capitalism: The Interaction-Recognition-Antinomy Thesis*. Leiden: Brill, 2018.
Furner, James. "Marx's Sketch of Communist Society in *The German Ideology* and the Problems of Occupational Confinement and Occupational Identity." *Philosophy and Social Criticism* 37, no. 2 (2011): 189–215.
Gardner, David P. "By Oath and Association: The California Folly." *Journal of Higher Education* 40, no. 2 (1969): 122–134.

Geras, Norman. "The Controversy About Marx and Justice." *New Left Review* 1, no. 150 (1985): 33–84.
Geras, Norman. *Marx and Human Nature: Refutation of a Legend*. New York: Verso, 1983.
Goldstick, Danny. "Marx, Marxism, Ethics." *Science & Society* 86, no. 1 (2022): 95–104.
Goldstick, Danny. "On Marxist Ethics." *Nature, Society, and Thought* 17, no. 1 (2004): 111–117.
Gordon, Daniel. "The Firing of Angela Davis at UCLA, 1969–1970: Communism, Academic Freedom, and Freedom of Speech." *Society* 57, no. 6 (2020): 596–613.
Greenwald, Emily. *Reconfiguring the Reservation: The Nez Perces, Jicarilla Apaches, and the Dawes Act*. Albuquerque: University of New Mexico Press, 2002.
Gregson, John. *Marxism, Ethics and Politics: The Work of Alasdair MacIntyre*. Boston: Springer, 2018.
Griffin, Nicholas. "Russell and Moore's Revolt Against British Idealism." In *The Oxford Handbook of the History of Analytic Philosophy*, edited by Michael Beaney, 383–406. New York: Oxford University Press, 2013.
Groff, Ruth. "Aristotelian Marxism/Marxist Aristotelianism: MacIntyre, Marx, and the Analysis of Abstraction." *Philosophy and Social Criticism* 38, no. 8 (2012):775–792.
Hacker, Peter M. S. "The Linguistic Turn in Analytic Philosophy." In *The Oxford Handbook of the History of Analytic Philosophy*, edited by Michael Beaney, 926–947. New York: Oxford University Press, 2013.
Hammen, Oscar J. "The Young Marx, Reconsidered." *Journal of the History of Ideas* 31, no. 1 (1970): 109–120.
Hart, H. L. A. "Bentham and the Demystification of the Law." *The Modern Law Review* 36, no. 1 (1973): 2–17.
Haslanger, Sally. "Failures of Methodological Individualism: The Materiality of Social Systems." *Journal of Social Philosophy* (Spring 2020): 1–23.
Hegel, Georg Wilhelm Fredrich. *The Science of Logic*. New York: Cambridge University Press, 2010.
Heller, Agnes. *The Theory of Need in Marx*. New York: Verso Books, 2018.
Henderson, George, and Eric Sheppard. "Marx and the Spirit of Marx." In *Approaches to Human Geography: Philosophies, Theories, People and Practices*, edited by Stuart C. Aitken and Gill Valentine, 64–78. Thousand Oaks, CA: Sage Publishing, 2014.
Hobsbawm, Eric. *The Age of Revolution: Europe: 1789–1848*. New York: Random House, 1962.
Hodges, Donald Clark. "Marx's Ethics and Ethical Theory." *The Socialist Register* 1, no. 1 (1964): 227–241.
Hodges, Donald Clark. "The Young Marx—a Reappraisal." *Philosophy and Phenomenological Research* 27, no. 2 (1966): 216–229.
Husami, Ziyad. "Marx on Distributive Justice." *Philosophy & Public Affairs* 8, no. 1 (1978): 27–64.
Irwin, Terence. *The Development of Ethics: A Historical and Critical Study*. 3 vols. New York: Oxford University Press, 2007.
Jaeck, Hans-Peter. *Die Französische Bürgerliche Revolution Von 1789 Im Frühwerk Von Karl Marx (1843–1846): Geschichtsmethodolog. Studien*. Berlin: Akademie-Verlag, 1979.
Jaeggi, Rahel. *Alienation*. New York: Columbia University Press, 2014.
Johnston, Adrian. *Prolegomena to Any Future Materialism: A Weak Nature Alone*. Vol. 2. Chicago: Northwestern University Press, 2019.

Johnston, Adrian. "The Triumph of Theological Economics: God Goes Underground." *Philosophy Today*, 64, no. 1 (2020): 3–50.
Kain, Philip J. "Aristotle, Kant, and the Ethics of the Young Marx." In *Marx and Aristotle*, edited by George McCarthy, 14–50. Totowa: Rowman & Littlefied, 1992.
Kain, Philip J. *Marx and Ethics*. Oxford: Clarendon Press, 1988.
Kain, Philip J. "Marx and the Abolition of Morality." *Journal of Value Inquiry* 18, no. 1 (1984): 283–297.
Kain, Philip J. "The Young Marx and Kantian Ethics." *Studies in Soviet Thought* 31, no. 4 (1986): 277–301.
Kamenka, Eugene. *The Ethical Foundations of Marxism*. Boston: Routledge & Kegan Paul, 1962.
Kamenka, Eugene. *Marxism and Ethics*. New York: St. Martin's Press, 1969.
Kandiyali, Jan. "The Importance of Others: Marx on Unalienated Production." *Ethics* 130, no. 4 (2020): 555–587.
Kant, Immanuel. *Groundwork of the Metaphysics of Morals*. Cambridge: Cambridge University Press, 1997.
Karim, Mahmoud Mofid Abdul. "Failure of Lehman Brothers." *Journal of Finance and Investment Analysis* 10, no. 4 (2021): 1–14.
Kautsky, Karl. *Ethics and the Materialist Conception of History*. Translated by John Askew. Chicago: Charles H. Kerr & Company, 1907.
King, Steve. *Remarks on Immigrant Farm Workers, before the House Judiciary Subcommittee on Immigration, Citizenship, and Border Security*. Captured by C-SPAN on September 24, 2010. https://www.c-span.org/video/?295639-1/immigrant-farm-workers.
Kirby, Mark. "An Interview with Erik Olin Wright." 2001. Accessed February 10, 2022. https://www.ssc.wisc.edu/soc/faculty/pages/wright/kirby_wright.pdf
Lebowitz, Michael. "Is Analytical Marxism Marxism?" *Science & Society* 52, no. 2 (1988): 191–214.
Lebowitz, Michael. *The Socialist Alternative: Real Human Development*. New York: Monthly Review Press, 2010.
Lenin, Vladimir. *Hegel Notebooks*. In *The Collected Works of VI Lenin*, Vol. 38. Moscow: Progress Publishers, 1961.
Levine, Andrew, Elliott Sober, and Erik Olin Wright. "Marxism and Methodological Individualism." *New Left Review* 162 (1987): 67–84.
Lewis, Sophie. *Abolish the Family: A Manifesto for Care and Liberation*. New York: Verso Books, 2022.
Locke, John. *Two Treatises of Government*. New York: Cambridge University Press, 1988.
Love, S. M. "Kant After Marx." *Kantian Review*, 22, no. 4 (2017): 579–598.
Lukács, Georg. *The Destruction of Reason*. New York: Verso Books, 2021.
Lukács, Georg. *History and Class Consciousness*. Cambridge: MIT Press, 1972.
Lukács, Georg. *The Ontology of Social Being*. London: Merlin, 1980.
Lukács, Georg. *Zur Ontologie Des Gesellschaftlichen Seins*. Darmstadt: Luchterhand, 1984.
Luxemburg, Rosa. "Social Reform or Revolution." In *The Rosa Luxemburg Reader*, edited by Peter Hudis and Kevin B. Anderson, 128–167. New York: Monthly Review Press, 2004.
MacIntyre, Alasdair. *After Virtue*. New York: Bloomsbury, 2013.
MacIntyre, Alasdair. "Hume on 'Is' and 'Ought.'" *The Philosophical Review* 68, no. 4 (1959): 451–468.

Malthus, Thomas Robert, Donald Winch, and Patricia James. *Malthus: "An Essay on the Principle of Population."* New York: Cambridge University Press, 1992.

Mander, William J. *British idealism: A History*. New York: Oxford University Press, 2011.

Marquez, Letisia. "Angela Davis Returns to UCLA Classroom 45 Years After Controversy." *UCLA Newsroom*, May 5, 2014. https://newsroom.ucla.edu/stories/angela-davis-returns-to-ucla-classroom-45-years-after-controversy

Marx, Karl. *Critique of Hegel's "Philosophy of Right."* New York: Cambridge University Press, 1970.

Marx, Karl and Friedrich Engels. *Karl Marx, Frederick Engels: Collected Works*. New York: International Publishers, 1975.

Marx, Karl, Friedrich Engels, and Institut fur Marxismus-Leninismus beim ZK der SED. *Erganzungsband: Schriften, Manuskripte, Briefe Bis 1844*. Berlin: Dietz, 1967.

Marx, Karl, Friedrich Engels, and Institut fur Marxismus-Leninismus beim ZK der SED. *Karl Marx, Friedrich Engels. Werke*. Berlin: Dietz, 1956.

McBride, William Leon. "The Concept of Justice in Marx, Engels, and Others." *Ethics* 85, no. 3 (1975): 204–218.

McCarthy, George. "German Social Ethics and the Return to Greek Philosophy: Marx and Aristotle." *Studies in Soviet Thought* 31, no. 1 (1986): 1–24.

McCarthy, George. *Marx and the Ancients: Classical Ethics, Social Justice, and Nineteenth-Century Political Economy*. Lanham, MD: Rowman & Littlefield, 1990.

McCarthy, George. "Marx's Social Ethics and the Critique of Traditional Morality." *Studies in Soviet Thought* 29, no. 3 (1985): 177–199.

McCumber, John. "Marx's Social Ethics and the Critique of Traditional Morality." *Studies in Soviet Thought* 29, no. 3 (1985): 177–199.

McCumber, John. *The Philosophy Scare*. Chicago: University of Chicago Press, 2016.

McCumber, John. *Time in the Ditch: American Philosophy and the McCarthy Era*. Chicago: Northwestern University Press, 2001.

McDowell, John. "Virtue and Reason." *The Monist* 62, no. 3 (1979): 331–350.

Meikle, Scott. *Essentialism in the Thought of Karl Marx*. London: Duckworth, 1985.

Mészáros, István. *Lukács' Concept of Dialectic*. London: Merlin Press, 1972.

Mészáros, István. *Marx's Theory of Alienation*. London: Merlin Press, 1975.

Mill, James. *The Collected Works of John Stuart Mill*. Vol. X. Toronto: University of Toronto Press and Routledge & Kegan Paul, 1969.

Miller, Dale E. "Mill's 'Socialism.'" *Politics, Philosophy & Economics* 2, no. 1 (2003): 213–238.

Mills, Charles W. *From Class to Race: Essays in White Marxism and Black Radicalism*. Lanham, MD: Rowman & Littlefield, 2003.

Mills, Charles W. "'Ideal Theory' as Ideology." *Hypatia* 20, no. 3 (2005): 165–183.

Mills, Charles W. "Marxism, 'Ideology' and Moral Objectivism." *Canadian Journal of Philosophy* 24, no. 3 (1994): 373–393.

Mills, Charles W. *The Racial Contract*. Ithaca, NY: Cornell University Press, 2014.

Myers, David B. "Marx and the Problem of Nihilism." *Philosophy and Phenomenological Research* 37, no. 2 (1976): 193–204.

Myers, David B. "Marx and Transcendence of Ethical Humanism." *Studies in Soviet Thought* 21, no. 4 (1980): 319–330.

Nasser, Alan G. "Marx's Ethical Anthropology." *Philosophy and Phenomenological Research* 35, no. 4 (1975): 484–500.

Nemeth, Thomas. "Althusser's Anti-Humanism and Soviet Philosophy." *Studies in Soviet Thought* 21, no. 4 (1980): 363–385.

Ng, Karen. *Hegel's Concept of Life: Self-Consciousness, Freedom, Logic*. New York: Oxford University Press, 2020.

Ng, Karen. "Ideology Critique from Hegel and Marx to Critical Theory." *Constellations* 22, no. 3 (2015): 393–404.

Nielsen, Kai. "Engels on Morality and Moral Theorizing." *Studies in Soviet Thought* 26, no. 3 (1983): 229–248.

Nielsen, Kai. "If Historical Materialism Is True Does Morality Totter?" *Philosophy of the Social Sciences* 15, no. 1 (1985): 389–407.

Nielsen, Kai. *Marxism and the Moral Point of View: Morality, Ideology, and Historical Materialism*. Boulder, CO: Westview Press, 1989.

Nielsen, Kai. "Marx on Moral Commentary: Ideology and Science." *Philosophy of the Social Sciences* 15, no. 1 (1985): 237–254.

Novakovic, Andreja. *Hegel on Second Nature in Ethical Life*. New York: Cambridge University Press, 2017.

O'Brien, M. E. *Family Abolition: Capitalism and the Communizing of Care*. Las Vegas: Pluto, 2023.

O'Connor, Brian, and Georg Mohr (eds.) *German Idealism: An Anthology and Guide*. Chicago: University of Chicago, 2007.

O'Rourke, James. *The Problem of Freedom in Marxist Thought*. Dordrecht: Reidel Publishing Company, 1974.

Paden, Roger. "Marx's Critique of the Utopian Socialists." *Utopian Studies* 13, no. 2 (2002): 67–91.

Pateman, Carol. *The Sexual Contract*. Palo Alto, CA: Stanford University Press, 1988.

Peffer, R. G. *Marxism, Morality, and Social Justice*. Princeton, NJ: Princeton University Press, 1990.

Pickford, Henry W. "*Poiêsis, Praxis, Aisthesis*: Remarks on Aristotle and Marx." In *Aesthetic Marx* edited by Samir Gandesha and Johan Hartle, 23–48. New York: Bloomsbury, 2017.

Proudhon, Pierre. *What Is Property*? New York: Cambridge University Press, 1993.

Roberts, Marcus. *Analytical Marxism: A Critique*. New York: Verso, 1996.

Rodriguez, Adrianna. "Texas' Lieutenant Governor Suggests Grandparents Are Willing to Die for US Economy." *USA Today*, March 24, 2020.

Rosen, Stanley. *Nihilism: A Philosophical Essay*. Ithaca, NY: Yale University Press, 1969.

Rousseau, Jean-Jacques. *The Social Contract and the First and Second Discourses*. New Haven, CT: Yale University Press, 2002.

Sayers, Sean. *Marxism and Human Nature*. New York: Routledge, 1998.

Sayre-McCord, Geoffrey, and David Hume. *Hume: Moral Philosophy*. New York: Hackett Publishing Company, 2006.

Shaw, Gary C. "Socialist Individualism." *Studies in Soviet Thought* 21, no. 1 (1980): 331–339.

Shelby, Tommie. "Afro-Analytical Marxism and the Problem of Race." Presidential Address Presented at the 117th Eastern Division Meeting of the American Philosophical Association. January 16, 2021. Virtual presentation.

Sherman, Howard. "Marx and Determinism." *Journal of Economic Issues* 15, no. 1 (1981): 61–71.

Shiell, Timothy. "On Marx's Holism." *History of Philosophy Quarterly* 4, no. 2 (1987): 235–246.

Shoikhedbrod, Igor. *Revisiting Marx's Critique of Liberalism*. New York: Springer International, 2019.

Siegel, Rachel. "The Gripping Sermon That Got 'Under God' Added to the Pledge of Allegiance on Flag Day." *Washington Post*, June 14, 2018. https://www.washingtonpost.com/news/retropolis/wp/2018/06/14/the-gripping-sermon-that-got-under-god-added-to-the-pledge-of-allegiance-on-flag-day/.

Singer, Daniel J. "Mind the Is–Ought Gap." *Journal of Philosophy* 112, no. 4 (2015): 193–210.

Smith, Sheldon. "Kant's Foundations for Newtonian Science." In *The Oxford Handbook of Newton*, edited by Eric Schliesser and Chris Smeenk. New York: Oxford University Press, 2017.

Sowell, Thomas. "Karl Marx and the Freedom of the Individual." *Ethics* 73, no. 2 (1963): 119–125.

Stepelevich, Lawrence S. "Max Stirner and Ludwig Feuerbach." *Journal of the History of Ideas* 39, no. 3 (1978): 451–463.

Stirner, Max. *Der Einzige Und Sein Eigenthum*. Leipzig: Verlag von Otto Wigand, 1845.

Stirner, Max. *The Ego and Its Own*. Translated by David Leopold. New York: Cambridge University Press, 1995.

Terence. *Terence*. New York: G. P. Putnam's Sons, 1920.

Thomas, Paul. "Karl Marx and Max Stirner." *Political Theory* 3, no. 2 (1975): 159–179.

Tomasello, Michael. *Becoming Human: A Theory of Ontogeny*. Cambridge, MA: Harvard University Press, 2019.

Townshend, Jules. *The Politics of Marxism: The Critical Debates*. London: Leicester University Press, 1996.

Trotsky, Leon, John Dewey, and George Edward Novack. *Their Morals and Ours: Marxist Versus Liberal Views on Morality*. 5th ed. New York: Pathfinder Press, 1973.

Troyer, John, ed. *The Classical Utilitarians: Bentham and Mill*. Indianapolis: Hackett Publishing, 2003.

Truitt, Willis H. *Marxist Ethics: A Short Exposition*. New York: International Publishers, 2005.

"U.C.L.A. Barred from Pressing Red's Ouster." *New York Times*, October 21, 1969, p. 35.

University Bulletin: A Weekly Bulletin for the Staff of the University of California. Berkeley: Office of Official Publications, University of California, 1969.

Ware, Robert X. *Marx on Emancipation and Socialist Goals: Retrieving Marx for the Future*. New York: Springer, 2018.

Weikart, Richard. "Marx, Engels, and the Abolition of the Family." *History of European Ideas* 18, no. 5 (1994): 657–672.

West, Cornel. *The Ethical Dimensions of Marxist Thought*. New York: Monthly Review Press, 1991.

Wilde, Lawrence. *Ethical Marxism and Its Radical Critics*. New York: Springer, 1998.

Wills, Vanessa. "Marx." In *A Companion to Atheism and Philosophy*, edited by Graham Oppy, 43–57. Hoboken, NJ: Wiley-Blackwell, 2019.

Wills, Vanessa. "Philosophy as a Virtuous Irritation: Can There Be Ruthless Criticism in Safe Spaces?" https://politicalphilosopher.net/2016/09/23/featured-philosopher-vanessa-wills/, September 23, 2016.

Wills, Vanessa. "PPE in Marx's Materialist Conception of History." In *The Routledge Handbook of Philosophy, Politics, and Economics*, edited by Chris Melenovsky, 43–51. Boca Raton, FL: Taylor & Francis, 2022.

Wills, Vanessa. "Towards a Concept of Revolutionary Admiration: Marx and the Commune." In *The Moral Psychology of Admiration*, edited by Alfred Archer and André Grahle, 113–129. Lanham, MD: Rowman & Littlefield, 2019.

Wood, Allen. *The Free Development of Each: Studies on Freedom, Right and Ethics in German Philosophy*. New York: Cambridge University Press, 2014.

Wood, Allen. *Karl Marx*. Boston: Routledge & Kegan Paul, 1981.

Wood, Allen. "The Marxian Critique of Justice." *Philosophy & Public Affairs* 1, no. 3 (1972): 244–282.

Wood, Allen. "Marx on Right and Justice: A Reply to Husami." *Philosophy & Public Affairs* 8, no. 3 (1979): 267–295.

Wood, Allen. "Marx's Critical Anthropology: Three Recent Interpretations." *Review of Metaphysics* 26, no. 1 (1972): 118–139.

Ypi, Lea. "From Revelation to Revolution: The Critique of Religion in Kant and Marx." *Kantian Review* 22, no. 4 (2017): 661–681.

Index

For the benefit of digital users, indexed terms that span two pages (e.g., 52–53) may, on occasion, appear on only one of those pages.

abolition
   of alienation, 65, 68, 72, 73, 74, 76, 112–13
   of capitalism, 13, 21, 24–25, 76, 164–65, 211, 223, 230–31
   of ideology, 24–28
   of morality, 2, 15, 57, 136, 138–39, 142, 143, 146–47, 193, 213, 214–15, 219, 220–21, 223–24, 225–26
   of religion, 173, 220
abstract, 4–5, 16–17, 22, 30–31, 37–38, 41, 46, 48, 52, 53, 54, 58, 59, 81, 90–91, 96, 103, 123, 125, 131, 162, 167, 169, 171, 180–81, 184–85, 198, 216, 218, 223–24, 229, 230, 232. *See also* concrete
abundance, 158, 160, 199, 200, 210–11, 243. *See also* resources, scarcity
activism, ix, 42–43, 244–45
actuality, 16–17, 18–19, 27–28, 47, 51, 60, 64–65, 66–67, 139–40, 141, 150, 151, 171, 172, 198, 220–21, 231–32, 234–35
Adler, Max, 2, 190
agency, 2–3, 80, 85, 97–98, 100–1, 112, 118, 136, 169, 190, 192, 234, 240
ahistorical, 9, 26, 73, 121, 167, 187
aim, 53, 64–65, 68, 70, 72–73, 75–76, 81, 88, 95, 112, 121, 126–27, 128, 149–50, 193, 226, 229, 239, 240, 242. *See also* end; teleology
alienation, 14, 29, 46, 58, 68, 72–94, 103, 125, 129–30, 132–33, 134, 144–45, 146, 164, 167–68, 172, 191, 216, 217, 236. *See also Entfremdung; Entäußerung*

Althusser, Louis, 11, 13, 14, 17, 28–30, 73–74, 190–91. *See also* interpellation
altruism, 44, 54–55, 135, 217–18. *See also* sacrifice
amoral, 2, 5, 49, 111, 144, 147, 149–50, 213
Analytical Marxism, 7–8, 37–38, 134, 137. *See also* Cohen, G. A.; Erik Olin Wright; Roemer, John; Rational Choice Marxism
analytical philosophy, 6–7, 8–9, 48, 96–97, 137, 139, 160
ancient Greece, 11, 88, 89, 101, 103, 122, 152. *See also* Aristotle; Epicurus
animals, 50, 51, 52, 59, 63, 67–68, 81, 82, 87, 102, 119, 126
antagonism, 66, 69, 96–97, 117, 124, 169, 221, 222. *See also* conflict
   class (*see* class conflict)
   social, 37, 136, 152, 163, 170
anthropocentrism, 60
anthropology, 3–4, 53, 54, 114–15, 121, 122–23, 125, 162. *See also* Morgan, Lewis Henry
Anti-Dühring, 10
antithesis, 214. *See also* antagonism; conflict; contradiction
appearance, 47, 48, 52, 53, 54–55, 64–65, 67–68, 69–71, 74–75, 102–3, 125, 151, 180, 201, 202. *See also* Essence
aristocracy, 41, 174. *See also* feudalism
Aristotle, 7, 49, 102, 104, 105, 191, 231–33, 236–37. *See also* De Anima
asceticism, 175, 243
atheism, 59–61, 131, 177

atomism, 74–75, 101–4, 118, 122–24, 125, 126, 132–33, 143, 150, 154, 159. *See also* Democritus; *Difference Between the Democritean and E.Picurean Philosophy of Nature, The*; Epicurus
Austro-Marxism, *See* Adler, Max
autonomy, 169–70, 179–80, 182, 183, 184, 189, 222. *See also* self-determination

Balzac, Honoré de, 108
Bauer, Bruno, 40, 87–88, 173, 174, 215
Bauer, Edgar, 40, 215
behavior, 52, 72–73, 95, 97, 100–1, 106–7, 111, 132–33, 139, 146, 226, 227, 229, 237–38
being, 7, 9, 36, 37–38, 59, 60, 102–3, 104, 105, 213–14. *See also* dialectics; social being; totality
belief, 31, 43–44, 59–61, 172, 173
Bentham, Jeremy, 142–43, 170, 171, 194–203, 205, 206, 207, 230
Bernstein, Eduard, 2, 160, 183, 185–88, 190, 191–92. *See also* evolutionary socialism; Karl Kautsky
biology, 50, 61–62, 63, 67, 69–70, 81–82, 113, 119, 126–27, 229, 242–43
biologism, 50
Blackledge, Paul, 49, 134, 177
blame, 95, 209, 210
bourgeois, *See* class, capitalist
Brenkert, George, 155, 160, 197
British Idealism, 6
Brown, Ricardo, 175
Brudney, Daniel, 2, 256n.19

capacities, 14, 27, 52, 57, 63, 66–67, 72, 76, 82, 89, 100–1, 119, 121, 122, 125, 128, 132, 156–57, 170, 233, 240
capital, 1, 2, 32, 34, 47, 93–94, 106–7, 110, 125, 144, 145, 148–49, 166, 199, 204–5, 211, 223, 229, 242
Capital: A Critique of .Political Economy, 36, 54, 92, 101, 105, 106, 108, 110, 121–22, 229, 239
Carver, Terrell, 262–63n.20, 270n.37, 274n.25
Categorical Imperative, The, 168–69, 180–82, 189, 191
causation, 93, 99, 103–4, 122, 179–80, 184–85, 187, 204

Celikates, Robin, 252n.38, 255n.4
children, 158, 260–61n.2. *See also* family
Chitty, Andrew, 61–62
choice, 106–8, 111, 113, 186, 187–88, 190, 240
Christianity, 166, 167–68, 173–74, 175–76, 191, 210. *See also* atheism; religion
Churchich, Nicholas, 209–10
citizenshi.P, 105, 148–49, 152, 153–54, 155, 222
civil society, 123, 124, 152, 153, 154, 214
"Civil War in France, The," 141
class, 26, 31, 56, 57, 73, 98, 136, 193–94, 205–6
  capitalist, 12, 18–20, 53, 76–77, 88, 99, 105–6, 107–8, 110, 136, 142, 144, 166, 193, 211
  class antagonism, 26–27, 31–33, 40, 144, 161, 163, 219, 220, 222, 223–24
  class consciousness, 17, 31–32, 36, 160
  class domination, 24–25, 27, 47, 222, 223–24
  class interests, 15, 17, 18–19, 31, 42, 43–44, 54, 56–57, 112, 134, 136, 151–52, 166, 182–83, 185, 193–94, 236
  class reductionism, 35–36
  class society, 4, 7, 10–11, 13, 18–20, 21, 24–25, 26–27, 33, 34, 35–36, 38, 39, 40–41, 47, 64, 65, 66–67, 76, 78, 84, 86, 88, 107–8, 109, 112–13, 135, 139, 150, 161, 162–63, 164–65, 170, 172, 197, 198, 210, 211, 220–21
  class standpoint, 18, 20–21
  class struggle, 5, 10–11, 23, 24–25, 41, 78, 111, 136, 139, 156, 163
  ruling, 12–13, 20–21, 23, 31, 32, 38, 40, 41, 151, 176, 236 (*see also* capitalist class)
  working, 4–5, 10, 12–13, 18–19, 20, 22–23, 24, 25, 31–32, 37, 41, 43–44, 47, 72, 76–78, 83, 98, 105–6, 107–8, 109, 135, 136, 147–48, 154, 155, 174, 186, 187–88, 193–94, 208, 214, 222
climate, x, 1, 12, 110, 113, 171
Cohen, G. A., 37–38, 137, 192, 206, 207. *See also* Analytical Marxism
collective, 1–2, 54, 133–34, 146–47, 156, 182–83, 190, 226, 243

commodity, 56, 74, 75, 78–79, 80, 86, 92, 142, 143, 145–46, 147–48, 156, 164, 204–5, 234–35
  commodity exchange, 142, 143, 145, 156, 206–7, 224–25, 228–29. *See also* exchange
  commodity fetishism, 175, 234
communism, 9–10, 24–27, 40–41, 42–44, 49, 58, 63, 69, 70–71, 72–73, 77–78, 96, 98, 99, 105, 109–10, 112–13, 121–22, 125, 130, 133, 140, 141, 147, 149–50, 155, 161, 162, 165, 175, 186, 192–94, 215–16, 217–18, 219, 220–21, 223–24, 226, 227–28, 237, 238, 240, 245
Communist Manifesto, The, 19–21, 37, 40, 84, 87, 101, 105, 109, 118, 136, 144–45, 219
compatibilism, 96–97. *See also* incompatibilism; determinism
compatibilism (dialectical), 14, 97, 100–1, 139, 187, 193
Competition, 46–47, 74, 78–79, 110, 111, 125, 144–45, 146, 150, 152, 155, 204, 206–7, 210–11
compulsion, 19–20, 51–52, 74, 77, 80–81, 83, 85, 88, 95, 99, 100–1, 105–6, 108, 110–11, 123, 143, 147–49, 154, 163, 164, 204, 223–24, 239. *See also* determinism
concrete, 8–9, 28, 29, 32, 40–41, 52, 53, 54–55, 57, 59, 64–65, 69, 97, 99–100, 103, 105, 114–15, 118, 121, 124, 132–34, 139, 141, 143, 148, 160, 167–68, 171, 175, 177, 179–80, 182, 188–89, 194, 196–97, 214, 215, 216, 223, 224–25. *See also* abstract
conflict, 7, 8–9, 10–11, 18, 22, 23, 24, 35, 37–38, 44, 47, 102, 126, 144–45, 147, 154, 169, 170, 171, 198, 210–11, 227, 238. *See also* antagonism
consciousness, 16–17, 25, 30, 31–32, 33, 34, 35, 36, 88, 160, 225
  class, 17, 31–32 (*see also* ideology)
consequentialism, 170, 182, 224–25
conservative, 19, 195, 210
consumption, 3, 67, 127–28, 158. *See also* production
contemplation, 10, 16–17, 30–31, 36, 97, 103, 131, 213–14, 232–33. *See also* .praxis

contract, 85, 142, 147–48, 161–62. *See also* Social Contract Theory
contradiction, 7, 11–12, 23, 25–26, 36, 37–38, 39, 47, 76–77, 97, 102–3, 105, 107–8, 109, 114, 135, 138, 143, 146, 149, 150, 151, 163, 180, 187–89, 204–5, 214, 219, 223–24, 236. *See also* antagonism; conflict
Contribution to the Critique of Hegel's Philosophy of Right, A, 30, 150, 151, 173. *See also* Philosophy of Right, The; Hegel
Contribution to the Critique of .Political Economy, A, 18–19, 35, 65–66, 92, 145, 237
cosmopolitan, 120–21
creativity, 4, 61–62, 72–73, 88, 89, 90, 100–1, 144–45, 177, 227–28, 229, 237
crisis, 1, 12, 23, 64–65, 113, 166, 186, 204, 239, 240, 242–43
Critique of the Gotha Programme, 85, 141, 157–58, 159

d'Holbach, Baron, 194, 195, 198. *See also* compatibilism; determinism; freedom; incompatibilism
Darwin, Charles, 210. *See also* Social Darwinism
Davis, Angela, 15, 244–45
De Anima, 231–33. *See also* Aristotle; sense-perception
democracy, x, 24–25, 41, 76, 88, 105, 118, 151–52, 155, 159, 198, 222, 227
Democritus, 101–2, 104, 121–22. *See also* atomism; *Difference Between the Democritean and Epicurean .Philosophy of Nature, The*; Epicurus
determinate, 46, 47, 52, 54–55, 103
determinism, 6, 12–13, 30, 95, 99, 100–1, 106, 111, 178–80, 192–93. *See also* compatibilism; freedom; incompatibilism
  economic, 11, 84, 95, 109, 116, 186, 207, 242
  freedom and, 14, 16, 49, 94, 96–98, 101, 122, 139, 144–45, 180, 187, 193
  mechanistic, 101, 104, 166–67, 188
dialectical materialism, 48, 161, 187–88. *See also* historical materialism

dialectics, 7–9, 14–15, 37–38, 47, 48, 50, 69, 134, 138, 160, 178, 220, 232–33. *See also* Hegel, G.W.H
dictatorship of the proletariat, 27, 33
Difference Between the Democritean and Epicurean Philosophy of Nature, The, 101, 121–22, 132–33, 150, 175. *See also* atomism; Democritus; Epicurus
distribution, 157–58, 202–4, 205, 206–7. *See also* redistribution
diversity, 66–67, 109, 201
dogma, 17, 195, 198–200, 205, 245
domination, 59, 75, 82–84, 113–14, 118, 142, 146, 150, 162, 167, 170, 172, 223–24. *See also* class, class domination
duty, 63, 163, 209, 216, 218, 226
dynamism, 6–7, 8–9, 32, 47, 52, 53, 54–55, 56, 68, 97, 126, 139, 140, 168, 228, 237, 239–40, 243

Eagleton, Terry, 59, 60–61, 63
ecology, 107, 113. *See also* climate
Economic and .Philosophic Manuscripts of 1844, The, 78, 84, 100, 141, 230
economic interests, 18–19, 43–44, 77, 111–12, 146, 156. *See also* class, class interests
economics, *See* political economy
egalitarianism, *See* equality
Ego and Its Own, The, *See* Stirner, Max
egoism, 74–75, 77, 123, 130–31, 132, 133–34, 135, 152, 154. *See also* individualism; Stirner, Max
Eighteenth Brumaire of Louis Bonaparte, The, 95–96, 111–12
Elster, Jon, 7, 137
emancipation, 5, 10, 39, 45, 68, 78, 83–84, 90–91, 95–96, 109, 113, 125, 135, 146–47, 153–54, 156, 193–94, 211–12, 214, 216, 221, 222, 223–24, 230–31, 233, 236. *See also* freedom
embodiment, 169, 211
emergence, 2–3, 16–17, 33–34, 50, 52, 72, 106, 119–20, 121, 126–27, 129, 134, 135, 236
empirical, 8, 33–34, 36, 45, 53, 55–56, 57, 59, 66–67, 162, 172, 183, 192

end, 27, 69, 81–82, 85, 86, 90, 125, 134, 147, 177, 181, 184, 200, 214, 229. *See also* aim; teleology
"End of History, The," 1, 237. *See also* Fukayama, Francis
Engels, Friedrich, 3–4, 10, 108, 109, 162–63, 215–16
enlightenment, 8–9, 20, 24, 162–63, 208, 230
Entäußerung, 75, 84, 90–91, 93. *See also* alienation; *Entfremdung*
Entfremdung, 84, 87–88. *See also* alienation; *Entäußerung*
entitlement, 150, 152, 156, 161–62, 165
Epicurus, 101, 121–22. *See also* atomism; Democritus; *Difference Between the Democritean and E.Picurean Philosophy of Nature, The*
epiphenomenalism, 13–14. *See also* causation
epistemic access, 225, 230, 232, 234
epistemology, 129, 232–33
equality, 4, 11–12, 93, 141, 142, 143–44, 156–58, 196, 198
equivalent, 142, 143, 146
essence, 47, 48, 51, 52, 53, 54–55, 58, 61–62, 64–65, 67–68, 69–70, 72, 73, 75–76, 81, 82, 83, 85, 88, 102–3, 105, 115, 119–20, 125, 131, 134, 150, 164, 174, 175, 180, 202, 206–7, 233–34. *See also* appearance
essentialism, 48, 117, 198–99, 231, 233
estates, 151, 214. *See also Contribution to the Critique of Hegel's Philosophy of Right, A*
"Estranged Labour," 75. *See also Economic and .Philosophic Manuscripts of 1844, The*
estrangement, 76–77, 79–80, 82–83, 85, 86. *See also* alienation; *Entfremdung*; *Entäusserung*
ethical life, 226, 227. *See also* Hegel; *Sittlichkeit*
Europe, 145, 273n.12
evolution, 50, 210, 260–61, 262n.4
Evolutionary Socialism, 183, 186–87, 188. *See also* Bernstein, Eduard
exchange, 18, 74, 85, 89, 93, 119, 126, 142, 146, 156, 175, 207, 222, 224–25, 230, 235
exchange value, 143, 229

existence, *See* being
existential, 177
experience, 32, 76, 85, 86–87, 120–21, 167–68, 171, 175, 191, 201, 222
  lived experience, 77, 114–15, 188–89
  sense experience, 129. *See also* sense-perception
  subjective experience, 77, 78, 79, 82, 83, 196–97
Exploitation, 5, 11–12, 19–20, 26, 32, 37, 54, 60–61, 78–79, 92, 113–14, 147–48, 157, 163, 200–1, 211, 214, 219, 222, 223–24, 225–26, 230, 236, 238, 245–46
  of the natural world, 243
expropriation, 160
external world, 51–52, 53, 64, 68, 85, 228–29, 230, 232–33, 241–42
extinction, 108, 113
eye, 230–32, 233–35. *See also* De Anima; sense-organ; vision

family, 126, 147–48, 220–21, 257, 273
Farneth, Molly, 227
fascism, 1, 43, 113
fatalism, 94, 95, 166–67, 178–79, 192, 240. *See also* determinism
feudalism, 11–12, 19–20, 23, 78, 105–6, 120–21, 145, 150, 159, 175. *See also* aristocracy
Feuerbach, Ludwig, 60, 73–74, 131, 132, 173. *See also* "Theses on Feuerbach."
Fichte, Johann, 177
flourishing. *See* human flourishing
forces, 41, 43, 44, 56, 58, 63, 98, 100–2, 124, 126, 132, 139, 142, 144–45, 172, 173, 187, 243
  economic forces, 97–98, 146, 163
  external forces, 101–2, 104, 179–80, 185. *See also* determinism
  forces of production, 18, 21, 22, 24, 66, 89, 91, 112–13, 124, 126–27, 128, 158, 204–5, 242
  historical force, 22–23, 98, 105–6, 242–43
  natural forces, 51–52, 89
Forst, Rainer, 191–92, 259
Fourier, Charles, 41
France, 39, 62, 99
  French Revolution, 66–67, 143–44, 148–49, 151–52, 182–83, 185

freedom, 4, 12, 14, 25–26, 79, 91, 95, 117, 121–22, 131, 134–35, 139, 169–70, 179, 180, 183, 187, 188, 206, 210–11, 212, 219, 220–21, 223–24, 228, 236, 241, 242. *See also* compatibilism, determinism, incompatibilism, unfreedom
  abstract freedom, 132–33
  academic freedom, 244–45
  bourgeois freedom, 14–15, 21, 166, 221, 223
  concrete freedom, 99–100
  and determinism (*see* determinism, freedom and)
  liberal freedom, 144–45
  negative freedom, 153
  positive freedom, 153
free will, 99–100, 142, 169–70, 179–80, 182, 184–85, 189, 190, 191, 211
friendship, 105, 227
Fromm, Erich, 68
Fukayama, Francis, 1. *See also* "End of History, The"
fulfillment, 12, 61–62, 63–64, 149–50, 167–68, 174, 210–11, 217. *See also* satisfaction
Furner, James, 8, 38

German Idealism, 30, 178, 179. *See also* Fichte ,Johann; Hegel, G. W. H.; Kant, Immanuel
Germany, 3–4, 39, 41, 42–43, 73–74, 115, 182–83, 185
globalization, 120–21, 222
gravediggers, 4–5, 47, 105–6
Greece (ancient), 11, 101, 122–23, 163. *See also* Aristotle; Democritus; Epicurus
Groff, Ruth, 228–29
Grundrisse, 2–3, 62, 67, 88–90, 93–94, 114–15, 119, 121–22, 125–26, 127–28, 137, 141, 143, 144–45, 194, 228, 240–42

habit, 226, 227, 237–38
happiness, 124, 128, 170, 176, 195–97, 202–3. *See also* Bentham, Jeremy; utilitarianism
Haslanger, Sally, 264n.42. *See also* methodological holism
heaven, 54–55, 123, 174, 175, 176, 210–11
hedonism, 198

Hegel, G. W. H., 73, 76-77, 99, 100, 150-51, 153, 178, 184-85, 214, 226-28, 230, 232-33, 237, 243, 245
  Hegelianism, 6-7, 30, 35-36, 47, 72-73, 104, 115, 134 (*see also* Young Hegelians)
Heller, Agnes, 61-62
Helvétius, 194, 195, 198, 201-2
hierarchy, 124, 163, 172
historical materialism, 3-4, 6, 8-9, 10, 13-14, 17-18, 29, 30, 31, 38-39, 45, 84, 92, 95, 97, 99, 109, 114-15, 117, 119-20, 162, 166-67, 169-70, 178, 183, 184, 187, 188, 191, 192, 215, 225-26. *See also* dialectical materialism
historicism, 2, 28, 134
historicity, 29, 134, 168, 213
historiography, 14, 60-61, 178
history, 16-17, 26, 28, 29, 95-96, 97, 98, 111-13, 125, 126
  The Science of, 6, 167
Hobbes, Thomas, 210, 274-75n.27
Hobsbawm, Eric, 145
holism, 7-8, 12-13, 37, 136. *See also* methodological holism; methodological individualism; totality
Holy Family, The (or Critique of Critical Criticism), 76, 83, 122-23, 141, 151-52, 174, 217-18
hope, 172-73, 193-94, 210-11, 243
Hudis, Peter, 221
human flourishing, 4, 14-15, 37, 44-45, 50, 53, 68, 70-71, 165, 177
humanism, 2, 11, 73-74, 93-94, 131, 132
human nature, 14, 72-73, 74, 76-78, 81, 83-84, 119-20, 121-22, 125, 127, 167-68, 172, 200-2, 208, 223-24, 233-34, 237. *See also* species being
Hume, David, 46-47, 48, 179
Husami, Ziyad, 157

idealism, 4-5, 34, 103, 132, 135, 178, 183-84, 235, 242
ideality, 34-35, 269-70n.34
ideals, 9, 94, 112-13, 134, 143, 144, 147, 174
ideology, 22, 24, 30, 94, 134, 147, 191, 192, 223-24, 225. *See also* consciousness
  bourgeois, 18-21, 23, 157-58, 209-10, 251
  proletarian, 18, 22, 24
ideology critique, 16-45, 182-83, 225-26
incompatibilism, 96-98. *See also* compatibilism
independence, 122-23, 152-53, 154, 223, 234
individualism, 68, 119, 132-33, 134, 136, 138, 139
individuality, 14, 103, 114-15, 117, 174, 175, 223-24, 240-41, 242. *See also* rich individuality; social individuals
individuation, 119, 122, 126-27
industry, 60, 127, 208-9, 239, 253-54n.55
inevitability, 98, 99, 105, 109-10, 139, 187, 192. *See also* determinism
interdependence, 48, 117, 120
interests, *See also* class, class interest; economic interest
  common, 56-57, 221
  objective, 216
  particular, 31, 99-100, 151-52, 169, 198, 214
  private, 142-43, 152, 154, 170, 180, 210-11, 214
  universal, ix, 19, 22-23, 37, 56-57, 99-100, 136, 193-94, 214-15, 216, 217
interpellate, 29. *See also* Althusser, Louis
irony, 99, 108, 135, 182-83, 220-21, 222
irrationalism, 12, 150, 172, 250n.7
is-ought fallacy, 48. *See also* Hume, David

Jaeggi, Rahel, 258-59n.1
Jewish Question, On the, 75, 153-54, 159
Johnston, Adrian, 256n.18, 261n.3
justice, 25-26, 131, 143-44, 213, 219, 244-45

Kain, Philip, 2, 57, 164, 183, 190-91
Kamenka, Eugene, 91, 98
Kandiyali, Jan, 218
Kant, Immanuel, 99, 122, 161-62, 224, 236-37. *See also* Categorical Imperative, The; German Idealism
  Kantian ethics, 2, 182-83
Kautsky, Karl, 188-90. *See also* Bernstein, Eduard
Kriege, Hermann, 215-17, 218

labor, 30–31, 32, 47–48, 55–56, 63–64, 67, 73, 74, 75, 80, 81–82, 83, 84–85, 87–88, 119–20, 127, 235, 243, 255n.12. *See also* wage labor
  alienated, 67, 112–13
  dead, 56, 80
  living, 90–91, 241
labor power, 56, 74, 75–76, 83, 85, 86–87, 88, 142, 143, 148
land, 78–79, 145, 160, 250n.7
law, 24–25, 142
  deterministic, 64–65, 97–98, 110, 111, 187
  natural, 105, 239
  physical, 169
  social, 65
lawlikeness, 2, 169, 179
Leibniz, Gottfried Wilhelm, 101
Lenin, Vladimir Ilyich, 255n.3
liberalism, 124, 135, 149, 166, 194, 205–6
liberation, 11–12, 60–61, 68. *See also* emancipation; freedom
liberty, 11–12, 93, 148–49, 152. *See also* freedom
  natural, 152–53
life activity, 52, 75, 86–87
Locke, John, 19, 123, 124, 147, 153, 161–62, 166
love, 168, 175, 210–11, 233–34
Love, S. M., 191–92, 193–94
Lukács, Georg, 63–64
Luxemburg, Rosa, 160, 240

MacIntyre, Alasdair, 49, 177
Malthus, Thomas Robert, 171, 199, 208, 209
Manifesto of the Communist Party, The, See Communist Manifesto, The
market, 56, 64, 74, 75, 145, 147–48, 235
material conditions, 1–2, 31–32, 34, 66, 128, 140, 173, 184–85
material interests, 5, 38–39, 167–68, 169, 184–85
materiality, 34, 100, 175
material resources, 63, 67, 78, 143, 153, 154, 200
matter, 13–14, 30–31, 101–3, 187, 231, 232–33, 234, 235

McCarney, Joseph, 35
McCarthy, George, 103, 104
McDowell, John, 275n.38. *See also* virtue ethics
Meikle, Scott, 231
Messianism, 68
Mészáros, István, 74–75
metabolism, 27, 50, 243. *See also* labor
metaethics, 188–89, 226
metaphysics, 122–23, 225, 269n.23
method, 136–37
  analytical, 8
  scientific, 59, 98
methodological holism, 7–8, 136–37, 138. *See also* being; dialectics; totality
methodological individualism, 136, 137–39, 140
Mill, James, 194, 198, 199. *See also* utilitarianism
Mill, John Stuart, 167, 170, 171, 194, 203, 204, 205, 206–7, 224–25. *See also* utilitarianism
Mills, Charles, 11–12, 13, 17, 32–33, 135
money, 63–64, 75, 85, 118, 171, 207, 224–25, 267
moralism, 17–18, 40–41, 42–44, 215–16, 218, 240, 247–48n.6, 248n.9
moral particularism, 275n.38. *See also* McDowell, John
Morgan, Lewis Henry, 3–4, 114–15, 162–63
Mystères de Paris, Les, 174, 175
mysticism, 7, 115, 178, 242
  mystification, 11–12, 17, 29, 34, 35–36, 115

Nasser, Alan G., 53
nationality, 221
nature, 18, 51–52, 55–56, 60, 89, 129, 233–34, 236, 241–42, 243
negation, 47, 72–73, 76–77, 100–1, 115, 146, 155, 220–21
  negation of the 223
neoliberalism, 1, 12
Newton, Isaac, 179
Ng, Karen, 227
Nicomachean Ethics, The, 7. *See also* Aristotle
Nielsen, Kai, 251n.18

nihilism, 5, 49, 129–30, 135
nonideological, 18, 25, 33, 34, 36. *See also* consciousness; ideology; objectivity
Novakovic, Andreja, 226, 227

objectivity, 5, 8–9, 29, 82, 100, 150, 183, 227, 229, 232, 236–37
obligation, 191, 225, 226
ontology, 82, 129
oppression, x, 11–12, 176
Origin of the Family, Private Property, and the State, The, 3–4, 114–15, 162. *See also* Engels, Friedrich; Morgan, Lewis Henry
Owen, Robert, 41, 107–8, 207

Paden, Roger, 41, 42–44
Paris Commune, The, 218. *See also* French Revolution, The
particularity, 37, 233
patriarchy, 11–12, 162–63
Peffer, R. G., 155, 160
perception, 60, 224–25, 230, 231–32, 233. *See also* De Anima; sense–perception
perfectionism (moral), 191, 236
Philosophy of Right, The, 99, 150, 151, 214. *See also Contribution to the Critique of Hegel's Philosophy of Right, A*; Hegel, G. W. H
Pickford, Henry, 233
political economy, 11, 105, 125, 138–39, 194, 205
political science, 25–26, 27, 219, 220
Popper, Karl, 98
positivism, 29, 105
poverty, 46–47, 100, 171, 208, 209
Poverty of Philosophy, On The, 20–21. *See also* Proudhon, Pierre
praxis, 5, 69, 105, 233, 236–37
private accumulation, 76, 88, 113–14, 145, 171, 199, 204, 211, 229
private property, 78–79, 124, 152, 154, 155–56, 159, 160, 196–97, 198, 230–31
production, 2–3, 55–56, 61–62, 64–65, 66, 67, 82–83, 88–90, 126, 175, 199, 200, 204, 239
  means of, 76, 92–93, 143, 146–47, 156–57, 199–200, 206, 235, 266
  mode of, 55–56, 57, 66, 106, 112, 113, 120, 127, 143, 146, 159, 203, 207, 221, 239
  relations of, 18, 22, 24, 29, 156–57, 203, 204–5
Profit, 74, 75–76, 107, 109, 110, 113, 127, 128, 200, 202, 204
progress, 7, 11–12, 18–20, 22–23, 24, 101, 108, 109–10, 121, 128, 155, 173, 208, 209–10
proletariat, *See* class, working
Proudhon, Pierre, 10, 143
Prussia, 150, 151, 175–76
psychologism, 72, 79

qualities, 102–3, 131, 184–85, 230–31, 234–35. *See also* abstraction; atomism; concrete

radical irreligion, 129, 173, 177. *See also* atheism; Christianity
Rational Choice Marxism, 137–38, 139. *See also* Analytical Marxism
reactionary, 16, 22, 24, 25, 35, 108, 166–67, 173, 239
realism, 108
Realm of Ends, The, 181–82, 184, 189, 236–37. *See also* Categorical Imperative, The; Kant, Immanuel
recognition, 12, 99–100, 115, 235, 264n.44
reconciliation, 46, 68, 96, 102, 137, 258–59n.1, 276n.46
redistribution, 196, 198, 202–3. *See also* distribution
Red Scare, 251n.8
reforms, 42–43, 107–8, 147, 186, 187–88, 200–1
religion, 24–26, 131, 153–54, 172–73, 176–77, 219, 220, 223–24, 225. *See also* atheism; Christianity; radical irreligion
reproduction, 52, 81–82, 127, 208, 217
revisionism, 187–88
revolution, 4–5, 40, 42–43, 70, 111, 148–49, 150, 151–52, 155, 156–57, 192, 218
rich individuality, 2–3, 119–20, 121–22, 126–28, 129, 228, 240, 241–42. *See also* individuality; social individuals
rights, *See* justice

Roemer, John, 7, 137. *See also* Analytical Marxism
Rousseau, Jean-Jacques, 79, 152–53, 161–62, 166, 208, 209–10
Ruge, Arnold, 59–60
ruling ideas, 12–13, 20–21, 31, 32, 144, 160. *See also* ideology

sacrifice, 45, 86, 87–88, 89–90, 130–31, 132, 133, 174, 175, 193, 214–15, 216
Saint-Simon, Henri, 41
saleability, 75
satisfaction. *See* fulfillment
 of needs, 13–14, 24–25, 27, 31, 48, 53, 54, 55, 56, 61–62, 68, 69–71, 74–75, 80–82, 83, 89–90, 106–7, 113, 114–15, 120, 125, 126–27, 128, 132–33, 149–50, 170, 200–1, 208, 211, 237
Sayers, Sean, 256n.16
scarcity, 150, 199, 202–3, 210–11. *See also* abundance
science, 5, 6, 8–9, 11–12, 19–20, 29, 35–36, 57, 60, 98, 113–15, 179, 217, 240–41, 242
 of history), 6, 47, 167
 natural science, 57, 60, 118
 scientificity, 10 (*see also* method)
 scientific socialism, 10–11, 14, 39, 44, 59, 92, 215–13
 social science, 57, 114–15, 118, 151, 161, 190
self-determination, 5, 185, 227. *See also* autonomy
self-realization, 10, 117, 218. *See also* flourishing
Semmig, Hermann, 40–41
sense-organ, 231–32. *See also* De Anima
sense-perception, 228–29, 230, 231–33. *See also* De Anima
Shelby, Tommie, 8–9. *See also* Analytical Marxism; analytical philosophy; method
Sherman, Howard, 106–7, 111
Shiell, Timothy, 138
Shoikhedbrod, Igor, 161–62, 163–64, 165
Silva, Ludovico, 220
Sittlichkeit, *See* ethical life
skepticism, 36, 46–47, 60–61, 69, 104. *See also* Hume, David

slavery, 77, 113–14, 141, 147–49, 152, 162–63, 166, 176
Smith, Adam, 35–36, 125
Sober, Elliott, 137. *See also* methodological individualism
social being, 6, 31–32, 33–34, 50, 54, 57, 61–62, 63–65, 67–68, 72, 81–82, 88, 119, 171, 223–24, 225–26
social contract theory, 11–12, 17, 161–62, 166
Social Darwinism, 210
social individuals, 117, 118, 121, 126, 127
socialism
 scientific, 10, 44
 Utopian, 17–18, 39, 44
social ontology, 138
sociology, 135, 157
solidarity, 26–27, 63, 70, 76, 134, 159, 188–89, 222, 236
Species, 12, 47, 52, 53, 70, 72, 75, 119, 127, 198, 211, 213–14
species-being, 52, 63, 229. *See also* essence; human nature
spirit, 30, 100, 167–68, 173
standpoint, 22–23, 89–90, 107–8, 126, 236. *See also* consciousness; ideology
Stirner, Max, 14, 44–45, 87–88, 129, 155, 173, 193, 216, 217–18, 230
subjectivity, 78, 79, 82, 83, 100, 196–97, 198, 232, 237–38
subordination, 133, 158, 171
subsistence, 10, 13–14, 30–31, 51, 63, 77, 92–93, 113, 119, 229
substance
 ideal/spiritual, 99
 metaphysical, 169
superstructure, 17, 34–36, 161, 248n.9, 252n.40
Szeliga (Franz Szeliga Zychlin von Zychlinsky), 174, 175. *See also* Holy Family, The; *Mystères of Paris, Les*

teleology, 49, 53, 64–65. *See also* aim; end; "end of History, The"
terence, 11. *See also* ancient Greece
Thatcher, Margaret, 12. *See also* neoliberalism

Theses on Feuerbach, 2, 9, 36, 48. *See also* Feuerbach, Ludwig
Thomas, Paul, 130, 131
Tomasello, Michael, 260–61n.2. *See also* evolution
totality, 6, 47, 52, 53, 54–55, 56, 57, 59, 89, 124. *See also* being; dialectics; methodological holism
Townshend, Jules, 98
transition (to communism), 43–44, 65, 216
True Socialism, 39, 40–41, 215. *See also* Utopian socialists
Truitt, Willis H., 99
Tucker, Robert, 157
Turner, Bryan S., 17, 31, 32

unfreedom, 111, 143, 144–45, 149
United States, 153, 215–16, 245, 272n.76
unity, 14, 50, 69, 155, 232–33. *See also* dialectics; totality
universality, 8–9, 37, 78, 89, 134–35, 227, 235. *See also* methodological holism; particularity; totality
use-value, 229
utilitarianism, 170–71, 194, 224–25, 229, 230. *See also* Bentham, Jeremy; Mill, James; Mill, John Stuart
Utopianism, 56, 58, 206–7. *See also* True Socialists; Utopian socialists

Utopian socialists, 41–44, 215, 218. *See also* True Socialists; Utopianism

vampire, 2, 147–48
Veräußerung, 75
violence, 42–43, 148
virtue ethics, 15, 48, 49, 177, 191, 275n.38
vision, 42, 98, 117, 205–6, 210–11, 230. *See also* De Anima; eye; sense-organ; sense-perception
voluntarism, 99, 240. *See also* free will

wage labor, 42–43, 53, 63, 77–78, 86, 87, 142, 148–49, 208
Wage Labour and Capital, 92
wages, 53, 63, 142
wealth, 89, 90–91, 92–93, 100, 105–6, 196–97, 200, 202–3, 233–34, 236
women, 21, 162–63
Wood, Allen, 91, 134, 135, 156, 157, 159, 160, 195–96, 202–3
work, *See* labor
worker, *See* class, working
worldview, 11, 19–20, 97, 101, 129, 171, 178, 240

Young Hegelians, 132, 173, 174. *See also* Bauer, Bruno; Bauer, Edgar; Feuerbach, Ludwig

Dear Reader,

We'd love your attention for one more page to tell you about the crisis in children's reading, and what we can all do.

Studies have shown that reading for fun is the **single biggest predictor of a child's future life chances** – more than family circumstance, parents' educational background or income. It improves academic results, mental health, wealth, communication skills, ambition and happiness.[1]

The number of children reading for fun is in rapid decline. Young people have a lot of competition for their time. In 2024, 1 in 10 children and young people in the UK aged 5 to 18 did not own a single book at home.[2]

Hachette works extensively with schools, libraries and literacy charities, but here are some ways we can all raise more readers:

- Reading to children for just 10 minutes a day makes a difference
- Don't give up if children aren't regular readers – there will be books for them!
- Visit bookshops and libraries to get recommendations
- Encourage them to listen to audiobooks
- Support school libraries
- Give books as gifts

There's a lot more information about how to encourage children to read on our website: **www.RaisingReaders.co.uk**

Thank you for reading.

---

[1] OECD, '21st-Century Readers: Developing Literacy Skills in a Digital World', 2021, https://www.oecd.org/en/publications/21st-century-readers_a83d84cb-en.html

[2] National Literacy Trust, 'Book Ownership in 2024', November 2024, https://literacytrust.org.uk/research-services/research-reports/book-ownership-in-2024

About the Author

Ted Kravitz is an experienced broadcast journalist who has reported on Formula 1 for nearly 30 years. During that time Ted has become something of an institution in the pit lane, working successively for ITV, the BBC, Channel 4 and Sky Sports and reporting for four BAFTA award-winning sports programmes in 2006, 2007, 2008 and 2021.

Ted's insider insights have made his on-the-spot reports essential viewing, while his widely acclaimed *Ted's Notebook* programme has become a fan favourite, explaining complex technical details for seasoned followers and taking new audiences behind the scenes with all the news from the sharp end of Formula 1. When not at the race track, Ted flies light aircraft. This is his first book.

Picture Credits

1a, 1c, 1b, 8b Ted Kravitz; 2a ©Sutton Motorsports/ZUMA Press/Alamy Stock Photo; 2b Swope/Sutton Images/Getty Images; 3a Edd Hartley/Sutton Images/Getty Images; 3b Darren Heath/Getty Images; 4a Clive Mason/Getty Images; 4b Mark Capilitan/Sutton Images/Getty Images; 5a Carlin; 5c Kym Illman; 5b Mark Capilitan/Sutton Images/Alamy Stock Photo; 6a Carl Bingham/LAT Images/Getty Images; 6b Mark Thompson/Getty Images; 7a Joe Portlock - Formula 1/Getty Images; 7b Kym Illman; 8a Mark Sutton/Sutton Images/Getty Images.

A special mention for Jennie Gow, my opposite number as BBC Radio's presenter and the only pit lane reporter to regularly join me in the actual pit lane during qualifying and the race. Following a stroke in 2023, Jennie has had to learn to talk and write again. The courage and determination she and her husband Jamie (one of my producers at Sky) have shown have been inspirational.

Which leaves one person who's piloted the F1 TV helicopter for nearly 30 years and that's 'the governor' himself, Martin Brundle. From ITV to the BBC to Sky, it's been an honour to be MB's comm box helper and reporter.

I owe a huge debt of gratitude to every F1 driver, team boss, technical director, engineer or mechanic past and present for answering my questions and to their press officers for their kind and professional collaboration. At Formula 1, thanks to Stefano Domenicali and Liam Parker, while I must reserve a special thanks to Bernie Ecclestone. 'You're not too bad nowadays,' he told me recently, 'since you grew up.'

But my professional life would be pointless without the people I do it for – any viewer, listener or reader, thank you for coming into the pit lane with me every week, and thanks to anyone who asked where I was.

Finally, much love, of course, to my family and friends. Thanks for letting me skip so many Sunday lunches. To my smart, funny, independent, bright, brilliant and beautiful daughters, thank you for not minding too much when I go away. Finally, to my 'executive producer', Kate, without whom this book wouldn't exist. Thanks for putting up with my author's travails and for editing the manuscript so brilliantly. I love what's in your head and cherish the daily joys of your companionship. I only hope my first effort is worthy of a mention on the Book Club Review podcast.

ACKNOWLEDGEMENTS

of Sky Group's Dana Strong. Thanks to my on-air colleagues, Simon Lazenby, Natalie Pinkham, whose sense of fun and charm has lit up our coverage, and Georgie Ainslie (née Thompson), whose mastery of the presenter's art saw me through my nerves at many a studio show. I began working with David Croft when we were both at the BBC and it's a pleasure to continue to listen to the voice of F1 in my headphones every week. Thanks to commentary colleagues Harry Benjamin, Ben Edwards and Alex Jaques. My two fellow reporters, Rachel Brookes, whose calm journalistic professionalism is complemented perfectly by Craig Slater, a brilliantly unconventional and idiosyncratic performer. I'm always grateful to our driver analysts for indulging my on-air questions. In alphabetical order: Jenson Button, Jamie Chadwick, Karun Chandhok, Anthony Davidson, Paul di Resta, Johnny Herbert, Damon Hill, Danica Patrick, Nico Rosberg, Naomi Schiff and Jacques Villeneuve. Not a racing driver, but I always value the quick intelligence of former engineer Bernie Collins when we're working the grid.

Thanks to our superb production team led by Tommy Herz, Jessica Medland and Jack McShane and to my pit lane technical troops – on cameras: Lee Kukor Morgan, Pete Velluet (a good man to have with you on an escalator), Keiran Startup, John Dalton, Simon Seager and Tom Basciano. On sound Dave Haigh, Tiger Harrigan, Jim Sefton and Carlton Waghorn; in the edit Tim Davis, Nick Cliff, Hugh Lutley and Simon Graham; writing online Sam Johnston, Nigel Chiu and James Galloway; and making the production happen, Laura Budd, Erin Cornwell, Georgia Constantinou, Chrissie Malone, Emma Chapman, Donald Begg, Gordon Roxburgh, Bridget Bremner and Jo Slennett. Thanks also to the directors and gallery team at Sky who cut the pictures, keep us to time, fade up the sound and roll the video.

Alan Hurndall, Valerie Garford, Sarah Needham, Anneliese Unitt and to Sally Blower for keeping the show on the road. Our lives were always enriched when we were joined by the Anglia Television power trio of Kevin Piper, Kevin Brown and Mr Steve Aldous. The ITV technical team, the exemplary camera ops Andy Parr, Mat Bryant and Keith Wilson, editors Chris Fells, Mark Jakeman and Dave Boyd Moss, comms Rob Walker, Bill Fievez, Tony Kennedy, Dave Hill and the much-missed Neil Crowland plus the graphics OGs John and Jeremy Tidy.

At ITV Network, thanks to the Controllers of Sport Mark Sharman and the great Brian Barwick for his pep talks. I'm indebted to the magnificent Murray Walker, to James Allen, who set the standard for telling stories from the pit lane, to my first co-reporter Louise Goodman, thanks for teaching me the subtleties of F1, and to the incomparable Steve Rider, 'the silver fox', thank you for your generous advice.

At BBC Sport, I'm indebted to Mark Wilkin for his wise editorship, to Barbara Slater and Ben Gallop at TV Centre and on the ground, to Andrew Benson, Sarah Holt, Sunil Patel, Tim Boyd, Richard Gort, Holly Samos, Jason Swales, Anne Somerset, Kay Satterley and Tom Gent. Thanks to the insanely talented editors Robin Nurse and Chris Denton and I loved working with the team of Lee McKenzie, Jonathan Legard, David Coulthard, Jake Humphrey and the irrepressible, irreplaceable Eddie Jordan. For the last decade and more, thanks to my friends and colleagues on the Sky Sports F1 team brought together by Martin Turner, whose encouragement and creativity always shone through. Huge thanks to Stephen Van Rooyen and Rob Webster for their leadership and impeccable judgement. And to the current Sky team, Billy McGinty, Yath Gangakumaran, Jonathan Licht and the unwavering support

Acknowledgements

I never planned on writing a book, but when literary agent Kerr MacRae suggested a 'greatest hits' compilation of F1 stories told from my viewpoint, a few ideas came together. That became more ideas when Cassell's Trevor Davies suggested something that takes the reader behind the scenes of F1. So, thanks to Trevor and Kerr for the idea and the team at Octopus: Mel Four, Erin Brown, Karen Baker, Jennifer Veall, Peter Hunt, Chris Stone and Scarlet Furness for guiding a first timer through the editing process. Hopefully this book has achieved most of its brief and for that, I'm indebted to my media centre, pit lane and paddock colleague Adam Cooper, for keeping the project on the track and out of the gravel trap.

I've been doing my day job full-time since 2002 after Neil Duncanson was brave and/or stupid enough to put an F1 obsessive with a face for radio on-air and into the pit lane. For that, I will be forever grateful. The Chrysalis Sport production team taught me many things – how to make great TV, how to put out a mixing desk that's on fire and how the best feature ideas come from a few Caipirinhas and a two-pence piece. Thanks to Rupert Bush, Dave Lewis, John Nolan, Gerard Lane, Jo Hybert, Malcolm Clinton, Andy Spellman, Andrew De Souza, Tim Breadin, Karen Raphael,

W Series 269–70; benefits of 270–3; financial difficulties 273

Walker, Murray 21, 24, 32, 35, 36, 46–7, 323–4; advice to TK 81; cue cards 46–7; 'Murray-isms' 68, 163; popularity of 39–42, 43, 54; retirement 69–70; and talkback 45–6; as a travelling companion 67; tributes to 71–7; warm-up routine 51–2; working style 48–9, 50–4

weather, disruptive 9, 94–6

Webber, Mark 107, 230, 233–5

Wheatley, Jonathan 307; Abu Dhabi GP 2021: 290–1, 296–7, 302, 306–7; and Masi 290–1, 296–7

White, Marcus 25–6

Whiting, Charlie 135, 174, 176, 191, 194, 288–90

Whitmarsh, Martin 188–9

Whitworth, John 25

Williams, Claire 269, 274

Williams, Frank 57, 212–31

Williams team 61–2, 213

Wirdheim, Bjorn 216

Wittich, Niels 307

Wolff, Susie 273

Wolff, Toto 16, 218, 220–1, 299, 307, 309–10

women: barriers to F1 participation 270–1; F1 Academy 273–4; sponsorship 274; supported by F1 teams 273–4; W Series 269–73

World Motor Sport Council 89–90, 160, 181

Wurz, Alexander 315–16

INDEX

Schumacher, Mick 207, 208–10, 294
Senna, Ayrton 21, 213
Shovlin, Andrew 191, 195, 198, 318
Silver Arrows 200, 206
Singapore GP, 2008: 42, 173–81
Sky Sports 218, 282; *The Notebook* 256–67; *The Qualifying Notebook* 258–60
Smedley, Rob 89–90
Spanish GP 1997: 58–61
Steiner, Guenther 276, 284–5
Stella, Andrea 223
Stepney, Nigel 157–9
Stoddart, Paul 73–5
support races 271, 273
Symonds, Pat 175–6; double diffuser issue 191, 194; Renault 'crash-gate' investigation 178, 180, 181–2

talkback 45–6
tape-logging 32, 33, 37
Taylor, Simon 35, 36
team bosses: competitive nature 211–12; interviewing 14–16; modern day 223; The Piranha Club 214
team orders: Ferrari controversies 84–91; open broadcast of 233–4
television. *see* broadcasting; individual stations
Todt, Jean 85, 86, 108
Toro Rosso 229–31
travel: F1 teams 117–20; spectators 127–8
tyre compounds 10
tyres. *see also* Bridgestone tyres;

Michelin tyres: changing 10–11; single set rule 131–2, 134–5; US Grand Prix 2005 131–42; wet conditions 94–6

United States GP 2005: 131–42
University Radio Exeter 24–5

Vasseur, Fred 15
Verstappen, Jos 325–6
Verstappen, Max 290–1, 307; Abu Dhabi GP 2021: 292–6, 298–9, 304, 306; career 324–9; and George Russell 328–30; and Hamilton 291–308; and Red Bull 325, 327
Vettel, Sebastian 169, 218–19, 279; Abu Dhabi GP 2010: 232; and Aston Martin 237, 282; and BMW Sauber 227–9; as a campaigner 237–8, 266; childhood 226–7; confidence 228–9, 231; and Ferrari 236–7, 246–7, 282; recklessness 226; and Red Bull 225–7, 229–32, 236; retirement 238; and Schumacher 227; and Toro Rosso 229–31; and Webber 230, 233–5
viewers, demographics of 283–4
Villeneuve, Gilles 56
Villeneuve, Jacques 37; and BMW Sauber 227–8; and Damon Hill 56, 57; and Eddie Irvine 60; and Schumacher 55–6, 57–8, 60; Spanish GP 1997: 60–3
Vowles, James 262–3, 294, 318

Piquet, Nelson Jr 42, 173–6, 178, 181
Piquet, Nelson Sr 21, 113, 176, 178
The Piranha Club 214. *see also* team bosses
pit lanes 7, 10, 14–15
pit reporting 6–8, 9, 255, 256–60. *see also* Allen, James; Goodman, Louise; live broadcasting; advice to TK 80–2; face to face communication 12; features 16–17; and media officers 12–13; notebooks 16–17, 259–61; post-race interviews 14–16, 90–1, 97, 105–7; practice sessions 7–10; qualifying 10; and team bosses 14–16
pit stops 10–11, 132, 134, 174
Powell, Alice 272
practice sessions 7–10, 48, 49
presenting 129–31, 137–8, 141
press officers 12–13
Pulling, Abbi 274

qualifying 10, 133–4, 152

race control, broadcasting 289–90, 307
race directors 289–90, 307
race strategy insights 11
radio journalism 23–5
Räikkönen, Kimi 109, 113–14, 165–6, 201, 279; world championship 2007: 161–2
Red Bull 218–19; Abu Dhabi GP 2021: 301, 302, 303–4, 306–7; Jaguar takeover 216–17; management style 247; and Renault 235, 245; and Vettel 225–7, 229–36
red flag usage 295, 303
Renault team: 2008 season 172–6; fixing Singapore 2008 GP 176–81; and McLaren 245; and Red Bull 235, 245
reporting. *see* pit reporting
Ricciardo, Daniel 235, 263
Rider, Steve 32, 33, 131, 149, 164
Roeske, Britta 264
ROKiT 269–70
Rosberg, Nico 16, 206, 314–16
Rosenthal, Jim 34–5, 36, 131, 136, 137–8, 141
Russell, George 263–4, 328–30
Ryan, Dave 150–2, 171, 272

safety cars 99, 174, 294, 295, 298, 300–1, 305
Sainz, Carlos 298, 330
Sauber. *see* BMW Sauber team
Schumacher, Michael 55–6, 76, 112–16, 131–2; and Barrichello 82–9; controversial Monaco GP 103–4, 107–11; and Damon Hill 55, 56; and Ferrari 82, 83–4; GP debut 214; and Jacques Villeneuve 55–6, 57–8, 60; and motorbikes 202; retirement 113–16, 143, 201–2; retirement, returns from 203–6; retirement, second 206–7; skiing accident 207–8; and TK 105–6; and Vettel 227

INDEX

and BMW Sauber 248; and
Ferrari 248–9; return to F1:
250–1

Latifi, Nicholas 294
Lauda, Niki 16, 221, 222, 319–21
Lazenby, Simon 129–30
LBC *Through the Night* 23–4
Lewis, Dave 31–2
Liberty Media 273
Liuzzi, Tonio 216
live broadcasting 9, 93–101; and accidents 96–8, 100–1; weather disrupting 9, 94–6
Lowe, Paddy 221–2

MACh1 32
Malaysian GP 2013: 232–5
Mansell, Nigel 21, 31, 164
Marchionne, Sergio 242–4
Marko, Helmut 215–16, 229
Masi, Michael: Abu Dhabi GP 2021: 292–308; and Jonathan Wheatley 290–1, 296–7; 'let them race' philosophy 292; as race director 289–90; rule breaking in Abu Dhabi 298–300
Massa, Felipe 89–90, 111; 2008 season 166–7, 168–71, 172, 180–1; accident in 2009: 203
Mateschitz, Dietrich 216
Mattiacci, Marco 240–2
McKenzie, Lee 184–5, 243, 262, 272
McLaren team 14, 58–9, 223; 2008 season 165–7, 168–72; Alonso/Hamilton rivalry 147–50, 152–7, 159; cars 165; and COVID-19: 275, 277–8; and Honda 188–9, 244–5; race fixing accusations 61–2; and Renault 245; 'spy-gate' scandal 157–61
Meadows, Ron 290, 318
Mercedes team 58; Abu Dhabi GP 2021: 300–3, 304–5; buys out Brawn GP 200, 206; buys out Honda 187; constructor's championships 309–10, 317–18; and hybrid V6 regulations 235; Spanish GP 1997: 58–60; Spanish GP 2016: 16; and Toto Wolff 221–2
Miami GP 2022: 253–5
Michelin tyres 131–5, 138, 142
Minagawa, Masayuki 190
Monaco GP 126; 2006: 103–4, 107–10; 2014: 97; 2024: 11
monoculars 13–14
Morrison, Stuart 260–1
Mosley, Max 159–60, 161, 176, 179

Netflix: *Drive to Survive* 93–4, 122, 211, 215, 283–6
Newey, Adrian 58, 262, 302, 318, 327
Nobels, Aurelia 274
Nolan, John 33, 37
Norris, Lando 164, 262, 330–1
Nürburgring 57–8

Park, Richard 26–7
Pérez, Sergio 293, 327
Piper, Kevin 79–80

championship 314–15; Abu Dhabi GP 2021: 292–6, 298–9, 304, 308; and Alonso 148–50, 152–7, 159; Australian GP 2020: 276–7; characteristics of success 310–13; competitive nature 311; and Ferrari 239, 310; GP2 career 144–6; and McLaren 146–7; and Mercedes 220–1; Mission 44 charity 313; and social justice 313–14; and Verstappen 291–308
Haug, Norbert 58
Hedges, David 27
helicopters, medical 9–10
Herbert, Johnny 22–3
Hill, Damon 29–30, 154; and Jacques Villeneuve 56, 57; and Schumacher 55, 56
Honda team: double diffusers 189–91; and McLaren 188–9, 244–5; and Mercedes 187; and Murray Walker 76–7; and Ross Brawn 15, 185–9
Horner, Christian 215–17; Abu Dhabi GP 2021: 296–7, 306–7
Hughes, Howard 28–9
Humphrey, Jake 130–1, 184
Hunt, James 41

IndyCar 56, 99, 271
Irvine, Eddie 60
ITV 31–7, 43, 183–4; advert breaks 35–6; *Development Corner* 265–6; *Ted's Notebook* 255, 256–67; *Testing Notebook* 265–6
Jaguar team 216–17, 321

Japanese GP 8; 1996: 40–1; 2011: 235
Jardine, Tony 35, 66, 75
Jordan, Eddie 213–15
Jordan team 213–15
journalism. *see* pit reporting

Kehm, Sabine 105, 108, 209
Kendrick, Jonathan 269, 274
Kovalainen, Heikki 165
Kravitz, Ted 43; Abu Dhabi GP 2021: 300, 304; applies for pit reporter role 79–81; and the BBC 193, 255–6; and Capital Radio 26–9; and cheese 266–7; childhood 19–21; and Chrysalis Sport 31–3, 36–8, 43–4; and COVID-19: 282; crowd interactions 167–8; and Dave Ryan 150–2; *Development Corner* 265–6; early passion for F1: 21–3; and Gemini FM 25–6; and ITV 31–3, 36–8, 43–4, 265–6; *Learn with Lewis* 267; *From the Pit Lane* 256; professional name 25–6; and Schumacher 105–6; spotter for ITV 44–50; and student radio 24–5; tape logging for ITV 31–3, 36–8, 43–4; *Ted's Lockdown Notebook* 283; *Ted's Notebook* 255, 256–67; *Testing Notebook* 265–6; and *Through the Night* radio programme 23–4
Kubica, Robert 227–8, 229; accident injuries 249–50;

INDEX

di Montezemolo, Luca 203, 240–1, 242
Domenicali, Stefano 15, 158, 240
double diffusers 190–4
Drive to Survive (Netflix) 93–4, 122, 211, 215, 283–6
drivers: characteristics of success 310–13; female 269–74; pressures on 330–1
Duncanson, Neil 33, 81–2

Ecclestone, Bernie 165, 184, 214, 216

F1: cost caps 118; media liaison 12–13; nature of 1–3, 323–4, 330–1; setting up races 123–5; support races 271, 273; travel & accommodation 117–23
F1 Academy 273–4
Ferrari, Enzo 56
Ferrari team. *see also* Bridgestone tyres: 2008 season 165–7, 168–72; cars 165–6, 240; controversial Monaco GP 103–4, 107–11; management style 247–8; popularity with world champions 239–40; and Schumacher 82, 83–4; Spanish GP 1997: 60–1; 'spy-gate' scandal 157–61; team orders controversy 84–91
FIA: Abu Dhabi 2021 investigation 304–5; aerodynamic testing restrictions 186, 189–90; double diffuser appeal 193–4; George Russell investigation 263–4; licensing of circuits 135; McLaren/Ferrari 'spy-gate' investigations 158–61; Renault 'crash-gate' investigation 176–9; safety car ruling 99, 174, 294, 295, 298, 300–1, 305; single tyre set rule 131–2, 134–5
Fontana, Norberto 61
FOTA (Formula One Teams Association) 188–9
Frentzen, Heinz-Harald 57

Gemini FM 25–6
German GP, 2008: 174–5
Ghosn, Carlos 172, 181
Glock, Timo 164, 168, 169, 170
Goodman, Louise 35, 47, 136
GP2 broadcasting 144–6
Grand Prixs. *see also* individual names: best to visit 126–7; garages 124–5; hospitality buildings 125; mechanics 125; practice sessions 7–10, 48, 49; qualifying 10, 133, 152; setting up 123–5; travel tips 127–8
Grosjean, Romain 100–1, 176, 284
ground-effect rules 266, 310, 327

Haas team: and COVID-19: 275, 277; and Guenther Steiner 284–5; and Mick Schumacher 209–10, 294; Stuart Morrison 260–1
Häkkinen, Mika 22, 61, 62–3, 76
Halo device 99–100
Hamilton, Lewis 16, 235, 304, 308; 2008 season 168–72; 2016 world

Bond Muir, Catherine 270, 272, 273, 274
Bottas, Valtteri 220, 317
Brawn, Ross 14–15, 85–6, 87–8, 90–1, 278; Brawn GP 187–200, 206; double diffuser issue 190–4; and Honda 15, 185–9; and Mercedes 221–2; and Schumacher 108, 111; and Toto Wolff 222
Brazilian GP: 1997: 37; 2008: 166–71; 2009: 196–9
Briatore, Flavio 42, 104, 160, 173–4, 177–9, 181, 212, 215
Bridgestone tyres 131–2, 134–5, 136–7, 142
British Touring Car Championship 164
broadcasting. *see also* pit reporting: commentating 44–7, 163–4; live 9, 93–101; post-race media briefings 289; presenting 129–31, 137–8, 141; team orders 84–91, 233–4
Brooks, Lizzie 269, 274
Brown, Zak 223
Brundle, Martin 35, 36, 43, 184; memorable lines 163–4; and Murray Walker 71; and TK 49–50; working style 48, 49–51
Bull, Clive 23–4
Bush, Rupert 31–2
Button, Jenson 185, 191, 192, 193; Brazilian GP 2009: 194–200; joins McLaren 200

Capital Radio 26–9
Carlton Television 32, 34
cars 7–8; aerodynamics 186, 189–90; double diffusers 190–4; explained using cheese 266–7; ground-effect rules 266, 310, 327; McLaren/Ferrari FIA investigations 158–61; safety cars 99, 174, 294, 295, 298, 300–1, 305; safety features 99–100
Chadwick, Jamie 269–70, 274
Channel 4: 24
Chinese GP: trackside fires 8
Chrysalis Sport 31–3
Clear, Jock 62, 191
commentary boxes 45, 48–9
commentating 44–5. *see also* Walker, Murray; cue cards 46–7; memorable lines 163–4; and talkback 45–6
Cook, Peter 24
cost caps on teams 118
Coughlan, Mike 157–9
Coulthard, David 231, 272
COVID-19: 274–82
Croft, David 163
cue cards 46–7

Daimler team 222
Davidson, Anthony 5–6
Dennis, Ron 14, 58, 62, 71, 189, 212, 214; Alonso/Hamilton rivalry 149–50, 153–4; and Max Mosley 161; McLaren/Ferrari 'spy-gate' controversy 159

Index

Abu Dhabi GP: 2010: 232–4; 2021: 287–8, 292–308
accidents and fatalities 96–9, 100–1; controversial 103–4, 107–8; helicopters 9–10; 'planned' 42; Renault 'crash-gate' investigation 176–9
air travel 117–20
Albon, Alex 330
Allen, James 31, 34, 35, 46–7, 61–2; advice to TK 105–6; successor to Murray Walker 70, 79
Allison, James 318–19
Alonso, Fernando 42, 89–90, 114–15, 116, 311; 2008 season 172–3, 175–7, 182; Abu Dhabi GP 2010: 232; and Aston Martin 246; and Ferrari 240, 242; and Hamilton 143, 147–50, 152–7, 159; leaves F1 temporarily 245; and McLaren 143, 162, 244; and Renault 172–3, 175, 245–6; and Schumacher 103–4, 107

Arden (team) 215–16
Arrivabene, Maurizio 242, 243, 247
Arrows (team) 29–30
Australian GP: 1994: 55–6; 1997: 36–8; 2020: 274–81; 2022: 168
Austrian GP 2002: 84–91
Azerbaijan GP 2021: 290–1

Bahrain GP: 2020: 100–1, 266
Barrichello, Rubens 15, 191, 193, 196; and Schumacher 82–9; and Williams team 200
Barwick, Brian 69, 80–1
Bauer, Jo 263–4
BBC 31, 130, 184–5, 193; F1 Forum 193; From the Pit Lane 255–6
Belgian GP 56; 2000: 65–7; 2024: 263–4
Bell, Bob 179–80
Ben Sulayem, Mohammed 304, 305
Bianchi, Jules 96–8
Bishop, Matt 272, 313
BMW Sauber team 193, 227–30, 248

tech, and keep on the good side of the team bosses – not to mention the sounds, the smells, the buzz, the roar of the crowd after an amazing overtake, the circuits and countries I get to visit.

If you've recently started following F1, welcome to the club. It makes me happy to think of new people coming in and discovering the sport I've loved so much for so long. I hope you've enjoyed reading some of the stories of the last few decades – the backstories, if you will. I've always been fascinated by the details, and when you put them together it makes those stories come to life. To those readers who've been as obsessed as I have, I hope you've enjoyed this trip through F1 eras past, from Schumacher and Alonso to Hamilton and Verstappen. The sport has evolved, but the essence remains the same. A unique combination of groups of people coming together to create extraordinary machines, raced by singularly talented individuals, with so many variables you never know what's going to happen in the next moment, much less across a season. The only thing I can be sure of is that I won't have long to wait before the next amazing story.

Thanks for reading, and I'll see you next time you switch on your television, tablet or phone and watch a race with us on a Sunday afternoon. I'll do my utmost to bring the pit lane into your front room, connect you with the drivers, take you behind the scenes and deliver as much access, news, gossip, information and entertainment from the paddock as possible. Come to think of it, everything you need to be an F1 insider.

generation. The money and the lifestyle might be one thing, but it's also evident that those things come at a cost.

It's hard to think of another sport that makes such demands of its participants. Although F1 is unquestionably a business, there are enough moments of pure sporting drama, passion, controversy and achievement taking place throughout the field to keep even the most cynical rev-head satisfied. The more you know about the personalities of F1 and the engineering technology of the cars, the more you want to know. That's sometimes hard, as it's a secretive sport, but the paddock thrives on gossip. Teams and the media arrive at the circuit early to beat the traffic, they leave late, and as there are only a few hours of track action each day, there's a lot of time for everyone to hang around and talk, about drivers, cars, teams, people and internal politics. Information is currency, and scraps are keenly traded. It's important not to lose perspective and not to forget that it's all just part of the show in the giant circus that is F1. A circus that pitches its tent, sprinkles its magic dust and performs, before packing up and moving on to the next town.

Which leads us back to the finish line, and what Anthony Davidson called my 'made-up job'. I hope you have a sense of what it entails and how addictive an environment it is, and the amazing stories I've witnessed. F1 has changed in so many ways over the last 30 years – more professional, more serious, more commercial and certainly more valuable. But it's also still fun, provided you don't take it too seriously.

F1 means as much to me now as it did back when I was in my parents' kitchen scouring the papers for snippets of information or the results tables. I'm still fascinated by the cars, interested in the drivers, enjoy the characters, try to keep on top of the ever-changing

'I've known Max for 12 years,' George said on camera. 'I've respected him all of this time, but now I've lost respect for him because we're all fighting on track, and it's never personal. Now he's made it personal, and someone needs to stand up to a bully like this. So far, people let him get away with murder.' Max called George 'a loser' and on it went – an old-fashioned grudge match that shows no sign of cooling down.

As for the other potential future world champions, Lando Norris, Oscar Piastri, Charles Leclerc and Carlos Sainz have all demonstrated that they know how to piece together winning race weekends. All could be champions if they get a chance in the right car, and certainly as of 2025 the McLaren duo of Piastri and Norris have the best package at their disposal. I'd add Alex Albon to that list, even though, at the time of writing, he's yet to win a Grand Prix, while Kimi Antonelli has the might of Toto Wolff and Mercedes behind him, and, at the start of the 2025 season, was the best-prepared rookie I've seen in years.

In many ways racing is the easy part of the job for the current generation of F1 drivers. Physically, they're top of the scale, able to withstand prolonged G-forces and attack from every dimension while trying to drive at speed and control a car that would happily kill them if not handled with care. Even though this is a sport practiced sitting down, they are incredible athletes. But they also have to balance driving with the fame and attention that comes their way, which can flick from acclaim to abuse in seconds in an era dominated by social media. As a result, they have developed different ways of coping with the pressure. Lando Norris has been particularly open about his mental health in a way that would have seemed inconceivable to the drivers of Senna and Schumacher's hearing, Russell said that Verstappen threatened to 'put him on his fucking head in the wall'. Verstappen denied he 'said it like that'. The next day, according to people who were present at the assembly point for the drivers' parade, Verstappen, still angry about the grid penalty, greeted Russell with 'I hope you're happy with yourselves, you and your FIA buddies.'

Compared to qualifying, the race was tame. As if to prove that an angry Max is a quick Max, or maybe he was just fired up because of his penalty, Verstappen took the lead from Russell at the start and never looked back, winning the Grand Prix by six seconds to Charles Leclerc. Russell was fourth.

One aspect of George Russell's character that many people miss is that, despite the gentlemanly exterior, he's a tough customer, completely comfortable fighting his corner when he feels he's in the right. For example, a week after Qatar, when Russell arrived at the Abu Dhabi track, he was in no mood to let the Verstappen situation lie. I'd spent the day interviewing drivers at the TV pen but hadn't yet heard any earth-shattering stories.

A minute before his time slot, up strode George. He called me over to the edge of the pen: 'Make sure you ask me a follow-up question.' 'What do you mean?' I asked. 'I'm going to give it back to Max, I've had enough of him bad-mouthing me in the press and I'm going to call him out on his bullying tactics. I know you're only supposed to ask one question, but never mind that, I'm up for as many questions as you like.' Before checking to see if he was wearing a *Drive to Survive* microphone, I asked him if he was absolutely sure he wanted to escalate what was essentially last week's story and start a new fight with Max, never an easy battle to win. He said he was positive, and away he went.

Essentially, the more time he can spend driving and racing, and the less time doing all the other tiresome tasks an F1 driver has to commit to, the better.

In the meantime, he has Grands Prix to contest, and rivalries to revisit. The very public spat with George Russell towards the end of 2024 was a good character study of both men. In the closing stages of qualifying for the Qatar GP, with both drivers on their build-up laps before starting proper qualifying laps, Russell accelerated through a couple of corners to find Verstappen on the racing line. George swerved to avoid an accident, and reported to his team on the radio what he saw as Verstappen's 'super dangerous' driving. As both were on out-laps, nothing much was thought of it, because no harm had been done to either driver's competitive result.

However, after the session the incident was investigated, and both Max and George were called to the FIA stewards to explain themselves. According to Verstappen, Russell tried his hardest to get Max a penalty, and succeeded – Max was duly given a one-place grid drop for 'driving unnecessarily slowly' on the racing line. There were two viewpoints. Russell claimed that Max was trying to slow his preparation lap down, which would cool the Mercedes W15's tyres, and compromise his lap. Verstappen insisted that he was courteously staying out of the way and preparing his tyres for his own lap. Max later said of George that he'd 'never seen someone try to screw someone over that hard,' and that he'd 'lost all respect' for him.

Verstappen and his team were furious with what they saw as an unjust penalty. Max was so determined to take the lead and seek justice for his grid drop that, coming out of the Saturday evening

THE FINISH LINE

The 2022 season saw the beginning of the ground-effect rules, which Red Bull's designer Adrian Newey understood better than anyone else. Max took advantage of the strong car and secured his second title with ease, winning 15 of the 22 races. However, that was a modest tally compared with 2023, when the RB19 was so dominant that Verstappen logged 19 victories, with teammate Sergio Pérez scoring two wins and only one escaping Red Bull, instead going to Ferrari's Carlos Sainz. It was a level of dominance that had not been seen since Michael Schumacher's Ferrari era. Then in 2024 Max got off to a flying start before McLaren and others caught up with Red Bull's pace, and thereafter he fought a rearguard action, still managing to secure his fourth title.

In a sense his approach to driving is akin to Schumacher's. Max doesn't give presents and he doesn't back down. He's incredibly skilful in wet weather conditions and has a fearless attitude in wheel-to-wheel battles, often going for an overtake at the first opportunity when his opponents realize that 'it's Verstappen' behind. He also has the Schumacher-style edge that can take his racing into the grey areas of fairness. Particularly evident in his on-track battles with Lando Norris, Charles Leclerc and Lewis Hamilton, Max knows the driving guidelines better than most, and is adept at putting them into practice in ways that are hard to penalize.

At the beginning of the 2025 season, Max was only 27 years old, an age that gives him the luxury of having enough time to achieve everything he wants to in F1, and then still have time to go and race in other categories. He's made no secret of his desire to try his hand at endurance races such as the Le Mans 24 Hours and the other major 24-hour races at Daytona and at the Nürburgring.

Driving alongside Schumacher, Jos had a couple of third places, but he was most famous for being engulfed in a fireball when a botched pit stop sent fuel spraying all over his car at the German GP. Like many TV viewers, I had been impressed by his insouciant wafting away of the fuel fumes at the time of the initial spill, only for the whole car to be set alight, forcing the Benetton pit crew to dive for cover. Jos suffered some minor burns, but was otherwise unharmed.

Spells at Arrows, Simtek, Tyrrell and Minardi followed, but Verstappen never got another chance at driving a potentially race-winning car. His hindsight has been Max's foresight – Jos learned the hard way about bad career moves, understood only too well the frustration of driving poor machinery and always looked for the quickest cars for his son.

Max's career gained even more momentum when he broke Sebastian Vettel's record as F1's youngest race winner, triumphing on his first outing with the senior Red Bull Racing team at the 2016 Spanish GP. He was only 18 at the time, but he has always looked grown up, unlike other young F1 drivers who seem to mature before your eyes, Lando Norris being a good example.

What has developed over his decade at the top level has been Verstappen's assured personality. He's focused on the few things that really matter to him in life – essentially family and racing. It's a refreshing character trait. He has no time for any of the off-track distractions that so often complicate life for F1 drivers.

The Verstappen era has been interesting, as the way he has won each title has varied so greatly. The 2021 season ended as previously described, and it came at the end of a gruelling year full of drama, forging a mental toughness that has since served Max well.

team for a year or so. In contrast, Red Bull had junior team Toro Rosso for just this purpose, and Helmut Marko and Christian Horner were only too ready to turf out an incumbent driver as soon as a potential megastar came along.

I spotted Jos and Max as they were leaving the back exit of the paddock. I'd known Jos since my first season in 1997. Indeed, my debut F1 television feature had been about Jos, following a great race in the wet 2001 Malaysian GP, when he drove brilliantly to finish seventh from 18th on the grid in an otherwise uncompetitive Arrows.

I greeted them and asked how things had been going. It was just a quiet little visit, Jos said, catching up with people and showing Max around. I introduced myself to Max, wished him good luck, and said that I was sure that he would make it into F1 quite soon. Jos, playing his cards close to his chest, said there was a long way to go before F1 was an option, that nothing had been decided. However, that day in Hockenheim had been very productive, and Max was announced as a Red Bull stable driver a month later. Having turned 17 he then drove in a practice session at that October's Japanese GP for Toro Rosso as part of the preparations for his debut season in 2015.

Jos 'The Boss' Verstappen's was a career that never quite fulfilled the promise it showed when he arrived in F1 in 1994 touted as the next big thing. He was viewed as a potential world champion, an image boosted by the fact that he drove for Willi Weber's F3 team three years after Michael Schumacher. He was signed as a Benetton reserve driver by Flavio Briatore, and soon graduated to a race seat as a substitute for JJ Lehto after the Finn fractured a vertebra in a testing accident.

race venues added to the schedule, or rule changes that threaten to disrupt the competitive order, F1 is always moving forward, always changing, creating new excitement every season that few other sports can match.

My grandfather, as he advanced towards the grand old age of 103, had an observation about the secret to a long and happy life: 'You always have to have something to look forward to.' Murray knew this better than anyone. At the first race you don't yet know what that new thing will be, or the story of the championship, but no question, you're looking forward to finding out.

One of my favourite things about the start of each new season is living through events that you will later come to recognize as significant. One of the big talking points of late has been whether Max Verstappen can add to his title tally in this, the Verstappen era. An era that saw its roots planted on Saturday 19 July 2014, qualifying day for that year's German Grand Prix.

At the time Max was only 16, but many people in the F1 world already knew how successful Jos Verstappen's boy had been in karting, how quickly he had adapted to F3 machinery, then blipped on the radar of the F1 teams. Hockenheim was the first time that Max had been in the F1 paddock, not as the young son of a driver, but as a driver in his own right, looking to break into the top level. It was the first time that he was there purely on business with the intention of walking away with a contract that would change the rest of his life.

Jos and Max had a meeting with Toto Wolff and Niki Lauda at Mercedes, but they couldn't offer him a race drive while Lewis Hamilton and Nico Rosberg were fighting for the world championship, and wouldn't be able to place him at a customer

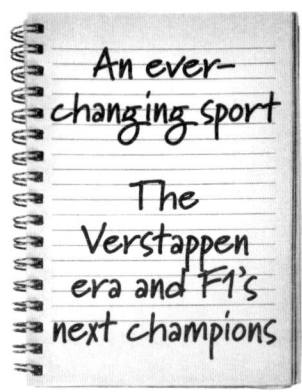

Chapter 22

The Finish Line

It was a beautiful March morning as race week began ahead of the 2000 Australian Grand Prix. Michael Schumacher was about to kick off what would become the first of his five straight world championships with Ferrari, and we had landed at Melbourne's Tullamarine Airport to start ITV Sport's fourth F1 season.

While James Allen, Louise Goodman and I stared out of the taxi-minibus window at the buildings that had sprung up since our last visit, a familiar voice from the front passenger seat burst the silence. 'You know the thing about F1? It has a unique ability to reinvent itself. Year after year, it finds a way to be new and interesting. Don't know how. Marvellous, really.' And with that, Murray Walker turned back to the windscreen and his thoughts, fingers drumming on his right knee.

Exhausted from the flight, I didn't think much of Murray's comment at the time. However, as the years have gone by, I've realized what an astute observation it was. Whether because of drivers moving teams, new drivers or new teams coming in, new

THE EIGHT-POINTED STARS

Boeing 777s to his private Bombardier Global 7000. But motorsport was never far away. Once Lauda Air had been sold, Niki received an offer from Ford to help run the Jaguar Racing team. His direct style worked wonders with drivers like Eddie Irvine, but didn't go down well at Ford's Dearborn HQ, and his bosses dispensed with the Austrian's services. He took a job as expert pundit with German broadcaster RTL where he originated the role of paddock insider, complete with forthright opinions, long before Eddie Jordan picked up a microphone. Niki frequently upset the thin-skinned, but he never lost anybody's respect.

The last race Niki Lauda attended was the British Grand Prix at Silverstone in June 2018, not long before his life-saving lung transplant. Ironically Mercedes was beaten that day by Ferrari and Sebastian Vettel, with whom he shared a natural affinity – the dirty jokes, the no-bullshit attitude, the stubborn refusal to accept an unsatisfactory situation. That was Lauda's way, not because he was a difficult person, but because his history had taught him to speak freely without fear of the consequences, aware there was a good chance the next day might be his last. We'll never see his like again, but every time I walk through the Mercedes garage and past his red cap on the radio rack, I hear his voice, in that thick Austrian accent: 'Hey, it's you again! Piss off back to the pit lane!'

As a driver Niki was very good, but he perhaps wasn't naturally gifted with raw speed in the style of Jim Clark, Ayrton Senna, Michael Schumacher or Lewis Hamilton. Rather, his strengths were in understanding his car's problems and knowing, with canny accuracy, how to resolve them. These days, Formula 1 engineers need banks of computers fed by thousands of sensors to tell them what the car is doing. With Niki, the computer was in his head.

The human computer worked. Having bluffed and bought his way into F1, Lauda won the 1975 and 1977 world championships for Ferrari, reaping what he'd sown in perfecting his cars. He would likely have won in 1976, too, were it not for the fateful accident at the Nürburgring, the resulting fire from which burned his face and choked him with noxious smoke. Doctors at the hospital didn't rate Lauda's chances of survival, and called a local priest to administer the last rites. But Niki wasn't ready to die that day. His injuries were just a problem he needed to fix.

It was the same for everything else in Lauda's life: from cars to airlines to wives. Married twice, Niki fathered five children and created three airlines. Lauda Air, which provided a focus when he first hung up his racing boots in 1979, was commercially successful (it was later bought by Austrian Airlines), but suffered a tragic crash in 1991 which killed 223 passengers and crew when a thrust reverser on a Boeing 767 deployed in flight. Lauda identified the cause with Boeing and made the American company fix it, ensuring a similar technical failure could never happen again.

He joked that he was running out of names after branding subsequent airlines Fly Niki and Lauda Motion. The discipline of flying appealed to the computer in his brain. An accomplished pilot, he flew every aircraft his companies operated, from huge person who, had he been alive in either world war, would have come up with a way of shortening it considerably, and who, if you worked for him, you'd be willing to jump off a cliff for, knowing that he would have invented some clever net device to catch you and that he'd be jumping too. Were he not colour-blind and too tall, he would have made an excellent Spitfire pilot. He scratches that itch flying vintage and not-so-vintage aircraft around the UK for fun.

I first met James when he was at Ferrari, leading the trackside aerodynamics team under Ross Brawn. I wondered who this guy was who spoke good Italian with a very British accent. It has been a great pleasure to know him ever since. If anyone can lead Mercedes out of the doldrums and back to brisk, blue skies it's Allison.

He has also been a valued sounding board for Toto Wolff in recent years, in much the same way that Niki Lauda used to be. However, the three-times world champion has proved to be completely irreplaceable in the Mercedes F1 camp, so much so that his trademark red cap still sits on top of his radio and headset on the rack inside their garage.

I used to interview Niki after most races, and like anyone who knew him, developed an immense respect for his many achievements. Having given the Grim Reaper the slip in 1976, death finally caught up with Lauda in 2019, when he succumbed to an illness related to his second set of kidneys. He was on his second set of lungs, too, following a transplant in August 2018. 'Whatever it takes to make things right.' This was Lauda's life philosophy, a time-efficient route to satisfaction – be it major organ transplant or perfecting race car setups, it made no difference. Something isn't right? Fix it. Quickly!

team unravelled, as F1 dream teams always tend to. First to step back was Andy Cowell, the head of the Mercedes engine division. After a spell on the sidelines, he became team principal at Aston Martin and is building his own dream team with Adrian Newey as technical partner. James Vowles is trying to do the same at Williams, his former role at Mercedes having developed far beyond that of head of strategy, before he left to become team principal of the Grove outfit at the start of the 2023 season.

Aldo Costa was a key engineer who had spent many years at Ferrari, and was known at Mercedes as 'Mr Suspension', thanks to having extensive experience of vehicle dynamics and getting the mechanical platform of a car to work smoothly with its aerodynamics. Costa's return to Italy and a new role at chassis builder Dallara was a key loss, as was Loic Serra, who worked on chassis design and general tyre dynamics. He joined Ferrari as its chassis technical director in 2024, and is now working once more with Hamilton. Also gone is Mike Elliott, a gifted aerodynamicist who was promoted to Mercedes technical director and then moved sideways to chief technical officer, neither of which really worked out.

Despite these departures, many key players remain in the Brackley camp, some of whom go back as far as the BAR, Honda and Brawn GP days. Sporting director Ron Meadows keeps the race team going and stays on top of the rules, while Andrew Shovlin heads up trackside engineering with Peter Bonnington. And then there's technical director James Allison. A self-confessed armed forces brat (his father being former Air Chief Marshal Sir John Allison), James is the kind of person who ought to go down in history as one of Britain's greatest engineers. He's the kind of working lives. Applying that standard to us more ordinary folk proves the point. We might go to work and do a decent job and come home feeling like we achieved something, but the reality is that most of us don't hit perfection every day. I certainly don't. However, that is what's demanded of F1 drivers, and when they don't achieve perfection, it gets noticed.

I tried to make the same point to Rosberg's Mercedes successor Valtteri Bottas at the end of a weekend spent filming with him in his hometown of Nastola in Finland. We were talking by the side of his local kart track, where he'd learned and honed his driving skills, in dry, wet and even snowy conditions. I thought it reasonable to observe that, just like Rosberg had found, Bottas might have to accept that on some days, Hamilton is simply unbeatable in the same car. And that's the way it is. 'No, I don't think that,' Valtteri said, his blue eyes narrowing against the cold. 'If I thought that, even for a second, I would just not show up in F1.'

I shouldn't have been surprised. Bottas put up a very decent fight against Hamilton over the five seasons they were teammates in 2017–21, winning ten races and millions of fans worldwide. He's one of the drivers of recent times who reminds me most of the seventies and the James Hunt era. That weekend in Nastola was one of my favourite road trips – enjoying some serious sauna time, before lowering ourselves slowly into the adjacent icy lake. Quite a buzz.

Bottas was a huge part of Mercedes winning those eight constructors' championships, and after a spell at Sauber he returned to the team as third driver. While he found many familiar faces, some of the key people with whom he previously worked are no longer in the Mercedes camp. As the years passed, so the dream his breadth of intelligence and knowledge about other things in life. He's a great guy.'

'Oh,' said Nico. And then, after a pause, 'What about current drivers?' I explained that there were things I liked and admired about all of them, but there wasn't one who was my favourite. 'I honestly don't have a preference who wins and who doesn't.'

'Yes, but . . .' he countered. 'Personally, you must have a view on who the current drivers are as people?' We discussed how Hamilton is an awesome driver but can be distant while he's lost in the focus of a Grand Prix weekend. How Fernando Alonso continues to impress and amuse, how Nico Hulkenberg is smart and quick, and how Daniel Ricciardo is generally lovely and adored by everyone he meets.

As the elevated motorway passed south of the city of Nara, I asked Rosberg how much of what we see of the drivers is their true character? They're heroes to many because they have skills the rest of us don't, and are expected to perform to their maximum potential, under intense pressure and scrutiny, every other Sunday afternoon. But do we ever really know them?

'Ah', said Nico. 'Definitely not. It's hard. People don't realize how difficult it is to be perfect, to be on top of your game, week after week. And how if you make one little mistake, whether it's a crash or a spin, not qualifying on pole, or a race where you're even the slightest bit off-form, everyone asks why you're suddenly useless.'

At that point the Mitsubishi fell silent as we both stared out the window and I tried to remember how many times I'd asked him something like that.

It's impossible to truly judge F1 drivers on anything but the most superficial level as we're asking for perfection every day of their were so intense as to be mentally unsustainable and certainly incompatible with an ordinary family life. His subsequent decision to retire shortly after winning his world championship seemed a fairly easy one.

These days Rosberg is much more relaxed. I suppose that having achieved your life's ambition and retired at the age of 31, financially secure for the rest of your days, means you can afford to be easy-going. More recently he has used everything he learned about himself and the power of human relationships to become a very successful businessman and investor.

One evening following the 2017 Japanese GP at Suzuka, Nico and I found ourselves in the back of a Mitsubishi Outlander for the two-hour trip from Suzuka to Osaka's Kansai Airport. I would have happily dozed off in the back of the car, or sat and listened to some music. However, typically for a racing driver, with brains used to processing information at speed, Rosberg gets bored quickly. So we soon got into conversation about a whole variety of subjects, from TV ratings to F1 teams, family to favourite airlines and flight routes. What caught Nico's attention was my answer to one particular question: 'Who's your favourite driver? Who do you really like?'

'Apart from Senna?' I replied. 'Erm . . . Alexander Wurz,' I said, namechecking the lanky Austrian who drove for Benetton, McLaren and Williams. 'Really?' said Nico, surprised. 'Why?' 'Well, I suppose because he was the only driver in my time working in F1 that I really identified with. We're the same age, and while he was very thoughtful about race strategy, setup and tactics during his driving career, when I interviewed him, he often surprised me with people's educational journeys, and provided 10 recommendations to address them. In 2024, the F1 organization, the FIA and all the teams adopted the recommendations of The Hamilton Commission in the form of a Diversity and Inclusion charter, the first of its kind in F1, and something that promises to get previously under-represented groups into motor sport. Nobody else – driver, team principal, team owner, administrator or governing body – has done as much as Lewis Hamilton to effect positive change in F1.

The 2021 controversy aside, the other title that got away from Hamilton was in 2016, when Nico Rosberg beat him to the world championship by five points, despite Lewis winning one more race. Reliability issues such as Hamilton's engine failure in Malaysia paired with Rosberg's consistency and an excellent drive under pressure at the deciding race in Abu Dhabi sealed the title, making Keke and Nico Rosberg the second father-son duo to win the F1 world championship after Graham and Damon Hill.

Nico is now a colleague on Sky F1, but we've known each other since his GP2 win in 2005 and his arrival in F1 at Williams in 2006. I'd often ask him questions about all sorts of topics, from Spy-gate to Crash-gate, largely because he could always be relied upon for a good answer. Nothing has changed in that regard, and as an analyst you can put any question his way and not only will you get an answer, but Nico will usually throw a question back, so take note that you have to be ready for it.

His approach to beating Lewis Hamilton in 2016 was forensic. He'd learned everything about Lewis that he didn't know already over the previous three seasons, including how to use the media in an attempt to get under his skin. It's hard to tell if that ever worked, but Rosberg's dedication and commitment over that 2016 season

7. Race craft. Lewis's father Anthony once said to me, 'The thing people don't fully appreciate about Lewis is that he's a mercenary. He's relentless, ruthless. A cold-blooded, merciless racer.' Again, not unique, but experience has given Hamilton such a massive databank of knowledge, of corner profiles, grip levels, hybrid power unit electricity generating zones – anything that can help predict who will be vulnerable to an overtake where and when. Plus, his technique, being clean, clinical and contact-free when he gets there; he remains one of the most effective racers and overtakers on the grid.

And to add to all of these, my own experience of Lewis has me agreeing with his ex-McLaren head of communications Matt Bishop, who called him 'a first-class human being'. It would be impossible not to admire the work Hamilton does when he's not at the track, using the power of his platform and status to effect positive change in the world. He has a heartfelt desire to help people less fortunate or in less advantaged positions achieve as much as possible in their lives. He established Mission 44, a charity that works to build 'a fairer, more inclusive future for young people around the world and to overcome social injustice'. I've seen kids and young people from every continent visit the F1 paddock on many occasions with Mission 44 and be inspired by what they see. It's already having an incredible effect.

Back in 2020 Lewis also put his own money into establishing The Hamilton Commission, which produced a report in 2021 titled Accelerating Change: Improving Representation of Black People in UK Motorsport. The report explores the barriers to recruitment and progression, which start in early life and last throughout young there's always more attention surrounding him at a race track than anyone else. A bigger crowd in the paddock, more fans lining up at the gate, always more of a fuss. It would be a huge drain on anyone's mental energy to absorb and react to that constantly, so with the exception of the drivers' parade, which Hamilton uses as a pre-race pump-up, he has an ability to shut out the rest of the world and remain laser-focused on his driving.

4. Consistency. This is by no means unique, but no driver has more experience than Hamilton at putting a world championship together in terms of scoring the points week in, week out. In a title fight there are few drivers better at maximizing their points and being consistent over 24 rounds. Even when he can't win, he's racking up the points – his seven world titles being the obvious result.

5. Work ethic. Lewis is honest with himself and habitually looks for areas that require improvement and then puts in the work to fix the deficiencies. Even at the beginning of his career the pace at which he would identify areas where he was weak and then improve them was particularly impressive.

6. Driving style. In this period of F1 when the races are predominately decided on who can get their tyres working best and lasting the longest, Hamilton has been adept at driving around the peculiar characteristics of the Pirellis. It's not a particularly sexy subject, but being a 'tyre whisperer' is something he can turn his skill set to when required.

are applicable to racing drivers. The time it takes for the eye to see, the brain to process and the body to react gets greater with age. These are well understood in such sports as downhill skiing, which is similar to motor racing in terms of reaction times and physical movements. We're talking tiny differences here, tenths of a second at most, and there are so many steering-wheel and throttle and brake inputs as to make the effect of age negligible. While Hamilton continues to try and rediscover his qualifying edge, Fernando Alonso, three years his senior, is proof that drivers don't lose their basic speed. And given that Hamilton's (and Alonso's, for that matter) natural speed started at a higher level than most in F1, any age-related loss is, in the races at least, yet to become a factor.

2. Thirst for success. Having reported on all of Lewis's championship seasons, what has consistently impressed me has been his relentless drive to achieve more. He's as competitive a personality as any other driver, but there's something about him that treats the beginning of each season, with 2025 at Ferrari being the best example, like it's his first. He has an ability to reset himself over the winter and always hit the first race with maximum motivation. Sure, we've occasionally seen him wanting to park his car in a hopeless race, only to be dissuaded by his team, but that intention was always to 'save the car' for better performance in a future Grand Prix. In the end, he never gives up if there's a chance of a win or points for the world championship.

3. Intensity of focus on a race weekend. Maybe it's because Hamilton is F1's only current worldwide household name (just as Michael Schumacher and Ayrton Senna were before him) but

he had just achieved something remarkable. Hamilton might have lost the drivers' title at the very last gasp, but nine years after writing that report for the Mercedes board about why their F1 team wasn't winning, Toto Wolff had led it to an eighth world championship. It was a phenomenal achievement. No team had ever won eight in a row – the closest anyone came was Ferrari's six titles from 1999 to 2004.

There were many stars in that team, both at the track and back at their Brackley factory. Most are still there, which makes their failure to master the ground-effect rule which lasted from 2022 to 2025 even more baffling. Lewis Hamilton won six of his seven titles with Mercedes and held out for another winning car for as long as he could, before electing to leave at the end of 2024 for a longer term deal at Ferrari. It was a move that sent shockwaves through the sport when it was announced, but it just felt right that the most successful driver of all time should drive for the most famous team of all time. Time will tell if he can win that eighth world title in red, but when I look back on the story of Sir Lewis Hamilton's F1 career – and I've reported on every season of it – a picture emerges of at least seven key characteristics that have kept him at the top.

1. Natural speed. When Lewis was struggling to match the single-lap qualifying pace of his teammate George Russell in 2024 he said, 'I'm definitely not fast anymore.' He would then deliver the kind of lap times in the races the next day that proved that he was definitely still fast. There are neurological and physiological reasons why athletes in their 40s are not as performant as those in their 20s. There's physical strength, balance, reaction speeds – all

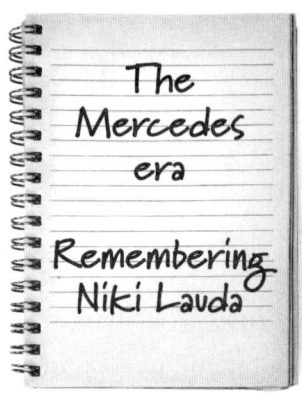

Chapter 21

The Eight-Pointed Stars

Pressure is a constant in F1. It's effective in terms of driving performance, but it's not healthy. So when Toto Wolff finally activated his personal pressure-relief valve in an Abu Dhabi nightclub just a few hours after that fateful 2021 Grand Prix, he really went for it. Lewis Hamilton might have lost the drivers' championship, but his 18 points for second place won Mercedes their eighth consecutive constructors' title.

As 'Freed From Desire' by Gala blasted out of the speakers, Toto crowd-surfed off the DJ decks into the waiting arms of his Mercedes mechanics, crisp blue shirt getting lost in the throng. There followed a group rendition of Queen's 'We Are the Champions', again. But there was something about the way Wolff threw himself into the celebrations that suggested a man more interested in burying his feelings of shock and outrage over the way the last race had unfolded, than savouring the actual championship they had won. He had clearly decided the only way to cope that night was to let go and blow off some steam. However, as a leader at Sauber/Audi. Christian Horner never left the spotlight and was subsequently sacked by Red Bull in July 2025.

As for Lewis Hamilton, he had been set to become the undisputed, greatest F1 driver of all time, beating Michael Schumacher to eight world titles. In the weeks and months after Abu Dhabi, he seriously considered quitting F1. With the support and advice of his family and friends, Lewis decided to return for 2022, not wanting the last word on his career to be what happened in Abu Dhabi. He wouldn't win again until the 2024 British GP, when the emotions came flooding back. After that race, Hamilton said, 'Honestly, when I came back in 2022, I thought that I was over it. And I know I wasn't, and it's taken a long time to heal that kind of feeling. And that's only natural for anyone that has that experience. I've just been continuing to try and work on myself and find that inner peace day-by-day.'

F1 has never been more popular, so it's difficult to judge to what extent the events of that night in Abu Dhabi damaged the image and integrity of the sport. Just like all the other great stories that make up F1's fascinating history, though, we shouldn't be afraid to talk about it.

different matter. The looks of surprise on their faces immediately after the race suggested to me that they never in a million years expected Masi to go along with their appeal of 'you only need one racing lap'.

Toto Wolff's belief was that Masi had been conditioned to accept Wheatley's suggestion because Wheatley had helped him out so many times previously – Wolff even described Masi and Wheatley's relationship as a 'bromance'.

As for Masi, for all his faults I don't believe (and there is no evidence that) he had a preference either way in terms of Red Bull or Mercedes, Verstappen or Hamilton, that he wanted one driver to be world champion over another. The FIA investigation concluded he was acting in good faith, and doing what he thought was the best thing to do in the situation. That is not to say that he made the right calls that day.

Wittich and Freitas took turns as race director in 2022, and this time the FIA was careful to keep both men well away from the media spotlight. There was also an abrupt end to the broadcasting of any pit wall intercom communications with race control – and team principals were banned from voicing their opinions. Henceforth only the sporting directors would be allowed to talk to the race director and then only to ask questions, not to suggest actions. Freitas soon departed, and Wittich was handed the race director job full-time. However, in November 2024, Wittich was himself sacked by Mohammed Ben Sulayem – a development that Masi may have watched from afar with interest.

Max Verstappen won every championship from 2021 until 2024. Jonathan Wheatley left Red Bull to become team principal

And that was it. Mistakes had been made, but Masi, it was felt, had acted in good faith and within his authority. This begged the question, though, if Masi hadn't done anything wrong in the FIA's summation, why was he removed from his job?

I have absolutely no problem with anything that Max Verstappen did in the car at the end of that race. It was the easiest strategic decision of the season for Red Bull to pit him under the safety car, and he drove perfectly to get the best advantage from the new soft tyres, performing a clean overtake on Hamilton, and winning the race to become a deserving world champion. On that night, he successfully played the hand that was dealt to him. Of course, had Latifi not crashed, Hamilton would have matched Verstappen's nine wins, and finished eight points clear to clinch his eighth world title. It was because of Masi and his officials' unusual actions that Lewis didn't win the race, so clearly, Hamilton would also have been a deserving world champion.

I also understand Horner and Wheatley (and later Newey) trying their luck with the referee. Granted, it's not the same as appealing for a penalty in football or an LBW decision in cricket, because in those instances, you're not encouraging the referee to enforce some rules of the game but not others – but the result is the same. Many people inside and outside the F1 paddock accused Wheatley and Horner of being unethical or unsporting in trying to influence Masi to improperly execute the rules. The Red Bull duo deny that and I can see their side of the argument – they had to try something. It was their job and their responsibility to their driver and team to try anything they could to help Max win. Whether Horner and Wheatley ever – for one single second – believed Masi was going to agree with them and carry out their suggestions is a been in a constructive dialogue with the FIA and F1 to create clarity for the future, so that all competitors know the rules under which they are racing, and how they will be enforced. Thus, we welcome the decision by the FIA to install a commission to thoroughly analyse what happened in Abu Dhabi and to improve the robustness of rules, governance and decision making in F1.' Ahead of the full result of the investigation Ben Sulayem announced in February that Masi had lost his job as F1 race director and would be replaced for the 2022 season by Niels Wittich and Eduardo Freitas, who were both race directors in other FIA series. Masi parted company with the FIA, to return to Australia and the local touring car scene.

The FIA's full report finally came out in March 2022. Among the conclusions was an acknowledgement that in effect Masi had been doing his best, noting that he 'was acting in good faith and to the best of his knowledge given the difficult circumstances, particularly acknowledging the significant time constraints for decisions to be made and the immense pressure being applied by the teams.' However, the standout admission was that there had been 'human error' in the calculation over which lapped cars should be allowed to unlap themselves. Intriguingly it was Masi's deputy, American Scot Elkins, who had the job of telling the race director which cars should be waved through – the report suggests Elkins simply didn't realize that there were three more lapped cars. Meanwhile, the FIA said the rule about cars unlapping themselves would be changed from 'any cars' to 'all cars'. The FIA found their stewards had been correct in their judgement regarding which rule overrode the other and that the famous rule 15.3 legitimized Masi's use of the safety car in the way he did.

were finally able to celebrate Verstappen's championship win. Mercedes lodged a notice of an intention to appeal, which meant that in theory the race outcome was still provisional, but that didn't stop Red Bull enjoying the victory.

On TV, we congratulated Verstappen, wrapped up our programme (noting the appeal and how this would not be the end of the matter), and went off-air. It was a weird feeling on the bus to Dubai Airport that night. We were happy with the comprehensive coverage we put out that evening (the programme later won Sky Sports F1 a BAFTA award). However, in all honesty we weren't sure what had just gone on, or how Article 15.3 could be used to justify Masi's actions. I remember on the flight from Dubai to Heathrow someone asked me about what had happened. 'I've got no idea,' I said. 'You'll have to ask me in about a year's time.'

We didn't have to wait a year. The FIA gala prizegiving, the event at which Verstappen would receive his championship winner's trophy, was coming up the following week. It would be completely unprecedented for Max to be crowned 'provisional' world champion while a legal process was still unfolding in the background. With that in mind, just before the FIA event, Mercedes withdrew its appeal, saying in explanation that it didn't want to damage the image of F1 by rendering the championship provisional. Hamilton didn't attend the gala to collect his second-place trophy and was fined €50,000 by the FIA for missing it. Meanwhile, new FIA president Mohammed Ben Sulayem, recently elected to replace Jean Todt, promised a full investigation in the form of a special commission.

In a statement Mercedes noted that the team had originally 'appealed in the interest of sporting fairness, and we have since control the use of the safety car, including its deployment and withdrawal. This was a curious decision based on a rule no one had paid much attention to before and certainly not relied on so heavily before, but there it was. In their judgement, the stewards acknowledged that 'although article 48.12 may not have been applied fully in relation to the safety car returning to the pits at the end of the following lap, once the message "safety car in this lap" has been displayed, it is mandatory to withdraw the safety car at the end of that lap', overriding the 'following lap' rule. It also agreed with Newey and Wheatley in ruling 'that Article 15.3 allows the race director to control the use of the safety car, which in our determination includes its deployment and withdrawal.'

Mercedes pointed out this was selective rule enforcing, that if the race had truly been run according to the rules, Lewis Hamilton would be world champion. Mercedes had called on the stewards to 'remediate the matter' by taking the positions of the cars at the end of the penultimate lap and determining that as the final race classification. This was an impossible ask. There was no mechanism in the rules to shorten a race retrospectively. The only time the classification from a previous lap can be taken is in the event of a red flag race stoppage that is not restarted, when the rules explicitly say that the result will be the race order at the end of the last lap before the red flag is shown (such as Brazil 2003, when Giancarlo Fisichella scored Jordan Grand Prix's last win).

With Mercedes's application to shorten the race by one lap rejected, the protest was dismissed, the race result made official and the 2021 world championship was decided. In the paddock we were all waiting for news. When it dropped, the atmosphere at Red Bull completely changed from one second to the other, as the team was fairly easily dismissed by the stewards – he drew alongside, but never had his car fully in front of Hamilton's.

The crucial part of that stewards' meeting was the discussion and the justification for Masi doing what he did with the safety-car rules. Mercedes was represented by Meadows, Andrew Shovlin and Paul Harris, a lawyer who the team had pre-emptively flown to Abu Dhabi just in case the championship had ended in controversy. Red Bull had Wheatley, Horner and Adrian Newey. According to people in the room, the Red Bull figure who was the most convincing and the most vociferous in defending their win wasn't Horner, or the rules man Jonathan Wheatley, but Newey. Frank Williams once called him 'the most competitive person in the pit lane' and here it was in action – Adrian Newey wasn't going to lose this fight.

After an initial exchange of opinions everyone went away to reflect and take the opportunity to gather more evidence. And it was Newey and Wheatley who found a hitherto little-known line in the FIA Sporting Regulations that transformed their case and could be used to get Masi off the hook for not adhering to rule 48.12.

Article 15.3 was, on the face of it, a simple confirmation of the split of responsibilities between the race director and the clerk of the course, the local official at each race who has responsibility for the marshals and track workers. It said that 'the race director shall have overriding authority in the following matters', and among the items listed was 'the use of the safety car'. It was this line that was highlighted by Red Bull, and was later relied on by the stewards to justify Masi's actions using the safety car as he saw fit.

This enabled the stewards to dismiss the Mercedes protest on the grounds that the race director has the overriding authority to the leader, the safety car will return to the pits at the end of the following lap.' That clearly hadn't happened.

Toto wasn't talking. I did a report into the commentary: 'They just don't understand what has happened at Mercedes, they're in a state of shock about what's going on.' I was trying to understand it as well, because we'd never seen the outcome of a race decided in this way, we'd only seen them decided according to how the rules were written. Meanwhile, at Red Bull, it was all kicking off. People were hugging each other and screaming, mechanics were dancing around the pit lane. One team had lost the 2021 world championship, and the other had won it. There were tears on both sides.

Mercedes immediately protested the result and then did something that seemed slightly strange: the team completely shut up shop. Wolff declined to be interviewed. Had Mercedes come out and been clear about which rules were not followed or had they even reminded Masi on the intercom during those last few laps of his obligations under rule 48.12, that would have been difficult for Masi to ignore and provided clearer context for everyone watching around the world.

Mercedes didn't do that. Emotions were running so high it was almost impossible to make cool-headed, detached public statements. Then there was a red herring the team pursued as part of the protest by suggesting that Verstappen had overtaken Hamilton under the safety car and he should be handed a five- or ten-second time penalty. All that did was divert everyone's attention off the main topic, which was that the race director had acted in such an unusual and unexpected way in his handling of the safety car. The issue of whether Max overtook Lewis under the safety car

Masi had a right to defend his decisions, but his use of the phrase 'motor race' – the very words that Wheatley had put in his head as a suggestion just a couple of minutes earlier – did not go unnoticed by those listening across the world.

I watched all of this unfold from my position in the pit lane between the McLaren and Aston Martin garages. I had a big screen in front of me, and I was listening intently to Martin Brundle and David Croft in my headphones. The traditional Abu Dhabi celebratory fireworks went off as the flag fell, but I hardly noticed them as I tried to process what had just happened and decide what questions I should now be putting to the key people. As team members and VIP guests poured into the pit lane, I ran towards the Mercedes and Red Bull garages.

At Mercedes I found a team completely shocked, bewildered, confused. I think I used the word 'befuddled' at the time. There was no one at Mercedes who could understand what mechanism had just been used to circumvent the rules they felt the race should have been concluded under, namely that all the lapped cars should have been allowed to overtake the safety car and unlap themselves, and only then should the race have resumed on the following lap.

Attention turned to Article 48.12 of the FIA Sporting Regulations, which among other things noted that 'any cars that have been lapped by the leader will be required to pass the cars on the lead lap and the safety car.' As was to become apparent, that word 'any' was suddenly up for discussion – most people in F1 had always assumed that *all* cars had to be allowed past. However, there seemed to be little doubt over the other part of rule 48.12 that said, and it's worth repeating, 'once the last lapped car has passed

THE 2021 ABU DHABI GP

Instead, by ignoring that part of the rule, Masi had found a way to squeeze in a final racing lap. It was then that we heard Toto Wolff's urgent appeal to Masi: 'Michael, this isn't right. Michael, that is so not right!'

As the cars prepared for the restart, Verstappen closed up on Hamilton and pulled alongside. From the onboard camera view, he appeared to briefly poke his nose in front, causing Mercedes sporting director Ron Meadows to tell Masi that Max had passed Hamilton under the safety car, although in fact he had not fully passed him.

Verstappen was right with Hamilton as the green flag flew for that crucial final lap. Now it was a simple matter of physics – Lewis was helpless on the old, hard compound tyres he'd been on since lap 14. Max was on new soft tyres, with far more grip, and sure enough the Red Bull dived past at the hairpin. Lewis, who over the radio made his feelings clear – 'This is being manipulated, man' tried to fight back, but Verstappen was comfortably ahead as the flag fell, winning the Grand Prix by 2.2 seconds and the world championship, with an advantage of eight points over his rival. It was then that Wolff voiced his utter frustration to Masi.

> Wolff: 'Michael, it was so not right. Michael, what was that? Michael? Race control?'
> Masi: 'Go ahead, Toto.'
> Wolff: 'You need to reinstate the lap before, that's not right!'
> Masi: 'It's called a motor race, OK?'
> Wolff: 'Sorry?'
> Masi: 'We went car racing.'

that the track was clear. It was then that he did indeed reverse his earlier decision and wrote on the timing screens that the lapped cars of Norris, Alonso, Ocon, Leclerc and Vettel could overtake after all. The message appeared as their race numbers, so cars 4, 14, 31, 16 and 5. This was Masi's first unexpected deviation from the rules in that he made no mention of the other lapped cars in the pack, which, crucially, included Daniel Ricciardo and Lance Stroll, who were running between Verstappen and third-placed Carlos Sainz. The rules referred to 'any car that has been lapped' but there were three cars that had been lapped who weren't being allowed to unlap themselves. So while Verstappen was now being allowed a clear run at leader Hamilton, Sainz was not being given the same opportunity to tackle the Dutchman. It meant that Max didn't have to worry about defending his position, and could focus entirely on Lewis ahead.

Radio messages went out to Norris et al. to the effect that they should overtake Hamilton and the safety car. They did – while Stroll, Ricciardo and Schumacher asked their engineers why they weren't being allowed to do the same. Masi then put the message 'Safety Car In This Lap' on to the timing screens and the official messaging system. The safety car duly turned its lights off and prepared to drive into the pits. It was the end of lap 57, and the race was heading into the final lap.

The timing of this instruction to the safety-car driver was Masi's second deviation from the rules. The rule stated (and the established procedure was) that 'once the last lapped car has passed the leader the safety car will return to the pits at the end of the following lap'. This would have coincided with the last corner of the race, allowing Hamilton to drive across the finish line safely in front.

THE 2021 ABU DHABI GP

receiving end of some urgent lobbying from the Red Bull camp. First Christian Horner got on the radio:

> Horner: 'Why aren't we getting these lapped cars out of the way?'
> Masi: 'Christian, just give me a second. OK, my big one is to get this incident clear.'
> Horner: 'You only need one racing lap.'
> Wheatley: 'Obviously those lapped cars, you don't need to let them go right the way around and catch up with the back of the pack.'

This was a perceptive point by Wheatley. Because he knew the race director's job so well, the Red Bull man was pointing out to Masi that he had the option to release the lapped cars and restart the race before they had circulated all the way round and rejoined at the back of the field. It was normal practice to allow the lapped cars to do this, but it wasn't a requirement. Bear in mind that at this point, Masi had already decided (and put on the FIA messaging system) that lapped cars would not be allowed to overtake. Wheatley was suggesting a way that Masi could reverse that decision and still have time to resume the race.

> Masi: 'Understood. Just give us a second.'
> Wheatley: 'You just need to let them go, and then we've got a motor race on our hands.'

All of this was happening in a matter of seconds while Masi was also checking that the Latifi wreck had been safely removed, and what was in effect a one-lap race after the restart. However, there was a consensus among team bosses in the F1 Commission (the body that, among other things, debates the rules) that there had been chaos at the restart on that day in Baku, so they would rather continue with the safety car if possible. Knowing this, Masi opted to continue under the safety car in the hope that the race would be able to resume.

Once he'd made that decision, the longer the marshals took to shift Latifi's wrecked car and sweep up, the safer the Mercedes call not to have pitted Hamilton looked. The team was banking on the remaining laps running out, allowing Lewis to finish the race in front. Red Bull, meanwhile, needed a restart and at least one racing lap to give Verstappen a chance to make use of his new tyres and get ahead of Hamilton. On the Red Bull pit wall, Wheatley and his boss Christian Horner were running out of time.

Masi's initial decision, which came up on the pit wall timing screens, was not to allow lapped cars to overtake, as he had done in Brazil two years previously. The intention behind this call was to avoid the time-consuming unlapping procedure which would help squeeze in one or two racing laps. This was Masi's preferred conclusion to the race, but it was bad for Red Bull. That outcome would make Verstappen's task of catching and overtaking Hamilton much harder, as he would have to get past the lapped cars of (in the order that he would reach them) Sebastian Vettel, Charles Leclerc, Esteban Ocon, Fernando Alonso and Lando Norris before finally being able to chase Hamilton, who, in the meantime, would have been scampering down a clear track, even on old tyres. Practically an impossible task, which is why Masi came on the

THE 2021 ABU DHABI GP

not have the luxury of pitting and staying ahead of Verstappen. It looked like quite a big crash, so might take a while to clear up. Six laps left. They made the call – stay out. As the second car, inevitably Red Bull did the opposite with Verstappen, and brought him in for new soft tyres. It was the easiest decision in the world for Red Bull's strategists Will Courtenay and Hannah Schmitz. Verstappen was so far ahead of the third-placed Ferrari of Carlos Sainz that he didn't even lose his second position – it was a free stop.

When Verstappen came out of the pits there were five lapped cars between him and Hamilton. They had stayed out, knowing that the way the safety-car rules were usually enforced would allow them to unlap themselves, leading to a better result at the end. This is a crucial point. Under a safety car Masi had the option not to allow lapped cars to overtake the leaders and unlap themselves. It was at his discretion – he could decide that everyone should hold station if he felt the unlapping procedure would use up too much time. Masi had done this before, at the final safety-car period of the 2019 Brazilian GP. Recovering Latifi's car took longer than was perhaps initially expected, with a brake fire occupying the marshals for a few crucial minutes. Getting the fire extinguished and the car removed was Masi's priority. Sorting out how to finish the race would come later.

It's worth noting that Masi did have the option of stopping the race by showing the red flag, which would have allowed the marshals to take their time. Under a red flag everybody can change their tyres, after which there would be a restart for the remaining laps with everyone on new tyres and on equal terms. This would have been the fairest way to decide the race. That's what happened in Azerbaijan earlier that year, when we had a late stoppage and

On lap 52, with just six laps left to run, Lewis was over 11 seconds clear. An eighth world championship was in his sights.

Further back in the race, Haas's Mick Schumacher was having a spirited fight with Williams's Nicholas Latifi for 15th place. Schumacher ran Latifi wide at Turn 9, which got the Williams's tyres dirty as he left the track. With poor grip, Latifi lost control of his car and crashed into the barrier on the exit of Turn 14, the left-hander after the circuit passes under the glitzy Yas Hotel. There's no run-off at that point, and with the damaged car stranded on the track, Masi was forced to neutralize the race by deploying the safety car, allowing marshals to clear up the heavily damaged Williams. The worst possible scenario for Lewis Hamilton and Mercedes had just become a reality.

It's a quirk of late-race safety-car periods that they often disadvantage the driver in the lead, because the second-placed man can react to what the leader does and do the opposite. Mercedes could see that the Red Bull mechanics were out in the pit lane with fresh new tyres for Verstappen, but that didn't mean Max was definitely going to pit. Had Mercedes brought Hamilton in, Red Bull would (probably) have told Max to stay out, which would have given him the lead of the race. What neither team could know was how long it would take to clear the Latifi crash, and whether the race would end before all the things that the rules said had to happen could happen before racing resumed. If the race finished under the safety car and Mercedes had handed Max the lead (and thus the world championship) by pitting Hamilton, the team would have looked pretty silly.

The Mercedes strategists led by James Vowles were under pressure and running out of time. Thanks to Sergio Pérez, they did

THE 2021 ABU DHABI GP

The drama began on the first lap. Hamilton got the better start and led into Turn 1, but Verstappen got a run on him down to the Turn 7 chicane. The Red Bull went for a pass down the inside and, like Brazil, walked the Mercedes to the outside kerb. Rather than concede the corner, Lewis drove across the run-off and rejoined the track ahead of Max. In the context of what happened in Jeddah, I expected Hamilton to voluntarily give the position back, looking to avoid a potential time penalty. As Verstappen was voicing his objection on the radio, Wheatley was already pleading his case to Masi, who referred the incident to the stewards, but they concluded that because Hamilton had been given no room and had reinstated the original gap to Verstappen, no further investigation was necessary. There was a radio message where Max was told that there would be no action, and he said, 'No surprise there.' In his eyes, he had been punished the previous week in Saudi for the same thing Hamilton had gotten away with now.

With better tyre usage and quicker pace Hamilton pulled away, but in the pit-stop phase, fell victim to a pre-planned Red Bull trap. When Hamilton rejoined following his pit stop on lap 14, Verstappen's teammate Sergio Pérez had been instructed to hold the Mercedes up for as long as he could. He managed to do so for nearly a lap before Lewis could get by, which, crucially, cost Hamilton nearly eight seconds. Max later called Sergio 'a legend' as he thanked him for his help. The time loss allowed Verstappen to close in on Hamilton. It wasn't the end of the world for Mercedes, they were still ahead and still quicker, but it did mean that in the event of a safety car, Lewis did now not have the handy 15-second time gap that would allow him to make a pit stop and rejoin ahead of Max. As long as there wasn't a late-race safety car, he'd be fine.

outside of Turn 4, Verstappen widened his line and eased the Mercedes off track. Not only was this permitted by the driving guidelines at the time, but Michael Masi had also committed to a general philosophy of 'let them race' whereby he preferred to allow the drivers to race each other hard, rather than referring every strongly defended move to the stewards.

Laudable though this aim was, it resulted in chaos, particularly in Jeddah a week before Abu Dhabi, when Verstappen was penalized twice, once for causing a collision with Hamilton and then for having left the track and gained an advantage. Hamilton declared Verstappen's racing to be 'over the limit' that evening while Max complained that 'F1 is more about penalties than racing'.

Hamilton's win in Saudi Arabia meant we headed into the final weekend in Abu Dhabi with the two title contenders on 369.5 points apiece. However, Verstappen had scored nine wins to Hamilton's eight, so if neither man scored in Abu Dhabi, the Dutchman would win the title.

Throughout practice the Mercedes was clearly quicker, and it was only a brilliant lap from Verstappen in the final part of qualifying that clinched him pole position. But on recent form everybody expected that Hamilton would have the faster car in the race and would be able to somehow get to the front and finish ahead. I remember sizing up the contenders in my *Notebook* on Saturday. I went up to random people in the paddock, and just asked, 'Hamilton or Verstappen?', and they gave their reasons as to which driver they thought was going to win the world championship. Certainly pace-wise it looked like Mercedes had the edge, but none of us could have predicted what a memorable race it would turn out to be.

THE 2021 ABU DHABI GP

cause appeared to be a rear-tyre failure. During the ensuing safety-car period Wheatley suggested that a red flag might be the best solution to allow everybody to stop racing and inspect or change their tyres, because Verstappen's crash had been so unexpected and had obvious safety implications. Lance Stroll had also suffered a suspected tyre failure earlier in the race. Wheatley's suggestion was timely, as Masi later said that he had already been thinking of stopping the race and allowing everyone to fit new tyres. The race restarted, and Red Bull went on to win with Sergio Pérez.

That 2021 season was Masi's third in charge, and it developed into an intense battle between Verstappen and Hamilton. There were plenty of dramatic incidents along the way, clashes between the two such as at Silverstone, when they battled for position into Copse Corner, which led to Verstappen having a huge crash and needing a trip to the hospital. Hamilton was given a 10-second penalty for causing the accident, which he overcame, going on to win the race. Mercedes's victory celebrations that day went down very badly with Red Bull and the Verstappen family, who felt them insensitive and disrespectful. Later in the season at Monza, Max and Lewis went into Turn 1 side by side. Neither would give ground and their wheels interlocked, flipping the Red Bull up to land on top of Hamilton's Mercedes. Verstappen was given a three-place grid penalty for the following race after the stewards judged he was to blame for causing the collision.

As the end of the season approached, Hamilton scored consecutive wins in Brazil, Qatar and Saudi Arabia, thanks to some late-season improvements that made his Mercedes significantly quicker than the Red Bull, but tensions ramped up between teams even further. In Brazil, as Hamilton was trying to overtake on the

There had long been an intercom channel between the teams and race control. Often the chat was about routine or mundane matters, such as why a session had been delayed or whether an extra formation lap would be needed. At other times the teams would report their rivals to the race director if they felt a rule had been broken. Whiting always took these appeals with a pinch of salt – it was part of the game, and he had a measured approach when it came to deciding which messages to act on. Charlie would hear mainly from team managers over the intercom, although team principals could ask questions and indeed did start doing so more often when, under Masi's tenure, the messages began being broadcast.

With all this change afoot, Michael Masi started to learn who he could lean on for support and advice. In Red Bull Racing's sporting director Jonathan Wheatley, he found a valued colleague and the two forged a professional relationship. Wheatley was one of the pit lane's leading experts on the rules, given that he'd been responsible for them at Red Bull since 2006. It was not only Wheatley – other team sporting directors such as Ron Meadows of Mercedes, Alan Permane of Renault/Alpine and Andy Stevenson of Racing Point/Aston Martin were also important sounding boards for Masi, as all had worked for many years with Whiting and knew the rule book by heart. However, I often saw Wheatley taking time to discuss matters with Masi, and he could be heard on the broadcasts taking a more collaborative, proactive tone with Masi than some of his fellow sporting directors.

One example of Masi showing that he was happy to accept Wheatley's advice occurred at the 2021 Azerbaijan GP when Max Verstappen's Red Bull crashed on the pit straight. The immediate

Masi had years of experience gained in the hectic world of the V8 touring car series in his home country and had been appointed as a deputy race director by the FIA in 2018.

The FIA issued a document naming Masi race director for the Australian GP. Initially engaged on a race-by-race basis, he was eventually awarded the job full-time. Replacing Whiting was an incredibly difficult task, and considering the scale of the challenge, Masi started relatively well. He played himself in, got to know the drivers and the teams, and worked to get F1 back on track during the Covid-19 pandemic in 2020.

During his tenure as race director, Whiting had agreed to requests from Formula 1 to grant their cameras more access to the rule-making and rule-enforcing side of the sport. F1 TV cameras were subsequently allowed into selected Friday evening drivers' briefings, which produced fascinating insights. Charlie had also agreed to hold post-race media briefings to discuss decisions he'd made during the weekend. After a period getting used to his new job, FIA officials began to make Masi available to the media, too. This both raised his profile and afforded much more scrutiny of his actions.

There was also a desire to make the mid-race decision-making process more transparent, so F1 asked for intercom messages between Masi in race control and the teams on the pit wall to be made available for broadcast – something I can't imagine Charlie agreeing to. This was new for F1, but a high degree of transparency was already common in sports such as rugby, cricket and tennis, where the referees or umpires routinely wear microphones so their decisions can be heard, and it was broadly accepted that it was good for F1 to follow suit.

the mere re-telling upsets one side or the other. However, if the study of history is to better understand, empathize and learn lessons for the future, and if you're interested in hearing the facts of what happened from someone who was there in the pits that evening and witnessed events unfold first-hand, here we go.

The story starts a couple of years earlier with the tragic death of veteran FIA race director Charlie Whiting. It was on the Thursday morning of the 2019 Australian Grand Prix that we learned the news that Whiting had died in his hotel room overnight at the age of just 66. It was a shocking occurrence, one of those events that sends the paddock into a very subdued place. Charlie's passing was the only thing that anybody was talking about on that day.

He had been a part of the F1 scene for over four decades, initially as a mechanic for Hesketh, and then for Bernie Ecclestone's Brabham team. He moved to the FIA in 1988, and over the years his role expanded to encompass a range of job titles alongside that of race director, including official starter, safety delegate and head of the technical department. A workaholic and perfectionist, he commanded respect across the paddock. Drivers and teams didn't always agree with his decisions, but they accepted them. Whoever you spoke to that day in the Albert Park paddock, be it mechanics, drivers, team bosses or journalists, everyone was shocked, especially as he'd been busy at the track with his usual pre-weekend duties just the previous day.

At the same time as dealing with the shock and making appropriate arrangements for Charlie's family, the FIA had to address how the race meeting could progress, given that he held such a crucial position. Few knew about it, but Whiting had been training up deputies in the race director's role. Australian Michael

Chapter 20

The 2021 Abu Dhabi GP

If you've read up to this point and been wondering when I was going to get to perhaps the most significant and important moment of my time in F1, and certainly the biggest story I've covered, well, here it is – the Abu Dhabi Grand Prix of 2021. It has become known as one of the most controversial moments in the sport's history, but since the facts of what happened that evening are known and generally accepted, why the controversy? No one disputes the course of events of this championship-deciding race, most of it was broadcast live and the players have all since had their say.

What is disputed is whether the result was fair – impartial and just, without favouritism or discrimination – and everyone is entitled to their opinion based on the evidence and facts. Of course, there is a feeling of injustice on one side and a defensive position on the other, all perfectly natural and understandable emotions. However, there's something about this race that makes people unwilling to even talk about it. Indeed, it would probably make my life easier not to write this chapter at all, for fear that present at all? After all, the *Drive to Survive* camera and sound crews don't live with the teams and drivers 24 hours a day – they have to be booked for a day's filming like any other service. Think about that process – would it start with a call from the team's press office to the *DTS* producers offering them a certain filming opportunity on the promise that something important is going to happen? Would that have been happening anyway or is it only happening in that way for the benefit of the cameras? And the team bosses? How have fame and recognition affected them and their decision-making process?

Finally, consider how much footage and how many behind-the-scenes stories didn't make the final edit, and what might happen to that material in the future. It's a fascinating thought that the cameras might have caught something that was too spicy or sensitive even for *Drive to Survive*, but which might be declassified and broadcast in 10 years when it's safe to do so. I'd watch that!

forgot he was being followed around by a camera and a microphone recording his every word, or just didn't care? The Netflix series made him famous, and even foretold his own departure from F1 when he explained that everyone is accountable and if the team doesn't perform, the buck stops with him. Steiner was relieved of his Haas duties on the eve of the 2024 season.

Like everyone, I love watching the episodes, but it's interesting to consider how they are put together, without many of the constraints in covering a race weekend that we are bound by at Sky. Firstly, the *DTS* cameras are everywhere and they film absolutely everything. There's a good reason for that – when the season starts the producers don't know what the stories are going to be. Midway through the season they're in a position to see what the emerging lead stories are, and what might make for a good episode, but until that point, you have to have the shots in the can. Secondly, Netflix are allowed in everywhere because the teams know that the footage won't be seen until the beginning of the following season, by which time it will be old news and not as sensitive. Final approval of *Drive to Survive* rests with Netflix and F1, but the teams and drivers are shown their sections ahead of broadcast and can make representations to the producers.

Thirdly, and media students will be writing theses on this well into the future, consider how the presence of the *Drive to Survive* cameras is affecting actual decisions being made in the F1 teams. Are events being created or staged when the cameras are rolling because the teams know it will guarantee them making it into an episode, giving their sponsors millions of eyeballs on this worldwide entertainment platform? What if there's something juicy about to happen but the cameras are somewhere else, or not younger age groups, two demographics that F1 had previously struggled to attract.

Much of this new audience was also in the USA and it's no exaggeration to say that, after decades trying to break the American market, F1 had *Drive to Survive* to thank for finally achieving it. It seems incredible now, but in the first season Mercedes and Ferrari had been reluctant to let the cameras go behind the scenes, and thus didn't allow the Netflix crews to fully embed themselves for a weekend. When they saw the final result and it dawned on them that it would be of benefit to their sponsors to be seen by such huge numbers of viewers, especially in the US, they opened their doors.

One of the early stars who came to worldwide fame thanks to *Drive to Survive* was the entertainingly sweary Guenther Steiner, at the time the team principal of the American-owned Haas F1 team. A favourite episode showed Guenther in his natural habitat, perched on his pit-wall command post. 'F**k!' Steiner barks at his monitors on the pit wall, watching his driver Romain Grosjean make a mistake in qualifying. 'I'm f**king speechless, I can't f**king believe it.' Grosjean is getting it in the neck and Steiner admits to the then chief engineer (and now team boss) Ayao Komatsu that his patience is wearing thin. 'Ach, f**k me. I can't keep finding excuses for him.' After hearing a string of Grosjean's own excuses for another race out of the points, Guenther responds, 'Just focus on driving, not f**king whinge.' Another episode shows Steiner hosting a team dinner at the French GP – Grosjean was absent. 'Maybe I didn't invite him because he doesn't deserve any food.'

It was deliciously entertaining stuff. And refreshing to see so much passion from an F1 team boss. Impossible to know if Steiner struggling to find ways of paying their staff, given that there was no appearance money coming in from the F1 circus. As soon as we were allowed out of our homes for a daily period of exercise, I offered my producers a weekly edition of *Ted's Notebook*, to round up all the bits and pieces of news I'd heard about. Given social distancing, I had to be my own cameraman, so I found a way to clamp my little pocket motion-stabilizing camera on to the end of a selfie stick, which seemed to work reasonably well as a technical solution to the problem of how to film myself while also walking round my local park. A couple of laps were enough to fill viewers in on the latest in F1 and what plans were afoot for the return to racing. I would never have imagined presenting *Ted's Lockdown Notebook*, and I sincerely hope I never do again, but in the absence of anything else to watch the shows were fairly popular and I still get people coming up to me from time to time saying how much they enjoyed them.

I'd like to think it was my lockdown rambles, but of course the thing that really skyrocketed F1's popularity during Covid was a new documentary series from Netflix called *Drive to Survive*. Commissioned by a television man, former ESPN executive Sean Bratches who moved to F1, the first season had aired with reasonable success but hadn't set the world alight. A second season had been commissioned, though, and the documentary makers had been out at the races filming all year. It was released worldwide on Netflix at the beginning of March 2020 and became a must-watch for people stuck at home, huge numbers of whom had never heard of or watched F1 before. They grew to love the drivers and team bosses through the stories showcased in such a vivid and compelling way. Many of these new viewers were female and from small cheer from the locals who were wondering why the guy on the screen was now standing there in front of them with a glass of the Yarra Valley's finest in his hand.

The last we'd see of each other was Sunday morning. My plan to fly around the world hit the buffers as the USA was starting to close its borders and there wasn't an assurance that when I got to San Francisco I'd be able to fly on to London. Pleasant as California is, I didn't want to be stranded there away from my family for the next three months, so flew back on Qatar Airways via Doha (indeed Qatar Airways never stopped flying during the Covid pandemic, providing an important lifeline to many). Two days after we got back to London, the UK closed its borders, told its population to stay at home, and that was it. I should have listened to Ben Hunt at The Nag's Head.

From breadmaking to online workouts, everyone went a bit stir-crazy during lockdown, but as a media company, we needed to figure out a way to meet the increased demand for our content. After a few weeks we pivoted to making programmes remotely and attempted to keep our audience informed and entertained by creating shows from our homes. We did 'watch-alongs' of classic races featuring the drivers who took part in them, a series called 'At home with . . .', where each of us on the Sky F1 team introduced three of our favourite features that had aired over the years, and told some stories about how they came to be, what happened during filming and so on. We filled out the schedule with extended highlights of previous races.

Things were still happening in F1. Sebastian Vettel split from Ferrari and was later confirmed at Aston Martin to replace Sergio Pérez, and there was worrying news from teams who were posterity before relocating to just outside the paddock entrance for probably the strangest press conference I'd ever attended. Then F1 CEO Chase Carey was joined by the AGPC chair Paul Little, its CEO Andrew Westacott, and FIA race director Michael Masi. They explained the situation and why they were left with no option but to cancel the event, stressing how sorry they were for the fans. Carey was asked for his response to Hamilton's suggestion that F1 had only travelled to Australia in a pandemic because 'cash is king'. 'I guess if cash was king, we wouldn't have made the decision we did today,' he replied. A fair response, but in reality, there was no alternative. Borders were being closed all over Europe, and it was only a matter of time before Australia did the same.

I broadcast a couple of reports from outside the paddock, one about what was going on with the teams and drivers and another reflecting on the news lines from the press conference. Simon Lazenby wrapped up our programme from the other side of the park, said goodbye to our viewers, and we went back to the TV compound to pack up our stuff. It was the strangest feeling knowing that the season had not even started but we were saying, 'Goodbye' and 'See you when all this blows over.' Then it was back to the hotel and try to figure out how to get home. The next day, while Helen Cox, Nick Warren and their team at Travel Places worked feverishly trying to find ways of getting all the UK-based teams and media home a few days early, the crew and I went for a very pleasant Saturday lunch on St Kilda Beach. There was a moment later that afternoon when we were in the restaurant's bar and the local news was on the TV. Suddenly it cut to one of my reports from the previous day about what the F1 teams would do next, and I got a although the gates were closed to the fans, the teams, media and officials were being allowed in. I'll never forget how bad I felt walking past a huge queue of ticket holders as we went through the gates. Some were asking us if we knew what was going on, and I answered as honestly as I could that it didn't look good, but there was still no official confirmation either way. The picture had been confused still further by various health and governmental agencies in the state of Victoria not wanting to be the ones who shut down the Grand Prix and offering last-minute solutions that were unlikely to work.

Mercifully the fans didn't have to wait outside too long. Around three hours after Seb and Kimi had taken off for Dubai, F1, the FIA and the AGPC announced the cancellation of the event. There was talk of a postponement, but this seemed unlikely when fans were offered a refund on their tickets. We were in our morning meeting in the TV compound when the news officially dropped. It was a real 'wow' moment. It wasn't what we came to Australia for, but we had a programme to make. For reasons I didn't understand, rather than stay at the track where the story was, our team was sent off-site to present a special programme from a café outside our hotel. As everyone else schlepped cameras, lights, tripods and sound equipment back across Albert Park, I put my radio mic kit on and headed for the paddock with Lee the marine.

Teams were already halfway through their pack-up procedures, unused fuel was being returned, tyres were being wheeled back to Pirelli. Equipment was being packed away with a bit more care than usual given the mechanics weren't sure when they were going to see it again. We filmed some of this activity for

Finally, at around 1am and following a day of further meetings in Europe, a decision was made. The race would be cancelled. Matters were left in the hands of the local authorities and lawyers to argue over liabilities. Ferrari's team principal Mattia Binotto could see that the race wouldn't take place, so called his drivers Sebastian Vettel and Kimi Räikkönen to tell them to get on the first flight out of Melbourne. They were only too happy to get back to their families, so packed their bags and arrived at Melbourne Airport at 4.45am for the 6.15am Emirates flight 409 to Dubai. Among the chaos and confusion, this was the clearest sign that the race was off. A 'whistle blower' posted a photo on social media of the flight manifest, printed, as they all still are, on a dot-matrix printer at the airport gate. The seat plan for flight EK409, on Friday 13 March 2020, was as follows: In 1A (with an Emirates gold card), Mr Sebastian Vettel, and in seat 3A (also with a gold card and a gluten-free meal request), Mr Kimi-Matias Räikkönen. There was the usual doubt when dealing with anything on the internet as to whether this was a fake, but as soon as I saw the dot-matrix detail and the use of Kimi's passport name of Kimi-Matias, I knew it was the real thing.

While we were sure that Seb and Kimi wouldn't be driving in the Australian GP, joining their McLaren and Mercedes colleagues Lando Norris, Carlos Sainz, Valtteri Bottas and Lewis Hamilton, the remaining 14 drivers woke up on Friday morning not knowing whether to head for the circuit or the airport. They were in good company. Tens of thousands of people turned up but weren't allowed into Albert Park. I had seen the Vettel/Räikkönen flight manifest picture over breakfast, which told me all I needed to know about the fate of the Grand Prix, but we were still at work, and calls by the local police, Victoria state health officials, lawyers and local government officials. Time was not on their side. Track inspections started at 7.40am and the gates to Albert Park were due to open at 8am. It was a tense meeting, and the financial stakes were high given how much money had already been spent and contractually promised. The only teams who committed to continuing with the Grand Prix and racing with or without McLaren were Red Bull, sister team Alpha Tauri and Racing Point.

Mercedes was diametrically opposed. On Thursday evening Mercedes wrote to F1 and the FIA requesting the cancellation of the race, reasoning that the team could not guarantee the safety of its employees if the event continued, it wasn't right to race if McLaren could not, while empathizing with the worsening situation in Europe, especially in Italy. Mercedes concluded by saying that it would pack up its equipment in the morning.

Clearly the situation was now turning legal. Mercedes couldn't say outright that it was withdrawing from the event, as it had legal obligations to continue, but that's effectively what the team was doing. Ferrari was equally very concerned about the state of affairs back home and was as keen as Mercedes to fly back before Italy locked down.

The team bosses argued about the legal and sporting aspects of the situation into the evening. Managing director of motorsport for F1, Ross Brawn, was in and out of the meeting as decisions swayed from carrying on to cancellation and back again. The organizers even considered continuing with local support events only, but abandoned that plan when it was pointed out that fans would not be too happy watching a touring car race while the F1 teams packed up their garages.

I don't feel like I should shy away from my opinion. The fact is we are here, and I just urge everyone to be as careful as you can be.' I'm not sure if Lewis meant the phrase 'cash is king' to be a throwaway line, but it made headlines around the world, hinting that as long as money was being generated by F1 for the teams and the circuits, it didn't matter about people's health. It was controversial but would be proved accurate in that when the money did stop flowing during the subsequent lockdowns, several F1 teams almost folded because of the lack of cashflow.

While all this was happening in the media centre, the team members' test results came in. The Haas mechanics only had common colds, but McLaren's test returned positive. F1 hadn't yet established procedures to follow in the event of a positive test, so when it did happen, McLaren suddenly had to isolate employees in a bid to prevent further transmission. As more and more people were identified as close contacts and were sent back to their hotel rooms, it quickly became clear to McLaren management that they didn't have enough people to crew their racing team. On Thursday evening the team announced that it was withdrawing from the Australian GP weekend. It was a big shock, and even people who thought they knew what was going on inside the paddock had no clue, such was the pace at which decisions were being made.

That evening a crisis meeting was held. The word 'stakeholders' is often overused in a mist of management speak, but it seemed particularly apt for this assembly of people at Melbourne's Crown Casino Hotel. In addition to the F1 team principals, the top people from Formula One Management, the FIA and the AGPC, the Australian Grand Prix Corporation, were joined on conference day. Guenther Steiner was the first interview of the day, and he sat in a corner of the team's paddock area with a table in front of him. Journalists placed their recorders on the table, behind which was a one-metre exclusion zone enforced by a retractable queue barrier. Behind that sat all the journalists, together. It was very odd. It seemed that the teams were afraid that the journalists would pass on the virus to the team members, when in fact, given the first reports of cases had been on the teams' side, the concern should have been the other way around.

The interviews continued throughout the day. At one point, I measured my arm to see if it was a metre long, so as to ascertain if I could hold a microphone close enough to any driver we were being socially distanced from. Everyone I spoke to had been pretty non-committal about whether they thought the race would be affected by the pandemic. Most wanted to fall back on the comfortable ground of lap times, setups and the FIA's recent response to questions surrounding Ferrari's engine.

Then came a bombshell. In the FIA press conference Lewis Hamilton, F1's biggest worldwide personality, had the courage to say what many were starting to think. 'I am really very, very surprised that we're here. I think it's great that we have races but for me it's shocking that we're all sitting in this room.' Hamilton added that he'd seen what the rest of us had in Australia, life going on as usual, and was concerned about how many people were gathered together in one place for the Grand Prix.

In an instant, the assembled journalists knew they had a massive story on their hands. A well-worded follow-up asked Hamilton, 'Why are we still here?', to which he replied, 'Cash is king. Honestly, I don't know. I can't really add much more to it.

trying to pad out with quotes.' Williams gave a straightforward answer about how everyone was keeping an eye on developments and trusted the FIA and F1 to make decisions about the calendar.

The press meeting wrapped up, I said my thanks and farewells, and mentioned to Jamie and Catherine how much I was looking forward to getting going with W Series for our second season. As I walked out of The Nag's Head into the spring sunshine I stepped over a floor mosaic by the entrance that read 'Established 1827.' 'This pub has been here for nearly 200 years,' I thought to myself. 'It's survived two world wars, a couple of global recessions, and whatever Covent Garden throws at it every Saturday night. A virus isn't going to hurt it.'

A few days later I flew to Australia via Singapore. I was particularly excited because I had booked a Star Alliance 'round the world' ticket with my return on United Airlines, flying across the Pacific from Melbourne to San Francisco. I was hoping to have seen Hawaii from the air before connecting on to a San Francisco to London flight to complete my circumnavigation of the globe. It was a longer route, but it appealed to my sense of adventure, as much as sitting in comfort on an aircraft can be adventurous. On landing, we'd seen the latest news about the virus – it already had a name, 'Covid-19', but on the Wednesday before the race, it had a classification: Pandemic.

Wandering around Melbourne, you wouldn't have known anything was different. Then that evening, news emerged that some members of the McLaren and Haas teams had displayed 'flu-like' symptoms on arrival in Australia, and had been quarantined in their hotel rooms and tested. With their results pending, the F1 paddock looked different when we arrived on Thursday for media some of whom race instead in consumer brand cars representing the series sponsors, for example Aurelia Nobels, who is supported by Puma. Other sponsors such as American Express, Charlotte Tilbury and Tag Heuer keep the money coming in.

Having been involved with getting W Series established on TV, I'm proud that its legacy lives on and we show every F1 Academy race live on Sky Sports F1. Wolff and her team are doing an amazing job in continuing to break down barriers and it's exciting to see some seriously talented drivers coming through. Abbi Pulling dominated the 2024 F1 Academy season and now races Formula 3 level cars in the British GB3 championship. Whether it's her or someone yet to come, it wouldn't surprise me to find a female driver racing full-time in F1 in the next decade.

On that day in 2020 at The Nag's Head, however, all Catherine Bond Muir and Jamie Chadwick were hoping was that their second season would get going without a hitch. Lizzie Brooks called the room to order; I popped my plate on the side and sat down to hear what everyone had to say. Jonathan Kendrick talked about his pleasure in sponsoring Williams after working for Sir Frank Williams as a tyre man in the 1980s. There were a couple of questions from the floor about the upcoming F1 season and to Felipe Massa on how he was enjoying his move to Formula E. Then *The Sun*'s F1 correspondent Ben Hunt piped up with a question for Claire Williams. 'There's a lot of talk about this virus that's coming out of China, and that's in Italy now. How concerned are you that it could affect sponsorships and sporting events with a lot of people gathering together, like at the Australian GP?'

'What a question,' I thought to myself. 'Some virus is hardly going to stop F1 from going ahead, is it? He must have a story he's

Finding that sponsorship money was for W Series to worry about. The organization attracted some great partners over the years, including Puma, Heineken and my pub hosts ROKiT, but rising costs and a year lost to the pandemic meant that by the end of its third season in 2022 W Series badly needed to find a new injection of money. By now it had joined the F1 travelling circus as a support racing series. While that was fantastic for prestige, publicity and the patronage of a few F1 teams, having to ship the cars all over the world was costing them millions.

At the start of 2023 Catherine Bond Muir's team had a new investor lined up, but at the last minute, unexpectedly, they withdrew, and she had to take the gut-wrenching decision to lay off staff and take the company into administration. There had been rumours of an opportunity around 18 months earlier for Sean Wadsworth and his fellow investors to sell the company to Liberty Media, owners of F1, but a deal never materialized. It wouldn't have taken much to keep the series alive – an F1 team's marketing budget would have done it – but time ran out and Bond Muir was forced to admit defeat.

What W Series did achieve was to prove beyond doubt that the concept worked, but that maybe a different financial model was required. Liberty Media certainly thought so, and asked Susie Wolff, the last woman to drive a Grand Prix car in a race weekend, to head up a new all-female championship by the name of F1 Academy. The drivers would have to pay €150,000 per season to compete, but that would be matched by Liberty. The existing Formula 2 teams would run the Formula 4-spec cars and the F1 teams got involved by supporting a driver each. Lia Block, for example, was selected to the Williams Driver Academy, so she races in Williams colours. But this system doesn't cover all the drivers, that there were so few female drivers coming through, and the barriers were so clear, that it seemed obvious some kind of positive action was needed to create new opportunities and broaden accessibility.

It was rare to find a startup that had such a strong group of people behind it. Founder Catherine Bond Muir had a decade's experience in intellectual property law and corporate finance. David Coulthard was on board, as was his friend Sean Wadsworth, chairman and cornerstone investor. Also involved were my old friend Dave Ryan from McLaren and Matt Bishop, former McLaren communications director, who had joined in a senior comms role because he believed in the project and liked working with good people. Lee McKenzie presented the broadcast coverage, I was the roving reporter, and Claire Cottingham was joined by Coulthard in the commentary box.

They came from a wide range of backgrounds with differing levels of experience, but the drivers were the stars. Alice Powell had been the first woman to win the UK Formula Renault championship and the first to score points in the GP3 series, but then she ran out of money. It was a similar story for Sarah Moore – she had won the Ginetta Junior Championship in 2009 (the same series in which five years later Lando Norris would finish third) but couldn't find the funding needed to move up the ladder. Other drivers like Naomi Schiff and Jessica Hawkins had more experience in GT cars but hadn't until this point been given a chance to drive many single-seaters. What W Series gave them and around 40 others who raced in it over three seasons was the opportunity to compete, and to showcase their skill and dedication without having to worry about where the next sponsor was coming from.

make it into F1, so a frequent hurdle was trying to raise a racing budget. W Series turned that on its head. The way the series was funded meant that all a driver had to pay for was their travel to their nearest major airport – W Series took care of the rest. On top of that, the drivers were actually paid, unheard of in the junior formulae. There would be prize money for everyone, and the championship winner received $500,000 with which to potentially fund their next drive.

Second was getting practice time in the cars. Any testing outside of a race weekend costs money, and these were not drivers with Formula 1 teams backing them up. The only way any driver improves is by practising, and W Series gave its drivers plenty of testing so they could sharpen their skills and compete at the higher levels. Thirdly, by being open, visible and publicizing the fact there was a series just for female drivers, W Series inspired a whole new generation of girls to see motor racing as something they could do, something that was open for them to try.

W Series's first season was held on the German Touring Car Championship support bill (anyone who has attended a major race will be familiar with the support races that keep the crowd entertained until the main event), and I saw first-hand how girls who came with little enthusiasm to Hockenheim or the Norisring with their families were suddenly entranced and inspired by these incredible female racers.

Surprisingly, there was some criticism of the series from a few female racing drivers including IndyCar drivers Danica Patrick and Pippa Mann, who felt W Series made it harder for female drivers to compete equally with men if they were segregated into a separate championship. But I would argue of the W Series (the world's first all-female racing series) and the CEO of that championship, Catherine Bond Muir.

Mini hamburgers were served at the back of the room, and we were given a particularly tasty German beer called ABK, one of the ROKiT brands, from a town southwest of Munich that I'd never heard of. I've since struggled to find ABK, which is a shame as I was quite taken with it, although only one of the three organizations present that day retained ROKiT's sponsorship, which indicated that the company may have had bigger issues on their hands than beer distribution.

I had been involved with the W Series since its debut in 2019, having found myself temporarily looking for work. Two of the questions I'm asked most, and that I used to ask myself, are, 'Why haven't there been more female F1 drivers?' and 'Will there be one in the next decade?' There is objectively no reason why there couldn't be a successful female F1 driver. Motor racing is one of the very few sports in the world in which women and men compete on equal terms. On average women are smaller and lighter than men (always a benefit in a racing car where mass slows you down), studies have shown that they process information faster and sports such as ultra running have proved that women can outstrip their male counterparts when it comes to endurance. Why then can I count on one hand the number of women who have driven in Formula 1? What has been holding them back? W Series was incredibly important, because while it might not have had all the answers, it did remove three of the barriers that were preventing female drivers from getting into single-seater motorsport.

The first was money. Based on the existing status-quo within the sport, most sponsors didn't think female drivers were likely to

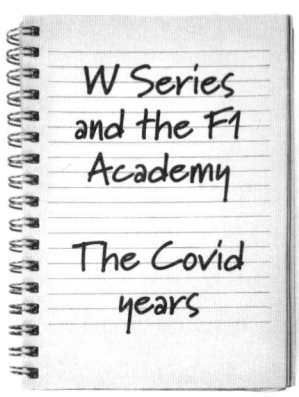

Chapter 19

Surviving, Driving

The Nag's Head, Covent Garden. A traditional English pub. Not your usual venue for an F1 sponsor day, but then this wasn't your usual sponsor. Organized by experienced motorsport PR Lizzie Brooks, it was hosted on a Monday in early March 2020 by a company called ROKiT, which has commercial interests in mobile phones, motorbike cleaning products, tequila and beer – hence the pub.

ROKiT chairman Jonathan Kendrick was there to talk about the company's upcoming sponsorship of the Williams F1 team, the Venturi Formula E team and the all-female W Series, which was just beginning its second season. 'JK' as he's known is a larger-than-life character. However, Lizzie had spent two years working for Eddie Jordan, so knew how to handle a character. Team principal Claire Williams was there with her former driver Felipe Massa (then at Venturi Formula E). Also present was Jamie Chadwick, Williams's development driver and inaugural champion

the Ferrari looked like the semi-circular wax casing of a Mini Babybel. So I put that to Carlos Sainz, who looked a little confused when I held up an example that I'd bought in a Barcelona supermarket – although after a demonstration, he had to agree.

I try not to keep too strictly to the format of *Ted's Notebook*, especially after 14 years. I like to shake it up now and then, and every year we do something a little bit different. In 2025 we're doing a *Learn with Lewis* section (when I remember to do it), where we acquire a new Italian phrase every week. He's learning Italian at Ferrari, so we're going to learn it with him. I'm looking forward to finding out how to say things like, 'Can we change the rear anti roll bar?'

Twenty-four years of what I'd like to hope are insightful contributions to practice, qualifying and race coverage, breaking stories and painstakingly crafting features, and yet I'm best known for a rambling, one-person, one-shot, live monologue – a programme I didn't think of, didn't name, reading off a notebook I didn't even pay for. However, if it is informing and entertaining the audience, I'm happy. Even if they are only watching to see Pete and me stack it on an escalator.

technology was in play or their purpose. And that became *Development Corner*, named simply because it was about developments and was presented in a quiet and dimly lit corner of the Barcelona media centre.

Finally, let me explain about the cheese. I have a fondness (fondue-ness?) for using cheese to illustrate complicated technical developments within F1, because it just works. This began in Bahrain in 2020, when the FIA removed a triangular section of the back of all the cars' floors to try and cut some of the downforce. It didn't seem like a big change, but it was in a crucial area of the car, and when I looked at the bit they cut out I thought it resembled a triangular slab of Swiss cheese. So on the way to the track I bought some Gruyère, used a ruler and knife to cut it to the exact dimensions of the bodywork in question, and took it into the paddock to hold up to camera and explain the rule change to the viewers.

A little later I turned up to an interview with Sebastian Vettel, still with this triangle of cheese in my carrier bag. We were familiar enough that I knew he'd say, 'What's in the bag?,' which was a perfect opportunity for me to ask if he wanted some of my cheese. Taking this evidence of my eccentricity in his stride, he added, 'What are you going to do with that?' I said, 'Well, I can't do anything. I can't eat it, it's been sweating in this plastic bag in the Bahrain sun all day.' The cheese had gone all wobbly, so Seb had a go at me for being wasteful!

When we got to the ground-effect era in 2022, in order to explain the downforce-generating venturi channels underneath the cars I used a block of Cheddar, and carved out channels in the correct dimensions. On another occasion I thought the sidepod scoops on

TED'S NOTEBOOK

Hopefully by now, I think most paddock regulars know what I'm doing when they see me wandering around with a microphone, seemingly talking to myself. Sometimes I notice people in my peripheral vision who look as if they might want to come and start a conversation. If I don't know them, or I can't predict what they're going to say, I'll turn my back and move away, hoping they'll get the message.

We can't edit a live *Notebook*. If you do see an edit or a cutaway on the Sky website or YouTube versions, it's probably because somebody has come and interrupted us or said or done something that we didn't want to include. A team boss's brother once leaned into my microphone and said something about a rival team that was potentially slanderous. It went out live, but we were able to edit it out of the replay. We also had to edit another one where a teenage fan in the paddock came and flicked the v's into the camera!

The regular race weekend *Notebook* has led to a couple of spin-offs. The first is the *Testing Notebook*, where we do a roundup of what happened at the pre-season test at the end of each day. Just as it's difficult for people to watch four hours of Grand Prix coverage on a Sunday, it's even harder for them to watch nine hours of testing coverage on a weekday, so I hope it serves our viewers to have a half-hour roundup of everything that happened. Then we have *Development Corner*, which started at a Barcelona test a few years ago. The track's media centre used to have little soundproofed booths where, before email existed, journalists would file their copy to their newspapers or magazines by telephone. Nobody used them anymore, but they remained in place, so I would pop into one with my laptop, the cameraman would join me, and I'd go through spy photos and pinpoint new aero parts on the cars, discussing what saying that there was a discrepancy in the minimum weight for car number 63. We happened to go to parc fermé at just the right time and saw the FIA officials wheeling the Mercedes on and off the scales, and the mechanics taking wheels and front wings on and off. Bauer and his colleagues were still in the process of confirming that Russell's car was indeed underweight, and we were there to bring the viewer into the moment, watching it play out in real time.

Post-race FIA investigations like these often take a while, and most don't get concluded before the *Notebook* finishes. With the Russell situation at Spa, for example, I couldn't say that he was definitely going to be excluded. For all we knew there was a valid explanation for the weight discrepancy, or Mercedes might have been able to show that a part fell off or something. So you can never call a stewards' decision in advance one way or the other, because there's always a chance that there won't be a penalty. If the results are still in question, I'll finish the programme encouraging viewers to check in with *Sky Sports News*, and we'll post the result on social media. That can be a bit frustrating, but there's only so long that we can stay on-air for, and the FIA don't consider TV schedules when they're conducting their investigations.

Because my cameraman is often some distance away from me, looking into motorhomes or garages, sometimes other people see me talking, don't realize that I'm actually live, and come up for a chat. The person who did this most often was Britta Roeske, Sebastian Vettel's media and general manager. She had a tendency not to notice that I was live and would say, 'Ah Ted, there you are. I have the details for next week's interview.' 'Thank you very much, Britta, but I'm in the middle of something.' 'Oh, you should have told me!'

TED'S NOTEBOOK

The conversation could have been about anything, but a couple of months later James was confirmed as the new Williams team principal, and I'm convinced that by chance we captured a crunch meeting.

When the opportunity arises, I stop and talk to drivers or team bosses, but those encounters are never planned. By the time we get on-air with the *Notebook*, a lot of the drivers are just about finishing their briefings and are heading back to their hotels or to the airport, and it's fair game to grab them on the way to the car park, if they are willing to talk. Nico Hulkenberg likes a chat, as does Lando Norris, whereas Alex Albon is normally very good at telling me to go and bother someone else! Going further back, Daniel Ricciardo was always prime *Notebook* gold, a flash of eye contact and that grin would play on his lips. He knew that there was mischief to be had on live, unedited TV.

Often while I'm doing the *Notebook* the team bosses are conducting press briefings in the motorhomes for the written media. We don't join those. It's not that we've been told not to, it's just not good form. It's a professional courtesy among the media that after TV has had its time with the team bosses, then it's the turn of the print and website journalists. However, if there's a massive story breaking, such as a big controversy, I've been known to nip into a motorhome and gatecrash a media session.

Sometimes after a race there's a big ongoing story such as a technical infringement and an FIA investigation playing out while I'm on-air. George Russell's eventual disqualification after he had won the 2024 Belgian GP on the road is a recent example. It wasn't exactly investigative reporting on my part, given that the FIA had already issued a document from technical delegate Jo Bauer

Cameramen Pete and Lee know what I'm after in terms of what to film during the *Notebook*. They tend to roam off by themselves while I'm talking, but I'll always have a mental picture of where they are, so I know where to find them if I need them to show something or someone. Sometimes you'll see Pete walking up the side of a team truck, and because I saw him go down there, I'm usually waiting for him when he walks back up the other side. My cameramen are like well-trained puppies in that regard, or perhaps I'm the puppy and they have me well trained!

Because we're just two people, we can cover more ground than a usual programme presentation crew which allows us to nab key people for a quick interview. The sheer joy and relief in Lando Norris when we spoke after his 2025 Monaco Grand Prix win made for a wonderfully human moment, while a swift encounter with Adrian Newey following the 2024 Japanese Grand Prix turned out to mark a turning point in his Formula 1 career.

Red Bull Racing had just dominated the race in Suzuka, finishing first and second with Max Verstappen and Sergio Pérez. The team were holding their victory photo on the grid, but as the champagne started to flow, I spotted Adrian and his wife Amanda slinking off the side of the grid into the pit lane. Dodging a forklift truck to get to them, I caught a very reflective Newey, crediting his team of engineers back in Milton Keynes. We'd later discover that it was on that weekend, maybe on that exact day, that Newey had decided to leave Red Bull Racing, hand the baton on to the team beneath him and head for pastures new.

In Mexico in 2022 I was talking about Alex Albon's race when the camera caught James Vowles, who was then still the chief strategist at Mercedes, chatting with the owners of Williams.

points in 2023, I'd ask about their race and he'd simply say, 'No pace, slow, that's it.' The whole exchange would take five seconds, and I had all I needed to know.

There is a provisional on-air start time for *Ted's Notebook*. We seldom hit it, as things tend to over-run after eventful races, but it doesn't matter. When we do get underway, what I do is pretty much unplanned, and that is by design. There have been various attempts over the years to make it into more of a polished TV programme, but the point of the *Notebook* is that once we start, it is live, it's one shot and we don't stop, even if I make a mistake or something goes wrong. We've even had a camera fail in the middle of filming and we've had to pick up with another camera. The shakier and less polished it is, the more I like it!

In deciding where to start I think carefully about how the previous programme ended. I don't want to pick up directly from what Simon Lazenby and the pundits were discussing in the post-race analysis, because I don't want people to start with something they've just seen. To my mind it's good to start somewhere fresh, and I'll have a quick think about what my top story is. It might not always be the race winner; if a team is doing a celebration photo with all the crew in the pit lane, I might start there – my choices are very much based on what's happening in the moment. Team photos are always a good watch, as every team member congregates in front of the garage around their drivers and there are always some amusing moments to witness.

I will always do a few minutes on the event and a few minutes on the winner, and after that I'm only left with around 30 or 40 seconds per driver, which isn't very long to explain what happened in their races, but I make sure I get all the best information in.

chief engineer interviews on the pit wall after the race. We'll usually do three or four of them for the post-race TV analysis, and I'll check in with others if there's something that happened in their races that should be explained. By then the drivers are in the interview pen, and we've already got our reporters there – Rachel Brookes, Craig Slater or Natalie Pinkham. In some ways it would be much simpler if I could also be there to listen to all the drivers and write down their quotes, but as most of the driver interviews are played out on our post-race show before the *Notebook* airs, there's no point just repeating that, unless they've said something particularly important.

My focus, then, is on researching extra background information from the teams – and it does happen that sometimes we're informed of things that the drivers themselves didn't know about during the race. Not everything goes out on the team radio. Sometimes if a driver doesn't have a good race you'll only find out later that they had some kind of technical issue, like a broken floor or an engine problem. Information like that obviously changes the whole story of their Grand Prix; I think it's important to get that information out to viewers so they can put the performance of that driver into context – otherwise they might be thinking, 'He only finished 18th, he was really slow today.'

This is where your contacts come in useful. When the pit lane clears, I'll go to each hospitality unit in the paddock to find anyone who can fill me in on any of the details. Usually, I only need a quick question answered. My first point of contact is usually the media relations or communications officers. I have a very good relationship with Stuart Morrison, the head of communications at Haas – he understands what I'm after. When his team wasn't scoring many

TED'S NOTEBOOK

season. One usually lasts for four or five weekends, but if there's a wet race and it gets soaked, I might have to change early! I'm often asked what I do with my old notebooks after they're full. If there's nothing in them that I might want to refer back to, I might throw them into the recycling bin when I get home. I do keep most of them, though, in a box file, waiting for me to rediscover them at some stage in the future and then throw them into the recycling bin after all.

If it's been an eventful race, the pages will be packed full of scribbles and notes, some bigger than others according to importance. I divide it up with five teams to a page and each driver in a sub-section of each team. There will be a couple of subjects at the top of each page to remind me of things that have happened during the weekend that I might want to start with, but otherwise the pages will pretty much be blank before the action starts. Throughout qualifying I'll fill in the results and events of Q1, Q2 and Q3 as they happen, and then the same for the race. If somebody drops out, I'll write DNF next to their name, put the reason for retirement if we know it, and then just write the odd note about what was happening before they stopped. By the time the qualifying session or race is done, my two pages are half full. I'll list where the drivers finished, and any other details about whether the result changes their position in the world championship. There'll also be a little arrow up or down next to the team name indicating whether the result has moved them up or down in the constructors' championship. I'll also remind myself to put dates and times of upcoming races that I might have to promote at the end of the programme.

The main way I get the information that fills the *Notebook* is by talking to people. The research starts with the usual team boss or going on in the paddock, and for it to be available after qualifying or the race had finished.

Secondly, it tells the stories of all 20 drivers. It's simply not possible for the TV director to follow every driver and the stories of their efforts in qualifying or the race. Directors have to decide if there's a frontrunning driver in danger of being knocked out in a qualifying session, or what the closest battle in a race is – these sorts of things tend to be the focus. However, every driver's story is interesting – even if they're having a lonely race. There's a story in every car, and the *Notebook* aims to tell it.

The *Notebook* also sheds light on the unexpected things that happen over a race weekend. Perhaps a pit stop went wrong, a driver's radio failed, the chequered flag was waved too soon, or something notable happened on the grid. I don't want anyone to go away at the end of the day wondering, 'What happened there?'

The *Qualifying Notebook* on Saturday is a bit more relaxed. I'll start with a general look around, giving a sense of the atmosphere at the track and in the host city, what the fan experience has been like, and what the main story of the weekend is. Then I get into the qualifying results, and while I'm reviewing those team by team, I keep an eye out for who I can find, or what I can show around the place.

In terms of notes, I don't use a tablet or phone, but an actual physical notebook in which I jot everything down by hand. What's not well known is that I don't even buy my own notebooks. Pirelli happens to supply the perfect pocket-sized, A6, ring-bound notebook, and they are available at every race in the tyre company's motorhome for anybody in the paddock, so I just pick up a new one when I've used all the pages. I'll use around five notebooks per worked hard to convince Sky and Formula 1 that rather than just producing coverage when practice, qualifying or the race was on (as had been done on the BBC and ITV), Sky Sports would create a dedicated Formula 1 channel, and he saw an opportunity with the *Notebook* to convey a sense of the last word on the day's events, as well as something that could be repeated on the channel after race replays throughout the week. He wanted the segment to be its own programme, with titles and a set duration. His view was also that you shouldn't have to be a Sky subscriber to watch the *Notebook*, it would also serve as an online promotional tool for the main programme – something to draw people into what had been happening, and which would hopefully make them interested in following the season with us on Sky Sports.

Following a modest start in 2012 the *Notebook* soon expanded to appear after qualifying as well as after the race, and eventually it grew to fit a commercial half-hour time slot – two parts of 13 minutes – with a total running time of around 26 minutes, in order to fit a four-minute advert break in the middle. It's been in that format ever since – as of 2025 we're into our 14th year.

The *Notebook* aims to do, or has evolved to do, two things. Firstly, (and I try to prompt myself to remind viewers of this at the start of at least one show per weekend), it's the programme that tells you what happened at the Grand Prix if you couldn't watch the Grand Prix. If you've got kids, or you've got things to do on a Saturday, or you've got the family round for a roast lunch on Sunday, it might not be possible to slip away to watch qualifying or a two-hour race with an hour's build-up and an hour of analysis either side. I wanted to make something that was easily accessible, a half-hour show that would sum up all the stories and give viewers a feel for what was the BBC. Secondly, after a year or so as a written column, the time needed to navigate an increasingly crowded race calendar was starting to affect my writing schedule. So together with programme editor Mark Wilkin, Andrew suggested that we turn the column into a video blog that we would record after qualifying or the race and publish on the BBC F1 website. 'Fine by me,' I said. 'But what shall we call it?' Benson said that since it was coming from the pit lane we should just call it *From the Pit Lane*. It ran for about 10 minutes, with me talking to camera, roaming around the pits and paddock, encountering some drivers, and relaying news and information from each team that hadn't made it into the main show.

I didn't come up with the name, and I didn't come up with the format. However, I did enjoy doing it. I felt excited yet comfortable, and I liked the element of surprise in that the viewers didn't know what was going to happen next, because neither did I. So it came to pass that when I joined the team at Sky Sports F1 in 2012, somewhere on our executive producer Martin Turner's 'to do' list was the subject of what he called my 'paddock ramble'. About two months into our pre-production phase Martin said, 'I liked what you were doing on the BBC website, we would like to do something similar – but there's no point calling it *From the Pit Lane with Ted Kravitz*, it's too long and cumbersome. Can you think of anything else we can call it?' I thought for a few seconds as if summoning up some creative spark. 'How about *Ted's Notebook?*'

Martin followed F1, but he clearly hadn't come across any of my earlier columns on the ITV Sport website, so he looked at me wide-eyed and said, '*Ted's Notebook*. Great name!', confirming in that moment that there are no new ideas in television. Turner had

Miami's long straight, yet still have the downforce to make up time in the corners. A blazing lap by Charles Leclerc put him nearly two-tenths of a second ahead of his teammate Carlos Sainz, and rival Max Verstappen. Three quarters of the way down now, and amazingly I'm not even out of breath – all that gym training is paying off! In my headphones I can just about hear some voices in the control room, possibly the words 'What is he doing?', but I can't say for certain. By that point, anyway, we've reached the bottom, jumped off the ramp and we're on our merry way down the paddock. We're still on-air, the radio camera picture was solid, no breakup on my microphone, and 21 minutes left on *Ted's Qualifying Notebook*. Sorted!

It's the only part of the weekend's coverage that I am fully responsible for, but weirdly enough, the *Notebook* wasn't actually my idea. It began life as a column for the ITV F1 website that its then editor Simon Strang asked me to write after every race. Simon had the notion that there must be little nuggets of information that I'd heard or observations I'd made that I'd scribbled down in my notebook but hadn't had time to use on TV. As it was a shame to waste them, couldn't I combine them into a column to help keep the numbers clocking up midweek? I agreed and he suggested that we call it *Ted's Notebook*, which seemed fitting.

The website column carried on for a year or so to no great acclaim. Some people must have been reading it, though, because when I moved to work for BBC Sport in 2009, assistant F1 editor Andrew Benson (who was primarily responsible for the BBC F1 website) was keen for me to carry on with it. However, he wanted two changes. Firstly, he didn't want to use the title *Ted's Notebook*, because ITV had done that, and it should be different if it was on in fact, stuck on this top level of the stadium. I need to be doing the next 22 minutes of the programme on ground level, where all the F1 team garages are, but I appear to have no way of getting back down there. There's a spiralling concrete ramp around the corner, but I'm already at the limit of our radio-frequency reception zone, and even if the picture did hold up, it would take a good three minutes to circle down the walkway to the bottom. Even if I ran down, we'd lose the sound and probably the pictures and effectively fall off-air. Not an option.

While half of my brain ponders this problem, the other half tells my mouth what to say about how this grid line-up should make for a fascinating race. Right. I've got to make a decision. We're live on-air – I don't have a choice. The camera and mic worked when we came up the escalator, so I know they will work when we go down. So what if it's still ascending? We'll just have to out-run it. I check that Pete is up for it. He shrugs his shoulders and nods. Good lad. He's always up for it – he's the kind of person I'd have gladly served alongside in any major conflict of the 20th century, and he wasn't an actual Royal Marine like my other most regular cameraman, Lee. We walk on to the landing zone and go for it. I had noticed on the way up that it was quite a fast escalator, so what worked in our favour around four minutes ago is now, annoyingly, demanding some rapid footwork. I decide to lead the way boldly, figuring that if Pete trips and falls, I'll be able to catch him, or at least catch his camera, which, he would agree, is the most important bit. I do check he's holding the handrail as he runs down after me. Safety first!

We're making good progress, so I launch into an explanation of how Ferrari managed to set their cars up perfectly to be quick on

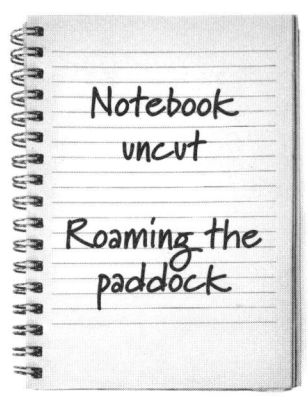

Chapter 18

Ted's Notebook

It's 6.35pm on a Saturday in May 2022, and I'm standing at the top of an escalator on the mezzanine level of the Hard Rock Stadium, home to the Miami Dolphins NFL team. To my left, cameraman Pete Velluet starts a slow pan across the famed playing field, from scoreboard to touchdown zone, as I enthuse about how well the new Miami Grand Prix venue has accommodated the Formula 1 circus for the weekend. The red light on top of Pete's camera confirms that we are live. The director is 'on' our pictures, and there are no replays or other shots going to air. I can hear myself in my headphones, which means that every word I say is, right at that moment, being heard by millions of people across not only the UK and Ireland but also Australia, New Zealand, South Africa, Canada and anyone tuning in here in the USA on the ESPN network. I try not to think about it.

I'm just finishing my explanation of what a success the first qualifying session has been and am starting to describe how Ferrari have locked out the front row of the grid when I realize that I am,

to land a Williams race drive for 2019. Eight years after the rally crash that nearly killed him, Kubica was finally back in F1.

He scored a symbolic point with a 10th place in Germany, but he was overshadowed somewhat by young teammate George Russell. He was then dropped by Williams at the end of that season and went instead to Alfa Romeo as a reserve driver, landing two further race outings in his second year there in 2021 when Kimi Räikkönen was ill with Covid-19. But it would be in 2025, 13 years after he should have made his Ferrari F1 race debut, that Robert's dream of winning for the Prancing Horse finally came true. Having moved to the World Endurance Championship, he and his teammates Yifei Ye and Phil Hanson won the Le Mans 24 hours, a remarkable achievement by an extraordinary racing driver.

Kubica was and remains hugely likeable. It's not often that someone gets a shot at redemption after fate has kicked them to the floor. His return was a great story not only because it was unprecedented in F1, but because it granted him a second chance at his F1 dream, and it went some way to putting right the tragedy of a career cut short.

training paid off, and he was able to drive a 2012 Renault reasonably quickly and without fundamental limitations. He could only change gear via a single paddle pushed or pulled by his left hand, and he lacked the fine-motor function to change steering-wheel dials with his right hand, so he also did that with his left. He did enough during initial running with the old car in Valencia and Paul Ricard to be given a proper test at the Hungaroring after the 2017 Hungarian GP. He was fourth fastest of those running, and completed an impressive 142 laps of Budapest's demanding, twisty track. He adopted a technique whereby most of the driving was done with his left hand, but when he needed to take that hand off the steering wheel to press a button or change a switch, he was able to drive by pushing his right palm on to the steering wheel and moving it with his shoulder muscles.

Renault made it clear that he would only be offered a race drive if he was good enough to win – anything else would be detrimental to both parties. It was close, but in the end, Renault passed on him. By then, though, Williams was interested, and after a good showing in end-of-season testing it looked like his shot at regaining F1 driver status was on, helped by some Polish sponsorship. I caught up with him in December at the Autosport Awards. At 32 he looked in great shape – a few grey hairs on his temples, but the sparkle in the eyes was still there. On stage he talked of how he was in better condition physically than in 2010. 'I have to work much harder now – I was a lazy guy in the past,' he joked, adding that 90 per cent of his driving ability was just as it was pre-accident.

In January 2018 he was confirmed at Williams in a reserve driver role, and that year he made his welcome return to Grand Prix weekends with three Friday practice outings. He did enough season as a potential replacement for Felipe Massa. All he had to do was see out one more year in a midfield Renault and he'd likely move to Ferrari. However, his life and his career path were to change in February 2011, just a few weeks before the start of the F1 season.

While his peers were sunning themselves on beaches or swooshing down alpine ski slopes, Robert was keeping his driving skills sharp. He entered a small Italian rally, the Ronde di Andora, on the country's north-western coast, only an hour's drive from Monaco. He was just as quick in a rally car as he was in F1 machinery. But on the very first stage, his Skoda went wide on one particular corner and hit a metal Armco crash barrier which punched a hole in the engine bay, pierced the cockpit and ripped into Robert's right side.

His co-driver was unhurt, but the injuries that Kubica sustained to his leg, arm and hand were so severe that his insurance company determined they would be career-ending, and it paid out on his loss of future earnings as an F1 driver. Kubica had other ideas. Through sheer bloody-minded determination, numerous medical procedures and operations, while suffering near-constant physical pain and requiring copious amounts of emotional grit, he focused on his recovery. He returned to rallying in 2013 and then moved to GT racing. Rally and sportscars had room in the cockpit for him to extend his elbow enough to have a good amount of movement in his right forearm and hand, but a single-seater was always going to be another matter.

He'd come this far, so nothing was going to put him off. Six years after the rally accident, Robert Kubica got a second chance at Formula 1. It was just a private test in a five-year-old car, but his

One driver who could surely have been a world champion for Ferrari in the 2010s was Robert Kubica. In many ways, Kubica is F1's greatest lost talent. He was quite simply incredibly quick. In his teens he moved from Poland to further his karting career in Italy. He learned the language, and the country became his second home. His speed meant that he was always going to find a place in F1, and his chance came with BMW Sauber when he replaced Jacques Villeneuve for the last third of the 2006 season.

The following year in Canada he suffered a setback when a small mistake – touching his front left tyre with Jarno Trulli's right rear – had a huge result. A high-speed smash into a concrete wall and a barrel roll down the track. I watched the accident from the McLaren garage, and every single person in there, hardened mechanics and engineers who'd seen it all in F1, could barely look at the sickening replays of the crash – the violence of the impact and the car's destruction was scary, especially as you knew that Kubica was right in the middle of it.

Exactly 12 months later at the same venue he could laugh about it – not only did he recover, but he returned to the track to win his first Grand Prix and took the lead of the 2008 drivers' world championship by four points. He believed that he had a shot at winning the title, but his BMW bosses halted development of the car in favour of the following year's contender, and the team's form faded. At the end of 2009, however, BMW pulled out of F1 and Kubica moved instead to Renault for 2010, picking up three podium finishes.

Ferrari appreciated how good he was and, encouraged by Fernando Alonso, offered Kubica a kind of provisional race contract to give the Maranello squad first call on his services for the 2012

NEARLY MEN

'I think I see what you mean,' I said, when the cameras had stopped rolling, and our sound man Dave Haigh had pulled the microphones from the inside of our shirts.

'Yeah, and it's fine,' replied Vettel. 'I'm a big believer that things happen for a reason.' Forgetting for a second that we weren't two friends down the pub, I replied, 'Sure, Seb, but you know the saying about everything happening for a reason? Sometimes that reason is that you're stupid and make bad decisions.' Vettel raised an eyebrow, turned and wandered off to his next media engagement. I wondered if I'd perhaps given him something to think about, although most probably he just thought I was a prat.

Vettel left Ferrari at the end of 2020 with an impressive tally of 14 wins, but no world title. There were many reasons why it didn't work out, but I felt one was that he missed the firm guiding hand of Christian Horner, and the even firmer hand of Helmut Marko. At Ferrari the drivers are the stars, and at the time, the bosses kept them on a much looser rein than Seb was used to at Red Bull. There was a lack of consistent leadership. Marco Mattiacci had signed Vettel, but he was moved aside shortly after, and his successor Maurizio Arrivabene had enough on his plate finding his own way, so he tended to leave the drivers to it. Mistakes started to creep into Seb's game, costing him points over the 2017 and 2018 seasons, and he started showing a level of impetuousness that hadn't been in evidence (and, knowing Horner and Marko, would have been cracked down on and prevented) at Red Bull. It is often evident in F1 teams that drivers' behaviour is affected by the example of the team boss. If drivers have a strong boss that they respect, and are a bit scared of, they stay in line. If they have a weak boss who they're not afraid of then they're much more likely to just do as they please.

2022 season he stunned the F1 world by signing for Aston Martin as replacement for the retiring Sebastian Vettel. As I write, he's still enjoying an astonishing career, and it's not over yet.

Alonso may have followed Vettel to Aston Martin, but at Ferrari it was the other way around. The German arrived at Maranello in 2015 and duly won his second race with the team. Unlike Alonso, Vettel did believe Ferrari could challenge for a world championship, but his 2017 campaign effectively ended on the damp streets of Singapore. He was on pole, but after a brief rain shower on the grid he drifted left off the start line and crashed into Max Verstappen and his own teammate Kimi Räikkönen. A week later in Malaysia an inlet manifold failed in qualifying, leaving him fourth in the race. Another retirement followed when a spark plug failed in Japan.

With at least 50 points dropped over three races, defeat was inevitable, but that didn't make it any easier to take. Ferrari people were in tears when Hamilton wrapped up the world championship in Mexico. Passion. It is Ferrari's strength, and its weakness.

Vettel was pretty down, too. He knew the unreliability wasn't his fault, but the unforced errors – a road-rage sideswipe on Hamilton in Baku that earned him a penalty, and the start line crash in Singapore – were. I asked him in an interview if he felt frustrated about those two lost opportunities. He made the distinction between frustration and disappointment. In Seb's mind, frustration would have been like some anxiety dream where he was in a position to win, but something was holding him back. Disappointment was when things simply went wrong, like crashing at the start or the car blowing up. So, he said he was disappointed, but not frustrated.

failed to meet them, which eroded McLaren's faith in their technology. And so, after three years, tacitly admitting that the 2015, 2016 and 2017 campaigns with Honda power had been a waste of time and money, McLaren decided to end the partnership.

The story of how they did it, especially considering Honda didn't want to leave, was F1 politics at its complicated best. Essentially it involved McLaren giving Red Bull the Honda engine (something that would work out very well), Red Bull giving Carlos Sainz to Renault (replacing poor Jolyon Palmer before Sainz himself left a year later to join McLaren) and McLaren finally getting a supply of Renault engines.

It had been only too easy for Eric Boullier to blame Honda, but the McLaren chassis had also fallen behind and the Frenchman left the team in the middle of 2018. Where was Alonso in all this? Fed up and disillusioned. He left F1 at the end of 2018, aiming to become the most versatile racing driver of the modern era. His talent, wasted over those three years at McLaren, turned to the Dakar Rally, the Indianapolis 500 and helped Toyota to win the Le Mans 24 Hours and the World Endurance Championship. His roving quest to become the 'most complete driver in the world' was entirely validated as he found job satisfaction in other categories of motorsport.

I thought he was done with F1 for good and even made a 'goodbye letter to Fernando' feature that we filmed in producer Jack McShane's flat. What I had underestimated was just how much Alonso still wanted Grand Prix victory number 33, and world championship number three. He returned to his roots at Renault (then under the Alpine brand) in 2021 for what was his third stint with the Enstone outfit. It wasn't a success, and in the middle of the being 6ft 5in, he looked down on most people. Marchionne died in 2018 from complications following shoulder surgery. He had his enemies, but I was saddened by his untimely passing.

By this point Fernando Alonso had left Ferrari. He had become convinced that the Scuderia could not, in the short-to-medium term, win the world championship, and that they did not have the leadership or the technical expertise with which to beat Mercedes. There didn't appear to be a seat free for him at Mercedes, even as a replacement for the retiring Nico Rosberg. It was felt that the pairing of Alonso and Hamilton would have created too much intra-team tension – a real pity for the rest of us who wouldn't get to see their 2007 McLaren rivalry re-kindled – and there wasn't a seat at Red Bull, who were focusing on Max Verstappen. That left Fernando with the unlikely option of a return to McLaren – quite astonishing given the circumstances under which he'd left eight years earlier. But by then Martin Whitmarsh had departed, replaced by Eric Boullier, who had done a decent job at the Enstone-based Lotus team, and Ron Dennis would lose a boardroom battle and effectively be forced out soon after. Besides, their new Honda engine couldn't be that bad, could it?

Sadly, it could. Honda rushed into their F1 return before their technology was really ready, and its engineers were forced to squeeze their power unit into McLaren's 'size zero' rear end to please the aerodynamics department. Achieving these constraints compromised the power unit's architecture, rendering it chronically unreliable. It was beset with high internal friction and vibration problems, plus the hybrid system kept failing. Engineers tried their best to fix the issues, but with little success. What made things worse was that Honda set ambitious targets, but then repeatedly for meetings and to inspect the Ferrari troops. My producers would pass this on with a 'we don't really need him, but keep across it' instruction. Anticipating a bit of an Italian media scrum, I'd wander down to the paddock with my cameraman Lee. You might well have heard me or Martin or Natalie talking about Lee, or 'The Marine'. Not difficult to guess from the nickname, but he served in one of the most feared fighting forces in the world, the Royal Marines, and saw action all over the globe. I'd trust him with my life.

An interview with Sergio Marchionne was never going to be too dangerous, but as a former Marine, Lee likes getting stuck in. So we always looked forward to being involved in the drama whenever Marchionne was around. We'd get ourselves in among the crowd outside the Ferrari motorhome, and when the boss came out, there would be a lot of jostling from his bodyguards. We'd allow ourselves to be pushed around by these guys in sunglasses a little bit before I would pipe up loudly, in as British an accent as I could muster, 'Ah, good afternoon, Mr Marchionne.' He would look up and say, 'Good afternoon,' and deign to give me a brief interview.

After the second or third of these encounters, he'd come to recognize me and Lee, and began to single us out and greet us with, 'Ah, hello, how have you been?' or some such pleasantry. Sometimes what he had to say was newsworthy, and we'd use a soundbite in our programme. When Arrivabene was appointed as Mattiacci's successor he would always be pinned to Marchionne's side during our interviews, and would literally stand there growling at me as I exchanged pleasantries with the man who could fire him at a moment's notice. Ferrari's corporate press liaison Stefano Lai (pronounced 'lie', a somewhat unfortunate name for a press officer) always looked down on proceedings with a little smile, although him at Ferrari either. He fell out with Alonso, and signed Vettel from Red Bull as his replacement. Vettel, then in his fallow period, with Hamilton and Mercedes winning consistently, had decided to try to succeed at Ferrari where Alonso had failed. Mattiacci hinted at a lack of energy from Alonso when he said of Vettel, 'He will bring the enthusiasm needed to go through certain difficult moments.' That prompted a terse response from Fernando, who noted that Mattiacci had 'only been here for a few months and has not seen the five years that I've spent here and how I've fought every single race.' Alonso had a point. After Monza, Di Montezemolo resigned as Ferrari president following disagreements with parent company FIAT's CEO, Sergio Marchionne. With his mentor Di Montezemolo gone, Mattiacci was also ousted as Ferrari team principal after just eight months, to be replaced by Maurizio Arrivabene, who had worked for many years with Ferrari sponsor Marlboro.

FIAT boss Marchionne was already a very powerful man in the motor industry, and after Di Montezemolo's departure he started to take more of a personal interest in F1. Everyone at Ferrari was terrified of him, and his occasional visits to the paddock would noticeably send the whole team into a mild panic. As I wasn't directly invested in the fortunes of Ferrari, to me he appeared more like a kindly uncle in his round glasses and trademark casual wool jumper, and I quite looked forward to his appearances. I have no idea how, but we struck up an unlikely professional relationship. It was probably because he wasn't my boss, and we never really needed an interview with him, so the stakes were low as to whether he told me to get lost or not.

This is what used to happen. We'd get word from our Italian colleagues that Marchionne was going to pay a visit to the paddock salesman. Given America's fondness for Ferraris and the fact that the company limited supply in order to maintain the brand's exclusivity, it was probably hard to underperform in such a role. However, after losing Domenicali, Di Montezemolo needed a new team boss in a hurry, and didn't think that Mattiacci's lack of technical knowledge or F1 experience would be a problem.

On a cloudy Shanghai Friday in April 2014 Mattiacci turned up for his first day at work. By any objective measure, he cut a stylish figure in the paddock, carrying a smart tan leather bag and wearing a pair of trendy yet practical sunglasses, the kind that fold up at the bridge for easy storage. Not that Mattiacci showed any sign of folding them up.

'Hey, the new Ferrari boss looks quite cool,' I remember remarking in our morning production meeting. The first practice session started, and the new boss watched from the garage. It got a bit darker as the day wore on, and Shanghai's famous smog hung in the air. The sunglasses stayed on. Ferrari's efficient media office invited us to a press conference with the new team principal. Mattiacci entered the room. We all looked around and smiled. 'We're indoors. Is he going to take the sunglasses off? No? Really?' It became quite the joke around the paddock, with some calling him 'Hollywood'. I preferred to imagine him taking cues from Enzo Ferrari himself, a man famously keen on dark glasses. Mattiacci was later asked directly why he had been wearing sunglasses all day, even indoors. Unfazed, the genial Italian replied: 'It's a very good question. In particular, if you do in less than four days almost 40 hours of flights, and you don't sleep, probably you need sunglasses!'

It was a decent enough explanation, and Mattiacci turned out to be a perfectly capable manager. However, things didn't end well for

Alonso had a habit of moving teams as he tried to position himself between cars that could win and team bosses he hadn't fallen out with. A victory on his Ferrari debut at the 2010 Bahrain GP set the scene for what ought to have been a third world championship that year, but for the ill-timed pit stop and Petrov's slippery Renault at the last race in Abu Dhabi that handed the title to Red Bull's Vettel. Ferrari then endured a shockingly disappointing 2011 season after a correlation problem between the Maranello wind tunnel and the track resulted in a car that was very difficult to drive. For the first half of the year Ferrari churned out new parts, but they didn't work. As Alonso said, 'We found ourselves in April with a car that was slower than what we had in February testing. We understood this too late, and that cost us the championship.'

Things improved in 2012. Alonso won three races and finished runner-up to Vettel by three points at the end of a season that saw seven different drivers win the first seven races. Fernando and his engineer Andrea Stella tried to make it work at Ferrari, but in subsequent years the team started to change. Stefano Domenicali took responsibility for the disappointing performance of the hybrid engine in 2014 and left the team. It was an honourable thing for him to have done, given that there had been pressure from the Ferrari president Luca di Montezemolo to sack engine chief Luca Marmorini for the power unit's deficiencies, something Domenicali refused to do. Marmorini left the team that summer anyway, to be replaced by Mattia Binotto – a name we'd hear more of further down the line. But when Di Montezemolo replaced Domenicali with a complete unknown, it signalled the beginning of the end for Alonso.

Marco Mattiacci had been head of Ferrari's operations in North America, and as such was essentially a successful road-car

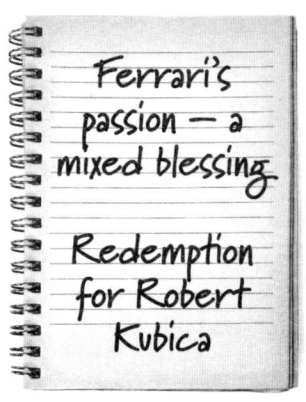

Chapter 17

Nearly Men

Former McLaren boss Ron Dennis always said that in F1 second place was just 'first of the losers'. He was right up to a point, but Dennis himself is proof that, just because you're not winning, doesn't mean that you're a loser. Every driver is competitive, but a common trait I've found in all the elite winners I've reported on – such as multiple world champions Fernando Alonso, Sebastian Vettel and Lewis Hamilton – is that they're so addicted to success and so used to that winning feeling that if they find themselves off the top of the podium for any length of time they are pretty quick to seize an opportunity to move teams, hoping to recapture winning form elsewhere.

All three of those drivers moved to the Scuderia Ferrari in search of their next world championship. On paper the iconic racing team promised Alonso and Vettel so much, but neither managed to win the title. In 2025 Hamilton followed in their footsteps, and at time of writing, alongside teammate Charles Leclerc, is finding it hard work to end a drivers' title drought that extends back to 2007.

crisis. However, he made a point of addressing his personal carbon footprint by offsetting his flights and even – when possible – travelling on public transport.

Vettel always did things his way, and he surprised everyone by creating his first social media account primarily to announce that he would retire from F1 at the end of the 2022 season, at the age of just 35. In each of his final seasons with Aston Martin he finished a modest 12th in the world championship, but his overall career statistics remain impressive – four world championships, 53 GP victories and 57 poles is quite an achievement by any standards. It could be argued that he retired too young, but when you've lived your life on fast-forward, things tend to come around earlier than you expect. Whether it's building bee hotels at Suzuka to promote biodiversity in Japan, or recycling plastic waste in Brazil, Sebastian enjoys being around enthusiastic, interesting people who are passionate about what they do. As far as I was concerned, that feeling was entirely mutual.

Ferrari fan.' We knew what he meant. Unfortunately, Vettel had the bad luck to be at Ferrari during a period of domination by Lewis Hamilton and Mercedes, and he never did win that fifth title, although it's easy now to forget that he finished runner-up in the championship in both 2017 and 2018, winning five races in each of those seasons. His stay at Maranello ended on a lower note with an uncompetitive car in 2020.

We saw a much more mellow Vettel in his final team, Aston Martin. He enjoyed two solid if unspectacular seasons alongside Lance Stroll. There were some good drives, including a second place in Baku in 2021 and another in Hungary that was then lost to disqualification for a minor weight infringement. What really caught the eye during those seasons was his emergence as an elder statesman of the sport. His work with the Grand Prix Drivers' Association on matters such as safety and governance began during his Ferrari years, and his experience gave him the power to achieve a great deal in those areas. He also became much more vocal about his wider interests in the environment, biodiversity and climate change, sometimes ruffling the feathers of those in authority with his outspoken campaigns on the issues he cared about. He wore a T-shirt at the Miami GP which read: 'Miami 2060 – 1st Grand Prix Underwater – Act Now or Swim Later'.

He was also active in using his platform to campaign for social justice, and was one of the first drivers to unhesitatingly 'take the knee' as a gesture against racism during pre-race ceremonies, while encouraging his fellow drivers to join him. In May 2022 he even appeared on the BBC political debate show *Question Time*, where he acknowledged the hypocrisy of being an F1 driver who effectively burns petrol for money campaigning on the climate

It was increasingly clear that his four title-winning seasons had taken a mental toll. He started to look around for a career change that would freshen him up. One slight problem was that he still had a year to run on his contract as a Red Bull driver, but crucially it had an exit clause that allowed him to leave at the end of 2014. The way Vettel exercised this over the weekend of the Japanese GP was dramatic.

It was shaping up to be an ordinary race weekend in the Red Bull camp, when completely out of the blue on Friday evening, Christian Horner received a text from Vettel asking him to come to his room at the Suzuka Circuit Hotel. According to Horner, Sebastian was close to tears, explaining how the season had really knocked his confidence and how he wanted to leave the team at the end of the season for a new challenge. It was difficult after all the success they'd enjoyed together, but as Vettel had wisely said on team radio after his third world-championship win in 2012, 'We have to remember these days, because there's no guarantee that they will last forever.'

So with Seb's tears drying on his pillow and after a late night for Red Bull's communications department, Saturday morning at Suzuka saw the news revealed. It was confirmed that Vettel would be leaving Red Bull to join Ferrari as teammate to Kimi Räikkönen, and that Toro Rosso's Daniil Kvyat would be his replacement.

A reboot is always good for a driver who has been with the same team for a few years, and Vettel slipped easily into his new home. He loved Ferrari, and they loved him. He created an F1 meme about how everybody is secretly a Ferrari fan when he joked with Lee McKenzie as she tried to conduct a serious interview with him in Canada. 'Everybody is a Ferrari fan. Even if they're not, they are a

SEBASTIAN

I thought: 'Good on you, Sebastian. That's a real racer's hard edge right there.' Vettel was still annoyed with Webber's unguarded remarks on the Malaysian podium, and how that had made him look. He had been back to the Red Bull Racing factory to apologize to the team, but now was clearly not in the mood to make nice.

It's not that Vettel didn't have a soft edge as well. He loved the fact that when he clinched his second world championship in 2011, he did it at Suzuka, where his heroes Senna and Schumacher had won in the past. He appreciated F1's history more than most of his contemporaries, as evidenced by the fact that he could name every world champion from 1950 onwards. He would make a little history himself by going on to win four titles in a row with Red Bull, which was a remarkable achievement, matched only by Juan Manuel Fangio, Michael Schumacher and Lewis Hamilton before, and Max Verstappen since.

Looking back, I think we didn't really appreciate how good Seb was, because he won so much so quickly. When he was in tune with the car, he would reliably qualify on pole, dominate the race, make his way through the pit stops, and close out the win. At the end of 2013 he was still on fast-forward, but the following season would see the pause button pressed. In the V8 engine era Red Bull's partnership with Renault had been very successful. But when Mercedes turned up in 2014 with by far the best power unit for the new hybrid V6 regulations, the Red Bull/Renault package was suddenly no longer capable of challenging for the world championship. Meanwhile, Daniel Ricciardo had replaced Webber and won the three races that were not claimed by Mercedes that year. Seb logged no victories, and had bad luck with mechanical failures.

Webber should let him pass. He initially ignored the instruction, responding on the radio, 'Which switch is that, mate? Which switch, where is "Multi?"', a delaying tactic that went down badly on the Red Bull pit wall.

Codewords were abandoned a few seconds later when Webber's engineer spelled it out on the radio. 'Let Sebastian go, please, Mark.' At the time, Vettel had not been particularly impressed with that, or with Webber's driving earlier during the race, when the Australian came close to putting his title-challenging teammate in the wall off the start line. Looking back on it years later on the F1 *Beyond the Grid* podcast, Christian Horner observed that it looked like Mark was driving for Ferrari that day, and confirmed that Sebastian had been furious with Webber about what happened in Brazil, and that ignoring 'Multi 21' in Malaysia was payback for it. For Vettel, revenge was definitely a dish best served cold.

At the race following 'Multi 21', in China, Red Bull had made Vettel available as usual on Thursday, and I remember walking into the team's hospitality building in the Shanghai paddock with Lee McKenzie. Based on the kind of repair job that the PR people had tried to do the week before, we were anticipating that Sebastian was going to be apologetic, saying something like, 'Well, maybe I made a mistake, and maybe I should have let Mark win, and I won't do it again.' Whether he was going to be apologetic or come out swinging, we knew we didn't want to miss it. Vettel didn't let us down. He was both business-like and totally unapologetic, saying: 'The bottom line is I was racing, I was faster, I passed him, I won.' Silence ensued in the room. I nudged Lee's arm. I'll always remember the unemotional way he said it, and at that moment to make it to the end of the race on their remaining sets of tyres, especially Webber's, which had already been lightly used when fitted. To protect both cars and their engines in the Sepang heat, Vettel was told to keep behind Webber for the run to the flag via the radio codeword 'Multi-map 21'. Meanwhile, the same coded message assured Webber that he would not come under threat from his teammate. Teams have radio codewords for all kinds of things – rivals are always listening, so anything that can be done to throw them off the scent is beneficial. To another team, 'Multi-map' could easily have referenced a switch on the steering wheel. It actually referred to the driver order, and '21' meant that car number two (Webber) was being told to finish ahead of car one (Vettel).

However, this was the day that Seb made it clear that he had no interest in team orders. After instigating a spectacular fight that lasted for several corners, he turned his engine up and overtook Webber, going on to win the race. On the podium it was clear that both men were unhappy with the way the race had been managed, with Vettel chafing at being told to stay behind, and Webber annoyed with Vettel for disobeying team orders and overtaking him. Mark then gave an explosive interview to Martin Brundle about how 'In the end, Seb made his own decisions today, and will have protection as usual, and that's the way it goes.'

Vettel looked embarrassed and angry at having been so publicly made to look the bad guy. But, as always in F1, there was a backstory that was just as fascinating. It went back a few months to the championship-deciding Brazilian GP at the end of the previous season, which was the last time Red Bull engineers had used the 'multi' team order codeword. That day, it was Webber who had been told 'Multi-map 12', i.e., that Vettel should be the lead driver and on top of the podium in F1 – and out came the finger. As the performance advantage of the Brawn waned, Vettel became a regular race winner, and he ended the year as title runner-up to Jenson Button.

The 2010 season featured one of F1's great championship showdowns in Abu Dhabi. After the penultimate race it looked like Fernando Alonso was headed for his third world title. The Spaniard was leading with 246 points, from Webber on 238 and Vettel on 231, while Lewis Hamilton was also still mathematically in contention on 222. Sebastian went into that final weekend very much as the underdog to win the championship. Being 15 points behind, his was a simple task – he had to win the race and not worry too much about what was going on behind him, or any other permutations of who finished where. In the event, he dominated from pole to take victory, while Ferrari famously made a bad strategy call that saw Alonso come out of the pits and get stuck behind the Renault of Vitaly Petrov. The Russian was quick on the straights, keeping Alonso behind him in seventh all the way to the flag, allowing Vettel – who hadn't led the championship all year – to score an emotional first-title success by a margin of four points.

The true greats of F1 all have a ruthless edge. They are mercenary creatures, hungry for success and selfish in pursuit of it. Vettel seemed to be an exception – an easy-going, funny, amiable young man with a social conscience. However, at the Malaysian GP at the start of 2013 we saw a side of Vettel that we hadn't seen before – a hard edge that was reminiscent of his close friend and mentor Michael Schumacher.

The pit stops played out and Mark Webber had just managed to stay in front of Vettel. However, it would be very tight for both men uncommon, but what happens in a wet qualifying often doesn't follow through once the weather has cleared up for the race. In this case the rain continued into Sunday, enabling Sebastian to put in a superb performance and win the Italian Grand Prix. It was one of those drives that convinces you, should you have any doubts, that here is somebody who is quite simply at one with an F1 car. As we marvelled at the sure-footed confidence he displayed in the near terrifying conditions, Martin Brundle felt sure he'd witnessed something special. 'This kid is going to be a world champion one day,' he said. It's no coincidence that F1 legends like Ayrton Senna and Michael Schumacher also scored their first victories in rain-affected races.

It was during 2008 that I really got to know Sebastian, usually by messing around with him at our Thursday catch-ups in the paddock. Before the win at Monza put him on everyone's radar there wasn't that much media interest in him, so often it would just be me and one German-speaking TV crew. Once they'd finished, Seb and I were left to exchange stupid jokes or discuss bits of news going on with other teams. He was still young, so I'd sometimes play tricks on him, such as asking his thoughts on FIA president Max Mosley, at that point very much in the news. Seb looked at me uncertainly, 'Erm . . .', then at the camera, then towards Toro Rosso press officer Fabiana Valenti who wasn't helping him out, then back to me again: 'You can't ask me that, you bastard!'

It was no surprise that when David Coulthard retired it was Vettel who replaced him alongside Webber at Red Bull Racing for 2009. Initially the car didn't have the double diffuser that was allowing Button and Barrichello to outpace everyone, but he still managed to score RBR's first win in China, Vettel's second time

American market, Speed was let go, and Vettel was handed his seat for the Hungarian GP. The move marked the end of his relationship with BMW Sauber – and he never looked back.

He settled in quickly at Toro Rosso, and learned from Tost and Berger, but it wasn't all plain sailing. At the soaking wet Japanese GP, colliding with any car wouldn't have been great, but Vettel made the mistake of taking out Mark Webber in the senior Red Bull while driving under the safety car, putting them both out of the race. The clash with the man who would later be Sebastian's teammate produced a great quote from the Aussie, who shared his exasperation live on ITV: 'Well, it's kids, isn't it?' he said. 'Kids with not enough experience to do a good job, then they fuck it all up for everyone else!' However, Vettel redeemed himself in the team's eyes with a fourth place the following week in China.

There were a few more incidents in early 2008, but he learned as fast as he drove, and soon became a regular points scorer with a decent car that was in effect a clone of Adrian Newey's design for Red Bull Racing. Veteran Toro Rosso engineer Giorgio Ascanelli had worked with Ayrton Senna during his last few seasons at McLaren, and the Italian was key in shaping Vettel into the finished product. Together they found a way of setting up the Toro Rosso which made everything click. After that, he was quick everywhere, and he truly announced his star quality at his team's home race at Monza.

It was a magic combination of factors. Many other drivers struggled in the rain, but that year's Toro Rosso was particularly good in the wet. This, allied with Vettel's pure talent, saw him become the sport's youngest pole sitter in one of the wettest qualifying sessions in memory. Saturday surprises are not

So it can't be that bad.' What I remember is going away from that interview thinking this guy has the kind of inner confidence and clear-headed thinking that you tend to notice in the very best drivers.

A day later Sebastian jumped into the Sauber and notched up the first of many records that he would hold in F1, and one that stands to this day. He became the driver who incurred the quickest penalty in an F1 career when he was clocked for breaking the pit lane speed limit just six seconds after he'd left the garage for the first time, but the rest of the session went well, and overall he made a good impression. At this point, however, there was no race drive available. After being BMW Sauber's Friday driver for the last four races of the season Vettel continued his testing role in 2007, while Red Bull also moved him full-time into the World Series by Renault.

An unexpected chance to step up to a BMW race seat came at that year's US Grand Prix. Kubica had a huge crash at the Canadian GP and was ruled out of the following week's event at Indianapolis. Vettel stepped in, finished an impressive eighth and set another record by becoming the youngest ever points scorer at the time (the record is currently held by Max Verstappen for his six points at the 2015 Malaysian Grand Prix). Kubica was fit and back in the car at the next race, but Vettel's performance had made it clear to longtime backers Red Bull they had a special talent on their hands, someone who should be driving full-time in F1. Red Bull's young driver supremo Helmut Marko rarely needed much encouragement to move his charges around. At the time Californian Scott Speed was having a few difficulties living up to his name and had a major fallout with Franz Tost and Gerhard Berger, bosses of Red Bull's junior team, Toro Rosso. Despite the importance to Red Bull of the weekend's press conference what he thought Sauber's reasons might have been in choosing him over Villeneuve. 'Maybe the pace,' he replied, to general laughter in the room. His promotion duly opened up a vacancy in the testing role, and BMW was quick to award it to Vettel.

My first encounter with him was at the Turkish Grand Prix, exactly a month after his Spa crash. With characteristic efficiency, the BMW press officers made Sebastian available for interview on Thursday. None of my producers at ITV had heard of him, so there wasn't much demand from the production. However, I was interested in him and the story with the finger, so I thought I'd go along anyway, just to meet him and find out a bit more. When I arrived, Sebastian had just finished with the print media and was ambling down the steps of the Sauber motorhome wearing faded jeans, a white BMW shirt that looked one size too big, with a mop of messy blonde hair underneath what appeared to be a borrowed team cap. I don't remember any other TV crews being present.

He looked like he'd just graduated from high school and was slight, like a stiff breeze would blow him over. My opening question was essentially, how old are you? He'd just turned 19, old by today's F1 rookie standards, but he looked younger. We talked about what his targets were, what he thought was going to be the plan for the weekend, the usual stuff. I asked him about the finger. His eyes brightened in a way I would come to know well over the next 15 years, and he seemed pleased to know that I'd done my research and was aware he'd injured it. He shrugged and said, 'Yeah, it's fine now,' although I could see that the fingernail was still in pretty bad shape.

What he said next really struck me: 'I still don't have much movement, but I came back and won both races at the Nürburgring.

and thought he'd give his oldest son a try in karting. Sebastian was a natural – he turned out to be one of those rare geniuses. There wasn't really anything to explain it, he was just incredibly quick, and was soon winning karting trophies. Red Bull were on the alert for promising young drivers, and in 1999, at the age of just 12, Sebastian was signed up for them as a junior driver. Later he would also attract the support of BMW, and thus early on he had two powerful organizations pushing his career – as well as a famous mentor by the name of Michael Schumacher. The two became close after Sebastian won a karting event at Michael's kart track in Kerpen, Germany, and there is a famous photograph of Michael in his prime next to a young Vettel nearly outsized by the two trophies either side of him.

The feeling I always got from Sebastian was that even for an F1 driver, he was a man in a hurry. It was like he'd pressed a fast-forward button on his life. Indeed, by the time of his Spa accident, he'd already tested an F1 car, BMW having arranged for him to drive a Williams at Jerez in September 2005. BMW moved to Sauber for 2006, and, it was clear, wanted Vettel to be part of its long-term plans, even though they already had three drivers on their books.

But Seb had a couple of lucky breaks. BMW had inherited Jacques Villeneuve's contract when it bought Sauber, but by the summer of 2006 the Canadian had fallen out with his new bosses, who had asked him to sit out a race so they could try out test driver Robert Kubica. Seeing the writing on the wall, Villeneuve made his decision and left the team abruptly after the German GP in July. Kubica was duly promoted to a race seat at the next event in Hungary. The Pole, never short on confidence, was asked in that of Eau Rouge. It spins and clouts the left-hand tyre wall, sending pieces of debris flying across the track. It's a nasty crash, but not life threatening. The driver jumps out and hops over the tyre barrier. He's holding his right hand as a rescue marshal escorts him down the hill to the circuit medical centre. 'This way,' instructs the marshal. 'What's your name?' 'Vettel. Sebastian Vettel.'

The crash was a real blow to Vettel given the career momentum he was enjoying. A piece of carbon fibre shrapnel had flown into the cockpit and sliced through his glove and index finger, taking the top of his fingernail off and leaving a cut that went right down to the bone. The Spa doctors stitched the wound, bandaged the hand, and sent him on his way. He was annoyed at being ruled out of racing for a few weeks, but not as annoyed as Alx Danielsson, a Swedish driver who was lucky not to be killed after hitting an errant wheel from the accident. 'Vettel was driving like it was a rental car,' the Swede told *Autosport* magazine. 'It was just a matter of time before he crashed.' It was a sentiment that would become a common theme in Vettel's early career.

The next day Sebastian drove back to the circuit to catch up with his team. After seeing the large white bandage and splint on his right finger, his mechanics quickly made their own outsize replicas from kitchen-paper rolls and stuck them on their right index fingers in an effort to cheer their driver up. It worked. As soon as the finger healed he was back winning F3 races again, holding up his still-mangled digit on the podium as a joke for his mechanics.

Born to a middle-class family in the small town of Heppenheim in the middle of Germany, Vettel's enthusiasm for motor racing was inspired by his father, Norbert. Much like José Luis Alonso, Fernando's dad, Norbert Vettel was a massive Ayrton Senna fan,

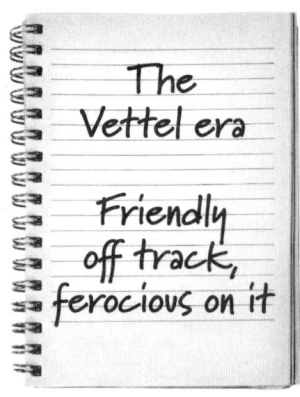

Chapter 16

Sebastian

It's 29 July 2006 at the Spa-Francorchamps circuit. As is so often the case even in the summer months, a passing rain shower has soaked what remains one of the sport's most challenging venues. However, this isn't the Belgian Grand Prix weekend – it's a sparsely attended World Series by Renault event, featuring a grid full of F1 hopefuls.

Among them is a young man who already knows that he's got a better chance of making it to the top than most of his fellow racers. Currently starring in the European F3 Championship, he's been parachuted into the Renault series by Red Bull, his sponsors who are actively nurturing his career, in order to gain some useful extra experience in a faster car. He's already won two races on his debut weekend at Misano in Italy, but Spa is a much tougher track to master.

The rain eases off, but as the race gets underway the track is tricky and wet. The Red Bull car runs slightly wide on the right-hand kerb on the steep slope of Raidillon, just after the compression

ex-engineers who have both leadership skills and an understanding of technical matters. The most successful of this new generation over the last couple of seasons has been Andrea Stella, once Fernando Alonso's race engineer at Ferrari, and now running the race team at McLaren.

Stella doesn't need to swim with the piranhas as he has the McLaren Group CEO Zak Brown to do that. Another former racing driver, Zak took a break from driving to start his own motorsport marketing business and did very well out of it. When McLaren's Bahraini owners needed someone to do the impossible and replace the man who defined McLaren, Ron Dennis, Brown stepped up. He has been very successful, recruiting the right people, getting the money in the door, and reserving just enough time in the day to think up ways to annoy and destabilize his fellow piranhas. The spirit of the club lives on.

Williams. So he proposed a deal to the Daimler board. He would agree to sell his stake in Williams and step away from the Grove team completely – but in recompense, Daimler would agree to sell him 30 per cent of the Mercedes team. Lauda was also up for investing if Daimler was selling, so he took a 10 per cent share. It was an incredible bit of negotiation that would, as Mercedes's value rocketed a few years later, make Wolff a billionaire.

Having swum alongside them for so long, at the end of 2013 Ross Brawn became a victim of the piranhas. In technical and sporting matters he was as ruthless as they come, but he was ultimately outmanoeuvred by Toto's business instincts, and he left the team (possibly relieved to go back to fishing in calmer waters). In Brawn's book *Total Competition*, written a few years later with ex-Williams CEO Adam Parr, Ross cited a breakdown in trust between himself, Wolff and Lauda. 'I was beginning to deal with people who I didn't feel I could ultimately trust; people within the team, who had let me down already in terms of their approach,' Brawn wrote. 'In early 2013, I discovered Paddy Lowe had been contracted to join the team and it had been signed off in Stuttgart. When I challenged Toto and Niki, they both blamed each other.' Brawn and Wolff duly went their separate ways only to find themselves working together again – somewhat awkwardly – when Ross became Managing Director (Motorsport) of the F1 management organization in 2017, a position that afforded him some power over Wolff and the other piranhas that must surely have given him a small sense of satisfaction.

F1 team principals are now a different breed compared to the days when they were owners rather than just hired hands. Aside from Horner and Wolff, most of the current crop are lights of Saalbach, deep in thought. 'Odd,' I thought, leaving him to it as I carried one of our tripods on my shoulder down to the hotel. I later found out that Wolff had rolled his snowmobile earlier that day, in practice for the evening's race. He was unhurt, but his team then lost in the final to the managing director of a haulage company. I later rationalized that odd moment by thinking that Toto must have been telling himself to calm it down with all the crashes.

But it wasn't that, and a few weeks later I found out why Toto had been behaving so strangely. He had been asked by the Daimler board and Mercedes F1 non-executive chairman Niki Lauda to assess why the works team's effort wasn't going to plan, and why it had struggled so much since winning the 2009 championship as Brawn GP. Toto had relayed his thoughts, and they had been impressed enough to offer him the job of team principal. However, Toto's way was not clear. Firstly, Mercedes already had a team principal – Ross Brawn. Wolff proposed that he would come in as 'executive director' in one of those opaque managerial structures that F1 teams adopt when they're deeply enmeshed in internal power struggles. Brawn would remain team principal, but as Wolff had also been appointed head of Mercedes-Benz Motorsport (Norbert Haug's old job), Ross would now report to him.

Secondly, Toto knew his limitations. He wasn't a technical genius, and to make the car quicker he needed help from the kind of boffin who could knock up a Large Hadron Collider in your back garden. Such a man was Paddy Lowe, whom Wolff recruited from McLaren for the role of Executive Director (Technical) – another impressive title. The third problem was a bit more personal. It was clear to all parties that if he was to be head of Mercedes, Toto couldn't still be a part-owner of

Barcelona). So we'll grab an interview with him, and it'll all be good.' Reassured, Alex told the Red Bull PR people that we wouldn't need DJ Ötzi's contact number after all, and we tucked into dinner. The next day was spent filming pieces to camera on the slopes with a final thought from me in a hot tub (mercifully never aired), before the climax of the snowmobile race and our opportunity to grab Toto, the only F1 interviewee we had. If he was curious as to why we were asking him so many questions about so many teams, effectively mining him for all the F1 content we had hoped we would be getting, he didn't show it. He delivered his interview in the impressive and authoritative style that we've all since become accustomed to. He even gave an early outing to his now famous 'like a bullet' catchphrase.

It was what happened afterwards that stuck in my mind. We had climbed a small hill in order to frame Toto's interview in a pretty way with the village in the distance. Once we had finished recording, rather than trudging back down the hill to a waiting glass of glühwein in the Red Bull Energy Station, Toto lingered to chat as the cameras packed up. We talked some more about Williams and its prospects, with Toto's own protégé Valtteri Bottas due to replace Bruno Senna. He then asked me what I thought about the Mercedes team, where they had gone wrong with Michael Schumacher's return, about Lewis Hamilton joining for 2013, and my thoughts on Ross Brawn.

I told him how motivated I thought Lewis would be, and that he would get on well with his friend from karting days Nico Rosberg, and that I thought Brawn was the perfect team boss to get the best out of both of them. Toto nodded, said his goodbyes, but still didn't leave: he just turned and stood, looking out down to the twinkling interrupt his own winter break by making an appearance, but with each successive conversation with every producer down the line, confidence somehow grew that he would show up. So two camera crews and a sound operator were booked, and I was put forward to go, along with producer Alex Rodger, for no greater reason than we could both ski.

A flight, two hire cars and five hotel rooms later saw us installed in the resort of Saalbach-Hinterglemm, warmly welcomed by some very nice people from Red Bull. They presented us with the list of the men and women, mainly winter-sports champions and Austrian celebrities, who would be attending the event, and whom we were welcome to interview. The list was alphabetical and I quickly scanned down, past a couple of skiers whose names I vaguely recognized from *Ski Sunday*, past Austria's legendary DJ Ötzi, all the way to the bottom. No Vettel. I checked back, not under 'Sebastian', either. For that matter, no 'Horner' or 'Marko' or anyone else from Red Bull Racing. However, there was someone related to F1 whose name I recognized at the bottom of the list: Wolff, Toto, at that time an increasingly active shareholder in the Williams team.

While Alex asked the Red Bull marketeers why they thought we had come all this way if no personalities from their F1 team were present, the crew and I melted away to the restaurant, ordered some Wiener schnitzels, and planned the next day's skiing. It's not like we ever had much of a plan A, but I had thought of a workable plan B. 'Don't worry,' I said, 'we can still make a nice feature out of this, the snowmobiles will look crazy buzzing through these tiny streets, this Toto guy is part owner of the Williams team and they won a Grand Prix this year (courtesy of Pastor Maldonado in

Toto Wolff does things differently. Unlike Christian Horner, Toto owns a third of the team he leads, the rest made up by Mercedes-Benz and Ineos, Jim Ratcliffe's chemicals-to-automotive conglomerate. Wolff came into Formula 1 on the business side, but there was racing in his past too, even if his lanky frame made it difficult to squeeze into single-seaters. He won some races in GT cars before an accident gave him cause to think about his attitude to risk. It happened at the unforgiving Nürburgring in 2009, when he had an idea that he could break the lap record of the Nordschleife in a sporty Porsche with just a foot full of throttle and a head full of belief. A blown tyre put Wolff into the barriers at 180mph, and the 27G crash gave him concussion and a trip to hospital. His career behind a desk has been much more successful. He presided over eight constructors' world championships between 2014 and 2021, although when I first met him, he was still figuring out how to manoeuvre himself into the top job at Mercedes.

We were coming to the end of our first year of F1 coverage on Sky Sports. Sebastian Vettel had signed off 2012 with his third world title, and the circus performers had packed their bags and returned home for the winter. As we still had an active F1 channel to fill with content, we tended to leap at every opportunity – and one such was an invitation from Red Bull. The company was organizing one of its typically attention-grabbing events where extreme sports athletes raced powerful snowmobiles around an old Austrian village. Somewhere along the line of communication we were made aware that Vettel might be attending, and that there could be an opportunity for a fireside chat with him about becoming a three-time world champion. Initially it seemed unlikely that Vettel would explained that he was keen to move into F1. He'd been in talks with Red Bull to be part of a takeover of Jordan, but the Austrian company had another interesting option in the Jaguar team currently delivering mediocre results under the ownership of the Ford Motor Company. 'So you might be interviewing me in the paddock next year,' concluded Horner, as I reached the front of the passport queue. 'Right, OK then,' I replied, in a 'Good luck with that, Christian' kind of way. I proceeded to do absolutely nothing with this little well-sourced news nugget. Several months later, to the surprise of everyone except me, it was announced that Red Bull, the Austrian fizzy drinks and marketing company, had bought the Jaguar team – and had employed the 31-year-old Horner as team principal.

Red Bull Racing's statistics under Horner's leadership were impressive: 8 drivers' and 6 constructors' world championships, 107 pole positions and 124 wins, but even this track record wasn't enough to convince Red Bull that he was the right man for the future. Just three days after the 2025 British Grand Prix, he was sacked by the Red Bull parent company in Austria. We've always sparred with one another, possibly because he is only four months older than me, and I see him as a contemporary, despite the fact that we're very different people. I think Christian sees the TV side of F1 as a game. He was intensively media trained before he started as team principal at Red Bull and developed into a savvy interviewee who would just about give you a straight answer if you asked the right question, much like a determined batsman dealing with a tricky delivery from a fast bowler. He made headlines of his own, and it remains to be seen how his next move in F1's Piranha Club works out.

team, buy the cars and employ mechanics and engineers to run them was rare, and hinted at greater ambitions.

Over his two unspectacular years in the category Horner's best achievement was a solitary sixth place in a field that included the likes of future F1 drivers Juan Pablo Montoya, Ricardo Zonta and Nick Heidfeld. He eventually concluded that he wasn't going to make it in his own right – reflecting years later on a podcast that it had been watching the way Montoya committed to high-speed corners that had made him realize he simply didn't have the racing bravery that the best of his rivals displayed. At the age of just 25 Christian hung up his racing helmet to focus instead on running Arden. Over the next few years the team developed into a well-respected and professional outfit, winning the drivers' F3000 title in 2003 with Bjorn Wirdheim. Clearly ambitious, Horner also became the representative of the F3000 team bosses in the F1 paddock, dealing with Bernie Ecclestone, who would become a friend and mentor. He also stayed close to Helmut Marko, who was becoming an increasingly powerful player in the sport as the right-hand man of Red Bull co-owner Dietrich Mateschitz. When Marko was looking for an F3000 seat for his protégé Tonio Liuzzi for the 2004 season, he went to Horner and Arden. It paid off for all parties, as the Italian dominated the championship, and the relationship between the team boss and the sponsor bloomed.

I'd often see Christian Horner in the F1 paddock when Arden had won an F3000 race, or he was going about some piece of business. It was in a passport queue at Milan's Linate Airport that he let me in on a little secret, hinting broadly that we might be seeing more of each other. As we got talking, Christian grandkids with all the zest that he put into his many years in F1. And to complain about trivial or petty things is something Eddie Jordan never did, just as he didn't have time for those who envied his success. He had a tattoo on his wrist – his sons Kyle and Zak have it too – the three letters FTB. It stands for EJ's favourite Irish motto: Feck the Begrudgers.

It's a pity that we didn't have *Drive to Survive* 30 years ago – cameras going behind the scenes with the likes of Eddie Jordan, Frank Williams, Ron Dennis, Tom Walkinshaw and Jean Todt would have been quite something. More recently, Flavio Briatore's surprise return to the paddock with the Alpine team in 2024 meant that we did get to see some of him in Season 7, and it was no surprise that he was immediately cast as a pantomime villain. The series has made unlikely TV stars out of the current generation of team bosses, and has highlighted just how highly motivated they are to beat each other, not least when documenting the intense rivalry between Toto Wolff and Christian Horner.

Born in 1973, Christian Horner embarked on a career as a racing driver, progressing through karting and winning a few races in British F3. In 1997, with help from his father, he opted to set up his own team for the step up to the next category, Formula 3000. Rather than use the family name he called the team Arden, after the area and forest made famous by Shakespeare, near his family home in Warwickshire. In need of a race transporter, he bought one that was surplus to requirements at Red Bull advisor Helmut Marko's RSM team. Horner is said to have gained the Austrian's trust by paying for the truck, sight unseen, with only Marko's word that it would actually be delivered. For his part, Marko may well have taken note. For a young driver to establish their own F3000

Schumacher his Grand Prix debut at Spa, Jordan was then ambushed by Flavio Briatore and Tom Walkinshaw from the bigger Benetton team. They had approached Schumacher to offer him a drive and, believing their car offered him a better chance of winning, Michael wanted to join Benetton. All Jordan had was a piece of paper signed by the German youngster saying he intended to sign 'a contract'. It was not an actual Jordan race contract, so legally, Eddie lost the fight to keep him. It was at this point Dennis is said to have welcomed Eddie to 'The Piranha Club'. The qualities of the South American fish to which he was referring were its powerful bite, sharp teeth and appetite to consume anything. Jordan was as canny an operator as anyone, having begged and borrowed his way from Dublin bank clerk to F1 team owner. But even he was astonished by the audacity of his fellow team principals in their willingness to screw over their rivals. Dennis knew what he was talking about – he'd savaged more than a few competitors himself.

The transfer was good for Benetton, good for Michael, and had met with the approval of Bernie Ecclestone, F1's benevolent dictator, at that time the owner of the lake in which the piranhas swam. Despite the fact that Ecclestone had sanctioned the swiping of Schumacher from under Jordan's nose, he and Eddie understood each other well, and were very close. In Eddie's years as a pundit at the BBC it was Ecclestone who was the source of many a good tip and inside story.

Jordan's F1 team would have been worth more than he got from Shnaider had he been able to keep it going for a few more years, but money was tight back then. He went on to enjoy his retirement and family life with his wife Marie and their children and many

I think most F1 fans have a soft spot for Williams Grand Prix Engineering Ltd, to give it its full name. The team won the constructors' world championship nine times between 1980 and 1997 along with seven drivers' titles with Alan Jones, Keke Rosberg, Nelson Piquet, Nigel Mansell, Alain Prost, Damon Hill and Jacques Villeneuve. Those numbers would surely have been even more impressive had Ayrton Senna not lost his life in a Williams at Imola's Tamburello corner in 1994.

I was always aware of this history any time I asked Williams for an interview, or talked to him in the team motorhome on some background enquiry. For all his achievements, Frank was an incredibly humble man, and it's a mark of the respect in which he is still held that the current owners of the team have never once considered changing the name above the factory door.

Sadly the same wasn't true for Eddie Jordan's team when he sold up to a Russian-born Canadian Steel magnate called Alex Shnaider, who only retained the Jordan name for the 2005 season, before re-naming it Midland F1 for 2006. I went to the final Jordan launch in Moscow's Red Square, a very curious occasion with lots of talk about wealthy Russian sponsors re-invigorating the team.

Jordan himself was another true racer. He'd actually been a relatively successful F3 driver before a big crash at Mallory Park turned him towards team ownership. Some people who dealt with Eddie thought he was primarily interested in money, but that was only because he never had any. Despite his many successes, Jordan Grand Prix was never awash with cash, and Eddie had to make what money he had work hard. But he was an ex-racer, and more than anything he loved the thrill of the sport and the drivers who raced in it. In 1991, having been responsible for giving Michael everyone else. And when I say everyone, I mean their drivers, other teams' drivers, rival team bosses, engineers, the F1 organization, the FIA and the media. There really isn't anyone that a team boss won't try to outface when the chips are down. And make no mistake, this is not only a ruthless power game between paddock competitors – it's about surviving at the top. If you can steal a rival's driver, lure away their technical director or seduce a sponsor, you not only strengthen your own team, you weaken the opposition. According to F1 lore, it was Ron Dennis who first coined the term Piranha Club, but we'll come on to that later.

The team bosses back in 1997, when I first arrived in the paddock, were a colourful bunch. Ron Dennis seemed calm and science-driven on the surface, yet underneath proved to be highly emotional. Flavio Briatore was (and remains) commercially driven and relatively unemotional. But Frank Williams was the one who made the biggest impression on me. What motivated him were his guiding principles of what was good for his company and his team, while also holding a strong belief in what was right for F1 as a whole.

You're probably familiar with the backstory, how Frank Williams followed his burning ambition to own and run a successful motor-racing team, how it almost broke him financially, how he managed to overcome every obstacle, how he eventually teamed up with talented engineer Patrick Head and finally found the budget with which to create a winning car. Then, in March 1986, came the road accident in France at the wheel of a Ford Sierra that did break him, physically at least. And yet Frank's incredible resilience and determination allowed him to remain in charge of his Williams team and lead it to even greater successes.

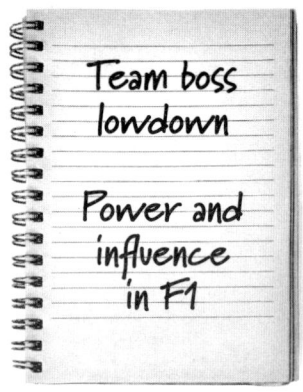

Chapter 15

The Piranha Club

There's a story that when the *Drive to Survive* producers started exploring the world of Formula 1 one of the first bits of advice received from an experienced press officer was, 'If you think the drivers are competitive, wait until you see the team bosses.' It's absolutely accurate – and has a very simple explanation. All team bosses share the qualities of being competitive and single-minded, but history has shown that many of the best were formerly drivers. Enzo Ferrari, Colin Chapman, Ken Tyrrell, Bernie Ecclestone and Frank Williams all came into the sport drawn to the life of the racing driver, but found in time that their true talents lay outside the cockpit. And the fact that they got tantalizingly close to success on the track may have sharpened their motivation even more.

The race drivers are the gladiators, the ones at the heart of the action. Team principals might be responsible for everything else, but the one thing they're not actually able to do is race the cars. They get keyed up watching their drivers fighting it out on track, and if their team hasn't done well, they tend to take it out on enough of Sabine's trust over the years to be comfortable giving an honest opinion. 'You need to be an island,' I said. Mick gave me a funny look, pursing his lips in a way so similar to Michael's it made me smile. 'OK, here's what I think. In Haas, you're joining the smallest team with the smallest resources both in terms of finances and factory. In Guenther Steiner you have a boss who is, essentially, a mad genius. He'll be busy keeping all the plates spinning, keeping Gene Haas happy, the team financially afloat, keeping the drivers out of trouble and hopefully scoring some points with you. You have a fellow rookie alongside, and the whole of Ferrari micro-analysing your every lap. This will create several whirlwinds over the season. You need to embed yourself as strongly as you can, be an island in the middle of it, and not get swept away in the storms to come.'

Whether this was more or less of the wisdom that he'd been hoping for I never knew, but Mick nodded his head and we said our goodbyes, aiming to have another chat when he started driving full-time at the start of 2021. His first full season with Haas was indeed a bumpy ride – there were more accidents than Schumacher and the team could afford. His best result that season was 12th at the Hungarian GP, just behind Daniel Ricciardo and Kimi Räikkönen. True to form, his second season was better, but there were more crashes, and a couple of points finishes weren't enough to save his seat. He was dropped by Haas at the end of the season and also left the Ferrari programme. He was hired as a test and reserve driver by Mercedes, his father's last team, but left at the end of 2024. Meanwhile, he forged a new career in sportscars, competing at Le Mans and other endurance races. In F1, being just an island is not enough.

SCHUMACHER'S SECOND COMING

driver programme, his time in F3 and F2 had followed a pattern, with the first seasons being learning years, before he stepped up his game and won both championships on his second attempt. With F3 and F2 titles under his belt and Ferrari's support behind him, an F1 graduation was inevitable. He tested the Alfa Romeo-branded Sauber in 2020, hoping to get the race drive, but with Kimi Räikkönen and Antonio Giovinazzi (a young driver one step ahead of Mick on the Ferrari ladder) already signed up he was placed instead into the Haas team for 2021, alongside fellow rookie Nikita Mazepin.

I'd seen Mick around the paddock and said hello, but it wasn't until the last weekend of 2020 when he'd been announced as a 2021 Haas driver that we sat down for our first interview. I walked down to the hospitality area with my cameraman Pete Velluet to find Mick already waiting for us, accompanied by the familiar face of Sabine Kehm, now the younger Schumacher's manager and media liaison.

After a quick exchange of pleasantries, the interview began. I asked him how he would be approaching the season, to which he answered that 2021 was his year to learn both the team and the circuits. He was really looking ahead to 2022, when a regulation change intended to make the cars less sensitive to aerodynamic turbulence and therefore easier to race had the potential to shake up the field, and perhaps result in some opportunities for smaller teams like Haas. The interview concluded, and Pete started packing away the camera and tripod. Mick took the opportunity to ask me how I saw the Haas team and its prospects for 2021, and how I thought he should play his hand.

Sabine kept a watchful eye on proceedings. It was only the second or third time I'd ever met Mick, but I felt I had earned

Over the next few months my thoughts about Michael's situation crystallized into two strands. Those of us in F1 who had watched him, worked with him, witnessed his triumphs and setbacks, had not the tiniest doubt that here was a man of such physical and mental strength, determination and stamina that he would be as well placed as anybody could be to recover from his injuries. If anyone could get through this, Michael could. One of the greatest champions Formula 1 has ever known, a charismatic and vibrant figure both on track and in the paddock, we sent him every best wish for the fight he had to come.

My second thought was on the cost of fame and stardom in F1. A guy from an ordinary background used his extraordinary gift to excel in his chosen sport. This attracted interest, appreciation and admiration. He had become so well known worldwide that there was an inexhaustible demand for information about him, particularly at this, his toughest moment. I watched the press conferences from the hospital in Grenoble and thought about all the similar setups where I'd seen Michael, sat behind some table, microphones spread out in front of him. Whether it was winning another world championship, giving his side of a controversy, or even letting us in at a vulnerable moment – Michael understood and appreciated that people were interested in him, and he wanted to give back. But now, when he couldn't give back, it felt to me as if people shouldn't be pushing for answers when there was so little to say. The fame and fortune of F1 stardom had a price, and it was being borne with strength and dignity by Michael's family.

When he began turning up regularly at Grand Prix weekends, Mick Schumacher carried himself lightly, seeming happy not to draw too much attention to himself. Signed up by the Ferrari young

SCHUMACHER'S SECOND COMING

It was the right time for Schumacher to retire for good. The mantle of 'best-current-driver' had already been passed on to Fernando Alonso, then Lewis Hamilton and coming through was Sebastian Vettel. Such is the speed at which F1 moves, even a name like Michael Schumacher was quickly consigned to the history books as the new drivers took centre stage.

Michael was free to spend time with his wife and kids, Gina and Mick, the latter of whom was continuing the family business. Mick Schumacher had started karting around the time of Michael's first retirement using his mother's maiden surname of Betsch in an attempt to divert attention and expectation. It didn't work. Everyone inside the karting community knew exactly who Mick's dad was, and anyone outside it would have been able to work it out pretty quickly just by looking at Mick's familiar facial features and consulting the internet. His results were good, and by 2013 Mick Schumacher was finishing in the top three of most karting championships he entered. There was good reason to think that Michael's genes and guidance would shape Mick into a champion of the future.

We had not long wrapped up our coverage of the 2013 F1 season on Sky Sports when, a few days after Christmas, we heard the news that Michael had been in a skiing accident in France while out on the slopes with Mick. We understood that he had hit his head on a rock. He was wearing a helmet, so when he was airlifted from Meribel to hospital in Grenoble initially we had no reason to be alarmed. Later that evening, however, Sabine Kehm sent an email saying that there would be no running updates regarding Michael's health, and a press conference the following day confirmed the seriousness of his brain injury.

take long for him to say yes. It was a dream signing. Jenson Button and Rubens Barrichello had both moved on. With fellow German Nico Rosberg as teammate in the re-born Silver Arrows, what could go wrong? 'You take the world championship-winning team at the end of '09, you take Mercedes and you take me,' explained Schumacher. 'So you think you've got to be fighting for the Championship.'

Unfortunately, the 2010 car proved not to be competitive. During the team's 2009 season Brawn GP had spent so much effort fire-fighting problems and trying to get both championships over the line that they had fallen behind in development and lost any advantage from the double diffuser as everyone else caught up. By the time Mercedes took over and the team began to build up its resources, the 2010 car trailed far behind the main opposition. It went from the front of the grid to scrapping for the minor points in the space of nine months.

Rosberg demonstrated that he was able to extract more from the Mercedes W1 than Schumacher, out-qualifying and out-racing the master over the course of 2010 and 2011. I had too much respect for Michael to ask him on-air why his comeback was going so badly. In reports I'd mention factors that could explain his performances, while everyone – the Mercedes team and the media – desperately searched for any glimmers of success. There was a brilliant lap in Monaco qualifying in 2012, and the only podium of his comeback in Valencia later that year, but that season would be Schumacher's last. The team poached Lewis Hamilton from McLaren for 2013. It was time for Michael's second farewell, which came in Abu Dhabi. I remember his wife Corinna looking forward to their family future outside F1. 'At last,' she said, 'we have him back.'

season could further damage this area of the skull, leading to long-term injury, or even paralysis.

Dr Peil said the tear could take another six or even twelve months to heal, or might never completely heal. Schumacher refused to completely rule out making a return to F1, but it would not be in 2009. Peil confirmed that aside from the neck issue, Michael was in top physical shape. An intensive workout regime had resulted in him losing 4kg, and his arm, shoulder and leg muscles were up to the job. It could have been a highly successful comeback.

Michael was visibly upset that it wasn't going to happen, saying that this was one of the toughest moments of his career. Weber remarked on how fast Schumacher had clicked back into the racing driver mindset.

After an hour and a quarter, the press conference came to a close. Michael thanked everyone for coming at short notice, stood up, had one last look around the room, puckered his lips up into a sad expression, and left by a side door. While my fellow reporters stood up to check additional details with Kehm, and my BBC cameraman arranged to feed the footage back to London, I reflected that while this had been a frustratingly unfulfilled episode in Schumacher's motor racing career, his comment about 'feeling back alive' when driving an F1 car was, for me, the big story. Michael Schumacher was burning to come back – and fight for that elusive eighth world championship.

A few months later the comeback became a reality – but not with Ferrari. Late in 2009 it was announced that Mercedes was buying the Brawn Grand Prix team and turning it into a full works outfit. When Brawn and Mercedes motorsport boss Norbert Haug asked Michael if he would like to join the newly re-named team, it didn't we had to cover it, so I jumped on a plane, met up with a BBC News cameraman in Switzerland, and set up ready for the conference. Before it started, we had the big announcement from Ferrari that Badoer would deputize for Massa after all, so the news that Schumacher's Ferrari comeback was not to be didn't come as a surprise.

It was clear as soon as Michael walked into the conference room that this was going to be tough. He looked miserable. Alongside him were his long-time manager Willi Weber, and his doctor of nine years, Johannes Peil, a tall, slim man with a kind face, a tidy moustache and a shock of blonde-grey hair. Schumacher began by saying how frustrated and sad he felt, and how disappointed he was not to be able to help Ferrari by standing in for the injured Massa. He then explained why. It was that motorbike accident in Cartagena, and only now did we discover how seriously he had been injured. He had broken a rib and fractured two vertebrae in the fall. They had since healed, but there was one remaining injury that had not healed, and it was the pain from that physical damage that made driving an F1 car for any length of time impossible.

As Michael sat listening intently and Willi Weber looked out into the room with a slight grimace, Dr Peil explained that there had been a tear in the left-hand side ligament that links the base of the skull to the first vertebra at the top of the neck, named the C1 or Atlas. This tissue around the Atlas played a highly important role in protecting the brain. This had not healed, and it was giving Michael so much pain that he was not able to drive the car. Schumacher admitted that if he'd had only a small pain in the neck, he'd have treated it with painkillers and got on with driving. However, Dr Peil also had concerns that any accident over the last half of the 2009 unsuspecting Felipe Massa's helmet, taking a sizeable chunk from the top left quadrant. It was a shocking accident. Massa was knocked unconscious, the car went head first into the tyre barrier and he narrowly escaped losing the sight of his left eye. It was impossible for him to race and he was out for the rest of the 2009 season.

It was assumed that Ferrari would call on their established test driver Luca Badoer as a stand-in for Massa, but we soon learned that Ferrari president Luca di Montezemolo and new team principal Stefano Domenicali wanted Michael back. He might nominally be retired, but his skill and experience vastly outclassed that of the journeyman Badoer. He initially said no when Di Montezemolo approached him with the offer, but was persuaded to test the 2007 car again. Nine days after Massa's crash, Michael pulled on the famous red race suit and headed to the Mugello circuit in Tuscany.

'He went into the racing department and was full of enthusiasm, like a kid or a young driver. Then he went to Mugello and did a very good test with the old car,' Di Montezemolo reported. Ironically it was Di Montezemolo himself who had done most to pressurize Michael into the decision to retire in 2006, but now he listened to the instinct that told him Michael was ready for all that ability, desire and motivation to come to the fore once again. For his part Schumacher confirmed that the Mugello test reminded him just how much he had been struggling with life outside F1. 'Although I was a retired race driver, still for a moment, I felt back alive.'

Just a few days after the Mugello test, Sabine Kehm invited us to a press conference with Michael and members of his team at the Intercontinental Hotel in Geneva, not far from his home. We knew was constantly evolving and seemed content enough to watch the ongoing rivalry between Alonso, Hamilton, Massa and Räikkönen.

When Schumacher was given the chance to sample the 2007 championship-winning Ferrari at the Barcelona post-season test he showed he'd lost none of his speed, but in general he was becoming more and more interested in two-wheeled motorsport. When he was racing, he would often be seen arriving at F1 paddocks on his custom Harley-Davidson and as part of a Ferrari-Ducati tie-up had even tested a MotoGP motorbike at Mugello, but being so focused on his F1 career, didn't have much more time for anything else. Once freed from his driving contracts, though, the idea of learning a completely new discipline appealed, and he enjoyed the sensations that racing motorbikes provided. He entered the German national Superbike series and was soon lapping within a couple of seconds of the top riders. Given that he was taller and more muscular than most motorbike riders tend to be and hadn't raced bikes all his life in the way they had, this was a seriously impressive performance.

Stories about his bike exploits would reach us in the F1 paddock, but at the beginning of 2009 news came through that he'd had an accident. It was at the Cartagena circuit, a small but well-used test track on Spain's southeast coast. Details were few and far between, but initial reports were that Michael had not been seriously injured.

The F1 season started and we all got wrapped up in the Brawn Grand Prix story. It wasn't until halfway through the year we discovered what that Spanish motorbike crash would mean for the rest of Schumacher's racing career.

At the Hungarian GP a rear suspension spring fell off Rubens Barrichello's Brawn, bounced down the track and hit an

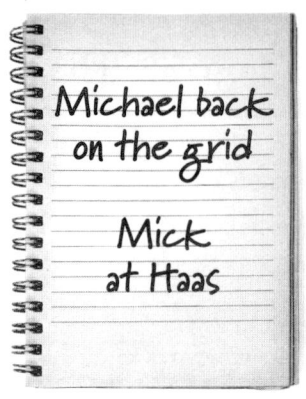

Chapter 14

Schumacher's Second Coming

Following his retirement at the end of 2006 Michael Schumacher was appointed a 'super advisor' to Ferrari by Jean Todt, keeping him connected to F1 during the 2007 season, but when he turned up in the paddock he always looked uncomfortable. Schumacher would typically watch the practice sessions from the pit wall but then retreat to the hidden racks of telemetry screens for qualifying and the race. His former teammate Felipe Massa was happy to have Michael around and ready to listen to his advice – Michael's replacement Kimi Räikkönen rather less so.

Michael could sense this, and I always observed the two keeping their distance, which just added to Michael's low profile. Whenever I'd pass him in the paddock, he'd give a quick 'howdy' (slightly odd, you might think, from a German speaker, but Michael liked the cowboy persona), but he wouldn't stop to chat. His manager Sabine Kehm would organize the occasional press conference in which Michael would handle questions about whether he was planning a comeback with a good-humoured 'no'. He knew that F1 chorus to Queen's 'We Are the Champions', slightly off-key. He was so openly ecstatic after the race that it was just as well he'd saved up some energy. The relief at getting the title wrapped up before the last round, the release of stress and pressure, and the sheer joy at not only winning, but doing it in such style were clear to see. Jenson had spent 21 years working on his dream of being world champion, and he had achieved it.

The story of Brawn GP was one of the greatest underdog tales that any sport has ever seen, but it could only last a single season. That sliding-doors moment when Martin Whitmarsh agreed that Mercedes could supply Brawn would come back to haunt him. Keen to have its own modern-day Silver Arrows team, Mercedes bought Brawn GP, renamed it, and began the process of withdrawing its works support from McLaren. The Woking team would not win another title until 2024.

Barrichello left to drive for Williams, and Button joined McLaren, where he had an enjoyable and successful end to his F1 career. He still races in other categories, and works as a pundit at Sky F1, and is every bit the lovely, easy-going, smart, sparky guy you'd think he is. His father John died in 2014, and is still missed and remembered with great affection. If you ever see me wearing a pink shirt on a race day, you'll know who inspired me.

hotel. He had a beer, checked in with his mum on the phone, and went to bed.

On Sunday morning, something clicked. By the time he got to the track, Jenson was up for the fight, and he knew that he had it in him to get the points he needed to close out the world championship. As he prepared for the race, he told Ross Brawn not to worry, and that he was going to make up for the lowly grid position. He then proceeded to drive like an absolute demon. Later, in his book *Total Competition* (2016), Brawn revealed he had been perplexed by Button's sudden aggressive precision: 'He came from behind, overtook people, he was decisive, he was really impressive. But then I thought, "Why can't you do that every race?"'

The truth was the sudden change in driving style took Button's opponents by surprise. Two overtakes in particular, on Romain Grosjean and Sauber debutant Kamui Kobayashi, were heart-in-the-mouth in terms of how risky they were, and how close to going wrong, and another on Sebastian Buemi, whom Button knew he had to take by surprise, because the Toro Rosso driver had very good straight-line speed and would be hard to pass. It's an often-used phrase, but it was a champion's drive, delivered at just the right time. By the chequered flag he had clawed his way up to fifth. There was one race in the season still to run, but Jenson Button had achieved the points he needed to win the 2009 world championship. By the time we got to him on the pit wall Brawn was in tears – in fact there was hardly a dry eye in the team's garage. Winning the constructors' world championship as well meant so much to the whole team because of what they'd been through together.

On the slowdown lap Button proved that the one thing he didn't have that weekend was a great singing voice as he belted out the

The car had been engineered with the beneficial characteristic of being easy on its tyres – it tended not to work them too hard or cause them to overheat and lose grip. In some of the hot, early races, and in Valencia in the middle of the summer, this was a positive attribute. However, at cooler track temperatures, such as those found at Silverstone, it meant that the car couldn't generate enough temperature to get the tyres in a sweet spot delivering grip to the driver. Couple that with Jenson's characteristic driving style, all smooth inputs and gradual steering, and you had a car that at some tracks could be completely different to the machine that had dominated the first third of the season.

One such circumstance was the drying track that presented itself in the second part of qualifying at Interlagos. A key bit of indecision in Shovlin and Button's communications meant that Jenson was left out on his full-wet tyres too long, when he should have pitted for intermediates. Shovlin had reasoned that since the car was generally easy on its tyres, the full-wets would last one more lap. They didn't – Button had no front grip, and the rear tyres overheated.

Explaining Button's sudden nervousness to me at the time, Ross Brawn said he believed that the consequences of making a potential mistake 'became prevalent in his thinking'. Martin Brundle described Button's qualifying problems as 'like a golfer with the yips'. In Brazil, Barrichello was on pole position. Yips or not, Jenson was starting a distant 14th on the grid. Maybe the ladder trick had worked after all.

That Saturday night, keen to avoid whatever hideous prank the Brazilian TV presenters had up their sleeves, Jenson had a quiet dinner with his entourage in the Japanese restaurant at his year before turned up and doubled down on Jenson. The prank occurred on the Tuesday evening before the race, when Button, his dad, his trainer Mikey 'Muscles' Collier and manager Richard Goddard drove to the Fogo de Chão steak restaurant, a venue beloved of the F1 paddock and a favourite stop for drivers. The two TV presenters, one wearing a chequered flag suit and the other a plastic wig and false teeth, set up a large A-frame ladder over the restaurant entrance, obliging Jenson to walk underneath if he wanted to get to his steak dinner.

Unlike crossing the path of a black cat, walking under ladders *is* usually considered bad luck both in the UK and in Brazil, so the pranksters thought their plan foolproof. Except they initially misidentified Collier as being Jenson, while the real man slipped round the back of them, therefore deftly avoiding the on-camera moment they'd hoped for. Jenson still had to walk under the ladder, but declared in his easy way that he wasn't superstitious, so the plan was wasted. Nothing if not determined, the jokers followed Button back to his hotel, where they repeated the trick, this time in the car park, where Jenson's whole car had to pass under the ladder once again. Adding insult to injury they then set off loud fireworks outside his hotel in an effort to disrupt his sleep. It made for a completely outrageous piece of TV, and Jenson did well not to react to it.

The weather in São Paulo is notoriously changeable, and a huge rain shower made for difficult conditions for everyone in qualifying. Neither Hamilton nor Vettel made it out of Q1, Vettel's misfortune being particularly good news for Jenson's championship chances. Then in Q2 a season-long characteristic of the Brawn BGP001 would prove troublesome once again, but at a crucial moment.

Japan kept the points coming. And then came Brazil, Barrichello's home event.

Button took a week off after the previous race in Japan. He had a few days in Tokyo with his partner Jessica Michibata before flying to Hawaii for a mini break. He spent the time eating, sleeping and training, knowing he'd need every bit of energy he had for the Brazilian GP weekend. It's quite difficult to get from Hawaii to South America, and for Jenson, it involved two whole days of air travel via Los Angeles and Miami to São Paulo. He had always enjoyed the Brazilian event, ever since his first race there with Williams in 2000. He loved the Interlagos circuit, the fans, the food and, like the rest of us, when the weekend's duties allowed, a caipirinha, the notoriously strong Brazilian cocktail. John Button was also a keen visitor, and I would sometimes find him taking a break at the back of the Interlagos paddock where the balcony looks out to the circuit below. He'd always joke about how it reminded him of Brands Hatch.

Unfortunately, the Brazilian reception extended to the Button clan in 2009 was not a warm-hearted one. Even with the emergence of Felipe Massa, who had come so close to winning the championship the year before, Brazilian fans still had a soft spot for the seasoned campaigner Rubens Barrichello. They understood that this was probably the last chance that he would have to win the world championship, and Barrichello had stoked the fire a few races earlier by publicly criticizing Brawn GP's race strategy, with the obvious subtext that he felt the British team with its British boss preferred their British driver to win, not the Brazilian.

After the black-cat prank on Lewis Hamilton hadn't proved effective, the same local TV show that pulled the stunt on Lewis the three reasons for this. Firstly, people. The champagne of Melbourne had barely dried when Fry and Brawn had to make a painful round of redundancies. The team was downsized from 750 to 400 employees as a cost-saving exercise, so Brawn GP was forced to operate with a smaller staff than its rivals.

Secondly, the development budget. The double diffuser had given Brawn a colossal early-season advantage, but there was no money to develop the car and maintain that sort of form. In an interview we did at one of the summer races, Button's engineer Andrew Shovlin was one of the first to publicly admit that, because Brawn GP didn't have much money, there was no development of the car happening. It was clear that the team was really struggling.

Thirdly, the opposition caught up. McLaren was the first rival to come out with its own double diffuser at the third race in Shanghai, and while Adrian Newey had a tougher challenge to incorporate it on to the Red Bull because of earlier gearbox and suspension design choices, the RB5 became increasingly competitive.

For these reasons, and some others, Jenson Button had something of a mid-season wobble. He became frustrated, made mistakes and generally lost the cool, calm and collected demeanour he'd had at the start of the season. The pressure was building – Vettel was catching up, as was Jenson's own teammate Barrichello, who won in Valencia.

After a mid-grid qualifying result in Belgium, Jenson tangled with Romain Grosjean on the first lap, and spun off into the barrier. That non-score looked like it might be a serious blow for his world championship chances, but luckily for Jenson it was Kimi Räikkönen who won at Spa, rather than Vettel or Barrichello. A crucial fifth place in Singapore and an eighth in quibbling over semantics. Not this one. It was a cracker, the star of the show being Nigel Tozzi QC, widely regarded as one of the pre-eminent barristers on the planet and engaged, just like he was in the Spy-gate hearings, by Ferrari. Tozzi (who had worked with Brawn when he was at the Scuderia) absolutely laid into Ross, accusing him of being 'a person of supreme arrogance', before criticizing Charlie Whiting for 'not understanding the point' and 'getting it wrong'. Whiting had seen this all before and, as I recall, knowing it was all bluster, found it quite entertaining.

Unfortunately for Tozzi and the other appellants the argument that the double diffuser was 'inconsistent with the spirit of the rules and the efforts of the FIA to facilitate overtaking' was completely torpedoed when Brawn proved that Renault had tried to do exactly the same with their double diffuser concept, so were hardly in a position to object. Pat Symonds must have wished he'd never asked Charlie Whiting's opinion!

Not only was that point dismissed, but all the others were too – including the legal debate over when a fully enclosed hole is classified as a hole, and when it's just a space created by discontinuations of surfaces, in which case it's not a hole! The intention of the rule was supposed to result in a flat, unimpeded area with no holes in it, but ultimately Brawn's (or Minagawa's) interpretation of the regulation as written was deemed legally correct. The appeal was dismissed, the Australian GP results stood, and the advantage swung firmly in Brawn's favour.

But it wasn't all plain sailing. Button's win in Melbourne was followed by victories in Malaysia, Bahrain, Spain, Monaco and Turkey, after which point (in early June in a season that would stretch to November) Jenson would not win again. There were see the car was the most developed of them all, and the double diffuser was so obviously different that I was willing to believe that Brawn would be a significant player in the mix. But I also thought there would be enough competition from the likes of Red Bull, Ferrari and BMW Sauber to make a close race of it in Melbourne.

In fact, Button would score a dominant victory from pole position, although it took Sebastian Vettel running into the side of Robert Kubica when battling for second place to allow Barrichello to recover from a bad start and come through to make it a Brawn GP one-two finish in the team's first race. I headed down to the team's garage to find Jenson's father John Button leading the celebrations in the pink shirt he always wore on race day. The mechanics and engineers looked ecstatic at what they'd achieved. Lee McKenzie grabbed a tearful Ross Brawn as he came off the podium with the winning constructors' trophy in his arms, and we analysed the race on the new BBC F1 'Forum' show until darkness descended on Albert Park.

In the emotion of that Sunday evening it was easy to forget that the result was still provisional pending a session of the FIA Court of Appeal. Ferrari, Red Bull, Renault and BMW Sauber had jointly protested the double diffusers on the Brawn, Williams and Toyota cars at the start of the weekend, but their protest had been rejected. Their next step was to escalate the case to the more formally legal surroundings of the appeal court. The teams that didn't join the protest were Brawn's fellow Mercedes-powered squads, McLaren and Force India – and Toro Rosso, because Red Bull was already represented.

FIA Court of Appeal sessions are often dreary affairs, with more lawyers than you'd ever want to have in a confined space

The team took some time to get the new car ready to run on that first morning, but once on track, it flew. Button's first flying lap was six-tenths of a second quicker than anyone else. He came back into the pits after a few laps of even better times and Shovlin said, 'No need to push, you're already a second quicker than everybody.' A disbelieving Jenson replied, 'I wasn't pushing!'

The car's performance wasn't just down to its double diffuser. When I first saw the Brawn chassis up close, it instantly struck me that it was much more developed for the new rules than any of the others up and down the pit lane. It had obviously had more time spent on it, and the detail was very impressive – the front wing endplates, the neat undercut below the sidepods. After those stunning first laps, Brawn subsequently focused on running heavy fuel loads in order to mask the car's pace and not attract too much attention. It thus appeared from the outside that those early fast laps were 'glory runs' set with a light car. This made it easier for Brawn's rivals to be sceptical about the BGP001's ultimate pace. We had a lot of people, from Christian Horner at Red Bull to Felipe Massa at Ferrari, wondering aloud in interviews whether Brawn had taken a lot of fuel out, or had not run any of the ballast to make the weight limit that most cars did, in order to be as quick as they were on those first laps.

There's a long history of F1 teams doing this in order to attract sponsors, but even though the car had not a single sponsor logo on it, to me it just didn't seem Ross Brawn's style to mess around with underweight cars in order to set deceptive lap times. Nevertheless, it is to my eternal regret that I didn't buy into the story of Brawn's stellar testing form, and remained sceptical of the hype that the team was going to dominate the first race in Australia. Yes, I could

BRAINS AND BRAWN

other teams if they thought that they should tighten up the rules. The consensus was 'no', so the loophole was not closed off. Brawn's conscience was clear. It was actually Renault's Pat Symonds who was the crucial player in declining to shut down the loophole, because his team was also working on a double diffuser. They had run their design past the FIA's Charlie Whiting, who gave an opinion that it was not legal, so the Renault engineers hadn't pursued it. However, Charlie's opinion was just that, an opinion. Brawn was more confident, and happy, should the need arise, to take the design to a higher legal authority. As a result Honda/Brawn and two other teams, namely Toyota and Williams, all incorporated a double diffuser on their 2009 models.

After a fraught winter of survival, Brawn GP wasn't ready to run at the first winter test because the team was still modifying the chassis and gearbox in order to accommodate the Mercedes engine. The Brawn BGP001 eventually turned its first wheel in a private shakedown at a misty Silverstone. Jenson Button wore his red, white and blue British Union Flag crash helmet which clashed horribly with the bright yellow of Brawn's new team identity. He'd have a new helmet in those colours ready for the first race – but that was the least of his concerns.

A few days later the Brawn team trucks rolled into the Circuit de Catalunya for the second pre-season test. On the first morning we walked down to the last garage to see all the familiar faces we'd known from Honda – Ross Brawn was in the pit lane, while Button, Rubens Barrichello and engineers Andrew Shovlin and Jock Clear hung out in the garage. They were wearing unbranded black clothing, as there was no proper team gear yet. McLaren's Dave Ryan would have been horrified.

watching them on track, we got used to the new, lower downforce bodywork.

Over the winter most teams estimated the downforce loss would make their cars a few seconds per lap slower. However, some months before they found themselves fighting for their survival, Honda's engineers had found a loophole in the rules that would enable them to claw back much of the downforce lost in the rule change. During that extensive aero research conducted in 2008 an aerodynamicist called Masayuki Minagawa, who had previously worked with Honda's second team Super Aguri, noticed that the wording of one of the rules referred to bodywork that is 'visible from beneath the car'. His literal interpretation was that this didn't apply to bodywork that wasn't visible from beneath the car. It gave Minagawa the scope to design a section of the floor ahead of the diffuser which had an increased surface area. It allowed more air into the actual diffuser, expanding and accelerating the all-important airflow. This in turn generated a high level of rear downforce – as much as 40 per cent of the total downforce of the car.

When we first started hearing about this design concept, rival teams called it a 'double deck' diffuser, because the two elements sat on top of each other, and worked together to generate extra downforce. The design later became known simply as the 'double diffuser'. However, it was almost done away with before it even raced at the suggestion of none other than Ross Brawn himself.

During 2008 Brawn had seen Minagawa's double diffuser idea, and had recognized that it was so effective that it was likely to claw back all the downforce that the new regulations were intended to cut. In the spirit of team unity fostered by FOTA, Ross brought up the issue in the FIA's Technical Working Group, where he asked the supplying Brawn, it would undermine the unity of the teams, and support Ecclestone's view that they were only out for themselves. Logically Whitmarsh has to have assumed that Brawn wouldn't be a threat, given that the team was scrabbling around just to stay alive, and it would also have to convert its new car to accept a Mercedes V8 instead of the Honda engine it was designed for. With this in mind, Whitmarsh duly waived McLaren's veto and gave permission for Mercedes to supply Brawn with their engine. My suspicion has always been that had Ron Dennis still been in charge of McLaren, he would not have been quite so willing to let Brawn have the Mercedes powerplant. However, he had recently handed day-to-day decision making to Whitmarsh and couldn't overrule him on his first big call. It would turn out to be a sliding-doors moment in F1 history.

While all this was going on, Brawn's engineers continued to work on the new car. The changes to the technical regulations from 2008 to 2009 had several intentions. There was a thought that the aerodynamic complexity of the cars had spiralled out of control, and in order to cut down on some of what was seen as wasteful spending on ever more weird and wonderful winglets, and to continue the FIA's constant quest to keep a cap on speeds, the 2009 cars were made to look a lot simpler than their immediate predecessors. It was also hoped that the reduction in downforce would make the cars less sensitive to turbulence, resulting in closer racing. The new regulations made the cars look quite strange, with wider and lower front wings paired with higher and narrower rear wings. Even now, the rear wings of those cars look out of proportion, and at the 2009 car launches I certainly thought so. However, after the first half hour of related to the Honda exit. The company may have sold the team to Ross Brawn, but it would not let him use its engine. The 2009 Honda V8 was expected to be an improvement on the woeful 2008 powerplant, but it was still likely to be less competitive than its rivals. Not being tied to using it was in one sense a bonus. However, Brawn now had to find, and pay for, an alternative engine supply.

As a rule, rival teams would be loath to help a fellow competitor, but there was a bigger political picture at play in F1 at the time that suspended the normal operating rules of the Piranha Club (the nickname by which the F1 team principals were known, alluding to the voraciousness with which they wanted to destroy each other). 2008 was a year of rare unity, in which the teams had allied to form the Formula One Teams Association, or FOTA. In essence they believed that as the circus performers, they were being undervalued and should be paid more via their commercial agreements with the ringmaster, Bernie Ecclestone. Teams were thus unusually open to the notion of assisting Brawn in order to maintain a show of unity, and to keep his two cars on the grid.

Ferrari boss Luca di Montezemolo offered an engine, but when Brawn discovered that what was on offer was the previous year's power unit, he declined. Then, a lifeline, when Mercedes put themselves forward as a possible partner but with a catch. McLaren was the works-backed Mercedes team, and until 2008 had exclusive use of its V8 engine. For 2009 a supply had been granted to Force India, with McLaren's permission, as part of a bigger technical deal. Now Brawn became an option as well – but only if McLaren would allow it to happen.

McLaren boss Martin Whitmarsh was very active in FOTA, and he understood that if he used his veto to stop Mercedes from was a reflection of the same global financial crisis that would also lead to both Toyota and BMW leaving the sport at the end of 2009.

Fry and Brawn managed to stall the closure of the team and persuaded Honda to keep things ticking over while they sought a buyer. Some serious players were interested, including Richard Branson's Virgin Group, Prodrive boss David Richards, and even Bernie Ecclestone. However, after careful consideration none was deemed to be the right fit. Eventually Honda resigned themselves to the fact that keeping the team alive via a Brawn and Fry management buyout would avoid the near $100 million cost of closing the doors and making everyone redundant. It would also be less embarrassing and more ethically correct, a highly important consideration for the Japanese company. As part of the deal, Honda would provide modest funding to keep the race team going.

It was a sensible resolution. Even though Fry and Brawn were taking on all the financial responsibility, they were still buying an F1 team for practically nothing. Well, not quite nothing. At the formal meeting to sign the ownership documents, Brawn reached into his pocket and pulled out a one-pound coin, which he gave to Honda's managing officer Hiroshi Oshima. Ross Brawn bought an F1 team for a pound! It was a gesture, but one appreciated by Oshima, who still has the coin. How Honda's financial people feel about that looking back on the deal is another matter. In 2010 Brawn sold the team to Mercedes for around £150 million, and the Mercedes F1 team is now worth an estimated £3 billion.

One of the first things to sort out was a team name. Fry had been keen on Pure Racing, but in the end it was decided to name the team after the boss, much like Ferrari, Williams or McLaren. And thus Brawn Grand Prix was born. There was one sting in the tail

Insomuch as there is a uniform for the pit lane reporter, I favour navy-blue shorts (which don't get as wet as trousers in the rain), and in hot weather, when permitted, my trusty Birkenstocks.

Flying wingman to George Russell in an RAF Typhoon.

Hamilton was defenceless against Verstappen's new soft tyres. Had the race been run to the rules as they were understood, the 2021 Abu Dhabi GP would have finished under the safety car and Lewis Hamilton would have been an eight-time world champion.

Azerbaijan, 2024. Even when things aren't going his way, Lando Norris has an easy charm that makes him a fan favourite.

An interview with W Series runner-up Alice Powell, 2019. All the W Series drivers were seriously quick and were pathfinders for the F1 Academy, which now seeks to discover the next female F1 driver.

Lewis Hamilton and Max Verstappen's intense rivalry ended with a race that damaged faith in Formula 1's referees.

Carlin mechanics attempting to cheer up Sebastian Vettel at Spa-Francorchamps, 2006, the day after he sliced the top off his finger. Vettel subsequently showed that famous finger on the podium every time he won.

Right Socially distancing from Valtteri Bottas. Formula 1 was the one of the first global sports to resume during the summer of 2020. We operated effectively in a bubble at the circuits, with no fans present, but the TV coverage brought a bit of normality and excitement to viewers kept indoors during Covid-19.

Right One of the Covid precautions distanced reporters from the pit lane. My trusty monocular was the only way to see what was happening in the garages.

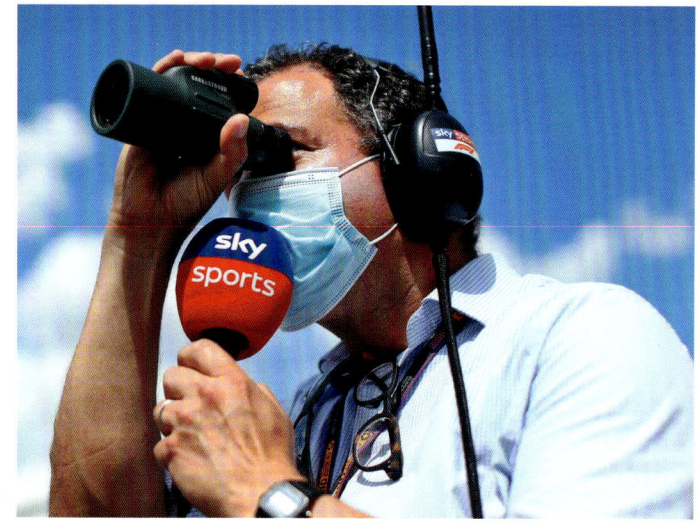

Jenson Button won the 2009 world championship in a Brawn car that was run on a shoestring but had the genius double diffuser from the start.

One of my frequent BBC interviews with Lewis Hamilton, but there wasn't much to smile about from 2009 to 2011: three seasons where Jenson Button and Sebastian Vettel shared the championship spoils.

All smiles between McLaren's Fernando Alonso and Lewis Hamilton before an explosive 2007 season characterized by threats, professional fouls and industrial espionage.

Putting the tumult of 2007 behind him, Lewis Hamilton, surrounded by his father, brother and the McLaren team, celebrates the pure joy of clinching the 2008 world championship on the last corner of the last lap of the last race.

Michael Schumacher demanded excellence from everyone around him. Interesting, well-considered questions were rewarded with an insightful answer. Jonathan Legard and Maurice Hamilton listen in behind, as Michael's media manager Sabine Kehm keeps an eye on proceedings.

The six-car race, Indianapolis 2005. The day we ripped up our running order and watched helplessly as Formula 1 dealt its popularity in the USA a heavy blow.

When Capital Radio issued me with a press pass in July 1996 I had no idea that it would lead me to a press conference with Damon Hill, a meeting with James Allen and my first job in Formula 1.

Murray's last race commentary for ITV, USA, 2001. When Murray and Martin were in full flow they used to sway together like windscreen wipers. Murray remained keenly in touch with the sport until his death in 2021, aged 97.

The ITV F1 team on Murray's last weekend. From top row to bottom, left to right: Jenny Bozson, Gerard Lane, Geoff Kay, Dave Boyd-Moss; Mat Bryant, Dave Hill, Kevin Chapman, Rob Walker; Les Horne, Bill Fievez, Tracy Rooney, Ron Trickett; Jon Pearce, Di Finch, Sally Blower, John Tidy; Kevin Piper, me, Andy Parr, Jo Hybert, Steve Aldous; Mark Blundell, Tony Jardine, Louise Goodman; James Allen, Jim Rosenthal, Murray Walker, Martin Brundle.

attempting to lure him back to F1 as Honda team principal, leaving Fry to concentrate on the commercial side and general administration.

It worked. Along with a very competitive salary, Fry convinced Brawn to join Honda because it was an interesting challenge and as team principal (a position Brawn had not been offered at Ferrari), his knowledge, methods and calm presence could have a transformative impact. Honda had finished a lowly eighth in the 2007 constructors' championship, and Brawn arrived too late to have any impact on the 2008 car. If anything, the RA108 was even less competitive than its predecessor, and it left Button and his teammate Rubens Barrichello struggling to get into the points.

What Ross could do straight away, however, was to take steps to improve the Honda F1 organization, and make big strategic decisions. The most significant was his call to halt any development of the hopeless 2008 car and focus instead on the following year's model and the opportunity that came with a blank sheet of paper, thanks to new aerodynamic rules that were coming in for that season.

This was the era before FIA aerodynamic testing restrictions put a limit on how much wind-tunnel running and Computational Fluid Dynamics research teams could do. The sky was the limit, and as 2008 progressed the Honda team worked on its future car in three wind tunnels, including one in Japan, with the aim of hitting the ground running in 2009. But at the end of November 2008 came a hammer blow. Fry and Brawn were called to a hurriedly arranged meeting with Honda executives and were stunned to be told that the company was pulling out of F1 immediately, and that the team was to be shut down. The decision of details. Lee would courteously hear me out, before turning back to camera to say, 'Yes, well, thank you very much for that, Ted, but just to confirm the main point, which is that Sebastian Vettel has avoided a grid penalty, and will start on pole position after all . . .'

For the first time since the end of 1996, F1 was back on the BBC and motorsport was about to gift it a 'phoenix from the ashes' story filled with grit and determination starring a car that came close to being mothballed: 2009 will forever be remembered as the Brawn GP year. The team's story began at the end of 2006 when Ferrari technical director Ross Brawn decided to take some long-craved time out. He'd been at the coalface at Maranello for a decade, and the pressure of the workload and competition had taken a toll. With Michael Schumacher retiring he wanted to spend more time with his wife Jean and their family, and to pursue the rather more relaxing hobby of fly fishing.

At the same time as Ross was thigh deep in waders in a chilly Scottish stream, the Honda Motor Company was growing frustrated with the lack of progress of its F1 team. Since graduation from engine suppliers to team owners with the purchase of the BAR team in 2005, Honda had invested heavily in F1, but only achieved a single victory with Jenson Button in the rain-affected 2006 Hungarian GP. In 2007 Honda's car was hopelessly uncompetitive. The unusual 'Earth Dreams' livery reflected the fact that there were few sponsors, and that Honda was underwriting the whole thing for little reward. Team boss Nick Fry couldn't fail to be aware that things weren't progressing under his leadership. A pragmatist, looking for a solution, he went on a charm offensive to Brawn, phoning him every week or so, sounding him out as to whether he felt he'd caught enough fish, moustache next to his very bushy, real one. It was excruciating viewing, but at least Hamilton, Sebastian Vettel, David Coulthard, Jenson Button, Rubens Barrichello, Alex Wurz and Murray Walker all took part, so I was in good company.

With ITV leaving, Bernie Ecclestone moved swiftly to offer the UK F1 broadcast rights back to the BBC. Given their licence-fee funding method, the corporation did not run adverts in the Grand Prix programmes, so it was a welcome return to uninterrupted coverage for our audience. The BBC Sport production team was led by Mark Wilkin, who had previously produced the coverage with Murray Walker and James Hunt in the years before ITV's stint. Jake Humphrey brought a fresh style to the presentation line-up alongside what grew to become a memorable punditry double-act between David Coulthard and Eddie Jordan. Martin Brundle was commentating, with Jonathan Legard, who had come in from BBC Radio 5 Live, and Lee McKenzie joined as my fellow pit lane reporter. Lee had a more personal connection to F1 in that her father Bob was the Grand Prix correspondent for British tabloid the *Daily Express* for many years, although he gained greater fame running around Silverstone on the 2005 British GP weekend wearing only body paint and a sporran after losing a bet with Ron Dennis!

As pit lane counterparts Lee and I developed an effective and enjoyable professional relationship that has endured to this day, despite the fact that we no longer work for the same broadcaster. In our stand-ups to camera we would follow up on incidents and stories that had come up over the weekend. Lee would introduce the topic, then I would get over-excited and go off into the deep end about why I thought it was the biggest story ever, bringing in loads

Chapter 13

Brains and Brawn

Lewis Hamilton's spectacular achievement on the last lap of the 2008 F1 season was the perfect way for ITV Sport to go out on a high. The financial crisis and slump in television advertising forced the broadcaster to make some hard decisions, and it opted to end its F1 coverage. The last programme we made for ITV ended with a music piece that pre-dated the American show *Lip Sync Battle* by a good seven years, albeit without the quality. Essentially it was the ITV presenters 'singing' along to 'Welcome to the Black Parade' by My Chemical Romance, the chorus of which began with the words 'We carry on'. True for F1, but sadly not for ITV, and most of the production team I had worked with for the past 12 years.

The producer responsible for the segment was Chris Holding, who did particularly well in persuading F1 drivers and team bosses to join in. 'Once a few start doing it, they'll all want to do it,' he told me while he was in the process of setting it up, basically inventing TikTok at that very moment. I roped in BMW Sauber team boss Mario Theissen, who took in good humour my wearing a false way he also spent a year on our team at Sky Sports as an expert analyst. And yes, it was awkward between him and me . . .

And the man who benefited most from that controversial evening in Singapore? How much Fernando Alonso really knew about Crash-gate remains a mystery to this day. If anything, it just adds to the mystique that has epitomized his F1 career.

A FIFTH AND A FIX

Years later, feeling so keenly that Singapore had contributed to his championship loss, Massa went on to file a lawsuit against the FIA for damages.

The other victim was the man who crashed. Nelson Piquet Jr was granted immunity from sanction by the FIA in return for his evidence, leaving him free to take another drive in F1 if he could find anyone who wanted to employ him. He could not and his F1 career was over, although he did continue to race in other categories, winning the inaugural Formula E title in 2015.

Briatore took the FIA to court in France, who ruled that the FIA and its World Motor Sport Council lacked the authority to impose Briatore's lifetime ban. The penalty was overturned and he was awarded €15,000 in damages. In the aftermath Briatore remained on the fringes of F1 as a sponsor finder, but in 2024 then Renault Group CEO Luca De Meo brought him back to Enstone in the role of 'executive advisor'. Meanwhile, the previous Renault boss Carlos Ghosn had a colourful fate. In 2018 he was arrested in Japan, charged with various crimes that centred on alleged improper financial conduct. Ghosn denied the charges, and was held under house arrest in Tokyo while awaiting a trial he felt would not be fair. He thus arranged to be smuggled out of Japan in a musical-equipment packing case via two private jets to his ultimate destination of Lebanon, his home country and one that has no extradition treaty with Japan.

Symonds also reached a settlement with the FIA which allowed him to return to F1, initially with the British team Manor. After a subsequent stint with Williams he was hired by the Formula 1 organization as its technical director, and in January 2025 he started work as a consultant to the new Cadillac F1 team. Along the your major title sponsor has walked out on you. How's your first week as team boss going?'

He answered with good humour: 'It can't get worse, can it! I can only look good in a situation like this whatever I do, so we'll deal with it.'

For a man who never wanted to be front and centre, being made team boss at such a moment was a poisoned chalice and one he dealt with admirably. In time he left Renault to join Mercedes, where he would play a key part in Lewis Hamilton's success. He later returned to Renault's Enstone base for another stint with the team before moving to Aston Martin in 2024.

Looking back at the roots of Crash-gate with the benefit of hindsight, it's clear that Pat Symonds was under immense pressure. He felt responsible for the hundreds of employees at the factory and feared that they could all lose their jobs. I'm not even sure Symonds would have considered what he orchestrated as such a terrible crime – Piquet wasn't risking his life in a slow-speed crash, and it was unlikely any marshals or spectators would have been hurt. Maybe he just saw it, to quote himself, as 'a bit of gamesmanship'. Maybe he succumbed to that pressure and hoped at least that it would be a victimless crime.

But it wasn't victimless: in the end the victims were two Brazilian racing drivers. Felipe Massa's Singapore race fell apart when, in the rush for pit stops under the Piquet safety car, a Ferrari mechanic gave Massa the green light to go while his fuel hose was still attached. Petrol sprayed everywhere from the severed fuel line, and Massa lost a minute and a half as the mechanics sprinted down to the end of the pit lane to retrieve the hose. He finished that race a lowly 13th, losing the points that would have won him the title.

guaranteed anonymity in return for his evidence so was known, dramatically, as 'Witness X' in the FIA hearing. The FIA ultimately judged that Flavio was indeed involved and banned him from motorsport for life.

Outside the hearing there was a media scrum. Mosley was challenged on the harshness of Briatore's sentence – the flamboyant, charismatic F1 showman, whose world had collapsed. 'It's sad to see a career end like that, but what else could we do?' he said. Max clarified that the FIA had not fined Renault as a team, nor kicked them out of F1 altogether. Despite his distaste for the power of manufacturers, Mosley knew that Renault's future participation was balanced on a knife-edge, and he didn't want to push Carlos Ghosn into shutting down the team.

The only real punishment Renault suffered was from its own title sponsor, the Dutch bank ING, whose management pulled their sponsorship and logos from the car, feeling they couldn't be seen to be associated with a team that had cheated.

With Renault understandably in scandal-management mode, Briatore and Symonds were relieved of their positions. The new team principal was a man who wasn't a fan of the limelight at the time, and possibly as a result of the events he steered the team through, hasn't been keen on it ever since: the likeable Northern Irish engineer Bob Bell. On his first weekend in the job, he was thrust in front of our BBC cameras. He looked like he would have rather been anywhere else, so I tried to put my question as nicely as possible, but there was no way around it:

'So Bob, your team has been embroiled in a race-fixing scandal, you've lost your team principal and your engineering director, and hadn't slept. He wasted no time in telling us that Piquet was just bitter and angry about being sacked, and that both his own and Renault's lawyers had commenced legal action against both Nelson Piquet Jr and Nelson Piquet Sr in the high court of Paris – for blackmail. The way he left the word 'blackmail' until last, and the portentous way he said it was pure theatre. 'How harmful have the accusations been to Renault's reputation?' I asked ('It's major damage') and then, slightly provocatively, knowing I'd get a testy response given that he'd already made his feelings clear, I asked how he felt towards his former driver, Nelson Piquet Jr. He turned to me with half a smile: 'The fact that we are taking him to court for blackmail, I think so is pretty much what is my feeling.' He could be incredibly charismatic when he wanted to be.

However, Flavio's charm didn't work when it came to the FIA's lawyers. At the hearing a week after Monza, having initially denied the whole plot, Symonds admitted that he had helped to fix the race. As a result, he was banned from all FIA sanctioned motorsport for five years. I had believed Symonds when he protested his innocence in Monza. He had been a regular contact of mine in the pits, and I trusted him, so when the truth came out, I had a keen sense of having been deceived. Briatore denied any involvement, but this was contradicted by Piquet, and by the testimony of a Renault engineer who alleged that Flavio knew about the plan, even if Flavio claimed it wasn't his idea and that he hadn't been involved in its execution. Such was Flavio's avowed lack of interest in anything technical such as race strategy, this seemed entirely plausible to the rest of the paddock. The engineer had been race victory, he was completely unfazed by the question and had no hesitation in answering.

> Fernando: 'Yes, I do.'
> Ted: 'Even though the team effectively manufactured it?'
> Fernando: 'Well, I think that's an interpretation. There are many interpretations [of] how you can win the race. That was in the very early stage of the race, and it was a long race to do. The car was performing well, I did no mistakes, and I still count it.'

Walking away from that interview I was impressed by Alonso's nonchalance. But looking back on it, Singapore is always such a hard race to win that I was willing to accept his point, or rather his 'interpretation'.

The extent of Briatore's involvement was very much open to interpretation, most of it created by the man himself. Piquet alleged that his former team boss was an active participant, and alongside Symonds had asked or instructed him to crash in Singapore. Briatore denied it and came out fighting. I was present at a tense media briefing Flavio gave in the Renault motorhome at Monza in 2009, the race before the FIA hearing. We were ushered in by his long-time media manager and right-hand woman Patrizia Spinelli, and by one of the many Renault company PR men who travelled the world with the team. It was a complete scrum, everyone crowded around a single table, and my BBC cameraman only just got a position.

In came Briatore, resplendent grey hair tumbling down to the collar of his trademark open-necked shirt. He looked like he lucky. We had no reason to suspect that there was anything untoward going on. Indeed Fernando went on to win the next race at Fuji, a chaotic rain-hit affair, proving his car was competitive.

And we were none the wiser until the middle of the 2009 season, at which point Piquet was fired by Briatore to make way for Romain Grosjean. Soon after, the Brazilian took the opportunity to come clean, telling the FIA in a sworn statement what exactly happened in Singapore, and an investigation immediately ensued. Coming just two years after the McLaren-Ferrari Spy-gate saga, the affair soon picked up the moniker Crash-gate.

Fixing a Grand Prix result is an incredibly risky thing to do, and the number of people who would need to be in on it tends to mean that eventually the true story comes out. In this case, it emerged that Nelson Piquet Sr had actually told FIA race director Charlie Whiting what had happened in Singapore at the end of the 2008 season in Brazil. Whiting had in turn told FIA president Max Mosley, but at that point the FIA didn't have enough evidence to do anything about it. It was only after Piquet Jr's statement that Mosley employed some ex-police investigators to interview Alonso and Pat Symonds and the truth started to emerge.

Alonso flatly denied knowing anything about the plan. I believed him, and so did the FIA's investigators. There was certainly no reason for him to have been aware in order for the plan to work. He might well have thought that lap 12 was a bizarrely early time to stop and made little sense as a race strategy, but his natural reaction in the cool-down room after the Grand Prix, where he immediately credited the safety car for his win, could not have come from someone who had been in on the plan to fix the result. When I asked him a year later whether he still counted Singapore '08 as a proper

A FIFTH AND A FIX

second and the podium in Germany. It was with this experience in their data memory banks that Renault sat down after qualifying in Singapore and thought hard about how to get Alonso to the front of the field, where he would be able to run at his true pace.

According to the evidence that emerged in the subsequent investigation, this is how things played out that Saturday night and Sunday. With Hockenheim in mind, Pat Symonds reasoned that if he could guarantee the timing of a safety-car period, Alonso could pit just before it, fuel up, gain track position at the front and use the inherent pace in the car to stay ahead and win. But how can you guarantee a safety-car period? Symonds figured that a crash in an area of the track that was hard for the marshals to reach would do the trick. Perhaps against his better judgement, Symonds came up with a plan to use Renault's second car to cause a safety-car period. He asked Piquet to crash. Under obvious pressure to keep his drive and please the team, the Brazilian agreed. The exit of Turn 17 was selected as the perfect spot, as it was difficult to access and recover a car quickly, a safety car being the certain consequence.

Whether in a coincidental foreshadowing of what was to come or because he was practising, Piquet spun his car on the formation lap to the grid. Once the race got underway Alonso made that early pit stop on lap 12, a move that made no sense at the time as generally those starting out of position, as he was, aim to run long in an attempt to work their way up the order. Then, on lap 14, coming out of Turn 17, Piquet spun and crashed, perhaps more heavily than planned, into the inside wall. The safety car was duly deployed, and with others pitting, Alonso eventually took the lead, and kept it. In the moment we thought that the timing of Alonso's stop had been but then spent 2007 on the sidelines as Renault's test and reserve driver. He had entrusted Flavio Briatore with managing his career, which paid dividends when he got the Renault race drive for 2008. However, he had a poor start to the season, retiring from six of the first nine races. But in Germany, he finished second, thanks to a lucky bit of pit-stop timing and the intervention of the safety car.

In 2008, there had been a significant change to the rules. The FIA weren't happy with the way that, as soon as someone crashed and it looked like there would be a safety-car period to slow the cars down, everyone would race hell-for-leather back to the pits to get their pit stop done without losing too much time. So race director Charlie Whiting inserted a rule that as soon as the safety car was deployed, the pit lane would 'close' (it wouldn't physically close, it just meant that if a car did come into the pits while the safety car was deployed it would get a time penalty). Once everyone was proceeding at a safe slow speed behind the safety car the pit lane would then 'open', allowing everyone to dive in. However, trying to solve one problem had created another with new dangers in the pit lane, one example of which would be crucial in deciding that year's world championship.

What Piquet and Renault learned from the German GP was that, should you have a lousy qualifying and start well down the grid, if you then happened to make a pit stop and fuel your car to the end of the race – and if someone then happened to crash and the safety car be deployed – you might well suddenly find yourself at the front, as the cars ahead of you make their pit stops. From that point, it would be a case of defending your newly found place at the head of the field, which is how Piquet went from 17th on the grid to

A FIFTH AND A FIX

With Hamilton and Massa still fighting for the world championship, the F1 circus left Europe and headed for Singapore and the sport's first ever night race. In free practice, there was a surprise for everyone in the pit lane: the Renault was actually quick. Alonso immediately clicked with the technically and physically demanding track, and once the engineers had made some adjustments, he was fastest across the race preparation runs of FP2, and the qualifying practice runs of FP3. The car was kind on its tyres and had good mechanical grip. Out of nowhere, Alonso was suddenly a real contender for a race win. But come qualifying, he had an unfortunate setback. A fuel-flow problem to the engine meant that his Renault came spluttering to a halt on track, and he couldn't set a time in Q2. Fernando was left watching helplessly as slower cars qualified ahead of him, and he ultimately wound up 15th on the grid. Alonso, Briatore, Symonds, chief engineer Alan Permane and the rest of the team were absolutely gutted. The car was worthy of running at the front, but was now out of position, starting three quarters of the way down the grid. It was an injustice – but given the fault was a technical glitch the Renault personnel had no one to blame but themselves.

Starting just behind Alonso on the Singapore grid was his teammate, Nelson Piquet Jr. The Brazilian didn't have the pace of Alonso and had failed to get out of Q1. It was an all-too-familiar story for the likeable Piquet, whom I'd got to know a little during his 2006 GP2 season as a result of all those interviews about his championship battle with Hamilton. Piquet was a quick driver. He had won the British F3 Championship and finished second to Hamilton in GP2, across towards Ron Dennis and Martin Whitmarsh on the pit wall. It was Hamilton's day, but Massa won just as many plaudits for the impeccable drive that had won him the race and the dignified manner in which he conducted himself once he had been told over the radio that the title had slipped out of his grasp.

As I mentioned, Felipe Massa lost valuable points at several key races before that day in Brazil, infamously at the Singapore GP, which later became known as the 'Crash-gate' race, but we would have to wait almost a year before the true facts came to light. Reporting on the race-fixing scandal for the BBC I called it 'one of the worst cases of cheating in sporting history'. I had debated with myself whether to word it so strongly, but the facts were undeniable, despite what we later found out about the timeline of events and the circumstances surrounding them that provided some mitigating context as to why those involved acted the way they did.

After his ill-fated 2007 season with McLaren, Fernando Alonso had returned to the Renault team where management were keen to show him that they were heading back to race-winning form in the hope they could keep their mercurial champion long-term. The Renault was a decent enough car, but it wasn't a winner, much to the disappointment of Carlos Ghosn, the Renault Group president and CEO.

Ghosn had a reputation for not being the most committed CEO among the F1 manufacturers and certainly (at least when it came to budgets) the most frugal, and re-iterated his demands that Renault perform 'at the top level' of F1 or the company's investment would have to be reviewed. That pressure to win was passed down from Ghosn to Briatore and on to the race team, which was headed by executive director of engineering Pat Symonds.

I'm sure that he's going to claim fifth place, which is all he needs to do to become . . .'

Martin: 'Yes!'

James: 'The 2008 F1 world champion – Lewis Hamilton! Well, the Ferrari boys are celebrating, they think they have won.'

Martin: 'They're wrong. You're wrong, guys.'

James: 'They absolutely haven't won. Hamilton finished fifth. . . . You will never see a more dramatic conclusion to any motor race, let alone a Grand Prix, than that. And the result of it all is that, in the most harum-scarum way possible, he doesn't make it easy for himself, does he? Lewis Hamilton is the world champion.'

Martin: 'Unbelievable.'

Hearts and heads sank in the Ferrari garage. The last corner of the last lap of the last race of the whole 2008 world championship! One Ferrari mechanic head-butted the garage wall so hard that it shattered. Hamilton himself didn't know if he'd done enough. He came on the radio: 'Do I have it? Do I have it?'

For Lewis to wait for confirmation of whether the championship was his must have felt like an eternity, but in fact took five seconds or so for his engineer Phil Prew to check with sporting director Dave Ryan, who gave the thumbs-up for Prew to confirm it on the radio. Hamilton had won the world championship by a single, solitary point. The McLaren mechanics already knew he had it, and they were on the pit wall cheering him home while the garage emptied into the pit lane, everyone screaming their heads off in pure joy. By that time cameraman Andy Parr had joined me, and we looked at each other, laughed and shook our heads in disbelief as we walked to the very real possibility that they were about to lose the world championship for a second year running. The 71st and last lap came, and I suddenly realized another reason I was cold. The wind had picked up in that way it does just before a rain shower – and at Turn 4, the Lake Descent, it was raining again, hard. As Massa came out of the last corner to win the Brazilian Grand Prix, Hamilton had just entered the twisty section of the track. Massa had done what he needed to do, and his family erupted with joy, only to be shushed by clued-up Ferrari mechanics, who knew the championship wasn't over until Lewis crossed the line. I looked across the pit lane, watching Ron Dennis on the McLaren pit wall, frozen to his seat, eyes glued to the TV screen, as I listened to Allen and Brundle in my headphones.

> James: 'Can Hamilton do anything? Can he run it up the inside of Vettel? Only a few corners to go now and desperation starts to creep in for Lewis Hamilton.'
> Martin: 'Räikkönen's third and . . . Is that Glock, is that Glock going slowly?'
> James: 'It is!'
> Martin: 'That's Glock!'

It was true, Glock's dry-weather tyres were suddenly useless in the wet conditions. He had no grip. Hamilton scythed past him.

> James: 'Oh my goodness me! Hamilton's back in position again. A hundred thousand local hearts sink in the grandstand. It's handed the place back to Hamilton. He comes through. And

A FIFTH AND A FIX

track ahead, and Felipe looked much more comfortable in the rain. Hamilton rejoined the track in fifth, now behind Glock, who had yet to come in. Coming up fast in sixth was Sebastian Vettel, who had proved, by brilliantly winning the Italian GP four races earlier, that he and his Toro Rosso made for a very quick package in wet conditions. Suddenly the threat to Hamilton was Vettel closing in behind. At a moment when Lewis went slightly wide, the German youngster overtook him. There were gasps and then shouts of frustration in the McLaren garage as the timing screen updated itself: Hamilton was now in sixth.

The layout of the McLaren garage was the same at every race. Mechanics sat in their fire suits and chrome stormtrooper-inspired helmets in an arc around a TV on each side wall, with tyres stacked in the middle where the drivers' families were allowed to stand and watch. (There was a viewing gallery in the middle of the back wall, but that was full of sponsors and guests.) From my spot in the front right-hand corner I couldn't see a TV screen, but I was listening closely to James Allen and Martin Brundle. Over my left shoulder I could see Lewis's step-mum Linda with his girlfriend Nicole Scherzinger alongside. They were bouncing on tip toes, hands either clenched by their sides or covering their eyes. Lewis's brother Nicholas sat with the mechanics, eyes riveted to the screens. Lewis's dad Anthony was not visible, as he preferred to watch from the computer racks behind a partition wall.

There was a lot of praying going on. Down at Ferrari, Felipe Massa's mother Ana, father Luis and brother Eduardo were cautiously optimistic. Felipe had kept the lead, and it wasn't raining hard enough for Glock's dry-weather tyres to lose grip just yet. I felt a chill run through the McLaren garage as everyone there faced up

I've had various hit-and-miss interactions with crowds of fans across my Formula 1 career. After the 2022 Australian GP the crowd ended up using me as a prop. Joining the post-race track invasion to give viewers a sense of the energy and enthusiasm of the Aussie crowd for Charles Leclerc's win, I was handed a shoe, by a fan, filled with warm beer, and encouraged to drink. As the crowd clearly sensed, while on live TV, I didn't really have the option to back out (and thanks to Daniel Ricciardo I did have some awareness of this Australian sporting tradition of the 'shoey'), with the result that viewers at home were treated to the unedifying spectacle of me downing the shoe's contents. And do you know what? It wasn't that bad.

Anyway, back to Brazil, and with my impertinence duly punished, I was fortunate that the beer was rinsed away by a heavy rain shower just before the start. This led to a delay so that the mechanics could fit intermediate tyres to the cars. When the race started, Massa led from the off, and as conditions dried out he kept the lead through the switch back to slicks. The fact that Hamilton didn't need to win outright – only finish fifth – understandably led to a cautious approach by the McLaren engineers. As I watched from the garage the team seemed to build a little inertia into their strategy calls, taking extra time to think through every decision. Lewis was a couple of laps late changing on to slicks, but he regained that vital fifth place on track. And there he stayed until, with 10 laps left, the rain came again, lightly at first. As everyone dived into the pit lane for a quick tyre change the Toyotas of Timo Glock and Jarno Trulli stayed out, the team having judged it wasn't damp enough for wets. That elevated Glock to fourth.

Like the rest of the field Hamilton pitted for intermediates, with frontrunner Massa stopping a lap later. The Ferrari had a clear

A FIFTH AND A FIX

had a lot to live up to (cue shots of Ayrton Senna), but that Massa had harnessed the adulation to raise his game. 'I've taken all the good energy around and exchanged it for extra power in the car,' he said, before we heard from former Brazilian champion Emerson Fittipaldi about how Felipe had matured. I ended the piece with an idea that I'd had the week before, although I hadn't quite figured out how it was going to work.

Knowing that the McLaren team had been carefully keeping a low profile in Brazil, travelling to and from the track in plain clothes (not unusual in São Paulo), I had the somewhat quixotic idea that I should see what happened if I deliberately attracted some attention. On Thursday I asked Massa what he thought would happen if I went out among the hugely partisan Interlagos crowd as a British TV presenter displaying a Union Flag. 'For me, it's not a good idea,' he cautioned. Despite this incredibly sound advice it was ITV's last F1 weekend before the BBC took over, and there was an end-of-term feeling in the air, so I decided to go for it. I stood on a wall overlooking the grid and did a little piece to camera next to the fans, separated from the crowd by a chain-link-fence which in retrospect probably saved my bacon given what I did next. I unfurled a modest Union Flag that I'd borrowed and waved it about, to see what would happen. For a second, nothing – astonishment, no doubt – but then the boos and whistles rang out, and someone in the third row lobbed a plastic cup half-full of (very tasty Brazilian Antarctica brand) beer over the railing and on to my shoulder. It was a great shot by the spectator, which is more than you can say for the TV piece.

On this occasion my attempt to keep things entertaining with the crowd's help may have gone slightly awry, but it's also true to say that actually developed the Ferrari F2008 even further away from Kimi's style and towards the preferences of teammate Felipe Massa, so it was the Brazilian who emerged as Hamilton's main title rival. Felipe was outstanding that year. He was driving less aggressively than in previous seasons and made fewer mistakes. Had the car been more reliable, he could have won the 2008 world championship comfortably. However, retirements from the first two races, an engine failure in Hungary and a botched pit stop in Singapore (more on that later) meant that Hamilton edged ahead, and Massa was left on the back foot going into the title decider in Brazil. Hamilton had a seven-point lead. In the days of the old 10-8-6-5-4-3-2-1 scoring system it was easy to work out that fifth place would guarantee Lewis the title even if Massa won the final Grand Prix.

Massa had a big home advantage at the decisive race of the season. His family and friends were in the paddock, and the crowd chanted his name throughout the weekend. There had even been support from the presenters of a Brazilian TV show that played practical jokes on people and filmed their reactions, a fashionable genre at the time. These two pranksters gatecrashed a McLaren sponsor function before the weekend began and handed a fluffy black toy cat to Lewis – black cats being a symbol of misfortune in Brazil – hoping to put some kind of curse on his race weekend. Hamilton laughed it off, pointing out that in the UK having a black cat cross your path is a sign of good luck.

No cats appeared, fluffy or otherwise, in ITV's final pre-race build-up. Louise and I flipped a coin to decide who was going to do which pre-race feature on the two contenders. I landed Massa. My piece started with the thought that Brazilian racing drivers

A FIFTH AND A FIX

In 2008, reeling from being thrown out of the previous year's constructors' world championship, McLaren was out for redemption. Having technically been classified last, the team was obliged to run the two car numbers of 22 and 23 at the bottom of the entry list (this was before drivers were allowed to choose their own race numbers). The team was at least saved the indignity of being relegated to a garage at the end of the pit lane after a moment of kindness (or pragmatism) from Bernie Ecclestone, who acknowledged that it would probably be better for the show and the TV coverage if the top teams competing for the world championship were near each other in the pit lane rather than separated by 10 other garages. The story went that Bernie had planned to give McLaren the third garage, but Renault objected. So they ended up in the fifth, next to Red Bull Racing. With Fernando Alonso gone, Heikki Kovalainen was brought in as a low-friction teammate for Hamilton, leading to a much more harmonious atmosphere in the McLaren camp.

The 2008 McLaren MP4-23 was a straightforward development of the car that should have won the previous year's constructors' title, and Lewis duly kicked off the season in style, winning from pole in Melbourne. Over at Ferrari a strange handling characteristic was taking the edge off Kimi Räikkönen's title defence. James Allison, one of Räikkönen's ex-technical directors, once described the Finn as having 'soft hands'. Not literally, unless Allison had some insight into Räikkönen's manicure routine that I'm unaware of, but in his particular sensitivity to a car's balance.

Too often Räikkönen found that he couldn't get his front tyres to work, losing him time as the car understeered into corners, the front end never biting and gripping up. A mid-season upgrade devastatingly simple, and yet became iconic, forming part and parcel of F1 lore: 'Is that Glock?' That simple question (and the confirmation that it was, indeed, Timo Glock, going slowly) encapsulated the dramatic end to Lewis Hamilton's first successful world championship campaign.

That 2008 season was a busy one. On top of an 18-race F1 calendar, Louise Goodman and I also presented ITV's coverage of the British Touring Car Championship, which meant we spent every weekend at a racing circuit. We'd go from Australia to Oulton Park, Snetterton to Singapore, and Budapest to Brands Hatch. It was great fun. I'd been a fan of the BTCC since Murray started voicing the highlights on BBC's *Grandstand* and had fond memories of Andy Rouse battling Frank Sytner, Nigel Mansell's escapades in a Ford Mondeo and Rickard Rydell's incongruous Volvo estate. Our Sunday coverage on ITV4 was, to say the least, comprehensive. It grew to encompass seven hours of live television from the opening race of the day for the Ginetta Junior Championship to the third and final BTCC round of the meeting. Incidentally, if you're hoping to spot the next F1 star, Ginetta Juniors is a great category to keep an eye on. With a minimum age of just 14, it is the first car series that many drivers graduate to on their way from karting up the racing ladder. Years later in 2014, when Steve Rider had taken back presenting duties on ITV's BTCC show, he passed on a tip – the only one he ever gave me – about a promising driver: 'Watch out for this kid in Ginetta Juniors called Lando Norris. He looks something special.' I'd worked with Steve for years and had never known him to single someone out like that before. Or since, for that matter, but Steve knows how to pick them.

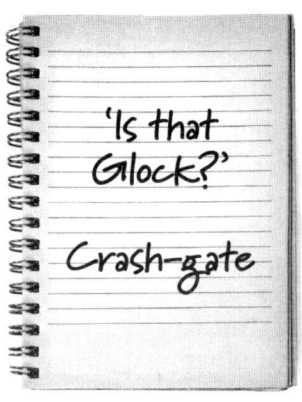

Chapter 12

A Fifth and a Fix

Sports commentators are a talented bunch. What makes a great commentator? I don't think there's a formula, but one important skill is the ability to come out with memorable lines, delivered completely off the cuff in the moment, and if you're lucky, come to be inextricably linked to the sport in question.

'Some people are on the pitch. They think it's all over. It is now!' was a line of genius from Kenneth Wolstenholme in the closing moments of the 1966 World Cup Final. In F1, Murray Walker had a gift for the right line at the right time. 'And colossally, that's Mansell,' when Nigel had his puncture in Adelaide in 1986, or 'I've got to stop because I've got a lump in my throat,' voicing the feelings of a nation when Damon Hill won the world championship in Japan a decade later. More recently, David Croft's 'Through goes Hamilton!' at the 2022 British GP was a reactive line judged and delivered to perfection.

However, there was one snippet of race commentary delivered by Martin Brundle on the last lap of the 2008 season that was

109 of Hamilton and Alonso. In the end Fernando had been right. The principle of supporting both drivers ultimately lost McLaren the drivers' title.

What was certainly clear after Spy-gate was that the Alonso-McLaren relationship was over. His contract was cancelled, and after just a year with the team he returned to his former home at Renault, leaving Hamilton clear to mount another championship challenge at McLaren in 2008. What a season. And little did we know, but the following year would see yet more drama surrounding the two men.

handed a staggering $100 million fine (although half was suspended). Mosley's view at the time was that looking back on the story 20 years hence, history would probably show that the FIA had been, if anything, too lenient on McLaren, and that not only should they have thrown Hamilton and Alonso out of the 2007 drivers' world championship, but they should have thrown the team out of the 2008 championship as well, because the information gleaned could have been used on the following year's car. McLaren would then have been able to start 2009 cleanly.

What complicated the picture was the well-known, long-running personality clash between Max Mosley and Ron Dennis, something Max talked about when the subject of the $100 million fine came up in Michael Shevloff's 2020 documentary *Mosley: It's Complicated*. Dennis always felt the aristocratic Mosley discriminated against him because of his humble family background and the fact he started in F1 as a mechanic. Mosley said that what really annoyed him about Spy-gate was that Dennis hadn't been straight with him on who in McLaren knew what and when.

In the fallout after Spy-gate McLaren had its shot at the 2007 constructors' title taken away, a championship it would have won. The team then contrived to lose the drivers' title as well. At the penultimate race, in Shanghai, Lewis Hamilton skated into a gravel trap at the pit entry having been kept out too long on old, wet tyres, which allowed Räikkönen to win the Chinese GP. This put the Finn up against the McLaren drivers in a three-way fight at the final race of the season in Brazil. Against the odds and with the help of Ferrari teammate Felipe Massa, Räikkönen got the job done, and clinched the world championship with 110 points to the

In any case, it turned out Max Mosley already knew about the emails – Bernie Ecclestone had told him about them (it was presumed Bernie's information had come from Flavio Briatore, Alonso's manager and confidant).

A much more detailed investigation than the first was then launched by the FIA. It confirmed the existence of the emails between Coughlan and McLaren test driver Pedro de la Rosa, and then between De la Rosa and Alonso, talking about such things as what gas Ferrari was using to inflate its tyres, and the F2007's weight distribution and ride heights – the sort of information that could be very useful for a rival team like McLaren.

As we covered the unfolding story on ITV F1, I became the 'Spy-gate' correspondent, updating the saga with features each race weekend. It was an exhilarating period as more information emerged, each snippet more incredible than the last. I suppose, like the frog in the pot of water, I didn't realize at the time what a big story it was becoming, because from my point of view it was new revelations and surprises, week after week. What frustrated me was that a lot of people in the paddock quickly tired of the story, and started dismissing it in terms of 'Oh, it's just F1 politics.' But it wasn't just politics, it was about unfair advantages. Ferrari had a highly justified grievance about the fact that its intellectual property had not only ended up in McLaren's hands but might also have been used to make the McLaren quicker.

The result of the FIA's second investigation and the verdict of the World Motor Sport Council came during the Belgian GP weekend in September. The McLaren team was found to be guilty of using and benefitting from Ferrari's IP and was punished by being excluded from the 2007 constructors' championship, and information had not been shared around the factory, and that it hadn't been used to any sporting advantage. This first FIA investigation therefore cleared McLaren of significant wrongdoing because while its chief designer had possession of the stolen information, the FIA could not prove that anything had been used to the team's benefit. Ferrari team principal Jean Todt was furious with the decision and promised to seek a judicial review.

This was all happening at the time of Hamilton and Alonso's pit lane bust-up. According to Ron Dennis, on the Sunday morning after the qualifying incident, Fernando Alonso came into his office in the McLaren motorhome. Alonso was furious that, having been recruited as world champion, he was not being given the advantageous treatment over Hamilton that he believed was his due. Dennis, it's worth noting, has always denied that he had promised Alonso number-one driver status.

As tempers rose, Alonso told Dennis of email documents he possessed that could be damaging to McLaren in their continued 'Spy-gate' investigation. This was the first Dennis knew of emails between Alonso and others at McLaren, which proved that there were more people within McLaren who had been aware of the Ferrari information than had been admitted to the FIA. Dennis called his deputy Martin Whitmarsh into the meeting where, it was alleged, Alonso threatened the McLaren duo that he would go to the FIA with these emails if they didn't do what he wanted. Rather than be dictated to by his driver, in a pre-emptive move Dennis called FIA president Max Mosley to inform him about the new disclosures. Later Alonso's manager told Ron that Fernando was sorry, that he had changed his mind and retracted what he had said. But by then it was too late – the call to Mosley had been made.

that time that something extraordinary happened. Stepney gave Coughlan a 780-page dossier detailing various parts of Ferrari's soon-to-be championship-winning car. Design files, drawings – a copy of what was in effect the 'owner's manual' for the Ferrari F2007. It was a detailed guide to the car and how to run it.

Coughlan said that he took it out of 'engineering curiosity', but somewhat naïvely then asked his wife Trudy to take the documents to his local print shop near the McLaren factory in Surrey to be digitized and copied on to compact discs. This was not a small job – it was almost 800 pages of confidential Ferrari information filling two binders. What the Coughlans couldn't have foreseen was that the manager of the print shop was not only an F1 fan, but a Ferrari fan. Noticing the prancing horse logos on car blueprints, the manager grew suspicious and began to realize the significance of what he'd been given to copy on to disc. Among the information was an email address. Following up on his suspicions that something wasn't quite right, the copy-shop manager sent an email to the address with his concerns. It was none other than Ferrari's then sporting director Stefano Domenicali. I like to imagine that Domenicali's reaction on reading the email was to spit out his morning cappuccino; he certainly took the information seriously – immediately contacting Ferrari's internal security team and the police, who took the matter from there. As this intellectual-property scandal duly erupted, it quickly became known as 'Spy-gate'.

McLaren was investigated by the FIA in an effort to determine to what extent the information in Coughlan's trove had been disseminated within the team. McLaren's response was that only a 'rogue' employee had possession of the documents, that the explain why Lewis said, 'I don't think Fernando has a great excuse for what happened today.'

The broader context for all this, of course, was Fernando's increasing frustration that his role as F1's kingpin was being challenged, and his sense that McLaren's management weren't doing enough to help him in his quest for a third world championship. Meanwhile, there was another story afoot, a story that turned out to be one of the most shocking and dramatic episodes to occur during my time in Formula 1.

In 2007, the Ferrari dream team was changing. Michael Schumacher had retired, Ross Brawn had followed him out of the door, and there was another key player who felt things weren't how they used to be. Nigel Stepney was a British mechanic-turned-team-manager who was known within Ferrari as 'The Enforcer'. He had been brought in by Brawn to help get the Maranello race team into shape, and he performed his role with military-grade efficiency. He was an imposing figure. Some people found him a bit scary, and he certainly had a ruthless streak, but he was extremely effective. He had learned Italian fluently, which helped him gain the respect of the mechanics. Although he was admired by many within Ferrari, he had also been passed over for promotion and felt he wasn't being properly appreciated.

Stepney had a friend at McLaren, chief designer Mike Coughlan. Coughlan had landed a plum job at the team's base in Woking largely off the back of a particularly good car he designed for the Arrows team, the A23. Despite his past success Coughlan found it difficult to flourish at his new team, so he, together with his friend Stepney, decided to offer their joint services as a kind of 'dream team' to the Honda F1 team, who were recruiting. It was around the scrubbed hard tyres, and the countdown, because in the camera shot you can see him looking over to Slade, his engineer, on the pit wall. There was an unlikely theory at the time that he might have been looking over at Fabrizio Borra, waiting for some kind of hand gesture signalling the perfect time to go, allowing him time to start his own lap but denying Hamilton the opportunity to do his. This falls down over the fact that there's no way that Alonso would have been able to see Borra, and even if he had, Borra wouldn't have been able to count the exact seconds. And, anyway, how would the two have known to pre-plan that before the session?

To this day, Alonso insists that his primary motivation was to follow the countdown and discuss tyres with his engineer over the radio, and not to stitch up Lewis. That there could have been so much doubt as to what really happened must seem surprising to a contemporary audience used to hearing full, unedited team radio exchanges between driver and engineer, but this was at a time when team radio was a closely guarded secret, digitally encrypted and not open to TV broadcasters (unlike today, where the regulations stipulate it must be accessible). I think Fernando didn't care that Lewis was behind him. I think he would have been perfectly happy to have a discussion with Slade about his tyres even at such an unusual and untimely moment, notwithstanding the fact that it might mean Hamilton struggled to get his lap in. If Alonso had done it deliberately, the mental agility required to have counted to the second precisely how long there was in the session and judge how long he needed to remain stationary to run Hamilton out of time, but not himself, would have been extraordinary. But it is possible that Alonso was thinking, 'Well, he screwed me over earlier on, so I'm quite at liberty to screw him over now.' And that would calculation'. What Fernando didn't explain, but which later emerged, was that he had been having an argument on the radio with his engineer about why he'd been given used, hard tyres for his last run, rather than the quicker new soft tyres.

This was all just about plausible, but the matter was far from over. Alonso, Hamilton, Dennis and Ryan were called to talk to the FIA stewards on Saturday afternoon to explain themselves, in an unusual investigation for an intra-team dispute. Some hours later the stewards showed that they weren't buying Alonso's explanation either, and found him guilty of an act 'prejudicial to the interests of the sport or competition.' He was demoted five places to sixth on the grid, and Hamilton inherited pole.

Like the stewards, most people inside F1 felt sure that it had been a bit of gamesmanship from Fernando. His former Renault engineer Pat Symonds even used that word when I spoke to him on Sunday. On our pre-race show we analysed the stewards' judgement that it had been a deliberate ploy by Alonso. In what had become his regular post-qualifying interview with Steve Rider, Hamilton said that he didn't think Fernando had a great excuse for what he did. Ex-driver and ITV pundit Mark Blundell echoed another popular view in the paddock – even if Fernando had stitched Lewis up deliberately, it was a team-on-team incident. No other team was disadvantaged, so why did the stewards get involved at all?

The feature I made covering the story on race day opened with 'McLaren say this is more a case of cock-up than stitch-up.' Looked at that way (and the stewards had acknowledged the role McLaren had played in the mess, docking their constructors' championship points for the weekend), I'm willing to believe Alonso's explanation that he was waiting while he argued about why he had been given it from there.' I followed up with a second question, but he wasn't budging. As a former racer, co-commentator Damon Hill was partly on Alonso's side: 'That's sport. That was tactics and timed to perfection,' he said over commentary. 'Alonso really, I'm afraid, stuffed it to Lewis.' 'I feel very strongly,' he added, 'that racing drivers should be allowed to race. Alonso did a little bit of a naughty thing there, it has to be said, but it was good tactics.' It was an observation borne of experience; Hill having been on the receiving end of a few 'naughty things' during his own time driving in F1.

Louise Goodman was covering Hamilton post-qualifying, so I headed to interview Fernando. The explanation he gave me that afternoon was that he could see Pete Vale telling him to go, but he was actually listening to a different count from his race engineer Mark Slade. 'We wait for the countdown in the radio, and we go,' said Fernando. 'Sometimes it's 10 seconds, sometimes 45 seconds, like the first stop of today. Sometimes 10 or 15, like the second. But I think the calculation was wrong, because my teammate didn't complete the lap and I crossed the line by two or three seconds. So it was really tight. These things unfortunately happened today to us.'

When I asked why he hadn't responded to the lollipop going up, Fernando had a ready explanation: 'Sometimes the mechanics, when they see another car [waiting] behind, they try to change the tyres and go. But I have the radio, 5-4-3-2-1, so I wait for the zero.' OK, I thought, but his team boss wasn't buying that. 'It's unfortunate that some people will jump to the conclusion that you did it deliberately,' I countered, to see how he'd react. 'I know,' replied Fernando, 'because I think the TV shows Ron not very happy, but I think he's not happy with the engineers, as they do the mechanic and lollipop man Pete Vale to re-enter a clear position on track. Meanwhile, Hamilton arrived behind Alonso and had to wait for his tyre change. Alonso was held for about 12 seconds, before Vale lifted the lollipop and told him to go, but Fernando sat there, not going anywhere. By the time he finally moved off and Hamilton could drive forward into the McLaren pit box for his new tyres there was only one minute and 25 seconds of the session remaining. An 'out' lap took one minute 30 seconds. It had been made impossible for Hamilton to get round in time to start his final lap, and thus he was unable to improve on his qualifying time. The session ended with Fernando on pole, and Lewis in second place.

Had Fernando deliberately screwed over Hamilton by making sure the time ran out and he couldn't get his lap in? Ron Dennis certainly thought so. The McLaren boss threw his headphones across the pit wall desk and marched straight to Alonso's physiotherapist Fabrizio Borra, who doubled up as the pit board man for Alonso when the cars were running on track. Borra was clearly shocked by Dennis's intervention, putting his hands up in a 'don't shoot me' gesture only for Ron to march him firmly down to the parc fermé area at the pit entrance, where Dennis knew Alonso and Hamilton would be shortly arriving.

Egged on by James Allen, avidly following events in the commentary box and, as my pit lane predecessor, frustrated not to be able to get in there and ask the questions himself, I dived in for a live interview with Ron, matching his pace as he strode along and ignoring the fact that he clearly didn't want to talk to me: 'What happened there?' Ron was visibly seething, and with his hand still firmly on Borra's shoulder said flatly, without slackening his pace or meeting my eye, 'We'll discuss it later within the team, and we'll sort stops you saying anything about our impending pit stops, that will be better for us.'

I thought about it for a beat before agreeing with a condition of my own that I be allowed to leave via the back of the garage and re-enter if there was a big story at another team that I had to follow up. 'OK, but it's not a bloody revolving door, mate,' said Ryan. I chuckled. The deal was done, and from then on there was a place for me in the far right-hand corner of the McLaren garage. The mechanics even offered me cold drinks at hot races! Thanks to that arrangement I had front-row access to what unfolded in many a key moment in F1 and in particular that explosive Hungarian qualifying session.

Hamilton had been told that when he and Alonso left the pit lane, he should allow Alonso to go in front of him in order that he could burn off some unwanted fuel. At the time, the rules made cars carry the fuel they needed for their first race stint in qualifying, but they could burn off some of this fuel before their qualifying lap because it would get topped up again before the race. However, Kimi Räikkönen came out of the pits at the same time, and in the moment Hamilton reasoned that it would be better for both McLarens that the Ferrari not overtake, so he ignored the instruction. All Fernando knew was that he was slower on that lap because Lewis hadn't done what the team had asked and allowed Fernando to burn off some fuel, meaning his car was heavier and therefore slower. He was furious but managed to set provisional pole on his next run.

With only two minutes and 15 seconds left before the end of the session, Alonso was fastest. He came in first, his tyres were changed, and then he was given a visual countdown by the chief walkways between the garages during a race, a useful spot I still use today, from where I could see the McLaren mechanics getting ready to receive one of their cars. James Allen threw down to me and I did a report along the lines of, 'McLaren are preparing themselves, they're getting ready for a pit stop, so this is the time for Ferrari to react.' All fairly standard stuff. After the race Ryan marched up to me. 'What the hell were you doing?' he demanded. 'You gave away information to Ferrari by saying that we were going to pit one of our drivers.' 'Well, I was just standing in the gap there,' I said. 'I could see your mechanics were getting ready. It's not difficult. If I could see it, Ferrari could see it too.' 'Well I'd rather you didn't do that,' he snapped. I didn't back down: 'Why shouldn't I? It's a good line.' Ryan grumbled in that way I had become familiar with, but then said something I didn't expect.

'Alright,' he stuck his hands on his hips, 'I'm going to offer you a deal. I will allow you to stand in the corner of our garage during every race and qualifying session. You will be the only non-McLaren person there. I will even make a little spot for you between the partitions, so that you can be behind the red line, but see everything you need to. But this way you will see stuff in the garage that is privileged information. The deal is, you can report on anything that you would have been able to see from your spot between the garages, but you will not broadcast any information that you have gleaned through being in this privileged position in our garage that might compromise our race operation. And in return you'll have a spot there to talk about anything outside of that.' I knew instantly I'd be able to see more and understand more about the race from inside the McLaren garage, even if I wasn't able to report all of it. The upside for Ryan was revealed in his next words to me, 'If this cars. Alonso appreciated Ron's position, but when he saw Hamilton starting to disobey team instructions, that was when things really started to fray. The most dramatic example was in qualifying for the 2007 Hungarian Grand Prix.

I was watching the session from a corner of the McLaren garage thanks to a longstanding deal I had with McLaren's then sporting director, Dave Ryan. A deal, you might wonder? Let me explain. In all my years in F1, I have found only one or two people more intimidating than Dave Ryan, a New Zealander who joined McLaren in the 1970s. One of my first tasks at ITV Sport in February 1997 was to connect our camera crew up with him at a Silverstone test in order that we could get some shots of David Coulthard for our programme titles. Familiar with Ryan from TV and the Ayrton Senna videos I'd grown up watching, I spotted him straight away, and enthusiastically approached as he emerged from the McLaren race truck. What followed can best be described as 'character-building' as Ryan proceeded to tear strips off me for wearing a North Face puffa jacket (which I had donned as a precaution against the famous Silverstone wind), rather than some (non-existent, I would take a second here to note) ITV Sport-branded uniform. He told me that I looked 'scruffy', 'unprofessional' and had 'failed to make a good first impression'. I tried to lighten the mood by assuring him that this was just our winter testing apparel, and we'd all be thoroughly logo-ed up in ITV F1 kit by the time of the first race. He muttered under his breath, told me where to find Coulthard, and stalked off.

By necessity we maintained a professional relationship over the following years, but it was another argument that gained me access to the McLaren garage. I was standing in one of the pit-lane young teammate and growing pretty annoyed at McLaren for not, as he saw it, helping him maximize his points. Hamilton was certainly aware of the situation, acknowledging later in the year, 'Nobody expected me to be as competitive as I am, leading the world championship, and having the current world champion chasing me.'

Any F1 newcomer who found themselves leading the championship in their rookie season, albeit driving the grid's fastest car, would have been a highly noteworthy story. As the UK's free-to-air broadcaster it was clear to us at ITV that we had a major new British sporting star performing every race week in our F1 coverage, someone our viewers were keen to know more about, and as a result we closely followed Hamilton's exploits.

After qualifying at most races, Steve Rider would do a sit-down interview with Lewis, which McLaren were keen to facilitate because it gave Vodafone and their other sponsors a generous amount of screen time. These days it's unimaginable that Lewis would do a 15-minute one-to-one interview with a broadcaster after each qualifying session, but as a rookie, he didn't know any different – the team wanted him to do it, therefore he obliged. And as we'd find out as the season went on, Rider's calm, reassuring manner allowed Lewis to feel comfortable enough that he revealed insightful details about what was going on at McLaren at the time.

We were of course equally focused on Fernando Alonso's role in the title fight, and could understand his conviction that he should be prioritized as team leader to contend for the drivers' title. However, his boss Ron Dennis had just as strong a resolve. Unlike Ferrari during the Schumacher era, one of the many principles Ron was committed to was that of equality between the two McLaren

British-based media representatives were told to report to Farnborough Airport that morning, and were ushered on to chartered jets to be flown to Valencia and back for the launch day. I sat with other F1 journalists admiring the 'Hemisfèric' planetarium and ooh-ing and aah-ing at the fireworks, while a series of acrobats, stilt walkers and break dancers entertained us all. Eventually out walked Alonso and Hamilton, and the new car was unveiled. It looked fantastic in its chrome and bright 'rocket' red livery and was, aerodynamically, very detailed. Everything was going swimmingly – Fernando spoke like someone who justifiably saw McLaren as his team to lead, and as reigning world champion he assumed that he would be afforded some level of seniority and preference in the way they went racing.

Alonso didn't have to wait long to find out that he wasn't going to get it. At the first race in Australia, Hamilton couldn't have announced his intentions more clearly, overtaking his more experienced teammate off the start line. Fernando did then pass him with pit-stop strategy, and they ultimately finished second and third, behind Kimi Räikkönen's Ferrari. However, it was obvious to everyone that Lewis had not come prepared to be a number two supporting act to Fernando. He was there to race and to win.

Alonso scored victories for McLaren in Malaysia and Monaco, while Räikkönen's Ferrari teammate Felipe Massa triumphed in Bahrain and Barcelona. But at every one of the first five races of the season, Hamilton was on the podium logging points. Lewis scored his maiden victory at round six in Canada, and followed up immediately with another in the USA. He took the lead of the world championship, while Alonso had a couple of poor results in Canada and France, and found himself lagging behind his been certain exactly what Ron meant, but he wanted to sound professional, so he just replied, 'OK, Ron, thanks very much'. What he hadn't fully realized was that Ron had decided that his protégé was indeed ready, and that Hamilton would be racing for McLaren in 2007. The team devised an extensive winter test programme for him, with way more mileage than young drivers can log these days under the current regulations.

From Fernando Alonso's point of view, Hamilton's appointment was something to take note of, but he didn't see it as a threat. My sense was he thought, 'Ah, a rookie alongside me, that's fine. He's not going to be a problem.' Alonso was at the height of his powers. He'd won two world championships, had signed a contract with McLaren for very much more money than he had been getting at Renault, and was set to be the star driver of his new team. What I also remember noticing at the time was how Alonso threw himself into what he thought was the McLaren way. He had his hair cut short, very neat and tidy, was clean-shaven every day, and unveiled a new crash helmet design which was predominantly silver and black. In effect he 'McLaren-ized' himself. Growing up, he had shared his father's admiration for Ayrton Senna and he'd always had a soft spot for the team. His dad had even built him a little pedal kart in the famous red and white Marlboro McLaren colours. Alonso made it clear how it was a dream come true for him to race for McLaren, and the team were equally enthusiastic about him in return.

One example of that was the choice of a Spanish venue for the team's car launch, the architectural marvel that is the City of Arts and Sciences in Valencia. McLaren's new title sponsor, Vodafone, was keen to make a splash, and money seemed to be no object.

Lewis's self-confidence was growing week by week. He'd had a breakthrough about a month earlier, when, following a tricky start to the season, he'd dominated both GP2 races at the Nürburgring. The Monaco win confirmed his form. There was a lovely moment just after Brundle's interview when Sir Stirling Moss came over to Lewis to say hello and congratulate him on his victory the day before. The two would get to know each other well over the coming years, with Moss often talking about how he admired Hamilton's racing skills.

As 2006 progressed it became less of a question of if Hamilton would graduate to F1, but more when, and with which team – specifically whether he was ready to be a full McLaren F1 driver. 'I don't expect to jump straight into a McLaren,' Lewis had said. 'I would have thought I would go into one of the lower teams, but we'll just have to wait and see.' The problem with that plan was McLaren didn't have any friendly teams lower down the grid that they could loan Lewis out to for a single season. As he kept winning in GP2, Ron Dennis and Martin Whitmarsh grew increasingly convinced that they had Alonso's teammate right there, ready to go. Although they didn't rush to tell Hamilton just yet. When I interviewed him at the start of the Turkish GP weekend in August, Lewis was clearly none the wiser, asking whether I thought McLaren were seriously looking at anyone else for Alonso's teammate, because as he was aware, they certainly had other options.

It was on the grid of the Italian GP two weeks later, after Hamilton had secured the GP2 title and his own racing season was over, that Dennis finally informed Lewis of his decision. 'I'm going to give you a chance,' he put it, simply. A year later in an ITV interview with Steve Rider, Lewis admitted that he hadn't as filling in his knowledge about the car's performance, any information that might help his career.

As that season went on, and Lewis started winning consistently, there was a sense of excitement whenever he was on the track. So much so that the GP2 races, often ignored in the F1 paddock, started to become essential viewing in team motorhomes – especially at McLaren. Ron Dennis and Mercedes motorsport chief Norbert Haug would sit downstairs in one of the glass-walled offices of their motorhome watching the races enthusiastically, to the obvious irritation of McLaren F1 drivers Kimi Räikkönen and Juan Pablo Montoya as they passed behind to get to their driver rooms.

In Monaco, Lewis appeared on the Grand Prix grid, having won that weekend's GP2 race in some style. Strange as it might seem today, Lewis didn't routinely get an F1 paddock pass, never mind grid access. He had been invited on as a result of his win, but he looked a bit self-conscious as he stood behind Räikkönen's car. Martin Brundle had just finished interviewing the Duchess of York, Sarah Ferguson, who had revealed that rather than either of the drivers she was 'a great supporter of Ron Dennis'. Martin then turned to find Lewis standing nearby.

> Martin: 'Lewis, do you think you might be standing here next year on the grid?'
> Lewis: 'Hopefully, it's a fantastic feeling to be here, I just hope I can sit there next year.'
> Martin: 'OK – and you think you'll be fully ready for it?'
> Lewis: 'I think so...'

Lewis Hamilton was a McLaren protégé and was still an F3 driver when Alonso first signed for McLaren in December 2005. Many observers of the junior categories had identified Hamilton as the next hot prospect and were keen to see what he did on his graduation to GP2, the next step up the ladder, in 2006. Possibly because of how promising Hamilton looked, and possibly as a favour to Bernie Ecclestone, who was keen to raise the profile and popularity of the GP2 series, ITV started covering it with a standalone programme, and asked me and Louise Goodman to present it.

Our GP2 coverage tended to be planned after we'd had our discussions about the F1 stories of the weekend. At the end of our Thursday morning meetings at European races with GP2 on the bill, we'd often be told that we had an interview with Hamilton in the support-race paddock. Generally Louise and I would take it in turns. We'd find a stack of tyres to sit on near his ART team's race truck and interview Lewis about how his season was going. The GP2 championship had quickly developed into a fight between him, a rookie, and the more experienced Nelson Piquet Jr. Hamilton came across as pretty shy back then, and even in those days clearly regarded interviews as a bit of a burden that he wished he didn't have to do. He was wary of saying the wrong thing with McLaren personnel listening, but he was also resigned to the fact that it was a necessary part of the job. On our side, sensing that, we tried to make interviews as enjoyable and efficient as possible, but it was when the cameras stopped recording that Lewis would perk up and grill either me or Louise for information about what was going on at McLaren, what we thought their thinking was on drivers and who else they were looking at alongside Alonso, as well

Chapter 11

From Ron to Ruin

Sometimes in F1, like the parable of the frog in the boiling pot of water, it's easy not to notice that significant events are happening around you. So much happens every day of every race weekend, it can be hard to see beyond details that feel like the continuation of ongoing stories. However, the transfer of eras in F1 between 2006 and 2007 was the kind of immediate event that would have that frog hopping right out of the pot.

Michael Schumacher was gone – manoeuvred into retirement, as we'd later discover, by Ferrari president Luca di Montezemolo – and for a few months at least, the Fernando Alonso era was at its peak. At the end of 2006, Alonso was a double world champion, and for 2007 he joined McLaren, the team of his hero Ayrton Senna, where his wish and expectation were to match the Brazilian legend's tally of three world titles. Unfortunately for Alonso the man who would dominate the next era of F1, and who happened to be his new teammate, had other ideas.

from all the key players and had the information to explain what was going to happen and why. The US Grand Prix lasted two more years at Indianapolis before falling off the calendar, while Michelin withdrew from F1 at the end of 2006, with Bridgestone becoming the sole supplier until Pirelli took over in 2011. Michelin has not subsequently been interested in returning to Formula 1.

THE SIX-CAR RACE

their cups of beer around.' Implicit in his tone was 'What have you stupid Europeans done here?'

Meanwhile, Schumacher beat Barrichello to win the race. The only tension was over which Jordan driver was going to be on the podium, but even that wasn't particularly close, the likeable Portuguese Tiago Monteiro beating teammate Narain Karthikeyan, who himself became the first Indian driver ever to score points in F1. The Minardis finished fifth and sixth, an outcome that the team could usually only dream about. However, none of it meant much to the fans, who made their displeasure clear, and the boos could be heard from the paddock.

Towards the end of the post-race part of the programme Jim Rosenthal had to do a promo for the upcoming *Coronation Street* episode. '*Coronation Street* is coming right up for you, more complications for Steve and Tracy. That is a soap opera worth watching. We had a bit of a soap opera here as well . . .' Jim ended the programme by saying, 'You've seen an F1 fiasco in peak time, and like David Coulthard I feel sick and embarrassed to my stomach. Circumstances beyond our control. We can only say sorry. Good night.'

It was quite strong stuff from Jim, but he was keenly conscious of the feelings of the viewers. That's what the presenter is there for – they need to ask the questions that the viewer wants answered, and to walk the viewer through events as they unfolded. Nobody else had offered an apology. Jim thought the viewers deserved one.

We went away from that race with mixed feelings. Frustrated, bemused and pretty disappointed, yes, but also content with the fact that as professionals we had stayed on top of the story, heard with a huge empty space between them. I remember watching the start of this six-car race, just staring at the monitor, not quite believing what I was seeing. In retrospect, everything that happened on Saturday night and Sunday morning had led inexorably to this point. The Michelin cars couldn't race without a chicane and a chicane couldn't be made.

The race was interesting for about a lap and a half, watching Schumacher get away ahead of Barrichello after an early tussle. On lap two, I realized that there wasn't going to be anything worth reporting on from the pits, so I headed into the paddock. Louise and I grabbed a few interviews with some of the Michelin drivers and team bosses expressing their disappointment with the outcome. And then it occurred to me that I should get out into the public areas to see what was going on there. It was the first time I'd done this in the middle of a race, but instinct told me that was the place I needed to be. Reassured by our tech people that my radio camera and microphone would work at that distance, off I went through the tunnel and out to the back of the grandstands.

There were many fans from around the world – and they were all confused. They didn't really know what was going on, or why there were only three teams racing. This was before the days of social media and internet on phones, so half my time was spent telling them the whole sorry story.

Some fans were shouting for refunds; others were starting to leave the grandstands. The bit I remember best was the strangest mid-race interview I'd ever done – with an Indianapolis police officer. He said, 'I don't know what's going on, but it's starting to get a bit sketchy down here. We've got a lot of angry people throwing

THE SIX-CAR RACE

big-picture questions about the impact on F1 in America and the future of Michelin in the sport. Bernie replied flatly: 'Not good in both cases.' Martin ended by asking, 'Surely we just have to have a sensible pill and say, "OK, this is the situation, let's take a sensible solution and go motor racing."' 'Tell me where to buy the pills,' said Bernie.

Sadly, the sensible pill never appeared. We could hardly believe what was about to happen. We still had some hope that at the last minute something was going to change. After all, everyone was on the grid. Surely they wouldn't be doing that if they were just going to head back into the pits? Even on the formation lap David Coulthard came on the radio to his Red Bull engineers: 'If it comes down to the drivers, I want to race.'

The cars were halfway around the formation lap when I noticed McLaren mechanics folding up all the chairs they had carefully laid out in the garage. I called through to our editor Gerard Lane, 'I've got a line from down here!' James Allen said, 'We don't know what's going to happen. Ted, do you have any more information?' 'James, I can see Renault and McLaren, they're both clearing two F1 car-sized spaces in the garage for their drivers to come in and retire.' There was also a radio message to Fernando Alonso from his Renault engineer Rod Nelson, who said, 'OK mate, you know what the plan is for the start, straight into the pits please.' Perhaps that was intended to discourage the world championship leader from going rogue!

Led by pole-sitter Trulli, all the Michelin runners peeled into the pit lane, leaving the six Bridgestone drivers to go the grid – the two Ferraris of Michael Schumacher and Rubens Barrichello in fifth and seventh spots, and the Jordans and Minardis at the back,

And that's the presenter's skill again. They need to know what's coming up while listening to the interview being played in, in order to be able to react to it and make more sense of it for the viewer. The hard thing about ripping up the running order and following where things went was that we never really knew where the story was going to go.

The drivers' parade took place, and the frantic meetings in the paddock offices continued. And then as the opening of the pit lane approached the drivers got ready to get in their cars. The confusing element for us in the pit lane was that as a result of all those interviews we were pretty certain that the Michelin runners would not be able to race. All the plans had failed, all the options had been exhausted. It would be a six-car race with the Ferraris, Jordans and Minardis. But when the pit lane opened, all the cars went to the grid. What we didn't know (not having access to the teams' contracts with Formula 1 and the FIA) was that the Michelin drivers had been told that legally, they had to drive to the grid to fulfil their team's contractual obligation to 'participate' in the event. They would then have to come into the pits and retire at the end of the formation lap.

This was going to hurt. Being six hours behind UK time, we were in a peak TV slot in the UK on Sunday evening, ahead of long-running British television soap opera, *Coronation Street*, so we had to explain to one of our biggest audiences of the year that they would be watching a six-car race. Martin did a brilliant grid walk. By now he knew from sources that the plan was for the Michelin teams not to race, despite there being no announcement of any kind. He pulled no punches in explaining what was likely to happen. He gave Bernie Ecclestone a good grilling, asking him

THE SIX-CAR RACE

Michelin teams weren't going to race, or they would run their own race and inevitably finish outside the points. The Bridgestone teams had equipment that wasn't going to fail. Ross Brawn made a clear point about how it would be the same with any other kind of component on the car. A team might come to a race knowing that their brakes weren't going to work, or the engine wasn't going to last beyond 10 laps, and tyres were no different. The decision for the Michelin teams was either not to take part, or to drive until the tyres failed, and then retire from the race.

As the Grand Prix approached, the meetings became increasingly frantic. There wasn't time for secrecy anymore, the paddock offices had huge windows, and from the outside it was easy to see everything that was happening. It was extremely entertaining to watch the team bosses arguing with each other – Ron Dennis shaking his head, Flavio Briatore waving his arms around, the drivers just standing there, looking like spare parts in this whole discussion, bemused, not knowing what was going on.

Meanwhile, we had a whole running order full of pre-recorded features lined up for our race show on ITV, including one that I had done on how F1's popularity in the USA was really picking up. That was the first piece to get dropped. And then one by one more features bit the dust. The running order was literally ripped up, replaced by Jim Rosenthal and Mark Blundell's analysis, and live interviews from Louise Goodman, me and Martin Brundle coming in from the paddock, as we tried to follow the unfolding story and keep viewers up-to-date with the drama.

I remember very well Jim's last instructions to our director Simon Dukes and editor Gerard Lane – keep the communication clear, keep it simple, and keep telling me where we're going next.

past the coffee and donut stands, anticipating an exciting race. Fans had travelled from as far as Colombia to see their hero Juan Pablo Montoya compete, and from across America and Europe, to get a feel for Formula 1 at the home of the Indianapolis 500, the USA's most famous race.

Aware discussions were still going on to try and find a solution to the Michelin problem, we had a quick production meeting, before Louise Goodman and I went into the paddock and started interviewing anyone we could find, to find out what was really going on. This was the moment Jim Rosenthal really came into his own. As the presenter, he knew how important it was for him to hold the whole programme together, processing that stringy cheese into mozzarella. So, he made a point of listening to all the interviews that Louise and I were getting in the paddock throughout the morning, with team bosses like Eddie Jordan and Minardi's Paul Stoddart, both Bridgestone runners, and McLaren's Martin Whitmarsh, whose cars were on Michelin. I remember interviewing David Coulthard on his way to the drivers' parade, and Mark Webber on his way back from it. All Michelin drivers were quite clear that they wanted to race, but that the chicane was the only realistic solution.

Meanwhile Louise got the other point of view. Ferrari was only too ready to race around the circuit the way it was. The other Bridgestone runners, Jordan and Minardi, were more open than Ferrari to finding a compromise solution. Yet Ferrari's position was not unreasonable. 'This has nothing to do with us, we'll leave it to the FIA' Jean Todt stated, while knowing full well that the FIA weren't going to allow any significant changes to the circuit. Every potential outcome was going to be beneficial for Ferrari – either the

THE SIX-CAR RACE

Todt might have been feeling somewhat victimized by the sudden 'one race, one set of tyres' rule and wasn't in any kind of mood to give the Michelin teams a free pass.

FIA president Max Mosley wasn't at the race, but he was being kept closely informed by race director Charlie Whiting about events and the chicane discussions. Mosley had a brilliant mind, which came with a mischievous streak, and when I interviewed him about the Indianapolis saga at the next race in France, he referred to the chicane off-camera as 'the chicken'. I never found out why, but I suspect he was referring to the affected teams 'chickening out' by not racing. Nevertheless, the FIA were perfectly within their rights to reject the chicane idea. There are strict rules concerning the approval and licensing of circuits for safety reasons, and everything must be homologated – legally signed off – by the FIA before the race weekend. Another factor was that the cars hadn't been fitted with gears suitable for a sudden decrease in speed. They were geared to pick up speed through the last proper corner and then go flat-out around Turn 13 and down the main straight.

Whiting's suggestion in turn was that the Michelin teams should simply decrease speed around Turn 13 in order to protect their tyres. He was willing to allow a white line to be painted around the corner – the six Bridgestone cars would be allowed to run at normal pace above it, and the Michelin cars would run below it with their speeds monitored by a radar gun. There would be, in effect, two parallel races. This was, at least, a workable if not desirable solution, but everyone went to bed on Saturday evening not knowing what tomorrow would bring.

Sunday morning at Indianapolis dawned bright and breezy. The 100,000-strong crowd of spectators made their way into the circuit, and therefore a quick lap time while not compromising your race by only having enough fuel to do a few laps, forcing an early pit stop while others with more fuel on board overtook you.

We expected the qualifying battle to be between title contenders Fernando Alonso and Kimi Räikkönen. Instead Jarno Trulli put his Toyota on pole position. The immediate assumption in the pit lane was that Toyota was trying to save face after its two practice incidents by running Trulli light, winning him pole. What we didn't realize at the time was that Trulli's engineers had indeed run him very light on fuel because they knew that their cars would either need to pit after a few laps or, worse still, would not be competing in the Grand Prix at all.

Following some more consideration and analysis after qualifying, Michelin's management raised the stakes. They told the FIA that they would not allow their teams to race around the circuit as it was, even if they made four pit stops. If the FIA wanted there to be a Grand Prix, stated Michelin, they would have to change the circuit's layout to slow the cars' entry and exit speeds at Turn 13. The easiest way to do this would be to paint new lines on the track and install a few bollards in order to create a tight chicane through which the drivers would have to pass at reduced speed.

Asking the FIA to change the track layout and create a new chicane just because one tyre manufacturer had supplied deficient material was unprecedented and unfair, a point that Bridgestone and Ferrari made vigorously. Bridgestone tyres were fine through the fast Turn 13, the loads causing no problems. Clearly, Ferrari also saw this as an opportunity to score some valuable points during what had been a difficult season, and to get themselves back into the championship hunt. It's also fair to say that Ferrari boss Jean

THE SIX-CAR RACE

that the sheer forces on the tyre on the banked Turn 13, combined with the way their tyres were made, were effectively rendering their product unreliable. Worse still, there was nothing that could be done to mitigate it.

On Saturday morning we had a production meeting. By then a few of us had heard from the teams that Michelin was concerned about the double tyre failures on the Toyotas. I remember interviewing Pierre Dupasquier, the charismatic Michelin competitions boss, and Nick Shorrock, who was the company's top engineer, but neither of them had let on that this was a problem that wasn't fixable. They were more upfront with the FIA and warned race director Charlie Whiting that their analysis suggested that the flaws seen in the rear tyres would likely lead to tyre failures after 15 laps at racing speed. The US Grand Prix at Indianapolis was a 73-lap race.

There were no easy solutions. The Michelin-shod cars would either need to change tyres four times in the race, which would look highly unusual and incur penalties for breaking the new 'single set of tyres' rule. Even if that rule was not enforced for one race due to *force majeure*, the consequence would be to create two separate races, between the one-stopping Bridgestone teams and the four-stopping Michelin teams. The only other option was to change the circuit – slowing the cars down into Turn 13 – which would reduce the loads that were damaging the tyres.

The F1 timetable doesn't stop for anything. While discussions continued and letters were going back and forth, we headed into qualifying. In those days you carried the fuel for your first race stint in qualifying, so qualifying as well as possible was a delicate balance, trying to use the absolute minimum of fuel for a light car

In 2005, in a move that would shake the championship up, the FIA introduced a dramatic rule change – drivers were required to use only one set of tyres for the whole race, and pit stops would be for fuel only. Michelin did a much better job of adapting to this new challenge than Bridgestone, who had previously been so good at making the 'sprint' tyres that had allowed Schumacher to run flat-out over short stints. The only major team affected was Ferrari, as the other remaining Bridgestone customers were backmarkers Jordan and Minardi. With Michelin suddenly dominant, the 2005 season quickly developed into a fight between Fernando Alonso of Renault and McLaren's Kimi Räikkönen. When we arrived at Indianapolis in June Schumacher was running fifth in the world championship, and Ferrari hadn't yet won a single race.

The weekend started like any other, but the first sign of trouble came in the first practice session when Toyota's test driver Ricardo Zonta had a spin into the gravel trap. Replays showed that he'd had a left-rear tyre failure, but that could have been caused by debris or any number of things, so there wasn't too much concern. What really got everyone's attention was when, in second practice, Zonta's teammate Ralf Schumacher had a high-speed crash at Turn 13. Indy's banked and extremely fast final corner had been a focus of attention since F1's first race at the venue five years earlier, but this time the TV footage indicated that he too had suffered a left-rear Michelin tyre failure just like Zonta's in the morning session.

Behind the scenes, this was Michelin's worst nightmare. After Friday practice the French company's engineers examined the rear tyres from all their teams, and to their horror, discovered that many of them had flaws in the sidewall – defects that were weakening the structural integrity of the tyre. Michelin suspected

THE SIX-CAR RACE

and many seasons of *Grandstand* to anchoring the last two years of Formula 1 coverage on ITV. Steve Rider presented F1 throughout my formative years when it was screened as part of *Sunday Grandstand* and his reporting from Imola in 1994 after the deaths of Roland Ratzenberger and Ayrton Senna had a huge impact on me. Rider retired midway through 2025 and, for me at least, was the doyen of sports broadcasting. As someone who had worked in print journalism before coming to television, his scripts and ability to find the perfect words were second to none, always matched by his flawless delivery.

But there was one race in particular that showcased better than any other the ability required of an F1 presenter to rip up the running order and wing it, and that was the 2005 US Grand Prix. The man in the chair for what became known as 'the six-car race' was Jim Rosenthal.

It had already been an interesting season. After winning five straight world championships, Michael Schumacher and Ferrari had been tripped up by a single rule change that left the Italian team struggling. This was the era of an intense tyre war between the two tyre suppliers Bridgestone and Michelin. Much of Ferrari's success over the previous seasons had been down to its close relationship with Bridgestone, whereby, as the driver most likely to win races and championships, Schumacher had been able to develop the tyres to his personal preference. Gradually the other big teams such as McLaren, Williams, Renault and Toyota all moved to Michelin, not wanting to be tied to Ferrari's tyre-development direction. The move to Michelin brought them a reasonable amount of success, but the Ferrari–Bridgestone bond was so strong that from 2000 to 2004 Michael won every drivers' championship.

Union coverage via a spell on a trading desk and running 'The Chilli Shack', a street food stall housed in an old fire truck. Simon is so good at what he does, he sometimes memorizes not only all his links (we don't use autocue) but also the whole running order and then hands his print-out to one of the camera crew. You know you're watching a master at work when you see Simon presenting one of our programmes holding just a microphone (and without a rolled-up running order in his back pocket). 'Not bad for a links man' is the general comment that I and our regular camera crew of Pete, Lee, JD and Keiran routinely throw Simon's way after he's successfully piloted a complex programme to its conclusion, sometimes accompanied by a slow hand clap if he's done really well. If he knew how full of admiration we are for his trademark smooth delivery, on-point questions and quick wit, we'd never hear the end of it.

Over the years I've worked with many different show anchors. During my time at the BBC, I saw Jake Humphrey move from presenting kids' TV to being one of the most sought after sports broadcasters in the country. Outside of some experience working on football, presenting Formula 1 on the BBC was the first major anchor role for Humphrey, and he brought a wide-eyed enthusiasm that perfectly countered the 'been there, done that' experience of David Coulthard and Eddie Jordan.

A Norwich lad, Jake was following in the footsteps of Steve Rider, who had performed the F1 presenter role at ITV. Rider's career path had gone from reporting from Norfolk's Snetterton circuit on the Formula 3 battles between Martin Brundle and Ayrton Senna, via the Olympic Games, several World Cups, European Championships, Commonwealth Games, Masters golf

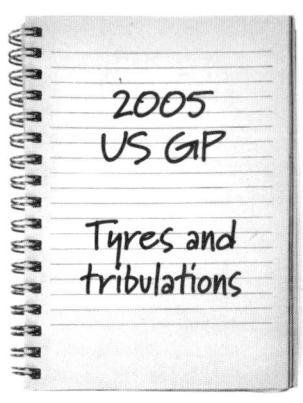

Chapter 10

The Six-Car Race

Reporting is easy. You come on, say your piece and then stop. Presenting the show is much harder. There's a good reason they call the presenter of a news or sport programme the 'anchor'. A live programme is like a swirling body of water, and there are strong currents that sometimes move things from where they're supposed to be. The anchor keeps everything stable. Or, to use more of a cheese-based metaphor (my preferred foodstuff for this sort of thing), being a successful presenter is like being able to take many strands of stringy cheese, process them together in your brain (while talking) and deliver them to the viewer as a perfectly shaped, easily understandable ball of mozzarella.

How do I know presenting is hard? I've tried it. Presenters need to have an incredibly good short-term memory so that they can remember their next link while listening to whatever is going out on-air and the instructions they're being given by the producer. Throughout my years at Sky Simon Lazenby has anchored our programme. He came to F1 from the broadcaster's live Rugby packing. If you're worried about your carry-on not being allowed in the cabin, invest in a soft bag that you will be able to squeeze into the annoying gauges that they have at the gate.

Public transport is always the best and often the quickest way of getting to and from airports and circuits, but if that's not possible then ride-share apps would be my preference for ensuring you won't get ripped off. Take a look at which side of a city the track is located, because there are often better options to stay in other areas. For the Miami GP, for example, it's more convenient to stay in Fort Lauderdale than Miami itself, while San Antonio is an affordable option for Austin. The city of Girona is within reach of the Barcelona circuit, as are many Catalan coastal resorts, while for the Dutch GP the town of Haarlem or Amsterdam itself are much better options than the small town of Zandvoort.

One last tip that I have never been able to do myself is to go with the flow and join in with the locals. No matter who your favourite team or driver, at the Dutch GP get yourself some Max Verstappen merchandise and hang out with the Orange Army for a weekend. Alternatively, feel the Ferrari passion, find some red trousers, and join the *tifosi* at Monza. You'll never be short of a friend to share a pizza with, and you'll have the time of your life. See you trackside!

scenery. Budapest is a beautiful city to visit in the middle of summer, and there's plenty to do in town for any family members less interested than you in F1. Baku's old town is worth discovering if you can find space on a flight to Azerbaijan. And then there's Monza – a late-summer gem of a Grand Prix, where the historic atmosphere is almost palpable, hanging between the trees and the old banking. Spa is impressive due to its sheer size – but bring your raincoat! Logistics are always a major consideration, of course. For many European races camping at or close to the track is a good budget option, and you can combine a race trip with a holiday.

Of the long-haul races if travelling from Europe, those I always recommend are Melbourne, Suzuka, Montreal, Austin, Singapore and my personal favourite, Interlagos in São Paulo, Brazil. Again, the city races are obviously easier logistically, and while Japan and Brazil have their challenges in terms of getting around, they are both fascinating places.

If you are travelling to a F1 race, here are some of my essential tricks of the trade to save time and money. Most importantly, as soon as the F1 calendar comes out, get booking! Most people wait, but you can snap up a bargain on flights and hotels before the operators realize there's going to be a Grand Prix in town. Sign up to the airline's frequent flyer programmes and their email marketing lists – they often have seat sales that you can use to fly to far-flung F1 destinations. It's the same for hotels in the destination city. Pack light – the key to saving time in airports is not to check in any hold luggage. That allows you to check in online, and head straight through security, and you'll also save time at the other end at baggage reclaim. If you're going away for a week or less, the only thing that's stopping you taking hand luggage is self-disciplined media the Sunday evening dash to make flights is often the most stressful part of the weekend, especially after a long and tiring race day. That's why it can sometimes be comforting to know that you're on a charter flight that at the very least shouldn't leave without you if the race has been delayed. Mechanics, meanwhile, usually spend Sunday evening working on the cars and preparing everything for its journey to the next GP, be it by air or road. They will usually fly home, or to the next venue, on Monday. In the case of triple-header races, therefore, it's likely that F1 mechanics won't see their families at home for 22 days straight.

If you're considering going to watch a race, which one should you go to? It's a question I'm often asked. In Europe, number one has to be Monaco. One of the oldest events, and the most prestigious, the sport's most famous street race never disappoints. The late spring weather is usually beautiful, the history and heritage are alluring, and the general glamour of Monaco is intoxicating, which is just as well when you find out how much it costs to buy a drink. Nowhere else allows you to get closer to the cars and the action than Monaco. During the build-up to the weekend, you'll frequently spot drivers, team bosses and other F1 luminaries as you walk around the principality. Monaco is also the only circuit that opens fully for the public to walk around every evening, even through the tunnel. It's no small thrill to stand on the start/finish line or place yourself on the pole-position grid box just a few hours before the Grand Prix starts. It might not be the cheapest race in terms of ticket prices, but being there is a pretty magical experience – and the tip for those on a budget is to stay in Nice and commute in by train.

Otherwise, the festival-like atmosphere of Silverstone is a lot of fun. Austria is always extremely well-organized amid breathtaking smooth enough to sticker with the team logo and the drivers' names and numbers.

Next to be constructed are the hospitality buildings used at European races, usually on the Tuesday before the race. We used to call them motorhomes, because that's exactly what they were, but these days they are elaborate structures that travel on 20 or more trucks and require a crane and crew to erect them and take them down. Each team's building is bespoke and has its own level of complexity. While Ferrari, for example, has a sleek Italian elegance with darkened windows and the iconic red trim, Aston Martin incorporates fine lines and classic leather and wood in the interiors. Once they have been constructed, they are ready for the hospitality staff to start preparing for the hundreds of team members and guests that they will serve over the weekend.

Next in are the mechanics, who will typically arrive on Tuesday, taking over from the setup crew, and start to prepare the two race cars on their perfect garage floor. Engineers arrive on Wednesday afternoon, while drivers will start appearing on Thursday lunchtime ready for their media and briefing commitments. The last members of the F1 race teams to arrive are usually the team bosses. With only a couple of exceptions (Ferrari's Fred Vasseur, McLaren's Andrea Stella), team principals don't feel the need to be at the circuit on the Thursday before track action starts, generally showing up on Friday morning having had a precious extra day in their office back at the factory.

Qualifying and race days come and go, and before the champagne is even dry on their race suits the drivers are whisked off by helicopter or driven under a police escort back to their private jets at the local airport. For the rest of the team members and the sometimes including local contractors, they are responsible for preparing the team garages ahead of the race weekend. Each team has multiple identical sets of non-performance critical equipment, such as garage walls, tyre trolleys and plastic chairs which travel by truck in Europe and by sea freight for the flyaway events. These would have been delivered some time before the race and have been stored ready for the setup crews' arrival.

The garage framework has to be bolted together before the overhead gantries are installed that provide the power, ventilation systems and air lines. The restricted areas in the back of the garage are set up for carbon-fibre fabrication, gearbox servicing and engine preparation, all secret technology that needs to be hidden away from prying eyes. In every garage there's a little pod for the fuel companies to do their petrol and oil analysis, too. There's also a complex network of cables linking the pit wall to the garage, looping in the engineering trucks where meetings are held, and all of it connecting via fibre-optic network back to mission control at the team's factory, from where engineers and strategists are in constant contact with their colleagues at the track. Connections to the FIA data system and F1 TV are also plumbed in.

Teams always want a perfect garage floor – as level as possible, so the cars can be laser scanned accurately, and the smallest nut or bolt can be spotted and won't roll away when a mechanic needs it most. Any imperfections are filled in by the setup crew, and the garage floor is freshly painted at the beginning of the week. It's not just because teams want to look smart – it's so that any fluid leaks will show up easily, or any stray nuts or fasteners can be identified after a rebuild. The surface must also be non-slip but

Yeongam district, close to the shipbuilding port town of Mokpo in the south-west of the country – a train journey or five-hour car ride from the capital. The brand-new circuit itself was fantastic, the facilities were top class, and despite the fact that it was somewhat out of the way, everyone enjoyed going there. Drivers, senior team personnel and the F1 and FIA top brass stayed in the nearby Hyundai Hotel, recently built on a hill with a fine view of the circuit and the neighbouring shipyard owned by the Korean conglomerate.

For the rest of us the only place to stay within an hour of the circuit was downtown Mokpo. There weren't many hotels there, or at least the kind of hotels that we were used to. What there were plenty of, as in many towns throughout South Korea, Japan and China, were establishments known colloquially as love hotels. In many cultures it's unusual for couples to live together before marriage, and while they're still residing in their family homes, it's difficult for them to get some privacy. That's where love hotels come in. The garishly decorated rooms are usually booked by the hour, so when 20 of us TV folk checked in, the receptionist (seated discreetly behind a screen) struggled to process the fact that we would be staying for five whole days and nights. Comparing the garish decor of the rooms (mirrored ceilings, theatrical lighting, no windows) and strange facilities (multiple computers and monitors in each room), the peculiarities of our respective love hotels were the main topic of conversation in the Korean International Circuit paddock. And were the rooms sub-let to young couples while we were at the circuit all day? We had our suspicions.

Assuming the F1 teams have their own hotels sorted, the first people at a circuit on race week are the setup crews, who arrive the weekend before the Grand Prix. Usually a team of five or six,

Drive to Survive in boosting fan attendance in places like Austin and Montreal accommodation is increasingly hard to come by. At the more rural track locations, notably Silverstone, Spielberg and Spa, finding somewhere to stay within easy reach of the circuit can be challenging. For the first few years that F1 returned to Austria, we couldn't find anywhere to stay less than 45 minutes' drive from the track, so our production team were split between some lovely guest houses in the beautiful town of Murau, which was located next to the river Mur and had its own brewery. It felt like a true home from home as the charming owner of our *Gasthof* cooked us something delicious every night, although every dish included asparagus, for reasons unknown.

In recent years many F1 drivers have made their lives easier by staying in huge and luxurious motorhomes at the European races. They don't have to commute to and from hotels, and thus avoid traffic, and they can stay later at the track for evening briefings with engineers. The drivers hire people to maintain these giant RVs and to drive them from track to track, staying in a shared compound. Sometimes this is within the confines of the circuit, or a scooter ride away if there's no space at the venue, but what's always true is that for a few days it is probably the world's most exclusive campsite, with ultra-tight security on the gate to ensure that they are not beleaguered by fans.

Surprisingly tricky in terms of accommodation was the Korean GP, which was held between 2010 and 2013 before it was removed from the calendar for financial reasons. You might think that Seoul would be the ideal location for an F1 race, and Bernie Ecclestone had been keen for the Grand Prix to be hosted there. However, the group financing the race had their own preference, insisting on the circuits they are expected to walk into the paddock in their race-team kit, so if they've had to drive straight from the airport to the track on a Thursday morning the only option is to change out of their travel kit in the airport car park. Many is the time I've walked past a load of mechanics in their underpants as they pack away their travel clothes and pop on the race-team kit, with full logos and branding, before getting into their minibus. The same is true at the other end of the weekend when team members must change back into their travel gear in the circuit car park before heading to the airport. If it has been raining this leads to all of them flying home in wet socks – truly the glamour of F1.

Luggage is also branded, usually provided by each team's official luggage partners. Fifty identical suitcases arriving at a baggage carousel would create chaos while people struggle to identify their bag, so they are all marked with a number allocated to each team member. Typically, a team principal gets 001, the drivers use their race number, the technical director tends to snap up 007 before anyone else can, and so on, in vague order of seniority. At one team this system caused such an argument among engineers that the pragmatic team boss ruled that bag numbers would be allocated at random to avoid resentment over who got the lowest numbers.

Having arrived, the next priority is somewhere to stay. Just as with the World Cup or Olympic Games, before a venue is selected to host a Formula 1 race a technical assessment is carried out, one element of which is ensuring there are enough hotel rooms within a reasonable distance from the circuit for the travelling personnel, VIP guests and attending fans. For races in or close to major cities such as Melbourne, Shanghai, Budapest, Singapore, Las Vegas or Barcelona it's rarely a problem, although thanks to the success of return flight from Sochi to Luton. We had been scheduled to take off at 9pm, but the local aviation authorities unexpectedly cancelled every foreign operator's pre-booked take-off slot before re-opening them for sale.

While negotioations took place, the rest of us could do nothing except wait it out. I remember young British driver Max Chilton sitting on the departure-gate floor, leafing through reams of data from the day's race with his engineers. TV producers stood around, gossiping about what they thought of the race. Others perused the duty-free shops, remembering that they'd promised to pick up a set of nesting Matryoshka dolls for their kids. The team bosses were the first to get away in their private jets, while our charter dropped to the back of the queue. We finally made it home at 4am.

If you happen to be at an airport either side of a race weekend and you spot a group of 40–50 people dressed identically, you can be pretty sure that they are part of an F1 team. All teams work closely with clothing partners, and typical travel kit is smart jeans or chinos with crease-proof polo shirts or jumpers, embroidered with a subtle team logo just about visible to the eagle-eyed fellow flyer. Ferrari travel in smart blazers with a prancing horse logo, making them hard to miss. The ostensible reason for travel kit is to ensure that team staff look professional while representing their employer in public. A secondary benefit in years past was that if staff were more easily identifiable it would discourage any extended periods spent in airport lounge bars that could lead to unwanted incidents on long-haul flights (which, without naming any names, did happen from time to time).

One challenge with F1 team travel clothes is where and how to change out of them. When mechanics and engineers arrive at

NUTS, BOLTS, BAGS AND FLIGHTS

It was won, incidentally, by Australian driver Mark Webber, who had the notion to go via Dubai, and from there to Nice, hopping on a train that took him the last leg into London. As the ash cloud was moving eastwards from Iceland over Europe I decided to try to outrun it, flying east over the Pacific, but then had to wait it out in New York for a week before eventually making it home via Lisbon. Lee McKenzie, Jake Humphrey and the rest of the BBC F1 production crew flew to Frankfurt and then drove home via Calais.

Even under ordinary travel conditions, F1 travel is far from ordinary. Teams and media make extensive use of charter flights – where the travel company hires out the plane – both in Europe, and for some flyaway trips that are not served by scheduled flights, such as the marathon Las Vegas to Doha, Qatar, route. At Sky we also often travel on these charters with F1 team personnel, the main benefit being that the departure time is set to allow everyone to make it to the airport after the race. I've found myself on Boeing 737s operated by the Dutch airline Transavia, the TUI Fly Belgium or Poland's Enter Air, and Airbus A320s from the UK's Titan Airways. They typically take 180 people back from European cities to London's Luton Airport, which is equidistant from McLaren in Surrey to the rest of the UK teams based in Oxfordshire and around Silverstone. I'm fond of Luton, as it's only a 20-minute drive from my parents-in-law's house, which has proved a handy pit stop when things have been running late or I've had an incredibly early flight.

Even with a chartered flight, though, you can't be sure the journey will go smoothly. The first visit to the Russian Grand Prix in 2014 went without a hitch until it came to the Sunday evening because travel is not covered by the FIA cost cap limits placed on all the teams, so any excess sponsorship or prize money that can't be used to develop the car can be used on flying privately. Max Verstappen has exclusive use of his plane while other drivers and team bosses lease time or are sponsored by business jet companies. It's not an environmentally friendly way to fly but does allow the top brass to make the most of their time at the circuits, or back home at the factory.

Before the cost cap, it was much more common to find yourself rubbing shoulders with F1 notables in the business-class cabin. It might be Sir Jackie Stewart, on his way to seat 1A, which was always reserved for him. Or imagine lying down for the night with Ross Brawn sound asleep not two feet away. Travel can lead to a strange intimacy with everyone enclosed in a pressurized tube at 39,000 feet – but the unsaid rule was always that work conversations stayed on the ground. Family holidays or the weather or the in-flight movie choices were all fine subjects to chat about, but the moment the plane touched down all that was forgotten as we got on with our jobs, hierarchy restored.

When British Airways still flew Boeing 747s, I remember dense fog once prevented us from landing in São Paulo and we were diverted to the city's third airport, Campinas. A moment of solidarity ensued as 30 F1 personnel all plotted furiously to figure out how to get from Campinas to downtown São Paolo – but luckily the fog lifted, and we were able to make the short hop back to the main airport, Guarulhos. There was also the Icelandic volcanic ash cloud of 2010 that grounded flights into and out of Northern Europe and left us all stranded in China, leading to a 'Great Race' style challenge for everyone to get back to the UK.

Chapter 9

Nuts, Bolts, Bags and Flights

One of the many lessons I learned from Michael Schumacher was that 'you take your journey with you', and in F1 this is especially true. With 24 Grands Prix on the calendar from March to December, and with most of them squeezed into double and triple headers that require you to go straight from one country to the next, a trouble-free travel experience can set you up perfectly for the working weekend – just as delays, cancellations and disruptions can ruin it before a car has even turned a wheel. Over a typical season I spend around 370 hours on airplanes. Mercifully, budgets allow a certain amount of our air travel to be spent in the more comfortable seats on the plane – flights over six hours will be spent in premium economy or business class. A luxury, but one that does ensure I arrive at circuits reasonably well rested and ready to do my job without the need for a day to recover from a flight with no sleep.

For the F1 drivers and team principals, in recent years air travel has become even more luxurious, with many more journeys taken by private jet. The cost of these has become easier to reconcile enough to go along with it and gave Martin a few thoughts about his F1 retirement.

Alonso duly finished the Brazilian GP in second position to become a double world champion, while Michael saw the chequered flag in his final outing for Ferrari, coming home in fourth place. His father Rolf was at the race, and over the weekend we learned that Michael's seven-year-old son Mick had recently started racing go-karts. As he left Brazil to begin his retirement, one thing seemed likely, that Michael Schumacher was not quite done with motorsport just yet.

to do at the last race in Brazil to win was finish. With the pressure off, Schumacher headed into his final race weekend as a Ferrari driver in a pretty relaxed mood.

One thing he insisted on at Interlagos made me think back to our encounters over the years: no interviews. He wanted to enjoy the weekend and concentrate on the slim chance he had of beating Alonso to the title (to achieve that he needed to win, with Fernando not finishing at all), so we were told he would only pre-record a few quotes that would be distributed to all broadcasters, and there would be no one-to-one interviews. Someone in our ITV Sport production team, however, had a bright idea. Like every F1 driver, Michael liked receiving awards, so if we were to give him a leaving gift (so the thinking went), he could hardly turn it down. And if he agreed to accept it on camera, we would be able to get our own interview with him on his retirement that way.

The idea itself, while a bit sneaky, wasn't terrible. Alas what points it gained for concept were unfortunately lost in the execution. Our producer bought Germany's most famous sportsman, the football-loving Michael Schumacher, a replica England shirt from the 1966 World Cup Final, signed by Geoff Hurst and the remaining members of the squad that won that match 4-2 over . . . West Germany. Seeing as he was Schumacher's Benetton teammate back in 1992, Martin Brundle was given the job of presenting Schumacher with the large, framed, cross-of-St George-emblazoned shirt. Martin was embarrassed enough over the choice of gift that he stressed repeatedly to Michael in the handover ceremony that it was given 'in good spirit'! Thankfully Michael accepted it the same way. The only way it could have been worse was if we'd given him a 'no parking' sign, but he was generous driver in 2007. The question still open was whether Schumacher or Massa would be his teammate.

The Monza paddock is always the best of the season, the late-summer sun superheating every rumour running between the motorhomes. By race day, it was clear that Michael had been forced into a decision. On the grid, Martin Brundle asked Ross Brawn whether Schumacher really was going to retire from F1. 'You'll find out after the race, Martin,' which was as much of a 'yes' as you would ever get from Brawn. Schumacher made his point in the Grand Prix by outpacing Räikkönen to win for Ferrari, to the delight of their home fans. After the chequered flag I headed over to the Ferrari pit wall to grab whatever interview I could when I was tipped off that Ferrari were confirming Schumacher's retirement. I raced through to the paddock to find that copies of a press release were being handed out in front of the Ferrari motorhome.

Sheet of A4 in hand, I ran back to the pit lane to catch the end of the podium ceremony where I was able to drop a report into the beginning of ITV's post-race coverage. I was mid-flow confirming Schumacher's retirement when his engineer Chris Dyer stopped to have a look at the document. It was too good an opportunity not to get him to comment. 'Well, it's been a fantastic time with him, and we'll be disappointed, but it's his decision and hopefully we can finish the job this year and send him out in the perfect way,' he said.

Unfortunately for Dyer and Schumacher, the grand send-off wasn't to be. Later that day, Räikkönen was announced as a Ferrari driver for 2007. A month later in Japan, Ferrari suffered their first in-race engine failure for five years, effectively ending Schumacher's bid for an eighth world championship. All Fernando Alonso needed have expected. But Michael's talent and dedication made things happen for him. A tug of war for his services saw Mercedes motorsport manager Jochen Neerpasch and Weber pull Schumacher out of Jordan and into Briatore's Benetton team after that debut race. There he was afforded a greater opportunity to win, but also exposed to a frosty reception from three-time world champion Nelson Piquet, furious that Schumacher had replaced his friend Roberto Moreno. Tough business deals, tough teammates, tough racing – Michael was learning this was the way things were in F1. When I asked him about some of his strong racing tactics Michael would often talk about not wanting to 'give presents' to rivals. That stuck with me, helping me understand not only Schumacher, but many of the great drivers who came after him who have shared his uncompromising mindset.

His work ethic and his ultra-competitive approach were still there towards the end of 2006, but his mental batteries were running low. At the beginning of the season, he had started to think about how long he wanted to continue. That year's Ferrari was a good car with which he felt that he could challenge for an eighth world title, but internally, the dream team was starting to unravel. Throughout the year Ferrari President Luca di Montezemolo had made little secret of his admiration of Kimi Räikkönen's speed and wanted the Finn at Ferrari. Team principal Jean Todt preferred stability and wanted Schumacher to continue alongside Massa or possibly even Valentino Rossi, the MotoGP world champion who had been testing for Ferrari in a potential move from two wheels to four. Deals were being discussed, and there were plenty of leaks to us reporters from both sides throughout the summer. But by the time we arrived at Monza for the Italian GP the word was that Kimi was going to be a Ferrari

That kind of strike rate compares favourably with the very top drivers that came before Michael. He was the natural successor to Ayrton Senna and shared the great Brazilian's commitment to do anything to win. I always felt that Schumacher's job was harder, though, in that he was bridging two generations. He learned from the tough, uncompromising tactics of Senna, Prost, Piquet and Mansell, but also raced at a time when principles were changing. Drivers who followed him like Alonso, Räikkönen, Button, Massa and Hamilton were of the generation who believed the way you won, with fairness, honour and respect, was just as important as whether you won at all.

For all that motorsport had turned Schumacher into a hard and ruthless racer, off track he was not a hard man. He was kind, sensitive and thoughtful. It was his motorsport life that gave him his tough edge. His parents Rolf and Elisabeth were from a working-class background, and had taken on considerable debt to finance Michael's motor racing, so he felt huge pressure to succeed. As a teenager he would often travel to races by himself and as a result developed a high degree of self-reliance.

With the help of Willi Weber and Mercedes, Michael made it to F1, but nothing he experienced in his early races taught him this was anything but a brutally uncompromising environment. In 1991 Weber famously had to exaggerate Michael's knowledge of the Spa circuit when Eddie Jordan asked if Schumacher knew the track. 'Oh yes, he's driven it many times,' assured Weber, not specifying to Jordan that Michael had never driven Spa in a car, only toured round it on a bicycle. Schumacher and Weber shared a youth hostel room on his debut F1 weekend, with a toilet and basin between their beds – a long way from the glamour they might

It was somewhat of a relief to finally get on with the race. If Schumacher was tired from Saturday's late night, it didn't show. Without help from any outside factors (a safety-car period actually hindered his race), Michael delivered one of the finest drives of his career to finish fifth from his pit lane start. He proved that you can indeed overtake in Monaco, and furthermore that he had no need to have performed the questionable parking manoeuvre at Rascasse. Even if he had started behind Alonso, his pace and that of the Ferrari and its Bridgestone tyres demonstrated he likely would have won the race. If he had done so he would have equalled Ayrton Senna's record of six Monaco victories.

Looking back on it with nearly 20 years of hindsight it's impossible to disagree with the judgement of the stewards, and the view that Michael used a racer's trick to gain a competitive advantage. In the 2020 Sky Documentaries programme *Race to Perfection,* Michael's 2006 teammate Felipe Massa revealed how 'causing a yellow flag' had been joked about in their pre-qualifying briefing, and how eventually, Schumacher came clean. 'It took one year for him to tell me he did it on purpose. One year. I said, "How can you do that?" It shows everyone makes mistakes in life.'

In the same documentary Ross Brawn gave this insight that forms a key part of understanding Michael Schumacher. 'Michael had occasional aberrations, things you could never give a logical explanation for,' Brawn said. 'He had this incredible competitiveness that drove him, and sometimes it would short circuit. Monaco pole, it's normally a given that you want it. But on that occasion, with the strategies, tyres and car we had, there was actually no need for it. It was just a stupid move. And one of those little glitches, short circuits that Michael had two or three times in his career.'

it, just locking the brakes and running out of road, Michael had cheated. Even though the penalty of disqualification from qualifying (while still being allowed to start the race from the back of the grid) was seen by many in the paddock as lenient given the transgression, the reputational damage was significant. This was yet another moment when this ruthless racer had crossed the line.

On Sunday morning the paddock was full of jokes about Michael being the only Ferrari driver able to find a parking spot in Monaco. The man himself stayed tight-lipped for the rest of race day. As the last opportunity to ask him questions had been before the stewards' verdict, I wanted to get something on record from his camp. Thus just 12 hours after I had left the previous night, I made my way on Sunday morning to the Ferrari motorhome. After a long wait Michael's long-time manager and mentor Willi Weber came out, adjusting his sunglasses against the morning sun. I didn't have to beg for an interview, though – Willi was keen to talk.

'You know Michael, he's not an emotional man, it takes a little while before he reacts so I cannot tell you anything about his reaction,' he said. 'I can tell you about my reaction: I'm pissed!' It was classic Weber. Michael might have had a media image of being somewhat of a machine, but he was very much an emotional man underneath. By Sunday morning Weber would have known well his friend's reaction, and I assumed this was his way of letting us know Michael's state of mind. Weber went on to deny that the stewards' judgement of Schumacher's incident and the paddock's near universal condemnation of his tactics would have any bearing on Michael's decision on whether or not he would retire from F1 at the end of the year.

attacks on his character, particularly those coming from 1982 world champion Keke Rosberg, who called Michael's manoeuvre 'the cheapest, dirtiest thing I have ever seen in F1'.

Schumacher had insisted in the press conference immediately after qualifying that it was a simple driving mistake. 'I was pushing, locked up and ran out of road, which is the consequence here in Monte Carlo,' he said. 'I didn't know what [lap times] the other guys were doing.' He added: 'You have your enemies and the people who believe in you. I won't be able to convince people. I've been here for many years, people should know better who I am and what I am.'

Maybe it was the lateness of the hour, but to me at least, Michael looked vulnerable. It wasn't like when he won the 1994 world championship in Adelaide by colliding with Damon Hill. On that occasion he had just realized his life's dream, and notwithstanding racing incidents along the way was on top of the world. It didn't even feel like the aftermath of Jerez in 1997 when, while eventually regretful, Michael was a little bemused at all the outcry, and even criticized rival Jacques Villeneuve for being too 'optimistic' in his overtake. This time, he was a third of the way through a season and was contemplating retirement, while his team was openly courting Kimi Räikkönen as a potential replacement. Nevertheless, he still had a realistic shot at an eighth drivers' title. The last thing Michael needed was everyone bringing up his propensity to go for an unfair advantage when the pressure was on.

When the stewards' verdict finally came, it was damning. Having analysed the speed at which Schumacher went into the corner, his 'excessive' braking and 'erratic' steering, and the TV footage seen by everyone, they effectively concluded that in 'deliberately stopping his car on the circuit' rather than, as he put

At Ferrari the famous loyalty and solidarity that Michael had worked so hard to foster was holding firm against the weight of evidence and the waiting reporters. In our interview after qualifying, I had put it to technical director Ross Brawn that the majority viewpoint in the pit lane was that Michael had parked his car deliberately to ruin Alonso's lap. Slightly mischievously, given Schumacher's track record, I asked whether Ross thought Michael would do that. 'Not the Michael I know,' replied Brawn, giving himself a sliver of wriggle room just in case the stewards found otherwise. As we waited into the evening, Ferrari's director of communications Luca Colajanni held court on the steps of the team's motorhome. Colajanni spoke for the Ferrari team and its boss Jean Todt, so while he, too, had to insist the incident was simply an accident, he was more interested in defending Ferrari's interests than just Michael's. Colajanni was in his element, picking apart arguments put forward by rival teams and drivers, getting into debates over their meaning, highlighting contradictions and hypocrisies and using his admirable grasp of semantics to re-frame how the sporting regulations may or may not have been broken at that moment at Rascasse. Inside the team motorhome Michael and Sabine Kehm knew they had a potential crisis to manage.

With most of his rivals safely in bed by this point, Schumacher appeared just after 10pm, with Jean Todt behind him, on the motorhome steps. We all held our microphones up as best we could (with the resourcefulness award going to the German-speaking crews who taped theirs together on to a boom pole and got a strong-armed sound engineer to hold them all directly under Michael's chin) and fired off questions. This was Schumacher's chance to have his say and to counter what he saw as overly harsh and personal beginning of any F1 interview, as it gives the camera operator time to press the record button and check that the focus is sharp before we begin. It also allows the interviewer to establish a kind of structure and take charge of the situation, something that Schumacher was keen on. Understandably he didn't like the chaos of a scrum of reporters and cameras, not least because he'd been in the middle of quite a few of them over the years. And at around 10pm on that Saturday in Monaco, he was about to be right in the centre of another.

The stewards were taking their time to come to a decision on whether Michael's accident was deliberate. Typically, in FIA stewarding, if it is decided that a rule has not been breached, or if it has and the decision is straightforward, any penalty will be handed down reasonably quickly. However, cases where the stewards must consider the kind of intent that will reflect badly on a competitor are naturally highly sensitive, resulting in longer deliberations to make sure that the outcome is the correct one. In Monaco, those deliberations entered their fifth hour while Schumacher waited for news in the Ferrari motorhome. Meanwhile, across Monte Carlo every other F1 driver was trying to dodge the Saturday night parties in search of a quiet dinner and an early night.

In his book *Edge of Greatness* James Allen tells the story about how Mark Webber and Fernando Alonso had bumped into each other at dinner that night. Alonso had just about calmed down from the silent rage he had displayed in the paddock earlier on, but he was concerned that the delay to the stewards' decision suggested they were looking to exonerate Michael, rather than penalize him. If that happened, Alonso declared he was 'going to pull up on the grid, get out of my car and lie down on the grid in front of his.'

angles that would make him think. This way he would perhaps get something from the interview too. I took that counsel very seriously, and for my first few encounters with Schumacher in 2001, I made sure that I asked the kind of question that made him ponder his answer. He had a bit of a tell when you'd asked a decent question – he'd purse his lips, look up to one side and then give a full response rather than just put the question away with the dreaded couple of words. The trick with the pithy questions was to leave them till the end of the interview. Michael, knowing the score, would usually oblige with a quick soundbite and then a wink at the camera. Generally he responded well to my lines of questioning. And before too long, I noticed camera crews from other broadcasters would come and stand next to me when I was about to interview Schumacher in the group media pen. One weekend I asked Fuji TV cameraman Ollie Parnham what was going on.

'Well, he seems to like you,' he explained. 'And you get good answers. So if Kaz [Kawai, legendary Japanese F1 broadcaster and my pit lane counterpart] isn't on site, we know we'll get what we need if we just pick up your interview.'

I was relieved that Michael hadn't decided I was a complete idiot at the start of our professional relationship, and I certainly respected him. We did get to know each other over the years despite the fact that we were never formally introduced. I assumed he wasn't particularly interested in who was asking the questions, so I hadn't wanted to waste his time by introducing myself when I first got the pit lane job. I had the feeling a quick 'hello' would suffice when he appeared for our first interview. For those of you taking notes on how to do the job of pit lane reporter, I'd mention here that there's always a side benefit of such a greeting at the priorities he ensured that anything else fitted exactly into its allotted time. He was helped in no small measure in this by Sabine Kehm, a Berlin-based journalist who joined Michael's management team in 1999 as media consultant and still works for the Schumacher family today. From the beginning of the race weekend Michael liked to stick to a routine. He'd always arrive at the circuit at the same time, just before lunch on Thursday morning. Meetings with engineers would follow before his media commitments, always at 4pm. He would allow time for some fitness training at the end of the day before the track action began on Friday morning. Time was his most valuable asset, and Michael guarded it carefully.

When it came to TV interviews, an activity he was obliged to do but which didn't make him or his car any faster, Schumacher was direct and to the point. James Allen had mastered the art of the Schumacher interview and gave me some tips. As he explained, most drivers get bored with always answering the same questions, such as 'What are your targets for the weekend?' or 'How do you expect the car to suit this track?' Most will just (figuratively) roll their eyes, give routine stock answers and move on, reasoning this will get the whole thing over and done with as quickly as possible. Not Schumacher. If he was obliged to answer questions, even in a brief TV interview, he demanded just as high standards from the interviewer as from everyone else in his professional life. And if you didn't demonstrate that you'd put in the effort to rise to those standards, he would give you a short and basic answer. You'd be left with practically no material for your news report and be in little doubt that he didn't think much of you or your question.

Allen advised me to take extra time to come up with questions for Michael that were intelligent, considered and original – specific lap behind him to slow down and abort. Alonso was one of the drivers affected, and as the session ended Michael had held on to his pole. I had been listening in to the commentary from my regular Monaco position – wedged between a stack of tyres and a marshals' cabin – and heard the drama unfold. I then walked down the pit lane accompanied by cameraman Andy Parr.

The first person we encountered was Alonso's team principal at Renault, Flavio Briatore. Schumacher was close to Briatore – they had won two titles together in the Benetton days – but on this occasion the team boss was furious with his former driver. The charismatic Italian practically had steam blowing out of his ears. He declared himself in no doubt that Schumacher had faked the accident to guarantee himself pole and to deny Alonso or anyone else the opportunity of beating him. 'This is the way Ferrari manage, you know,' he fumed, before ending our interview by stalking off to prowl the garage. He wasn't alone. The FIA race stewards agreed that the incident looked suspicious. They called Michael and his team representatives to a hearing, and examined closely the telemetry data from Schumacher's car.

As their deliberations dragged on all anyone could do was wait, and outside the Ferrari motorhome seemed as good a place as any. Ironically, waiting for Michael Schumacher was not something I was used to over the six previous seasons covering his Ferrari career. One of Michael's many qualities was his immaculate timekeeping, a consequence of his famous self-discipline which extended just as much to media time as it did to physical or technical preparation. He was always very clear that his two top priorities were his fitness training and driving. Of course, he had other commitments, so to make sure he could focus on his

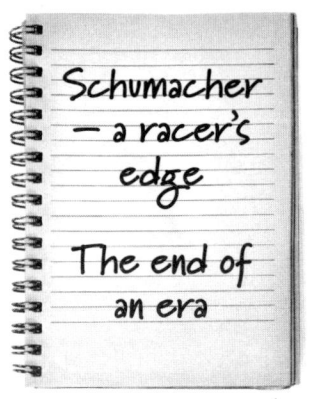

Chapter 8

Michael

It's a pleasant May evening in Monaco and journalists, reporters and camera crews have gathered outside the Ferrari motorhome a few hours after qualifying for the 2006 Monaco Grand Prix. Earlier that afternoon we had witnessed Michael Schumacher shunting his car into the barrier at the penultimate corner, La Rascasse, causing yellow flags to be brought out and wrecking his championship rival Fernando Alonso's final chance of clinching pole position. This is motor racing, and accidents can and do happen. This one, however, had a distinctly dubious look to it – the way Michael's car ended up just short of damaging itself against the barrier yet still effectively blocking the track had suggested to many observers that this wasn't an accident at all.

Schumacher was sitting in provisional pole position. Knowing Alonso had the chance for another hot lap, on his final run Schumacher, a driver renowned for his finesse and skill, seemed to clumsily wrestle with his car at the Rascasse corner until it came to a stop, blocking half the track and forcing anyone completing a

DEALING WITH DISASTER

Later that evening, after the race had finished and we knew Grosjean was safe and well in the medical centre, my producer asked me to go down to the crash site to file a report on what the scene was. The exit of Turn 3 was easily accessible from the paddock, and just within the range of our microphones and camera.

Grosjean's wrecked chassis had long since been transported away, but the first thing that struck me most forcefully was the smell of burning plastic and carbon fibre hanging in the air. It was a sobering sight to see the discarded sections of damaged barrier, temporarily replaced for the restart by a section of concrete wall. Seeing the aftermath in person made it even more incredible to think that Grosjean had been able to survive such a horrendous accident.

Such are the perils of live broadcasting. Motorsport is inherently dangerous, and the speeds involved are so high that any accident has the potential to be fatal. It gets safer every year as lessons are learned from incidents and near misses, but the nature of F1 is its unpredictability. Just as the drivers accept that risk when they put their helmet on and step into a car that in the wrong circumstance could kill them, so we also accept the risk when we turn on our cameras and broadcast live TV.

got used to it and recognized its value. Since its introduction the Halo has certainly saved the lives of drivers, not just in F1, but in the other formulas in which it was adopted. Perhaps the most notable example was another accident where we were left shocked and desperate for information – but which ultimately had a much happier outcome.

Having started the 2020 Bahrain Grand Prix from near the back of the field, Romain Grosjean was clipped by Daniil Kvyat's Alpha Tauri on the straight that followed Turn 3. His Haas speared right, slammed into the Armco barrier at high speed, and exploded in a ball of flame. The chassis punched right through the metal barrier, snapping the rear of the car housing the engine and gearbox clean off. It was a shocking, sickening crash.

As with the Bianchi accident, the F1 world-feed director quickly cut away, and there followed an agonizing period during which neither those in the pit lane nor viewers around the world knew what had happened. After around 30 seconds, we finally saw shots of Grosjean. Not only had he made it out of the car but he was being walked to the medical car. Replays showed how he had twisted his body and pulled himself up through the Halo device as the fire blazed all around. He was then helped over the barrier by the FIA medical delegate Dr Ian Roberts while medical-car driver Alan van der Merwe sprayed them both with fire extinguishant. Grosjean suffered burns to his hands but the fire-resistant race suit, balaclava and underwear did their job. It was a miraculous escape, but the Halo device had been crucial. Without it Grosjean would surely have suffered a severe head injury on impact with the metal barrier and have been helpless to escape the subsequent fire.

In the immediate aftermath of the accident the FIA announced an investigation. Under scrutiny was the speed at which Bianchi had been driving through the corner under the double yellow flags when he lost control, but there was equal scrutiny of whether more could have been done to prevent the circumstances leading to the incident, and quite rightly the sport learned lessons, as is so often the case following a serious accident. The investigation led directly to the introduction of the virtual safety car – much like an average speed zone on a motorway, a read-out on the dashboard forces all drivers to reduce their speed equally, and removes the discretionary element following an incident. It was trialled over the remaining races of 2014, before becoming a standard procedure, particularly when marshals are engaged in recovering cars from the track.

Bianchi's crash also added impetus to the FIA's research into a head-protection system for F1 cars. Various options had been under development, including a laminated polycarbonate windscreen – something that was later adopted by IndyCar – and two metal bars either side of the driver's head, aimed at deflecting large objects like wheels. There was a fair amount of resistance to the concept. Some drivers spoke of their concern that F1 would lose the essence of being an open-cockpit category, while others didn't like the idea of having their vision partially obscured.

The FIA would eventually settle on what became known as the Halo, a cast titanium wishbone-shaped device that is mounted either side of the driver's cockpit and secures to the front bulkhead of the chassis just in front of the steering wheel. Opinions were mixed when it was introduced at the beginning of 2018. But just like the HANS device – the Head And Neck restraint System that was made mandatory in F1 a few years earlier – the drivers quickly

The contrast with the tense atmosphere post-race at Suzuka just a few months later could not have been more marked. There were a lot of rumours going around, and everyone was hungry for accurate information. It was Matteo Bonciani, then the FIA's head of communications, who eventually came out to speak to us. He was met with an impatient rush of microphones and cameras, and I felt I had to implore my colleagues to step back and give Bonciani some space. It was a very intense moment. Bonciani gave us a prepared statement to the effect that Bianchi had sustained a head injury, and that he had been transferred to hospital in Yokkaichi. And there was simply no more news to give us than that.

In the case of information from the teams or the FIA, it's important to focus on facts and not speculate. There's not much that can stop the internet, however. In this case, videos taken by spectators at the Dunlop corner began to emerge on social media that gave us the best indication yet of just how the accident had happened and how serious it really was. We had the statement from the FIA, we had limited information from the team, and from the pictures online we had a pretty good idea of the nature of the accident and the injury Bianchi had suffered. The crash was a stark reminder of how exposed the drivers really were. We still had limited official news at the time we went off-air, which is where our live element ended and the pre-recorded programmes picked up. It was a very sombre flight back to London.

After several months in a Japanese hospital Bianchi was eventually transferred back to France. Sadly he never regained consciousness from his brain injury, and passed away in July 2015, aged just 25.

covering it. Everyone watching the live coverage was looking for news about Bianchi's condition. His team told us that they hadn't received any response on the radio, so at that point they didn't know anything more than we did.

Jules Bianchi was a young Frenchman who had seemed to have it all – incredible skill in a racing car, a great personality, movie-star appearance, and a bright future ahead of him. His parents were friends with the Leclerc family, so much so that Bianchi had been named godfather to the young Charles Leclerc, who in 2014 was racing in Formula Renault. Bianchi was generally regarded as one of the future stars of F1. A protégé of Ferrari, he was in his second year with Marussia, and was set to move up to the Sauber team in 2015. Ferrari planned to nurture him in such outfits that ran Ferrari engines until a place opened up for him at the main team.

There had been many moments where Bianchi had demonstrated that promise, none more so than his eighth-place finish at the 2014 Monaco GP. The aftermath of that race particularly stands out in my memory. The pit reporter's job is to quickly interview the winner and then look for what's going to be the second story of the post-race programme's recap, most regularly a surprise placing or a feel-good result from someone in mid-field. In this case Bianchi had scored the first points for both himself and the Marussia team. I headed down to the garage, where I found the mechanics hugging each other in celebration. Team patriarch John Booth was walking around, slapping everyone on the back. It was a joyous celebration, because it meant the team would move off the back of the constructors' championship and begin to earn prize money that would guarantee their survival in F1.

Dunlop Curve. It wasn't a particularly hard impact, and it was quickly clear that Sutil was out of the car and OK. Race control told the marshals to wave double yellow caution flags as the recovery workers dispatched a small crane to move the stranded car. Double waved yellow flags were standard practice and generally considered sufficient for this type of incident. The rules stated that drivers under waved yellow flags had to reduce their speed and be prepared to stop.

Then, at the very same spot where Sutil had spun off, Jules Bianchi lost control of his Marussia. He slid across the wet grass at high speed and hit the heavy counterweight of the recovery crane with such force that it jolted up momentarily. The incident wasn't shown on the world feed, and initially we were confused as to what had transpired. The world-feed director would have seen what happened, but the general principle is that serious accidents are not shown until they are sure the driver is alive and well. When the director did cut to a distant shot of the scene, we could just about tell through the murk that a second car had gone off at the position where the crane was working on Sutil's car. The Marussia wasn't clearly visible, but the activity of the marshals and medical team did not bode well.

Furthermore there were no replays – a sure sign that something serious had happened. Realizing this, David Croft immediately shifted the tone of the commentary down several gears. Our worst fears were confirmed when, after the cars had circulated for a couple of laps under the safety car, there was a red flag, and the race was stopped.

Our first job as broadcasters was to try to figure out what had happened so that we could calibrate how we were going to deal with

DEALING WITH DISASTER

I remember at Suzuka, Japan, in 2017 – mechanics floating paper boats they had made down the flooded pit lane. Under more extreme circumstances the qualifying session might be abandoned, postponed until Sunday morning, or even a race time suddenly moved forward to avoid an incoming storm, as happened at Interlagos in 2024. As broadcasters we know a rainy weekend usually leads to good TV, as racing in the wet tends to bring out some amazing performances from the very best drivers. Memorable wins for Lewis Hamilton at Silverstone in 2008 and Max Verstappen in Brazil in 2024 are just two that come to mind, races where in each case in the wet, these drivers were simply in a class of their own.

But inclement weather can also lead to weekends where things go very wrong indeed. One such was the Japanese GP of 2014. We'd been warned of a typhoon approaching the Nagoya Bay area, near to where the Suzuka circuit is situated. Typhoons aren't uncommon in Japan, especially in the autumn, and so, despite forecasts that the weather was due to get worse over the course of Sunday afternoon, there had been no adjustment to the schedule, and no amendment to the race's 3pm start. F1 boss Bernie Ecclestone, who wasn't actually present at the track that weekend but was in touch by phone, was reluctant to interfere with the broadcast slots scheduled around the world, and the Japanese organizers had made the decision to go ahead, believing that they could get the race completed before the worst of the rain reached land.

Conditions were tricky and wet as the race went ahead. As the daylight began to fade, it looked as if the 53-lap race would be completed without serious incident. But then, on lap 41, Sauber driver Adrian Sutil spun off into the barrier on the outside of the figured out the story arc for the season, but what that means is that most of what they film will never be seen or heard.

For F1 personnel it's important to know who's live and who isn't. If there is any professional code among the F1 paddock media, it's that the broadcasters who are going out live, with no opportunity to stop or edit, are afforded a higher priority than those who are not. Of course, the non-live (recorded or 'off-tape') camera crews still need their interviews, so an interview scrum, whether around a driver or team principal, usually comes down to a ballet of split-second timing to make sure that everyone gets what they need, and nobody is left with a hole in their programme. One final point to note is that it's generally good policy to let the drivers know before an interview starts whether they're live or not, so they don't swear (although if you make a point of mentioning it to Australia's Daniel Ricciardo he won't miss a beat before replying with a swear word just for everyone's amusement).

Getting any live broadcast to work takes a huge amount of preparation and, given that triumph or disaster is only ever a split-second away, broadcasting F1 is exceptionally demanding. It's the typical swan paddling on a lake scenario. Things might look serene from the surface, but out of view under the water everyone is working furiously to make the programme happen. To me, live TV is a bit of an art form. There is so much that could go wrong at any point, it's remarkable we don't have more disasters than we do.

When plans go out of the window, it's usually because of circumstances beyond anyone's control. The most familiar culprit is the weather. Every once in a while rain means we get a delayed or interrupted session or race which leaves us trying to fill the air time, grateful for shots of marshals dancing in the rain, or – as

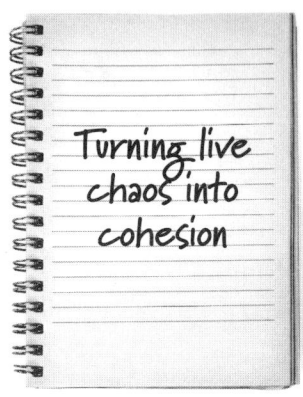

Chapter 7

Dealing with Disaster: The Pitfalls of Live Broadcasting

Hang around behind the Formula 1 garages for long enough with a TV camera and you're guaranteed to hear one question: 'Are you live?' Most frequently asked over a Grand Prix weekend by reporters to other reporters, and by mechanics, engineers, team press officers and drivers, it essentially means, 'What exactly is going on here, with this TV camera?' They want to know whether the moment is being beamed out to millions, or whether they can afford to be slightly more relaxed, the equivalent of standing to attention or standing easy. In my case, the answer is almost always, 'Yes, we're live.'

It's not just me. F1 has around 35 broadcasters at the circuit presenting all or some part of their programmes live. There are others who are there with film crews, but who are not live, a good example being the crew filming the Netflix documentary series *Drive to Survive*. Netflix aim to try and capture as much as they can, editing it all down to the most compelling stories once they've

'Oh, so you want to talk to me now, do you?' Brawn said, with a trademark raised eyebrow.

'Yes, I always want to talk to you, what do you mean?'

'Well, you didn't seem too keen on listening to my answer or concluding the interview when you just turned and walked off on me in Austria.'

It belatedly dawned on me how it must have looked to Brawn at the time. As I turned away the TV audience would have heard me say into my microphone, 'Well thanks for explaining, Ross' or something along those lines, but crucially Ross hadn't heard it. Viewers also couldn't see Brawn's point of view as he watched me duck away from him and out of the scrum. That taught me the important lesson that you should always end any interview politely and directly, thanking the interviewee to their face. And if you can avoid giving them any indication as to whether you agree with them or not, then so much the better.

Michael Schumacher won the 2002 world championship with a massive total of 144 points, almost double Barrichello's 77 and nearly triple Montoya's final tally of 50 points. Jean Todt needn't have got the frights after all.

Realizing that he had just been designated the support act at Ferrari, Massa duly let Alonso through. Smedley's subsequent message to Massa of 'OK mate, good lad. Just stick with him now, sorry', provided a further indication that the order had come from the team. Alonso went on to win the race while Massa fended off a charge from Red Bull's Sebastian Vettel to finish second.

This set of radio messages once again landed Ferrari before the FIA race stewards, accused of breaking sporting regulations, and the team was again found guilty and fined. A later investigation by the World Motor Sport Council upheld the stewards' decision and the fine, but stopped short of taking any further sporting sanctions. Behind the scenes the WMSC directed F1's Sporting Working Group (a committee made up of F1 team managers and FIA officials) to take another look at the regulation banning team orders due to it being unenforceable. And so, in 2011, eight years after it had first been brought in, article 39.1 of the FIA Formula 1 Sporting Regulations banning 'team orders which interfere with a race result' was deleted from the statutes.

As for me, the aftermath of Austria 2002 gave me reason to consider the dangers of bringing one's feelings about a racing decision into an interview. Brawn could tell by the tone of my questions that, like most people watching, I felt that his and Todt's decision had been unfair, unnecessary and unsporting. At the end of our interview in the Spielberg pit lane I had turned away from the mêlée surrounding Brawn to allow another reporter in to ask their question. It was only at the following race in Monaco when I approached Ross for a post-qualifying interview that I discovered he was annoyed.

summon both the team's representatives and drivers to the World Motor Sport Council at their Paris headquarters. Under the gaze of the camera crews lined up outside, in walked Todt, Brawn, Schumacher and Barrichello to face the music, but the problem for the FIA was that Ferrari hadn't actually broken any rules in switching the positions – team orders have a long history in Grand Prix racing, and at that time they were not outlawed.

What the World Motor Sport Council was able to penalize, however, was the breach in protocol when the drivers had switched positions on the podium. In the FIA's eyes this had 'confused and embarrassed' the podium dignitaries (a bit of a stretch given they are recorded on TV smiling and applauding Schumacher's gesture), but it was nevertheless against the rules. Ferrari avoided a points penalty in place of a $1 million fine, half of which was suspended against future good behaviour. The FIA also decided to make a stand in order to deter future team-order controversies, and from 2003 the practice of F1 teams instructing one driver to let the other pass for a race position was banned.

The rule lasted until 2011, when it was quietly dropped, in essence because the teams had found so many ways of subverting it, most obviously if it was the driver's decision. The most famous example came at the 2010 German GP, once again involving Ferrari. Felipe Massa was leading teammate Fernando Alonso when his engineer Rob Smedley sent a highly unsubtle coded request for a swap of positions. 'OK,' Smedley began with audible reluctance, signalling that it was a decision he was being made to execute. Never has an 'OK' done so much heavy lifting. After a beat, Smedley continued. 'Fernando is faster than you. Confirm you understood the message.'

the nugget of information unavailable to us throughout the Grand Prix, an added detail from Brawn that changed the story. He revealed that Michael hadn't been racing Rubens at all, and that in fact, such was their dominance over Montoya's Williams the drivers had been instructed to back off, turn down their engines and manage their pace, coasting to the end – both cars were merely on a cruise to the finish. This raised two additional questions that we would go on to debate long into the evening. If the Ferrari drivers were so much quicker than Montoya, then why was Todt so worried about Williams closing up in the championship? And, second question, if both had been allowed to push flat-out, would Schumacher really have been able to outpace and overtake Barrichello – something he had been unable to do all weekend?

Brawn was being scrupulous in his honesty, perhaps reasoning that if people understood the cars hadn't really been racing they might mind less about the team orders – but his statement mixed uncomfortably with the result, and viewers were left wondering, if there hadn't actually been a race, what exactly it was that they had been watching for the last hour and a half? Furthermore, by switching positions at the most awkward and embarrassing moment, only yards from the finish line, Barrichello had most publicly signalled his frustration with the decision, which suggested that all was not rosy in the Ferrari garden.

Things were about to get much less rosy still on the podium. Embarrassed by the crowd's hostile reaction, and keen to offer an olive branch, Michael refused to take his place on the top step, insisting instead that Rubens take the winner's position. The move was taken in good faith by the local dignitaries handing out the trophies, but the FIA was less impressed and would go on to close behind him, to power past to the finish line. Unlike Lando Norris, who years later would do the same to let Oscar Piastri win the Qatar GP sprint race in 2024, this wasn't Barrichello's choice – and loud boos rang out from the crowd, objecting to the apparent manipulation of the race result.

What really made Ferrari's decision baffling for most observers was that while it was in line with the way the team generally raced, they hadn't needed to do it. Any reasonable projection could see that Schumacher was likely to win the world championship easily, and in no way needed the extra four points that separated first from second. Allowing Barrichello to take his first win of the year would have given him a huge confidence boost after his poor start, and that would in turn have helped the team overall in its battle for the constructors' title. Instead, Ferrari was now in the firing line, with even the most loyal fans upset by what they had witnessed.

With the negative reaction from the Austrian crowd ringing in his ears, Michael was apologetic in the post-race interviews. Barrichello by contrast had already made his point in the most public way, so was actually pretty relaxed about the result. In the moments before the podium ceremony, it was down to me to make some sense of Ferrari's decision for ITV's viewers. Ross Brawn stepped off the pit wall into a throng of reporters. I had positioned myself second in line behind home broadcaster ORF. Ross was besieged and looked slightly taken aback as to why the result had caused such controversy.

He turned to me. 'Rubens had won the race, hadn't he?' I demanded. 'Why did you swap?' Ross conceded Barrichello had the race effectively won. 'But in the interests of Ferrari and the drivers' championship,' he said, 'we made the decision.' Then came of 71 laps. Again and again, Rubens passed by the pits, retaining his lead. I was watching the drama on the Ferrari pit wall play out in real time. This was before the current era of fully open team radio channels, so as broadcasters we had little idea of what was going on from the drivers' point of view, but what I could see from the pit lane was a highly unusual amount of back-and-forth communication between Todt and Brawn. Notes were being pointedly passed across the carbon fibre-lined desk, and there were intense discussions between Brawn, Delli Colli and Todt. Conscious of eyes and TV cameras upon them, they were just about staying outwardly calm, but one person wasn't playing ball.

Ten years later, in an interview with Brazil's TV Globo, Barrichello described the closing stages of the race. 'It was eight laps of war. It's very rare that I lose my temper but I was screaming on the radio. I kept going to the end, saying I would not let him pass.' Whether Barrichello's reasoning for disobeying the team order was that he felt the swap was unnecessary given Schumacher's championship lead, or that he thought it was simply unsporting, didn't matter. On the radio, Barrichello said he was told that he must 'comply or face stiff consequences.' Looking back on it, Rubens referred to a 'broad form of threat', but this was not revealed by the F1 TV camera now trained on Todt. What we did observe was Todt's final, slightly desperate radio call which was played out on the main TV feed. 'Rubens – last lap. Let Michael pass for the championship. Let Michael pass for the championship, Rubens, please.'

At the last minute, Barrichello complied. To make it absolutely clear this was a team order, and at what was clearly the worst possible moment for Ferrari in PR terms, Rubens lifted his accelerator coming out of the last corner, allowing Schumacher, rewarded a more precise approach and favoured Barrichello's driving style.

The Brazilian led away from pole position, and for most of the race he ran comfortably ahead of Schumacher and a chasing Juan Pablo Montoya. But rather than just sit back and let the race play out, at around half distance Jean Todt got the frights. Worrying was something that Todt did quite a lot of during races. I often saw his fingernails wrapped in medical tape to prevent him biting them to the quick. Even though Schumacher's lead in the drivers' championship was a healthy one, experience told Todt that things could change very easily over the rest of the season. All it would take was some of Barrichello's mechanical unreliability to strike Schumacher's car and the German's lead could be wiped out. Whether those concerns were well founded or not, Todt was in charge, and he wasn't about to let Barrichello take four points off Schumacher, no matter how much Rubens deserved the win.

He duly instructed Ferrari's technical director Ross Brawn to execute the driver swap so that Schumacher could take the full 10 points (the score for a win at that time) and further extend his lead in the world championship standings. Ross in turn told Barrichello's engineer Gabriele Delli Colli to order his driver to give up the lead. Team orders were nothing new and were an established part of motor racing at this time – it was just another routine race decision at Scuderia Ferrari. But someone wasn't listening. For lap after lap, Barrichello ignored the instructions from the pit wall, and stayed in the lead. Brawn even tried talking to him directly – with no response.

Spielberg is a short circuit, so to complete the mandated 305-kilometre Grand Prix distance, the drivers had to drive a total

People even went so far as to suspect that Michael had these advantages formally included in his contract with Ferrari, something that he always firmly denied.

All of this notwithstanding, Schumacher certainly had the better start to the 2002 season, winning in Melbourne, São Paulo, Imola and Barcelona. By complete contrast, Barrichello's campaign had started disastrously. He retired from the first three races and failed even to start the Spanish GP from his second place on the grid, thanks to a gearbox failure on the formation lap. In his darkest moments of paranoia Rubens might indeed have imagined that these misfortunes had been created by Ferrari to ensure that Michael could rack up the points untroubled, satisfying the supposed conditions of the number-one driver. If Barrichello suspected that, he never said it publicly, and even the lightest investigation of his technical issues confirmed that they were simply a run of bad fortune. This was recognized by the Ferrari team principal Jean Todt, who sympathized with his travails, and appreciated his loyalty in his reluctance to blame the team. Todt had rewarded Barrichello with the early contract extension, and the Brazilian flew into Austria full of confidence and ready to reboot his championship challenge.

The Spielberg track, a shortened version of the original Österreichring built in the late 1960s, was and remains a stunningly beautiful and technically challenging venue. Some drivers always went well there, some did not. Schumacher was in the latter camp, having never previously won in Austria. It was one of the very few tracks where his ability to throw the car into corners and then sort out the sliding rear end was rendered fruitless, as the circuit layout what he was thinking, largely because he'd tell you. From tears of joy at winning to tears of despair when things went wrong, over an 18-year, 326-race career, Rubens did a fair bit of crying. But he wasn't just emotional, he was also honourable.

His reasoning in renewing his deal with Ferrari was simple. Would it be better, he asked himself, to be a number-one driver in a less competitive team, driving a car that wouldn't necessarily allow him to win races, or to be a 'team' driver at Ferrari where he did in theory have a chance to challenge for the world championship? Of course, to do that he'd have to beat Schumacher. That was a big ask, but Rubens had proved himself an excellent driver and knew that it wasn't impossible. From Ferrari's point of view, the number-one and number-two philosophy began with a simple concept – both drivers started the season on zero points. Whoever scored the most points early on and therefore showed themselves as most likely to win the world championship would become the team's focus, and the other driver would take a supporting role. In Schumacher's previous seasons alongside Barrichello he had taken the lead-driver role by the time the European season started, or at least by the time of the Monaco Grand Prix at the end of May, and then as a result had enjoyed number-one status for the rest of the season with Rubens acting as his rear-gunner, racing in the team's – and Michael's – interest, which included obeying team orders when they were issued.

The more cynical in the paddock believed Ferrari would find ways to make sure that Schumacher was the points leader by the time the European leg of the championship started, whether that was down to a car advantage over his teammate, favourable race pit-stop strategies, or some other preferential treatment.

the details I'd need to fully immerse myself into the world of the pits, paddock and media centre.

'Stay out of the TV compound,' Duncanson warned. 'You'll never learn anything from broadcast trucks and the production office. Get out into the paddock. Make friends and contacts. Talk to drivers and engineers, team principals and FIA officials. Get a feel for their backstories and motivations, find out what they're thinking, and how they're approaching the weekend.'

Neil's advice is as valuable now as it was back then. Indeed, it's still how I approach every race weekend. But while I was thrilled with my new role, in terms of what was happening on track, my first season as pit lane reporter was proving to be less than thrilling – Michael Schumacher's Ferrari was dominant and he was winning practically every race. Until, that was, a sunny May day in Austria, when I had my first big F1 controversy to report on.

2002 was no flash in the pan for Ferrari. With hindsight it's clear they were in the middle of the five-season-long stretch of dominance that ran from 2000 to 2004. Michael Schumacher was the team's designated number-one driver. Early in the year there had been flashes of pace from a resurgent Williams team and their promising BMW engine, but Michael had won four of the first five races, and round six in Austria found him 21 points clear of his nearest rival. The feeling in the paddock was that Williams weren't quite ready to win consistently, and that Schumacher was a solid bet for the title. Ferrari had just re-signed Michael's teammate Rubens Barrichello, providing stability on their side, while Barrichello was pleased to have the security of a two-year deal.

Rubens didn't so much wear his heart on his sleeve as carry it around like a giant helium balloon. You always knew immediately reporter's role full-time. And that was it. I've been in the job ever since!

With the exception of some early risers who might have caught me on Capital FM's breakfast news bulletins, I was completely unknown to a British audience. Barwick gave me some advice: to play myself in quietly, not to try to make a big splash, to do the basic things consistently and well, and to give myself time to become established in the role. Helpful, but by far the most useful advice I received was from the previous pit lane reporter, James Allen himself. 'The best reports from the pit lane essentially drop little golden nuggets of information into the race commentary, and then allow the commentators to get on with it,' he said. 'Viewers can't always hear every word you say from a noisy pit lane, so keep it simple, be precise, get the information out there, and then shut up and focus on anything else going on in the pits that the commentators can't already see for themselves.'

Murray Walker also threw me some advice: 'Inform and entertain' was his golden rule. His feeling about the art of live reporting was that it's as important to think about the way you say things as the detailed content. He was right. You can take your time finessing pre-prepared packages until they are frame-perfect, but a reporter will always be judged on the quality of their contribution to the race and qualifying commentary. So the trick was firstly to make sure it was informative, and secondly, if possible, entertaining. But of all the advice I received, perhaps the most memorable came from Neil Duncanson, who simply told me to 'be a sponge'. I knew what he meant. Even though I'd been coming to the races for five years, and knew my way around, I also knew that to really delve into had also been part of our production since the start. He had previously been Head of Sport at Anglia TV, and he was a highly experienced and accomplished journalist. Grand Prix racing had a long and distinguished history in the Anglia region. Lotus was based in Hethel in Norfolk, not far from the Snetterton circuit, where local boy Martin Brundle had sparred with Ayrton Senna as they both learned race craft competing in F3, and Kevin, or 'Pipes', as he was widely known, had reported regularly on F1 stories over the years. Before joining Chrysalis Sport to produce the F1 shows for ITV, Kevin also had the honour of playing himself in the opening scene of the football comedy film *Mike Bassett: England Manager*.

In 2001, while James Allen was trialling to take over from Murray, Kevin and I each had an opportunity to try out for the pit lane reporter's role. My first chance came at the Brazilian Grand Prix. It was more than a little nerve-wracking. Starting as I was expected to go on, my first ever report was live and broadcast instantly to millions of people in the UK and around the world. The subject was the ever-changeable São Paulo weather and, in particular, as I gamely pointed to it on camera, 'that cloud, over there'. In the end, the cloud in question wasn't rain-bearing but the threat of it had been enough to affect the teams' strategies. What I was attempting to do was convey the mood of tension among the teams, and communicate the possible consequences of the rain that never fell.

This and subsequent contributions from me must have not been entirely awful because at the end of the year Neil Duncanson recommended to ITV's Brian Barwick that I be given the pit

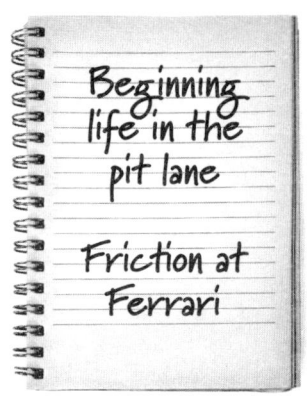

Chapter 6

Learning the Ropes

It's hard to think of any other sport where one person was for so long its voice and effective figurehead. Murray Walker's professional longevity meant a 50-year wait for the job of commentator to come up. However, at the end of 2001 that opportunity finally arose. Waiting in the wings was James Allen. Deputizing for Murray alongside Martin Brundle three times during the 2001 season, James had proved himself a perfect fit for the role and for the viewers was a known and trusted voice. Thus, he was duly promoted from pit lane reporter to the role of ITV F1's lead commentator. All sorted, then. Apart from one detail – who was going to replace James as pit lane reporter?

It is, as you're hopefully learning from this book, a job that requires a very particular set of skills. James had successfully defined the role and I had watched and learned as he did it. I was already part of the team, had reporting experience from my radio days and, by now, a decent spread of F1 knowledge, so I made the shortlist to replace him. The other frontrunner, Kevin Piper,

and first-hand stories about his time in F1. He went to quite a few races in a Honda shirt and cap, which always felt a bit strange, but it was lovely to see him around and enjoying life. He was happy to remain involved in F1. He told me he feared that had he stayed at home and sat and read books, or gone cruising around the world with Elizabeth, he would have lost his mental sharpness. And as it turned out, the commentary box hadn't seen the last of Murray because he came back for one final F1 commentary at the 2007 European Grand Prix at the Nürburgring, when he filled in at BBC Radio 5 Live for David Croft, who was attending the birth of his son. That really was the last one for Murray, performed at the grand old age of 84. He had an extraordinary life and career in the sport he loved so much. I'll be forever grateful for the time I spent with him and to this day there isn't a race weekend that goes by that I don't think of him, and hear the echo of that voice of his, reverberating around the race track.

It wasn't a particularly significant race. While Mika Häkkinen won for McLaren, Michael Schumacher had wrapped up both the drivers' and constructors' championships three races earlier in Hungary. Almost before I realized it, we had come to the end of the show. I remember Murray's last sign-off as vividly as if it were yesterday. There were four of us in the commentary box; Murray, Martin, cameraman Mat Bryant and myself. With the post-race analysis all done, at around 9.30pm UK time, Jim Rosenthal handed back for Murray to say farewell, and to take the programme off-air. And in typical Murray fashion, he kept it straightforward and direct. 'That's the last from me,' he concluded. 'All I can say is that it always has been a pleasure, and I hope you will enjoy Grand Prix racing from now on. Goodbye.' That was it.

The director cut to a package we'd prepared, a musical tribute edited to the Cole Porter song 'You're the Top'. Murray put down his microphone and had a little hug with Martin. He then quietly gathered up his stuff, stowing it in the vintage 'Shell Oils Grand Prix of Europe' bag that he carried everywhere, left the commentary box, and walked down the stairs with Martin. There weren't any tears, it was just a very matter-of-fact sign-off. It was obviously a moment of huge significance for him, and for all of us, but unlike Murray we would be going on to the season finale in Japan. Murray got a car back to the hotel, stayed Sunday night, just as he had done that evening in Brussels the previous year, and flew home the next day to get on with the rest of his life.

Over the next couple of years, I wondered if Murray had retired too soon, because he showed no signs of being done with F1, or of being ready to stop working. He signed up to be a Honda ambassador in 2005, providing their guests with paddock insights who had to re-package and stow the emergency slide that night the next day off!

Then, all too soon, came the United States GP at Indianapolis, Murray's last race as commentator. This had been his choice, as he felt it might have been somewhat of an anti-climax had his last race been the final round of the season in Japan, which traditionally, due to the time difference, doesn't attract as large an audience as the US races. North American races are generally shown at prime time in the UK, and as everyone knew it was to be Murray's last race, early evening would make for an easier time for people to watch.

It was an emotional weekend. Our production manager, Sally Blower, helped to organize a surprise farewell event for Murray on the Saturday evening after qualifying. The event was being held in the Paddock Club, Formula 1's VIP hospitality area, but no one wanted Murray to twig what was going on, so we all sneaked up the back stairs to the club. When Murray was brought in through the main entrance, he was stunned to see so many people from the F1 paddock: all the ITV crew, other members of the media and key people from the teams, including most of the drivers. Bernie Ecclestone was there, along with Michael Schumacher, David Coulthard, Mika Häkkinen, Jenson Button, Juan Pablo Montoya and many other famous names. Host Tony Jardine did a charming review of some of Murray's most famous quotes and 'Murray-isms'. He asked the drivers to come up and read theirs out with Murray standing alongside. Indianapolis Motor Speedway owner Tony George presented Murray with one of the bricks from the famous original track. It was all done with a huge amount of affection.

Race day came, but as the Grand Prix was the first big sporting event held in the USA after September 11 the tone was subdued.

memories'. He had also invited a few more people to come along for the celebratory flight in addition to the returning crowd of mechanics and engineers. To my eternal gratitude my producer Rupert Bush asked myself and Andy Parr, our top cameraman at ITV F1, to go along to document the occasion. Throughout the weekend we all had to keep the planned celebration a secret from Murray. We left the circuit before him and joined the other passengers to line up on the tarmac at Bergamo Airport wearing special 'Thanks for the Memories' T-shirts. I still have mine. When Murray arrived, he was delivered straight to the side of the plane and found all of us in a guard of honour waiting for him. I think he may have suspected something was up when he was chauffeur-driven to the door of the aircraft, but the sight of all of us clapping him in our T-shirts, and discovering his name and picture emblazoned on the side of the BAC 1-11 was something he would never forget.

Andy captured the moment of Murray receiving his guard of honour, but after take-off, the fun really started. As soon as the seatbelt signs were turned off the cabin erupted into one big party, with champagne being served by one Murray Walker OBE, dressed in the European Aviation cabin crew uniform of blouse, scarf and skirt! Eventually Andy gave up trying to film the proceedings, knowing that none of it could be used. The whole flight was by far and away the most memorable F1 party I've experienced in nearly 30 years, and it was topped off by Stoddart, on landing back in the UK, opening the forward door when it was still set to 'automatic'. That popped the emergency slide, and he then beckoned all of us – including Murray, hip replacements notwithstanding – to disembark the aircraft by jumping on to the slide and bouncing down to ground level. I like to think Paul gave the airline mechanics when, on race day, the FIA and Bernie Ecclestone sent him out on the drivers' parade once again.

But Murray's most raucous send-off during that 2001 season came appropriately enough from Paul Stoddart, the gregarious Australian entrepreneur, then owner of the Minardi team. 'Stoddy', as he was known, was a firm friend of Murray's. Alongside his F1 interests he ran European Aviation, a charter and cargo airline based out of Bournemouth Airport. As a side note for anyone as interested in the world of aviation as I am, the airline exists very successfully to this day. It's now known as European Cargo, and operates a fleet of Airbus A340-600s, massive four-engined aircraft bought at good prices from Virgin Atlantic. In 2020, Stoddart and European Cargo made a significant contribution to the UK's Covid-19 pandemic response, ferrying testing kits and protective equipment from China to the UK when they were needed most.

As Murray's house in the New Forest was only 20 minutes from Bournemouth Airport, Murray was a regular on Paul Stoddart's passenger aircraft, a BAC 1-11 that first entered service with British European Airways in 1969. From Bournemouth, the aircraft would hop up to Coventry to collect mechanics and engineers from various teams before flying on to whatever European race was being held that weekend. This arrangement saved Murray hours of travelling time.

Monza was the last European F1 race for Murray, so for the homebound leg after the race on Sunday, Stoddart pulled out all the stops to make it a flight to remember. He decorated the side of his BAC 1-11 with a giant decal reading 'Goodbye Murray and thanks for the priceless. 'Well, I can tell you this,' he said once he'd got his breath back. 'If you ever think that life is dull and ordinary, and that things are passing you by, you should try this.'

We wanted to make Murray's last home Grand Prix as special as possible, but with so much having been done already we found ourselves slightly at a loss as to what that something special could be. From getting Murray a ride with the Royal Air Force Red Arrows to lowering him out of a Royal Navy Sea King helicopter on an abseiling rope to land at the front of the starting grid, some seriously wild ideas were being considered.

At this point one of the producers asked me to run to the tape library and pull out a VHS recording of the previous year's race so we could assess how big the area was at the front of the grid for a potentially abseiling Murray Walker to land. Watching the tape we noticed something. The British fans loved to bring their own handmade banners and flags supporting their favourite teams and drivers to Silverstone, hanging them on the fences or the grandstands around the track. Why not ask the fans to bring their own flags and banners with messages written on them for Murray? Jim Rosenthal put out an on-air call for F1 fans to get involved. And the Silverstone public really did rise to the occasion. Come race weekend the grandstands were lined with 'Murray Walker' flags and banners with amusing Murray quotes. As the host broadcaster at the British GP (before F1 standardized and centralized the main race feed coverage) we were able to make the most of it by choosing the perfect moments to cut to these banners on the coverage when Murray was watching from the commentary box. He found the messages from the fans very touching and was full of emotion

MURRAY'S LAST SEASON

The commemorations and special events continued throughout the season. One of Murray's goodbye presents was a ride in the McLaren two-seater, a racing car well ahead of its time – it even had its own chassis designation, the MP4/98T. McLaren boss Ron Dennis and his marketing maestro Ekrem Sami had invested a lot of time and money into the two-seater project. They recognized that it was a huge PR opportunity for McLaren to be able to put their sponsors and VIP guests in a car in which they could experience the thrill of Formula 1, but with state-of-the-art safety standards. The two-seater was well engineered, well built (with a race-grade Mercedes V10 engine) and was driven most often by David Coulthard, Mika Häkkinen or Martin Brundle.

Murray's outing in the MP4/98T took place at Silverstone, a few weeks ahead of the British GP. ITV had a crash helmet specially designed for him, and it was my job to go and collect it from a company called Grand Prix Racewear. It had Murray's name on the side and the Union Flag on the top. Martin Brundle was going to drive Murray, and if I'm honest, there had been some qualms about putting this elderly legend in the back of an F1 two-seater. What would happen if he passed out due to the G-forces? What if something broke and they crashed? Murray had driven a McLaren himself back in 1981, but that had been years before, and maybe his body wouldn't be up to it now. As a precaution there was a panic button, which if pressed would alert Martin to slow down and return to the pits. Need we have worried? Of course not. Murray had the time of his life; he absolutely loved it. Brundle didn't hold back, and really gave his passenger a flat-out lap. The edited film aired over the build-up to the British GP, and you can still watch it online. The look of delight on Murray's face afterwards was

The outcome of that meeting was the mutual decision that Murray would be given a year's farewell tour, and if 2001 was to be his final season behind the microphone, it would be a celebration. Murray also agreed to miss three races out of the 16 that year, essentially so that ITV could field test his successor, none other than current pit lane reporter James Allen. And, significantly, as it turned out for me, they also planned to try out a couple of candidates for James's old job.

Over the winter, Murray's retirement became public knowledge. Within the F1 community and particularly, of course, within our ITV production, there was sadness at the end of an era, but also determination to send Murray off in style. Murray's swansong year kicked off memorably at the first race of the season in Melbourne, where the organizers went to town for him. Murray was hugely popular in Australia, and he returned the nation's regard. He would usually fly out there a fortnight before the race with his wife Elizabeth, and they would tour around a different part of the country or spend a week on a cruise before making their way to Melbourne. On Sunday morning the grandstands of the 2001 Australian Grand Prix were packed with well-wishers as the drivers emerged for the routine track parade.

Murray had been doing some research in the pits when Stuart Sykes from the Australian Grand Prix Corporation tapped him on the shoulder and suggested he might like to go out on to the grid. Intrigued, Murray crossed the pit lane to discover that one of the vintage cars had been stickered up with 'Murray Walker' across the windscreen sun strip. A gobsmacked and delighted Murray was driven round at the back of the parade and received as big a cheer as any of the drivers.

MURRAY'S LAST SEASON

It was a happy time to be a part of the ITV F1 team. By the end of 2000 we'd had three different world champions, and we were just entering the Michael Schumacher era, when the great man would win five straight drivers' championships and return Ferrari to the top of the sport. Viewing figures were good, and people even seemed to be getting used to the mid-race advert breaks. Thus, when a rather nasty column about Murray appeared in the British tabloid the *Daily Mail*, none of us on the production team paid much attention to it. It was followed up the next day by a readers' poll on whether it was 'time for Murray Walker to hang up the microphone'. It wasn't, of course, but Murray used to buy the *Daily Mail*, and perhaps because it was a newspaper he read, it wasn't so easy for him to dismiss it as just 'next day's chip wrapping'.

In his autobiography *Unless I'm Very Much Mistaken*, Murray later revealed that, being 'a sensitive soul', the article had seemed like a warning shot across his bows. Annoyed with himself for a mistake in which he'd mixed up Michael Schumacher and Rubens Barrichello at the German GP a few weeks earlier, Murray had begun seriously to think about whether it was better to stop when he felt he 'was still at the top of the tree rather than tumbling down it'. With retirement in mind, Murray went to see ITV's controller of sport at the time, Brian Barwick, a genial Liverpudlian who later became more widely known as the chief executive of the Football Association. Barwick told Murray that it had to be his decision, and that the network would support him either way. In hindsight, I believe Murray went to see Brian hoping he'd be talked out of the idea of retiring, but if that was the case he got no such response. If they're not going to beg me to stay, Murray may have reasoned, maybe it is the right time to go.

made, the so-called 'Murray-isms', but as I'd find out in my own time on-air, we all make mistakes, it's just when you make them on television, everyone knows about it!

For a commentator, accurate driver identification is the most important thing to perfect, even though the commentator has a much less favourable viewing environment with sunlight coming in from all angles of the average commentary box, and only, in those days, a small 4:3 cathode-ray tube TV to watch, amid constant requests on talkback providing multiple distractions. The viewer, sitting in comfort at home watching on a massive TV, is always going to have an easier time identifying cars than those in the broadcast booth. That's why, as Murray's commentary-box producer, I tried hard to limit the distractions, leaving him free to concentrate on his world feed monitor and the timing screen on top of it. If Murray did mis-identify a driver, I'd wait for Martin to gently put him right, or if it was important, I'd press the little talkback button I had going into his headphones, and just say the name of the driver. Murray would then correctly identify whoever we were looking at, and we'd all move on. It really wasn't a big problem.

Having said that, Murray cared very much about maintaining his own professional high standards. He'd been doing the job for over 50 years. Despite having had two hip replacements, he was physically active and as fit as a fiddle. The only things he did suffer from health-wise were the occasional coughs and colds he picked up because of all the air travel. Long before any of us started cleaning surfaces with antibacterial wipes, Murray had noticed the cause and effect between long-haul flights and minor illnesses, which I remember he found annoying.

a Brussels Airport hotel, so it mattered not one iota to him that we were moving at a snail's pace out towards the motorway.

Murray was a fantastic travelling companion, because he loved to pass comment on everything – on the race that he'd just commentated on, or the particular performance of a certain team or driver, or sometimes the standard of road driving in the queue around us. Usually, it was in his conversational voice, but sometimes he'd amuse his fellow passengers with a burst of 'and it's go, go, go!' when the traffic lights turned green.

In this instance we had been turned away from our usual route towards Liège, and were being vectored into an unfamiliar direction. In the front, Louise and James were poring over the map we'd been given by the hire-car company and trying to figure out a new route (younger readers, this is what we did before Google Maps and SatNav). While the driver and her navigator were getting more and more frustrated in the front, I noticed Murray gazing out of his window. He then theatrically leaned across me to look out of my window. Louise and James had given up complaining about the diversion and settled into a 'We'll get there eventually' mode. Only then, with perfect timing, did Murray lean forward and say, 'Do you know, I think I drove my tank through here in 1944 . . .'

We laughed, as it put our minor squabbles about the vagaries of Belgian traffic into perspective. Here was a man who at the age of 76 was not only still very much at the top of his game as the voice of F1, but in his younger days had served in World War Two as an officer in the Royal Scots Greys regiment.

Murray's age was never an issue as far as the ITV production was concerned. He was consistently brilliant at what he did, and was adored the world over. Sure, there were little mistakes that he

Rosenthal, Tony Jardine or ITV's technical producer, Roger Philcox, a legend on the production crew. Roger's job was to book all the satellite lines for ITV's F1 programmes, and he used to travel around the world with a briefcase stuffed full of US dollars in case he needed to pay for an extension to a satellite booking at short notice. Back then there wasn't the ability to transfer money instantly at the click of an app, so in the event of a race overrun or a red-flag stoppage, Roger would save ITV from falling off-air by running to the uplink van and paying in person for the satellite fees with wads of the network's cash.

Unusually for Spa-Francorchamps, the 2000 race hadn't overrun, which had enabled Roger, Jim and Tony to escape eastbound to Cologne Bonn Airport across the border in Germany, from where they had a flight back to Heathrow. (From Spa, it's actually easier to get to Cologne than Brussels, despite it being in a different country.) In fact, due to his many frequent flights keeping ITV's outside broadcasts on-air worldwide, Roger Philcox held such high status with British Airways that he was able to phone a special number to request that the plane he was booked on not leave without him – thus making travelling alongside him extremely advantageous. To my knowledge Roger never missed a flight.

Murray preferred a more relaxed kind of race weekend getaway, often electing to stay Sunday night near the circuit or in an airport hotel to rest after the day's exertions, rather than rushing to get home that evening with all the stress that entailed. He also factored in the fact that if his flight was to arrive back at London Heathrow, that meant there was still a 90-minute drive south to his home in the New Forest. Best make that journey when you're not absolutely knackered, Murray reasoned. In this case, he was overnighting at

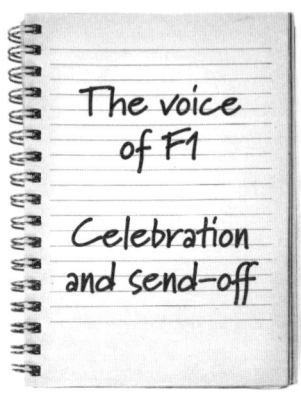

The voice of F1

Celebration and send-off

Chapter 5

Murray's Last Season

The Belgian GP at Spa-Francorchamps has always struggled with traffic problems. It's not the organizers' fault, it's just that there's a huge number of spectators to get in and out. The race is enormously popular among Dutch, German, British and French fans. In fact, the only country that doesn't appear to be well represented at the Belgian GP is Belgium! It's a circuit with one road in and one road out. Sometimes, if the police are in a good mood and if there's a 'T' in the month, they might open some of the single-track lanes that lead out of the back of the huge five-mile circuit, allowing better dispersal to all points south and east. But most of the time everyone is funnelled into the same massive traffic jam northbound towards the motorway. And it was after the 2000 race that I found myself in this very traffic jam, occupying the back of a hire car with Murray Walker, on the way to Brussels Airport.

Louise Goodman was driving with James Allen alongside and Murray was next to me in the back. It was rare for Murray to travel in our reporters' car – usually he'd get a lift with Jim

following year. For Villeneuve, meanwhile, Jerez was all about the release of a season's-worth of pressure and an opportunity to celebrate achieving his long-held dream of winning an F1 Championship. On his return to the pits, Villeneuve hugged Clear, whose own ambition to beat Schumacher (a driver he would later work with closely at Mercedes) had also been well and truly achieved. 'We did him! We fucking did him!' screamed Jock, as the Williams mechanics, sporting yellow-blonde wigs to mimic Jacques's peroxide hairstyle, carried the Canadian on their shoulders down to the podium and a moment that, although brief, would remain bright in my memory and that of millions of other F1 viewers worldwide. Jacques was now a champion in his own right, no longer just Gilles's son.

and filmed the ensuing chat. Ron Dennis shielded his mouth from the camera. Patrick Head was known to be hard of hearing, but Ron was also in the habit of covering his mouth to shield his words when he spoke, and this wasn't by any means the first or the last time I observed him doing this.

It was a highly unusual thing to happen and naturally viewers suspected that some kind of deal for Villeneuve to let the McLaren duo through was being confirmed. Upon investigation, however, the FIA found there was no case to answer and Williams simply called it 'good communication'. McLaren denied there had ever been a pact and maintained that in fact they had simply been honouring an informal understanding not to get involved in the championship decider. This claim was then supported by the second event: a team radio message, that came to light some time after the race, which revealed engineer Jock Clear advising Villeneuve of the closing McLarens. On tape you can hear Clear asking Villeneuve to 'remember what we discussed' and reitcrating, several times, how Häkkinen had been 'helpful' to the Williams cause.[1]

For Mika Häkkinen the race victory was the start of a winning streak that would lead him to his first world championship the

---

1   Jock Clear (to Villeneuve): 'Keep concentrating, Jacques. Keep concentrating. Häkkinen up to position two. Häkkinen quite quick and very helpful. (Later) Be aware that Häkkinen is now in position two. He probably wants to win. Very helpful. (Later) DC [David Coulthard] is controlling [Eddie] Irvine. Häkkinen immediately behind you, Jacques. Immediately behind you, Häkkinen.'

Clear (Later): 'Keep concentrating, Jacques. Häkkinen is immediately behind. Last lap. Last lap. Häkkinen has been very helpful. Jacques, position two. Don't let me down, Jacques. We discussed this . . .'

In the race, too, Ferrari had allies. Halfway through, Villeneuve lost time as he was held up behind Sauber driver Norberto Fontana, which led to this exchange between Murray Walker and Martin Brundle in the commentary box that made me smile:

> Murray: 'Case of champagne from Ferrari to Sauber for Norberto Fontana because the Argentine newcomer really, really helped Michael Schumacher on his way there.'
> Martin: 'What engine have they got in that Sauber, Murray?'
> Murray: 'Er...'
> Martin: 'Isn't it a Ferrari?'
> Murray: 'Well, it is, yes. Oh Martin, you are a cynical chap!'

Following the lap 48 clash with Schumacher, Villeneuve led the race until the last lap. Villeneuve then allowed both McLarens through, giving Mika Häkkinen an emotional maiden win just two years after a qualifying accident in Australia that had nearly cost the Finn his life. Afterwards Villeneuve explained that he had needed to protect his car following the clash, and that he wasn't bothered about finishing on the podium: he had the points he needed to be world champion. There were, however, two key events that prompted the FIA to briefly investigate McLaren and Williams for collusion or 'race-fixing' once the season was over.

First was the appearance of Williams technical director Patrick Head in the McLaren garage, a few laps before the end of the race. James Allen had positioned himself to watch the race from the same garage and ITV cameraman Keith Wilson was also on hand matter – Villeneuve had set the time first, followed by Schumacher and then Frentzen, so that was the grid.

As for the race, while it ended for Michael Schumacher in that controversial block on Jacques Villeneuve, that was by no means the final twist. After it had been struck by Schumacher's front-right tyre, Williams were concerned about the integrity of Villeneuve's car. Rightly, as it turned out – post-race inspections revealed that the on-board battery keeping Villeneuve's electronic systems alive had become dislodged by the impact of the Ferrari and was left hanging by its red-and-black connection wires inside the car. The thought of this battery, weighing half a kilo or so, dangling freely in the Williams's left-hand sidepod, secured only by a couple of wires, must have given Jacques chills for years after. Driving to achieve maximum speed while protecting his car as he did meant the battery survived the race and he emerged the world champion. Had he not done that, Michael would have won Ferrari's first drivers' title since 1979.

As all F1 viewers of that season cannot fail to have been aware, Michael had some assistance in the form of a couple of friendly drivers. His Ferrari teammate Eddie Irvine irritated Villeneuve by holding him up in practice several times. Springing vividly to mind is the moment Jacques hopped out of his car at the end of Friday practice, strode down the pit lane and confronted Irvine, who was still in his Ferrari, being wheeled back into the garage. It's hard to convey anger when your face is hidden by a crash helmet, but no viewer could be in any doubt that Villeneuve was furious and that Irvine got the message. Years later, Jacques claimed his was an intentional overreaction, as he wanted to draw attention to what he saw as Ferrari's 'games'.

itself more like a science-lab-style F1 operation, a paragon of excellence and efficiency, the pinnacle of Formula 1 technology.

Selling that idea was down to good old-fashioned marketing and McLaren had its own well-financed marketing division headed up by Ekrem Sami, a legend in F1's commercial world. On the eve of the Jerez weekend, McLaren Mercedes held a lavish party for their team and sponsors at one of the town's sherry wineries. The travelling F1 media were sent an invite which read 'Take the Bull by the Horns'. Nobody really knew what this meant: some assumed it alluded to McLaren's determination to end the season on a high, while others saw it as a reference to Spain's bullfighting tradition. It was only years later I found out it pointed towards a design detail of the McLaren's car livery that had remained practically unnoticed for years: in the negative space in the middle of the car's front wing was a silhouette of a bull's head and horns. The party was a great success, enlivened by McLaren's team co-ordinator Jo Ramirez, a proud Mexican who lived in southern Spain, holding court with stories of the explosive battles between Ayrton Senna and Alain Prost of F1 seasons past.

From a memorable party to a memorable qualifying session. For the first time in Formula 1 history, three drivers set identical lap times in qualifying, a 1.21.072. Murray Walker called it 'almost unbelievable' and there were plenty of cynics in the F1 world who spoke of timing glitches or some kind of manipulation designed to increase the tension ahead of the race. Williams later published the telemetry data proving definitively that Jacques Villeneuve and Heinz-Harald Frentzen had completed their laps with exactly the same lap time, to the thousandth of a second. Ferrari didn't release the data from Michael Schumacher's car but in the end, it didn't rental cars every morning. We stayed in a town called Blankenheim, which had the Eifel mountains on one side and the 'Schloss Blankenheim', an imposing medieval castle, on the other. Should you be curious to experience it for yourself, you can stay there – it's now a youth hostel.

After the Nürburgring there were only two Grands Prix left in the 1997 season and Villeneuve well and truly drew a blank at Suzuka. Already compromised by a suspended race ban imposed for failing to slow down sufficiently in an accident zone at the Italian GP, Jacques repeated the offence and was disqualified from the Japanese GP – a penalty so harsh as to be unheard of these days. For Jacques it meant that having gone into the Suzuka weekend nine points ahead of Michael, he started the final round in Jerez one point behind.

In previous years the season had ended at an Asian or Australasian race, but this year we finished in Europe, giving the F1 teams an opportunity to achieve the maximum marketing impact in their home territories, and none were keener than McLaren, who had launched their car eight months previously at the Royal Albert Hall with an exclusive performance by one of the biggest musical acts of the nineties, The Spice Girls. McLaren were on the verge of something big, competitively speaking. Having left Williams for McLaren at the end of 1996, Adrian Newey had designed a car that was now reaching full potency and Mercedes were getting on top of the small reliability issues that had previously been their undoing. McLaren boss Ron Dennis and the amiable Norbert Haug, motorsport director of Mercedes, were Formula 1's power couple. In sharp contrast to the 'tyre-marks on the garage floor', 'oily rag' aesthetic of Williams, McLaren was positioning down to preserve his engine, handing Hill the win. Villeneuve gave Hill a good run for his money that season, making the top step of the podium four times, but Damon's eight wins saw him eventually crowned champion at the end of the year in Japan.

Was it the seeming ease with which Villeneuve was able to match Hill's pace that led Frank Williams to lose faith in Damon? Although Frank remained convinced of the British driver's race craft and consistency, he decided, in a move that surprised everyone, that he saw more natural ability in Heinz-Harald Frentzen, a funeral director's son from Mönchengladbach who had matched Michael Schumacher lap for lap when they competed in German Formula 3 (in the sort of detail that delights me you might be interested to know that Frentzen returned to the undertaking business after his retirement from Formula 1). In 1997, with Frentzen replacing Damon Hill at Williams, Villeneuve had a new set of variables affecting his own championship challenge.

Things started off well enough. Jacques won two out of the first three races, but Frentzen was on the pace and pushing hard. Meanwhile, McLaren's (first) partnership with Mercedes engines was starting to bear fruit and the car was quick, if not particularly reliable. As the battle with Schumacher ebbed and flowed, Villeneuve won his seventh race of the season at the Nürburgring on a chilly late September day. It would turn out to be his final race win in Formula 1, the beneficiary of an embarrassing double-engine failure for McLaren duo Mika Häkkinen and David Coulthard on Mercedes's home turf.

I loved the Nürburgring. The F1 circuit was well laid-out, the expert organization highly efficient and we would drive past the final straight of the old circuit, the famed Nordschleife, in our

Murray's approach to race commentary than anything I've read before or since) and Martin Brundle, whose cool racer's reaction precisely summed up the desperate manoeuvre: 'That didn't work, Michael, you hit the wrong part of him, my friend.'

The cars may have collided in that championship-deciding race, but the story of the Villeneuve–Schumacher clash began at the start of the 1996 season when they found they shared a common adversary in Hill, Schumacher's victim from Adelaide '94, now Villeneuve's teammate. Jacques came in hot to the Williams Renault team from IndyCar in the USA, where he had won both the 1995 title and the famed Indianapolis 500. He was at the top of his game in the American racing scene, but the lure of Formula 1 had been irresistible, not least because of his F1 heritage.

Jacques's father was Gilles Villeneuve, French-Canadian but European in spirit and adored by F1 fans for his flamboyant, acrobatic driving style, his sheer speed, his intense competitive spirit and his affection for Enzo Ferrari, who, in turn, loved Gilles like a son. Tragically, Gilles was killed after an accident in his Ferrari during the qualifying session for the Belgian Grand Prix of 1982. Jacques was just 11 years old and grew up with the double burden of missing his father, but also, when he himself started racing, with the weight of expectation that came with being the son of the great Gilles Villeneuve. Added to this was the pressure he put on himself, wanting to win the F1 championship his father never did.

The Adrian Newey-designed Williams FW18 was quick, and a winter of intense testing saw Villeneuve extremely well prepared for his debut season, so much so that he led the first race of 1996 in Melbourne from pole position before an oil leak forced him to slow

Chapter 4

Jacques, Gilles and Jerez

Not only was I now travelling with the Grand Prix circus and in a position to watch the races from the commentary box, but my first season ended with one of the all-time great stories of F1. Before Lewis Hamilton was out of karting and Max Verstappen was out of nappies, this was the season when Michael Schumacher failed to pull off the trick he'd been successful with three years previously: running into the side of a Williams to try to win the world championship.

In 1994, at the Australian Grand Prix, the Williams in question had been Damon Hill's, its front suspension damaged beyond repair following a sideswipe from Schumacher's Benetton. This time it was Jacques Villeneuve's Williams that was hit by Schumacher's Ferrari as the Canadian was trying to overtake for the lead of the European Grand Prix. I watched the whole thing unfold from the commentary box at the Jerez Circuit in southern Spain, with Murray Walker, trousers metaphorically on fire (a description first coined by Clive James that more perfectly sums up third gear, Murray was careful never to say too much, or to give the listener an overwhelming amount of information. 'So, lap 45 in Hungary. Ayrton Senna leads for McLaren with Nigel Mansell 2.3 seconds behind. Gerhard Berger is third, a further 5.8 seconds behind the Williams Renault.' A typical succinct Murray recap with information gleaned from the timing screen, but it tallied with what the viewers could see on track, and reassured the audience that Murray was on top of the whole situation.

When he'd finished a top six rundown Murray used to physically push his microphone away from his mouth, a signal for Martin to pick up. If there wasn't much overtaking or racing to get excited about, that was when Murray would turn to the stories that he'd researched on Thursday. Choosing three or four topics of conversation in the paddock that weekend, Murray would collate and prioritize which stories to share, for instance the latest moves in the driver market, or if a team principal or chief designer was being appointed or replaced. These topics were usually delivered in first or second gear.

Finally, there was that voice. Not before or since has there been a voice that was so naturally suited to the sport it covered. It was powerful, it had immense physical volume, and it had a recognizable and repeatable tone. Generations of viewers can, to this day, immediately conjure up Murray Walker's voice. To listen to Murray in top gear was the next best thing to being trackside yourself. Through Murray you knew that what you were watching was exciting, significant and important, that it meant as much to him as it did to you, and that is why he was so loved by his audience.

THE MURRAY AND MARTIN SHOW

Go, Go, Go,' which worked well with his inimitable voice. Honestly, it didn't really matter what he said, all Murray needed was to buy a few seconds to allow the cars to move off the line so that he could establish whatever order they were in. The fact that he used to mix it up always felt, to me at least, that he was having fun, and wanted the flexibility to call the start of the race in whatever way he liked.

And there you have the key aspect of Murray Walker's commentary style – he liked what he was watching. That description of Murray's enthusiasm having a 'childlike quality' is true in part and goes some way to explaining the connection he made with young viewers who got hooked on F1. I would add that he simply had a genuine passion for motor racing and thoroughly enjoyed what he was doing. His responses to events were unrehearsed: 'Oh my goodness, look at that!,' or 'This is the worst start to a Grand Prix that I have ever seen *In The Whole Of My Life.*' Murray's use of language was always exhilarating.

Giving yourself time to think when you're talking consistently for hours on end is an art, and Murray managed to achieve this by slowing down and carefully managing all the available content. If you listen back to any of his race commentaries you'll notice that, like one of his beloved BMWs, he had his own personal six-speed gearbox. He would start in fourth, go into fifth for the start, before dropping down through the gears as the race progressed. He'd be able to ratchet back up to fifth and even sixth gear if the action was particularly significant, but knew very well that the audience would find a commentary constantly in sixth gear completely exhausting to listen to, so he used that mode sparingly.

Gearbox perfectly tuned, a certain economy with words allowed him to think about what to say next. Purring along in second or performance. After that it was time for the mouth exercises. The story goes that a famous theatre actor (I recall Sir John Gielgud being mentioned) once told Murray that the mouth contained a hundred muscles, all of which need warming up if one was to deliver one's best vocal performance. Murray would duly go through the most rigorous contortions of his mouth to get all those muscles well and truly warmed up. I must admit, it works, and if your job depends on you using your voice it's worth noting. Most of the time our mouths are shut, and we talk from our lips. To really enunciate fully and not trip over your words, you have to warm up your mouth. It's a practice I learned from Murray, and I make sure to do it before every session.

A few more shoulder rolls and neck stretches, and then the F1 titles played, signalling five minutes until the race start. 'Cue Murray!' and we were off. I never knew how Murray was going to begin the commentary, but what you could expect was that it would be dramatic. *'Stand By Because This Is The Big One!'* Murray might have said that at the first race of the season, or at Silverstone, or at the world championship decider – to him they were all big ones! He would set the scene, talk about what had been happening leading up to the race and recapping qualifying for those who hadn't seen it. All of this allowed Martin time to come up to the box after his live grid walk. Once he was settled Murray would bring his co-commentator into the conversation for the first time.

As Murray might have said, with 'tension so thick you could cut it with a cricket stump', the cars lined up on the final starting grid, and it was 'go' time. The FIA only started using the current five lights on-hold-and-off system at the beginning of 1996, so Murray used to mix up his 'lights out' phrases. He was most well-known for 'And it's

THE MURRAY AND MARTIN SHOW

Martin: 'Charlie's got a Bobcat.'
Murray: 'What?'
Martin: 'Look, Charlie's got a Bobcat.'
Murray: 'Oh, yeah.'

And with that, they both put their headphones back on, stared back at the screen, and settled into another 20 minutes of silence.

I smiled. Only in F1 could the words 'Charlie's got a Bobcat' make any sense. Martin was pointing out that FIA (Fédération Internationale de l'Automobile) race director Charlie Whiting had deployed an additional recovery vehicle, a small crane made by the Bobcat company. Martin hadn't seen Whiting sanction the use of a Bobcat before, and clearly thought it was of note. Murray was less interested but I loved that little exchange, and I'll never forget it. Charlie's got a Bobcat. Great name for a rock band.

The next day, it was showtime. Murray had a very specific warm-up routine. With about five minutes to go before the F1 introduction that signalled it was nearly time to start commentating, Murray would stand up and take off his headphones. This was my cue to remove his chair to the back of the commentary box or place it outside. He wouldn't be needing it again. Then he would start his exercises. He proceeded to stomp his feet three or four times left to right, and then began a vigorous upper-body aerobic warm-up session. Arms out to the side, five times. Alternate forward punches, five times. Elbows back to stretch and open up the rib cage. A few more tightened fist pumps and he was ready for action.

Murray's commentary was a physical performance. As he commentated from a standing position he felt a warm-up opened up his chest, which delivered a better, more powerful vocal box. From that point, Martin and I developed a kind of unspoken communication system over the years – we can catch each other's eye for a second across a grid or paddock and know exactly what we're each thinking. His nickname in the TV compound is 'The Guv'nor'. I don't know why, it just fits. Probably because he is the best in the world at what he does.

But back to my early commentary-box days and I was concentrating on everything so hard I sometimes had to remind myself to enjoy the little behind-the-scenes moments. One year at Japan's Suzuka circuit Martin came up to watch the second free practice session with Murray. It wasn't a particularly eventful session, so we all sat there in silence. After 10 minutes or so Martin shared an observation with Murray about a particular racing line a driver was taking. 'Oh yeah,' said Murray, before they both lapsed into silence for another 15 minutes. We were all battling the effects of a plus nine-hour time difference, and the soporific engine noise made it difficult for Martin and me to beat the jet lag and stay awake. Murray, though, was glued to that TV. Another 15 minutes passed and just as our eyelids were starting to droop, the race feed cut to a car spinning off, fast, at the 130R corner. 'WHAM!' exclaimed Murray at full volume, shattering our drowsy silence. 'Oh, crikey!' A pause to check the driver was conscious. 'Dear oh dear, he's made a right mess of that one, hasn't he?'

Martin nodded in agreement as the Japanese marshals ran to help the unfortunate driver who had flung his Grand Prix car into the gravel. Murray made a note of who and when. Another couple of minutes into the recovery process passed before Martin, lifting off one side of his headphones, had something to say.

THE MURRAY AND MARTIN SHOW

In the middle of the commentary box was a monitor showing the ITV programme output, so Murray and Martin could watch our pre- and post-race coverage. Martin had his own world feed and timing screens centre right, and squeezed into the far-right corner was my little spot with a talkback panel to communicate with the producer and director in the gallery, volume knobs to listen to James and Louise in the pits, and switches to talk via the headsets to Murray and Martin.

Once everything was set up to Murray's satisfaction he would sit and watch the practice sessions with an intensity that took me a while to understand before I realized that he was practising too. He was watching the cars, making sure he was spot-on with his identification, and noting features of the circuit itself. He had a copy of the track map, and he would annotate it, marking which advertising billboards were on which corner. This was important, because if he saw a car stop, or if there was an accident, his first job would be to identify the car and driver. The second job would be to identify the corner, and if for example there was Foster's signage in the background then Murray knew from his sponsor marked-up map that the incident was at Turn 5, or if there was a Rolex billboard, it had to be Turn 10, and so on. When first practice ended, Murray would take his headphones off, slap his thigh and say, 'Right! That's lunch,' and we would both make our way back to the TV compound.

I have been lucky enough to parallel Martin on his second career journey through broadcasting. We first got to know each other at ITV Sport, and then moved together to the BBC, and on to Sky Sports. In another life, I would love to have been his race engineer, but in this one we started out having to communicate by looks and gestures alone, as we stood shoulder to shoulder in the commentary

I'd hung on to every other weekend for years, and Martin Brundle, the new star of F1 broadcasting. And whether it was spotting a spin, or a quick sector time on the timing screen, or giving Murray a steer on which driver the visual feed had cut to if he'd been looking elsewhere, I was helping. As you might well imagine, the four years I spent in the commentary box remain the most enjoyable time I've had in my professional life.

As the season continued, I'd spend more time in the box on Fridays, setting up the TVs and fixing sun-screening material to reduce the light glare from the windows. Murray would watch every practice session from the box (live coverage of free practice only started in 2012), and he used the time to prepare for qualifying and the race. Martin might join us for the second or third practice sessions, but would generally alternate between watching the action trackside, from the media centre, or from a motorhome over coffee with a team member. For Murray, practice sessions were a vital part of his preparation, research and thinking time.

He would get to the commentary box around half an hour before first practice and get it set it up just the way he liked it. It was identical at every race. His preferred commentary-box layout was simple. He'd always be on the far left of the box with his notes and statistics stuck to the left-hand wall or window. Directly in front of him was the main F1 world feed (the stream of images produced by F1 and fed out to broadcasters around the world) on a high-quality TV placed on a packing case, so it was just below his eye level. The timing screen was then put on top of the main monitor, and in front of that we placed a solid plastic tripod case that came up to Murray's midriff. This acted as a very handy little writing table on which Murray would take note of who pitted on what lap.

if I started to wave the sign up and down, that meant something urgent was happening in the pit lane, and Murray or Martin should try to throw down to James as soon as they could. I had what's called a 'snoop' of James Allen's and Louise Goodman's microphones through my headphones, so I could hear everything they said to the producer. Very useful, as it helped me gauge whether something was urgent or not, and very useful training for my next job!

THROW TO LOUISE: Unlike James, Louise wasn't always in the pits. Often, she was with a driver in the paddock or a team boss in a garage, so we felt a more generic 'throw' was best.

WRAP UP COMMENTARY: I'd considered 'STOP', but feared, Murray being Murray, he would just stop talking immediately. I'd thought long and hard about 'NO MORE COMMENTARY', but that sounded a little curt, so 'WRAP UP COMMENTARY' won the day.

The cue cards worked perfectly. Most of the time they would be greeted by a thumbs-up 'received and understood' acknowledgement from Murray, but sometimes he was so engrossed in his commentary that he would either not notice or ignore the cards. At which point I'd start to move them gently up and down in his field of view, much to Martin's amusement.

That first weekend in the Hockenheim commentary box, with the huge swathes of Schumacher fans below us in the grandstand enjoying the German GP, was a markedly different experience to logging the race in a windowless broadcast truck. I was standing alongside Murray Walker, my TV hero, the man whose every word an interview, or leading to the next part of a programme. However, if he was interrupted when he was concentrating and commentating in full flow he would usually stop talking and look at me as if to say, 'Who was that, what were they saying, and why the blazes were they interrupting me?' All important thoughts, but with no words emerging at the same time it did leave a bit of a gap in the commentary.

I had noticed that he was fine with talkback if it was simply telling him to start ('Cue Murray') or to stop ('Wrap it up please Murray'), but anything outside of that was a problem. I wondered if a series of handwritten signs might be a more effective alternative.

I got through 50 sheets of A4 paper during that first weekend in Hockenheim. On my return to London I decided to print out the five most common instructions in big, bold, capital letters, and get them laminated for regular use. Those five cue cards were:

START: An obvious one, I thought. I could have put 'GO', but Murray might have bolted for the door!

LEAD TO BREAK: This was a difficult one, as we tried to make the throw to in-race advert breaks as subtle as possible, and if I'd put 'GO TO BREAK', Murray might have said, 'So, it's lap 35 and we're going to a break', whereas 'lead' reminded him to gently wrap up his sentence or thought and take a pause in order for the production gallery to roll in the advert break.

JAMES IN PITS: Our pit reporter James Allen was always in the pits, but this sign had a dual meaning. If I held it still, it meant James's report wasn't urgent or particularly time sensitive, whereas didn't get missed. Starting at the 1997 German GP, I was sent to the commentary box. If I could find it.

Commentary boxes are interesting little things. At older circuits they're usually located in a position that allows the commentator to see a large portion of the track. Circuits like Silverstone, Hockenheim or Monza run race meetings year-round, and most of these aren't televised live, which means that any commentator present needs to be able to see the action out of the window with a pair of binoculars. Most club-racing circuit commentators only have a timing screen and a good view to work from, and if all the TV pictures go down, that's what F1 commentators need to be able to work from, too.

At Hockenheim the commentary boxes were on a gantry on top of the main grandstand, which meant plotting a route out of the TV compound, which as usual was situated near the paddock on the inside of the circuit. I had to go through a tunnel under the track, come out behind the main start/finish line grandstand, find the security guard by the gate, and then climb up four storeys to the top.

Once there, my instructions were no more detailed than simply to 'give Murray and Martin a hand'. I soon realized that having an extra pair of eyes on the timing screens and somebody to act as a halfway house between producer and commentator was going to be a big help. Not least because, while Murray could commentate accurately and entertainingly for the duration of a Grand Prix, the moment somebody talked to him through his headset he would grind to a halt, looking around the box as he listened. In TV terms, Murray couldn't take talkback.

That's not entirely fair because, as a TV professional, Murray *could* listen to a director's voice in his ear when he was conducting session, I was allowed to lean out the back of the truck and watch the F1 cars speed past.

The view varied. In Monaco we were on the outside of the Swimming Pool exit – a truly breathtaking vantage point from where you could have reached out and touched the cars if you were stupid enough to try. At the Circuit de Catalunya in Barcelona we were on the outside of the last corner, which saw some seriously impressive speeds.

Seeing the cars on track was great fun, and it at least gave me a brief glimpse of the F1 world in which I worked. But after 10 minutes it was back into the cool, dark TV truck for more tape logging. The job that took me to TV compounds in circuits all around the world, requiring hours and hours of my time logging F1 sessions, pit lane camera footage and driver interviews is now done by an AI-powered plug-in to our media library. In 1997 we were a long way off this technological development, but nonetheless halfway through the season there did come a significant change to my job.

Imagine being in the commentary box commentating on the race. You'll need to be keeping an eye on multiple screens showing race positioning and technical data, feeds from cameras following individual cars on track and also watching the parts of the track and pit lane that can be seen from the commentary-box window. You'll be keeping across 20 cars and debating events with your co-commentator as well as listening to information from the production team and your pit lane reporters. What you'd probably wish you had is an extra pair of eyes. And so my boss Neil Duncanson decided to use me as a spotter, helping Murray and Martin filter the huge range of information and ensuring things

THE MURRAY AND MARTIN SHOW

Alongside Murray there was the reluctant genius: Martin Brundle. Reluctant because he hadn't been ready to start his TV career so soon, and genius because he's the most knowledgeable, most authoritative, quickest-witted communicator in broadcast sport. In his day Martin was a very good racing driver – he was quick, consistent, versatile, mentally tough and smart. When it came to commentary, all that gave him authority, but what he also brought to his television career was an easy charm, a sharp sense of humour and a team ethic worth its weight in gold. Perhaps because he was part of so many good (and bad) F1 outfits over the years, Martin, it turned out, found much to enjoy about being part of a close-knit TV production.

In that first 1997 season the dynamic between Murray and Martin in the commentary box quickly established them both as the stars of our show. I'd been systematically logging their interviews and their recorded links for features. In all the time I spent watching them I was able to learn about how they worked, and about their respective characters. Murray had the habit of beginning his links with a little laugh, to ensure he had a smile on his face when the viewer first saw him, 'making a friendly first impression,' as he put it. Martin wasn't used to this 'TV lark', as he used to call it, and I saw him working away at his takes to achieve something he was happy with.

Up to this point I hadn't really left the TV compound at any of the tracks we visited. I didn't even have a paddock pass, because there wasn't any need for me to go there. I'd arrive at our outside-broadcast truck every morning, log tapes, help out with edits and, when the sessions were on, sit and log those as well. If I was lucky and one of the producers took over logging duties for 10 minutes during a

However, he also kept an open mind. Murray was initially suspicious of Flavio Briatore, who had been appointed from the fashion world by the Benetton family to run their F1 team. Murray questioned what someone who had never been to a Grand Prix could possibly know about operating a team. As it turned out, Flavio's work ethic and demonstrable success at Benetton (later Renault) eventually convinced Murray that the Italian's intentions were for the greater good of F1, rather than just himself. Although it was probably a good thing that he wasn't still commentating at the time of the Renault Crash-gate scandal of Singapore 2008 (involving Nelson Piquet Jr and an 'accidental' crash that put his teammate Fernando Alonso in a position to win the race, a crash that later emerged to have been planned). Murray would have thought that 'a very rum do!'

Murray was by no means an apologist for the many occasions F1 didn't exactly show itself in the best light. He would be front and centre in reporting a controversial piece of driving, or a rule breach by a team. He was as disappointed as any F1 fan by an uneventful race, although he'd save his true personal opinion for when we had gone off-air, when he would wrap up the commentary over the podium celebrations, put his microphone down and say, 'Well, that's not going to have them tuning into the highlights, is it?' That would be the extent of his criticism. Murray wouldn't ever call a race boring. Firstly, to him no F1 race could be boring, as viewing these incredible cars going at amazing speeds, driven by heroic drivers, could only ever be 90 minutes of pleasure. Secondly, while there might not be much going on among the frontrunners, there would always be some story or battle further down the field that would hold Murray's interest – and he'd make the rest of us care about it, too.

he stayed there. And Damon Hill exits the chicane and wins the Japanese Grand Prix – and I've got to stop, because I've got a lump in my throat.' But Murray was never naïve. He knew that his authentic passion and honesty were the best approach, because he understood the power of marketing, selling and promotion from his many years working in the advertising industry (in his former career he had been responsible for advertising Trill budgie seed. His clients had a problem in that their product was so successful, everyone was already using the seed to feed their birds. Murray's solution? 'An only budgie is a lonely budgie.') He knew that in F1 broadcasting, as in any market, you're not selling the steak, you're selling the sizzle, and he understood the psychology behind building tension, conveying excitement and in knowing how get people to feel invested in the outcome. Outside of the drivers I think he did the most to further the popularity and therefore the success of F1.

On screen, Murray never had a cross word for anyone and he served as a moderate foil to some of the strong views voiced by his co-commentator of the day, British ex-F1 champion James Hunt, not known for his discretion ('The problem with Jarier is that he is a French prat, always has been, always will be.') However, off-screen there were some people who were not Murray's cup of tea. He didn't have much time for those who he felt had come into F1 to make a quick buck for themselves while not particularly caring about the sport. Sometimes over dinner the subject of conversation would turn to one of these figures, whether they be brash, arrogant or particularly full of themselves – attributes hardly in short supply in the F1 paddock. Murray would pipe up, 'Oh, him. If he was made of chocolate he'd eat himself,' before breaking out into his huge laugh.

the F1 paddock and be instantly recognized, welcomed and accommodated in whatever he was looking for.

Most of the time, that was information. Murray always put a great deal of work into his preparation, and he covered a lot of ground on a race weekend. I'd often see him on Thursdays scouring the paddock and media centre, catching up on stories from the week between races, and getting inside information from the teams that he might need to refer to in commentary.

I say 'might' because Murray's style wasn't simply to bombard his audience with facts and figures or stories of an encounter with a driver in a lift. Despite having been at the job for so long, his magic ingredient was that he remained so charmingly enthusiastic about the pure motor-racing aspect of the F1 circus. His enthusiasm was often described as 'childlike', which I think is fair in that, despite having all the answers, he approached the viewing of every Grand Prix from a completely fresh perspective, as a child might have done watching from home. Not letting on that he had a pretty good idea beforehand of what was going to happen in the race, or that he might know the inside story about why a team or driver's performance was set to be the way it was, allowed Murray to connect with his audience, and to share those moments of discovery with them.

That's what made all his emotional reactions so genuine. All of the classic Murrayisms – 'There's nothing wrong with the car, except it's on fire', 'The lead car is unique, except for the one behind it, which is identical' – were instinctive. He said what he was really thinking at the time, and his emotions were never far from the surface. British viewers of a certain age will always remember his lines at the end of the 1996 Japanese Grand Prix, 'He fought from second on the grid, he passed Jacques Villeneuve, he took the lead,

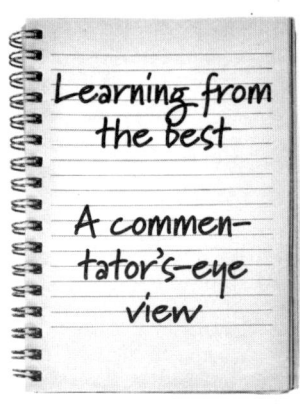

Chapter 3

The Murray and Martin Show

It is a truth universally acknowledged that no one can go through a career in Formula 1 and be respected by everyone – it's just too competitive an environment for that. However, there was one notable exception, and that was Murray Walker.

Everyone loved Murray, for a whole host of reasons. He was a kind, generous, witty, thoughtful, talented man – qualities which were evident to anyone he met. As a professional, he was widely respected within the F1 paddock, while his irrepressible passion, enthusiasm and joy in the sport communicated itself to viewers at home who responded in kind. Then there was his sheer longevity. Most people who work in F1 enjoy the sport, and probably grew up watching it on TV. If they watched it in the UK, or the USA or Canada, South Africa, Australia, New Zealand or pretty much any other English-speaking country, they would have been listening to Murray Walker's commentary. That inherent familiarity, that people already felt they knew him, meant Murray could walk into any garage or team motorhome or pretty much anywhere else in night, with my first F1 weekend over, I sat in the middle of a block of four seats at the back of a Swissair MD-11 en route from São Paulo to London via Zurich. I couldn't have been happier.

THE START LINE

spent most of the day filming features to fill the pre-race airtime we now had, but had only been able to get started on editing in the late afternoon. I was working on the first race of the season from London, so wasn't on-site to log the tapes and, since the producers hadn't had time to log their own tapes, if they needed some 'paint' shots to cover edits or show examples of what the interviewee was talking about, they had no idea if the two cameramen had shot the required footage, or if they had, where those clips were. Edits, therefore, were taking much longer than they should.

What they needed was someone to log the tapes, someone who knew where every shot was, and on which tape to find it. My job, in fact. Starting from the second race of 1997 in Brazil, it was decided that I would travel to the circuits. To downplay this slightly, the fact was I wouldn't get out much, I wouldn't see any cars on track or be able to leave the TV compound. I was there to manage all the tapes, log them, know where every shot was, log the practice sessions, qualifying and the races and be on hand for as long as was needed. If John 'Noz' Nolan was editing a piece about Ferrari, for example, he would shout through to me, 'Hey, Tedos [his nickname for me], I need a shot of Michael looking happy at the back of the garage, helmet off,' and I'd know that our cameraman Andy Parr had filmed that the day before, or at a previous race. I'd race to the tape shelf, grab the tape and cue the shot up for Noz's approval or rejection. This way, the edits rocked along at a much quicker pace, and not only were there no more all-nighters, but on some nights over that second race weekend in Brazil we actually made it back to our hotel for a Caipirinha and a steak.

Jacques Villeneuve won the Interlagos race, his first victory of the season on the way to the world championship. And on Sunday advert break, a 90-minute to two-hour Grand Prix is a completely different matter. In Formula 1 anything can happen at any time on track; how could viewers be sure they wouldn't miss key moments in the action due to an ad break? As there was no way of knowing until we had tried it, we were all a little apprehensive.

We didn't have long to find out. Thankfully, Australia went well, Murray was his brilliant best, while Martin was a revelation, a natural talent, adding a completely new dynamic with his energy and level of knowledge to the co-commentator's role. His star was well and truly born. There was some of the expected negative reaction to the advert breaks, but looking back on it we didn't exactly help ourselves. Ordinarily if any sport programme misses something in a break, they replay it when they come back to the action, and the commentator voices it. However, like the BBC in the past, ITV had sold Murray and Martin's commentary on to networks around the English-speaking world, not all of whom took advert breaks at the same time we did, if at all. There was a concern that Murray re-voicing something wouldn't make sense for people in other countries who hadn't missed it, and so it was decided that if we did happen to miss something significant, Jim Rosenthal would come in after the break, and hand over to analyst Simon Taylor who would voice the action. A reasonable idea, but in practice all it did was draw more attention to the fact we'd missed something in a break. It took a year or so for the producers to abandon the protocol and revert to the original idea of getting Murray to recap.

The only thing that didn't go well in Melbourne was what would now be called 'extended workflows'; back then it was known more simply as 'pulling an all-nighter in the edit'. The producers had three-hour show running – no easy task – and know to ask the pundits the right questions.

The year 1997 started with a pre-season press launch outside ITV's headquarters in Gray's Inn Road, unveiling the full presentation team: Murray Walker and ex-F1 driver Martin Brundle commentating, Jim Rosenthal anchoring, with Tony Jardine (who had previously worked in motorsport PR) and Simon Taylor (writer and columnist) as expert analysts, plus James Allen and Louise Goodman (formerly Eddie Jordan's press officer at Jordan Grand Prix) as reporters. I remember how delighted Murray was to be there, knowing he would still be commentating on the sport he adored. As I later learned Martin had more doubts, feeling uncomfortable moving into a TV role when he still wanted to be driving. Thinking he'd been pushed out of F1 too soon by Eddie Jordan, for whom he raced in 1996, Martin hadn't given up, and continued to hunt for an F1 drive while he was commentating throughout '97.

It was a pleasant enough press conference. The main points of interest seemed to be that Murray would be continuing as the voice of Formula 1, and Louise's groundbreaking role as the first full-time female F1 reporter. More unwelcome were the headlines the next day, which focused on the negative impact for F1 viewers of the races being shown on a commercial channel. It had been revealed that ITV would have to squeeze five two-minute advert breaks into each Grand Prix. For ITV, it wasn't negotiable. A commercial channel makes money from putting ad breaks in their programmes, that's how it works. But while a 45-minute half of a football match is just about long enough to air without an find the UK's next F1 presenter. The three candidates were all racing fans: Mike Smith, a well-known TV presenter and sometime racing driver; David Smith, who used to read the news on Channel 4's *Big Breakfast* ; and David 'Kid' Jensen, the Radio 1 DJ. Our setup was basic to say the least. I set up a table in a small studio with some tablecloths and a chequered flag, and the three candidates did their screen tests. Their task was to introduce the viewers to the programme, perform some links, read out the world championship standings and throw to James Allen, signed-on with Chrysalis as pit lane reporter, who would be on the other side of the studio with a camera and microphone, ready to do a pretend report.

As the day wore on James suggested we move out of the building, so I found myself in Foubert's Place, looking after the cameraman's back and the cable that trailed into the studio. While James was doing his mock pit report a dog came up and peed against a lamp post. 'This could mean trouble,' James said, without missing a beat, 'the car has sprung a leak,' to much hilarity in the gallery.

The three presenters were all very good. However, in the end ITV stepped in with their choice of Jim Rosenthal, who was their well-known main anchor for boxing and a presenter on some football programmes. As noted, Carlton had also seen Jim as the man for the job; he had been signed up to present for them had they won the bid. Being a football man at heart, Jim was always quite honest about the fact that he was not an F1 aficionado. He kept up with the main stories, but he wasn't an expert and didn't pretend to be. In fact, it's not essential that your main presenter has that expertise: that's what your guests and reporters are for. You need the presenter to be a rock-solid steady pair of hands to keep a live,

THE START LINE

Now they had to deliver. I got the call I had been hoping for, and was offered a job to join the production team as junior researcher. I met the top boss Neil Duncanson and the rest of the team: field producer Alan Hurndall, VT producer John 'Noz' Nolan and production managers Tim Breadin and Karen Raphael. A small group, now about to produce a big sport.

There was so much to do in just a few months that I didn't have time to think about the fact I was now working in F1. I spent the winter of 1996–97 in a darkened room with a TV and a tape machine logging all the tapes of the previous season's racing that Chrysalis had received from Formula One Management, the company headed at the time by Bernie Ecclestone, that controls the commercial and broadcast rights of Formula 1. I was in heaven – the opportunity to come into work, sit down in front of a TV, put on tapes of races and write down what I was seeing was bliss. I couldn't believe that I was being paid for it!

Chrysalis had some problems to solve. Earmarked for the presenter's job, Steve Rider decided that he wasn't quite ready to leave the BBC just yet. As he told me many years later, when we worked together, at the time he'd had the feeling that the senior executives at ITV weren't particularly keen on bringing in a major signing from a rival network, preferring to use their own people. Chrysalis boss Neil Duncanson pushed back against that, arguing that F1 needed a fresh start with a knowledgeable presenter, rather than an existing ITV name brought in from football. But for now, Rider had decided to stay at the BBC, and if he was out, who could do it?

So it was that, in November 1996, I found myself at Molinare Studios in London's Carnaby Street, helping out at a screen test to cut together. Before searchable digital video libraries, the only way to know what shots were where was for somebody to physically watch all the tapes and log it down on pieces of paper (which you then slotted into the tape box, or a central file, so that anyone could look through it and find the shots they needed). A tape-logger was a good place to start for a junior and was the way lots of people found their way into the television industry.

I turned out to be more than competent at watching back the races and writing a description of the shots and the audio or commentary with timecodes, and Dave and Rupert told me to stay in touch. At that point they were waiting to find out if they had won the production contract, or if it had gone, as most TV sport industry insiders predicted it would, to the in-house production arm of Carlton, ITV franchise licence holders for the London region. Carlton had already lined up BBC legend Murray Walker to continue to be lead commentator for ITV, and had chosen Jim Rosenthal to present. I never found out if Carlton was aware, but Chrysalis had also signed up Murray. Smart operator as he was, I think Murray had told every bidder that he was on their team! Chrysalis (whose bid partnered up with the Meridian and Anglia ITV franchises, creating the neat production name MACh 1) had Steve Rider – seasoned BBC sports presenter, who anchored prestige shows such as *Sportsnight* and *Grandstand* – optioned to present the ITV F1 show if they won the contract.

And much to everyone's surprise, they did. Suddenly MACh 1 had to organize one of the hardest jobs in TV sport – live, on-site presentation of F1 on a grander scale than had previously been seen on the BBC. Arguably, Chrysalis had won the bid because they convinced ITV they could do it bigger and better than anyone else.

THE START LINE

myself, the BBC had lost the rights to televise F1 to the ITV network, who were preparing to appoint a production company to make the programmes for them. I didn't know it at the time, but I was about to meet someone at that press conference who would change my life. I had been aware of James Allen through his news editorship of *Autosport* magazine and as the presenter/reporter on *Nigel Mansell's IndyCar 1993*, a programme I and many F1 fans had enjoyed, documenting Nigel's championship-winning season with Newman-Haas in the USA. That programme had been made by a production company called Chrysalis Sport, and I guessed that James might also be involved in their bid to produce ITV's F1 coverage for the 1997 season.

I spotted him watching the press conference scene from the back of the room, so afterwards I went up and introduced myself. We fell to chatting about the Chrysalis Sport bid and I asked if they might be looking for someone junior who could tell Jacques Villeneuve's helmet from Damon Hill's. James smiled. He couldn't speak for Chrysalis, but what he did do was tell me who to write to (and I do mean a written letter – email was in its infancy in 1996). This was the producers Rupert Bush and Dave Lewis. I wrote, and wrote again, then phoned to follow up, and then phoned again. If only to stop me bothering them, Dave and Rupert finally took my call and invited me into their office, a converted church on Camden Park Road, for a chat. In fact, were it not for the patience and kindness of Valerie Garford and Sarah Needham, who had to field my many calls to the Chrysalis Sport producers, I might never have got through the door.

As a trial task Dave and Rupert gave me a race to log. When you're editing a video feature you need to have footage – clips – to

Arrows chaps next season, team boss Tom Walkinshaw having convinced him to join what was then a back-of-the-grid team. My editor wasn't aware Damon had been dropped by his current team, Williams, despite the fact that he was about to win them the championship, and he cared even less about Arrows. However, I managed to convince him that even though my shift had finished, I should go and record the audio from the press conference, just in case they did want to run a clip that evening. With my Capital FM press card, and a tape recorder and microphone, I hopped on the tube down to Chelsea Harbour.

Damon looked understandably miffed at the whole situation. Most likely his mind was on the world championship-deciding race in Japan, which was still a fortnight away. His manager Michael Breen was there, looking rather happier than his client, probably because the multi-million-pound contract with Arrows would result in a nice commission for him. All the F1 correspondents from the newspapers I had scoured for F1 news for so long were present, including Derick Allsop (*The Independent*), Stan Piecha (*The Sun*), Ray Matts (*Daily Mail*) and Bob McKenzie (*Daily Express*). They asked Damon questions along the lines of 'Why Arrows?' and more forthrightly 'You know you're not going to be winning any races with Arrows, how much of a come down is this for a guy who looks like he's about to become the 1996 world champion?' Damon went from looking a bit miffed to increasingly pissed off as the press conference went on.

While Damon grappled with the implications of his team move, there was also a significant change going on in the world of F1 broadcasting in the UK. After 20-odd years of showing occasional qualifying sessions and most of the races to devoted viewers such as

THE START LINE

Something else Howard understood was about the times that people would be listening to the radio. Bear in mind this was the mid-nineties, when the first thing people did to find out what was happening in the world when they woke up in the morning was turn on the radio, rather than picking up their phones.

'What's the point in doing this early breakfast news at 5am?' I once asked. 'Why don't we just take the feed from Independent Radio News?' Howard replied, 'There are more people listening to Capital FM at 5am than there are at 5pm, and that's why it's important to read our own news.' Hard to believe, but the listening figures showed he was right.

I loved it at Capital. The Euston Tower and Leicester Square studios were always exciting places to be. I thought that I was going to carry on working in radio. I enjoyed doing it, and I'm blessed with a decent enough voice. I still loved F1, but there was no real opportunity to work in the sport as far as I could see. It was on the BBC, Murray Walker did the commentary and that was that. It wasn't even a realistic dream, or something I ever thought I could get into. That all changed on an otherwise ordinary day in September 1996.

I was coming to the end of my early breakfast shift, which included a handover meeting with the day newsreaders and a planning meeting for that evening's edition of Capital's news show *The Way It Is*. An alert popped up on the Press Association's planning schedule: 'Arrows F1 team press conference at Chelsea Harbour.' The rest of the newsroom had never heard of Arrows. The sports team had, but even they weren't particularly interested.

So with my metaphorical F1 anorak on, I explained that this was going to be an announcement that soon-to-be world champion and household name Damon Hill was going to be driving for these man with a booming voice called Howard Hughes, for whom I wrote those 90-second bulletins at 6.50am each day.

Howard was a radio nut. He loved all things radio and was blessed with one of the best voices of all time. He was also very, very funny and had a few highly individual quirks, one of which was reciting his own, unrepeatable, voiceover introduction to the ITV news. Another was his affection for an aftershave called Jazz. It came in a bottle with a black and white cap, and Howard would always spray about five squirts around his neck before he left the newsroom to go on-air. Was it that the alcohol in the aftershave helped his voice sound more booming and resonant? Or did he just really like the scent?

Every day Howard would burst into the office at 6.50am. 'Ted, good morning!' he would boom. 'What are you leading with today?' Most of the time I had what he considered the correct top story, or he would say, 'That's fine, I'll just change this a bit', before going into the studio and reading the 7am news with small alterations to the script that I'd prepared. One particular day there had been a storm overnight in London, and as I was driving in at 3am I had seen that some scaffolding had come down and fallen billboards and other debris were lying around the streets of the West End. This seemed to me important news for listeners on their way to work that morning, so I made that the top story. It was the one time Howard wasn't happy with my choice. He didn't exactly say, 'This is weather, not news,' he just said, 'Hmm, interesting choice. No, I don't think we'll lead with that, I think we'll lead with another story today.'

Gradually, through moments like that, I was learning about telling a story, painting a picture, the importance of headlines and the priority that stories should get – the nuts and bolts of editorial.

THE START LINE

wanted to work at Capital Radio. Was there anybody I could talk to at their Euston Tower base about some shifts?

Sizing me up (my decent voice, the fact that I'd gone up to him to ask for a job), Park gave me the phone numbers of the news editors at Capital, David Hedges and Patrick Johnston. As a regular listener to 95.8 Capital FM (Capital's on-air name), I already knew of Patrick. He was a superb news presenter and, together with Hedges, delivered it in the distinctive and accessible style that was proving so popular as an alternative to the traditional BBC news offering.

Hedges had a few early breakfast news-reading shifts that, for obvious reasons, his usual pool of reporters weren't that keen on filling. He agreed to try me out on a few to see if I was up to it. Early breakfast sounds quite dynamic, but really, it was a night shift. I had to wake up at 3am to be in the newsroom on the ground floor of the Euston Tower by 4am. I would then read the news wires, look at the morning's papers (the first editions of which were already strewn around the newsroom) and from those, write a one minute to 90-seconds long bulletin, and then read it out on the air at 5am. There was no time for nerves or to think about how many people were listening. The 5.30am headlines came up quickly, and then it was on to the 6am and the 6.30am slots, before writing another updated bulletin for the main breakfast newsreader.

All breakfast shows are the most listened-to programmes on their radio stations. At a time when Capital Radio was the biggest commercial radio station in Europe, *Chris Tarrant in the Morning* was its headline show. We were all a bit in awe of Chris, as he really was a very famous household name and absolutely at the top of his game. More approachable was Tarrant's newsreader, a wonderful

I should mention at this point that Marcus White had a lisp, and he may have had more interest than most in avoiding names beginning with S.

I thought for a second and said, 'Well, my mother's maiden name is Kravitz.'

He sounded it out a few times. 'Kravitz, Kravitz. Ted Kravitz. That'll do!'

My true passport name is no secret, but professionally I've taken my mother's maiden name ever since that day. There wasn't any great discussion about it. I wasn't going to invent a cool name, this happened to be the only other name I had. My maternal grandfather, Richard Kravitz, was delighted. He was in the media world, publishing *Esquire* in the UK and *Boxing News*. In fact, I used to go with my uncle Pete to sell copies of *Boxing News* outside the York Hall in Bethnal Green when there were fights on.

With some on-air reporting for Gemini FM under my belt, I now had some demo tapes with which to try and secure more work in what was increasingly looking like my chosen career. The Radio Academy ran a training weekend with an opportunity to submit a half-hour radio documentary that would be judged by a panel. I'd pulled an all-nighter to get mine edited. The next day's talk was being given by one of the heaviest hitters in radio broadcasting, Richard Park. At the time Richard was programme director at London's Capital Radio, then the most popular and successful commercial radio station in Europe. Ordinarily I would have been too terrified to approach him, but with the usual alerts in my sleep-deprived state not quite working perfectly, I found myself walking up to him. I introduced myself and told him that I'd been working in Devon but lived in London, and that I really

THE START LINE

I would watch the races together in the student union bar and then have a go ourselves at a karting track that had been set up inside Exeter's Westpoint Arena. Unfortunately, I got my finances wrong, and having paid to hire the karting venue at a fee of around £500, discovered that only six people had showed up for the kart race, and that they couldn't afford to pay more than a tenner each. The sponsorship income for untalented university students being non-existent, I ended up funding the rest of the track-hire fee from my savings.

University Radio Exeter was much better run and maintained high standards, so full training in microphone technique, editing, reporting, writing and general presenting was supplied by the older students and by John Whitworth, a radio professional known affectionately as 'Frog'. Once you had learned the ropes there was an informal talent-scouting relationship with the professional local radio stations, who were open to finding new voices for freelance reporting or presenting on those shifts at times when nobody else wanted to work. I never really felt like a BBC kind of person (although much later I did end up working for the corporation for three happy years), so I focused on trying to get in the door at the local commercial station, Gemini FM. A meeting with news editor Marcus White led to a couple of try-outs and then a shift reporting on *The Devon County Show*. But before my voice could appear on-air Marcus wanted a word about my name.

'Right, Ted, what's your surname again?'

'Slotover,' I replied.

'Well, we can't call you Ted Slotover, it's too awkward for radio. Have you got any other names?'

going to call up next, and neither did Clive. Comedian, writer, actor and author Peter Cook was a regular caller under the pseudonym Sven from Swiss Cottage, purporting to be a visiting Norwegian whose wife Jutta had walked out on him and was at large somewhere in Continental Europe. Sadly, Sven never found her, instead distracting himself with late-night complaints to Clive about the national obsession with fish in his native Norway. I recommend a documentary made for the UK's Channel 4, easily found online, called *Night Caller*, all about Clive Bull's *Through The Night*. It's well worth your time.

Radio would eventually lead me to Formula 1, but it was Exeter University that led me to working in radio. I had chosen to study politics, a subject I found pretty interesting and, crucially, pretty easy to pass exams in. Thus, A-Levels followed by a degree in political science made sense. Exeter was a fine place to do a politics degree, but my real interest in applying there was the student radio station, University Radio Exeter, or URE for short – at that time one of the best in the country. My course only required four hours of lectures and four tutorials per week, so I spent the rest of my three years there learning how to present and produce radio, while spending my Sunday afternoons in the company of Steve Rider and Murray Walker (and thanks should be offered at this point to the patience of my fellow Mardon Hall residents who were kind enough not to mind too much that I regularly commandeered the shared TV room on Sunday afternoons).

While at university I also learned the hard way how difficult it was to make any money in motorsport when I set up the extremely unsuccessful and ultimately loss-making Exeter University Motorsport Club. The plan was that like-minded petrolheads and the roar of the V8 engine was like nothing I'd ever encountered. By now, F1 was firmly my life's passion. Not for one second, though, did I ever think that I would work in it. I just didn't see a way in. And at this point, I was focused on a more realistic career prospect, radio journalism.

My fondness for radio developed in my teens. I was a bit of a night owl, and I loved the immediacy and intimacy of a radio programme – the thought that there was someone else on the other end of an airwave, awake at the same time, making us listeners feel we were not alone. In the late eighties and early nineties nobody did that better than LBC's *Through the Night* show.

The programme, on-air from 1am to 4am, was presented most often by Clive Bull, who created a society of listeners. His regular listeners might not have had the same interests or opinions, but what we did have in common was that we were all awake at that time of night, some working, some not, but all listening out for each other.

As much counsellor, lawyer and therapist as he was the presenter, Bull usually devoted the first hour to 'calls on the topic of your choice', which allowed regulars like Babs from Bermondsey or Charles from Camden to phone in with updates on their lives. As members of the club, fellow listeners were always interested to hear their stories. Clive would introduce segments like 'guess the mystery noise', which was usually made by some office accessory that he had picked up in the deserted LBC newsroom, or 'the rolling quiz', where a caller would set a question and the first person to answer it correctly would then set the next question, and so on, carrying on throughout the night. These kept me listening into the early hours, the other hook being that you never knew who was

When I turned 17 and learned to drive, I became even more interesting in the physics of forward motion, of acceleration, of braking, the difference between understeer and oversteer, or, in the case of my Peugeot 106, chronic understeer. Knowing what 50 or 70mph actually felt like from a driver's perspective only deepened my motor-racing obsession.

I could never persuade any of my family or friends to go with me to a Grand Prix, and even back then it wasn't affordable. The first time that I saw F1 cars on track was in 1992 at an *Evening Standard*-sponsored racing day at Brands Hatch, free to attend with the voucher in the newspaper. Brands Hatch was the closest circuit to my home in London and I was old enough to get there by myself on the train, voucher in hand. The star attraction among the Minis and Formula Fords was a special appearance by Team Lotus. Johnny Herbert was the home hero, and his enthusiastic fans followed him around the paddock chasing for an autograph. His teammate Mika Häkkinen was quietly keeping to the sidelines. When I spotted him, I was quite excited. I was probably one of the few people there who knew who Mika was, as I had been keeping an eye on his early career. I went to meet him. He was sitting on a tool chest handing out autograph picture cards to those who'd been disappointed not to meet Johnny, although he hadn't actually signed any. He was as taciturn then as he would go on to be in his future racing career, although as we would later find out, his emotions ran deep.

The highlight of the day was a set of laps from the Lotus-Ford F1 car, and when Johnny booted it out of the last corner, Clark Curve, the acceleration and the sound of that engine brought a huge smile to my face. To experience the drama of an F1 car on track with

THE START LINE

It's not really any different from what I do today. Much as I love numbers, I'm not great at remembering them. *Ted's Notebook* was partly born from the notebook I always have in hand where I've recorded numbers to the thousandth of a second.

As a kid at that kitchen table I found that F1 had a curious pull on me – the more I read, the more I wanted to read. The more I learned about these teams and their drivers, the more I wanted to learn. It got to the point where I would scour every newspaper every day to see if they had an F1 story buried in the back pages, and I'd devour even the smallest article. Thursday morning's trip to the newsagent to pick up a fresh copy of *Autosport* magazine was a weekly highlight. My family weren't the least bit interested in F1, and were often heard to wonder where this fascination had come from.

Looking back, it was probably Nigel Mansell's exploits in the mid-eighties that hooked me in. I particularly remember watching the 1987 British GP on BBC television, and Nigel's famous charge to overtake and beat his nemesis and Williams teammate Nelson Piquet. Drawn to Nigel as I was (at the time a British household name), I found myself more intrigued by drivers from faraway lands with interesting names and flamboyant characters. As I grew older the Brazilian driver Ayrton Senna started winning races regularly, and I realized I'd found my racing idol. His skill, his flair, his handsome features, the fact he was so good, the best of his era, all that pulled me in. I watched all the races. Whether they were broadcast live into *Sunday Grandstand* or were just a 45-minute highlights show, I would be glued to the screen. Murray Walker became the soundtrack of my weekends, with James Hunt and then Jonathan Palmer alongside the great man.

wasn't interested in my preferences, I spent my free time after school reading the papers on our kitchen table. Those hours must have left their mark, because I came to appreciate the way the news was reported, the prominence that certain stories were given, and the skill of the journalists in telling the reader why they should care, all of which gave me the first sense that I might enjoy a career in journalism.

Reading and enjoying the political coverage in newspapers like *The Times*, *The Daily Telegraph*, *The Independent* or *The Guardian* set me up for my university degree in politics. But the stories I looked forward to reading most were to be found in the sport section. I was interested enough in the three or four pages of football news and results, and as you now know, I was very happy reading the numbers in a league table – matches played, won, lost, drawn, goal difference and points – and if a big tournament or championship was on, I loved reading about the competitors' stories. But what I really wanted to read about was Formula 1. F1 coverage in the newspapers was pretty hit and miss when I was growing up; if you wanted to read those stories you had to hunt for them. And so that's what I did.

The race or qualifying reports were always welcome, but what I wanted most were the numbers. Growing up pre-internet and even pre-regular TV coverage, the only place you could access the full lap-time qualifying results or race classifications was the following day in the newspapers. Happily my parents would generally have a copy of every Sunday paper and thus Sunday mornings would find me forensically examining the lap times from the previous day's qualifying and building my own story of what had happened – who did well, who did badly, what the gaps between the drivers were, and what stories the lap times told.

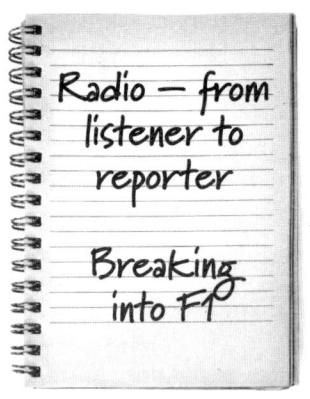

Chapter 2

The Start Line

Strangely for someone who is terrible at maths, I find comfort in numbers. I was one of those children who found that engaging with them helped me make sense of things I didn't fully understand. I found numbers pleasing to look at and to write, I knew where I was with them. If numbers represent order in the world, F1 is full of numbers and, growing up, I found that very reassuring. Even today, in an anxiety-inducing world, I find much comfort in a neat table of motor-racing finishing positions, lap times and points scored.

The rest of my family are literary and artistic types. My father ran an agency representing classical musicians, conductors and opera singers, while my mother worked for many years in book publishing, and – so that they could keep across the reviews – we always had stacks of newspapers around the house. After my mother had taken the books section, my father the music reviews and my eldest brother exercising his right as firstborn to the TV guide, I was left with the news, politics and sports pages. And because my middle brother had control of the TV remote and

disproportionate amount of our time over a weekend, because they're highly crafted, tightly edited pieces of work. They are devised mainly by our production team and myself, before being scripted, filmed and edited, just in time for transmission before the race.

And finally, the aspect of the pit reporter's job I did truly invent: *Ted's Notebook*. The essential ethos is simple. It's one shot. One take. Once we start, we're going out live, and we don't stop, so anything can happen and often does. It came about because I realized so many of the stories about the drivers who were not the frontrunners were getting lost. And so the purpose of the notebook is to tell the story of every driver's day.

So there you go, Anthony Davidson, that's my made-up job. But it's quite a fun one, and if we can make it feel like a little race club, with all of us rev-heads watching together based upon our shared interest in F1, a club that anyone can be a part of and feel included in, then it won't seem quite so ridiculous.

yield the best results. I'm all for being direct if the situation demands it, but most of the time, you'll get a worse interview if you go in with a 'Why on earth did you do that?' approach. In general, a bit of empathy and a sympathetic request for an explanation will almost always yield a more informative answer for the viewer.

Sometimes bosses can go into defensive mode if they anticipate they're going to be under attack from the fans or the media, whereas others are less guarded. In 2016 Mercedes teammates Lewis Hamilton and Nico Rosberg collided on the first lap of the Spanish GP. In the immediate aftermath I found F1 legend Niki Lauda, who since 2012 had been attached to the Mercedes team in the chairman role, pacing around outside the back of the garage, clearly furious. He wasted no time in telling me how angry he was with the drivers. In his view it was completely unacceptable. One had forced the other on to the grass, only for the other one to turn in, and make sure the two crashed. By contrast, after the race, in damage-limitation mode, team principal Toto Wolff was more measured, arguing there was blame on both sides, that the drivers were generally free to race but that he would be having words with them.

These post-race interviews are key to understanding the outcome of the Grand Prix. They often reveal newsworthy stories that change the viewers' perception of the events they've just spent a couple of hours watching. It's my job to ask the questions that I believe our viewers at home would ask if they were in the pit lane at that moment.

I'm yet to mention two final aspects of the job, namely features, as we call them – three- or four-minute pre-made video stories that run pre- and post-race, and the notebook, my pit-lane roundup that goes out live after qualifying and the race. Features take up a engineers. Whether his team had done something incredibly good, like win a championship, or something incredibly bad, like ordering Rubens Barrichello to give up the win of the 2002 Austrian GP, Ross was always as close to being an emotional flatline as I've seen. The exception was when, having saved the former Honda team from going out of business, he won both the 2009 drivers' and constructors' titles with a car bearing his name. On that memorable afternoon in Brazil Ross was in pieces.

To get the interviews you need, it's vital to learn everyone's preferences. Ferrari's Fred Vasseur leaves the pit wall extremely quickly, sometimes before the chequered flag has even fallen. By the time you get to the Ferrari pit, he's long gone, usually across to the garage, or back to his office, so you can only ever catch up with him later on in the paddock. One of his predecessors at Ferrari, Stefano Domenicali, now the boss of the F1 organization, had a set routine, of which his interview with me was a part. He would congratulate or have a chat with colleagues on the pit wall, then go into the garage and shake hands with his mechanics. He'd then come out front to grant an interview that just happened to have the Ferrari garage and its sponsors' logos visible in the background. Clever man!

Once you know your team bosses and they know you, they become the easiest interviews to get. It's almost like they're expecting you to be there, and they're disappointed if you're not. The hardest interviews tend to be when the team bosses have had a very bad day, when their drivers have collided with each other, or they've lost a race or a championship. Or even worse, when it's the team that is at fault, rather than the driver. In those instances it's very rare that a two foot forward 'sticking the boot in' question will wide field of vision) in my back pocket that is brilliant for seeing details far away down the pit lane. For example, if I'm watching from a midfield garage, and a Red Bull or McLaren comes in with a problem at the far end of the pit lane, with the trusty monocular I can see if there's a mechanic topping up the engine air system, or removing some debris from a radiator duct. Very useful, that little telescope. In addition, I have the live timing app running on my iPhone, which is really all you need to read a race without pictures. It gives race positions, lap times, gaps to the leader, intervals between cars, and sector times and speeds.

Once the race is over and the last car has returned to the area of the pits reserved for technical checks, reporters are allowed into the pit lane proper to grab some interviews with the team principals or top engineers as they come down from their pit wall gantries. This is always a highly charged and emotional time for the team personnel. You, meanwhile, need an interview, and so you need to pick your moment carefully. I've seen many race victories, championship wins, near misses, race losses and the aftermaths of accidents from here. Everyone deals with triumphs and tragedies differently, and you have to know how to treat each team boss.

McLaren's Ron Dennis was, for all his vaunted self-discipline and self-control, often surprisingly emotional when he came off the pit wall. I've experienced him both with eyes filled with tears, and lip curling with anger. By contrast, Ross Brawn (Ferrari, Brawn Grand Prix and Mercedes) kept his emotions firmly in check. He would give his colleagues a handshake, briefly look through some data on the pit wall, and then turn in my direction to grant an interview, usually, I suspect, because he wanted to get it out of the way in order to go and discuss things in further depth with his times is to present their teams in the best possible light. Protocol demands that rather than talking directly to a mechanic, engineer or technical director during the race, I consult the press officers first. I'm trying to keep across what's going on with 20 drivers and how they're all doing in the race – the fact that team press officers are only interested in their two drivers is helpful because they can fill me in on anything I might have missed while I've been covering other cars. They will always have a line about what the intention is for their driver in this stint, or explain whether they are saving tyres, engine or going flat-out.

It's pretty rare that you go into a garage and you can instantly see that something's wrong. So what are you looking for? The most obvious clue something isn't right is when you see a technical director leave the pit wall and cross the pit lane to the garage. If they go back and forth, you'll know that something's up with one of the cars.

Let's say you've done your work beforehand and convinced a team press officer to let you into their garage for the race. Well done, but you then have to be mindful about what you're reporting. For example, back in the days when we had refuelling I could sometimes see the figure revealing how many kilos of fuel they were about to put in the car, but obviously I couldn't broadcast that as it would be tactically useful for rival teams. So there's always an element of give and take.

If I can't see the pictures, how do I follow the race? By listening to it. I'm always listening to the commentary, effectively treating every word with the value a radio listener does, concentrating on the descriptions in the absence of visuals. And as a bit of an aid, I carry a fairly powerful monocular (basically a telescope with a race coverage and looking at the same timing screens as the commentators – they've already got that covered. At the more modern circuits like Yas Marina in Abu Dhabi there's a big screen temptingly visible from the pits, but beware – if you end up just watching the race like everybody else, you'll be missing the stories the cameras don't see.

Even without a big screen to watch it's a mistake to stay put in the same location for the whole race. Going from garage to garage, talking to your contacts in the teams directly rather than by text message, will always result in quicker, better, fresher information that will be of value to the listener. Texts or WhatsApp groups can be an effective way for teams to keep every broadcaster and journalist informed at the same time, but where possible it's always better to get that information face to face. Plus, if you're the only reporter consistently going from garage to garage, as I seem to have been over the last 23 years, you'll find you tend to get the story before anyone else.

The first job is getting past the security guard at the back of the garage, and you're only going to do that if you have been granted special permission to watch from there. It might surprise you to learn that some of the most secretive and guarded teams are not the frontrunners – they're actually the teams whose cars are the slowest, which makes me smile, when I encounter their stonewalling, and wonder what it is they're so anxious to protect. Mercedes, McLaren and Ferrari, on the other hand, are comparatively open. The teams employ press officers or, as they're known more generally, communications managers – effectively media liaisons – to deal with enquiries from the written and broadcast media and it's worth remembering that their aim at all

A MADE-UP JOB

waiting for the resumption (as happened in the 2024 Monaco GP), every car will have to make at least one in-race pit stop. Obviously, a load of time is lost having to slow down to come into the pit lane, have your tyres changed by 20 motivated mechanics in two seconds flat, and then get going again, and therefore drivers try to make as few pit stops as possible. But sometimes the tyre wear makes the car so slow that it's actually quicker to make another pit stop to take on fresh rubber for the race to the end. Who does what in these situations is called race strategy, which for obvious reasons the teams want to keep secret. A fundamental part of the pit lane reporter's job, therefore, is trying to figure out what they're up to and reporting back to explain it during the race.

It's also my job to tell the commentators if one of those pit stops has been particularly slow – or fast – and how that might affect the remainder of that driver's race. The key is to provide the viewers with as much relevant information as possible. If you approach the pit lane reporter's job that way, you won't go far wrong.

What complicates matters is that at most circuits I can't actually watch the race when I'm in the pits, and unless there's a big screen situated above the start/finish line grandstand, I have no way of seeing the race coverage. Now I realize this might seem odd for someone whose job is literally to tell people what happened in that day's Grand Prix, but it's true. At the majority of events the first time I watch qualifying or the race will be when I get home on Sunday night or Monday morning, or if I manage to catch any snippets on social media on the bus to the airport.

There's a very good reason why this is not problematic. Given that the pit reporter is there to tell the commentators what they *can't* see on their TV screens, there is no point in watching the same powerful enough to be able to broadcast live from these helipads, which I'm only too happy to do, more often than not brimming with the vital news that nothing continues to be happening.

With the practice sessions complete, or not, the next task for the pit reporter is qualifying. It's often the most exciting part of the weekend, where the cars are as light on fuel as possible in order to achieve the quickest lap time. The aim in qualifying is to deliver information into the commentary about any driver who has a car problem that is preventing them from getting out on track, keeping an eye on which compound of tyres everyone is using, and whether drivers are using a new set for best performance, or an already used set which means that their lap time won't be quite as good. Since there's more frantic activity in the pit lane than in the more relaxed practice sessions, reporters are required to stand in line with the front of the garages, on an actual, painted red line that has 'PIT LANE' helpfully added in white letters. You can move up and down the line, but only from the garage side – you're not allowed to step over it. From whichever part of the pit lane you choose, you can see what's coming out of three or four garages either side, but you can only see directly into the ones either side of you, unless you have a periscope on the end of a very long pole (not a bad idea, actually!).

Most drivers and engineers will tell you that qualifying is the most intensely pressurized part of the entire race weekend, and they're only too happy when it's all over, and they've not made some huge and costly mistake.

Once a driver has qualified on pole, the race is a doddle. OK, that's not quite true, as the current iteration of the rules demands that at least two different tyre compounds are used. Unless there is a race stoppage which allows everyone to change their tyres when

A MADE-UP JOB

While random trackside grass fires would be a good example of something that would call a halt to proceedings midway through, some sessions never get going in the first place, and the usual cause for this is the weather. F1 drivers are happy to practice, qualify and race in the rain, but there are complicated medical contingencies that need to be met if one of those cars were to crash and the driver to need transferring from the circuit medical centre to a more comprehensively equipped hospital. If the race track is in a city where the nearest hospital is only a mile or so away, such as Melbourne, Jeddah, Monaco, Monza or Singapore, then a regular road ambulance can be used. The problem is that most permanent race tracks are situated away from urban conurbations on account of the noise they tend to generate, so in the cases of Silverstone or Austria, Spa or the Nürburgring, a medical helicopter needs to be able to fly from the track to the nearest hospital and needs to be able to see where it is going. If there's low cloud, rain or fog, the helicopter cannot fly according to visual flight rules, and so to ensure nobody crashes their F1 car in the first place, a track session may be delayed indefinitely or even cancelled, leaving us on TV with some time to fill.

Time to fill is no cause for panic, as there are plenty of interesting things going on outside of the pit lane. You might head out to join the spectators in the grandstands, you might take the opportunity to talk to bored trackside marshals, or make the trek to one of my favourite spots to report from: the circuit helipad. It is almost always adjoining the medical centre, for obvious reasons. Why do I like it? Mostly because I like helicopters and talking to their pilots about the weather, and whether the practice session can start or not. Luckily the radio microphones and cameras we use are winning everything is now fighting for the minor placings. So much is learned and achieved by research and development over a season that an F1 team can often find significant seconds worth of lap time from March to December. Your best opportunity for identifying the bits that have achieved those performance gains is during the free practice sessions, which has made watching what is essentially 'training' a very popular part of F1 fans' weekend viewing. They also provide the commentators with an opportunity to familiarize themselves with each corner, the angles from which they are being filmed and what they look like on screen. These sessions are as crucial for the commentator and reporter as they are for the driver. This is your best opportunity to acquire essential knowledge and gather the thoughts that will help you read the story of the race to come.

The practice sessions also give us broadcasters the opportunity to get out more: to report from parts of the race track that will add insight into the prospective form of each car and to explain weird things that inevitably crop up, such as the trackside fires in the grass verges at the Japanese and Chinese Grands Prix, among others. The first time it happened in Shanghai we were surprised: there was no obvious reason for this seemingly spontaneous combustion. It was only when I walked down to the corner that I saw that there was a bump – invisible to the TV cameras – over which the cars were bottoming out, which was sending particles of burning titanium off the cars' skid blocks into the air, only for the wind to drift them on to the dry grass. In Japan, Sky Sports News's Craig Slater and I witnessed the marshals pre-emptively dousing the grass to make it less combustible, using anything that could hold water, from empty Bento boxes to upturned traffic cones.

sport, the instrument with which the athlete performs in F1 is not as simple as a bat or racquet. It is a car made up of nearly 15,000 individual components, each playing a specific and vital role in keeping the thing going. Since Formula 1 cars cannot and do not carry any redundant parts – as the weight of these would cost performance – every bit has to fulfil its function, so it also helps to have an understanding of what those components do. In addition, an understanding of the physics of aerodynamics and the laws of mechanical engineering is desirable, although there will be ample on-the-job training opportunities to learn about aspects of F1 you had no clue even existed, usually five minutes before you need to sound like an expert on the subject in front of millions of people.

So, if that's what the pit reporter actually does, where do they do it? It starts with the first, second and third free practice sessions of an ordinary Grand Prix weekend, which you'll be spending walking up and down the pit lane. It is, after all, where all the garages are, where the engineers work, where the cars are built and repaired after the drivers have broken them, polished with the most expensive microfibre rags money can buy and then meticulously disassembled at the end of the weekend. It's also where most of the drama and intrigue happens, where plans are hatched, where snooping on rivals takes place and where drivers often lose their metaphorical rags with their competitors.

Additionally, the practice sessions have become part of the art of pit reporting, in that they are very useful for spotting new parts on cars. Upgrades, as we call them, have become a crucial part of telling the story of how a Formula 1 season evolves, explaining why the car that was once slow is now fast and why the car that was the race. No one let me stand in their garage. Crap phone signal, way too much hiss through the headphones and I had to lug around that high-powered radio mic pack and battery you use. Unbelievable! I couldn't see a thing and didn't contribute to the commentary once. But here you are, and you've somehow managed to turn all that into a job. A job that you've basically made up! I don't know how you do it!'

Ah, Anthony, the job does exist, but what is it exactly? A pit lane reporter contributes information, explanation and observation into a race commentary from a position other than the commentary boxes. Usually this is around the garages in the pit lane, where race-critical pit stops take place and strategic decisions are made by the teams or the race officials. Having a roaming reporter able to go to where the stories are rather than being tied to a commentary box offers on-the-ground insight that, it is hoped, enhances the viewer's understanding and enjoyment of the race. It happens to be a pit lane in motorsport, but the job is similar to that of a reporter from a touchline, boundary, technical area or even from the 18th hole.

Building up to a golf, football or cricket event, reporters will often do 'stand ups' by the side of the playing area, ideally to inform viewers about an aspect of the field of play that will affect one side or the other. You can point something out on camera, in vision, but once the match, game or race gets going, a reporter will be a voice you hear over the main feed. In this respect, it's not dissimilar to a radio commentary, which is useful, as radio was my first professional love and the medium in which I'd planned a career before the lure of the F1 circus drew me in. As in any area of journalism, having a curious mind and the ability to understand and explain things are prerequisites for the job, but unusually in

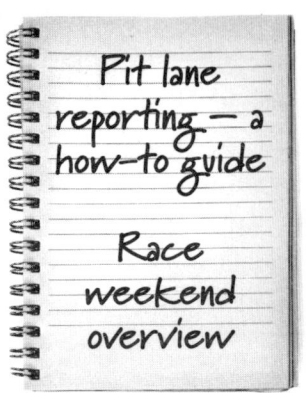

Chapter 1

A Made-Up Job

I'm standing in a gap between garages in the pit lane of the Suzuka circuit in Japan. It's raining, as usual. Mechanics from the McLaren Formula 1 team rush off the grid, pushing stacks of tyres into positions ready for the first pit stop. As I watch, there's a chug-chug from over my shoulder as members of the Sauber team force generator trolleys over a drain cover through to the paddock behind us. The trolleys are stuffed with bottles of compressed air, engine oil and tins of hydraulic fluid – crucial equipment on the grid, but useless to their cars once the race starts.

'Ah, here you are, ready to do your ridiculous, made-up job,' teases a passing Anthony Davidson, former World Endurance Car champion, Toyota Le Mans driver, and as an ex-Honda F1 driver, somewhat of a celebrity in Japan. This weekend, he's my Sky Sports F1 colleague.

'What do you mean?' I reply. 'I tried to do your job in Zandvoort,' he explains, 'and it was impossible. Nowhere to stand in the pit lane. Teams utterly unhelpful in giving out any information during

INTRODUCTION

Prix that has viewers jumping up and down around their living rooms, that has spectators trackside screaming encouragement at their heroes and even applause ringing out in the media centre. Sometimes it's caused by a brief rain shower, sometimes by a genius strategy, but these racing performances always rely on the skill and courage of the drivers. What particular combination of events got them to that point, nobody really knows – it's a mystery.

I've spent my professional life looking for the why's, the where's and the how's, piecing together little details that might be missed. Add them up, though, and you'll start to get a picture of what's *really* going on, and in this book I'm going to be sharing them with you. In these pages you'll be joining me behind the scenes in the pit lane and if you're curious to know how I do my job, consider this your handbook. But first, how did I get there?

ring. What actually happens in the performance – the result – is newsworthy, so journalists inform those who weren't fortunate enough to get a ticket for the big top as to what happened and why. There's always something going on, so for those there to report, observation, curiosity and an eye for detail are key attributes in order to fully understand the action and the movements behind the scenes.

It's been this way for 75 years in the form of the official Formula 1 world championship and for nearly 50 years of Grand Prix racing before that. And in each of those seasons, remarkable events have always happened. Stories that belong more in the theatre than a circus, often defying explanation as to how they came about. In searching for a reason as to how these stories – these legends – are made, I'm often reminded of a scene from the 1998 film *Shakespeare in Love*, featuring Geoffrey Rush as Philip Henslowe, owner of the Rose Theatre in London. Pursued by his patron Hugh Fennyman, played by Tom Wilkinson, Henslowe attempts to explain the conundrum of how the theatre business seeks to overcome its inherent 'insurmountable obstacles on the road to imminent disaster':

Fennyman: 'So what do we do?'
Henslowe: 'Nothing. Strangely enough it all turns out well.'
Fennyman: 'How?'
Henslowe: 'I don't know, it's a mystery.'

It's the same in Formula 1. Just as it looks like the championship is uncompetitive or the same team or driver is winning everything or the racing isn't as exciting as it used to be, along comes a Grand

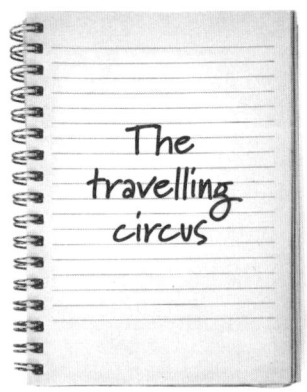

Introduction

'Hi, Ed.'

'Hi, Ted.'

I don't quite know how this has happened, but I'm walking down the pit lane of the Miami International Autodrome alongside singer-songwriting superstar Ed Sheeran.

'What do you make of Formula 1?' I ask him.

'It's nice, man. It's a circus, though.'

He's come a long way from South Suffolk to South Miami with many a packed stadium tour on the way, but even Ed Sheeran can see that F1 is a circus and in that, he's exactly right.

The Formula 1 world championship is essentially its own circus. It transports a show from town to town, performs to an excited audience, there's interest for the locals as the circus sprinkles its magic dust for a weekend, but come Sunday evening, it packs up and moves on.

The drivers and teams are the performers. Back in the day, Bernie Ecclestone was the ringmaster. Now it is the F1 organization, making sure the show starts and finishes on time. Media companies from around the world film and broadcast what happens in the

CONTENTS

Chapter 17: Nearly Men	239
Chapter 18: Ted's Notebook	253
Chapter 19: Surviving, Driving	269
Chapter 20: The 2021 Abu Dhabi GP	287
Chapter 21: The Eight-Pointed Stars	309
Chapter 22: The Finish Line	323
Index	333
Acknowledgements	341
About the Author and Picture Credits	345

Contents

Introduction	1
Chapter 1: A Made-Up Job	5
Chapter 2: The Start Line	19
Chapter 3: The Murray and Martin Show	39
Chapter 4: Jacques, Gilles and Jerez	55
Chapter 5: Murray's Last Season	65
Chapter 6: Learning the Ropes	79
Chapter 7: Dealing with Disaster: The Pitfalls of Live Broadcasting	93
Chapter 8: Michael	103
Chapter 9: Nuts, Bolts, Bags and Flights	117
Chapter 10: The Six-Car Race	129
Chapter 11: From Ron to Ruin	143
Chapter 12: A Fifth and a Fix	163
Chapter 13: Brains and Brawn	183
Chapter 14: Schumacher's Second Coming	201
Chapter 15: The Piranha Club	211
Chapter 16: Sebastian	225

First published in Great Britain in 2025 by Cassell, an imprint of
Octopus Publishing Group Ltd
Carmelite House
50 Victoria Embankment
London EC4Y 0DZ
www.octopusbooks.co.uk
www.octopusbooksusa.com

An Hachette UK Company
www.hachette.co.uk

The authorized representative in the EEA is Hachette Ireland,
8 Castlecourt Centre, Dublin 15, D15 XTP3, Ireland (email: info@hbgi.ie)

Text copyright © Ted Kravitz 2025
Design and layout copyright © Octopus Publishing Group Ltd 2025

F1, FORMULA 1, GRAND PRIX and related marks are trade marks
of Formula One Licensing BV, a Formula 1 company.

Distributed in the US by Hachette Book Group
1290 Avenue of the Americas, 4th and 5th Floors, New York, NY 10104

Distributed in Canada by Canadian Manda Group
664 Annette St., Toronto, Ontario, Canada M6S 2C8

All rights reserved. No part of this work may be reproduced or utilized in any form or by any means, electronic or mechanical, including photocopying, recording or by any information storage and retrieval system, without the prior written permission of the publisher.

Ted Kravitz asserts the moral right to be identified as the author of this work.

ISBN (Hardback): 978-1-78840-570-6
ISBN (Trade Paperback): 978-1-78840-571-3
eISBN (eBook): 978-1-78840-572-0

A CIP catalogue record for this book is available from the British Library.

Typeset in 11.25/16.5 pt Miller Text by Six Red Marbles UK, Thetford, Norfolk.

Printed and bound in Great Britain.

7 9 10 8 6

Publisher: Trevor Davies
Editor: Scarlet Furness
Copy Editor: Chris Stone
Creative Director: Mel Four
Picture Research Manager: Jennifer Veall
Senior Production Manager: Peter Hunt
Additional Text By: Adam Cooper

This FSC® label means that materials used for the product have been responsibly sourced.

For Jill and Robert,
with love and thanks for buying the papers.

F1 INSIDER
NOTES FROM THE PIT LANE

TED KRAVITZ